Colombia

San Andrés & Providencia p170

Caribbean Coast p120

Pacific Coast p255

Boyacá, Santander & Norte de Santander p83

Medellín & Zona Cafetera p186

Bogotá p42

Cali & Southwest Colombia p224

Amazon Basin p270

THIS EDITION WRITTEN AND RESEARCHED BY

Alex Egerton, Tom Masters, Kevin Raub

PLAN YOUR TRIP

ON THE ROAD

VIVIAN OSORIO/LONELY PLANET ©

BLUE-AND-YELLOW MACAW
P303

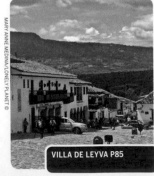

MARY ANNE MEDINA/LONELY PLANET ©

VILLA DE LEYVA P85

Contents

UNDERSTAND

SURVIVAL GUIDE

SPECIAL FEATURES

Welcome to Colombia

Soaring Andean summits, unspoiled Caribbean coast, enigmatic Amazon jungle, cryptic archaeological ruins and cobbled colonial towns. Colombia boasts all of South America's allure, and more.

Diverse Landscapes

Colombia's equatorial position affords it a diversity of landscapes. A slight tinkering in altitude takes you from sun-toasted Caribbean sands to coffee-strewn, emerald-green hilltops in the Zona Cafetera. Continue to climb and there's Bogotá, the bustling cradle of Colombia and third-highest capital city in the world. Go up another few thousand meters for snowcapped peaks, high-altitude lakes and the eerie, unique vegetation of the *páramo* (high mountain plains). The bottom drops out as the Andes give way to Los Llanos, a 550,000-sq-km swath of tropical grasslands shared with Venezuela.

Outdoor Adventures

Colombia's varied terrain is fertile ground for outdoor adventurers to dive, climb, raft, trek and soar. San Gil is the undisputed adventure capital, but Colombia boasts alfresco pleasures in all corners. Some of the continent's most iconic trekking is here: a multiday jungle walk takes you to the ancient ruins of the Tayrona Ciudad Perdida, while numerous ascents inside Parque Nacional Natural El Cocuy places intrepid hikers on the highest reaches of the Andes. Providencia's world-class reef spells aquatic heaven for scuba divers, and whale-watchers on the Pacific coast can see majestic humpbacks in the wild.

Ancient Culture

A wealth of ancient civilizations left behind a fascinating spread of archaeological and cultural sites throughout Colombia. The one-time Tayrona capital, Ciudad Perdida, built between the 11th and 14th centuries, is one of South America's most mysterious ancient cities, arguably second only to Machu Picchu. Also shrouded in mystery is San Agustín, where more than 500 life-sized ancient sculptures of enigmatic origin dot the surrounding countryside. And then there's Tierradentro, where elaborate underground tombs scooped out by an unknown people add even more mystique to Colombia's past.

Colonial Charm

Led by Cartagena's extraordinarily well-preserved old city, Colombia offers an off-the-radar treasure trove of cinematic cobblestoned towns and villages that often feel bogged down in a different century, content to carry on as they have since the departure of the Spanish without a care in the world. Unweathered Barichara and happily sleepy Mompox feel like movie sets, impossibly unspoiled by modern progress; while whitewashed Villa de Leyva appears stuck in 16th-century quicksand – and these are just the villages that people *do* visit.

Why I Love Colombia

By Kevin Raub, Author

It was a much different country the first time I came to Colombia in the early 2000s, but the stellar hospitality of Colombians had me at arrival. Today, the security situation has improved dramatically, helping Colombia to become South America's phoenix from the flames. But that initial reception has always stuck with me: without a five-star tourism magnet – no Machu Picchu, no Iguazu Falls, no Patagonia – Colombia works harder for its money, and that begins and ends with the people, who ensure you leave with a different impression than the one you landed with.

For more about our authors, see page 352

Above: Cabo San Juan del Guía (p151), Parque Nacional Natural (PNN) Tayrona

Colombia

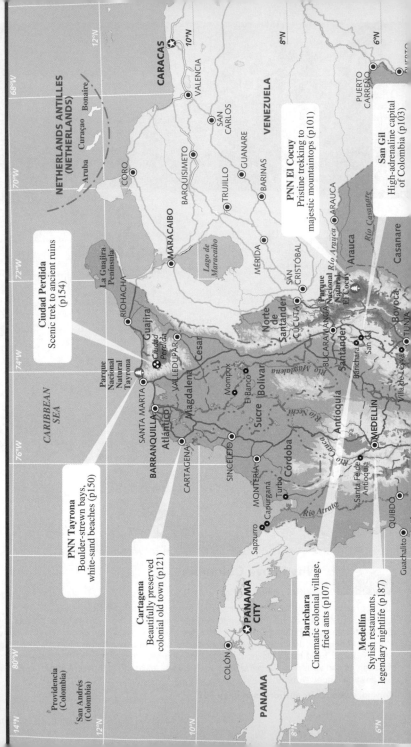

Ciudad Perdida
Scenic trek to ancient ruins (p154)

PNN Tayrona
Boulder-strewn bays, white-sand beaches (p150)

Cartagena
Beautifully preserved colonial old town (p121)

Barichara
Cinematic colonial village, fried ants (p107)

Medellín
Stylish restaurants, legendary nightlife (p187)

PNN El Cocuy
Pristine trekking to majestic mountaintops (p101)

San Gil
High-adrenaline capital of Colombia (p103)

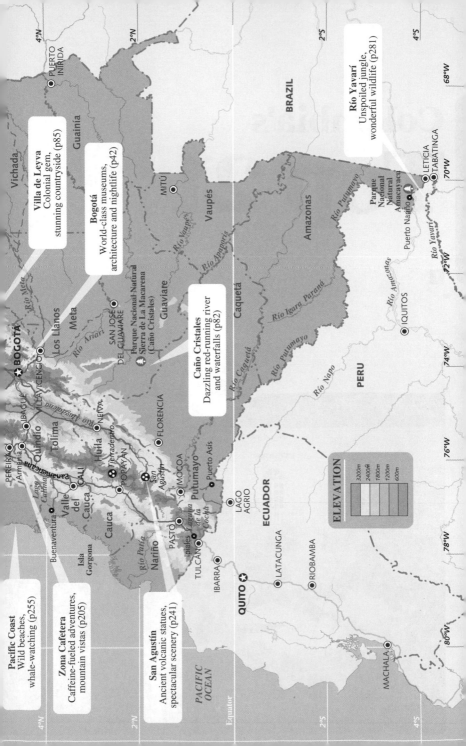

Villa de Leyva
Colonial gem, stunning countryside (p85)

Bogotá
World-class museums, architecture and nightlife (p42)

Caño Cristales
Dazzling red-running river and waterfalls (p82)

Río Yavarí
Unspoiled jungle, wonderful wildlife (p281)

Pacific Coast
Wild beaches, whale-watching (p255)

Zona Cafetera
Caffeine-fueled adventures, mountain vistas (p205)

San Agustín
Ancient volcanic statues, spectacular scenery (p241)

ELEVATION
3200m
2400m
1800m
1200m
600m

PUERTO INÍRIDA

Guainía

Vichada

MITÚ

Vaupés

BRAZIL

LETICIA
TABATINGA

Parque Nacional
Natural
Amacayacu

Puerto Nariño

Río Putumayo

Amazonas

Río Vaupés

Río Apaporis

Guaviare

Parque Nacional Natural
Sierra de La Macarena
(Caño Cristales)

SAN JOSÉ
DEL GUAVIARE

Río Ariari

Meta

Los Llanos

Río Meta

BOGOTÁ

IBAGUÉ
VILLAVICENCIO

Tolima

Quindío
ARMENIA

PEREIRA

Lago
Calima

Valle
del
Cauca

CALI

Buenaventura

Isla
Gorgona

PACIFIC
OCEAN

Río Patía

Cauca

Nariño

PASTO

Ipiales
TULCÁN
Laguna de la Cocha

IBARRA

QUITO

LATACUNGA

RIOBAMBA

ECUADOR

LAGO
AGRIO

Putumayo

MOCOA

Puerto Asís

Río Napo

Río Putumayo

Río Caquetá

Caquetá

Río Igara Paraná

PERU

IQUITOS

Río Amazonas

Río Yavarí

Huila

NEIVA

FLORENCIA

Tierradentro

POPAYÁN

San
Agustín

Panamericana

Río Magdalena

Río Cauca

Equator

Equator

MACHALA

Río Napo

2°N

4°N

2°N

4°N

2°S

4°S

2°S

4°S

Equator

68°W

70°W

72°W

74°W

76°W

78°W

80°W

Colombia's
Top 21

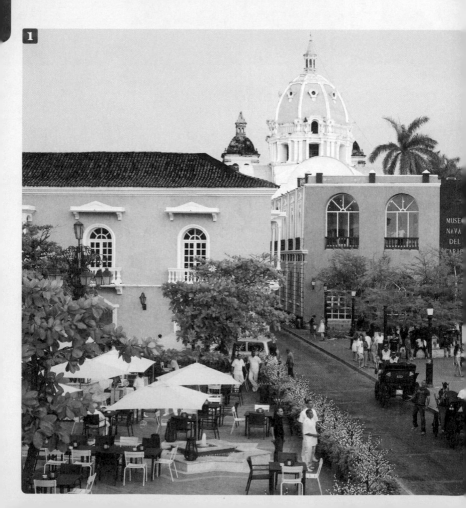

Cartagena's Old Town

1 The hands of the clock on the Puerta del Reloj wind back 400 years in an instant as visitors enter the walled old town of Cartagena (p124). Strolling the streets here is to step into the pages of a novel by Gabriel García Márquez. The pastel-toned balconies overflow with bougainvillea and the streets are abuzz with food stalls around magnificent Spanish-built churches, squares and historic mansions. This is a living, working town that just happens to look a lot like it did centuries ago.

Journey to Ciudad Perdida

2 The trip to Ciudad Perdida (p154) is a thrilling jungle walk through some of the country's most majestic tropical scenery. It has become renowned as one of Colombia's best multiday hikes. Surging rivers pump faster than your pulse can keep pace as you ford them, waist deep, against the otherwise quiet beauty of the Sierra Nevada. Your destination is awe-inspiring – an ancient lost city 'discovered' by graverobbers and gold-digging bandits deep in the mountains, laid out in mysterious, silent terraces – but it's as much about the journey itself.

GUIZIOU/FRANCK / HEMIS.FR / GETTY IMAGES ©

2

FELIPE MESA / AGESTOCK ©

La Guajira's Dunes & Deserts

3 Reaching this remote desert peninsula (p157) may be fun or arduous, depending on how you like to travel, but everyone who makes it to South America's most northerly point is blown away by the stunning simplicity of it all. Pink flamingos, mangrove swamps, sand-dune beaches and tiny Wayuu settlements dot the vast emptiness of this most magnificent and little-visited corner of Colombia. Come here to swap the noise of cities for the reverent silence of nature.

Trekking in El Cocuy

4 Parque Nacional Natural (PNN) El Cocuy (p101) is one of South America's most coveted stomping grounds – and for good reason. In season (December to February), everything throughout the region is characterized by burnt-auburn sunrises that bounce off craggy peaks and the glacial valleys, mountain plains, high-altitude lakes and rare vegetation of the *páramo* (high mountain plains) ecosystem. On clear days, entire swaths of Los Llanos can be seen before you from any number of surrounding 5000m-high peak viewpoints.

Caño Cristales

5 Held hostage by guerrillas for two decades, Caño Cristales (p82) is once again open for business. One of Colombia's most fascinating natural wonders, this gorgeous river canyon, flanked by the verdant jungle and mountainous terrain, explodes into an astonishing sea of red for a couple of months between July and November. This unique phenomenon is caused by an eruption of kaleidoscopic algae along the riverbed. Trekking between waterfalls and natural swimming pools is a fabulous experience.

The Museums of Bogotá

6 There are few places in the world where you can get a sense of what finding a long-lost buried treasure might be like. Bogotá's Museo del Oro (p49), one of South America's most astonishing museums, will floor you with a sensation of Indiana Jones proportions – and it's merely one of countless museums in the city. Whether you dig portly Boteros, presidential helicopters, cocaine-kingpin firearms, Bolivarian swords, exquisitely tiled bathrooms or broken vases, Bogotá has a museum for you. Above: Artifact, Museo del Oro

GEORGE HOLTON / GETTY IMAGES ©

Ancient Statues of San Agustín

7 Scattered throughout rolling green hills, the statues of San Agustín (p241) are a magnificent window into pre-Columbian culture and one of the most important archaeological sights on the continent. More than 500 of these monuments, carved from volcanic rock and depicting sacred animals and anthropomorphic figures, have been unearthed. Many statues are grouped together in an archaeological park, but many more are in situ, and can be explored on foot or by horseback along trails interspersed with waterfalls and steep canyons.

Pacific Coast Whale-Watching

8 There are few sights in nature as impressive as watching a 20-ton whale launch itself through the air against a backdrop of forest-covered mountains. Every year hundreds of humpback whales make a 8000km-plus journey from the Antarctic to give birth and raise young in Colombia's Pacific waters. These spectacular mammals come so close to shore in Ensenada de Utría (p261) that you can watch them cavorting in shallow waters from your breakfast table. To get even closer, sign up for a boat tour.

Salsa in Cali

9 Cali might not have invented salsa, but this hardworking city has taken the genre to its heart and made it its own. Going out in Cali (p226) is going out to dance salsa – it's how *caleños* express themselves. From the tiny barrio bars with oversized sound systems to the mega *salsatecas* (salsa dance clubs) of Juanchito, salsa helps to break down social barriers and unites this sprawling city. If you know how to dance, this is the place to show off your moves and, if not, there is nowhere better to learn.

Colonial Barichara

10 There is something immediately transcendent about stepping foot in stunning Barichara (p107), arguably Colombia's most picturesque colonial village: its rust-orange rooftops, symmetrically cobbled streets, whitewashed walls and pot-plant-adorned balconies contrast against a backdrop of postcard-perfect Andean green. Barichara is a slow-paced marvel – its name means 'place of relaxation' in the regional Guane dialect – and finding oneself wandering its streets in a sleepwalker's daze, blindsided by its beauty, wouldn't be unusual.

Fantasy Island: Providencia

11 It might be a little tricky to reach, but the effort pays off before you even land on this mountainous, jaw-droppingly beautiful slice of Caribbean fantasy: the view from the plane or cata-maran window is that good. With some of the best beaches in the country, superb diving possibilities, excellent hiking, wonderful cuisine and a unique English Creole to get your head around, Providencia (p180) is a little-explored, off-the-beaten path favorite, where you won't find a single all-inclusive resort.

10

11

Coffee Fincas in the Zona Cafetera

12 Jump in a classic WWII jeep and go on a caffeine-fueled coffee-tasting adventure. Many of the best *fincas* (farms) in the Zona Cafetera (p205) have thrown open their gates and embraced tourism – eager to show visitors what sets Colombian coffee apart and to share a little of their hardworking culture. Strap on a basket and head into the plantation to pick your own beans before returning to the traditional farmhouse to enjoy the end product.

Beaches of PNN Tayrona

13 The beaches at Parque Nacional Natural (PNN) Tayrona (p150) near Santa Marta on the Caribbean coast are among the country's most beautiful. Tayrona's limpid waters heave against a backdrop of jungle that sweeps like a leafy avalanche down from the soaring Sierra Nevada de Santa Marta, the world's highest coastal mountain range. The picturesque white-sand beaches are lined with palm trees and strewn with vast boulders, some cleaved in half, as if a giant has had a geological temper tantrum.

CHRISTIAN HEEB / GETTY IMAGES ©

DAMIAN TURSKI / GETTY IMAGES ©

Cañon de Río Claro

14 A majestic canyon carved in marble, the Reserva Natural Cañon de Río Claro (p205) is one of Colombia's top natural destinations and lies just 2km off the main Bogotá–Medellín highway. Through the middle runs a crystal-clear river, which forms numerous refreshing swimming holes. Fly along a zipline over the river; explore bat-filled caves; or go rafting. In the evening, as the setting sun paints the rocks in warm tones, flocks of birds spring to life and the canyon fills with the sounds of the jungle.

Colonial Villa de Leyva

15 Big, wide blue skies hover over the high-altitude valley that forms the backdrop of impressive Villa de Leyva (p85). Just 165km north of Bogotá, Villa is a sleepy colonial village, and has one of the largest and prettiest main squares in the Americas. Lazy Villa and its picturesque center are flush with international gastronomic pleasures, rich history, ancient churches, interesting museums and artisan shopping. You'll also find a wealth of low-key outdoor adventures in the surrounding countryside.

Hiking in PNN Los Nevados

16 The snow-covered peaks of Parque Nacional Natural (PNN) Los Nevados (p212) have long been revered by indigenous cultures and visitors alike. Covering a total of 583 sq km, the reserve is home to some of the most breathtaking stretches of the Colombian Andes. The southern reaches of the park offer fantastic trekking through diverse ecosystems ranging from humid cloud forests to rare *páramo*. Keen hikers can summit both Nevado Santa Isabel and Nevado del Tolima on one high-altitude adventure.

KIM SCHANDORFF / GETTY IMAGES ©

Wildlife Lodges on the Amazon

17 The sheer size of the Amazon is nearly incomprehensible to the average person – Colombia's portion alone is bigger than Germany – so it goes without saying there are many places to bed down on a once-in-a-lifetime trip. But those in the Parque Nacional Natural (PNN) Amacayacu (p279) and along the Río Yavarí are the best places to see the greatest variety of wildlife and ecosystems. Here you can swim with dolphins, fish for piranha and see alligators, monkeys and frogs up close. Above: Titi monkey

Outdoor Adventures in San Gil

18 San Gil (p103) isn't much to look at, but what it lacks in natural beauty, it more than makes up for in high-octane amusements. Peddle, paddle, rappel, spelunk, bungee or paraglide – whatever your preference, San Gil is Colombia's go-to outdoor-adventure playground, most famous for heart-stopping Classes IV and V rapids on the Río Suárez, but boasting a résumé far beyond white-water rafting. Get wet, get airborne, get your courage boots on – San Gil will test your limits.

Exploring Medellín

19 Get a bird's-eye view of life in the real Medellín (p187) as you soar in the city's award-winning metrocable system above working-class neighborhoods clinging precariously to steep mountainsides. The maze of haphazard red-brick abodes below is the beating heart of a city where difficult terrain is no obstacle to growth. After dark, check out the other end of the spectrum by visiting the chic restaurants, bars and clubs of El Poblado, the center of Medellín's legendary nightlife, popular with the city's well-heeled, fashionable crowd. Above: Medellín's Metrocable (p200)

Desierto de la Tatacoa

20 An otherworldly anomaly, the Desierto de la Tatacoa (p247) is a striking landscape of ocher and gray sands, sculptured cliffs and clumps of cacti. Surrounded by mountains, the semi-arid landscape sits in a rain shadow formed by the towering Nevado de Huila and is a silent, spiritual place with an ecosystem unlike any other in Colombia. The lack of cloud cover and light pollution make it the best place in the country for stargazing, either with the naked eye or at the local observatory.

The Páramos of Lago de Tota

21 Fewer than a handful of countries boast alpine tundra ecosystems formed by glaciers known as *páramo* – and Colombia hogs the majority. The area around sky-high Lago de Tota (p94) lays claim to one of the most rewarding hikes in Colombia: the Páramo de Ocetá is a 19km jaunt through landscapes of peat bogs, wet grasslands peppered with signature *frailejón* (yellow-flowering shrubs), colorful flowers, waterfalls, spectacular lagoons and a natural city made of stone. Some say it's the most beautiful moor on earth.

20

21

Need to Know

For more information, see Survival Guide (p307)

Currency
Colombian peso (COP$)

Language
Spanish (and English in San Andrés & Providencia)

Money
ATMs *(cajeros)* widely available in all cities and towns. Credit cards widely accepted in urban areas.

Visas
Not required for stays up to 90 days for citizens of the Americas, Australia, New Zealand, Japan, South Africa and most of Western Europe.

Cell Phones
Cell phone and 3G coverage is excellent. Most unlocked cell phones will work with a local SIM card.

Time
Colombia is five hours behind GMT. There is no daylight savings.

When to Go

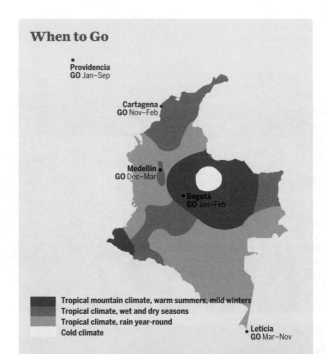

Providencia
GO Jan–Sep

Cartagena
GO Nov–Feb

Medellín
GO Dec–Mar

Bogotá
GO Jan–Feb

Leticia
GO Mar–Nov

Tropical mountain climate, warm summers, mild winters
Tropical climate, wet and dry seasons
Tropical climate, rain year-round
Cold climate

High Season
(Dec–Feb)

➡ Sunny skies and warmish days throughout the Andes

➡ Dry everywhere but the Amazon

➡ San Andrés and Providencia are gorgeous

➡ Prices countrywide are at their highest

Shoulder
(Mar–Sep)

➡ Bogotá, Medellín and Cali suffer a secondary rainy season in April/May

➡ Best whale-watching is July to October on the Pacific coast

➡ Cartagena shines through April, hard rains begin in May

Low Season
(Oct & Nov)

➡ Flash floods often wash out roads in the Andean region

➡ Cartagena and the Caribbean coast is disproportionally wet in October

➡ Low water levels in the Amazon means excellent hiking and white-sand beaches

➡ Prices everywhere are at their lowest

Useful Websites

This Is Colombia (www.colombia.co/en/) A superb website aimed at promoting Colombia to the world.

Proexport Colombia (www.colombia.travel) The official government tourism portal.

Colombia Reports (www.colombiareports.co) Top English-language news source.

BBC News (www.bbc.com/news/world/latin_america/) The Beeb has excellent South American coverage.

Parques Nacionales Naturales de Colombia (www.parquesnacionales.gov.co, in Spanish) Detailed parks information.

Lonely Planet (www.lonelyplanet.com/Colombia) Information, forums, hotel bookings and online shopping.

Important Numbers

Country code	✆57
International access code	✆00
Directory assistance	✆113
Ambulance	✆125
Fire & police	✆123

Exchange Rates

Australia	A$1	COP$1909
Brazil	R$1	COP$818
Canada	C$1	COP$2023
Euro Zone	€1	COP$2657
Japan	¥100	COP$2077
New Zealand	NZ$1	COP$1896
UK	£1	COP$3691
USA	US$1	COP$2481

For current exchange rates see www.xe.com

Daily Costs

Budget:
Less than COP$50,000

➜ Dorm bed COP$18,000–25,000

➜ *Comida corriente* (set meal) COP$5000–12,000

➜ Self-catering in supermarkets

Midrange:
COP$100,000–200,000

➜ Double room in midrange hotel COP$70,000–100,000

➜ Mains in decent local restaurant COP$20,000–30,000

Top end:
More than COP$200,000

➜ Double room in a top-end hotel from COP$160,000

➜ Multicourse meal with wine from COP$50,000

Opening Hours

Opening hours vary enormously. Unless stated otherwise in reviews, the following are open at these times:

Banks 9am–4pm Monday to Friday, 9am–noon Saturday

Restaurants noon–3pm and 7pm–10pm

Cafes 8am–8pm

Bars 6pm–3am

Clubs 9pm–3am

Shops 9am–5pm Monday to Saturday

Arriving in Colombia

Aeropuerto Internacional El Dorado (Bogotá; p76) Buses (COP$1400–1700) run every 10 minutes, 4am to 11pm. Taxis (COP$25,000–37,000) take 45 minutes to the center.

Aeropuerto Internacional José María Córdoba (Medellín; p199) Buses (COP$8600) run every 15 minutes, 5am to 9pm. Taxis (COP$60,000) take 45 minutes to the city

Aeropuerto Internacional Rafael Núñez (Cartagena; p138) Buses (COP$2000) run every 15 minutes, 6:50am to 11:45pm. Taxis (COP$9000-12,000) take 15 minutes to the old town.

Getting Around

Transport in Colombia is cheap, though prices rise quickly if you want to travel in comfort.

Air The easiest (and most expensive) way to cover the huge distances between big cities. Air travel has become more accessible lately with the advent of budget airlines, and booking in advance can make it a very reasonable way to travel. Nearly all cities have airports, as well as many smaller, more remote towns.

Bus The main way to get around Colombia, buses range from tightly packed *colectivos* (shared minibuses or taxis) to comfortable air-conditioned long-distance buses, and connect most towns in the country.

Car Useful for traveling at your own pace, or for visiting regions with minimal public transport. Cars can be hired in major cities, but it's generally not cheap. Driving is on the right.

For much more on **getting around**, see p324

If You Like...

National Parks

Colombia has carved out 12% of its national territory for its Natural National Park (Parques Nacionales Naturales; PNN) system, which includes almost 60 protected areas covering cool Caribbean waters, soaring Andean peaks, tropical grasslands and expansive Amazon jungle.

PNN Tayrona One of Colombia's most popular parks; palm-lined white-sand beaches at the foot of the Sierra Nevada de Santa Marta mountains .(p150)

PNN El Cocuy Commanding peaks, mountain lakes, icy glaciers and views to Venezuela highlight Colombia's best high-altitude jaunts. (p101)

PNN Sierra de La Macarena A former guerilla stronghold, the now-accessible PNN Sierra de La Macarena is home to the unique Caño Cristales. (p82)

Santuario de Iguaque Steeped in Muisca legend, this 67.5-sq-km national park is easily reached from Villa de Leyva and offers beautiful *páramo* (high-mountain plateau landscapes. (p93)

PNN El Tuparro Off the beaten path in the Los Llanos nature reserve, boasting sandy river beaches, green grasslands and some 320 bird species, plus jaguars, tapirs and otters. (p82)

Museums

A fascinating clash of indigenous culture, colonization and conflict means Colombia has a wealth of history to cull for its plethora of museums. Bogotá is Colombia's museum epicenter with more than 60 venues.

Museo del Oro One of South America's most extraordinary museums; home to the biggest collection of pre-Hispanic gold work in the world. (p49)

Museo de Antioquia Along with Bogotá's Museo Botero, this is one of Colombia's best museums to admire the portly works of *paisa* Fernando Botero. (p191)

Museo Nacional Housed in a building in the shape of a Greek cross, designed as a prison by an English architect, Colombia's national museum offers an exhaustive look at the nation's heritage. (p53)

Palacio de la Inquisición Call it macabre, but the frightening instruments of torture on display at this 1776 Cartagena palace will have little trouble commanding your attention. (p124)

Wildlife

Pristine Amazon jungle accounts for more than a third of Colombia's total area – it's the best spot to observe wildlife in its natural habitat. But along with the jungle, there are many interesting opportunities throughout Colombia, one of the world's most biodiverse nations.

Río Yavarí Technically straddling Brazil and Peru, the lodges along this Amazon tributary, reached from Leticia, are surrounded by abundant fauna. (p281)

PNN Amacayacu Home to 500 bird species and 150 mammals, including a brilliant outpost of rehabilitating monkeys, deep in the Amazon rainforest. (p279)

PNN Ensenada de Utría This is whale-watching central on Colombia's Pacific coast, a pre-served inlet visited by humpbacks from July to October. (p261)

Reserva Ecológica Río Blanco You'll find 13 of Colombia's endemic bird species in this undeveloped bird-watchers' paradise near Manizales – and 362 other species to boot. (p210)

Santuario de Flora y Fauna Los Flamencos A vibrant colony of pink flamingos descends on this 700-hectare nature reserve in La Guajira Peninsula – some 10,000 in the wet season. (p158)

Top: Jaguar, Leticia (p271)
Bottom: Capurganá and Sapzurro (p166)

Hiking

Colombia's varied terrain has some of the world's most stunning hikes. You'll find jungle terrain, sky-high mountains and snowcapped Andean peaks, including the abundant *páramo*, a rarity found in just a handful of countries.

PNN El Cocuy Commanding peaks, mountain lakes, icy glaciers and views to Venezuela highlight this week-long, high-altitude jaunt. (p101)

Ciudad Perdida A chance to make a multiday jungle trek across surging rivers to one of the largest pre-Columbian cities discovered in the Americas. (p154)

PNN Los Nevados Hike through the *páramo* to the glacier at the summit of Nevado Santa Isabel in a challenging one-day trek. (p212)

Valle de Cocora Gawk at giant wax palms (Colombia's national tree) strewn about verdant valleys and misty green hills on this half-day hike. (p223)

Tierradentro Take in all of Tierradentro's pre-Columbian underground tombs surrounded by gorgeous hillsides on this full-day hike. (p245)

Memorable Food

Colombian gastronomy won't satiate foodies in the way of Peru's famed cuisine, Brazil's multicultural fare or Argentina's gaucho grill culture, but there is amazingly fresh seafood here, succulent steaks and no shortage of unique culinary curiosities.

Leo Cocina y Cava Take a fine-dining trip through creative Colombian cuisine via a tasting menu at this fiercely local top-end treat in Bogotá. (p64)

Punta Gallinas No restaurants, but how does fresh lobster grilled by the Wayuu people sound? (p160)

Mini-Mal Culinary introspection at its finest: the country's most interesting regional ingredients form gourmet goodness at this Bogotá trendsetter. (p65)

Central Cevicheria This Bogotá hipster hangout serves some of the most innovative ceviche in Colombia. (p66)

Asadero de Cuyes Pinzón Throw yourself mouth-first into Pasto culture by dining on the local delicacy: grilled guinea pig. (p251)

Mercagán Some say it's the nation's best steak. (p113)

La Cevicheria This is Cartagena's tiny, hidden gem serving world-renowned ceviche and seafood. (p133)

Beaches

Colombia is more famous for mountains than beaches, but as the country is blessed with both Caribbean and Pacific coasts, sun-toasted stretches of sand are never more than an overnight bus or quick flight away.

Playa Taroa Slide down a towering sand dune onto Colombia's most beautiful – and emptiest – beach in Punta Gallinas. (p160)

Capurganá & Sapzurro La Miel, on the Panamanian side, and Colombia's Playa Soledad are palm-strewn patches of paradise straddling the border. (p166)

Playa Morromico Flanked by waterfalls crashing down from jungle-covered mountains, this secluded private beach is one of Chocó's most romantic destinations. (p264)

PNN Tayrona Preserved and very popular, this national park has serene golden-sand bays and cerulean waters. (p150)

Playa Guachalito This is one of the Pacific coast's most idyllic beaches, flush with orchids, heliconias and wild jungle encroaching its gray sands. (p264)

Playa Blanca A novel 3015m-high white-sand lakeside beach deep in the Andes. (p95)

Month by Month

January

Colombia's equatorial position means temperatures fluctuate by altitude, not season, so almost anytime is a good time to visit. January could be considered ideal for its dissipating holiday crowds coupled with lingering festivals and parties.

✺ Carnaval de Blancos y Negros

Pasto's uproarious post-Christmas bash, originating during slavery times, sees drunken crowds throwing grease, talcum powder, flour and chalk on each other until everyone is coughing up powdery mucus and doused in gunk. Leave the *haute couture* at the hotel. (p251)

February

The Andean region remains pleasant and Cartagena almost drought-stricken, making February a great time to beach-hop along the Caribbean coast. With kids back in school and domestic merrymakers returned to the grind, Colombia is *tranquilo*.

✺ Fiesta de Nuestra Señora de la Candelaria

A solemn procession is held in Cartagena on 2 February to honor the town's patron saint at the Convento de la Popa, during which the faithful carry lit candles. Celebrations begin nine days earlier, the so-called Novenas, when pilgrims flock to the convent.

✺ Carnaval de Barranquilla

Held 40 days before Easter, Barranquilla's Carnaval is the continent's second-biggest after Rio de Janeiro. A spectacular four-day bash of drinking, dancing, parades, costumes and Colombian music concludes on Mardi Gras with the symbolic burial of 'festival icon' Joselito Carnaval. (p141)

March

As with most Catholic countries, Easter is big business. Whether it falls in March or April, the country is seriously tuned in. Expect crowds, high prices and weather taking a turn for the worse.

✺ Semana Santa in Popayán

The most famous Semana Santa (Holy Week) celebration is held in Popayán, with nighttime processions on Maundy Thursday and Good Friday. Thousands of the faithful and tourists take part in this religious ceremony and the accompanying festival of religious music.

✺ Semana Santa in Mompox

Colombia's second-most important Semana Santa celebration is in the sleepy river town of Mompox, near the Caribbean coast.

☆ Festival Iberoamericano de Teatro

Held during Semana Santa, this biennial festival of Latin American theater takes place every even-numbered year, and ends with a fireworks spectacular in

Bogotá's football stadium. Check out www.festival deteatro.com.co for more information.

June

After a respite in April and May, storm clouds once again loom. Bogotá is at its driest, though, and humpback whales begin arriving on the Pacific coast. Prices rise for summer school vacations.

☉ A Whalin' Good Time

June marks the beginning of the spectacular whale-watching season (p255) on Colombia's Pacific coast, when hundreds of humpback whales arrive from Antarctica, some 8500km away, to give birth and raise their young in Colombia's tropical waters. (p255)

August

Relatively mild August can be drizzly, but excellent festivals more than make up for impending rains. Bogotá, Cali and Medellín all soak up the end-of-summer atmosphere with a bonanza of music and culture.

☆ Festival de Música del Pacífico Petronio Álvarez

This Cali festival celebrates the music of the Pacific coast, which is heavily influenced by African rhythms introduced to Colombia by the slaves who originally populated the region. (p227)

🎇 Feria de las Flores

This week-long feria is Medellín's most spectacular event. The highlight is the Desfile de Silleteros, when up to 400 campesinos (peasants) come down from the mountains and parade along the streets carrying flowers on their backs. (p192)

September

Showers hit most of the country, but Amazonian river levels are low, making it an excellent time for wildlife viewing, hiking or just kicking-back on a sandy river beach.

☆ Festival Mundial de Salsa

Don't miss this classic Cali festival. Despite the name, it's not really a worldwide festival, but you'll see some amazing dancers, and there are often free salsa shows at the outdoor amphitheater, Teatro al Aire Libre Los Cristales. (p227)

🍴 Congreso Nacional Gastrónomico

Every year top chefs from different countries are invited to cook up a storm in tiny colonial Popayán for the gastro-fueled Congreso Nacional Gastronómico. Jump online to see what's on the menu. (p236)

☆ Jazz Festival

Jazz aficionados get psyched for the annual Festival Internacional Mede Jazz (http://festivalmedejazz.com), which often features prominent musicians from North America, Europe and Cuba. Concerts

usually take place at Teatro Universidad and El Tesoro shopping mall, and some of them are free.

☆ Festival Internacional de Teatro

Held since 1968, Manizales' theater festival is Colombia's second-most important theater festival (after Bogotá's Festival Iberoamericano de Teatro). It features free shows in Plaza de Bolívar. (p207)

October

On average, October is one of Colombia's rainiest months. Bogotá, Cali, Medellín and Cartagena are all at the mercy of the weather.

☆ Festival de Cine de Bogotá

With a 20-year history, the city's film festival attracts films from all around the world, including a usually strong Latin American selection. Check out www.bogocine.com for info and year-by-year selections.

☆ Mompox Jazz Festival

This relatively new festival began in 2012 and has helped attract visitors to Mompox, a beautiful but remote colonial town in northern Colombia. Its program includes international jazz performers, and the festival even attracted the Colombian president in 2014.

☆ Rock al Parque

Three days of rock, metal, pop, funk and reggae bands rocking out at Parque

Simón Bolívar in Bogotá. Rock al Parque is free and swarming with fans – it's now Colombia's biggest music festival. Did we mention it's *free*? (p58)

November

November is wet, wet, wet throughout Colombia. Your best refuge from the deluge is Bogotá, but you'll still be breaking out the umbrella regularly.

🎇 Concurso Nacional de Belleza

Also known as the Carnaval de Cartagena or Fiestas del 11 de Noviembre, this beauty pageant and festival, Cartagena's most important annual bash, celebrates the city's independence day and the crowning of Miss Colombia. Festivities include street dancing, music and fancy-dress parades. (p130)

Top: Desfile de Silleteros, Feria de las Flores
Bottom: Alumbrado Navideño (Christmas Lighting), Medellín

December

The rains begin to recede and the country is awash instead in holiday festivals, spectacular light displays and spur-of-the-moment partying. Expect crowds and cries of joy throughout Colombia.

🎇 Christmas Lighting

Every Christmas, Colombian cities compete in the annual Alumbrado Navideño (Christmas Lighting) to see who can put up the most elaborate lighting display along their respective rivers – Medellín's colorful display often wins and is well worth a detour.

Itineraries

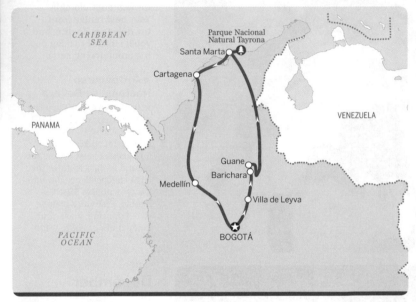

 Bogotá to Bogotá

Welcome to Colombia! Cosmopolitan cities, looming mountains, colonial villages, verdant jungles and Caribbean beaches await. Pulling off this itinerary requires fifth gear and copious amounts of caffeine – good thing you're in the land of coffee!

Take a day or two in **Bogotá**, admiring La Candelaria (its colonial center), the best of myriad museums, and world-class food and nightlife. Shake off the hangover a few hours north in the calming colonial villages of **Villa de Leyva** and **Barichara**, both miraculously preserved and picturesque. Take a day to walk the historic El Camino Real to **Guane**. Bus to San Gil to pick up the long bus ride to **Santa Marta**, from where you can access **Parque Nacional Natural (PNN) Tayrona** – linger on the park's otherworldly beaches for a few days. Continue southwest along the Caribbean coast to **Cartagena**, Colombia's crown jewel – a postcard-perfect old city chock full of colonial romance. It's another long bus ride (or a quicker flight) to **Medellín**, where again you're faced with Colombia on overdrive: culture, cuisine and Club Colombia, *paisa*-style. Raise a toast to El Dorado and exit via Bogotá, bowled-over by Colombia's hospitality.

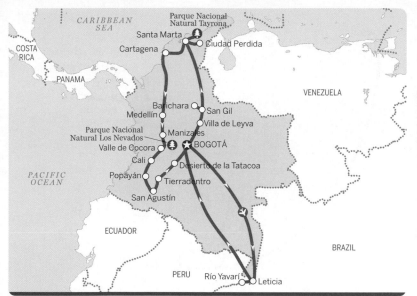

 The See-(Almost)-Everything Route

The beauty of Colombia's diverse landscapes is that you can choose to fully immerse yourself in just one – Caribbean beaches, wildlife-rich jungle or soaring Andean highlands – or you can go for the full monty! Hit the ground running with three or four days in **Bogotá**, Colombia's Gotham, and don't miss its Museo del Oro, one of the continent's most fascinating museums, and the city's atmospheric colonial center, La Candelaria. From there head north to **Villa de Leyva**. Explore its cobbled streets and enjoy some colonial charm for a day or two, then visit **San Gil** for hiking and rafting, making time for nearby historic **Barichara**. Pass through Bucaramanga to catch a long-haul bus to **Santa Marta**. It's worth moving quicker than normal up to this point in order to free up some time for the sweaty, multiday trek to **Ciudad Perdida** or blissing-out for a day or two in the beach-riddled Parque Nacional Natural (PNN) Tayrona, Colombia's most popular national park. Next stop, **Cartagena** – you'll need a few days to fully indulge this exquisite colonial city.

From the Caribbean, take a bus or fly south to spend a week exploring **Medellín** and the Zona Cafetera. Enjoy some time in the nature reserves around **Manizales** before testing your fitness among the spectacular peaks of **PNN Los Nevados**. Next stop, the breathtaking **Valle de Cocora** outside Salento. Want to take a piece of Colombia home with you? Visit a coffee *finca* (farm) near Armenia and stock up on single-origin coffee beans direct from the source.

Spend the night in **Cali** to experience the city's hopping salsa joints. Travel down through colonial **Popayán** to the archaeological ruins at **San Agustín** and **Tierradentro**, two of the country's most important pre-Columbian sites worth a few days. Return to Bogotá via the startling **Desierto de la Tatacoa** and catch a flight to **Leticia**, where a wildly different Colombia exists. Spend a few days exploring the three Amazonian ecosystems: *terra firme* (dry), *várzea* (semi-flooded) and *igapó* (flooded) along the **Río Yavarí**, the best spot in Amazonia to observe wildlife in its natural habitat. Fly back to Bogotá, or, from Tabatinga across the Brazilian border from Leticia, head deeper into the Amazon via adventurous river-boat rides to Manaus (Brazil) or Iquitos (Peru).

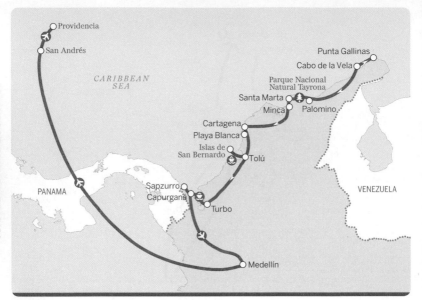

3 WEEKS Complete Caribbean

This is the ultimate beach adventure; Colombia's northern coast and islands serve up slices of luminous Caribbean waters backed by an astonishing variety of landscapes.

Start out east of Santa Marta with a few days at **Cabo de la Vela** on La Guajira Peninsula, a striking panorama where the desert meets the sea at the top of the continent. Don't skip South America's northernmost tip, **Punta Gallinas**, where you can sleep in a hammock and feast on local lobster near towering dunes somersaulting into remote beaches.

Heading southwest, make your way to lovely **Palomino**, where you'll find a crystal clear river running down from the majestic Sierra Nevada to a wild palm-studded beach. A short drive away is **Parque Nacional Natural (PNN) Tayrona**, very popular among aspiring beach bums. Giant boulders frame pretty coves and you can ride horses through the jungle to the ruins of a pre-Hispanic settlement. Spend a couple of days, then pass through **Santa Marta** and take a break from the heat with an overnight side-trip to the charming mountain town of **Minca**.

Next spend a leisurely couple of days exploring the colonial splendor of **Cartagena** before getting your tanning plans back on track with a trip to **Playa Blanca**. Hit the road again and make your way to **Tolú**, where you can take a trip in the mangroves before boarding a boat to the **Islas de San Bernardo** for three days of white sands, crystalline waters and tiny fishing communities.

Suitably relaxed, make the arduous journey southwest via Turbo to spend a few days in **Capurganá** and **Sapzurro**, two cute beachside neighbors surrounded by jungle right on the border with Panama, which offer excellent diving.

If you're hungry for more, take a flight via **Medellín** to **San Andrés** to experience Raizal culture with its British Caribbean roots. The next day, head over to **Providencia** to soak up the tranquillity and reflect on your journey, while reclining beside some of Colombia's most idyllic stretches of sand.

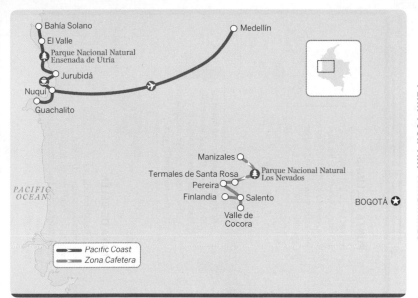

Pacific Coast
Zona Cafetera

 ## 2 WEEKS Zona Cafetera

In this arabica-fueled region, hearts are pumped with caffeine as much as blood. Visiting coffee farms will keep you hyped for exploring the region's highlights. Start by spending a few days in the nature parks around **Manizales** – Los Yarumos, Recinto del Pensamiento and Reserva Ecológica Río Blanco, the latter a bird-watching favorite. Indulge in a coffee tour just outside town at Hacienda Venecia, for an excellent overview of all things coffee. Return to Manizales to organize a hiking trip among snow-covered volcanic peaks in **Parque Nacional Natural (PNN) Los Nevados**. Spend a night in the *páramo* (high-mountain plains) beside the mystical Laguna de Otún before heading down the mountain to **Termales de Santa Rosa** to reinvigorate tired muscles. Suitably revitalized, pass through **Pereira** to spend four days in coffee-crazy **Salento**, full of quaint charm and typical *bahareque* (adobe and reed) architecture. Take a classic jeep up to the impressive **Valle de Cocora**, one of Colombia's most beautiful half-day hikes. Finally, make the short trip across the highway for a couple of days in slow-paced **Filandia** and toast your tour from its towering *mirador* (lookout), which offers some of the best views in coffee country.

 ## 10 DAYS Pacific Coast

Colombia's ultimate off-the-beaten-path destination boasts tropical jungle, diving, whale-watching, world-class sportfishing and black-sand beaches. It isn't cheap – all transportation is by small plane and boat – but it's worth it. Start by flying in for a couple of days at **Bahía Solano**, where you can get used to the pace of El Chocó while lounging in a hammock at Punta Huína. After a spot of diving or a jungle trek, take a taxi south for a night in **El Valle**, where in nesting season you can observe turtles laying eggs and swim beneath a thundering waterfall. Hike south to **Parque Nacional Natural (PNN) Ensenada de Utría** and take a row boat to the visitor center, where you can spend the night. During whale season you can spot the magnificent mammals playing in the inlet.

Next hire a boat to take you to the friendly village of **Jurubidá** and visit the thermal pools hidden in the jungle. Yet another boat will take you to **Nuquí** for an overnight stay. From here you can pick up transport to **Guachalito**, a top-class beach with several comfortable eco-lodges. After three days, return to Nuquí to take a quick flight back to Medellín.

Colombia: Off the Beaten Track

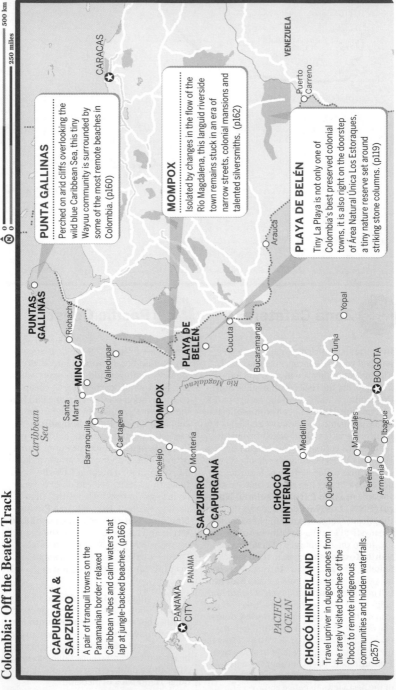

CAPURGANÁ & SAPZURRO

A pair of tranquil towns on the Panamanian border: relaxed Caribbean vibes and calm waters that lap at jungle-backed beaches. (p166)

CHOCÓ HINTERLAND

Travel upriver in dugout canoes from the rarely visited beaches of the Chocó to remote indigenous communities and hidden waterfalls. (p257)

PUNTA GALLINAS

Perched on arid cliffs overlooking the wild blue Caribbean Sea, this tiny Wayuu community is surrounded by some of the most remote beaches in Colombia. (p160)

MOMPOX

Isolated by changes in the flow of the Río Magdalena, this languid riverside town remains stuck in an era of narrow streets, colonial mansions and talented silversmiths. (p162)

PLAYA DE BELÉN

Tiny La Playa is not only one of Colombia's best preserved colonial towns, it is also right on the doorstep of Área Natural Única Los Estoraques, a tiny nature reserve set around striking stone columns. (p119)

DESIERTO DE LA TATACOA

Hike around the striking barren landscapes, checking out fossils and towering cacti before indulging in a spot of stargazing in the evening. (p247)

MACIZO COLOMBIANO

Travel among the misty peaks and *paramó*-covered plateaus of this remote region straddling Cauca and Huila that is the birthplace of three great rivers. (p242)

SAN CIPRIANO

The only way in or out of this isolated Afro-Colombian town in the jungle is on one of the motorcycle-powered wooden carts that speed along the old railway line. (p268)

MOCOA

Entrance point to the Putumayo, a natural wonderland sandwiched between the Andes and the Amazon that is covered in dense forest punctuated by roaring waterfalls and isolated swimming holes. (p244)

Obando

BRAZIL

Río Amazonas

Leticia

Mitú

San José del Guaviare

Villavicencio

DESIERTO DE LA TATACOA

Río Caquetá

Río Magdalena

SAN CIPRIANO

Cali

Neiva

Silvia

Popayán

MACIZO COLOMBIANO

Florencia

MOCOA

PERU

QUITO

ECUADOR

Plan Your Trip

Colombia Outdoors

Exploring Colombia's dramatic landscapes, from glacier-topped peaks to lowland jungles, is a highlight of any visit. Discover the best ways to experience these natural wonders to the fullest, whether on foot, in the water or soaring on thermal winds.

Best Treks

Ciudad Perdida (p154) The most popular trek: a four- to six-day, 44km-long walk through jungle to the remarkably preserved ruins of the lost city of Tayrona.

Parque Nacional Natural (PNN) El Cocuy (p101) Best high-altitude trek: the four-day Paso del Conejo circuit will take your breath away in more ways than one as you pass through high-mountain plains surrounded by towering snow-covered peaks and icy glacier lakes.

Valle de Cocora (p223) The best half-day trek: the towering wax palm (the world's tallest palm, and Colombia's national tree) juts through misty green hills on this hike in coffee country.

Best Diving

San Andrés & Providencia (p178) A 35km reef in warm Caribbean waters is home to spectacular colored corals, large pelagic fish, portly eels and long-lost shipwrecks.

Best White-Water Rafting

Río Suárez (p105) Near San Gil, Classes IV and V rapids await on the country's wildest river.

Hiking & Trekking

Colombia has some of South America's best trekking opportunities. The casual hiker looking for good one-day walks also has many options to choose from – most of which, such as Laguna Verde and Valle de Cocora, can be done independently without a guide. Guided day-hike prices range from COP$40,000 to COP$80,000. For multiday treks expect to pay COP$100,000 to COP$150,000 per day, depending on the difficulty and the guide's experience. The best times of year for a walk are February on the coast, and December to February in the mountains.

Where to Go

Ciudad Perdida On the Caribbean coast; this long trek involves a sweaty, multiday hike through the jungle and across waist-high rivers. At the end you arrive at the long-forgotten ruins of the Tayrona civilization.

Parque Nacional Natural (PNN) El Cocuy With at least 12 peaks above 5000m and phenomenal high-altitude landscapes, this national park offers rich rewards for intrepid trekkers. Those with the lungs for it should not miss a trek here.

Parque Nacional Natural (PNN) Tayrona Offers accessible short hikes through tropical dry forest with the opportunity to eat, drink and swim along the way.

Valle de Cocora Near Salento; the country's best half-day hike takes you up into the national park amid wax palms.

Tierradentro A spectacular one-day walk in the south that traverses a triangular ridgeline and visits all of the nearby tombs.

Volcán Puracé Near Popayán; can be summited in one day (weather permitting).

Parque Nacional Natural (PNN) Farallones de Cali Near Cali; offers a day-long hike to the summit of Pico de Loro.

Laguna Verde Between Pasto and Ipiales; this five-hour hike takes you to a stunning green lake hidden in the crater of a rugged volcano.

ORGANIZED ADVENTURES

If you fancy joining up with local outdoor enthusiasts while exploring Colombia, check out the following nonprofit organizations that arrange group excursions into the countryside.

Sal Si Puedes (p54) Runs weekend walks in rural areas around Bogotá.

Ecoaventura (⌨300-645-0232; www. ecoaventura.org) ✆ This organization from Cali offers a variety of outdoor activities all over southern Colombia including night hikes and abseiling trips.

Diving & Snorkeling

Colombia's Caribbean coast offers clear waters and bright coral formations, while the Pacific region offers close encounters with large marine animals.

On the Caribbean coast you'll find diving at budget prices with two tank dives starting from around COP$175,000. Prices in the Pacific tend to be significantly higher.

Where to Go

San Andrés & Providencia Classic Caribbean diving, with excellent visibility, fine coral reefs and a variety of marine life. There are even two sunken ships you can visit. The snorkeling is also top-notch with a lot of marine life in shallow waters.

Taganga On the Caribbean coast, Taganga offers some of the cheapest diving courses on the planet. Here you can get your PADI or NAUI certification from around COP$590,000 for a four-day course. The diving itself is second-rate, but at these prices, it's hard to complain.

Cartagena Boasts good diving around Bocachica, Tierrabomba and Punta Arena.

Islas del Rosario Famous for its diving and snorkeling, although warm-water currents have somewhat damaged the reef.

Capurganá and Sapzurro These small Pacific-coast towns are just minutes from the Panamanian border and offer good diving in clear Caribbean waters.

Isla Malpelo A small Pacific island 500km west of the continent that's home to schools of more than a thousand sharks. It can only be reached by joining a minimum eight-day live-aboard dive cruise from Buenaventura, on Colombia's Pacific coast, or Panama.

Playa Huína There are some diving opportunities near Bahía Solano, where a warship that survived Pearl Harbor has been sunk to create an artificial reef.

Hyperbaric Chambers

There are several hyperbaric chambers around the country – including at the Hospital Naval (p136) in Cartagena – should you experience decompression sickness (ie 'the bends').

At the time of research the government had just committed to installing new facilities in Taganga, Providencia, San Andrés and Bahía Solano to improve access for leisure divers.

In an emergency, your first response should be to contact local emergency services (⌨123) who will stabilize the diver and help to locate the nearest treatment facility. For additional advice contact the **Divers Alert Network** (⌨emergency hotline in US +1-919-684-9111; www.diversalertnetwork. org).

White-Water Rafting, Canoeing & Kayaking

Rafting trips cost from COP$30,000 to COP$180,000 depending on length and adrenaline-level.

Canoeing and kayaking aren't especially popular in Colombia, but opportunities are growing. Experienced paddlers can rent kayaks in both San Gil and San Agustín for white-water runs. In Ladrilleros, you can rent sea kayaks for a paddle around Bahía Malága. For some high-altitude paddling, rent a kayak in Guatape to explore its extensive artificial lake.

Where to Go

Top rafting spots include the following:

San Gil This is the white-water rafting capital. The Río Fonce is fairly leisurely while the Río Suarez offers some serious thrills on Classes IV and V rapids.

San Agustín A close second to San Gil. Here you can go white-water rafting on the Río Magdalena, one of Colombia's most important rivers. There are easy Class II and III trips, and longer, more difficult trips for experienced rafters.

Río Claro Offers a quiet paddle through the jungle with some minor Class I rapids. It's a fine spot to admire the flora and fauna instead of obsessing about falling out of the raft.

Río Buey and Río San Juan Wild water and great mountain vistas outside Medellín.

BIRD-WATCHING IN COLOMBIA

Clocking in at 1903 bird species (the number so far recorded; new species are still being discovered), Colombia is the world's number-one country in bird diversity and easily holds its own against Peru and Brazil in endemic species. The Andean mountains are full of hummingbirds (more than 160 species); the Amazonian jungle is full of toucans, parrots and macaws; and Parque Nacional Natural (PNN) Puracé, near Popayán, is home to condors, which the wardens will tempt down with food so you can see them up close. The Pacific coast is flooded with swarms of pelicans, herons and other water birds.

Some 70% of the country's birds live in the Andean cloud forest, one of the world's most endangered ecosystems. The single-best bird-watching spot in the country is Montezuma Peak, located inside Parque Nacional Natural (PNN) Tatamá in the Cordillera Occidental between the departments of Chocó, Valle del Cauca and Risaralda. Here you'll find the best mix of Chocó and Andean birds in the country; it's packed with endemics, regional specialties and mega-rare birds. Access to the park itself is often restricted; fortunately nearby Planes de San Rafael is a reliable alternative.

Other great bets include Reserva Ecológica Río Blanco near Manizales, and Km18 near Cali. The Amazon basin near Leticia is also an excellent spot for jungle birds, as is the Chocó. Colombia also features the western third of the Los Llanos area, shared by Venezuela, and it's a fine spot to see the diverse mix of birds this region attracts.

ProAves (☏1-340-3229; www.proaves.org) is a Colombian nonprofit organization dedicated to preserving vital bird habitat. It runs a number of private reserves in Important Bird Areas (IBAs) around the country. For more details on IBAs, check out the Red Nacional de Observadores de Aves (www.rnoa.org).

Finding bird-watching guides in Colombia can be difficult. In many remote areas, locals can take you where they know birds are, but it'll be up to you to find them. For Andean bird-watching, you may be able to find a guide through Mapalina (www.mapalina.com), a nonprofit initiative based in Cali.

One reputable bird-watching tour company is **Colombia Birding** (☏314-896-3151; www.colombiabirding.com), run by a bilingual Colombian whose network of local guides can show you around many of the country's most popular bird-watching areas. It charges US$100 per day plus expenses. Its website has information on birds by region.

Robin Restall's *Birds of Northern South America* (2007) is the essential bird-watcher's field guide to Colombian birds, with full-color plates for every bird you're likely to see. For online information, check out Colombia's official tourism portal, www.colombia.travel, which does a surprisingly good job with bird-watching.

San Andrés (p172)

Rock Climbing & Abseiling

The birthplace of Colombian rock climbing is Suesca, a quick day trip from Bogotá. You'll find 4km-long sandstone Guadalupe formations and more than 400 climbing routes, both traditional and bolted. Suesca-based DeAlturas (p79) offers five-day climbing courses for COP$500,000, or day climbing (including equipment) for COP$120,000. In Medellín, Psiconautica (p192) runs a rock-climbing/ abseiling/canyoning school as well.

If you want to test your skills before committing to a full-on rock-climbing adventure, Gran Pared (p54), in Bogotá, offers a challenging climbing wall where you can get a feel for the sport.

Canopying

Sometimes called 'ziplines' in North America, canopying involves strapping yourself into a harness and zipping around the forest canopy on cables. You use a heavy leather glove on top of the cable to brake. The last several years have seen an explosion in popularity of this sport in Colombia, particularly in the mountain regions.

Where to Go

One of the best is in Río Claro, halfway between Medellín and Bogotá, where a series of canopy lines zigzags across the river.

Other spots where you can go canopying include Los Yarumos near Manizales, the shores of Embalse Guatapé, near Medellín, and Termales San Vicente near Pereira. There are also canopy lines near Villa de Leyva.

Paragliding

Colombia's varied mountain terrain means there are lots of great thermals to ride if you want to try *parapente* (paragliding). Tandem flights in Bucaramanga are cheap – starting from a mere COP$50,000. You can also enroll in a 10-day paragliding course for COP$2,800,000 and become an internationally accredited paragliding pilot.

Where to Go

Bucaramanga Arguably the country's paragliding capital, attracting paragliders from around the world.

Parque Nacional del Chicamocha One of the most spectacular spots, with longer rides ranging from 30 to 45 minutes of gliding.

Medellín Urban paragliders can test their wings on Medellín's outskirts, where a number of schools offer tandem flights and instruction.

Horseback Riding

With their deep rural roots, Colombians love riding horses. In almost every town that's frequented by locals you'll find rentals and guided tours. While most tours are short half-day trips to local attractions, there are also some epic multiday adventures on offer, especially in the south of the country where the rolling green hills and temperate climate make for fantastic rides.

Where to Go

San Agustín Travel between remote pre-Columbian monuments in stunning natural settings. Most horses here are strong and in excellent condition.

Jardín Ascend steep, narrow mountain paths on the way to the spectacular Cueva del Esplendor.

Providencia Pick up your mount in Southwest Bay and trot along beaches and rural paths all over the island.

Desierto de la Tatacoa Bring your spaghetti Western fantasies to life among striking arid landscapes.

Laguna de Magdalena Ride from San Agustín high into the *páramo* (high-mountain plains) of the Macizo Colombiano to the source of the mighty Río Magdalena on this multiday expedition.

Valle de Cocora Make your way beneath wax palms on the short circuit to Reserva Natural Acaime.

Filandia Explore local coffee farms on horseback.

Mountain Biking

Cycling is very popular in Colombia, although most of it is road cycling. Prices for bike rental vary across regions, depend-

Paragliding near Medellín (p192)

ing on the quality of the bike – expect to pay anywhere from COP$10,000 to COP$50,000 per half-day bike rental.

Where to Go

There's something about mountains that makes cyclists want to conquer them. Mountain biking per se is most popular in San Gil and Villa de Leyva, where several adventure companies and bike-rental shops can facilitate your adrenaline fix.

Some other great routes:

Minca Offers exciting mountain-bike runs in the Sierra Nevada mountains.

Coconuco to Popayán Take a dip in the thermal pools then cruise back down the mountain.

Otún Quimbaya to Pereira The run from Santuario de Flora y Fauna Otún Quimbaya back to town passes through spectacular scenery.

PNN Los Nevados A longer, challenging ride. Kumanday Adventures (p206) in Manizales offers four-day mountain-biking trips through the *páramo* of PNN Los Nevados. Because of the remoteness and altitude (above 4000m), a guide and support vehicle are mandatory.

A WHALE OF A VIEW

Every year whales living near Chile's Antarctic waters make the 8000km-plus journey to Colombia's Pacific coast to give birth and raise their young. These are humpback whales (yubartas, sometimes called jorobadas), and more than 800 have been recorded off the Colombian coast. They grow to 18m long and weigh up to 25 tons; there are few things cuter than spotting a *ballenato* (baby whale) already the size of a small truck, nosing its way through the surface.

The best whale-watching is from July through October, though arrivals begin in June. Whales can be seen all along the Pacific coast, and there are comfortable resorts where you can relax before and after a boat tour. Sometimes whales come so close to shore they can be seen from the beach, or from lookouts in the hills. Most whale-watching tours last 1½ to two hours and cost around COP$30,000 to COP$80,000 per person (although these prices can vary widely depending on the operator).

Where to Go

Humpback whales can be seen all along Colombia's Pacific coast but are not always easy to spot from the beach. We list the best places to observe whales up close.

Bahía Solano & El Valle While it's possible to spot whales right from the beach here, there are also a number of lookouts in the hills that offer better vantage points. Alternatively, organize a boat trip for an even closer look.

Parque Nacional Natural (PNN) Ensenada de Utría This narrow inlet of water, in the Chocó, is one of the best places to see whales up close while staying on dry land. During the calving season the whales enter the *ensenada* (inlet) and play just a few hundred meters from shore.

Ladrilleros The most accessible option, this popular destination, a short boat ride from Buenaventura, is great for budget whale-watching tours.

Isla Gorgona Whales come very close to the shore at this island national park, and boat trips are available.

Guachalito There are a variety of accommodations ranging from rustic to high-end on this long beach near Nuquí and all can arrange whale-watching trips.

Kitesurfing & Windsurfing

Colombia's vast water resources and tropical climate make it an ideal place for kitesurfing (kiteboarding) and windsurfing.

The casual traveler will find the learning curve for windsurfing much shorter than for kitesurfing; it's also a fair bit cheaper. Prices vary considerably. Expect to pay roughly COP$60,000 per hour for windsurfing instruction and COP$90,000 to COP$100,000 per hour for individual kitesurf instruction (prices are lower in groups). Kite rentals go for around COP$60,000 per hour. If you've got your own gear, you'll pay COP$20,000 to COP$30,000 for each water entrance.

The most comprehensive guide to kitesurfing in Colombia can be found at www.colombiakite.com.

Where to Go

On the Caribbean coast, winds are best from January to April. Good spots include the following:

Lago Calima The star kitesurfing spot is not where you might think: Lago Calima is an artificial reservoir (elevation 1800m) lying 86km north of Cali. The appeal is year-round 18- to 25-knot winds, which attract world champions to its competitions held every August and September. There's no beach here; access to the water is via the grassy slopes along the lake.

La Boquilla Just near Cartagena.

Cabo de la Vela Terrific remote beaches; stunning backdrops.

San Andrés Launch from the island's famous white-sand beaches.

Regions at a Glance

Boyacá, Santander & Norte de Santander

....

Villages
Adventure
Nature

....

Colonial Villages

This region has four of Colombia's most striking colonial villages: Barichara and Villa de Leyva, both well-established tourist haunts preserved with precision; and sleepier Monguí and Playa de Belén, which receive few tourists and remain unspoiled.

Thrilling Adventures

Whether seeking a challenging high-altitude trek or white-knuckle adventure, Boyacá and Santander deliver. In Parque Nacional Natural (PNN) El Cocuy, visitors can scale at least 12 peaks above 5000m, while the small town of San Gil is ground zero for outdoor adventure and extreme sports.

Great Outdoors

Nature enthusiasts should flock to Villa de Leyva and Barichara for their excellent natural surroundings. Lago de Tota (Colombia's largest lake) ups the ante with *páramo* (high-mountain plains) trekking and a sky-high beach.

p83

Bogotá

....

Architecture
Museums
Wining & Dining

....

Colonial Epicenter

Bogotá's historic colonial center of 300-year-old homes, churches and buildings known as La Candelaria is a preserved mix of Spanish and baroque architecture. It commences in the grand Plaza de Bolívar, a picture-perfect living museum for Colombia's Andean showpiece.

World-Class Museums

Anchored by one of South America's most brilliantly curated and designed museums, the fascinating Museo del Oro, Bogotá boasts more than 60 museums, many of which hold rank among Latin America's best.

Wining & Dining

Eating well in Bogotá is as distinguished a pursuit as anywhere. From its classic regional specialties such as *ajiaco* (an Andean chicken stew with corn), to modern takes on gourmet fare that have begun to employ Colombia's wealth of native ingredients, the city is on the cusp of a bona fide foodie resurgence.

p42

Caribbean Coast

Beaches
Architecture
Trekking

Beaches

The idyllic beaches of Colombia's Caribbean coast and islands are Colombia's best. Here, white sands are fringed with seething jungle, dramatic deserts or – for the purists – plenty of palm trees. Whatever your poison, there's sun and sand for all.

Colonial Architecture

The walled city of Cartagena offers ornate churches and romantic, shaded squares, while hidden Mompox has a restored colonial heart. Santa Marta's faded grandeur kindles a half-forgotten memory of an imperial dream.

Trekking

The multiday trek to Ciudad Perdida (the Lost City) is one of the continent's classic hikes – four to six days in the jungle, fording rivers and creeping through the canopy; the destination is a mysterious ancient city belonging to a disappeared culture.

p120

San Andrés & Providencia

Diving
Beaches
Hiking

Diving

Both islands have extensive coral reefs totaling 50km with a biodiversity that equals any in the region. Sharks are the standout, but there are also turtles, barracudas, stingrays, manta rays and eagle rays just offshore.

Beaches

Take your pick of idyllic beaches bordering the archipelago's famed sea of seven colors. While those in San Andrés offer vibrant atmosphere and water sports, the real stars of the show are the tranquil, remote stretches of sand on Providencia.

Hiking

San Andrés and Providencia don't just cater for beach bums and divers: the island's interior is mountainous, and El Pico Natural Regional Park on Providencia offers walkers a breathtaking, crow's-nest 360-degree view of the Caribbean.

p170

Medellín & Zona Cafetera

Coffee
Nightlife
Hiking

Coffee Fincas

Throughout Caldas, Risaralda and Quindío departments, some of Colombia's best coffee *fincas* (farms) welcome visitors onto their plantations. Learn all about the growing process and the rich culture that has developed around it.

Nightlife

Going out in Medellín is all about seeing and being seen. *Paisas* (people from Antioquia) love to dress up and go out, and from the bright discos of Parque Lleras to the bohemian bars downtown, you can pretty much find a party for all tastes, any day of the week.

Mountain Treks

With high-altitude treks in PNN Los Nevados and more sedate strolls through regional nature reserves, the Zona Cafetera offers hikes to match all energy levels. Don't miss the Valle de Cocora, near Salento, with its towering wax palms.

p186

Cali & Southwest Colombia

....

Archaeology
Culture
Architecture

....

Pre-Columbian Ruins

Less than 100km apart amid stunning Andean panoramas sit two of Colombia's most important archaeological sites. More than 500 mysterious stone statues are scattered around San Agustín, while at Tierradentro, archaeologists have unearthed more than 100 underground tombs.

Salsa

From small barrio bars to the sweaty *salsatecas* (salsa dance clubs), high-energy salsa is the beat that drives Cali. Let the pros show you how it's done at the World Salsa Championships or take classes at one of the city's many academies.

Architectural Grandeur

Boasting whitewashed mansions and splendid churches, Popayán is a superb example of Spanish-colonial architecture. Continue the colonial theme in Cali's Barrio San Antonio or head to Ipiales to check out the immense neo-Gothic Santuario de Las Lajas.

p224

Pacific Coast

....

Marine Life
Beaches
Nature

....

Whales & Turtles

Get close to massive humpback whales at Parque Nacional Natural (PNN) Ensenada de Utría or head out at night to watch sea turtles lay their eggs near El Valle. Divers can swim among hundreds of sharks at Islas Malpelo and Gorgona.

Beaches

Framed by jungle-covered mountains, the rugged gray beaches of the region are breathtaking and mostly deserted. Guachalito and Playa Almejal both have fine resorts wedged between the jungle and the sea. Surfers will find excellent breaks around Arusí and El Valle.

Natural Wonders

Often overlooked by hikers, the Chocó boasts fantastic off-the-beaten-track treks to waterfalls deep in the jungle. On the water, check out the region's amazing biodiversity while paddling up the Río Joví or Río Juribidá in a dugout canoe.

p255

Amazon Basin

....

Wildlife
Jungle
Ecovillages

....

Wild Kingdom

While human encroachment, both legal and otherwise, have pushed the Amazon's wildlife population in the wrong direction, it remains an incomprehensibly gigantic hotbed of biodiversity, the world's largest collection of living plants and animal species.

Jungle

The mother of all jungles, no word conjures up a more alluring mix of enigmatic rainforest, enormous rivers, indigenous folklore and tropical wildlife than the Amazon. The sheer scale of it is mind-blowing; if there ever was a place where imagination meets reality, it's in this endless sea of green.

Ecovillages

The ecological village of Puerto Nariño – a living model for a sustainable existence in the middle of the world's largest jungle – is a charming, architecturally interesting, near-perfect place to chill out in the rainforest.

p270

On the Road

Bogotá

1 / POP 7.4 MILLION / ELEV 2625M / AREA 1587 SQ KM

Best Places to Eat

➡ Central Cevicheria (p66)
➡ Mini-Mal (p65)
➡ La Condesa Irina Lazaar (p63)
➡ Agave Azul (p64)
➡ Sant Just (p63)

Best Places to Stay

➡ Orchids (p60)
➡ Casa Deco (p60)
➡ Casa Platypus (p59)
➡ La Pinta (p60)
➡ Hotel Click-Clack (p61)

Why Go?

Bogotá is Colombia's beating heart, an engaging and vibrant capital cradled by chilly Andean peaks and steeped in sophisticated urban cool. The city's cultural epicenter is La Candelaria, the cobbled historic downtown to which most travelers gravitate. Here, preciously preserved colonial buildings house museums, restaurants, hotels and bars peppered amid 300-year-old homes, churches and convents. Nearly all of Bogotá's traditional attractions are here – radiating out from Plaza de Bolívar – and gorgeous Cerro de Monserrate is just east.

The city's grittier sides sit south and southwest, where the working-class barrios continue to battle well-earned reputations for drugs and crime. In the ritzier north, you'll find boutique hotels and well-heeled locals piling into chic entertainment districts such as the Zona Rosa and Zona G. Here, rust-tinted sunsets dramatically bounce off the bricks of upper-class Bogotá's Andes-hugging residential buildings – a cinematic ceremony that begins the city's uproarious evenings.

When to Go
Bogotá

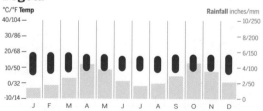

Jun & Jul Temperatures aren't as high as May, but rainfall drops dramatically in the capital.

Aug Fiesta free-for-all: Salsa al Parque and the Festival de Verano get the city's hips shaking.

Dec *Bogotanos* fall hard for Christmas, when the city sparkles in a festival of lights.

Bogotá Highlights

1 Ponder Colombia's El Dorado myths among glittering displays at one of the continent's top museums, **Museo del Oro** (p49).

2 Step through the looking-glass into the surreal nightlife world of **Andrés Carne de Res** (p67) in Chía.

3 Trek up the towering **Cerro de Monserrate** (p48). with the Sunday pilgrims for sweeping capital views.

4 Appreciate the beauty of heft at the free **Museo Botero** (p45).

5 Genuflect at the striking interiors of **Iglesia Museo de Santa Clara** (p45) and **Iglesia de San Francisco** (p52).

6 Soak up the village colonial feel of food-centric **Usaquén** (p67).

7 Attack Bogotá by bike on a fascinating two-wheel tour with **Bogotá Bike Tours** (p55).

History

Long before the Spanish Conquest, the Sabana de Bogotá, a fertile highland basin which today has been almost entirely taken over by the city, was inhabited by one of the most advanced pre-Columbian indigenous groups, the Muisca. The Spanish era began when Gonzalo Jiménez de Quesada and his expedition arrived at the Sabana, founding the town on August 6, 1538 near the Muisca capital, Bacatá.

The town was named Santa Fe de Bogotá, a combination of the traditional name, Bacatá, and Quesada's hometown in Spain, Santa Fe. Nonetheless, throughout the colonial period the town was simply referred to as Santa Fe.

At the time of its foundation Santa Fe consisted of 12 huts and a chapel where a Mass was held to celebrate the town's birth. The Muisca religious sites were destroyed and replaced by churches.

During the early years Santa Fe was governed from Santo Domingo (on the island of Hispaniola, the present-day Dominican Republic), but in 1550 it fell under the rule of Lima, the capital of the Viceroyalty of Peru and the seat of Spain's power for the conquered territories of South America. In 1717 Santa Fe was made the capital of the Virreynato de la Nueva Granada, the newly created viceroyalty comprising the territories of present-day Colombia, Panama, Venezuela and Ecuador.

Despite the town's political importance, its development was hindered by the area's earthquakes, and also by the smallpox and typhoid epidemics that plagued the region throughout the 17th and 18th centuries.

After independence the Congress of Cúcuta shortened the town's name to Bogotá in 1821 and decreed it the capital of Gran Colombia. The town developed steadily and by the middle of the 19th century it had 30,000 inhabitants and 30 churches. In 1884 the first tramway began to operate in the city and, soon after, railway lines were constructed to La Dorada and Girardot, giving Bogotá access to the ports on the Río Magdalena.

Rapid progress came only in the 1940s with industrialization and the consequent peasant migrations from the countryside. On April 9, 1948 the popular leader Jorge Eliécer Gaitán was assassinated, sparking the uprising known as El Bogotazo. The city was partially destroyed; 136 buildings were burnt to the ground and 2500 people died.

Tranquil life in Bogotá was rocked again on November 6, 1985 when guerrillas of the M-19 (Movimiento 19 de Abril) revolutionary movement invaded the Palace of Justice in Bogotá and made hostages of the 300-plus civilians in the building. By the next day, 115 people were dead, including 11 supreme court judges.

In the 1990s and 2000s, Bogotá has made many surprising advances – the city managed to reduce its homicide rate from 80 murders per 100,000 residents in 1993 to just 17 in 2013, making it one of the safest urban areas in Latin America, though muggings are on the rise. And a host of progressive projects under successive mayors (eg the 350km of CicloRuta bike lanes) have made major strides toward the city positioning itself as a cultural capital.

◎ Sights

Most attractions are in historic La Candelaria, where Bogotá was born, and you'll probably want more than a day to look around the area.

If you're thinking of going to a museum on a Sunday, think twice – Bogotá has half-a-hundred options, and most get crammed with locals, particularly on free day (the last Sunday of the month); we've seen 45-minute lines outside modest museums that we don't even list! It's quieter during the week.

When walking about, pop into random churches, too. Most are beauties, often dating from the 17th and 18th centuries, and often with more elaborate decoration than the exterior would suggest. Some show off a distinctive Spanish-Moorish style called Mudejar (mainly noticeable in the ceiling ornamentation) as well as paintings of Colombia's best-known colonial-era artist, Gregorio Vásquez de Arce y Ceballos.

◉ La Candelaria

Blissfully alive and chock-full of key things to see, La Candelaria is Bogotá's colonial barrio, with a mix of carefully restored 300-year-old houses, some rather dilapidated ones, and still more marking more modern eras.

The usual place to start discovering Bogotá is **Plaza de Bolívar** (Map p50; Plaza de Bolívar btwn Calle 10 & 11), marked by a bronze statue of Simón Bolívar (cast in 1846 by Italian artist Pietro Tenerani). It was the first public monument in the city.

The square has changed considerably over the centuries and is no longer lined by colonial buildings; only the Capilla del Sagrario dates from the Spanish era. Other buildings are more recent and flaunt different architectural styles.

Some of La Candelaria's most popular sights, as well as the Centro Cultural Gabriel García Márquez, are within a couple of blocks east of the plaza. The slightly confusing web of museums run by the Banco de la República, including Museo Botero, Casa de Moneda, Colección de Arte and Museo de Arte del Banco de la República, are essentially one massive and labyrinthine interconnected museum complex and form what is easily one of Bogotá's top attractions. Plan ahead: the complex's last entrance is 30 minutes before closing.

It's best to avoid walking alone here after dark, and keep your wits about you during the day as well.

★ **Museo Botero** MUSEUM
(Map p50; www.banrepcultural.org/museo-botero; Calle 11 No 4-41; ☺9am-7pm Mon & Wed-Sat, 10am-5pm Sun) **FREE** The highlight of Banco de la República's massive museum complex is several halls spread over two floors dedicated to all things chubby: hands, oranges, women, mustached men, children, birds, Fuerzas Armadas Revolucionarias de Colombia (FARC) leaders. All of these are, of course, the robust paintings and sculptures of Colombia's most famous artist, Fernando Botero (Botero himself donated these works).

The collection also includes several works by Picasso, Chagall, Renoir, Monet, Pissarro and Miró, and some hilarious sculptures by Dalí and Max Ernst. Audio guides in English, French and Spanish (COP$6000) are available from the museum complex's main entrance on Calle 11.

★ **Iglesia Museo de Santa Clara** CHURCH
(Map p50; www.museoiglesiasantaclara.gov.co; Carrera 8 No 8-91; adult/child COP$3000/500; ☺9am-5pm Tue-Fri, 10am-4pm Sat & Sun) One of Bogotá's most richly decorated churches and also its oldest (along with Iglesia de San Francisco). It's now run by the government as a museum. Considering all the other churches from the same era that can be seen for free, many visitors pass on this one, but it is a stunner.

Built between 1629 and 1674, the single-nave construction features a barrel vault coated in golden floral motifs that looks down over walls entirely covered by 148 paintings and sculptures of saints.

Catedral Primada CATHEDRAL
(Map p50; www.catedraldebogota.org; Plaza de Bolívar; ☺9am-5pm Tue-Sun) This neoclassical cathedral stands on the site where the first Mass *may* have been celebrated after Bogotá was founded in 1538 (some historians argue it happened at Plazoleta del Chorro de Quevedo, just east). Either way, it's Bogotá's largest. It's also the main plaza's most dominating building, facing from the northeast corner.

BOGOTÁ IN...

Two Days
Start in La Candelaria, with a snack at **La Puerta Falsa** (p61), a look at **Plaza de Bolívar** (p44), then see sculptures of chubby bodies at the **Museo Botero** (p45). Lunch at **Quinua y Amaranto** (p61), then walk over to take in Colombia's golden past at **Museo del Oro** (p49). Grab dinner in **Zona G**, **Zona Rosa** or **Parque 93**, where you can eat and drink until your heart's content.

On your second day, you'll want to leg it up **Monserrate** (p48) for massive capital views, and then grab a nap. At night, enter the surreal world of **Andrés Carne de Res** (p67), a 23km taxi ride north in Chía.

Four Days
Follow the two-day itinerary, then take a day trip to the salt cathedral at **Zipaquirá** (p55), easily reached by public transportation. On your last day, start out with a brunch in **Usaquén** (p67) before heading to the city for a tour on two wheels to otherwise no-go neighborhoods with **Bogotá Bike Tours** (p55). Afterward, grab a hot cup of *canelazo* (made with aguardiente, sugarcane, cinnamon and lime) in a cafe in **La Candelaria** (p68), and have a lovely farewell meal at an innovative Colombian restaurant in the bohemian foodie neighborhoods of **Chapinero Alto** (p64) or **Macarena** (p64).

Greater Bogotá

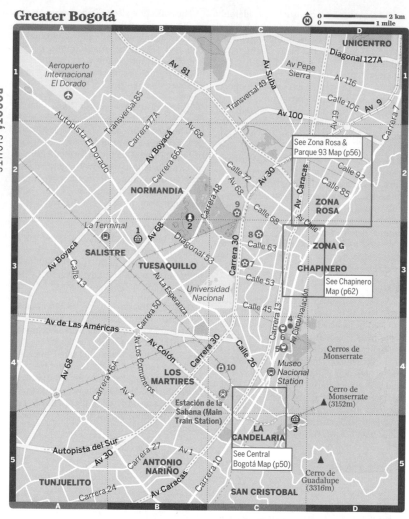

The original simple thatched chapel was replaced by a more substantial building from 1556 to 1565, which later collapsed due to poor foundations. In 1572 the third church went up, but the earthquake of 1785 reduced it to ruins. Only in 1807 was the massive building that stands today initiated and it was successfully completed by 1823. It was partially damaged during the Bogotazo riots in 1948. Unlike many Bogotá churches, the spacious interiors have relatively little ornamentation. The tomb of Jiménez de Quesada, the founder of Bogotá, is in the largest chapel off the right-hand aisle.

Capitolio Nacional HISTORIC BUILDING
(Map p50; ☑ 383-3000; Plaza de Bolívar; ⊘ closed to public) On the southern side of the plaza stands this neoclassical seat of Congress. It was begun in 1847, but due to numerous political uprisings was not completed until 1926. Its square-facing facade was built by English architect Thomas Reed. To visit, call ahead; otherwise you can wander around the stone courtyard.

Palacio de Justicia HISTORIC BUILDING
(Map p50; Plaza de Bolívar; ⊘ closed to public) On the northern side of the plaza, this massive,

Greater Bogotá

rather styleless edifice serves as the seat of the Supreme Court.

It's seen its troubles. The first court building, erected in 1921 on the corner of Calle 11 and Carrera 6, was burnt down by a mob during El Bogotazo in 1948. A modern building was then constructed here, but in 1985 it was taken by M-19 guerrillas and gutted by fire in a fierce 28-hour offensive by the army in an attempt to reclaim it. The new building was designed in a completely different style.

Casa de Nariño　　　HISTORIC BUILDING
(Map p50; www.presidencia.gov.co; Plaza de Bolívar) On the south side of Plaza de Bolívar, beyond the Capitolio Nacional and reached via Carrera 8 or 7, this is Colombia's neoclassical presidential building, where Colombia's leader lives and works. To visit, you'll need to email or go to the website and scroll down to 'Visitas Casa de Nariño' under 'Servicios a la Ciudadanía.' No permission is needed to watch the changing of the presidential guard – best seen from the east side – held at 4pm Wednesdays, Fridays and Sundays.

The building is named for Antonio Nariño, a colonial figure with ideas of independence who secretly translated France's human-rights laws into Spanish – and went to jail for it, a couple of times. In 1948 the building was damaged during El Bogotazo riots and only restored in 1979.

Note: guards around the president's palace stand at barriers on Carreras 7 and 8.

It's OK to pass them; just show the contents of your bag and stay clear of the fence-side sidewalks.

Casa de Moneda　　　MUSEUM
(Mint; Map p50; www.banrepcultural.org; Calle 11 No 4-93; ⊙9am-7pm Mon-Sat, 10am-5pm Sun) 🆓 This historic museum inside the Banco de la República complex houses the **Colección Numismática**. The exhibits start with pre-Columbian exchanges of pots and lead chronologically to misshapen coins, the introduction of a centralized bank in 1880, and the making of the cute tree art on the current 500 peso coin in the late 1990s.

Colección de Arte　　　MUSEUM
(Map p50; www.banrepcultural.org; Calle 11 No 4-14; ⊙9am-7pm Mon-Sat, 10am-5pm Sun) 🆓 Most of Banco de la República's permanent Colección de Arte, which features 800 pieces by 250 different artists spread over 16 exhibition halls at two addresses, is reached via elaborate staircases within the same museum complex as Casa de Moneda and Museo Botero. The collection has been reorganized into five time periods spanning the 15th century to the modern day, each separately curated. The collection's contemporary art exhibition is located inside Biblioteca Luis Ángel Arango on Calle 12.

Most of it sticks with modern splashes of oils by Colombian artists, including giant figurative paintings by Luis Caballero (1943–95) on the 1st floor. A bit at odds with the rest are the two 1st-floor halls toward the east, which focus on 17th- and 18th-century religious objects, including two extraordinary *custodias* (monstrances). The largest was made of 4902g of pure gold encrusted with 1485 emeralds, one sapphire, 13 rubies, 28 diamonds, 168 amethysts, one topaz and 62 pearls. But who's counting?

Museo Histórico Policía　　　MUSEUM
(Museum of Police History; Map p50; www.policia.gov.co; Calle 9 No 9-27; ⊙8am-5pm Tue-Sun) 🆓 This surprisingly worthwhile museum not only gets you inside the lovely ex-HQ (built in 1923) of Bogotá's police force, but gives you 45 minutes or so of contact time with English-speaking, 18-year-old local guides who are serving a one-year compulsory service with the police (interesting tales to be heard).

The best parts otherwise follow cocaine-kingpin Pablo Escobar's demise in 1993 – his Harley Davidson (a gift to a cousin) and his personal Bernadelli pocket pistol, otherwise known as his 'second wife.'

DON'T MISS

CERRO DE MONSERRATE

Bogotá's proud symbol – and convenient point of reference – is the white-church-topped 3150m **Monserrate peak**. It flanks the city's east, about 1.5km from La Candelaria, and is visible from most parts across Sabana de Bogotá (Bogotá savannah; sometimes called 'the valley'). The top has gorgeous views of the 1700-sq-km capital sprawl. On a clear day you can even spot the symmetrical cone of Nevado del Tolima, part of the Parque Nacional Natural (PNN) Los Nevados volcanic range in the Cordillera Central, 135km west.

The **church** up top is a major mecca for pilgrims, due to its altar statue of the Señor Caído (Fallen Christ), dating from the 1650s, to which many miracles have been attributed. The church was erected after the original chapel was destroyed by an earthquake in 1917. You'll also find two restaurants and a cafe – make a day out of it.

The steep **1500-step hike** – past snack stands – to the top (60 to 90 minutes' walk) has reopened from 5am (closed Tuesdays). It is a popular weekend jaunt for *bogotanos;* on weekdays it can be dangerous, as thefts occur, so take the regular *teleférico* (cable car) or funicular, which alternate schedules up the mountain from **Monserrate station** (www.cerromonserrate.com; round trip from COP$16,400 Mon-Sat, COP$9400 Sun; ⊘7am-midnight Mon-Sat, 6am-6pm Sun). Generally the funicular goes before noon (3pm on Saturday), the cable car after. If you do decide to leg it during the week, head up before 10am; after that, you won't have strength in numbers for personal safety.

The funicular is a 20-minute walk up from the Iglesia de las Aguas (along the brick walkways with the fountains – up past the Universidad de los Andes), at the northeast edge of La Candelaria – but again you're best off doing it on weekends, particularly in the morning, when many pilgrims are about. During the week the trail and the short walk between Quinta de Bolívar and Monserrate has seen an increase in knife-point muggings.

Museo de la Independencia – Casa del Florero
MUSEUM

(Casa del Florero; Map p50; www.quintadebolivar.gov.co/museoindependencia; Calle 11 No 6-94; adult/student COP$3000/2000, free Sun; ⊘9am-5pm Tue-Fri, 10am-4pm Sat & Sun) Just after Napoleon overcame Spain in 1810, local Creole Antonio Morales supposedly came to this late-16th-century home and demanded an ornate vase from its Spanish owner, which led to a fistfight on the street (plus one shattered vase) – eventually spurring a rebellion. In these hallowed halls you can see the broken vase in question. The story is known as 'the broken vase was heard around the world.'

Museo de Arte del Banco de la República
MUSEUM

(Map p50; www.banrepcultural.org/museodearte.htm; Calle 11 No 4-21; ⊘9am-7pm Mon & Wed-Sat, 10am-5pm Sun) **FREE** Though indistinguishable as its own museum, this is the space inside Banco de la República's museum complex used for temporary exhibitions. Its auditorium hosts many free events.

Museo de Arte Colonial
MUSEUM

(Museum of Colonial Art; Map p50; ☑341-6017; www.museocolonial.gov.co; Carrera 6 No 9-77; adult/student COP$3000/2000; ⊘9am-5pm Tue-Fri, 10am-4pm Sat & Sun) This museum occupies a one-time Jesuit college and traces the evolution of how religious and portrait art pieces are made, particularly by Colombia's favorite baroque artist, Gregorio Vásquez de Arce y Ceballos (1638–1711). At time of research, it was closed for renovations and expected to open again in 2016.

Capilla del Sagrario
CHURCH

(Sagrario Chapel; Map p50; Plaza de Bolívar; ⊘7am-noon & 1-5pm Mon-Fri, 3-5pm Sun) This small baroque cathedral has more to see than its bigger brother next door, the Catedral Primada, including six large paintings by Gregorio Vásquez.

Plazoleta del Chorro de Quevedo
PLAZA

(Map p50; cnr Carrera 2 & Calle 12B) No one agrees exactly where Bogotá was originally founded – some say by the Catedral Primada on the Plaza de Bolívar, others say here, in this wee plaza lined with cafes, a small white church and many boho street vendors (or hacky-sack players).

It's a cute spot at any time of day, but particularly as dark comes – when students pour onto the scene – in the narrow funnel-like alley leading past pocket-sized bars just north. On Friday afternoons (at 5pm) there are Spanish storyteller sessions – well worth a visit for the atmosphere.

Teatro Colón
THEATER

(Map p50; ☎284-7420; www.teatrocolon.gov.co; Calle 10 No 5-32; ⊗box office 10am-5pm Mon-Sat, to 3pm Sun) The Teatro Colón, with its adorable Italian-style facade, has had various names since its birth in 1792; this latest version opened as Teatro Nacional in 1892 and was designed by Italian architect Pietro Cantini. Fresh off a mid-2014 reopening after its lavish interiors underwent a six-year makeover, the theater hosts concerts, opera, ballet, plays – and even electronica DJ sets.

Starting in 2015, day tours will be instituted – check at the box office.

Museo Militar
MUSEUM

(Military Museum; Map p50; Calle 10 No 4-92; ⊗9am-4pm Tue-Fri, 10am-4pm Sat) FREE This two-floor museum is run by military guys in fatigues, and may be interesting to some for its playful models sporting the history of military uniforms (note the 'antiterrorist' outfit); a Korean War room; and a courtyard of artillery and aircraft including a presidential helicopter. ID required.

Edificio Liévano
HISTORIC BUILDING

(Map p50; Plaza de Bolívar; ⊗closed to the public) On the western side of the plaza, this French-style building is now home to the *alcaldía* (mayor's office). The building was erected between 1902 and 1905.

Palacio de San Carlos
PALACE

(Map p50; Calle 10 No 5-51) This massive edifice has seen a few lives, notably as the presidential HQ of Simón Bolívar, who narrowly escaped an assassination attempt here in 1828 when his friend-with-privileges Manuelita Sáenz tipped him off and became known in Bogotá circles as 'the liberator of the Liberator.' A (dramatically worded) sign in Latin under his window (to the right) retells the story.

Centro Cultural Gabriel García Márquez
CULTURAL CENTER

(Map p50; ☎283-2200; www.fce.com.co; Calle 11 No 5-60; ⊗8am-8pm Mon-Sat, to 4pm Sun) FREE A modern addition to La Candelaria, opened in 2008, this expansive complex pays homage to Colombia's most famous author in name, but its events span the cultural spectrum way past literature. There's also a giant bookstore (with a few English titles), a small space for rotating exhibitions, a great hamburger restaurant and a Juan Valdéz cafe.

⊙ City Center

Bogotá's scrappy business center – busiest along Calle 19 and Carrera 7 – is easiest to deal with on Sundays, when Ciclovía shuts down Carrera 7 for cyclists and pedestrians, and the Mercado de San Alejo flea market is in force. Some of its most visited parts (notably the Museo del Oro) cluster near La Candelaria by Av Jiménez.

★Museo del Oro
MUSEUM

(Map p50; www.banrepcultural.org/museo-del-oro; Carrera 6 No 15-88; COP$3000 Mon-Sat, free Sun; ⊗9am-6pm Tue-Sat, 10am-4pm Sun) Bogotá's most famous museum and one of the most fascinating in all of South America, the Gold Museum contains more than 55,000 pieces of gold and other materials from all the major pre-Hispanic cultures in Colombia. It's all laid out in logical, thematic rooms over three floors – with descriptions in Spanish and English.

Second-floor exhibits break down findings by region, with descriptions of how pieces were used. There are lots of mixed animals in gold (eg jaguar/frog, man/eagle); and note how female figurines indicate how women of the Zenú in the pre-Columbian north surprisingly played important roles in worship.

The 3rd-floor 'Offering' room exhibits explain how gold was used in rituals. Displayed *tunjos* (gold offerings, usually figurines depicting a warrior) were thrown into the Laguna de Guatavita; the most famous one, actually found near the town of Pasca in 1969, is the unlabeled gold boat, called the Balsa Muisca. It's uncertain how old it is, as generally only gold pieces that include other materials can be carbon dated.

There's more to understanding the stories than the descriptions tell, so try taking a free one-hour tour Tuesday through Saturday (in Spanish and English; 11am and 4pm), which varies the part of the museum to be highlighted. Audio guides are available in Spanish, English and French.

BOGOTÁ'S TOP MUSEUMS

➡ Museo del Oro (p49)

➡ Museo Botero (p45)

➡ Museo Nacional (p53)

➡ Casa de Moneda (p47)

➡ Iglesia Museo de Santa Clara (p45)

BOGOTÁ SIGHTS

Central Bogotá

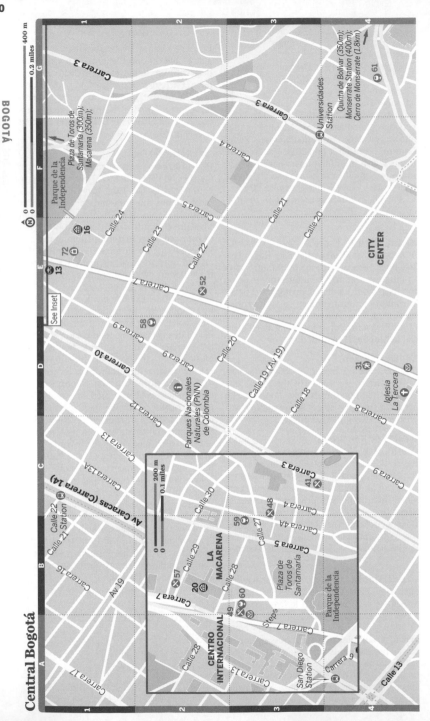

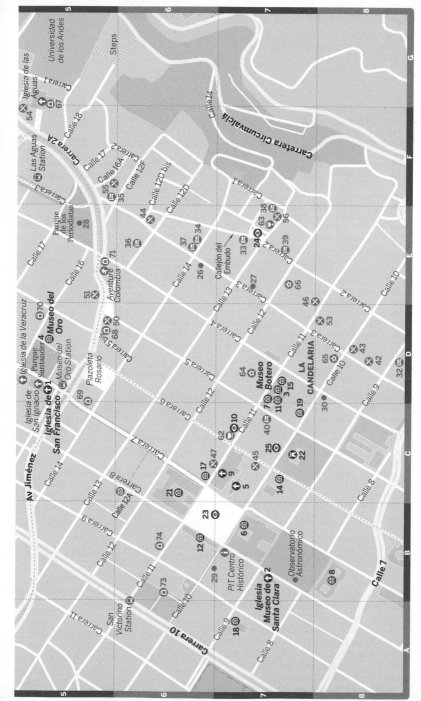

Central Bogotá

★ **Iglesia de San Francisco** CHURCH
(Map p50; www.templodesanfrancisco.com; cnr Av Jiménez & Carrera 7; ⊙ 6:30am-10:30pm Mon-Fri, 6:30am-12:30pm & 4-6:30pm Sat, 7:30am-1:30pm & 4:30-7:30pm Sun) Built between 1557 and 1621, the Church of San Francisco, just west of the Museo del Oro, is Bogotá's oldest surviving church. Of particular interest is the extraordinary 17th-century gilded main al-

tarpiece, which is Bogotá's largest and most elaborate piece of art of its kind.

Quinta de Bolívar MUSEUM
(Map p46; www.quintadebolivar.gov.co; Calle 20 No 2-91 Este; adult/child COP$3000/1000, free Sun; ⊙ 9am-5pm Tue-Fri, 11am-4pm Sat & Sun) About 250m downhill to the west from Monserrate station, this lovely historic-home museum is

set in a garden at the foot of the Cerro de Monserrate. The mansion was built in 1800 and donated to Simón Bolívar in 1820 in gratitude for his liberating services. Bolívar spent 423 days here over nine years. Its rooms are filled with period pieces, including Bolívar's sword. Less is said about its later days as a mental institution.

There's an English- and French-language brochure available for COP$2500, English-language audio guide for COP$1000 or guided tours in English Wednesday at 11am.

Mirador Torre Colpatria VIEWPOINT
(Map p50; Carrera 7 No 24-89; admission COP$4500; ⊙6-9pm Fri, 2-8pm Sat, 11am-5pm Sun) From the 48th-floor outside deck of the Colpatria Tower you can catch a superb view of the decommissioned bullring, backed by office buildings and the mountains – there are also fine 360-degree vistas across the city. The 162m-high skyscraper – Colombia's tallest – was finished in 1979.

Museo de Arte Moderno MUSEUM
(MAMBO; Map p50; www.mambogota.com; Calle 24 No 6-00; adult/student COP$4000/2000; ⊙10am-6pm Tue-Sat, noon-5pm Sun) Opened in the mid-1980s in a spacious hall designed by revered local architect Rogelio Salmona, MAMBO focuses on various forms of visual arts (painting, sculpture, photography, video) from the beginning of the 20th century to the present. Exhibits change frequently, often highlighting Latin American artists.

◉ Centro Internacional

Business offices look over Carrera 7 in this busy pocket of the city, where you'll find a few attractions and lots of business meetings.

Museo Nacional MUSEUM
(National Museum; Map p50; www.museonacional.gov.co; Carrera 7 No 28-66; ⊙10am-6pm Tue-Sat, to 5pm Sun) FREE This museum is housed in the expansive, Greek-cross-shaped building called El Panóptico (designed as a prison by English architect Thomas Reed in 1874). Walking through the (more or less) chronological display of Colombia's past, you pass iron-bar doors into white-walled halls. Signage is in Spanish only, but each floor offers handy English placards that you can take along with you for the highlights.

The ground floor looks at pre-Columbian history, with rather oblique references to past groups and some gripping Muis-

ca mummies that may date as far back as 1500 years. On the 3rd floor, room 16 gives the best sense of prison life – with old cells now done up in various exhibits. The first on the right regards Jorge Gaitán, the populist leader whose 1948 assassination set off the Bogotazo violence – and coincidentally delayed the opening of this museum!

Afterward, check out the lovely gardens and their nice glass Juan Valdéz cafe; and there are many good eating options on nearby Calle 29bis.

◉ Northern Bogotá

Museo El Chicó MUSEUM
(Map p56; www.museodelchico.com; Carrera 7A No 93-01, Mercedes Sierra de Pérez; adult/student COP$7000/5000; ⊙10am-5pm Tue-Sun) Housed in a fine 18th-century *casona* (large, rambling house) surrounded by what was once a vast hacienda. It features a collection of historic objects of decorative art mostly from Europe – the exquisitely tiled bathroom is worth a visit alone – and a picnic-perfect park.

Plaza Central de Usaquén PLAZA
(Los Toldos de San Pelayo, Carrera 6A, btwn Calles 119 & 119A) It's best coming on Sunday for the flea market (from 10am to 5pm).

◉ Western Bogotá

Parque Simón Bolívar PARK
(Map p46; Calle 63 & 53, btwn Carreras 48 & 68; ⊙6am-6pm) At 360 hectares, this is slightly larger than New York's Central Park, something that more than a few of the weekend

---

GREEN-PEOPLE-WATCHING FROM ABOVE

While walking around La Candelaria, try keeping one eye down for fresh dog feces and missing pothole covers, *and* another one up for a unique art project that peers down from rooftops, window ledges and balconies. Made in the past decade, the artworks – green figures made from recycled materials representing local *comuneros* (commoners) – come from local artist Jorge Olavé.

Note the guy watching over Plaza de Bolívar from atop the **Casa de Comuneros** at the southwest corner – best seat in town.

draw of 200,000 local park-goers like to point out. It's a nice spot, with lakes, bike paths and walkways, public libraries, stadiums and many events including the beloved Rock al Parque in October or November. The 'Simón Bolívar' station on TransMilenio's E line reaches the east end of the park (at Av Ciudad de Quito and Calle 64).

🏃 Activities

If you're looking for a place to kick around a football or go for a jog, try Parque Simón Bolívar, or go for a climb up Monserrate (p48) on weekend mornings.

To get out on two wheels, nothing beats Bogotá's incredible 376km network of **CicloRuta** – separate bike lanes that cross the city. **Ciclovía** (www.idrd.gov.co) opens about 121km of city roads to cyclists and pedestrians from 7am to 2pm on Sundays and holidays for a well-run event that gets Bogotá out on two wheels. Fruit-juice and street-food vendors, performers and bike-repair stands line the cross-town event, which has a street party vibe with or without a bike. If you have wheels, Wednesday nights' **Ciclopaseo de los Miercoles** is a good-time free bike ride that meets at **Plaza CPM** (Map p56; Carrera 10 at Calle 96) at 7pm.

Sal Si Puedes   HIKING
(Map p50; ☎283-3765; www.salsipuedes.org; Carrera 7 No 17-01, Oficina 640; ⊗8am-5pm Mon-Thu, to 2pm Fri) 🌿 This is an association of outdoor-minded people which organizes weekend walks in the countryside (COP$45,000 per person, including transportation and

---

Spanish-speaking guides). Most last nine or 10 hours. Drop by for a yearly schedule.

Gran Pared   ROCK CLIMBING
(Map p62; ☎285-0903; www.granpared.com; Carrera 7 No 50-02; full day COP$25,000; ⊗10am-9:45pm Mon-Fri, 8am-7:45pm Sat, 10am-5:45pm Sun) Bogotá rock climbers head off to nearby Suesca, but if you want to hone your skills in town, this towering climbing wall is challenging and well organized.

Courses

Spanish in Colombia comes with a clearer pronunciation than some Latin American destinations.

**International House
Bogotá**   LANGUAGE COURSE
(Map p50; ☎336-4747; www.ihbogota.com; Calle 10 No 4-09; ⊗7am-8pm Mon-Fri, 8am-1:30pm Sun) Offers group Spanish-language courses in La Candelaria (US$220 per week for five four-hour morning classes) or private tutors (US$30 per hour).

**Escuela de Artes y
Oficios Santo Domingo**   CRAFTS COURSE
(Map p50; ☎282-0534; www.eaosd.org; Calle 10 No 8-65; courses from COP$221,000; ⊗shop 8am-5pm Mon-Sat) This donation-sustained organization offers one- and two-month (and beyond) courses in woodwork, leatherwork, silversmithing, embroidery and weaving in a gorgeous restored building in La Candelaria. And, though technically not a store, its shop is the best spot in town for well-made, gorgeous handicrafts.

Nueva Lengua   LANGUAGE COURSE
(Map p62; ☎861-5555; www.nuevalengua.com; Calle 69 No 11A-09, Quinta Camacho) This language school offers a number of study programs, including at its branches in Medellín and Cartagena. A 25-hour week with a private teacher costs US$850; a 20-hour week in a small class costs US$200; and a four-week (minimum) study-and-volunteer program, including work at an orphanage or hospital, costs US$800.

**Universidad Javeriana's Centro
Latinoamericano**   LANGUAGE COURSE
(Map p46; ☎320-8320 ext 4620; www.javeriana.edu.co/centrolatino; Transversal 4 No 42-00, piso 6) Bogotá's best-known school of Spanish language offers private lessons (COP$97,000 per hour) or 80-hour courses (COP$2,080,000 per person).

BOGOTÁ FOR CHILDREN

Some Bogotá attractions are particularly kid-friendly. **Maloka** (Map p46; ☎427-2707; www.maloka.org; Carrera 68D No 24A-51; museum/cinemas/both COP$15,500/10,500/24,000; ⊗8am-5pm Mon-Fri, 10am-7pm Sat & Sun) is a child-oriented science museum with a dome cinema, and **Museo El Chicó** (p53) has a kids' park and library. In the **Museo Nacional** (p53) you can see mummies and old jail cells. Vendors sell bird seed for the (many) pigeons in **Plaza de Bolívar** (p44). And you can marvel at the funny hats of the changing of the presidential guard at nearby **Casa de Nariño** (p47).

ZIPAQUIRÁ

Far and away the most popular day trip from Bogotá is to head 50km north of Bogotá to the **Salt Cathedral** (☑594-5959; www.catedraldesal.gov.co; adult/child COP$23,000/16,000; ☉9am-5:30pm) of **Zipaquirá**. This underground cathedral carved out of salt is one of only three such structures in the world – the other two are in Poland.

In the mountains about 500m southwest of Zipaquirá there are two salt cathedrals: the first opened in 1954 and was closed in 1992 for safety reasons, but you can visit its stunning replacement. Between 1991 and 1995, around 250,000 tonnes of salt were cleared away to carve out the moody, ethereal underground sanctuary, heralded as one of Colombia's greatest architectural achievements. You'll descend to 180m below ground through 14 small chapels representing the Stations of the Cross – Jesus' last journey – each a maudlin-lit triumph of both symbolism and mining. But nothing prepares you for the trail's culmination in the main nave, where a mammoth cross (the world's largest in an underground church) is illuminated from the base up, like heaven itself. The tradition of mixing religion with salt has logical roots: work in the mines was dangerous so altars were made.

All visitors must join regularly departing groups on hour-long tours – you can leave the tour once you're inside if you want. The 75m-long mine can accommodate 8400 people and holds services on (very busy) Sundays at noon. In addition to the Salt Cathedral, there is a Brine Museum and other minor attractions on the premises; and Zipaquirá's main plaza is lined with cafes and has a lovely church worth peeking into.

To head to Zipaquirá, hop on a frequent bus from the Portal del Norte TransMilenio station at Calle 170, which is about a 45-minute ride from the city center. From here, buses to Zipaquirá (COP$4300, 50 minutes) leave every four minutes or so until 11pm from inside the portal's Buses Intermunciples platform. You can also catch an hourly direct bus from *módulo* 3 (red) at Bogotá's bus station (COP$4200, 1½ hours). Alternatively, take the **Turistren** (☑375-0557; www.turistren.com.co; round trip adult/child COP$43,000/27,000), which runs Saturdays and Sundays from Bogotá to Zipaquirá. The train departs Bogotá's main train station, **Estación de la Sabana** (Calle 13 No 18-24), at 8:30am, stops briefly at Usaquén Station at 9:20am and reaches Zipaquirá at 11:30am.

From Zipaquirá it's possible to catch a few daily buses on to Villa de Leyva.

A round-trip taxi from Bogotá should run about COP$180,000 plus COP$25,000 per hour waiting.

About 15km northeast of Zipaquirá, the town of **Nemocón** is also home to a smaller (and less touristy) salt mine that can be visited daily. This one has been in use for 400 years, and once served as the town hall. Head there by taxi.

⚲ Tours

Free walking tours depart daily at 10am and 2pm (in English at 2pm Tuesday and Thursday) from the Punto de Información Turística (PIT; p74) branch in La Candelaria.

★**Bogotá Bike Tours** CYCLING
(Map p50; ☑281-9924; www.bogotabiketours.com; Carrera 3 No 12-72; tours COP$35,000, rentals half-/full day COP$20,000/35,000) Run by California bike-enthusiast Mike Caesar, these tours are a fascinating way to see Bogotá, especially the neighborhoods that would otherwise be a no-go. Tours leave daily at 10:30am and 1:30pm from the La Candelaria office.

Typical highlights include La Candelaria, a fruit market – watch those spice vendors with their superhot wares! – the Plaza de Toros de Santamaría, the Central Cemetery and the Red Light district. Mike also rents bikes.

Bogotá Graffiti Tour ART TOURS
(Map p50; ☑321-297-4075; www.bogotagraffiti.com) **FREE** A fascinating 2½-hour walking tour through Bogotá's considerable and impressive urban art daily at 10am starting from Parque de los Periodistas. The tour itself is free but a COP$20,000 to COP$30,000 gratuity is recommended for the guide.

5Bogotá CULTURAL TOURS
(☑313-278-5898; www.5bogota.com) This upstart agency run by young *bogotanos* takes a hands-on approach to exploring the city and stands out among the standard fare. It creates sensorial experiences from the daily activities of everyday people. Unique tours include exploring truly local markets rather

Zona Rosa & Parque 93

N

500 m
0.25 miles

Calle 93

Carrera 30

AV 30

Calle 97A

Carrera 9A

Carrera 9

Carrera 8A

Calle 97A

Carrera 9A

Calle 96

Calle 95

Calle 94A

Carrera 10

Calle 94 (Av 94)

Hacienda Santa
Bárbara (3.5km);
Usaquén (4km)

Carrera 7

Calle 93

Chicó
Oriental
Bus Stop

Carrera II

Carrera 11A

Calle 96

Calle 95

Calle 94A

13

21

29

Ministerio de Relaciones
Exteriores (400m)

PARQUE
93

Calle 93A

Carrera 10

Carrera 11A

Carrera 10

Calle 92 (Av 92)

7

Carrera 15

Carrera 14

Calle 93B

Calle 93

Carrera 13

Parque
93

17

Calle 93

9

Carrera II

CHICÓ

Carrera 14

Calle 93B

Centro
93

19

Carrera 16

Carrera 14

Calle 90

Carrera 13

3

Calle 86A

Carrera 13

Carrera 13A

Calle 94 (Av 94)

Calle 93B

Carrera 17

Carrera 16

Carrera 14

6

Carrera 13A

Calle 85

Carrera 15

30

18

Calle 93B

Carrera 19

Carrera 18

Calle 92 (Av 92)

Carrera 17

Carrera 16

Calle 87

Carrera 19

Carrera 16

Calle 85

Calle 93

Calle 93B

Carrera 20

Carrera 19

Carrera 18

Calle 87

Carrera 22

Carrera 19A

Carrera 21

Calle 88A

Virrey
Station

Transversal 21

Autopista del Norte (Av 13)

Calle 85
Station

POLO
CLUB

Calle 87

Transversal 21

Diagonal 85A

Transversal 22

Diagonal 83

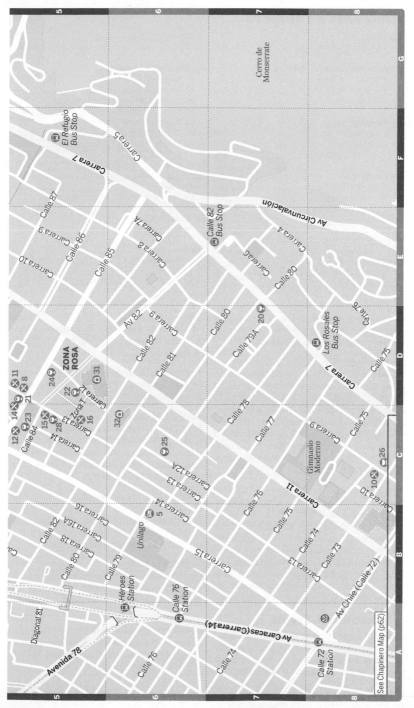

Cerro de Monserrate

El Refugio Bus Stop

Carrera 7

Carrera 5

Calle 87

Carrera 9

Calle 86

Carrera 10

Calle 85

Carrera 8

Carrera 7A

Av Circunvalación

Calle 82 Bus Stop

Carrera 4

Carrera 6

Calle 80

Calle 75

Av 82

Carrera 9

Calle 80

Los Rosales Bus Stop

Calle 76

ZONA ROSA

24

11

8

21

14

12

23

15

28

22

16

31

32

25

20

Calle 82

Calle 81

Calle 79A

Carrera 7

Carrera 12

Carrera 13

Carrera 14

Carrera 16

Calle 84

Zona T

Carrera 12A

Carrera 13

Calle 78

Calle 77

Carrera 9

Calle 75

Calle 79

5

Calle 82

Carrera 16A

Carrera 18

Calle 80

Unilago

Calle 76

Carrera 14

Carrera 13

Carrera 11

Gimnasio Moderno

10

26

Calle 76

Calle 75

Calle 74

Carrera 13

Calle 73

Carrera 15

Diagonal 81

Héroes Station

Avenida 78

Calle 76 Station

Av Caracas (Carrera 14)

Calle 76

Calle 74

Carrera 10

Av Chile (Calle 72)

Calle 72 Station

Carrera 15

See Chapinero Map (p62)

Zona Rosa & Parque 93

than touristy ones; learning how to make empanadas; taking graffiti lessons from a *grafitero;* and drum yoga sessions.

Destino Bogotá GUIDED TOURS
(☎753-4887; www.destinobogota.com) Offers many playful city and area tours including Haunted Bogotá, salsa lessons and club-hopping; more standard fare such as a worthy Guatavita/Zipaquirá day trip; and rarer options including East Hills hiking and a coffee-masters tour. New themes focused on beers, literature and gay nightlife are in development.

Andes Ecotours ECOTOURS
(Map p50; ☎310-559-9729; www.andesecotours.com; Carrera 3 No 12B-89) 🌿 Andes offers nature-focused day trips in and around Bogotá (Choachi cloud-forest hike, Sumapaz Páramo and Chingaza National Park hikes) as well as more far-flung multiday trips to Lago de Tota and coffee agrotourism adventures. All have a strong emphasis on sustainable tourism and community development.

🎉 Festivals & Events

A mix of local and national festivals takes place constantly throughout the year. The following is a selection of the best. Also ask around as smaller festivals are held each month.

Salsa al Parque SALSA
(www.festivalsalsaalparque.blogspot.com; ⊙Aug) A salsa extravaganza in Parque Simón Bolívar.

Festival de Verano CULTURAL
(⊙Aug) Ten days of free music and culture in Parque Simón Bolívar.

Festival de Jazz JAZZ
(www.culturarecreacionydeporte.gov.co/jazz_al_parque; ⊙Sep) Organized by Instituto Distrital de las Artes, this festival features local and national Latin jazz artists, plus an occasional US or European star.

Festival de Cine de Bogotá CINEMA
(www.bogocine.com; ⊙Oct) With a 30-year history, the city's film festival attracts films from all around the world, including a usually strong Latin American selection.

Hip Hop al Parque MUSIC
(www.culturarecreacionydeporte.gov.co/hiphop/; ⊙Oct) Two days of hip-hop taking over Parque Simón Bolívar.

Rock al Parque MUSIC
(www.rockalparque.net; ⊙Oct & Nov) Three days of (mostly South American) rock/metal/pop/funk/reggae bands at Parque Simón Bolívar. It's free and swarming with fans.

Expoartesanías   ARTS & CRAFTS

(www.expoartesanias.com; ⊘ Dec) This crafts fair gathers together artisans and their products from all around the country. Crafts are for sale and it's an excellent place to buy them.

🛌 Sleeping

Bogotá recently experienced a boutique hotel boom and there are now plenty of trendy options and high-end choices mainly in the north. If you are in town on business, appreciate the finer things or just want peace of mind from a security standpoint, you may be best served by the hotels scattered north of Calle 65, many of which are within walking distance of the lively scene of Zona G, Zona Rosa or Parque 93, and there is a hostel scene on the cusp as well. Sleep here and visit La Candelaria during the day.

If travel's your game and time's short, La Candelaria is where most of Bogotá's attractions and budget lodgings are located.

🛌 La Candelaria

In the past couple of years, the historic suburb of La Candelaria has seen an explosion in hostels. Generally private rooms in hostels are better than cheapie rooms in the several dated, grubby hotels around here. Higher-end travelers can choose from a couple of fine locales with more colonial spirit than you'll find anywhere else in the capital.

Cranky Croc   HOSTEL $

(Map p50; ☑ 342-2438; www.crankycroc.com; Calle 12D No 3-46; dm from COP$23,000, s/d/tr COP$56,000/74,000/105,000, without bathroom COP$66,000/90,000/120,000; @ 🛜) One of our favorite hostels in town. It's run by a friendly Aussie and offers six dorms and seven rooms around several communal areas, including a chef-driven kitchen with made-to-order breakfasts and excellent coffee. Dorm beds get lockers, reading lamps and individual electric outlets for device charging. And those newly renovated bathrooms? You'd think you were in a boutique hotel.

Lima Limon   HOSTEL $

(Map p50; ☑ 281-1260; www.limalimonhostel.com. co; Carrera 1 No 12B-15; dm from COP$22,000, s/d without bathroom COP$40,000/60,000, all incl breakfast; @ 🛜) Set around a colorful internal courtyard, this cozy hostel has tonnes of character. Its small size and chilled, artistic vibe make it feel more like a houseshare than a big-city hostel and there is an excellent kitchen for preparing communal meals. Bonus: 24-hour reception and hot water all day.

Casa Bellavista   HOSTEL $

(Map p50; ☑ 334-1230; www.bellavistahostelbogota.com; Carrera 2 No 12B-31; dm from COP$18,000, s/d COP$60,000/70,000, all incl breakfast; @ 🛜) You'll find good value and loads of antiquated character at this small, family-run choice in a historic house steps from Plazoleta del Chorro de Quevedo. Creaky hardwood floors lead to colorful dorms that have their own bathrooms, and the two spacious private rooms are chock-full of detail such as original tile flooring.

⭐**Masaya Intercultural Hostel**   HOSTEL $$

(Map p50; ☑ 747-1848; www.masaya-experience.com; Carrera 2 No 12-48; dm from COP$20,000 r with/without bathroom from COP$100,000/70,000; @ 🛜) Taking flashpacker luxury to a new level, this large French-owned hostel has notably comfortable dorms, with privacy curtains, bean bags, and fluffy pillows and duvets, while the private hotel-quality rooms are very spacious and boast first-rate wardrobes and flat-screen TVs. You'll also find great common areas, piping-hot high-pressure showers and a wealth of cultural activities.

Casa Platypus   GUESTHOUSE $$

(Map p50; ☑ 281-1801; www.casaplatypus.com; Carrera 3 No 12F-28; dm/s/d/tr COP$44,000/ 144,000/166,000/188,000; @ 🛜) This upscale guesthouse is the flashpacker choice. Simple rooms have masculine hardwoods and private bathrooms, a narrow terrace perfect for watching the 5pm weekday university fashion show in the street below, and a wonderful rooftop terrace with Montserrat views.

Anandamayi Hostel   HOSTEL $$

(Map p50; ☑ 341-7208; www.anandamayihostel. com; Calle 9 No 2-81; s without bathroom COP$40,000/110,000/160,000, d COP$180,000, all incl breakfast; @ 🛜) South of most hostels, this lovely whitewashed and turquoise-trimmed colonial home has very well-furnished rooms with wood-beam ceilings, plenty of wool blankets and colonial furniture. Rooms and the 13-bed dorm surround a few semi-leafy central stone courtyards with hammocks. A top Candelaria choice for those seeking peace and quiet in their hostel and a less gringo-centric experience.

★ **Orchids** BOUTIQUE HOTEL **$$$**
(Map p50; ☑745-5438; www.theorchidshotel.
com; Carrera 5 No 10-55; r COP$550,000, ste
COP$660,000; @ 🛜) Behind the mauve fa-
cade hides La Candelaria's most discerning
and posh choice, an intimate eight-room
boutique hotel absolutely beaming with his-
toric character. Every generously spacious
room dabbles in a different design scheme,
but period furniture (some original to the
historic mansion), four-poster beds, porce-
lain sinks and thick wooden writing desks
are just some of the details on display here.

The stylish staff is decked out in
purple-accented butler-type fare (think
Latin Downton Abbey!) and the by-
reservation-only restaurant serves a menu
created by Harry Sassoon, one of Bogotá's
most famous chefs.

★ **Casa Deco** BOUTIQUE HOTEL **$$$**
(Map p50; ☑282-8640; www.hotelcasadeco.
com; Calle 12C No 2-36; s/d incl breakfast from
COP$190,000/229,000; @ 🛜) A 21-room gem
run by an Italian emerald dealer (no pun in-
tended), this discerning option is a serious
step up from the sea of hostels surrounding
it. Rooms come in seven bright colors and
are laced with bespoke hardwood art deco-
style furniture, desks and futon beds.

There's a guitarist at breakfast, adorable
staff, and a mesmerizing terrace with Monserrate and Cerro de Guadalupe views.

🛏 Chapinero

★ **La Pinta** HOSTEL **$$**
(Map p62; ☑211-9526; www.lapinta.com.
co; Calle 65 No 5-67; dm from COP$26,000,
s/d COP$90,000/120,000, without bathroom
COP$70,000/96,000; @ 🛜) In an unmarked
residential home in a great Chapinero lo-
cation just steps from La Séptima (Car-
rera 7), this spotless little secret offers a
fantastic back garden; big, modern bath-
rooms; and colorful down comforters in
hardwood-floored rooms that approach
boutique-hotel levels. There's a large, com-
munal kitchen; a cozy new bar; and a
whacky, lovable dog. Room 304 is the best
double with a garden view.

Fulano Backpackers HOSTEL **$$**
(Map p62; ☑744-2053; www.fulanobackpackers.
com; Carrera 10A No 69-41; dm from COP$24,000, r
with/without bathroom from COP$110,000/86,000,
all incl breakfast; @ 🛜) An Italian-Colombian
affair inside a historic Quinta Camacho

mansion, this boutique hostel is easy on
the eyes. It calls on juxtapositions of hard-
woods, minimalist design schemes and
artistic bathroom tilings to foster an aesthet-
ically impressive environment for a hostel.
DJs, live music sets and spontaneous BBQs
on the custom-built grill aren't uncommon,
and an air of cultural awareness pervades
throughout.

12:12 Hostel HOSTEL **$$**
(Map p62; ☑467-2656; www.1212hostels.com;
Carrera 4 No 66-46; dm COP$26,000-40,000, r
COP$116,000; @ 🛜) 🌀 This artsy new hostel
epitomizes the cutting-edge Chapinero Alto
scene: recycled materials such as discarded
bikes, which climb the walls like funhouse art
installations, and tossed-aside books, which
pepper the walls instead of wallpaper, are the
backbone of this design-forward choice.

The colorful dorm beds are Bogotá's most
comfortable, with cozy down comforters,
reading lamps and privacy curtains; and
the big, modern, communal kitchen and
slate bathrooms are above and beyond for
a hostel.

Casa Rústica GUESTHOUSE **$$$**
(Map p62; ☑210-0023; www.casarusticabogota.
com; Calle 70 No 9-41; s/d incl breakfast & lunch
COP$115,000/195,000; 🛜) 🌀 This quirky
choice in Quinto Camacho has the neighborhood talking. The somewhat eccentric owner
specializes in Art Réco, a movement that follows the philosophy of one's person's trash is
another person's treasure. To that end, 80%
of this 1950s home is furnished with recycled, discarded and rescued objects.

The six rooms are cozy – think of writers
tucking away from civilization for a few days –
and the idea is novel. Our favorite is the El
Altillo, an attic room with exposed brick,
slanted ceiling and rooftop views.

🛏 Zona G

La Casona del Patio GUESTHOUSE **$$$**
(Map p62; ☑212-8805; www.lacasonadel
patio.net; Carrera 8 No 69-24; s/d incl breakfast
COP$125,000/170,000; @ 🛜) This tranquil
guesthouse in a historic home has grown to
24 rooms and feels a bit like an adult hos-
tel. Old rooms surrounding a small court-
yard now boast LCD TVs in addition to faux
wood floors and are picture-themed for area
attractions. Newer rooms in a second, at-
tached home are more modern.

🛏 Zona Rosa & Parque 93

Chapinorte Bogotá　　　　HOSTEL **$$**
(Map p56; ☑ 317-640-6716; www.chapinortehostelbogota.com; Calle 79 No 14-59, Apt 402; s/d/tr COP$85,000/100,000/145,000, without bathroom COP$60,000/80,000/120,000; @ 🛜) In a nondescript residential building just beyond the northern edges of the Chapinero, this eight-room guesthouse on two floors is a great anti-Candelaria choice. Run by a friendly Spaniard, some of the hostel's stylish rooms have enormous bathrooms and cable TVs, and surround a cute island kitchen in the living room. No breakfast.

★ Hotel Click-Clack　　　BOUTIQUE HOTEL **$$$**
(Map p56; ☑ 743-0404; www.clickclack.com; Carrera 11 No 93-77; r COP$280,000-470,000; ✳ @ 🛜) This high-design newcomer is the boutique hotel of choice for hobnobbing with Colombia's trendsetters. The urban, sophisticated aesthetic here is vaguely based around vintage TVs and photographic equipment. The best of the five room sizes (extra small to large) are the 2nd-floor mediums, which open up to spacious outdoor patios with small patches of grass and a vertical garden.

There's no spa or fitness center – everything here from Apache, the high-class mini burger bar on the roof with stupendous views, to 100 Grams, the trendy basement restaurant where everything is served in 100 gram portions (like larger-sized tapas), is focused on a good time, not on R&R. There's both a Lust kit and a Hangover kit in each room, depending on how things go.

Cité　　　　　　　　　　BOUTIQUE HOTEL **$$$**
(Map p56; ☑ 644-4000; www.citehotel.com; Carrera 15 No 88-10; r incl breakfast from COP$560,000; ✳ @ 🛜 ≋) Part of a small Bogotá chain, this newish business-hip boutique hotel located between Zona Rosa and Parque 93 boasts rarely seen advantages such as a heated rooftop pool, extra-large rooms with lots of natural light and even some with bathtubs, a true rarity. Perhaps coolest of all is that there are bicycles for guests to use for free – handy as you are on a CicloRuta bike path.

🍴 Eating

Fusion is the word today for many restaurateurs in Bogotá, who are running Mediterranean, Italian, Californian or pan-Asian influences through typical Colombian dishes. Peruvian seems to have taken off at an obnoxious level. After being ruled by chains (albeit great ones) for years, the burger scene in Bogotá has finally received its requisite makeover and now boasts a plethora of gourmet burger hot spots. The best dining destinations include Zona Rosa, Nogal and Zona G; also recommended is Macarena's slightly boho scene, just north of La Candelaria, where many restaurants close up the kitchen and continue on into the night with drinks for the lively student scene.

🍴 La Candelaria

Quinua y Amaranto　　　　VEGETARIAN **$**
(Map p50; www.blog.colombio.co/quinua-y-amaranto.html; Calle 11 No 2-95; set lunch COP$14,000; ☺ 8am-4pm Sat & Mon, to 7pm Tue-Fri; ☑) This sweet spot – run by ladies in the open-front kitchen – goes all vegetarian during the week (there's often chicken *ajiaco* – soup with chicken, corn, potato, cream and capers – on weekends), with tasty set lunches and empanadas, salads and coffee. A small section of coco leaves, baked goods and tempting chunks of artisanal cheese (on Saturdays) round out the homey offerings.

La Puerta Falsa　　　　　FAST FOOD **$**
(Map p50; Calle 11 No 6-50; candies COP$1500-2000, snacks COP$3500-6300; ☺ 7am-9pm Mon-Sat, 8am-7pm Sun) This is Bogotá's most famous snack shop. Displays of multicolored candies beckon you into this tiny spot that's been in business since 1816. Some complain it's nothing but foreigners with their Lonely Planet guides these days, but don't buy it – there were no other gringos on our visit.

The moist *tamales* and *chocolate completo* (hot chocolate with cheese, buttered bread and a biscuit; COP$6500) remain a Bogotá snack of lore.

**Café de la Peña
Pastelería Francesa**　　　　　CAFE **$**
(Map p50; Carrera 3 No 9-66; items COP$2700-5800; ☺ 8am-7pm Mon-Sat, 9am-6pm Sun; 🛜) Colombians run this fabulous French-style bakery, but you'd never know it. They make some of the nicest sweets and *pan de chocolate* in the area; and they roast their own excellent coffee. Local art adorns the walls of the garden and there are a couple of seating areas.

Hibiscus Cafe　　　　　　BREAKFAST **$**
(Map p50; Calle 12D No 2-21; breakfast COP$3400-7900; ☺ 7am-6pm Mon-Sat, 8am-3pm Sun; 🛜) Splitting its breakfast trade evenly between

Chapinero

N 0 _____ 400 m
0 _____ 0.2 miles

See Zona Rosa & Parque 93 Map (p56)

Calle 73

Av Chile (Calle 72)

Bellavista
Bus Stop

Calle 68

Calle 71

Calle 70A

Flores
Station

2 ● KIIA

5

4

Av Chile
Bus Stop

Calle 68

Calle 69

Carrera 11

Calle 70

16

Calle 70

Calle 67

Carrera 9

Carrera 8

Carrera 7A

6

Calle 69A

Calle 66

Calle 69

ZONA G

11

Av Caracas (Carrera 14)

Calle 64

15

Carrera 13

Calle 68

Calle 63

Calle 67
Bus Stop

Calle 63
Station

17

Calle 63

3

Carrera 7

Carrera 11

Calle 62

7

8

13

Carrera 9A

Calle 65

Carrera 4

Calle 61

Calle 64

Carrera 5

Calle 60

Calle 62

Av Caracas (Carrera 14)

Calle 59

Universidad
La Salle
Bus Stop

19

Calle 58 bis

Carrera 9

CHAPINERO
ALTO

18

Calle 57
Station

20

Calle 57

Carrera 13

21

Calle 59

Carrera 4

Carrera 8

Parque
Portugal

14

Calle 55

Bosque
Calderón
Bus Stop

10

Carrera 3A

Calle 56

9

Carrera 7

Calle 54A

Av Circunvalación

Calle 53

Calle 54

12

Transversal 3

Calle 51

Calle 51A

C 51

1

Chapinero

locals and backpackers, this simple and cute corner pad has great, quick set breakfasts that up the ante on what some simpler accommodations may offer in the morning.

★**Sant Just**   FRENCH $$
(Map p50; Calle 16A No 2-73; mains COP$14,000-32,000; ⊙noon-4pm Mon-Sat; 🛜) 🍽 This wonderful French-owned cafe serves a daily changing menu of Colombian-leaning French fare presented tableside via chalkboard. Whatever the kitchen churns out that day – fresh juices, sustainably caught seafood, wonderful lamb served alongside previously out-of-favor veggies such as *cubio* (an Andean root) – it nails, both in the presentation and the comfort-food-goodness quotient. Expect a wait. Cash only.

Trattoria Nuraghe   ITALIAN $$
(Map p50; Calle 12B No 1-26; mains COP$14,000-28,000; ⊙11:30am-9pm Tue-Sat, noon-5pm Sun) Absolutely excellent home-style Italian served up by a friendly Sardinian family in a narrow and intimate space. This place is perfect for a long and leisurely wine-fueled lunch, especially on Sundays, when it's one of the few great choices open.

Real-deal Sardinian dishes such as *malloreddus alla campidanese* (shell-like pasta with Italian-style chorizo and pecorino) and *spaghettino allu ollu e bottarga* (pasta with garlic, parsley and bottarga) are the way to go.

Capital Cocina   COLOMBIAN $$
(Map p50; Calle 10 No 2-99; mains COP$15,500-25,000; ⊙noon-3:30pm & 6:30-10pm Mon-Sat) Prepare to fight for tables at this quaint cafe serving a few takes on simple Colombian comfort food – fish of the day, pork chop, steak, *pollo suprema* – that are in fact anything but simple. The daily menu (COP$16,500) is a three-course steal considering the quality of Chef Juan Pablo's food; and there are artisanal beers, decent wines and single-origin coffee. For dinner in La Candelaria, it's tough to beat.

La Hamburguesería   BURGERS $$
(Map p50; www.lahamburgueseria.com; Calle 11 No 2-78; burgers COP$13,500-25,000; ⊙11am-10pm Mon-Sat, to 6pm Sun; 🛜🍽) Some of the city's best burgers are found at the Candelaria outlet of this trendy burger chain, born a little more north in Macarena. Thick, gourmet patties are beefed up with an international flare (Mexican, Mediterranean, Middle Eastern, including several vegetarian options) and served alongside five housemade relishes and sauces. There's also live jazz on Friday nights from 8pm.

★**La Condesa Irina Lazaar**   AMERICAN $$$
(Map p50; 📋283-1573; Carrera 6 No 10-19; mains COP$25,000-40,000; ⊙noon-3:30pm Mon-Fri & 7-10pm Thu-Sat; 🛜) 🍽 This small, unsigned 10-table eatery run by a hands-on Mexican-American from California caters to bohos, judges, Congressmen and ambassadors in the know. It's named after a character in a forgettable American Western, *Shalako*. Thankfully, the food is way better than the film. Chef Edgardo dishes out fantastic comfort food, going organic where possible.

From line-caught fish to organic chicken, beautiful ham steak and wonderfully spicy shrimp *étouffée*, every choice from the small menu is a knockout and the entire experience is easily Candelaria's best.

✕ City Center

Pastelería Florida   COLOMBIAN $
(Map p50; Carrera 7 No 21-46; snacks COP$1100-22,000, chocolate completo COP$8600) Those

needing a bit of pomp or history with their *chocolate santafereño* (hot chocolate served with cheese) should make the hike to this classic snack shop–restaurant (a legendary spot for hot chocolate since 1936), where uniformed waiters serve up a variety of cakes.

Olimpica
SUPERMARKET $

(Map p50; Av Jiménez No 4-70; ⊗7am-9pm Mon-Sat, 9am-4pm Sun) About a five-minute walk from most hostels in the area.

Restaurante la Pola
COLOMBIAN $$

(Map p50; Calle 19bis No 1-85; ajiaco COP$17,000-19,000; ⊗11am-5pm Mon-Sat) This rambling classic on the road to Monserrate has a mix of old-style rooms and a small courtyard. It offers some great lunch grills, or you can order à la carte for some of the city's best *ajiaco*.

✕ Macarena

Macarena is an up-and-coming dining district – with a stream of excellent, stylish choices – holding true to its local roots. It's the kind of place where passersby are likely to pop in and chat with diners. Macarena is a dozen blocks north of La Candelaria (east of Carrera 7 from Centro Internacional and on up the hill).

There are also many worthy choices on Calle 29bis, just northeast of the Museo Nacional.

La Tapería
TAPAS $$

(Map p50; www.lataperia.co; Carrera 4A No 26D-12; tapas COP$9900-27,000; ⊗noon-3pm & 6pm-late Mon-Fri, 1-11pm Sat, to 4pm Sun; ⊛) To the delight of nearly everyone in the know, delectable tapas such as cherry tomatoes wrapped in blue cheese and bacon with a balsamic reduction (our fave!) are churned out under the guidance of a Dutch music fiend in this cool, loft-aesthetic Macarena lounge. There's live flamenco (Thursdays and Saturdays) and Friday's neighborhood-curated Musica del Barrio playlist draws the young and restless.

★ Agave Azul
MEXICAN $$$

(Map p50; ☑315-277-0329; www.restaurantagaveazul.blogspot.com; Carrera 3A No 26B-52; meals COP$70,000; ⊗noon-3pm & 6-10pm Tue-Fri, 1-4pm & 7-10:30pm Sat; ⊛) This outstanding restaurant is a trip, both literally and figuratively, through truly authentic Mexican cuisine by way of Chicago, New York and Oaxaca. Chef Tatiana Navarro has no menu – just a daily open-ended tasting menu – and no sign. It's

hidden away inside a residential home on a difficult street in Macarena. Take a taxi.

Once you're safely inside, a culinary coup awaits: possibilities include slow-braised Jalisco shortribs with chile ancho, black lasagna with *huitlacoche* (corn fungus) or mini *carnitas* sandwiches with *chicharones* (pork cracklings), avocado and marinated onions, but it's always a surprise. Chase it with outstanding chipotle margaritas (COP$19,000) – surely Colombia's best – and you have reached nirvana *cocina Mexicana*.

Leo Cocina y Cava
COLOMBIAN $$$

(Map p50; ☑286-7091; www.leococinaycava.com; Calle 27B No 6-75; mains COP$29,000-46,000; ⊗noon-4pm & 7-11pm Mon-Sat) Chef Leo Espinosa is the go-to culinary priestess for Colombian fine dining. Her classic (COP$140,000) and seasonal (COP$130,000) tasting menus are a journey through exotic regional ingredients, much of which are ignored by most Colombian kitchens. A meal here is revelatory – bold colors, striking flavors – and triggers a 41-word glossary to explain it all! A foodie must.

✕ Chapinero

The established Chapinero Alto artistic community is close-knit and boasts all kinds of quaint neighborhood cafes and shops.

Arbol de Pan
BAKERY $

(Map p62; Calle 66 No 4A-35; items COP$1500-6500; ⊗8am-8pm Mon-Sat; ⊛) Forget about breakfast at your hotel or hostel, as this all-natural bakery and pastry shop pumps out a long list of daily just-baked breads (multigrain, dates and oats, etc) and a slew of delectable pastries. There's also heartier breakfast fare, such as croissants stuffed with poached egg, ham and spinach (COP$12,500).

The sunlit patio is perfect for lingering in the aroma of baked goodness from the open kitchen.

Salvo Patria
CAFE $$

(Map p62; www.salvopatria.com; Carrera 54A No 4-13; mains COP$16,000-32,000; ⊗noon-11am Mon-Sat; ⊛) This hip cafe's popularity outgrew its original location. Now having moved a few blocks away, it remains a Chapinero Alto stalwart of coolness and quality. It's one part very serious coffeehouse (the *bogotano* owner honed his barista skills in Australia, so even Australians don't complain about the coffee!), and one part

BOGOTÁ CHAINS

We're not accustomed to touting chains, but Bogotá has some surprisingly worthy ones. You'll find them in most neighborhoods, particularly in the north.

Wok (www.wok.com.co; mains COP$13,900-31,900) Choosing your dish at this hip chain with a social/environmental bent is as agonizing as deciding which of your children to throw to the wolves: excellent Chinese, Vietnamese, Indonesian and Cambodian dishes abound (including line-caught sushi), and attract a steady stream of cool locals. Everything is great. There are several branches: Centro Internacional (Map p50; www.wok. com.co; Carrera 6 No 29-07, Centro Internacional; mains COP$13,900-31,900; ⊗noon-10pm Mon-Thu, to 10:30pm Fri-Sat, noon-6pm Sun; 🕾🗷) Parque 93 (Map p56; www.wok.com.co; Calle 93B No 12-28, Parque 93; mains COP$13,900-31,900; ⊗11am-10:30pm Mon-Wed, noon-11pm Thu-Sat, to 9pm Sun; 🕾) Zona Rosa (Map p56; www.wok.com.co; Carrera 13 No 82-74; mains COP$13,900-31,900; ⊗noon-10:30pm Mon-Wed, to 11pm Thu-Sat, to 10pm Sun; 🕾).

El Corral (Map p56; www.elcorral.com; Calle 85 No 13-77; burgers COP$10,300-18,900; ⊗24hr; 🕾) Part of the El Corral and El Corral Gourmet empire – some of the best fast-food burgers you'll ever stumble across – this 24-hour outlet is requisite refueling for the restless set. There's another branch at Centro Cultural Gabriel García Márquez (Map p50; Calle 11 No 5-60; mains COP$17,500-46,900; ⊗noon-8pm Mon-Sat, to 5pm Sun; 🕾).

Bogotá Beer Company (Map p56; www.bogotabeercompany.com; Calle 85 No 13-06; pints COP$10,900; ⊗12:30pm-2:30am; 🕾) These pub-style, upscale beer joints are a godsend for beer lovers, with some 12 seasonal microbrews on tap (though many are often unavailable). The Usaquén and Macarena locales are a bit more laid-back than most; and Chapinero Alto's smaller take-away La Bodega serves pints 40% cheaper than a normal BBC. Branches: Usaquén (www.bogotabeercompany.com; Carrera 6 No 119-24, Usaquén; pints COP$10,900; ⊗12:30pm-1am Sun-Tue, to 2:30am Wed-Sat; 🕾) Macarena (Map p50; www.bogotabeercompany.com; Carrera 4A No 27-04; pints COP$10,900; ⊗12:30pm-late; 🕾) Chapinero Alto (La Bodega; Map p62; www.bogotabeercompany.com; Calle 59 No 4-15; pints COP$4300-5900; ⊗10am-9pm Sun-Wed, to 11pm Thu-Sat; 🕾) Zona Rosa (Map p56; www. bogotabeercompany.com; Carrera 12 No 83-33; pints CP$10,000; ⊗11:30am-1am Sun-Tue, to 2am Wed, to 3am Thu-Sat; 🕾).

Crepes & Waffles (Map p56; www.crepesywaffles.com.co; Carrera 9 No 73-33; mains COP$9900-24,400; ⊗11:45am-10pm Mon-Thu, to 11pm Fri, to 10:30pm Sat, to 9pm Sun; 🕾) Of the 35 Bogotá locations of this ever-busy chain – which employs women in need – we like this one best: a two-story brick home with sidewalk seats between Zona G and Zona Rosa. Like the others, it serves up veggie, meat and seafood crepes, plus irresistible ice-cream-topped waffles (COP$6300).

Juan Valdéz (Map p50; www.juanvaldezcafe.com; Carrera 6 No 11-20, Centro Cultural Gabriel García Márquez; coffee COP$2900-6000; ⊗7am-6pm Mon-Sat, 10am-6pm Sun; 🕾) One of two big Starbucks-like chains here (Oma is the other), Juan Valdéz does as a reliable a job with a *tinto* (black coffee), cappuccino or cafe americano as nearly anyone in town. Try the following branches: Museo Nacional (Map p50; Carrera 7 No 28-66, Museo Nacional; coffee COP$2900-6000; ⊗10am-6pm Tue-Sat, to 5pm Sun) Zona G (Map p62; www.juanvaldezcafe.com; Calle 70 No 6-09; coffee COP$3400-6800; ⊗7am-10pm Mon-Sat; 🕾) Zona Rosa (Map p56; www.juanvaldezcafe.com; cnr Calle 73 & Carrera 9; coffee COP$2900-6000; ⊗7am-8pm Mon-Fri, 8am-8pm Sat-Sun; 🕾). You'll find them all over town; the north has the most, including a boutique version specializing in single origin coffees (Zona G).

bar-restaurant dishing up sophisticated Mediterranean-French bistro fare to artsy hipsters in the know. Great cocktails, rarer Colombian craft beer and great-value *menú del día* (COP$18,500).

★**Mini-Mal** COLOMBIAN $$$
(Map p62; www.mini-mal.org; Carrera 4A No 57-52; mains COP$16,900-32,900; ⊗noon-10pm Mon-Wed, to midnight Thu-Sat; 🕾) 🖋 You'll be hard-pressed to find a more creative

Colombian menu than at this excellent Chapinero Alto hot spot, which has resurrected some of the country's more interesting regional ingredients – sourced sustainably and fiercely artisan – and breathed new life into contemporary Colombian cuisine.

Beef braised with *tucupi* (a spicy, *adobo*-like sauce sourced from poisonous yuca root); green-curried seafood on a thin wafer made from coconut, demerara sugar and lemon; plaintain sushi with coastal cheese – it's all outstanding and totally without precedent. Chase it down with cocktails made with *viche* (a smoky sugarcane moonshine) and kick yourself for not moving beyond *arepas* (corn cakes) and *ajíaco* sooner. Sweets are given equal attention a block away at **Dulce Mini-Mal** (Map p62; www.mini-mal.org; Calle 57 No 4-09; items COP$700-6500; ◎11am-8pm Mon-Fri, 9am-8pm Sat, to 5pm Sun; 🛜).

✕ Zona G

Bogotá's primo dining area fills a couple of blocks of converted brick houses and offers a mix of excellent eateries (Argentine, Italian, French), about 10 blocks south of Zona Rosa.

Nick's   SANDWICHES $$
(Map p62; www.nicksbogota.com; Carrera 4 No 69-23; sandwiches COP$10,000-18,900; ◎10am-11pm Mon-Thu, to 3am Fri & Sat, to 5pm Sun; 🛜) Nick honed his deli skills in Boston and, recognizing a niche in his hometown, now presides over a killer deli-sandwich kingdom in Bogotá. This Zona G hot spot is the hippest of the four locations, which include El Nogal, Chicó and **La Candelaria** (Map p50; www.nicksbogota.com; Carrera 5 No 12C-85; ◎10am-10pm Mon-Sat; 🛜).

Almost 30 sandwiches are churned out on soft ciabatta, feeding a frenzy that turns the multi-level indie-vintage space (flush with enough retro props to support a period film) into a full-on bar at night.

✕ Zona Rosa & Parque 93

Within the Zona Rosa, the 'Zona T' is named for its T-shaped pedestrian zone filled with bars, restaurants and a few chains; there are also oodles more options on surrounding blocks. Ten blocks north, the more-sedate Parque 93 and Calle 94 have even classier spots. For shoppers, high-class foodies or the boutique-hotel and club crowd, this is your part of town.

You'll see a few food trucks, but shipping containers seem to be all the rage. There's a small congregation of **gourmet food containers** (Map p56; Calle 95 btwn Carreras 11A & 12) that serve up ceviche, bagels, sandwiches and sweets; an entire gourmet shipping-container food court, **Container City** (Map p56; Calle 93 No 12-11; ◎11am-11pm), has opened nearby as well.

La Areparia Venzolana   FAST FOOD $
(Map p56; Calle 85 No 13-36; arepas COP$11,00-13,500; ◎9am-10pm Mon-Thu, to 4am Fri & Sat; 🛜) Firmly rooted late-night hot spot for drunken munchies right off Zona Rosa. Venezuelan-style *arepas* (better than the Colombian corn cakes) are stuffed with all manner of fillings.

La Paletteria   DESSERTS $
(Map p56; cnr Carrera 13 & Calle 84; popsicles COP$4000-5000; ◎11am-9pm Mon-Fri, to 10pm Sat) If you're as serious about your popsicles as some *bogotanos*, come to La Paletteria for the 36 flavors standing sentinel like a kaleidoscopic tutti-frutti army of sweets in a display case. They're divided by base: yogurt, water or cream. It's painstaking to choose, but *guanabana* (soursop) with *arequipe* (a sweet dessert of milk and sugar) won us over.

★ Central Cevicheria   SEAFOOD $$
(Map p56; ✆644-7766; www.centralcevicheria.com; Carrera 13 No 85-14; ceviche COP$17,800-19,800; ◎noon-11pm Mon-Wed, to midnight Thu-Sat, to 10pm Sun; 🛜) This good-time, high-concept cevicheria is the real deal: Bogotá's high and mighty ogle over the superb ceviches, split into spicy and nonspicy categories, of which there are a dozen inventive offerings. Reservations are recommended.

We opted for the kick-laced *picoso,* swimming in two peppers, cilantro and fresh corn. But it doesn't stop there: there are numerous *tiraditos* (long-cut ceviches without onions), tartares, fresh seafood main dishes and burgers. It's Colombian coastal cuisine on overdrive. Save room for the dense and delicious coconut flan!

Di Lucca   ITALIAN $$
(Map p56; www.diluccatogo.com; Carrera 13 No 85-32; pizza COP$19,900-29,900; ◎noon-midnight Mon-Sat, to 11pm Sun; 🛜) Locals unanimously gush over this smart trattoria and its soothing prices. Pizza, pasta and risottos rule. Solo travelers could do much worse than bellying up to the hardwood bar and ordering a perfectly executed off-menu *medium*

ANDRÉS CARNE DE RES

You cannot describe the indescribable but here goes: the legendary **Andrés Carne de Res** (☑863-7880; www.andrescarnederes.com; Calle 3 No 11A-56, Chía; mains COP$16,700-75,500, cover Fri & Sat COP$10,000-15,000; ⊙11am-3am Thu-Sat, to midnight Sun) bar-restaurant is an otherworldly entertainment cocktail that's equal parts Tim Burton, Disneyland and Willy Wonka – with a dash of junkyard kitsch and funhouse extravaganza. No, wait. A Swedish tourist said it better: 'It's like eating dinner in a washing machine.' *Whatever.* Andrés blows everyone away – even repeat visitors – for its all-out-fun atmosphere with awesome steaks – the menu is a 70-page magazine – and all sorts of surreal decor. For most, it's more than a meal, but an up-all-night, damn-the-torpedoes spectacular.

The catch is that it's out of town – in Chía, 23km north toward Zipaquirá. A taxi from Bogotá costs about COP$70,000, or COP$140,000 for the round trip plus COP$25,000 per hour waiting. A party bus to Andrés on Saturday nights leaves at 10pm from **Hostal Sue Candelaria** (Map p50; ☑344-2647; www.suecandelaria.com; Carrera 3 No 12C-18; dm COP$23,000, s/d without bathroom COP$45,000/60,000, r COP$70,000, all incl breakfast; @☎), returning at 4am (COP$60,000 – includes admission and booze on the bus). Alternatively, save a bit of money getting there by catching a Chía-bound bus from inside the TransMilenio's 'Portal del Norte' station from the Buses Intermuncipales platform; buses leave every two minutes until midnight (COP$2300, 30 minutes). See for yourself if Andrés' isn't the most insane night you have ever had.

For a more sedate location closer to town, **Andrés D.C.** (Map p56; ☑863-7880; www.andrescarnederes.com; Calle 82 No 12-21, Centro Comercial El Retiro; mains COP$16,700-70,700, cover Thu & Sat COP$10,000-20,000; ⊙noon-3am) is also an option, but it lacks that certain indescribable something.

prosciutto pizza for just COP$17,600. Great food, low bills, fun crowd *and* open on Sunday nights!

🍴 Usaquén

Once a village to the north, Usaquén has been overtaken by Bogotá – but still lives at its own quiet pace. You'll find a smorgasbord of chic dining all within a few blocks of the tranquil plaza.

★Abasto
BREAKFAST $$

(www.abasto.com; Carrera 6 No 119B-52; breakfast COP$5800-19,900, mains COP$19,600-33,900; ⊙7am-10pm Mon-Thu, to 11pm Fri, 9am-10:30pm Sat, 9am-5pm Sun; ☎🖊) A weekend pilgrimage to Usaquén is in order to indulge in the creative breakfasts and delectable mains and desserts at this rustic-trendy restaurant. Inventive *arepas* and seriously good egg dishes such as *migas* (scrambled eggs with bits of *arepas* and *hogao,* a concoction of onion, tomatoes, cumin and garlic) are washed down with organic coffee by true morning-sustenance connoisseurs.

Whatever you order, sprinkle a bit of the punch-packing Wai Ya organic Amazonian pepper in it. Down the road, the new **La Bodega de Abasto** (www.abasto.com; Calle 120A No 3A-05; mains COP$6500-26,800; ⊙9am-5pm Tue-Sun; ☎) 🖊 is similar, but more focused on gourmet products and simpler (but scrumptious) lunches such as country rotisserie chicken.

🍷 Drinking & Nightlife

Some of the city's most atmospheric bars – that is, if you're into 300-year-old homes with corner fireplaces and old tile floors – are in La Candelaria, a great spot to try a hot mug of *canelazo* (a drink made with aguardiente, sugarcane, cinnamon and lime). Watering holes get way more trendy and upscale around Zona Rosa or Parque 93.

Strap yourself in: Bogotá boogies. There's all sorts of ambience and musical rhythm on offer – from rock, techno and metal to salsa, vallenato and samba. If you don't know how to dance, be prepared to prove it. Strangers frequently ask each other to dance and everyone seems to know the words to every song played.

The relatively laid-back club scene of La Candelaria caters to local students, but is seedy at night and isn't always a great option for drunken foreigner revelery. Macarena draws a more sophisticated, thirtysomething crowd of newlyweds, latent singles and those looking for more of a lounge experience than a club. Further north, particularly in the chic scene around the sparkling and vibrant (if pretentious) *salsatecas* (salsa dance clubs) and clubs of Zona Rosa and Parque 93, you may be turned away for not being dressed up to the part.

New laws allow some spots within Zona Rosa, Chapinero and Parque 93 to stay open until 5am on weekends. Cover charges vary from free to COP$20,000 or so.

La Candelaria

Considering the student scene in the area, La Candelaria cafes focus on drinks alone after-hours. Our favorite congregation of bars is Callejón del Embudo ('Funnel') – the tiny alley north of Plazoleta del Chorro de Quevedo – which is lined with sit-and-chat cafes and bars selling *chicha* (an indigenous corn beer).

Pequeña Santa Fe   BAR
(Map p50; Carrera 2 No 12B-14; canelazo COP$6500-7000; ⊙noon-1am) A cozy, historic two-story home with a fireplace by the bar and a softly lit loft upstairs sits next to the evocative Plazoleta del Chorro de Quevedo. It's one of a few great spots where you can sample a hot mug of '*canelazo* Santa Fe' (a yerba-buena tea with aguardiente), or a beer.

City Center

A Seis Manos   BAR
(Map p50; Calle 22 No 8-60; cocktails COP$8000-14,000; ⊙8am-11pm; 🛜) This contemporary, cool cultural space and bar lures the artistically inclined, who mingle at communal tables in the industrial, warehouse-like space. People eat, drink, work, read, flirt and unwind with good mojitos and standard bar fare.

El Goce Pagano   CLUB
(Map p50; www.elgocepagano.co; Carrera 1 No 20-04; ⊙7pm-3am Fri & Sat) Pushing 40, this divey salsa and reggae bar near Universidad de Los Andes is a smoky place with DJs and sweat-soaked bodies from all over Colombia, moving to ethnic rhythms.

Macarena

The Centro Internacional business district west of Carrera 7 tends to clear out after dark. You'll find several bars along Macarena, home to a growing conglomerate of laid-back and cozy nightlife options, frequented by crowds who appreciate hip loungy music at less deafening volumes.

★El Bembe   BAR
(Map p50; www.elbembe.co; Calle 27B No 6-73; cover Fri & Sat COP$20,000; ⊙noon-3pm & 5-10pm Tue & Wed, noon-3pm & 5pm-3am Thu, noon-3am Fri & Sat) Head up the Cuban-colored stairs to this little piece of *tropacalia* on a magical cobbled street in the Macarena. You'll discover what Havana would be like if there were no US embargo: bright colors; breezy, beautiful balconies; and outstanding salsa. The mojitos (COP$22,000 to COP$25,000) flow freely on Fridays, when all-out salsa *revolución* carries into the wee hours.

Chapinero

The edgy, sprawling, bohemian district of Chapinero with its many gay bars and theaters sits south of the high-end eateries of its more polite northern neighbor, Zona G. Start on Calle 60, between Carreras 8 and 9, and head south on Carrera 9. Further south, Calle 51 between Carreras 7 and 8 is something of a 'student street' with half-a-dozen flirt-all-day glassed-in bars and a couple of dance clubs. This is where alt-urbanites and teenage anarchists go to party, and there are some great cafes to ease the hangover the morning after.

Taller de Té   TEAHOUSE
(Map p62; www.tallerdete.com; Calle 60A No 3A-38; tea COP$3000-9000; ⊙10am-8pm Mon-Sat; 🛜) 🍃 This adorable cafe is unique in Bogotá for serious tea. Owner Laura sources more than 50 teas and infusions from plantations around the world and blends with Colombian teas; and there are organic, vegetarian and vegan light bites from trusted culinary artisans around Colombia to pair with them.

Amor Perfecto   CAFE
(Map p62; www.amorperfectocafe.net; Carrera 4 No 66-46; coffee COP$3500-11,000; ⊙8am-9pm Mon-Sat; 🛜) This seriously hip Chapinero Alto coffeehouse is for serious coffee lovers. Pick your single-origin regional Colombian specialty bean; select your method of preparation (Chemex, Siphon, AeroPress or French press); and let the highly knowledgeable baristas do the rest. You can also pop in for a tasting and a course. Hardwood floors and sexy red booths complement the evolution of Bogotá's caffeine scene.

Mi Tierra   BAR
(Map p62; Calle 63 No 11-47; ⊙6pm-late) Find a space among the busted typewriters, sombreros, moose heads, musical instruments

GAY & LESBIAN BOGOTÁ

Bogotá has a large and frequently changing gay-nightlife scene. It's mostly centered in Chapinero, nicknamed 'Chapi Gay,' between Carrera 7 and 13 from Calles 58 to 63.

Browse www.guiagaycolombia.com/bogota for details on dozens of varied clubs and bars, or check online listings from **Colombia Diversa** (www.colombiadiversa.org), a not-for-profit organization promoting gay and lesbian rights in Colombia. Lesbian-only places haven't really caught on here yet, so most gay bars and clubs attract a mix crowd.

Theatron (Map p62; www.theatron.co; Calle 58 No 10-32; ⊗9pm-late Thu-Sat) On a small road between Carreras 9 and 13 in the heart of Chapinero, the classic Theatron is carved from a huge converted film house. It draws gays and straights – some 3000 on weekends – among its eight different environments. Some areas are men-only.

El Recreo de Adán (Map p56; Carrera 12A No 79-45; ⊗5-11pm Sun-Thu, to 12:30am Fri-Sat) In the north, El Recreo de Adán is a classic chill lounge with karaoke and board games.

El Mozo (Map p56; www.elmozoclub.com; Calle 85 No 12-49/51; cover COP$15,000-20,000; ⊗5pm-3am Wed-Sat) El Mozo is an upscale hot spot, divided into two musical environments (crossover and electronica); it has a retractable rooftop, and serves good cocktails and food.

and TVs at this friendly Chapinero bar that resembles a licensed flea market. It's popular with a chilled crowd so you don't need to be overly concerned about the collection of old machetes; and the music is particularly well curated.

Latora 4 Brazos CLUB
(Map p46; Carrera 8 No 40A-18; cover from COP$30,000; ⊗8pm-3am Wed-Sat) A seedy and cryptic neon-lit '4' marks the entrance to this figuratively underground club that draws artistically inclined thirtysomethings to its musically noncommittal atmosphere. DJs unleash a sonic hopscotch of Latin, indie, soul, funk, afrobeats, indie reggaeton and tropical that bounces off the sparsely decorated walls of this multiroom house. The laid-back atmosphere is a nice change from laser lights and smoke screens.

El Titicó BAR
(Map p62; Calle 64 No 13-35; cover COP$10,000) Inspired by the classic *salsatecas* in the south of the country, this sexy hidden bar in Chapinero is like a piece of Cali in the capital with its plush red booths and a big octagonal dance floor. Get your salsa on.

🍷 Northern Bogotá

North of Calle 72 is the trendiest area for sophisticated mixology, jolts of excellent caffeine or pints of microbrews, especially around Zona Rosa or Parque 93. In the former, the pedestrian mall (Zona T) offers Bogotá's highest concentration of noctur-

nal diversion and pub-crawl potential, though some might say it's quantity over quality.

★**Cine Tonalá** CINEMA, CLUB
(Map p46; www.cinetonala.com; Carrera 6A No 35-27; films COP$7000-9000; ⊗noon-3am Tue-Sun; 🎬) Bogotá's only independent cinema champions Latin and Colombian films and international cult classics, but this Mexico City import refuses to be categorized. The multifaceted cultural center, set in a renovated 1930s La Merced mansion, is the city's newest shelter for artistic refugees, who retreat here for a very hip bar scene, excellent Mexican food and rousing club nights from Thursday to Saturday.

El Coq BAR
(Map p56; Calle 84 No 14-02; cover Fri & Sat COP$20,000; ⊗7pm-3am Wed-Sat) This unsigned see-and-be-seen spot evokes a French country greenhouse, complete with basketball goalposts and Spanish moss that's strewn across the retractable ceilings. It counts legions of indie creative types (ad folks, actors, film crews, music biz peeps) as devotees. The electro/indie soundtrack skips happily between Phoenix and Friendly Fires, then throws you for a loop with '80s hip-hop.

Andrés Juan, a Colombian actor who isn't afraid to throw down with the cool kids, runs the show. Good ginger mojitos for the Straight Edge crowd.

Azahar Cafe
CAFE

(Map p56; www.azaharcoffee.com; Carrera 14 No 93A-48; coffee COP$3000-5000; ⊗8am-9pm Mon-Sat, noon-9pm Sun; 🛜) 🍴 Extreme exportation means coffee snobs have more than a little bit of trouble finding a passable cup of Joe in Colombia, but this dead-serious java joint serves single origin, micro-lot coffee prepared in all the ways only considered routine by serious caffeine fiends: Aero-Press, Chemex and the like.

The hardwood outdoor patio is immensely pleasant and your beans are handled with way more care than the ubiquitous chains.

Uva
JUICE BAR

(Map p56; www.uvabar.co; Carrera 13 No 94A-26; juices COP$5200-8900; ⊗8am-5:30pm Mon-Fri, 9:30am-4:30pm Sat; 🛜) 🍴 This adorable little juice bar near Parque 93 liquifies all manner of organic concoctions, including the most popular choice, 'super salamontes' (celery, kale, bok choy, apple, pear and lime). There are also great veggie bowls and salads.

Armando Records
CLUB

(Map p56; www.armandorecords.org; Calle 85 No 14-46; cover Thu-Sat COP$15,000-20,000; ⊗8pm-2:30am Tue-Sat) Still all the rage in Bogotá after several years, this multi-level hot spot features the 2nd-floor Armando's All Stars, which skews younger for crossover tunes and includes a back garden packed in with the young and the restless; and the 4th-floor retro rooftop, where the tunes guide your evening – think LCD Soundsystem and Empire of the Sun.

Bistro El Bandido
BAR

(Map p56; 🖉212-5709; Calle 79B No 7-12; mains COP$29,000-36,000; ⊗noon-1am Mon-Sat; 🛜) Step back in time at this popular high-end bar and brasserie hidden behind residential shrubbery in Nogal. DJs spin oldies (think Big Band, Elvis) between live jazz sets while a well-heeled crowd laps up classic cocktails (from COP$16,000). An excellent menu of brasserie standbys, including a chorizo appetizer, *coq au vin* and fish *meunière*, comes highly recommended.

It all surrounds a big and beautiful social bar – somewhat of a novelty in Bogotá. Reservations essential after 7pm.

Yumi Yumi
COCKTAILS

(Map p56; www.yumiyumi.com.co; Carrera 13 No 83-83; cocktails COP$25,000-29,000; ⊗3pm-3am Tue-Sat; 🛜) Travelers, twentysomething nightlife hounds and cocktail connoisseurs

pile in to this Zona Rosa hot spot for excellent, high-value drinking. Cocktails are two-for-one as a general rule and three-for-one four days a week until 6:30pm (until 9:30pm Saturday!). It's owned by an expat Brit, who does a mean Thai curry special on Tuesdays and Thursdays (COP$15,800 including a beer).

☆ Entertainment

Bogotá has far more cultural activities than any other city in Colombia, including dozens of cinemas offering the usual Hollywood fare. Check out the online 'Entretenimiento' section of local paper *El Tiempo* (www.eltiempo.com/entretenimiento), a what's-on section listing events, and Plan B (www.planb.com.co) and Vive.In (www.vive.in). For cultural events and commentary in English, pick up the free monthly *City Paper* (www.thecitypaperbogota.com).

For schedules and tickets to many events (theater, rock concerts, football games), check Tu Boleta (www.tuboleta.com).

Theater

Bogotá is big on theater and has more than a dozen options. Left-leaning, politicized troupes dominate La Candelaria, while more mainstream options linger 'uptown' in the north.

Teatro Colón
THEATER

(Map p50; www.teatrocolon.gov.co; Calle 10 No 5-32) La Candelaria's most famous theater – and the city's loveliest – reopened in 2014 after a six-year renovation. It hosts a repertoire of large-scale opera, concerts, ballet and plays for a dressed-up, high-end crowd. There's also traditional Colombian music on Mondays at 7:30pm and children's plays on Sundays at 11am.

Teatro la Candelaria
THEATER

(Map p50; www.sigtemedia.net/teatro; Calle 12 No 2-59; tickets adult/student COP$12,000/8000) One of the edgiest theaters in the city center, presenting a mix of political shows (often left-leaning, sometimes covering women's rights issues) that always know when to insert a joke to defuse any tension.

Fundación Gilberto Alzate Avendaño
CULTURAL INSTITUTE

(Map p50; www.fgaa.gov.co; Calle 10 No 3-16) This cultural institute in La Candelaria hosts many events (including dance and theater, and also some concerts). In 2008 a Goya painting was stolen during an art exhibit here.

Live Music

Clubs across town stage live music nightly in Bogotá, and outdoor festivals such as Rock al Parque are huge events that attract fans from all over the continent. Posters around town tout big-name acts, who play at Estadio El Campín, Parque Simón Bolívar or Parque Jaime Duque (on the way to Zipaquirá, north of the city).

Latino Power LIVE MUSIC
(Map p62; Calle 58 No 13-88; cover COP$10,000; ☺9pm-2:30am Wed-Sat) Despite this graffiti-covered disco space undergoing an unfortunate name change (from the far-superior Boogaloop), its mantra perseveres: a shelter for indie-rock kids to take in eclectic alternative DJ sets and energetic live performances (ska, punk, vallenato) by talented local musicians.

Gaira Café LIVE MUSIC
(Map p56; ☑746-2696; Carrera 13 No 96-11; ☺noon-2am Mon-Sat, to 5pm Sun; ☏) Vallenato legend Carlos Vives' ultrafun dancehall and restaurant hosts live vallenato, cumbia and porro – or modern takes on them. Locals pack in for food and rum drinks, and dance in the tight spaces around tables to an 11-piece band.

Biblioteca Luis Ángel Arango LIVE MUSIC
(Map p50; www.banrepcultural.org; Calle 11 No 4-14) This huge La Candelaria library hosts a selection of instrumental and vocal concerts each month; Wednesday events are more expensive (from COP$20,000) than other days (COP$4000 to COP$6000).

Sports

Many outsiders equate Colombia's national sport – football (soccer) – with the shooting of Andrés Escobar after his own goal eliminated Colombia from the 1994 World Cup; but seeing games here is generally a calm affair (perhaps wearing neutral colors isn't a bad idea though). The two big rivals here are the (blue-and-white) **Los Millonarios** (Map p46; www.millonarios.com.co) and (red-and-white) **Santa Fe** (Map p46; www.independientesantafe.co).

The principal venue is the 36,343-seat **Estadio El Campín** (Map p46; ☑315-8726; Carrera 30 No 57-60). Games are played on Wednesday nights and Sunday afternoons. Reserve your seats online in advance (COP$35,000 to COP$180,000) for big matches; otherwise, turn up at the ticket window before match time. For international matches, check with **Federación Colombiana de Fútbol** (www.fcf.com.co) for locations that sell tickets.

Bullfighting was banned in Bogotá in 2012 by Mayor Gustavo Petro, relegating the city's 1931 red-brick ring, Plaza de Toros de Santamaría, to little more than an impressive historical circle. The decision was overturned by a Colombian constitutional court in 2014, however. Check ahead for the current situation.

🔒 Shopping

Locals love malls – **Centro Comercial El Retiro** (Map p56; www.elretirobogota.com; Calle 81 No 11-84; ☺10am-8pm Mon-Thu, to 9pm Fri-Sat, noon-7pm Sun) and **Centro Comercial Andino** (Map p56; www.centroandino.com.co; Carrera 11 No 82-71; ☺10am-8pm Mon-Thu, to 9pm Fri-Sat, noon-6pm Sun) are the two best – but Sunday flea markets and the crusty Plaza de Mercado de Paloquemao are more inviting attractions. Also look along Carrera 9, south of Calle 60, for Chapinero's antique shops.

If you're looking for cutting-edge Colombian fashions, there's a small cluster of boutiques in the Chapinero on Carrera 7 between Calles 54 and 55.

Mambe HANDICRAFTS
(www.mambe.org; Carrera 5 No 117-25; ☺8:30am-4:30pm Tue-Thu, 10am-6pm Fri, 2-6pm Sat & Sun) ✏ This excellent Usaquén shop houses a limited but extremely well-done selection of weekly rotating Fair Trade handicrafts from 40 artisan-driven communities around Colombia.

Artesanías de Colombia HANDICRAFTS
(Map p50; www.artesaniasdecolombia.com.co; Carrera 2 No 18A-58; ☺9am-6pm Mon-Fri) ✏ In a hacienda next to the Iglesia de las Aguas, this classy shop has higher-end crafts (lots of home accessories, plus purses, toys, hammocks and some clothing), and 70% of the profits go directly back to the village artisans.

Brincabrinca CLOTHING
(Map p56; www.brincabrinca.com; Carrera 14 No 85-26; ☺10:30am-2pm & 3-7:30pm Mon-Sat) Designer T-shirt addicts should head straight here for some of Bogotá's most stylish tees (COP$60,000), designed by a bastion of Colombian and international contest winners.

La Casona del Museo HANDICRAFTS
(Map p50; www.lacasonadelmuseo.com; Calle 16 No 5-24; ☺9am-7pm Mon-Sat, 10am-5pm Sun) This old building near Museo del Oro houses a convenient, cheerful collection of souvenir

ℹ HOW TO BUY EMERALDS

Some of the world's highest quality emeralds are mined chiefly in the Muzo and Chivor areas of Boyacá. Colombia is the world's largest exporter of emeralds, making these precious stones a coveted item on tourists' 'To Buy' lists when visiting Bogotá and surrounding regions.

In years past the beauty of Colombia's emeralds had been overshadowed by the dangerous conditions in which they were mined. Some locals compared Colombia's emerald market with the diamond industry in Africa. In 2005 the government abolished tariffs and taxes associated with mining, effectively ending the power of the black market and associated elements.

Travelers can now buy emeralds in good conscience. In the capital, emeralds are sold in the flourishing **Emerald Trade Center** (Map p50; Av Jiménez No 5-43; ☉7:30am-7pm Mon-Fri, 8am-5pm Sat), where dozens of *comisionistas* (traders) buy and sell stones – sometimes on the sidewalks. You will also be offered emeralds on the street. Don't do it – glass imitations these days look a lot like emeralds (and, even if they are real, you will surely overpay)! Serious buyers should consider a tour with **Colombian Emerald Tours** (☎313-317-6534; www.colombianemeraldtours.com). This outfit runs a two-hour tour in the city that introduces you to the *comisionistas* as well as schools you on cut, quality and the like inside the Emerald Trade Center. There's no pressure to buy but if you do, the COP$60,000 tour price is credited back. It also offers a long day trip into the emerald mine in Chivor, Boyacá, an ecotourism initiative run by the local community there (from COP$320,000 all-inclusive).

Here are a few tips to keep in mind while shopping for emeralds:

➡ When looking at emeralds, you have to inspect the person selling you the emerald as closely as the emerald itself. Find a seller that you feel comfortable with. You will be surprised at how obvious it is to either run away or relax when you just place some attention on the seller.

➡ Gems and jewelry are very subjective and often when looking at emeralds in the shops or from dealers your first impression is the best and most reliable impression. Don't be in a hurry when buying. The quality of the gem in any Colombian shop is regulated by the tourist industry and there are never disputes as to quality, so just concentrate on the price. Don't be afraid to walk away if you feel the price is too high.

➡ When looking at a stone, you have to assess the harmony between the color, clarity, brightness and size.

➡ Colombians are convivial and often comical. If you find a jeweler or dealer you like, invite him for tea or a *tinto* (black coffee). You will hear good stories and will have an ally in the emerald business.

One reliable emerald dealer in Bogotá is **Gems Metal** (Map p50; ☎311-493-1602; Carrera 7 No 12C-28, Edificio America, oficina 707; ☉8am-5pm Mon-Fri). Dealer Oscar Baquero has more than 35 years experience in the emerald industry. English is spoken. Price ranges run the gamut from US$50 into the stratosphere.

stands and two nice cafes (the upper level one, La Fuente, does good coffee by a trickling fountain).

Plaza Central de Usaquén   MARKET
(Los Toldos de San Pelayo, Carrera 6A btwn Calles 119 & 119A; ☉8am-6pm Sat & Sun) Just north of the main square in the village-like Usaquén, you'll find stallholders selling food, colorful purses, assorted handicrafts and bamboo saxophones – there's a satellite area a couple of blocks east, too.

Pasaje Rivas   HANDICRAFTS
(Map p50; cnr Carrera 10 & Calle 10; ☉9am-6pm Mon-Sat, to 3pm Sun) A couple of blocks west of Plaza de Bolívar, this craft market is a good spot for cheap nontouristy buys, including lots of straw hats, T-shirts, toy figurines, baskets and *ruanas* (Colombian ponchos). The entrance next to Iglesia de la Concepción reads 'Pasaje Paul.'

Librería Lerner BOOKS
(Map p50; ☎334-7826; www.librerialerner.com.
co; Av Jiménez 4-35; ⊙9am-7pm Mon-Fri, 7am-
2pm Sat) Stocks many Spanish-language
guidebooks on Colombia and the full gamut of maps, including the *Movistar guía
de rutas por Colombia* (a color map/
guide; COP$15,000) and the 12-map series
of national routes *Mapas de ruta* (sold individually for COP$1000, or as a packet for
COP$14,000).

Plaza de Mercado de Paloquemao MARKET
(Map p46; www.plazadepaloquemao.com; cnr Av 19
& Carrera 25; ⊙8am-1pm) A real-deal, messy
Colombian market. Go early on Friday or
Sunday – flower days!

Mercado de San Alejo MARKET
(Map p50; Carrera 7 btwn Calles 24 & 26; ⊙7am-
5pm Sun) This city-center classic fills a
parking lot with a host of yesteryear items
(posters, books, knickknacks) that are fun to
sift through.

Camping Amarelo OUTDOOR EQUIPMENT
(Map p62; ☎217-4480; www.campingamarelo.
com; Calle 57 No 9-29, oficina 301; ⊙9am-5:30pm
Mon-Fri, to 12:30pm Sat) This small shop sells
and rents all the camping gear you'll need,
including tents, which start at COP$8000
per day, and boots. It takes bookings for
rooms in its *refugio* at Suesca (rooms from
COP$45,000).

San Miguel HATS
(Map p50; ☎243-6273; Calle 11 No 8-88; ⊙9am-
6pm Mon-Sat) Open for more than 70 years,
this classic milliner is the best of the bunch
on the block. Mostly felt fedoras and cowboy
hats, pressed before your eyes.

Hacienda Santa Bárbara MALL
(www.haciendasantabarbara.com.co; Carrera 7
No 115-60; ⊙10am-8:30pm) This mall is built
around a colonial *casona* (1847), making
the place a fine combination of historic and
modern architecture, and it's quieter than
the Zona Rosa scene. It's the initial/final
stop on the L80-M80 TransMilenio hybrid
bus line along Carrera 7.

ⓘ Orientation

Sprawling Bogotá stretches mostly north–south
(and west in recent years) with the towering
peaks of Monserrate and Guadalupe providing
an easterly wall.

Locating an address in the city is generally
a breeze...after getting your head around the
mathematical precision of it all. Calles run east–
west, rising in number as you go north, while
Carreras go north–south, increasing in number
as they go west (away from the mountains).
Handily, any street address (almost) always
indicates the nearest cross streets; Calle 15 No
4-56, for example, is on 15th St, 56m from the
corner of Carrera 4 toward Carrera 5.

Central Bogotá has four main parts: the partially preserved colonial sector La Candelaria
(south of Av Jiménez and between Carreras 1
and 10), with lots of students, bars and hostels;
the aged business district 'city center' (focused
on Carrera 7 and Calle 19, between Av Jiménez
and Calle 26); the high-rise-central of Centro
Internacional (between Carreras 7, 10 and 13
from Calles 26 to 30); and, just east toward the
hills, the bohemian eatery district Macarena.

Northern Bogotá is known as the wealthiest
part of the city. The north, more or less, begins
2km north of Centro Internacional. A scene of
theaters, antique shops and many gay bars, the
sprawling Chapinero (roughly between Carrera
7 and Av Caracas, from Calle 40 to Calle 67 or
so) is scruffier than areas further north, which
begin with Zona G, a pint-sized strip of high-end
eateries (east of Carrera 7 and Calle 80). Chapinero Alto is an artsy mini-enclave in Chapinero
between Carrera 7A and Av Circunvalar from
Calles 53 to 65.

Ten blocks north, lively Zona Rosa (or Zona T,
stemming from the 'T-shaped' pedestrian mall
between Carreras 12 and 13, at Calle 82A) is a
zone of clubs, malls and hotels. A more sedate
version – with many restaurants – rims the
ritzier Parque 93 (Calle 93 between Carreras 11A
& 13), part of the Chicó neighborhood, and the
one-time *pueblo* plaza at Usaquén (corner Carrera 6 and Calle 119). The rather unappealing modern buildings of the so-called 'financial district'
line Calle 100 between Av 7 and Carrera 11.

The most popular links between the center and
north are Carrera Séptima (Carrera 7; 'La Séptima') and Carrera Décima (Carrera 10), which
are crowded with many city buses. Av Caracas
(which follows Carrera 14, then Av 13 north of
Calle 63) is the major north–south route for the
TransMilenio bus system. Calle 26 (or Av El Dorado) leads west to the airport and bus terminal.

ⓘ Information

DANGERS & ANNOYANCES

Despite great progress over the course of two
decades, security in Bogotá has taken a con-
cerning step backwards of late, though the city
is still relatively safer than it once was. La Candelaria is generally safe during the day, but tourist
muggings (even stabbings) have been far from
rare of late. If you opt to stay in La Candelaria,
choose accommodations not only based on your
general criteria but security as well and avoid

walking alone or with anything valuable at night in the area, when the very-evident police presence from the day inexplicably packs it in. There has been a dramatic increase in muggings since 2013 or so (500 more than average) and Calle 9 up the hill nearer the poorer neighborhood of Barrio Egypto is a notable hot spot – this area is best avoided entirely (do not stray beyond Carrera 1). At its north end, Parque de los Periodistas (Av Jiménez and Carrera 4) has seen knife-point muggings – as well as some drug sales – and the road between Universidad de Los Andes and Monserrate should also be avoided by solo travelers. This seemingly innocent walk, either on the mountainside trails, or the short walk between the cable-car station and Quinta de Bolívar just below, is quite risky.

It's also a very bad idea to wander aimlessly around Macarena (take a taxi and stick to the main restaurant streets) – La Perseverancia barrio, just north of Macarena, has a very dodgy reputation and it's not difficult to stray into it if you are unfamiliar with the area.

Overcrowding and snarling expansion projects have caused dramatic increases in crime on the TransMilenio public transit system – always be on guard to avoid pickpocketing while riding the buses.

Additionally, escalations between the government and National Liberation Army (ELN) rebels means Bogotá has seen an increase in bombings in the last few years, though tourists are not specifically targeted.

The north is, on the whole, a different story. Many locals walk well after dark between, say, Zona Rosa and Parque 93's club and restaurant scene. That said, the area has seen a few isolated bombings.

Obviously, don't fight back if you've been targeted – hand over your money and move on. Meanwhile, avoid deserted streets and take taxis after hours.

EMERGENCY

For ambulance services, dial ✆125. For police and fire, it's ✆123.

Tourist Police (✆280-9900) Bilingual staff.

MEDICAL SERVICES

It's preferable to use private clinics rather than government-owned institutions which, though they are cheaper, may not be as well equipped.

Fundación Santa Fe (✆603-0303; www.fsfb. org.co; Calle 119 No 7-75) Very professional private hospital.

Immigration Medicals (✆311-271-6223; Carrera 11 No 94A-25, oficina 401; ⊗9am-noon Mon-Fri) Dr Paul Vaillancourt is an English-speaking half-French-Canadian doctor who is extremely friendly and highly recommended. He charges COP$160,000 per consultation

(medical insurance isn't accepted, but can refer to hospitals that do, if needed). If you're looking for a yellow fever vaccine, this is the quickest and easiest spot to get it as well (COP$56,000).

MONEY

There are two exchange houses in the Emerald Trade Center (p72), but it's best to use an ATM, which are plentiful.

Bancolombia (Carrera 8 No 12B-17) Changes traveler's checks.

Western Union (www.westernunion.com; Calle 28 No 13-22, local 28; ⊗9am-5pm Mon-Fri, to 1pm Sat) Can wire money.

POST

Courier Box (Map p50; Carrera 7 No 16-50; ⊗8am-6pm Mon-Fri, 9am-noon Sat) FedEx, DHL, TNT and UPS rep.

Post Office (4-72; Map p50; www.4-72.com. co; Carrera 7 No 27-54, Centro Internacional; ⊗8am-6pm Mon-Fri, 9am-1pm Sat) Branch of 4-72, Colombia's postal service.

Post Office (4-72; Map p56; www.4-72.com.co; cnr Av Chile & Carrera 15, Chapinero; ⊗8am-6pm Mon-Fri, 9am-2pm Sat)

Post Office (4-72; Map p50; Carrera 8 No 12A-03, La Candelaria; ⊗8am-5:30pm Mon-Fri, 9am-1pm Sat)

TOURIST INFORMATION

Colombia's energetic **Instituto Distrital de Turismo** (✆800-012-7400; www.bogota turismo.gov.co) is making visitors feel very welcome, with a series of Puntos de Información Turística (PIT) branches opening at key locations around Bogotá, operated by very friendly English-speaking staff. A couple of PIT locations offer free walking tours (scheduled separately in English or Spanish). There are PITs at each of the airport terminals and a few select TransMilenio stations, among other locations around the city.

Parques Nacionales Naturales (PNN) de Colombia (Map p50; ✆353-2400 ext 138; www.parquesnacionales.gov.co; Carrera 10 No 20-34; ⊗8am-6pm Mon-Fri) This central office has good information on Colombia's national parks and community ecotourism opportunities. It looks abandoned – knock on the big black door and it will open.

PIT Centro Histórico (Map p50; ✆283-7115; cnr Carrera 8 & Calle 10; ⊗7am-6pm) Inside the Casa de Comuneros facing Plaza de Bolívar, this tourist office has walking tours in English at 2pm Tuesdays and Thursdays.

PIT Terminal de Transporte (✆295-4460; Transversal 66 No 35-11, La Terminal, módulo 5) At the arrival hall of the main bus terminal.

VISA INFORMATION

Visa extensions are handled by the Migración Colombia (p320) office north of Parque 93. To reach the office, catch the M80 TransMilenio from 'Museo Nacional' to the 'Escuela de Caballería' bus stop (Carrera 7 and Calle 100) and walk four blocks west. For details on the process, see p320.

⊕ Getting There & Away

AIR

Bogotá's shiny new airport, **Aeropuerto Internacional El Dorado** (Map p46; www.el-nuevodorado.com; Av El Dorado), which handles nearly all domestic and international flights, is located 13km northwest of the city center and is fresh off a massive US$900 million facelift. Future plans could include the integration of the two terminals.

Terminal T1, which replaced the old El Dorado terminal, serves all international flights, Avianca's main domestic routes (Barranquilla, Bucaramanga, Cali, Cartagena, Medellín, Pasto, Pereira and San Andrés) and domestic routes from other airlines.

Terminal T2 (Puente Aéreo), 1km west of T1 and reached by airport shuttle, serves the remainder of Avianca's domestic routes (Armenia, Barrancabermeja, Cúcuta, Florencia, Ibagué, Leticia, Manizales, Montería, Neiva, Popayán, Riohacha, Santa Marta, Valledupar, Villavicencio and Yopal).

Most airline offices in Bogotá are in the north; some have more than one office. There are plenty of domestic flights to destinations all over the country. For a list of domestic airlines serving Colombia, see p324.

BUS

Bogotá's main bus terminal, **La Terminal** (Map p46; ☑ 423-3630; www.terminaldetransporte.gov.co; Diagonal 23 No 69-11), about 5km west of the city center in the squeaky-clean planned neighborhood of La Salitre, is one of South America's best, most efficient and is shockingly unsketchy. It's housed in a huge, arched red-brick building divided into five *módulos* (units). Southbound buses leave at the west end from *módulo* 1 (color-coded yellow); east- and westbound from *módulo* 2 (blue); and northbound from *módulo* 3 (red). *Colectivo* vans leave for some nearby towns such as Villavicencio from *módulo* 4, while all arrivals come into *módulo* 5 (at the station's eastern end).

There are plenty of fast-food options, ATMs, left-luggage rooms, (clean) bathrooms and even showers (COP$6500), and a PIT information center in *módulo* 5, which will help you track down bus times or call for accommodations.

Each *módulo* has a number of side-by-side ticket vendors from various companies, sometimes trying to hassle you for their buses. For some long-distance destinations – particularly to the Caribbean coast – you can sometimes haggle in low season. The usual type of bus is the *climatizado*, which is air-conditioned. Various companies are not the best at displaying destinations, fares and departure schedules – the best resource for that is La Terminal's official website.

Domestic Buses

For most domestic destinations, there are frequent departures during the day (for destinations such as Medellín, Cali or Bucaramanga it's usually half-hourly) by a few different companies. Shop around for prices and departure times, as they will vary wildly depending on season, company and quality of service.

Expreso Bolivariano (☑ 800-011-9292; www.bolivariano.com.co) is Colombia's best national bus company with comfortable buses.

International Buses

Buses for cities around South America depart from *módulo* 2 (blue) in La Terminal. **Expreso Ormeño** (☑ 410-7522; www.grupo-ormeno.com.co) with Friday and Sunday departures and **Cruz del Sur** (☑ 428-5781; www.cruzdelsur.com.pe; La Terminal) with Monday departures sell tickets for most destinations.

SAMPLE INTERNATIONAL BUS FARES & ROUTES

DESTINATION	PRICE (COP$)	DURATION	DEPARTURE
Buenos Aires	810,000	6-7 days	11am Mon, 9pm Fri & 9pm-midnight Sun
Caracas	208,000	36hr	Wed 7-11pm
Guayaquil	230,000	41hr	11am Mon, 9pm Fri & 9pm-midnight Sun
Lima	390,000	2½ days	11am Mon, 9pm Fri & 9pm-midnight Sun
Mendoza	726,000	5½ days	9pm Fri & 9pm-midnight Sun
Quito	170,000	36hr	11am Mon, 9pm Fri & 9pm-midnight Sun
Santiago	650,000	5-6 days	11am Mon, 9pm Fri & 9pm-midnight Sun
São Paulo	923,000	8 days	9pm Fri & 9pm & midnight Sun

ℹ Getting Around

Rush hour in the morning and afternoon can really clog roads – and space on the buses.

TO/FROM THE AIRPORT

The most economical and efficient route from the airport is the TransMilenio (p78), but it's tricky: the bus doesn't accept cash. You need a *Tarjeta Tu Llave* or *Tarjeta Cliente Frecuente*, which, in a tremendous feat of ingenuity, weren't being sold at the airport at time of research.

For those staying in Chapinero or points to the north, bus M86 departs from outside Puerta 8 in the arrival's hall every seven minutes between 4:30am and 11pm Monday to Friday, 5am to 11pm Saturday and 9am to 6pm Sunday and heads toward Centro Internacional before turning north and carrying on up Carrera 7 to Calle 116. If you don't have a *Tarjeta Tu Llave* or *Tarjeta Cliente Frecuente*, you'll need to instead catch the free '16-14 Aeropuerto' shuttle bus, which departs between Puerta 7 and 8 every 10 minutes from 4am to 11pm, to TransMilenio's Portal El Dorado, where you can then buy a card and carry on with the M86 from there (ATMs are located across from Puerta 5 in the arrivals hall). The same line operates as K86 from the north to the airport.

If you are staying in La Candelaria, you will need to switch buses. From the airport, catch the aforementioned '16-14 Aeropuerto' shuttle bus to Portal El Dorado, and switch to TransMilenio J6 to Universidades, which is attached to Las Aguas station via an underground tunnel. To the airport, catch K6 from Universidades to Portal El Dorado and switch to the airport shuttle.

SAMPLE DOMESTIC BUS FARES & ROUTES

DESTINATION	PRICE (COP$)	DURATION	MÓDULO (NO)	COMPANIES
Armenia	51,000	7hr	yellow (1)	Flota de Magdalena, Expreso Bolivariano
Barranquilla	70,000	17-20hr	red (3) & blue (2)	Copetran, Expreso Brasilia, Berlinas
Bucaramanga	40,000	8-9hr	red (3)	Libertadores, Copetran, Transporte Reina
Cali	59,000	8-10hr	yellow (1) & blue (2)	Flota La Magdalena, Expreso Bolivariano, Velotax
Cartagena	90,000	12-24hr	blue (2) & red (3)	Copetran, Expreso Brasilia, Berlinas
Cúcuta	100,000	15-16hr	red (3)	Expreso Brasilia, Berlinas
Honda	20,000	4hr	blue (2)	Flota Aguila, Rapido Tolima
Ipiales	121,000	22hr	yellow (1)	Continental Bus
Manizales	50,000	8-9hr	blue (2)	Expreso Bolivariano, Rapido Tolima
Medellín	55,000	9hr	yellow (1) & blue (2)	Expreso Brasilia, Expreso Bolivariano
Neiva	30,000	5-6hr	yellow (1) & blue (2)	Flota La Magdalena, Rapido Tolima
Ocaña	88,000	12hr	red (3)	Copetran, Omega
Pasto	110,000	18-20hr	yellow (1)	Continental Bus, Flota La Magdalena
Pereira	50,000	7-9hr	yellow (1)	Expreso Bolivariano, Flota La Magdalena
Popayán	80,000	12hr	yellow (1)	Flota La Magdalena, Velotax
Riohacha	100,000	18-19hr	red (3)	Copetran, Expreso Brasilia
San Agustín	464,000	9-10hr	yellow (1)	Taxis Verdes, Coomotor
San Gil	40,000	6-7hr	red (3)	Berlinas, Omega, Copetran
Santa Marta	70,000	16-17hr	blue (2) & red (3)	Berlinas, Omega, Copetran
Sogamoso	23,300	4hr	red (3)	Libertadores, Autoboy
Tunja	19,000	3hr	red (3)	Libertadores, Copetran
Villa de Leyva	23,000	4hr	red (3)	Libertadores, Rapido El Carmen
Villavicencio	21,000	3hr	blue (2)	Flota La Macarena, Expreso Bolivariano

Either way, plan on a solid hour ride during the best of times, cushioning for longer during rush hour.

From the airport, **Taxi Imperial** (www.viajesimperialsas.com/taxiimperial) manages the airport taxis – look for the folks in orange jackets. Estimated fares from the airport include La Candelaria (COP$25,000 to COP$30,000), Chapinero (COP$35,000 to COP$37,000) and Zona Rosa (COP$35,000 to COP$37,000). The (usually lengthy) taxi line is right outside the main terminal. You pay a *sobrecargo* (surcharge) of COP$3600 for taxi trips to or from the airport and there is also sometimes a nominal add-on fee for luggage.

TO/FROM THE BUS TERMINAL

The fastest and most convenient option to the main bus station, La Terminal (p75), is a TransMilenio–short walk combo. El Tiempo station, on the TransMilenio M86-K86/J6-K6 line to the airport, is 950m from the terminal. To reach La Terminal, exit El Tiempo station on the footbridge to the right and then head right again down to the sidewalk. Walk straight along for 1½ blocks to Carrera 69 and turn left (between the Cámara de Comercio Bogotá and World Business Port buildings). Walk five blocks, passing Maloka on the left and crossing over two pedestrian footbridges (over Calle 24A and Av La Esperanza, respectively), then continue on the sidewalk 300m toward the 't' tower. Follow the directions in reverse to leave from La Terminal.

Módulo 5 of La Terminal has an organized taxi service; it has outrageous lines but you pay by the meter. Rates are around COP$12,500 to La Candelaria, COP$9500 to Chapinero Alto and COP$12,500 to the Zona Rosa. There is a COP$1700 surcharge between 8am and 5am.

BICYCLE

Bogotá has one of the world's most extensive bike-route networks, with more than 350km of separated, clearly marked bike paths called CicloRuta. Free Bogotá maps from PIT information centers show the CicloRuta paths.

In addition, about 121km of city roads are closed to traffic from 7am to 2pm on Sundays and holidays for a citywide Ciclovía (p54), a well-run event to get Bogotá out on two wheels. You can rent a bike at Bogotá Bike Tours (p55). Ciclovía runs along Carrera 7 all the way from La Candelaria to Usaquén – it's worth witnessing even if on foot.

BUS & BUSETA

In addition to its TransMilenio (p78), Bogotá's public transportation is operated by buses and *busetas* (small buses), though the latter are being phased out, replaced with more official **SiTP** (Sistema Integrado de Transporte Público; www.sitp.gov.co) blue buses, nicknamed '*azules.*'

These are being implemented to integrate with TransMilenio and wrangle the entire city transportation system under one efficient umbrella. To help make sense of it all, TransmiSitp (www.transmisitp.com) is a popular app that coordinates routes between TransMilenio and SiTP. They all run the length and breadth of the city, usually at full speed if traffic allows. At the time of writing, about half of the *busetas* remained in operation.

Except on a few streets, there are no bus stops – just wave down the bus. Board via the front door and pay the driver or the assistant; you won't get a ticket. In buses you get off through the back door, where there's a bell to ring to let the driver know to stop. In *busetas* there's usually only a front door through which all passengers get on and off. When you want to get off, tell the driver '*por acá, por favor*' (here, please).

Each bus and *buseta* displays a board on the windscreen indicating the route and number. For locals these are easily recognizable from a distance, but for newcomers it can be difficult to decipher the route description quickly enough to wave down the right bus. It's just a matter of persevering.

Flat fares, regardless of distance traveled, are posted, and are generally around COP$1400. It's sometimes slightly higher at night (after 8pm) and on Sundays and holidays.

Minibuses called *colectivos* also operate on major routes. They are faster than the buses and *busetas* and cost about COP$1600.

TAXI

Bogotá's impressive fleet of Korean-made yellow taxis are a safe, reliable and relatively inexpensive way of getting around. They all have meters, and drivers almost always use them. When you enter a taxi, the meter should read '25,' which relates to a coded pricing scheme (a laminated card should be hanging on the front passenger seat showing the pricing). The minimum unit fare is '50,' which equates to COP$3600. The meter should change every 100m. Taxi trips on Sundays and holidays, or after dark, include a COP$1700 surcharge; trips to the airport have a COP$3600 surcharge. There is a COP$600 surcharge for booking taxis.

If you're going to make a couple of trips to distant places, it may be cheaper to hire a taxi for about COP$18,200 per hour.

Don't even think about waving down a taxi in the street unless you are with a local. When you do so, you're not registered and therefore forfeit all the security measures put in place to protect you, exponentially increasing your chances of robbery. You can call numerous companies that provide radio service such as **Taxis Libres** (📞 311-1111; www.taxislibres.com.co) or **Taxi Express** (📞 411-1111; www.4111111.co), but popular

❶ TAXI TIPS

After soliciting a taxi via phone or the booking app Tappsi (www.tappsi.co), you'll need to give the driver a password (clave), which is normally the last two digits of the phone you used. Without it, the driver cannot begin the meter.

During rush hour, taxis are scarce: unless you add a tip from the app, most taxi drivers won't accept your solicitation. On Tappsi, click 'More,' enable 'VIP' and add an amount to help encourage their response (COP$2000 to COP$3000 should do it).

Bogotá taxi app **Tappsi** (www.tappsi.co) is even better and eliminates the language barrier.

Naturally, don't ride with a driver that refuses to use a meter. Most drivers are honest, but it's worth confirming the final fare with the price card. Some drivers, particularly in late hours, will round fares up a bit. Drivers don't often get tips.

TRANSMILENIO

The ambitiously named **TransMilenio** (www. transmilenio.gov.co), modeled after a similar groundbreaking system in Curitiba, Brazil, has revolutionized Bogotá's public transportation. After numerous plans and studies drawn up over 30 years to build a metro, the project was eventually buried and a decision to introduce a fast urban bus service called TransMilenio was taken instead. Today, it is the largest BRT (Bus Rapid Transit) system in the world.

It is, in essence, a bus system masquerading as a subway. Covering 112km with a fleet of 1400 buses, TransMilenio counts 12 lines and 144 dedicated self-contained stations at time of writing, which keeps things orderly and safe (and some have wi-fi). Buses use dedicated lanes, which keeps them free from auto traffic. The service is frequent and cheap (fares, either COP$1400 or COP$1700, fluctuate throughout the day according to peak and off-peak time frames). Most lines operate from 4:58am to 12:15am Monday to Saturday, 5:55am to 11:15pm Sunday.

Tickets are bought at the entrance of any TransMilenio station. There are several types of frequent rider cards in operation to avoid waiting in line every time. Of most use to tourists and nonresidents is the *Tarjeta Cliente Frecuente* (COP$2000), which can be loaded with up to 50 rides or COP$85,000 and covers nearly every TransMilenio route plus SiTP buses. The *Tarjeta Tu Llave* is essentially the same thing but can only be used for newer Phase III TransMilenio stations and SiTP buses, which were built and operated by a different company and (ingeniously) do not play nice with the rest of the system.

TransMilenio serves up to 2.2 million people daily – well over capacity – so buses get *very* crowded at rush hour (locals jokingly refer to it as the *TransmiLLENO,* which would translate to the *TransFULL*); transfers at Av Jiménez resemble punk-rock mosh pits. TransMilenio's current plans project completion by 2031 with lines canvassing a total of 388km.

On posted maps in stations, routes are color coded, with different numbered buses corresponding to various stops, but it's all very confusing (even for locals). The main TransMilenio lines of interest to visitors run north–south along Av Caracas between Av Jiménez and Portal del Norte stations; northwest–southeast along Av Dorado between Portal El Dorado and Universidades (access to the bus terminal and airport); and north–south along the new hybrid line (part dedicated BRT, part regular city bus) introduced in 2014 along Carrera 7, which facilitates access to Chapinero, Zona Rosa and Usaquén. This route (M80-L80) begins at Bicentenario and operates on dedicated lanes to the shiny new Museo Nacional station, then continues in regular traffic lanes along Carrera 7 to Calle 114. There are nine terminuses, but the only one of real use to travelers is the **Northern Terminus** (Carrera 45 with Calle 174, Portal del Norte).

It takes practice to understand which bus to take. Ruta Facil routes, for example, stop at every station on a line, while others zip along some sort of express route – leapfrogging, in confusing patterns, several stations at a time.

You can preplan your routes online at SuRumbo (www.surumbo.com); click on your departure and destination station for options. Most key north-central routes change in Calle 22, and Av Jiménez has many more transfers (sometimes involving an underground walk between neighboring stations).

The B74/J72 express lines are being phased out of La Candelaria in order to make it a pedestrian-only zone and only run to/from Av Jiménez outside rush hour. Both *centro histórico* stations – Las Aguas and Museo del Oro – were slated to close as part of this plan, though protest over this means their future remains uncertain.

Key routes (subject to change depending on day and time):

La Candelaria to Portal del Norte Take F23 from Museo del Oro to Av Jiménez; switch to B74 to Portal del Norte (last stop).

La Candelaria to Chapinero From San Victorino, take M7 to Museo Nacional; switch to M80 to Universidad La Salle or Calle 67.

La Candelaria to Zona G Take M7 from San Victorino to Museo Nacional; switch to M80 to Av Chile.

La Candelaria to Zona Rosa Take B74 from Las Aguas or Museo del Oro to Calle 57; switch to B23 to Calle 85.

Portal del Norte to La Candelaria Take J72 from Portal del Norte to Av Jiménez; switch to F23 to Museo del Oro.

Chapinero to La Candelaria Take L80 from Calle 67 or Universidad La Salle to Museo Nacional; switch to L7 to San Victorino.

Zona G to La Candelaria Take L80 from Av Chile to Museo Nacional; switch to L7 to San Victorino.

Zona G to Zona Rosa Take M80 from Av Chile to Calle 82.

Zona Rosa to La Candelaria Take K23 from Calle 85 to Calle 57; switch to J72 to Av Jiménez.

AROUND BOGOTÁ

Most *bogotanos* looking for a break from the city also look for warmth. Some towns within a couple of hours of the city, such as Villavicencio, rest way below Bogotá's elevation and have higher temperatures. Outside the capital there are also significant changes in landscape, where you can find lakes, waterfalls, cloud forests, mountains and a maze of small towns and villages, many of which hold on to their colonial fabric.

North of Bogotá

Many day-trippers out of Bogotá head this way. You can combine a trip to Zipaquirá and Guatavita in a day – agencies such as Destino Bogotá (p58) offer combo day trips.

Suesca

☑ 1 / POP 14,000 / ELEV 2584M

One of Colombia's most popular rock-climbing destinations lurks just south of this colonial town, 65km north of Bogotá. Arriving by car or bus, you'll pass the 4km-long sandstone Guadalupe formations standing up to 370m high along the Río Bogotá, home to 400 (and counting) routes.

Many visitors come for day trips from Bogotá, particularly on weekends, when the half-a-dozen (or so) outfitters open their doors to greet a couple of hundred climbers daily. There are also rafting options, but the water is much warmer in Tobía.

🏃 Activities

Veteran climber and mountaineer Rodrigo Arias (p102), who lives in Suesca when not climbing PNN El Cocuy, is a great guide in the area and can arrange multiday rock climbing, mountain biking and hiking excursions. Climbing school **DeAlturas** (☑ 301-642-6809;

www.dealturas.com) offers a five-day course for COP$500,000 and a day climb (including equipment) for COP$120,000, as well as accommodations for COP$20,000 per person.

🛏 Sleeping

There are many camping options, or you can rent a full cabaña from Camping Amarelo (p73) in Bogotá for COP$45,000 per person.

El Vivac Hostal HOSTEL $$
(☑ 311-480-5034; www.elvivachostal.com; campsites per person COP$15,000, dm COP$25,000, d COP$70,000) El Vivac Hostel is a farm turned hostel run by a local woman climber and pioneer, who arranges climbs and rents bikes (from COP$10,000).

ℹ Getting There & Away

To get to Suesca, take the TransMilenio to its northern terminus at Portal del Norte, and catch a frequent direct Alianza bus (COP$5100, one hour), which departs inside the Portal's Buses Intermunicipales platform every 20 minutes to 11pm.

West of Bogotá

Those who go west from Bogotá are heading to the beach, Medellín or coffee country. Many don't stop, but there are a few places that qualify as destinations. If you're traveling by your own means, note that two highways head out of Bogotá – take the northerly route via La Vega (west on Calle 80), a nicer drive than the southern route via Facatativa, which hooks up with the La Vega route (after many suburbs and truck jams) at Villeta, about 65km west.

Bosque de niebla (cloud forest) hikes await only 20km west of Bogotá in the gorgeous privately owned **Parque Natural Chicaque** (☑ 1-368-3114; www.chicaque.com; admission COP$14,000; ☺ 8am-4pm). The 3-sq-km area features half-a-dozen walks (about 8km altogether), which are among the nation's best marked. During rainy season, walks lead to waterfalls. On weekends you can hire a horse to ride back up the steep hill paths.

You arrive above the trails, and below – a steep hike down – you'll find various **accommodations** (campsite/dm/bungalow incl all meals COP$56,300/92,350/298,4000), including a nice bungalow for two (advance reservations require a bank deposit, which is a pain for foreigners). You can also camp up at the entrance for COP$13,500 (no meals).

The reserve is a few kilometers off the Soacha–La Mesa road. To get there from

Bogotá's center, take the TransMilenio to Terreros, where buses leave for the park at 8am, 9:30am, 11am, 2pm, 3:45pm and 5:15pm (COP$5000), returning at 8:45am, 10:15am, 1pm, 3pm, 4:30pm and 6pm. If you call ahead other days, a pickup from an agreed-upon location can also be arranged.

South of Bogotá

Travelers mainly venture south from Bogotá on their way to Villavicencio and Los Llanas beyond, but there are other attractions out this way, including mummies.

San Bernardo

The unique climate conditions of the Andean highlands have been conducive to the preservation of mummies across parts of Colombia – some of which have been relocated as far away as the British Museum in London. One place you can see some is the 'mummy town' of San Bernardo, about 87km southeast of Bogotá. A century ago, several dozen bodies were unearthed from the cemetery after interment fees were not paid and diggers, surprisingly, found mummies – a product of the unique soil and the local diet of guatila fruit. Some are on view in glass cases in the cemetery crypt in town.

LAGUNA DE GUATAVITA: LAKE OF (FOOLS') GOLD

Traditionally, the Muisca believed that Laguna de Guatavita – once set in a perfectly round crater rimmed by green mountains – was created by a crashing meteor that transported a golden god who resided in the lake's floor. Turns out, it's now believed, volcanoes are more likely to be the lake's creator. Many hopes of finding El Dorado once converged on this small, circular lake about 50km northeast of Bogotá. Lovely Guatavita was the sacred lake and ritual center of the Muisca people. Here, half a millennium ago, the gold-dust-coated Zipa – the Muisca *cacique* (indigenous tribal head) – would throw precious offerings such as elaborate *tunjos* (ornate gold pendants and figurines) inscribed with wishes into the lake from his ceremonial raft. He'd then plunge into the waters to obtain godlike power. You can see many such *tunjos* at Bogotá's Museo del Oro.

This led to a frenzy for gold for the Spaniards, and many other outsiders, who felt they'd reached a watery El Dorado. Over the years many painstaking, fruitless efforts were made to uncover the treasures lurking below. In the 1560s a wealthy merchant, Antonio de Sepúlveda, cut a gap on one side – still visible today – to drain the lake, yielding a mere 232 pesos of gold. Sepúlveda died bankrupt. By the late 19th century an English company managed to drain the lagoon, finding only 20-odd objects – not nearly enough to pay off the UK£40,000 and eight years invested in the project.

In the 1940s US divers with metal detectors searched out treasures, and the Colombian authorities – finally – banned such activities in 1965. Not to say that all treasure seekers obeyed. In the 1990s access to the lake required a permit in order to keep track of visitors (illegally coming with scuba gear to search out fortunes).

Despite its fame, Guatavita never yielded much gold. Colombia's best-known piece – the Balsa Muisca (housed at the Museo del Oro) – was actually found in a cave near the village of Pasca.

Today you can't follow the Zipa's lead (no swimming allowed), but there are several lookouts on a trail above the water. The area is higher up than Bogotá – and you'll feel the difference in altitude on the 15-minute hike up to the lakeside hilltops from the site entrance (Colombian/foreigner COP$9500/14,000; ☺ closed Mon).

Laguna de Guatavita isn't the most convenient destination to reach by public transportation. From the TransMilenio northern terminus – Portal del Norte – in northern Bogotá, buses leave every 20 minutes or so from inside the Portal's Buses Intermuncipales platform (COP$8000) to the town of Guatavita, via Sesquilé. About 11km north of town, the bus passes the 7km uphill road to the lake – no public transportation. Ask to get out, and walk or hitch (follow the signs to the right near the Escuela Tierra Negra). Alternatively, go on to the town of Guatavita, where on Sundays *colectivos* (shared transport) head directly from the central plaza to the lake. Taxis are scarce here.

The price for a round-trip taxi from Bogotá is up for negotiation. Expect around COP$150,000 including waiting time.

You're best off having your own transportation to get here.

Los Llanos

As you head southeast away from Bogotá, the jagged, Andean terrain soon drops and flattens out as if a giant guillotine dropped down across the mountains, revealing an endless sea of green grasslands. This is Los Llanos (The Plains).

Sometimes called the Serengeti of South America, Los Llanos is teeming with wildlife. It harbors more than 100 species of mammals and more than 700 species of birds, about the same number of birds as found in the entire USA. According to the Nature Conservancy, Los Llanos is also home to some of the most endangered species on Earth, including the Orinoco crocodile, the Orinoco turtle, giant armadillo, giant otter, black-and-chestnut eagle and several species of catfish.

The flat, grassy plains make this region ideal for cattle grazing. *Llaneros* (Colombian cowboys) spend long hours herding cattle in grueling conditions on mega ranches, some of which are thousands of hectares in size. This hard, isolated life inspired a unique culture very different from 'mainstream' Colombia. *Llaneros* are associated with their distinctive straw hats, *coleo* rodeos, the *joropo* dance and their bluegrass-like genre of folk music known as *música llanera*.

Los Llanos occupies the Colombian departments of Arauca, Casanare, Guainía, Meta and Vichada. As recently as 2003, much of this area was off-limits to foreigners. Today many of the bigger cities are safe and open for business. Serious wildlife seekers should head to Casanare, which offers wildlife on par with Brazil's Pantanal or Los Llanos on the Venezuelan side.

Despite many recent Colombian military victories, FARC rebels and other guerrilla groups still control swaths of Los Llanos. At the time of writing, independent travel was slightly dicey but relatively fine if you stick to the towns of Villavicencio, Inirida, Puerto López, Puerto Gaitán, Orocue and Puerto Inirida. It's also relatively fine in Puerto Careño – though the road from Puerto López to Puerto Careño on the Venezuelan border remains problematic; Yopal – though it has seen some issues with violent protests and devastating agricultural consequences from 2014's El Niño drought; and San José del Guaviare – but note the area south of San José del Guaviare remains very dangerous.

> ### ⓘ DON'T WANDER OFF...
>
> It is important to note that in all of Los Llanos you cannot wander off on your own. The security situation in Colombia is very fluid and can change very quickly – always check current situations with authorities and/or travel agencies before embarking anywhere in this region.

De Una Colombia Tours (p326) in Bogotá organizes guided tours to Parque Nacional Natural (PNN) El Tuparro as well as Cerros de Mavecure, Casanare, Guanía and Raudal Alto, among others.

VILLAVICENCIO

☑ 8 / POP 385,000 / ELEV 467M

The heavily militarized highway heading south from Bogotá leads to Villavicencio – 'La Puerta al Llano,' the gateway to the Llanos – 75km to the southeast. It's a bustling though not particularly interesting city with a serious penchant for nightlife and grilled meat. The city is a good base for exploring the plains; and though no longer a requisite jumping-off point for trips to Caño Cristales, it does offer the most thrilling ride there: in an ancient and creaky, white-knuckle-inducing 1940s-era DC-3!

🛏 Sleeping & Eating

Asaderos (restaurants serving roasted or grilled meats) serve the regional specialty, *mamona* (baby beef).

Mochileros Hostel HOSTEL $
(☑ 667-6723; www.mochileroshostel.com; Calle 18 No 39-08; dm COP$24,000, s/d COP$45,000/75,000, without bathroom COP$35,000/65,000, all incl breakfast; 🛜) The only hostel in town is a nice option in the upscale neighborhood of Barrio Balatá near loads of nice shopping, restaurants and bars. Good-value private rooms come with flat-screen TVs and cable (but no hot water); and there's a breezy patio in front for socializing. The vibe is a work in progress.

Three-night Caño Cristales trips can be arranged for COP$1,040,000 per person.

El Ranchón del Maporal COLOMBIAN $$
(www.ranchondelmaporal.com; Vía A Restrepo, Km1; mains COP$18,500-41,300; ⊘ kitchen 5pm-midnight Tue-Fri, 11am-10pm Sat & Sun; 🛜) This trendy restaurant on the edge of town does great steaks, seafood and regional cocktails

in an open-air atmosphere. On weekends, don't miss the *Llanero* seafood specialties, such as *amarillo monseñor,* a sort of cowboy riverfish chowder. It swarms with beautiful people as the night wears on and morphs into a bar/club with DJs (and cover charges) on weekends.

ℹ️ Information

Turismo Villavicencio (📞 670-3975; www.turismovillavicencio.gov.co; Calle 37 No 29-57, 6th fl) Operates three tourist information points: at the airport, at the bus station and in Plazoleta Los Libertadores.

ℹ️ Getting There & Away

Numerous daily buses serve Villavicencio from Bogotá (COP$21,000, three hours) and cities further afield in Los Llanos such as Yopal (COP$30,000, five hours), Puerto Gaitán (COP$25,000, three hours), Puerto López (COP$13,000, 1½ hours) and San José del Guaviare (COP$40,000, six hours).

Charter flights to La Macarena (COP$450,000), for Caño Cristales, leave from here in six-seat Cessnas; and on Saturdays in a 1940s-era DC-3.

CAÑO CRISTALES

It's been a long time since anyone visited one of Colombia's most impressive ecological wonders on a regular basis. Guerrilla, paramilitary and army activity in the department of Meta over the last few decades has meant that **Parque Nacional Natural (PNN) Sierra de La Macarena**, better known as **Caño Cristales**, has been closed to tourism since 1989. And, officially, it still is. But some pioneering tour agencies with an eye on preservation have secured authorization to visit the site, and began offering carefully crafted tours to the area in 2009, despite continued FARC presence in the greater surrounding areas.

Caño Cristales, located in the Macarena Mountains, has been called everything from 'The River of Five Colors' to 'The Liquid Rainbow.' Why all the superlatives? Well, for most of the year, you'd be right to inquire, but for a couple of months some time between July and November, water levels are just right for a unique biological phenomenon: an eruption of algae produced by a unique species of plant called *Macarenia clavigera.* The algae forms an underwater blanket of bright red, transforming the crystal-clear water into a river of cabernet that contrasts with the lunarscape of an-

cient, hollowed-out riverbed rock and surrounding savannah-meets-jungle landscape, dramatically altering the whole area into a thousand shades of awe.

Not only that, but there are numerous swimmable waterfalls and natural pools along the river, and the 10-minute ride from La Macarena along the Río Guayabero yields impressive wildlife, from sizable turtles and iguanas to macaws, and *aguilas* (Colombia's national bird, not the beer) to hoatzins (fascinating tropical pheasants with sinister faces!).

You cannot yet visit Caño Cristales on your own – you are obligated to go with an agency or guide. **Aventure Colombia** (📞 702-7069; www.aventurecolombia.com; Av Jiménez No 4-49, oficina 204, Bogotá) offers three- (COP$1,150,000) or four-day (COP$1,300,000) packages to the region that include flights, hotel, food, local transportation and a professional guide. **De Una Colombia Tours** (📞 1-368-1915; www.deunacolombia.com; Carrera 24 No 39B-25, oficina 501, Bogotá) offers fascinating tours to the region from COP$750,000. But it is possible to make your way to La Macarena independently: Satena (p324) now offers direct flights from Bogotá three times a week (Wednesday at 9:30am, Friday and Sunday at 10:30am; round-trip fares hover around COP$450,000) in high season (July to November). Alternatively, get yourself to Villavicencio (an easy bus ride from Bogotá; COP$21,000, three hours) and contact **Ecoturismo Sierra de La Macarena** (📞 8-664-3364; www.ecoturismomacarena.com; Aeropuerto Vanguardia, Villavicencio) at the airport, which can arrange charter flights, including (rather adventurous!) Saturday outings in an aged DC-3 to the small, otherwise inaccessible base town of La Macarena, and guides.

Caño Cristales is no secret – Colombians swarm to it on long weekends (called *puentes*) when the maximum daily visitor count of 180 isn't always enforced; these holiday weekends are best avoided.

PARQUE NACIONAL NATURAL (PNN) EL TUPARRO

The **Parque Nacional Natural (PNN) El Tuparro** (www.parquesnacionales.gov.co; Colombian/foreigner COP$12,000/35,000) is a 548,000-hectare nature reserve on the Venezuelan border. This biosphere of sandy river beaches and green grasslands is home to some 320 species of birds plus jaguars, tapirs and otters. Getting here won't be easy, but it could be very rewarding.

Boyacá, Santander & Norte de Santander

Best Places to Eat

➜ Mercagán (p113)

➜ Mercado Municipal (p91)

➜ Ristorante Al Cuoco (p111)

➜ Gringo Mike's (p106)

➜ Piqueteadero Doña Eustaquia (p103)

Best Places to Stay

➜ Refugio La Roca (p116)

➜ Suites Arco Iris (p89)

➜ Color de Hormiga Posada Campestre (p109)

➜ Renacer Guesthouse (p89)

➜ Finca San Pedro (p95)

Why Go?

Boyacá, Santander and Norte de Santander together form one of the first areas settled by Spanish conquistadores and its calling as Colombia's heartland cannot be understated. It's here that the seeds of revolution were sowed, culminating in the victory at Puente de Boyacá that ultimately led to Colombia's independence.

Amid its deep gorges, fast-flowing rivers and soaring, snowcapped mountains, extreme is the game in Colombia's outdoor adventure capital, San Gil, and the glacial peaks of Parque Nacional Natural (PNN) El Cocuy. But it's the region's bucolic colonial villages evoking life inside a living museum that forge the most lasting impressions – immensely beautiful Villa de Leyva and its massive main plaza; fiercely authentic Monguí burrowed near the *páramo* of Lago de Tota, Colombia's largest lake; unadulterated Playa de Belén, saddled up against the eroded brownstone pedestals of Área Natural Única Los Estoraques; and cinematic, perfectly preserved Barichara.

When to Go
Bucaramanga

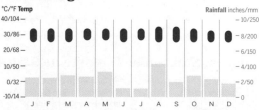

Jan The driest, clearest days in PNN El Cocuy, Colombia's most coveted park for trekking.

Feb & Mar The pre–Semana Santa (Holy Week) season has less crowds and full-bloom parks.

Dec Like elsewhere in Colombia, a festival of lights illuminates the region's charming villages.

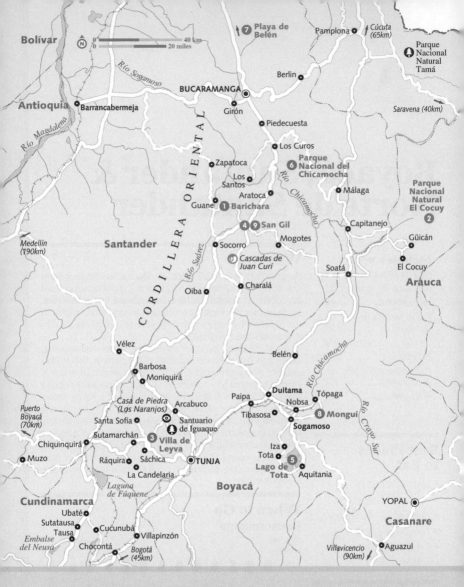

Boyacá, Santander & Norte de Santander Highlights

1 Wander the colonial village of **Barichara** (p107).

2 Ogle Los Llanos from **Parque Nacional Natural (PNN) El Cocuy** (p101).

3 Juggle sophisticated restaurants, colonial cobblestones and prehistoric fossils in pristinely preserved **Villa de Leyva** (p85).

4 Tackle the epic Cañon del Río Suárez in **San Gil** (p103) via white-water rafting or extreme mountain biking.

5 Trek the extraordinary *páramo* wetlands around sky-high **Lago de Tota** (p94).

6 Paraglide over **Parque Nacional del Chicamocha** (p112).

7 Explore rock formations around the postcard-perfect **Playa de Belén** (p119).

8 Lose yourself in the color-coordinated, stuck-in-time village of **Monguí** (p95).

9 Take on **tejo** (p106) in San Gil, an alcohol-fueled game of pucks and explosions born in Boyacá.

History

The Muiscas (Boyacá) and the Guane people (Santander) once occupied the regions north of what is now Bogotá. Highly developed in agriculture and mining, the Muisca traded with their neighbors and came into frequent contact with Spanish conquistadores. It was their stories of gold and emeralds that helped fuel the myth of El Dorado. The conquistadores' search for the famed city also sparked settlements and the Spanish founded several cities, including Tunja in 1539.

Several generations later, Colombian nationalists first stood up to Spanish rule in Socorro (Santander), stoking the flames of independence for other towns and regions. It was also here that Simón Bolívar and his upstart army took on Spanish infantry, winning decisive battles at Pantano de Vargas and Puente de Boyacá. Colombia's first constitution was drawn up soon after in Villa del Rosario, between the Venezuelan border and Cúcuta.

❶ Getting There & Around

The region is easily accessible by public transportation. Most of its cities are located along the safe and modern highway that stretches from Bogotá in the south to the Caribbean coast. Buses are frequent, comfortable and economical. There are regular buses along the main highway from Bogotá to Bucaramanga and beyond. Cúcuta is a major entry point for travelers coming from Venezuela.

Within the region intercity buses and minivans depart frequently. By plane, many cities, including Bucaramanga and Cúcuta, are increasingly served by low-cost airlines; and an airport in San Gil is supposedly opening in 2015.

BOYACÁ

The department of Boyacá evokes a sense of patriotism among Colombians; it was here that Colombian troops won their independence from Spain at the Battle of Boyacá. The department is dotted with quaint colonial towns; you could easily spend a few days bouncing between them. Boyacá's crown jewel is the spectacular Parque Nacional Natural (PNN) El Cocuy, located 249km northeast of the department capital, Tunja, though access has been cut back by park officials.

Villa de Leyva

📋 8 / POP 9645 / ELEV 2140M

One of the most beautiful colonial villages in Colombia, Villa de Leyva is a city frozen in time. Declared a national monument in 1954, the photogenic village has been preserved in its entirety with cobblestone roads and whitewashed buildings.

The city's physical beauty and mild, dry climate have long attracted outsiders. The town was founded in 1572 by Hernán Suárez de Villalobos, who named it for his boss, Andrés Díaz Venero de Leyva, the first president of the New Kingdom of Granada. It was originally a retreat for military officers, clergy and nobility.

In recent years an influx of wealthy visitors and expats has slowly transformed this once-hidden gem. Boutique hotels, gourmet restaurants and tacky tourist shops are replacing many of the old family *hosterías,* cafes and the authenticity. The 2007 *telenovela* (soap opera) *Zorro: La Espada y la Rosa* was filmed here, bringing further publicity to the city. On weekends the narrow alleys can get downright crammed with day-trippers from Bogotá. But thankfully on weekdays the city reverts to a peaceful, bucolic village, one of the loveliest places in Colombia.

◉ Sights

Villa de Leyva is a leisurely place made for wandering around charming cobblestone streets, listening to the sound of church bells and enjoying the lazy rhythm of days gone by. Villa de Leyva is also famous for its abundance of fossils from the Cretaceous and Mesozoic periods, when this area was underwater. Look closely and you'll notice that fossils have been used as construction materials in floors, walls and pavements.

As you stroll about, pop into the **Casa de Juan de Castellanos** (Carrera 9 No 13-15), **Casona La Guaca** (Carrera 9 No 13-57) and **Casa Quintero** (cnr Carrera 9 & Calle 12), three meticulously restored colonial mansions just off the plaza that now house quaint cafes, restaurants and shops.

★ Plaza Mayor   PLAZA

At 120m by 120m, Plaza Mayor is one of the largest town squares in the Americas. It's paved with massive cobblestones and surrounded by magnificent colonial structures and a charmingly simple parish church.

Villa de Leyva

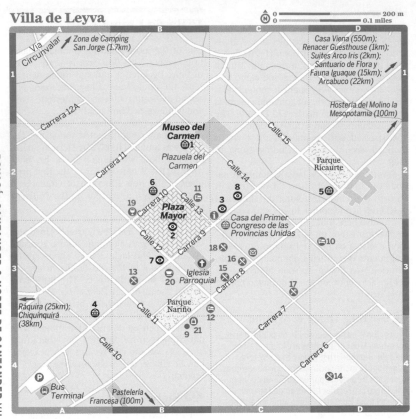

Only a small Mudejar fountain in its middle, which provided water to the village inhabitants for almost four centuries, interrupts the vast plaza. Unlike most Colombian cities where the main squares have been named after historic heroes, this one is traditionally and firmly called Plaza Mayor.

★**Museo del Carmen** MUSEUM
(Plazuela del Carmen; admission COP$3000; ⊙10:30am-1pm & 2:30-5pm Sat & Sun) One of the best museums of religious art in the country, Museo del Carmen is housed in the convent of the same name. It contains valuable paintings, carvings, altarpieces and other religious objects dating from the 16th century onward.

Casa Museo de Luis Alberto Acuña MUSEUM
(www.museoacuna.com.co; Plaza Mayor; adult/child COP$4000/2000; ⊙9am-6pm) Featuring works by one of Colombia's most influential painters, sculptors, writers and historians,

who was inspired by sources ranging from Muisca mythology to contemporary art. This museum has been set up in the mansion where Acuña (1904–93) lived for the last 15 years of his life and is Colombia's most comprehensive collection of his work.

Casa Museo de Antonio Ricaurte MUSEUM
(Calle 15 No 8-17, Parque Ricaurte; ⊙9am-noon & 2-5pm Wed-Sun) FREE Antonio Ricaurte fought under Bolívar and is remembered for his act of self-sacrifice in the battle of San Mateo (near Caracas in Venezuela) in 1814. Defending an armory and closely encircled by the Spaniards, he let them in, then set fire to the gunpowder kegs and blew up everyone, including himself. The battle was won. Casa Museo de Antonio Ricaurte is the house where Ricaurte was born in 1786.

It's now a museum displaying period furniture and weapons, and has pleasant gardens.

Villa de Leyva

Casa Museo de Antonio Nariño MUSEUM
(Carrera 9 No 10-25; ⊙9am-noon & 2-5pm Thu-Tue) **FREE** Antonio Nariño was known as the forefather of Colombia's independence and Casa Museo de Antonio Nariño is the house where he spent the last two months of his life before succumbing to a lung infection in 1823. Nariño was a fierce defender of human rights and is also revered for translating Thomas Paine's *Rights of Man* into Spanish. The house has been converted into a museum containing colonial objects and memorabilia related to this great man.

🏃 Activities

There are many **hiking** possibilities all around Villa de Leyva, as well as some longer treks in the Santuario de Iguaque. In town, there's a great hike that begins directly behind Renacer Guesthouse, passing two waterfalls to reach a spectacular bird's-eye view of the village; the round-trip hike takes less than two hours.

The alternative to foot power is **cycling** or **horseback riding**; both can be booked from one of the tour operators. Bikes cost about COP$15,000/25,000 per half-day/full day; horses are COP$30,000 per hour with a guide (folks in town will offer them cheaper, but they neglect to mention the price of the guide isn't included).

Swimming holes can be found beneath many of the nearby waterfalls or just outside town at **Pozos Azules** (admission COP$5000; ⊙8am-6pm). The most spectacular falls in

the area are El Hayal, Guatoque and La Periquera, but the last of these was officially closed at time of research after too many accidents and deaths over the years. More extreme-sporting options in the area include **rappelling, canyoning** and **caving**.

☞ Tours

Taxis at the bus terminal offer round trips to the surrounding sights. The standard routes include El Fósil, El Infiernito and Convento del Santo Eccc Homo (COP$134,000), and Ráquira and La Candelaria (COP$134,000). Prices, which include transportation, guide and insurance (but not entrance fees), are per person based on two people and drop with larger groups.

Colombian Highlands ECOTOURS
(📱310-552-9079, 732-1201; www.colombianhighlands.com; Av Carrera 10 No 21-Finca Renacer) 🍃 Run by biologist and Renacer Guesthouse owner Oscar Gilède, this agency has a variety of offbeat tours including ecotours, mountain trips, nocturnal hikes, bird-watching, rappelling/abseiling, canyoning, caving and hiking, and rents bikes and horses. English spoken.

Ciclotrip BICYCLE RENTAL
(📱320-899-4442; www.ciclotrip.com; Carrera 8 No 11-32; ⊙9am-5pm Mon-Fri, 8am-8pm Sat & Sun) This highly recommended bike outfitter/tour agency gets you out on two wheels to all the usual suspects, but also to more obscure waterfalls and points of interest,

TUNJA'S ENIGMATIC CEILING PAINTINGS

Tunja, founded by Gonzalo Suárez Rendón in 1539 on the site of Hunza, the pre-Hispanic Muisca settlement, is the capital of Boyacá and a bustling student center. It is often ballyhooed by Colombians and overlooked by travelers rushing on to Villa de Leyva. The city is a trove of colonial-era churches noted for their Mudejar art, an Islamic-influenced style developed in Christian Spain between the 12th and 16th centuries. It's particularly visible in the ornamented coffered vaults.

Several colonial mansions in Tunja, including the **Casa del Fundador Suárez Rendón** (Carrera 9 No 19-68; admission COP$2000; ⊘ 8am-noon & 2-6pm Mon-Sat) and the **Casa de Don Juan de Vargas** (Calle 20 No 8-52; admission COP$2000; ⊘ 9am-noon & 2-5pm Tue-Fri, 9am-noon & 2-4pm Sat & Sun), have ceilings adorned with unusual paintings featuring a strange mishmash of motifs taken from very different traditions. They include mythological scenes, human figures, animals and plants, coats of arms and architectural details. You can spot Zeus and Jesus amid tropical plants or an elephant under a Renaissance arcade – you probably haven't seen anything like this before. In fact, there's nothing similar anywhere in Latin America.

The source of these bizarre decorations seems to be Juan de Vargas himself. He was a scribe and had a large library with books on European art and architecture, ancient Greece and Rome, religion and natural history. It seems that the illustrations in the books were the source of motifs for the anonymous painters who worked on these ceilings. Since the original illustrations were in black and white, the color schemes are by the design of these unknown artisans.

For information on Tunja's colonial-era churches, such as **Capilla y Museo de Santa Clara La Real** (☑ 320-856-3658; Carrera 7 No 19-58; admission COP$3000; ⊘ 8am-noon & 2-6pm), **Iglesia de Santo Domingo** (Carrera 11 No 19-55) and **Templo Santa Barbara**, stop by the city's friendly **Tourist Office** (☑ 742-3272; www.turismotunja.gov.co; Carrera 9 No 19-68; ⊘ 8am-6pm) on Plaza de Bolívar.

If you come through, dress for the weather: Tunja is the highest and coldest departmental capital in Colombia. You'll find the best budget sleeps at **Hostería San Carlos** (☑ 742-3716; hosteriasancarlostunja@gmail.com; Carrera 11 No 20-12; s/d/ tr COP$40,000/60,000/75,000; 🛜), in a rambling colonial home and run by a friendly matriarch; and at **Hotel Casa Real** (☑ 743-1764; www.hotelcasarealtunja.com; Calle 19 No 7-65; s/d COP$62,000/86,000; 🛜), a step up with smartly furnished rooms surrounding a pleasant courtyard and extra sweet staff.

Buses to and from Bogotá (COP$19,000, 2½ to three hours) depart every 10 to 15 minutes, respectively. Moving on from Tunja, northbound buses to San Gil (COP$25,000, 4½ hours), Bucaramanga (COP$35,000, seven hours) and beyond run at least every hour. There is one 9:15pm bus to Güicán. Minibuses to Villa de Leyva (COP$6500, 45 minutes) depart regularly between 6am and 7pm, and to Sogamoso (COP$6500, 1½ hours) from 5am to 8pm.

including a winery. The owner, Francisco, is a good guy and trained in first-aid and mountain rescue. Day trips run COP$21,000 to COP$50,000. Also rents bikes.

✪ Festivals & Events

Encuentro de Musica Antigua   MUSIC
(Semana Santa) Old-school *Barroco* music festival with concerts at local churches including Iglesia Parroquial and Iglesia del Carmen.

Festival de las Cometas   KITES
(⊘ Aug) Locals and foreign kite fans compete in this colorful kite festival.

Festival de Luces   FIREWORKS
(⊘ Dec) This fireworks festival is usually on the first or second weekend of December.

🛏 Sleeping

Villa de Leyva has a large selection of hotels in all price ranges. Note that prices rise on weekends, when it may be hard to find a room. During high seasons, including Semana Santa and December 20 to January 15, prices can more than double. Plan ahead. Camping around the area runs about COP$15,000 per person, including at the extraordinary **Zona de Camping San Jorge**

(📧 732-0328; campingsanjorge@gmail.com; Vereda Roble; campsite per person high/low season COP$17,000/15,000; 🛜), a huge and impressive space for 120 tents with lovely views of the surrounding mountains.

★**Renacer Guesthouse**   HOSTEL $
(📱 732-1201, 311-308-3739; www.colombianhighlands.com; Av Carrera 10 No 21-Finca Renacer; campsite per person with/without tent rental COP$20,000/14,000, dm COP$22,000-24,000, s/d from COP$60,000/70,000; @🛜🏊) Located about 1.2km northeast of Plaza Mayor, this delightful 'boutique hostel' is the creation of biologist and tour guide extraordinaire Oscar Gilède of Colombian Highlands (p87). Everything about this place feels like home – hammocks surrounding an immaculate garden, a communal, open-air kitchen with brick oven, and spotless dorms and rooms.

There's also a natural swimming pool in the back and an outsourced cafe. Oscar will credit guests' first taxi ride from the bus terminal (COP$5000).

Casa Viena   HOSTEL $
(📱 314-370-4776; www.casaviena.com; Carrera 10 No 19-114; dm COP$15,000, s/d without bathroom COP$28,000/38,000, r COP$45,000; @🛜) Hans and family of Cartagena's Casa Viena fame fled the Caribbean heat and opened this small guesthouse just outside the village. They spend a lot of time on their nearby farm, though, so the vibe has suffered, but the four simple rooms are still a good-value bed down, especially for long-term stays.

★**Suites Arco Iris**   BOUTIQUE HOTEL $$
(📱 311-254-7919; www.suitesarcoiris.com; Km2 Vila la Colorada; r mountain/village view incl breakfast COP$152,000/264,000; 🛜) Perched on a hilltop above town, this romantic 26-room

hotel tops the charts in Villa de Leyva for pizzazz and personality. The massive rooms, all unique but equally drenched in colors, art and character, are snazzy affairs with Jacuzzis, terraces, kaleidoscopically tiled bathrooms and fireplaces. Views, be them mountain or town, are stupendous.

The bummer here is if you don't have your own wheels, you'll drop an additional COP$24,000 to COP$30,000 round-trip going to and from town.

Hospedería La Roca   GUESTHOUSE $$
(📱 311-895-6470; jucasato9@hotmail.com; Plaza Mayor; r per person incl breakfast COP$65,000; 🛜) Located directly on Plaza Mayor, the well-lit La Roca offers 23 pleasant rooms surrounding a gorgeous, plant-filled courtyard in a spacious space that feels way bigger than its room inventory. All rooms have high ceilings, flat-screen TVs and modern bathrooms with hot water. Taking quality and location into account, you aren't going to find better value.

Hospedería Don Paulino   GUESTHOUSE $$
(donpaulino@hotmail.com; Calle 14 No 7-46; r per person incl breakfast COP$50,000; 🛜) This great-value midrange sits on a quieter end of the village but is still just two and a half blocks from Plaza Mayor. There are 15 rooms, mostly around a bright courtyard and past arched hallways. Rooms are simple but well presented and maintained enthusiastically by the friendly manager, with clean, modern bathrooms, TVs and the occasional carefully chosen antique.

Hostería del Molino La Mesopotamia   HISTORIC HOTEL $$
(📱 732-0235;   www.lamesopotamia.com; Carrera 8 No 15A-265; s/d/tr incl breakfast COP$127,155/170,690/210,776; 🍴🛜🍽) Built in

BOYACÁ, SANTANDER & NORTE DE SANTANDER VILLA DE LEYVA

BOLÍVAR'S BRIDGE

The **Puente de Boyacá** is one of the most important battlefields of Colombia's modern history. On August 7, 1819 and against all odds, the armies of Simón Bolívar defeated Spanish troops led by General José María Barreiro, sealing Colombia's independence.

Several monuments have been erected on the battlefield. The centerpiece is the **Monumento a Bolívar**, an 18m-high sculpture topped by the statue of Colombia's hero and accompanied by five angels symbolizing the so-called *países bolivarianos*, the countries liberated by Bolívar – Venezuela, Colombia, Ecuador, Peru and Bolivia. An eternal flame for Bolívar burns nearby.

The Puente de Boyacá, the bridge which gives its name to the battlefield and over which Bolívar's troops crossed to fight the Spaniards, is just a small, simple bridge reconstructed in 1939.

The battlefield is on the main Tunja–Bogotá road, 15km south of Tunja. Any bus passing along this road will drop you off.

DON'T MISS

SUTAMARCHÁN

While traveling about around Villa de Leyva, it's worth stopping in **Sutamarchán**, the *longaniza* capital of Colombia, 14km west of Villa on the road to Ráquira. *Longaniza* is a regional sausage similar to Portuguese *linguiça*. In town, it's grilled up everywhere – follow your nose. The best spots to try it are **Fabrica de Longaniza, Piqueteadero y Asadero Robertico** (Carrera 2 No 5-135, Sutamarchán; from COP$15,000; ⊗8:30am-7:30pm Mon-Fri, 7am-8pm Sat & Sun) – the more rustic, spicier version – and **El Fogata** (Carrera 5 No 5-55, Sutamarchán; grills per 1/6 persons COP$14,000/78,000; ⊗8am-8pm Mon-Fri, from 7am Sat & Sun), a more clean-cut operation.

1568, this old flour mill is four years older than Villa itself and one of the most beautiful buildings in town. It's not gone without complaints from travelers, mainly about dampness in some rooms, but it's still worth considering for its colonial architecture, furnishings and artwork. You can sleep with history here.

Posada de San Antonio   BOUTIQUE HOTEL **$$$**
(☑732-0538; www.hotellaposadadesanantonio.com; Carrera 8 11-80; s/d incl breakfast COP$203,448/231,000; @🛜) Natural light permeates all the nooks and crannies of this antique-packed, charismatic 1860 colonial home, one of Villa's most discerning choices. Rooms feature exposed glimpses of original brick and there's a lovely open kitchen, a character-filled restaurant/living room, a small portable altar and, of course, a lovely courtyard. A new spa offers massages (COP$80,000), steam room and atmospheric Jacuzzi, the last two of which are included in rates outside holidays.

✖ Eating

Villa is the most sophisticated foodie destination in Boyacá. There are a few gourmet food courts in the village, with Casa Quintero and Casona La Guaca offering the best and most diverse options.

★ Pastelería Francesa   BAKERY, FRENCH **$**
(Calle 10 No 6-05; items COP$1500-3600; ⊗8am-7pm Thu-Sun, closed Feb & Sep) You can smell the sweet scent of baked goodness a block away from this authentic French bakery with croissants (oh, those almond ones!), baguettes, tarts, quiches, mini-pizzas, coffees and hot chocolate. It's great if you can catch it open – the owner likes his vacation time – and a classy redo of the place approaches legitimately chic.

Restaurante Estar de la Villa   COLOMBIAN **$**
(Calle 13 No 8-75; set meals COP$10,000; ⊗9am-5pm Mon-Fri, 8:30am-8pm Sat & Sun) Honest to goodness, clean-cut cheapie serving up wholesome daily set meals with just the right amount of motherly love. There's a menu but why bother – just go for the set meal, especially if it's serving *sopa de colí* (green banana soup). It's tucked away inside the Luna Lunera Centro Comercial.

Don Salvador   COLOMBIAN **$**
(market; meals from COP$7000; ⊗6am-3pm Sat) Dig into regional *boyacense* cuisine at Villa's bustling Saturday market. Look for this stall, where Don Salvador does the best *mute* (puffed corn soup, served with a side of cow's feet or chicken thigh) and *carne asada* (grilled steak).

Barcelona Tapas   SPANISH **$$**
(Carrera 9 No 11-57; tapas COP$5500-12,000, mains COP$8500-34,500; ⊗6-9pm Wed & Fri, noon-1am Sat & Sun) Ignacio and Nina, a lovely Catalan couple who fled Spain for economic reasons, do lovely work at this five-table restaurant just off Plaza Mayor. Perfect meal: grilled prawns with crunchy fried garlic followed by Catalan-style buffalo medallions, smothered in an extraordinary pepper sauce.

Restaurante Savia   VEGETARIAN, ORGANIC **$$**
(Carrera 9 No 11-75, Casa Quintero; mains COP$13,500-33,400; ⊗noon-7pm Tue, Sun & Mon, to midnight Fri & Sat; 🖋) The delightful Savia specializes in inventive vegetarian, vegan and organic fare and local eco-artisanal products of the same ilk. Carnivores aren't left behind, though – there's fresh seafood and poultry dishes (but no red meat). A plaque outside commemorates the last concert performed by former Elvis Presley drummer Bill Lynn before he died in Villa de Leyva in 2006.

Restaurante Casa Blanca   COLOMBIAN **$$**
(Calle 13 No 7-16; set meals COP$9500, mains COP$15,000-25,500; ⊗8am-9pm) One of the better midrange restaurants in town. Prepare to wait.

★ Mercado Municipal COLOMBIAN $$$

(Carrera 8 No 12-25; mains COP$28,000-52,000; ☺noon-5pm Sun, Mon & Wed, to 9pm Thu, to 10pm Fri & Sat) This chef-driven outdoor restaurant around the gardens of a 1740 colonial house has resurrected ancient techniques of cooking meats in a 1m-deep underground wood-burning *barbacoa* (barbecue) on its way to becoming Boyacá's most interesting restaurant. The rich pork shank in blackberry reduction is a mountainous *chicharrón* of carnivorous love, the tender meat effortlessly sliding off the crispy skin.

But the varied menu goes gourmet beyond meat. There's agnolotti pasta with ricotta and honey, rustic lentil soup and some wonderful desserts, including a ridiculous coconut caramel pie. *Buen provecho!*

La Bonita MEXICAN $$$

(cnr Carrera 9 & Calle 12, Casa Quintero; mains COP$11,000-42,000; ☺noon-10pm Sun-Tue, Thu & Fri, to 11pm Sat) This upscale Mexican hot spot does a bang-up job with tacos (COP$25,000 to COP$26,000) – *cochinita pibil* (achiote-rubbed pork tacos) rivaling the Yucatán, with pretty decent *carnitas* (braised pork), too – and great tortilla soup (COP$12,000). It's located inside the gourmet Casa Quintero.

miCocina COLOMBIAN $$$

(www.academiaverdeoliva.com/micocina-restaurante-villa-de-leyva; Calle 13 No 8-45; mains COP$17,000-48,000; ☺11am-4pm Sun-Thu, to 9pm Fri & Sat; 🖥) This colorful restaurant/ culinary school prides itself on being 100% Colombian and is indeed the best place to sample Colombian gastronomy at levels beyond *sancocho* and *patacones*. There's a set lunch menu (COP$10,000) as well as à la

carte options. The basil-based salad dressing is hands-down best in town.

🍷 Drinking & Nightlife

The drinking scene in Villa centers around the charming plaza – locals and visitors alike plop down on the steps along Carrera 9, which turns into a full-on street party, and there's more cafes than German World Cup goals!

Bolívar Social Club BAR

(cocktails COP$14,000-18,000; ☺3-10pm Thu, to 1am Fri & Sat, 1-6pm Sun) Inside Mercado Municipal, Villa's first attempt at a legitimately trendy bar is a semi-circle number under the watchful eye of a Simón Bolívar rabbit head. There's draft microbrews and creative cocktails, all knocked back to tunes that jump from Eddie Vedder to '60s kitsch pop and back again. Live jazz and rock on weekends and DJs in high season.

La Cava de Don Fernando BAR

(Carrera 10 No 12-03; ☺2pm-1am Sun-Thu, to 2am Fri & Sat; 🖥) A cozy bar on the corner of Plaza Mayor with excellent tunes, atmospheric candles and one of the better beer selections in town.

Sybarrita Cafe CAFE

(Carrera 9 No 11-88; coffee COP$1600-5000; ☺8:30am-9pm) Villa de Leyva's most serious java joint, serving daily-changing single-origin coffees from around Colombia's best regions in an old-school environment that feels a lot more classic than this upstart cafe's age. The few tables are usually crammed with village old-timers mingling with nomadic caffeine connoisseurs.

JUST ANOTHER CERAMIC SUNDAY...

Twenty-five kilometers southwest of Villa de Leyva, **Ráquira** is the pottery capital of Colombia, where you'll find everything from ceramic bowls, jars and plates to toys and Christmas decorations. Brightly painted facades, a jumble of craft shops and stacks of freshly fired mud and clay pots make a welcoming sight along the main street of this one-horse town. There are many workshops in and around the village where you can watch pottery being made. There are also dozens of craft shops around the main square, all selling pretty much the same stuff, including pottery, hammocks, baskets, bags, ponchos, jewelry and woodcarvings. The best day to visit is Sunday, when the market is in full swing.

Ráquira is 5km off the Tunja–Chiquinquirá road, down a side road branching off at Tres Esquinas. Four minibuses run Monday to Friday between Villa de Leyva and Ráquira (COP$5500, 45 minutes, 7:30am, 12:45pm, 3pm and 4:50pm), with a fifth added on weekends. A round-trip taxi from Villa de Leyva with an hour or so to explore will set you back about COP$60,000 to COP$70,000. A handful of buses from Bogotá also call here daily.

WORTH A TRIP

IT'S A MIRACLE!

Chiquinquirá is the religious capital of Colombia, attracting flocks of devoted Catholic pilgrims due to a 16th-century miracle involving a painting of the Virgin Mary.

The *Virgin of the Rosary* was painted around 1555 by Spanish artist Alonso de Narváez in Tunja. It depicts Mary cradling baby Jesus and flanked by St Anthony of Padua and St Andrew the Apostle. Soon after it was completed, the image began to fade, the result of shoddy materials and a leaky chapel roof. In 1577 the painting was moved to Chiquinquirá, put into storage and forgotten.

A few years later, Maria Ramos, a pious woman from Seville, rediscovered the painting. Though it was in terrible shape, Ramos loved to sit and pray to the image. On December 26, 1586, before her eyes and prayers, the once faded and torn painting was miraculously restored to its original splendor. From then on its fame swiftly grew and the miracles attributed to the Virgin multiplied.

In 1829 Pope Pius VII declared the Virgen de Chiquinquirá patroness of Colombia. Dubbed 'La Chinita' by locals, the image was canonically crowned in 1919, and in 1927 her sanctuary declared a basilica. Pope John Paul II visited the city in 1986.

Dominating the Plaza de Bolívar, the **Basílica de la Virgen de Chiquinquirá** houses the **Sacred Image**. Construction of the huge neoclassical church began in 1796 and was completed in 1812. The spacious three-naved interior boasts 17 chapels and an elaborate high altar where the painting is displayed. The painting measures 113cm by 126cm and is the oldest documented Colombian painting.

There are eight buses a day between 7am and 4pm from Villa de Leyva to Chiquinquirá (COP$7500, one hour). Buses to Bogotá depart every 15 minutes (COP$17,000, three hours).

Shopping

Check out the colorful market held every Saturday on the square three blocks southeast of Plaza Mayor. It's best and busiest early in the morning. There is also an organic market there on Thursdays.

Villa de Leyva has quite a number of handicraft shops noted for fine basketry and good-quality woven items such as sweaters and *ruanas* (ponchos). There are some artisan shops around Plaza Mayor. A number of weavers have settled in town; their work is of excellent quality and their prices are reasonable. Most craft shops open only on weekends.

La Tienda Feroz ARTS & CRAFTS
(www.latiendaferoz.com; Carrera 8 No 11-32; 9am-5pm Mon-Fri, 8am-8pm Sat & Sun) This great little shop features the unique art of 27 Colombian artists (and a few Mexican ones sprinkled in) and is the spot to pick up items that *aren't* typical tourist wares. The owners have backgrounds in illustration, animation and industrial design, so they know their creativity.

Information

There are several ATMs in and around the plaza.

4-72 (www.4-72.com.co; cnr Carrera 8 & Calle 13; 10am-10pm) Not a full post office but rather a postal representative inside a souvenir shop.

Police (732-0236; cnr Carrera 10 & Calle 11) Villa's police station.

Tourist Office (Oficina de Turismo; 732-0232; Carrera 9 No 13-11; 8am-12:30pm & 2-6pm Mon-Fri, 8am-6pm Sat, 9am-5pm Sun) Provides free maps, brochures and information in Spanish.

Getting There & Away

The bus terminal is three blocks southwest of Plaza Mayor, on the road to Tunja. Minibuses run between Tunja and Villa de Leyva every 15 minutes from 5am to 7:45pm (COP$6500, 45 minutes). More than a dozen direct buses travel daily to Bogotá (COP$22,000, four hours) between 4:30am and 5pm (5am and 5pm on Sunday). For San Gil, connect in Tunja (not Arcabuco as some would have you believe – it will take longer).

Around Villa de Leyva

Don't leave town without exploring some of the many nearby attractions, including archaeological relics, colonial monuments, petroglyphs, caves, lakes and waterfalls.

The area is completely safe. You can walk to some of the nearest sights, or go by bicycle or on horseback. You can also use local buses, go by taxi or arrange a tour with Villa de Leyva's tour operators. If you choose to go by taxi, make sure you confirm with the driver all the sights you want to see and agree on a price before setting off.

Founded by the Dominican fathers in 1620, the **Convento del Santo Ecce Homo** (admission COP$5000; ☺9am-5pm Tue-Sun) is a large stone-and-adobe construction with a lovely courtyard. The floors are paved with stones quarried in the region, so they contain ammonites and fossils, including petrified corn and flowers. There are also fossils in the base of a statue in the chapel.

The chapel boasts a magnificent gilded main retable with a small image of Ecce Homo, and the original wooden ceiling is full of fascinating details: note the images of pineapples, eagles, suns and moon – used to help convert indigenous peoples; the images of a skull and crossbones with a Bolivian-style winter cap in the Sacristy; and the crucifix in the Capitulary Hall showing Christ alive, a rarity in South America (his eyes are open). Look out for the drawing of Christ in the west cloister – from different angles it appears that the eyes open and close.

The convent is 13km from Villa de Leyva. The morning bus to Santa Sofía will drop you off, from where it's a 15-minute walk to the convent. A round-trip taxi (for up to four people) from Villa de Leyva to El Fósil, El Infiernito and Ecce Homo should cost about COP$60,000 to COP$75,000, including waiting time.

El Fósil (www.museoelfosil.com; adult/child COP$6000/4000; ☺8am-6pm) is an impressive 120-million-year-old baby *kronosaurus* fossil and the world's most complete specimen of this prehistoric marine reptile. The fossil is 7m long; the creature was about 12m in size but the tail did not survive. The fossil remains in place exactly where it was found in 1977. The fossil is off the road to Santa Sofía, 6km west of Villa de Leyva. You can walk there in a bit more than an hour, or take the Santa Sofía bus, which will drop you off 80m from the fossil. Don't miss the new **Centro de Investigaciones Paleontológicas** (CIP; www.centropaleo.com; adult/child COP$8000/4000; ☺9am-noon & 2-5pm Tue-Thu, 8am-5pm Fri-Sun) just across the main road from El Fósil – a sleek facility that combines an open-window research facility with even more impressive fossils, including an amazing full-body *plesiosaurus* (a Jurassic sea dragon) and the only tooth of a saber-tooth tiger ever discovered in Colombia. Everything is signed in English.

The **Estación Astronómica Muisca** (El Infiernito; adult/child COP$6000/5000; ☺9am-noon & 2-5pm Tue-Sun) dates from the early centuries AD and was used by the Muiscas to determine the seasons. This Stonehenge-like site contains 115-odd cylindrical stone monoliths sunk vertically into the ground about 1m from each other in two parallel lines 9m apart. By measuring the length of shadows cast by the stones, the *indígenas* were able to identify the planting seasons. The site is 2km north of El Fósil. There's no public transportation, but you can walk there from the fossil in 25 minutes. Bicycle, horse and taxi are other means of transportation.

Santuario de Iguaque

High above the surrounding valley and shrouded in mist is a pristine wilderness that Muiscas consider to be the birthplace of mankind. According to Muisca legend, the beautiful goddess Bachué emerged from Laguna de Iguaque with a baby boy in her arms. When the boy became an adult they married, bore children and populated the earth. In old age, the pair transformed into serpents and dove back into the sacred lake.

Today this Muisca Garden of Eden is a 67.5-sq-km national park called **Santuario de Flora y Fauna de Iguaque** (Colombians/foreigners COP$14,500/38,000; ☺8am-5pm). There are eight small mountain lakes in the northern reserve including Laguna de Iguaque, all sitting at an altitude of between 3550m and 3700m. This unique *páramo* (high-mountain plains) neotropical ecosystem contains hundreds of species of flora and fauna but is most noted for the *frailejón*, a shrub typical of the highlands.

It can get pretty cold here, with temperatures ranging between 4°C and 13°C. It's also very wet, receiving an average of 1648mm of rain per year. The best months to visit are January, February, July and August. Come prepared. Only 50 people are allowed to enter the sanctuary per day.

The **visitors center** (dm per person COP$38,000, campsite per person COP$10,000; ☺8am-5pm), 700m up hill from the ranger station, is under concession to **Naturar** (☎312-585-9092, 318-595-5643; naturariguaque@yahoo.es), which runs a restaurant (meals COP$11,000 to COP$16,000) and simple accommodations in rather nice dorm facilities, with 48 wool-blanket-covered beds (soon to be less as they are planning on creating two private doubles). They also have camping facilities with cold-water bathrooms and a kitchen nearer to the ranger station. Lodging reservations via Naturar are required in December, January, June, the second week of October and any holidays; otherwise, you can stroll up. It's a supreme place to chill out in the mountains, with nightly visits from wild turkeys!

To get to the park from Villa de Leyva, take the Arcabuco-bound bus (departs 6am, 7am, 8am, 10am, 10:30am, 3pm and 4pm) and tell the driver to drop you off at Casa de Piedra (also known as Los Naranjos; COP$4000) at Km12. From here, walk up the rough road to the visitors center (3km). The hike from the visitors center to Laguna de Iguaque takes about three hours. A leisurely round trip takes five to six hours, or longer if you plan to visit some of the other lakes. Colombian Highlands (p87) runs full day tours from Villa de Leyva for COP$134,000 per person for two people, less for larger groups.

La Candelaria

⚡ 8 / POP 300 / ELEV 2255M

This tiny hamlet set amid arid hills, 7km beyond Ráquira, is noted for the **Monasterio de La Candelaria** (admission COP$5000; ⏱ 9am-noon & 2-5pm). The monastery was founded in 1597 by Augustine monks and completed about 1660. Part of it is open to the public. Monks show you through the chapel (note the 16th-century painting of the Virgen de la Candelaria over the altar), a small museum, a stunning courtyard flanked by the cloister with a collection of 17th-century canvases, and the cave where the monks originally lived. Some of the artworks were allegedly painted by Gregorio Vásquez de Arce y Ceballos and the Figueroa brothers.

A round-trip taxi from Villa de Leyva to Ráquira and La Candelaria can be arranged for around COP$90,000 to COP$100,000 (up to four people), allowing some time in both villages.

Another option is to walk along the path from Ráquira (one hour). The path begins in Ráquira's main plaza, winds up a hill to a small shrine at the top and then drops down and joins the road to La Candelaria.

Lago de Tota & Around

Heading some 130km east of Villa de Leyva, you'll encounter the largely unexplored region known in the indigenous Muisca language of Chibcha as 'Sugamuxi' – the Valley of the Sun. Ecotourism is blossoming in this area, which remains locked in traditions and offers a side of Colombia relatively unaffected by massive tourism (Monguí being the belle of the ball). Nature rules here, with astonishing treks in and around Lago de Tota, Colombia's largest lake; numerous colonial villages in the vicinity nearly untouched by international tourism; and an out-of-the-blue white-sand Andean beach, the 3015m-high Playa Blanca, sweetening the deal.

The area's *páramo* ecosystem, which is a rare glacier-formed tropical ecosystem that exists between 3000m and 5000m in the mountains, characterized by lakes and plains rich with peat bogs and wet grasslands mashed with shrub lands and forest patches, only exists in a few countries in the world, with a large portion in Colombia. Like Parque Nacional Natural (PNN) El Cocuy to the north, where the *páramo* also thrives, there are naturally excellent trekking opportunities here.

Worthwhile treks in the region include Páramo de Ocetá, 18km through the *páramo* ecosystem to a spectacular lookout over the Laguna Negra; and Gran Salto de Candelas, 8km through tropical forest to a beautiful 250m-high waterfall.

The region is also a particularly good place to spy endangered Andean condors, reintroduced here to increase the Colombian population. The recently carved La Ruta del Condor, a 17km trek through Páramo de Guantiva, is your best chance to spot them.

For more information on activities in the region, check out www.visitsugamuxi.com, which supports a local NGO that helps protect the lake from contamination.

Sogamoso

⚡ 8 / POP 106,000 / ELEV 2569M

Sogamoso is a distinctly uninspiring working-class Colombian city, but it was a religious center of the Muiscas and is the jumping off point for explorations further afield around Lago de Tota and its environs. That said, the city does boast the only archaeological museum of the Muisca people in Colombia; and travelers and yogaphiles often lose themselves for days on end at the town's one great place to stay.

◉ Sights & Activities

Finca San Pedro arranges all activities around Lago de Tota, including rock climbing, high-altitude diving, condor viewing, paragliding, horseback riding and bird-watching.

Museo Arqueológico
Eliécer Silva Célis   MUSEUM
(Calle 9A No 6-45; adult/child COP$6000/5000; ⊙9am-noon & 2-5pm Mon-Sat, 9am-3pm Sun) This very well-done archaeological museum was built on the remains of Sogamoso's Muisca cemetery and highlights this most important of Chibcha-speaking cultures – among others – through art, ceramics, sculpture, music, paleontology etc. The most interesting exhibits include the mummified remains of a *cacique* (head of tribe) and the spine-shivering shrunken-head techniques of the Jivaros and Shiworas tribes.

The grounds include a replica of the Temple of the Sun, the Muisca necropolis destroyed by the Spanish (by accident, according to the chronicles, while inspecting its dark interior with torches) in 1537.

Playa Blanca   BEACH
(☑312-241-5616) This white-sand Andean beach on the southwestern shore of Lago de Tota is one of the highest beaches in the world (3015m). You can camp here for free but the facilities leave something to be desired. There is a good restaurant serving trout right on the beach.

In 2014 the mayor brought in outside sand for a beach volleyball tournament, tarnishing Eden a bit here by manipulating nature for commercial gains (the town was working on a fix to bring the beach back to its natural state). To reach the beach, there are several bus options; the *easiest* is catching a Cootracero bus from Sogamoso's bus terminal (COP$6000, 1½ hours, hourly).

Agama Yoga Colombia   YOGA
(☑312-567-7102; www.agamayogacolombia.com; Km2 Via Lago de Tota (Aquitania), Sogamoso) Travelers rave about this independently operated yoga school on the grounds of Finca San Pedro that offers serious yoga and tantra courses in English as well as complete facilities for long-term study, including lodging, kitchen and hang space. Owner and instructor Juan Ananda honed his Zen throughout Asia. First day free.

🛏 Sleeping

★Finca San Pedro   GUESTHOUSE $
(☑312-567-7102; www.fincasanpedro.com; Km2 Via Lago de Tota (Aquitania); dm from COP$25,000, s/d/tr/q incl breakfast from COP$50,000/70,000/100,000/120,000; @🛜) This excellent, family-run farm-turned-hostel located just 1.5km outside Sogamoso is wonderfully appointed and dripping in country charm – bougainvillea, Phoenix palms and Araucaria trees dot the landscape – and the English-speaking hosts enthusiastically plot your excursions in the area and make you feel like part of the family. Inquire about yoga and volunteer opportunities.

ℹ Getting There & Away

Regular buses serve Sogamoso from Bogotá (COP$23,000, three to four hours, hourly) and Tunja (COP$5500, one hour, every 15 minutes). From Sogamoso, **Cootracero** (☑770-3255; www.cootracero.com) serves Iza (COP$2600, 40 minutes) and Monguí (COP$3500, one hour) every 20 minutes. There are six buses a day to San Gil (COP$35,000, six hours), most of which depart with **Concorde** (☑314-324-1233; www.cootransbol.com).

Monguí

☑8 / POP 5000 / ELEV 2900M

Surrounding Lago de Tota is a series of picturesque colonial villages, highlighted by Monguí, 14km southeast of Sogamoso, once voted the most beautiful village in Boyacá. The first missionaries appeared in the region around 1555 but the town was not founded until 1601 and later became a catechetic center of the Franciscan monks – as evidenced by one of the town's most striking buildings, the Convento de los Franciscanos, which dominates the gorgeous plaza. Today, this Christmas-colored village boasts uniform green and white colonial architecture only broken by occasional newer brick constructions that evoke the English countryside. Either way, the beautiful facades are all dripping with colorful red rose-scented geraniums and ivy. It's a truly lovely *pueblo* adhering to a fiercely authentic ethos, a sort of mini–Villa de Leyva if nobody had ever heard of it.

The idyllic village is famous for more than good looks, though: since the beginning of the 20th century, *monguiseños* have engaged in a tradition of hand-sewn leather footballs. These days, the town exports over

WORTH A TRIP

SUGAMUXI'S POSTCARD-PERFECT VILLAGES

When it comes to picturesque time-trapped villages, Sugamuxi is hardly a one-trick pony. Though limited, **Monguí** has the most traveler infrastructure, but there are several other villages in the region well worth a visit, with **Iza**, 15km southwest of Sogamoso, leading the way. The immensely quiet town is particularly notable for its desserts. It all started with *merengón* (meringue with local fruits) sold from the back of cars and grew into a tradition, especially on weekends, when it's a sweet-tooth free-for-all in the plaza. The rest of the week, Iza is supremely tranquil, and is worth bedding down in for a night if you're looking to bliss out in a colonial hamlet untouched by big tourism. There are some popular hot springs, which are particularly atmospheric under the moonlight, when locals often take a dip across the road in the completely natural and unguarded pools (technically illegal). If you do stay the night, the best spot is the boutique *cabañas* at **Casitas Barro** (☑ 314-472-6272; www.casitasbarro.com; Carrera 6 No 3-57; s/d/tr COP$80,000/100,000/170,000; ☜). The budget choice would be **La Posada del Virrey** (☑ 312-567-7373; www.laposadadelvirrey.galeon.com; Calle 4A No 4A-75; s/d/tr COP$40,000/70,000/90,000), the most traditional in town. Bring your own food just in case – there are several restaurants around the plaza, but most only serve lunch (for now).

If you dig the idyllic village sort of thing, there are more in the area: **Tópaga** (famous for its devil sculpture inside the local church and handicrafts made from coal); **Nobsa** (well known for Boyacá handicrafts); and **Tibasosa** (the *feijoa* – pineapple guava – capital of Colombia). Or, check out all of them at once at **Pueblito Boyacense** (www.pueblitoboyacense.co; Calle 29 No 26-75; admission COP$500; ⊙ 8am-10pm), a somewhat Universal Studio-y but well-done re-creation of all of Boyacá's most beautiful villages in one convenient theme park. It's a nice spot for a cafe and live music in the evenings, and there are good handicrafts shops. Perhaps most interesting is that people actually live there!

300,000 footballs to Latin countries and the industry creates over 100 jobs for peasant families.

◉ Sights & Activities

There are several *fabricas* (factories) around the plaza where you can pop in and see how they make the famous *monguiseño* footballs and pick up a football for yourself. Monguí is also one of the starting points for the excellent 8km Páramo Ocetá trek (the other is 12km northeast in similarly named Mongua).

Convento de los Franciscanos
MONASTERY

(Plaza Principal) Construction on this Franciscan monastery, the most dominating building in Monguí, began in 1694 and took 100 years to complete. The stunning red stone marvel is attached to the Basílica Menor de Nuestra Señora de Monguí, whose three-nave interior boasts a richly gilded main retable, and the image of the Virgen de Monguí, crowned in 1929 as the patron saint of Monguí. The Museo de Arte Religioso is also housed inside the convent.

A fussy priest presides over the inconsistent opening hours of the temple and convent, which were closed for renovations at time of research.

🛏 Sleeping & Eating

Calicanto Real Hostal　　GUESTHOUSE $
(☑ 311-811-1519; calicantoreal.hostal@gmail.com; Carrera 3; r per person COP$30,000; ☜) Overlooking one of Monguí's most magical scenes – the stone Puente Real de Calicanto bridge and grumbling Morro river – this six-room guesthouse in a stuck-in-time *casona* (large, rambling old house) is chock-full of colonial character and period-style furnishings. Many of the rooms have outstanding views over the bridge.

Hospedaje Ville de Monguí　　GUESTHOUSE $
(☑ 311-260-2736; hostalvillademongui@gmail.com; Calle 5 No 4-68; s/d/tr COP$35,000/65,000/90,000; @) There is better value elsewhere, but this simple five-room guesthouse one block from the plaza has a guest kitchen, so if you fancy yourself the next Top Chef, this might be a good choice. Although rooms are a tad too cramped for the price, it's friendly enough.

La Casona GUESTHOUSE **$$**

(✏311-237-9823; la_casona_mongui@hotmail. com; Carrera 4 No 3-41; r per person incl breakfast COP$45,000; ☎) The festive bedspreads jump out at you at this clean and concise midrange option in a very friendly family home. Not only that, but each of the well-maintained six rooms offer TVs, hot water and little above-and-beyond touches like half bottles of wine and better towels than you're used to at this price range.

The town's best restaurant is here as well (mains COP$12,000 to COP$26,000), and offers à la carte Colombian specialties, a great COP$9000 lunch menu and even cocktails like mojitos and *canelazos* (hot drink made with aguardiente, sugarcane, cinnamon and lime). Check those views!

❶ Information

The nearest ATM is in Sogamoso.

Monguí Tourist Office (Calle 5 No 3-24; ◷8am-noon & 2-6pm Mon-Fri, 10am-noon & 2-4pm Sat & Sun) Has basic info in Spanish and a nice town map.

❶ Getting There & Away

Minibuses to Sogamoso (COP$3500, every 20 minutes) depart from Monguí's plaza. There are two daily buses for Bogotá, but a *Super Directo* from Sogamoso is a much quicker bet.

Sierra Nevada del Cocuy

Relatively unknown outside of Colombia, the Sierra Nevada del Cocuy is one of the most spectacular mountain ranges in South America. This gorgeous slice of heaven on earth has some of Colombia's most dramatic landscapes, from snowcapped mountains and raging waterfalls to icy glaciers and crystal-clear blue lakes.

It is the highest part of the Cordillera Oriental, the eastern part of the Colombian Andes formed by two parallel ranges. A chain of beautiful valleys is sandwiched in between. The Sierra Nevada del Cocuy contains 21 peaks, of which 15 are more than 5000m. The tallest peak, Ritacuba Blanco, reaches 5330m.

Because of its climate and topography, the Sierra Nevada del Cocuy ecosystem has a striking abundance of flora, representing some 700 species. It is especially noted for its *frailejóns*, many of which are unique to the region. Fauna includes spectacled bears, pumas, white-tailed deer and the famous Andean condor, a symbol of Colombia. This area is also the ancestral home of the indigenous U'wa people, who still make their home in this harsh terrain.

In 1970 a large swath of this pristine land was set aside for the creation of Parque Nacional Natural (PNN) El Cocuy. With a massive 306,000 hectares, PNN El Cocuy is the fifth-largest national park in Colombia, stretching across the departments of Boyacá, Arauca and Casanare.

The mountains are quite compact, relatively easy to reach and ideal for trekking, though rather more suited to experienced hikers. The starting points for these hikes are the pretty villages of Güicán and El Cocuy. The two rival towns have good food and lodging facilities, and scenic beauty that even nonhikers will appreciate.

El Cocuy

✏8 / POP 5400 / ELEV 2750M

Dramatically surrounded by soaring mountains, the pretty colonial village of El Cocuy is the most traveler-friendly entry point to PNN El Cocuy, with several hotels, restaurants and a few bars. El Cocuy has preserved its colonial character; nearly every building in town is painted white with sea-green trim and topped by red Spanish tiled roofs.

🛏 Sleeping & Eating

There is a good selection of hotels in El Cocuy, all located within three blocks of the town square. Most restaurants are located inside hotels. In the evening, street vendors sell *comida corriente* (fast food) in the square.

★**La Posada del Molino** HISTORIC HOTEL **$**

(✏789-0377; www.elcocuylaposadadelmolino. com; Carrera 3 No 7-51; r per person high/low season COP$40,000/25,000, cabaña high season COP$250,000; ☎) This 225-year-old renovated colonial mansion gives a whole lotta atmosphere for the peso. The building's Swedish-colored (ie blue-and-yellow) interiors evoke its colorful history – and the hotel is reputedly haunted (our TV popped on by itself at 2:49am. No, we weren't sleeping on the remote)!

Some rooms are decorated with tasteful wooden furnishings, while simpler, newer cabañas offer five beds each. Upgrades like satellite TV, wi-fi, hardwood floors and renovated bathrooms are bonuses, and the gorgeous fossil-strewn courtyard with a babbling brook will lull you to sleep. It's also the best place to eat (meals COP$6000).

Sierra Nevada del Cocuy

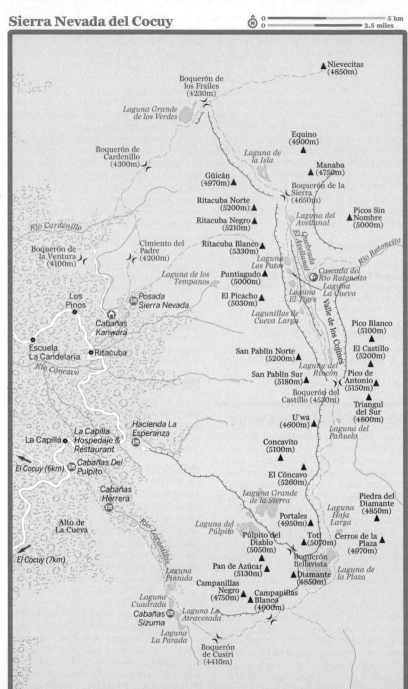

0 — 5 km
0 — 2.5 miles

Nievecitas (4850m)

Boquerón de los Frailes (4230m)

Laguna Grande de los Verdes

Equino (4900m)

Boquerón de Cardenillo (4300m)

Laguna de la Isla

Manaba (4750m)

Güicán (4970m)

Boquerón de la Sierra (4650m)

Ritacuba Norte (5200m)

Picos Sin Nombre (5000m)

Ritacuba Negro (5210m)

Laguna del Avellanal

Río Cardenillo

Cimiento del Padre (4200m)

Ritacuba Blanco (5330m)

Quebrada El Avellanal

Río Ratoncito

Boquerón de la Ventura (4100m)

Laguna Los Patos

Cascada del Río Ratoncito

Laguna de los Tempanos

Puntiagudo (5000m)

Laguna La Cueva

Los Pinos

Posada Sierra Nevada

El Picacho (5030m)

Laguna El Tigre

Valle de los Cojines

Cabañas Kanwara

Lagunillas de Cueva Larga

Pico Blanco (5100m)

Escuela La Candelaria

Ritacuba

San Pablín Norte (5200m)

El Castillo (5200m)

Río Cóncavo

San Pablín Sur (5180m)

Laguna del Rincón

Pico de Antonio (5150m)

Boquerón del Castillo (4530m)

Triangul del Sur (4800m)

Hacienda La Esperanza

U'wa (4600m)

Laguna del Pañuelo

La Capilla Hospedaje & Restaurant

La Capilla

Concavito (5100m)

El Cocuy (6km)

Cabañas Del Pulpito

El Cóncavo (5260m)

Cabañas Herrera

Laguna Grande de la Sierra

Piedra del Diamante (4850m)

Alto de La Cueva

Laguna del Púlpito

Portales (4950m)

Laguna Hoja Larga

El Cocuy (7km)

Río Lagunillas

Púlpito del Diablo (5050m)

Tott (5070m)

Cerros de la Plaza (4970m)

Laguna Pintada

Pan de Azúcar (5130m)

Boquerón Bellavista

Diamante (4850m)

Laguna de la Plaza

Campanillas Negro (4750m)

Campanillas Blanco (4900m)

Laguna Cuadrada

Cabañas Sizuma

Laguna La Atravesada

Laguna La Parada

Boquerón de Cusiri (4410m)

Casa Vieja HISTORIC HOTEL $
(☑313-876-8783; Carrera 6 No 7-78; r per person without bathroom COP$12,000) As the name suggests, this cheapie is located in an old colonial house. Owner and artist Roberto Arango has decorated the courtyard garden with his original paintings and often performs live music for guests. The character of the building makes up for the barren rooms.

Hotel Casa Muñoz HOTEL $
(☑789-0328; www.hotelcasamunoz.com; Carrera 5 No 7-28; r per person low season COP$25,000, d/q high season COP$80,000/120,000) Located on the town square, this newer hotel has clean, comfy rooms with cable TV, firm beds and private bathrooms with hot water, all surrounding a haphazard concrete courtyard filled with geraniums. The 2nd-floor rooms have hidden lofts that can sleep larger groups, and there's also a precious, slipshod common area with plaza views.

Hotel Villa Real HOTEL $
(☑789-0038; Calle 7 No 4-50; s/d with bathroom COP$15,000/30,000, without bathroom COP$12,000/25,000) A rambling hotel around the corner from the town square with basic rooms and a popular lunchtime restaurant that serves set meals for COP$6000.

ℹ Information

Banco Agrario de Colombia (cnr Carrera 4 & Calle 8) The only ATM in town.

Internet Central (Carrera 5 N 7-72; per hr COP$1500; ◷8am-noon & 2-8pm) Four computers with internet on the plaza.

Parque Nacional Natural (PNN) El Cocuy Headquarters (☑789-0359; cocuy@parquesnacionales.gov.co; Calle 5A No 4-22; Colombians/foreigners COP$25,000/50,000; ◷7-11:45am & 1-4:45pm) All park visitors must report here to register their itineraries, prove insurance coverage above 4000m and pay the admission fee.

ℹ Getting There & Away

All buses arrive and depart from their respective offices (many of which are convenience stores) on the town square along Carrera 5.

Luxurious **Libertadores** (☑313-829-1073; www.coflonorte.com; Carrera 5 No 7-28/32; ◷8am-noon & 2-8pm) buses to Bogotá depart from the square's Hotel Casa Muñoz at 5:30pm and 8pm daily (COP$45,000, nine hours); in Bogotá buses depart from the main terminal for El Cocuy at 6pm and 8:50pm. **Concorde** (☑313-463-0028; Carrera 5 No 7-16; ◷6am-noon & 2-7pm Mon-Sat, 6am-noon & 3-7pm

Sun) buses depart the square at 4am and 6pm (COP$45,000, 11 hours) for Bogotá. **Fundadores** (☑310-787-3394; www.expresopazderio.com.co; Carrera 4 No 7-60; ◷8am-noon & 2-8pm) busetas to Bogotá depart at 4:30am, 6am, 11am, 5pm and 7:30pm (COP$40,000, 11 hours); they depart Bogotá to El Cocuy at 5am, 6am, 2pm, 6pm and 8:30pm daily.

Alternatively, you can catch a Cootradatil bus to Soatá (COP$15,000, four hours) at 7:30am, noon and 12:30pm, where you can catch more frequent connections to Bogotá.

To Güicán, **Cootradatil** (☑321-403-2465; Carrera 5 No 7-72; ◷6am-8pm) buses depart at 11:30am, 4pm and 8pm (COP$3000, 30 minutes). You can also catch the Fundadores buses going from Bogotá to Güicán, which you can hop on in El Cocuy for the final leg (COP$3000, 30 minutes) at 4:30am and 6pm.

To Bucaramanga, take the Concorde bus to Capitanejo (COP$15,000, two hours, 4am and 6pm) and then change buses. The total trip takes about 14 hours along mostly unpaved roads that are prone to landslides and delays. You are normally better off returning to Tunja and catching the frequent northbound buses to Buca and beyond.

Güicán
☑8 / POP 7416 / ELEV 2880M

Though not as photogenic or traveler friendly as its rival El Cocuy, the chilly village of Güicán has nevertheless become the main starting point for trekkers heading up to the mountains, mainly because it provides a closer and easier hike to PNN El Cocuy. And for nonhikers, Güicán offers plenty of sights and tourist attractions that don't necessarily involve walking uphill. Güicán is the heart of the indigenous U'wa community. Religious tourism is also a major source of revenue, associated with the miracle of the Virgen Morenita de Güicán.

◉ Sights & Activities

Güicán's most famous attraction is the **Virgen Morenita de Güicán**. The shrine to the Morenita is located inside the **Nuestra Señora de la Candelaria** church on the town square, Parque Principal. The brown brick and faux marble church isn't much to look at outside, but inside it's richly decorated and painted in pastel pinks, greens and blues.

East of town is a 300m-high cliff known as **El Peñol de los Muertos**, where U'wa people jumped to their deaths upon the arrival of the conquistadores rather than live

VIRGEN MORENITA DE GÜICÁN

Güicán is known throughout Colombia for the miracle of the Virgen Morenita de Güicán, which was an apparition of the dark-skinned Virgin Mary that appeared to the indigenous U'wa people. The story begins in the late 17th century when Spanish conquistadores arrived in the area and set about converting the U'wa to Christianity. Rather than bow to Spanish rule, U'wa chief Güicány, for whom the town is named, led his tribe to their deaths by leaping off the cliff now called El Peñol de Los Muertos. Güicány's wife Cuchumba was spared because she was pregnant. Cuchumba and a handful of survivors fled to the mountains and hid in a cave. On February 26, 1756 an apparition of the Virgin Mary mysteriously appeared on a cloth. The image of Mary had a dark complexion and indigenous features, just like the U'wa, who quickly converted to Christianity.

A small chapel was built in Güicán to house the Virgen Morenita. During one of the many civil wars between the rival towns of Güicán and El Cocuy, the Virgen was stolen and hidden in El Cocuy, supposedly behind a wall in what is now La Posada del Molino hotel. The family residing there was haunted until they returned the Virgen to Güicán, where it resides today under lock and key.

The grand Festival of the Virgen Morenita is celebrated yearly from February 2 to 4, attracting faithful religious pilgrims from far and wide.

---

under Spanish rule. The trail to the cliff begins at the end of Carrera 4. A hike to the top of the cliff takes about two hours. The **Monumento a la Dignidad de la Raza U'wa** depicting this mass act of suicide is located at the entrance of town.

🛏 Sleeping & Eating

Hotel El Eden　　　　　　　GUESTHOUSE $
(📞311-808-8334; www.guicanextremo.com; Transversal 2 No 9-58; campsite/r per person COP$5000/25,000) More Noah's Ark than El Eden, this family-run guesthouse is a favorite with foreigners. The garden is filled with ducks, goats, rabbits, parrots, gerbils and a trout pond, and the wood-filled rooms smell of forest. Most have private bathrooms and some have lofts. Eden is a 12-minute walk north of the plaza. To get here, walk north up Carrera 4, turn right on the road leading past the artificial football pitch on your left, take your first right past the national park office and then your second left.

Brisas del Nevado　　　　　　　HOTEL $
(📞789-7028; www.brisasdelnevado.com; Carrera 5 No 4-59; r per person COP$35,000, without bathroom COP$20,000-25,000) The comfiest hotel in town also houses Güicán's best restaurant – great *huevos pericos* (scrambled eggs with tomatoes and scallions) for breakfast. Most rooms have private baths and TV. The best rooms are the two private cabañas located in the garden behind the main building. Meals run COP$10,000 to COP$17,000.

Casa del Colibri　　　　　　　GUESTHOUSE $
(📞311-517-1736; sirenamario@gmail.com; Calle 2 No 5-19; r per person COP$20,000) You're on your own here, but if you're looking for a cheap room, these four, surrounding a flowery courtyard with a Virgin Mary statue, are simply appointed but huge, with modern bathrooms. The caretaker can deliver meals as well (COP$6000 to COP$7000).

ℹ Information

Banco Agrario de Colombia (Carrera 5) The town's only ATM, next to the Hotel Brisas del Nevado hotel half a block from the plaza.

Cafeteria La Principal (Carrera 5 No 3-09; per hr COP$2000; ◷8am-8pm; 📶) Doubling as the Fundadores bus company office on the plaza, this small convenience store has internet on four computers and wi-fi.

Parque Nacional Natural El Cocuy (📞789-7280; cocuy@parquenacionales.gov.co; Transversal 3 No 9-17; Colombians/foreigners COP$25,000/50,000; ◷7-11:45am & 1-4:45pm) All park visitors must pay the park admission fee here and register their itinerary. You must also present proof of insurance that covers you above 4000m; otherwise, you must purchase the park's insurance for COP$7000 per day, which will not include helicopter rescue (in other words, bring your own!).

To find the office, walk north up Carrera 4, turn right on the road leading past the artificial football pitch on your left, then your first right up the hill northeast of town.

ℹ Getting There & Away

All buses arrive and depart from their respective offices on the plaza except Libertadores, whose office is just off the plaza on the Carrera 5 side of the Casa Cural.

Luxurious **Libertadores** (🗷 314-239-3839; www.coflonorte.com; Carrera 5 & Calle 4, Casa Cural) buses to Bogotá depart from the plaza at 4:30pm and 7pm daily (COP$50,000, 11 hours); buses from Bogotá to Güicán depart Bogotá's main bus terminal at 6pm and 8:50pm daily (COP$45,000, 11 hours). Less-comfortable **Concorde** (🗷 314-340-0481; www.cootransbol. com; Calle 4 No 4-20) buses to Bogotá depart the plaza at 3am and 5pm (COP$45,000, 11 hours), and at 3:30am, 5am, 9am, 4pm and 6:30pm (COP$45,000, 12 hours) with **Fundadores** (🗷 314-214-9742; www.expresopazderio.com.co; Carrera 5 No 3-09; ☺ 8am-8pm); departures from Bogotá to El Cocuy call at 5am, 6am, 6:50am, 5:50pm, 6pm, 7:30pm, 8pm and 8:30pm.

To El Cocuy, local **Cootradatil** (🗷 320-330-9536; Carrera 3 No 4-05) buses depart at 7am, 11am and 2pm (COP$3000, 40 minutes). Alternatively, take one of the Bogotá-bound buses, which all pass through El Cocuy on their way to the capital. To go to Bucaramanga, Cúcuta, Santa Marta or other points northwest, take a Bogotá-bound bus to Capitanejo and change buses there (there's an 11pm Copetran bus that's popular with travelers); or catch a 20-minute charter flight from Capitanejo's nearest airport in Málaga (COP$150,000).

Parque Nacional Natural (PNN) El Cocuy

Parque Nacional Natural (PNN) El Cocuy is the main attraction of the Sierra Nevada del Cocuy region. Established in 1977, the park covers a massive 306,000 hectares. The western boundary of the park begins at the 4000m elevation line; the eastern half drops to just 600m elevation to the Colombian *llanos* (plains).

Most of PNN El Cocuy is made up of a diverse ecosystem known as the *páramo*. This glacially formed, neotropical system of valleys, plains and mountain lakes includes the largest glacier zone in South America north of the equator. Sadly, the park's glacier fields are rapidly melting due to climate change. At the present rate, park officials believe the glaciers will be gone within 20 to 30 years.

Despite the harsh environment, PNN El Cocuy is home to diverse species of flora and fauna. Animals you might encounter include the spectacled bear, also called the Andean bear, deer, eagles, condors, mountain tapirs, chinchillas and the beautiful spotted ocelot. The mountaintop plains are covered in a variety of shrubbery, the best known being the yellow-flowered *frailejón* that is native to the area.

The park has 15 peaks that are at least 5000m. The highest is Ritacuba Blanco at 5330m. The park's most famous landmark is an unusual rock formation called the Púlpito del Diablo (5120m; Devil's Pulpit). This outdoor playground is popular for hiking, trekking, mountaineering, camping, climbing and paragliding, though the last is not commercially available (that is, only for private flyers).

From 1985 until early this century PNN El Cocuy was occupied by ELN guerrillas until the Colombian army moved in. Today the park is once again safe for visitors (the little-used eastern plains area of the park in Arauca and Casanare is still questionable). Colombian soldiers have a base in the mountains and regularly patrol the trails. This peace has quickly brought visitors back to the peaks. In 2003 fewer than 100 people climbed PNN El Cocuy; that figure jumped to an estimated 9000 in 2010 and a whopping 14,147 in 2013, according to park officials.

The park's popularity has proved problematic. In 2013, the main attraction, the Güicán–El Cocuy Circuit Trek, was closed to visitors. Depending on with whom you speak, the reasons are park officials who do not like dealing with the added workload that tourism brings; U'wa Indians along the route fed up with tourists trekking through their land; or the popularity of the trek and all the associated infrastructure doing too much damage to the park, its trails and the surrounding environment. The reality is likely a combination of all three, but whatever the reason, at the time of research the circuit was indefinitely closed – check ahead before your journey to see if the situation has changed by the time you visit. Meanwhile, other parts of the park and at least 12 peaks over 5000m remain open to visitors.

ℹ Climbing Cocuy

The mountains of PNN El Cocuy are relatively compact and easy to reach. The complete Güicán–El Cocuy Circuit Trek, which traverses passes that top out at Boquerón de la Sierra (4650m) and takes in the park's most transcendent attraction, Laguna de la Plaza, was indefinitely closed at the time of research. However, there are many shorter day hikes and at

BOYACÁ, SANTANDER & NORTE DE SANTANDER SIERRA NEVADA DEL COCUY least one recently developed four-day trek. The hike to the snowline is only about three hours from the northern park boundary.

There is no special experience required. However, due to the elevation and terrain, park officials recommend that hikers have at least some previous trekking experience and be in good health. Park entry is prohibited to children under 12 years, pregnant women and people with heart or lung ailments.

The starting points for hiking PNN El Cocuy are the archrival villages of Güicán and El Cocuy. All visitors to the park must first report to the PNN El Cocuy offices in either Güicán or El Cocuy, register their itineraries, prove insurance coverage and pay the park admission fee (foreigners/Colombians COP$50,000/25,000). Don't forget to check back in after your hike; if you don't show up by your return date, park officials will launch search and rescue operations (by donkey, one mountaineer scoffed!).

Guides, while not required, are highly recommended.

ⓘ When to Go

The only period of reasonably good weather is from December to February. The rest of the year has a varied climate and there is snow at high altitudes and on the highest passes. The weather changes frequently. The Sierra Nevada is known for its strong winds.

ⓘ What to Bring

All park visitors must be totally self-sufficient. There are no residents or services inside the park. That means bringing all your own high-mountain trekking equipment, including a good tent, a sleeping bag rated to below 10°C, warm and waterproof clothing, good hiking boots, flashlights, first-aid kit, gas stove and food. You cannot buy outdoor equipment in El Cocuy or Güicán, but you may be able to find camping gear in Bogotá. The circuit (sadly) no longer traverses a glacier, so you won't need any special equipment.

If you don't have a tent or basic trekking gear, the only way to explore the mountains is in a series of short, one-day walks from a base at one of the cabañas. This, however, will only whet your appetite for these magnificent mountains.

⌂ Tours

You can hire guides from any of the cabañas near the mountains or at Ecoturismo Comunitario Sisuma in El Cocuy. Expect to pay about COP$80,000 a day for a campesino (who can merely show you the way) for up to eight people; or COP$100,000 to COP$150,000 for an actual accredited trek-

king guide for up to six people. Porters cost about COP$60,000 to COP$80,000 per day (horses were banned above 4000m in 2013). Solo hikers and small groups can be paired up with others to keep costs down.

While the main circuit is closed, there are plenty of day and multiday treks available. The main event now is the four-day Paso del Conejo circuit, which crosses from Valle de Lagunillas (3974m) to Laguna Grande de la Sierra (4444m). It's possible to add various peaks to this trek, mainly El Cóncavo (5260m) and Pan de Azúcar (5130m). The best day treks are to Laguna Grande de la Sierra from Hacienda La Esperanza (moderate; around 10 hours); from Cabañas Kanwara to Cimiento del Padre (4200m) and on to Boquerón de Cardenillo pass (moderate; 4300m; around six to seven hours); and Cabañas Kanwara to the base of Ritacubas (4800m) or Laguna de los Tempanos (difficult; 4600m). Anyone who's not an experienced mountain trekker should hire a guide for the last of these, which has a very steep and loose section and a less obvious trail.

Veteran climber Rodrigo Arias of **Colombia Trek** (☑320-339-3839; www.colombiatrek.com) is an experienced, highly recommended guide and one of the few English speakers in the mountains. He can arrange personalized tours and all-inclusive packages for individuals or groups. For the four-day Paso del Conejo trek expect to pay from COP$1,350,000 per person for two people and an English-speaking guide, or COP$1,100,000 if there are four of you (with two English-speaking guides), excluding transportation from Bogotá or elsewhere. For individual peaks, prices range between COP$1,280,000 to COP$1,700,000 per person all-inclusive with English-speaking guides, depending on the peak and number of days. He also rents camping gear and equipment.

Ecoturismo Comunitario Sisuma (☑321-345-7076; www.elcocuyboyaca.com) 📶 is a community-driven concession of guides and services, who also operate the only cabañas within the park boundaries at Laguna Pintada. They can also give you a ride from El Cocuy to the top of the mountains – Hacienda La Esperanza or Cabañas Lagunillas-Herrera – for COP$100,000.

🛏 Sleeping

After a visit to El Cocuy or Güicán, most hikers choose to acclimate to the altitude by staying overnight at one of several cabañas located just outside the park boundaries.

The most comfortable are located in the north end of the park near Güicán. The best-known is **Cabañas Kanwara** (☑311-231-6004, 311-237-2660; kabanaskanwara@gmail.com; r per person COP$40,000). Its A-frame cabins each have between eight and 14 beds, a fireplace, kitchen and bath. Less recommended but functional is **Posada Sierra Nevada** (☑311-237-8619; www.posadaenguican.com; r per person COP$40,000, meals COP$15,000); it's also the highest at 3960m.

Halfway between El Cocuy and Güicán at Alto de la Cueva you'll find the **Cabañas Del Pulpito** (☑313-309-9734; turismococuy@gmail.com; r per person COP$30,000) and the rustic working farmhouse of **Hacienda La Esperanza** (☑313-473-0990, 310-209-9812; haciendalaesperanza@gmail.com; r per person incl breakfast COP$35,000).

At the southern end of the park, **Cabañas Lagunillas-Herrera** (☑310 294 9808; sierranevadaelcocuy@gmail.com; campsite/r per person COP$5000/30,000) has four rooms with private bath and a camping zone. Further on than Lagunillas-Herrera, within the park's boundaries at Laguna Pintada, **Cabañas Sizuma** (☑321-345-7076; www.elcocuyboyaca.com; r per person with/without bathroom COP$40,000/35,000) is run by a local concession of guides.

❶ Getting There & Away

From Güicán, it's a five-hour hike straight up to Cabañas Kanwara, where the northern circuit trails begin (though you're not allowed to go beyond the Boquerón de Cardenillo pass at 4300m). Private car hire to one of the cabañas will set you back about COP$80,000 to COP$100,000. Some cabañas also offer transportation; prices vary depending on destination and group sizes. A cheaper, last-resort alternative is to hop a ride on a *lechero* (COP$5000 to COP$12,000), one of the morning milk trucks that make the rounds to the mountain farms, though this shouldn't be considered comfortable or safe. The *lecheros* leave Güicán plaza at 5am, reach El Cocuy plaza at 6am and make a counterclockwise circuit back to Güicán. There are several *lecheros,* so you'll have to ask around to find the one going to your destination. Most *lecheros* do not stop directly at the cabañas; you'll be let off at the nearest intersection where you must hike up the rest of the way.

SANTANDER

The north-central department of Santander is a patchwork of steep craggy mountains, deep canyons, plummeting waterfalls, raging rivers, unexplored caves and a temperate, dry climate. Mix them together and it's easy to see why Santander has become a favorite destination for outdoor lovers. Extreme-sports nuts can choose from white-water rafting, paragliding, caving, rappelling, hiking and mountain biking. Visitors with more sanity can enjoy exploring the rustic charms of colonial Barichara, shopping in Girón or getting their dance on in the nightclubs in the department capital city of Bucaramanga.

San Gil

☑7 / POP 44,561 / ELEV 1110M

For a small city, San Gil packs a lot of punch. This is the outdoor capital of Colombia and a mecca for extreme-sporting enthusiasts. The area is best known for white-water rafting, but other popular pastimes include paragliding, caving, rappelling and trekking. Closer to earth, San Gil has a quaint 300-year-old town square and Parque El Gallineral, a beautiful nature reserve on the banks of the Río Fonce.

San Gil may not be the prettiest town in Colombia, but dig beneath the exterior shell and you'll discover a wonderful city of natural beauty and friendly, welcoming residents. San Gil definitely lives up to its motto, 'La Tierra de Aventura' – the land of adventure.

◉ Sights

Cascadas de Juan Curi   WATERFALL
(entrance COP$7000-10,000) Take a day trip to this spectacular 180m-high waterfall where you can swim in the natural pool at its base or relax on the rocks. Adventure junkies can rappel the sheer face of the falls; book this activity with one of the tour companies. Juan Curi is 22km from San Gil on the road to Charalá. Charalá buses depart twice hourly from the local bus terminal.

Ask to be let off at 'Las Cascadas,' where two 20-minute trails lead up to the falls. Most travelers choose the cheaper (though slightly less adventurous) trail at Parque Ecológico Juan Curi. If you like food, combine a trip here with a stop in Valle de San José for the famous *chorizo* cooked in *guarapo* (fermented sugarcane juice) at **Piqueteadero Doña Eustaquia** (Calle 3 No 5-39, Valle de San José; chorizo COP$1300; ☺7am-8pm).

Pescaderito   OUTDOORS
FREE This free group of five swimming holes is a great little place to relax the day

San Gil

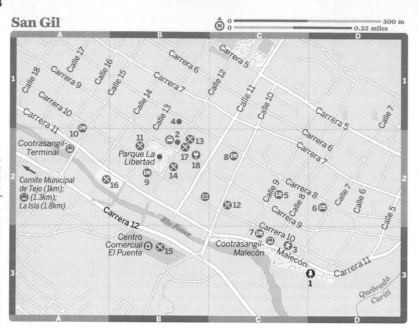

San Gil

away. Skip the first one; they get better the further up you go (the fifth is the best, no diving from the third!). To reach here, catch a bus from the local bus terminal to Curití's main square (COP$2400, every 15 minutes), walk four blocks past the church and take the road leading out of town about 40 minutes upriver.

It's also a nice camping spot.

Parque El Gallineral PARK
(☏724-4372; cnr Malecón & Calle 6; adult/child COP$5000/3000; ⊙8am-5:30pm) San Gil's showpiece is the mystical Parque El Gallineral, a 4-hectare park set on a triangle-shaped island between two arms of the Quebrada Curití and Río Fonce. Nearly all of the 1876 trees are covered with long silvery tendrils of moss called *barbas de viejo* (old man's beard), hanging from branches to form translucent curtains of foliage and filtered sunlight. It's like a scene set in JRR Tolkien's Middle Earth.

Several paths and covered bridges snake through the urban forest and over the rapids. After your hike, relax with a swim in the pool or sip a *cerveza* (beer) at one of the pricey restaurants and cafes.

🏃 Activities

Several tour agencies in San Gil run white-water rafting on local rivers. A 10km run on Río Fonce (Class 1 to 3) costs COP$30,000 per person and takes 1½ hours; experienced rafters can tackle the extreme rapids of the Río Suárez (COP$125,000, up to Class 5). Most operators also offer paragliding, caving, horseback riding, rappelling/abseiling, mountain biking, bungee jumping and ecowalks.

★ Colombian Bike Junkies

MOUNTAIN BIKING

(☑ 316-327-6101; www.colombianbikejunkies.com; incl breakfast & lunch COP$175,000) Modeled after Gravity in Bolivia, this recently Colombian/Ecuadorean-owned extreme mountain bike company offers a 50km downhill adrenaline overdose on two wheels through the Cañon del Río Suárez, with catering by Gringo Mike's. It's a high-adrenaline, all-day affair that takes in absolutely epic countryside. If you don't own padded cycling shorts, consider stuffing your pants with household sponges!

Colombia Rafting Expeditions

RAFTING

(☑ 724-5800; www.colombiarafting.com; Carrera 10 No 7-83; ⊙ 8am-6pm) The rafting specialist for the Río Suárez; also offers hydrospeeding and kayaking. The more centrally located satellite **office** (Calle 12 No 8-32; ⊙ 8-11am & 4-9pm Mon-Sat) is open late.

Macondo Adventures

ADVENTURE SPORTS

(☑ 724-8001; www.macondohostel.com; Carrera 8 No 10-35) Organizes all the usual suspects, plus a great regional foodie tour that takes in local specialties like *cabra* (goat) and *carne oreada* (sun-dried beef).

🍃 Courses

Connect4

LANGUAGE COURSE

(☑ 724-2544; www.idiomassangil.com; Carrera 8 No 12-19) Offers a 10-hour Spanish crash course geared toward travelers (from COP$198,000) and private lessons (from COP$32,000 per hour).

🛌 Sleeping

San Gil has plenty of downtown budget and moderately priced lodging options. Private rooms in most hostels are so nice, it's not usually necessary to splurge for a midrange. In addition to the options here, there are many basic cheapie hotels on Calle 10. Folks looking for a little more pampering should check out the luxury hotel-resorts on the outskirts of town along Vía Charalá or Vía Mogotes.

Macondo Guesthouse

HOSTEL $

(☑ 724-8001; www.macondohostel.com; Carrera 8 No 10-35; dm COP$20,000-25,000, s with bathroom COP$55,000-65,000, d with bathroom COP$65,000-75,000, s/d without bathroom COP$45,000/55,000; @ 🛜) This San Gil classic remains a laid-back but secure (CCTV) hostel that's a bit like crashing at a friend's place. The space offers a wonderful leafy courtyard with a 10-person Jacuzzi, and there's a variety of dorm and room options, including three upgraded privates that outpunch their hostel weight class. Not the flashiest choice, but nails the San Gil vibe.

The Australian owner and staff are a treasure trove of information and can book all of your adventures in the area. Don't miss Tejo Tuesdays and don't even think about showing up without a booking.

La Posada Familiar

GUESTHOUSE $

(☑ 724-8136; laposadafamiliar@hotmail.com; Carrera 10 No 8-55; r per person COP$35,000; @ 🛜) Señora Esperanza dotes over guests at this most Colombian of choices, a lovely six-room guesthouse wrapped around a plant-jammed courtyard with a gurgling fountain. Well-maintained rooms are unembellished, but offer modern bathrooms and hot water and there's a small but nice guest kitchen with a hardwood sink.

If you want to escape the foreigner hostel scene and get down with locals, you could do much worse.

Santander Alemán TV

GUESTHOUSE $

(☑ 724-0329; www.hostelsantanderaleman.com; cnr Carrera 10 & Calle 15; dm COP$18,000-20,000, s/d COP$40,000/60,000; @ 🛜) The best guesthouse of Santander Alemán's three in town, this spot boasts a terrace with views (hence the name: Terrace Vista) around the corner from *terminalito* (the local bus terminal). The eight double rooms are clean and comfortable and a great choice as a step-up from a hostel but with the same traveler camaraderie.

Hostal de la Nueva Baeza

GUESTHOUSE $

(☑ 724-2606; hostaldelanuevabaeza@hotmail.com; Calle 9 No 8-49; r with/without air-con COP$40,000/35,000; ❄ 🛜) Early risers looking for a very comfortable room in a quiet colonial house without all the fuss should consider this 10-room guesthouse. Attention is limited, but rooms feature vaulted bamboo

DON'T MISS

TIME FOR TEJO!

Gunpowder, lead weights, alcohol? That's a dream mix anywhere, and in Colombia, it's perfectly legal. *Tejo,* a rural tradition with roots in Boyacá, is a loud and rambunctious pre-Columbian game where 2kg puck-like weights (once made of solid gold called *zepguagoscua,* nowadays made of lead) are tossed to a clay pit to hit a metal ring known as a *bocin,* which is surrounded by ready-to-explode gunpowder-filled triangular pieces of wax paper called *mechas.*

Macondo Guesthouse (p105) in San Gil runs a *tejo* night every Tuesday at 8pm (open to nonguests as well) where they block out a few lanes at **Comité Municipal de Tejo** (724-4053; Carrera 18 No 26-70) and organize a guide to help explain the rules and make sure you don't blow anything up that isn't meant to be blown up! Sign up in advance (the group fills up quickly and is limited to 32). The outing and *tejo* itself is free, but guests are expected to purchase drinks (or make a donation; beers run COP$1800 and are usually purchased by the crate). Although well-behaved foreigners are welcome other days of the week (Wednesdays and Fridays are best for getting a court), it's not recommended unless you are educated in all things *tejo.*

ceilings, new flat-screen TVs and very nice bathrooms. It's a step-up despite the price, but you'll hear those church bells a ringin'. Prices spike in high season.

Hostal Le Papillon
HOSTEL $

(723-6350; hostallepapillon@hotmail.com; Calle 7 No 8-28; campsite per person COP$10,000, dm COP$17,000, s/d without bathroom COP$25,000/40,000; @) This quiet hostel on a quieter street than most is a good choice for peso-pinchers. It's run by a nice Colombian-Swiss couple and has good dorms, a few private rooms with shared bathrooms and a grassy area out back for camping and hammocks. Two cute cats and a dog have the run of the place. English and French spoken.

Sam's VIP
HOSTEL $$

(724-2746; www.samshostel.com; Carrera 10 No 12-33; dm COP$22,000, s/d with bathroom COP$60,000/80,000, without bathroom COP$40,000/60,000; @) San Gil's shiniest hostel is right on the plaza and wins accolades for approaching boutique levels with its furnishings and decor. The staff is very friendly – invite them into the small pool with wonderful mountain views, or for a drink on the expansive terrace overlooking the plaza. There is also a superb, straight-out-of-suburban-USA kitchen for guests.

Eating

San Gil isn't the most gastronomically inclined area of Colombia, but it does have some decent restaurants serving home-cooked local cuisine. For self-catering there is **Autoservice Veracruz** (Calle 13 No 9-24; 8am-9pm Mon-Sat,

to 2pm Sun) on the plaza (better for fresh fruit and veggies) and **Metro** (8am-9pm Sun-Fri, to 10pm Sat) – San Gil's biggest; better for dry goods – inside Centro Comercial El Puente, San Gil's modern new shopping center.

★ Gringo Mike's
AMERICAN $

(www.gringomikes.net; Calle 12 No 8-35; burgers COP$11,000-18,000; 8am-noon & 5-10pm Sun-Thu, to 11pm Fri & Sat;) What *isn't* good? In a moody, candlelit courtyard, you'll find this US-UK operation thrilling homesick travelers with a surplus of American-portioned gourmet burgers, bacon-heavy sandwiches, breakfast burritos and French Press coffee! Highlights are deep and long: the spicy jalapeño burger; the mango, peanut and blue cheese salad with prawns; the Mexican bacon burrito. Great cocktails and veggie choices, too.

Having lived and traveled in South America for over a decade, this author is baffled by how the hell he pulls it off!

★ El Maná
COLOMBIAN $

(Calle 10 No 9-42; set meals COP$11,500; 11am-3:30pm & 6-8:30pm Mon-Sat, to 3:30pm Sun) This popular, word-of-mouth favorite is the best Colombian restaurant in town. You can taste the extra love in its fantastic set meals – seven or so to choose from daily – they feature traditional dishes like chicken in plum sauce, *estofado de pollo* (chicken stew) and grilled mountain trout. The bummer is it closes early if you're out all day.

La Casa del Balcón
COLOMBIAN $

(Calle 12 No 9-19, 2nd fl; breakfast COP$1500-4000; 8am-11pm Mon-Sat, 9am-10:30pm Sun;)

This cute little Colombian spot with a balcony overlooking the plaza is very pleasant for a tasty and cheap breakfast – *arepas,* eggs a few ways, espresso, cappuccino – or late afternoon beers with views.

Plaza de Mercado   MARKET $
(Carrera 11; arepas COP$1500-1800; ⊙ 6am-3pm Mon-Wed, to 2pm Thu & Sun, to 4pm Fri & Sat) For a true locals' experience, head to this bustling covered market where you can grab plenty of *comida corriente,* tamales and fresh-squeezed juices. Don't miss the stuffed *arepas* that a few kiosks do in the middle aisle nearest the Calle 13 side entrance – one of the tastiest breakfasts in town.

Sam's Gastro Pub &
Steakhouse   STEAKHOUSE $$
(Calle 12 No 8-71; mains COP$8000-22,000; ⊙ noon-2pm & 6-10pm Mon-Sat; 🍴) Attached to a second hostel from Sam of Sam's VIP fame, this traveler favorite dishes out pork ribs and burgers but it's all about the excellent filet mignon, served in his (400g) and her (250g) sizes and doused with a variety of sauces (pepper and parmesan are faves). Presentation is better than expected, too. A solid bet for carnivores.

🍸 Drinking & Nightlife

If you are looking for an espresso, several cafes on the plaza now have proper machines, but the best coffee is in Centro Comercial El Puente (try Doto's or Cinnamon Gourmet). Cold beers in the lively main square is also a very popular pastime.

La Habana   BAR
(Carrera 9 No 11-68, Local 212; ⊙ 6pm-midnight Mon-Thu, to 2am Fri & Sat) Located on the 2nd floor of Centro Comercial Camino Real, this hot nightspot is a hidden local gem. Besides being the best bar, its high-reaching walls are decorated in canvas artwork by local artists.

La Isla   BARS
(Vía San Gil-Bogotá, Km1) This glorified gas pump on the way out of town is the hottest after-hours ticket in town. There's One Shot (loud and hip bar), Caña Brava (karaoke lounge) and Rodeo (Latin crossover disco). There is also a great food court for late munchies, full of locals sitting around drinking. Go early and grab a bite at the proper Mexican restaurant.

ℹ️ Information

There are several ATMs in and around the plaza (avoid the problematic Banco Agrario one). The official tourism website is www.sangil.com.co.
4-72 (Carrera 10 No 10-50; ⊙ 8am-noon & 1-6pm Mon-Fri, 9am-noon Sat) Post office.
Tourist Police (☑ 350-304-5600; Carrera 11 at Calle 7) Police.

ℹ️ Getting There & Away

San Gil has numerous bus stations with numerous names, but you'll most likely arrive at the intercity bus terminal (known locally as *terminal principal*) located 3km west of downtown on the road to Bogotá. Local buses shuttle regularly between the terminal and the city center, or take a taxi (COP$3400 to COP$3600).

Frequent buses depart to Bogotá (COP$35,000, six hours), Bucaramanga (COP$15,000, 2½ hours), Barranquilla (COP$55,000, 13 hours), Cartagena (COP$70,000, 15 hours), Santa Marta via Bucaramanga (COP$60,000, 13 hours), Sogamoso (COP$30,000, five hours), Medellín (COP$85,000, 12 hours) and Cúcuta (COP$50,000, nine hours). **Copetran** (☑ 313-333-5740; www.copetran.com.co) has a (sometimes) direct service to Santa Marta at 7:30pm (COP$60,000, 12 hours). Otherwise, most folks change in Ciénega, about 40 minutes from Santa Marta.

Cootrasangil operates two local terminals. **Cootrasangil – Terminal** (☑ 724-2155; www.cotrasangil.com; cnr Calle 15 & Carrera 11) – known locally as '*terminalito*' – has frequent buses to Barichara (COP$4200, 45 minutes) from 6am to 6:45pm. This terminal also serves Guane (COP$6000, one hour, eight per day) and Charalá (COP$5000, one hour, every 30 minutes from 6:30am to 4pm), among others. **Cootrasangil – Malecón** (☑ 724-3434; www.cotrasangil.co; cnr Carrera 11 & Calle 8) – known locally as 'Terminal Cootrasangil' – has buses to Bucaramanga (COP$15,000, two hours) via Parque Nacional del Chicamocha (COP$8000, one hour) every 20 minutes from 4:30am to 8pm.

Barichara

☑ 7 / POP 7651 / ELEV 1336M
Barichara is the kind of town that Hollywood filmmakers dream about. A Spanish colonial town saturated with atmosphere, it boasts cobblestone streets and whitewashed buildings with red-tiled roofs that look almost as new as the day they were created some 300 years ago. It's no wonder that many Spanish-language films and *telenovelas* are shot

Barichara

here. Granted, the movie-set appearance owes a debt to considerable reconstruction efforts made since the town was declared a national monument in 1978.

Barichara is located 20km northwest of San Gil high above the Río Suárez. According to legend, in 1702 a farmer discovered an apparition of the Virgin Mary on a rock in his field. The locals built a small chapel here to commemorate this miracle. Three years later Spanish Captain Francisco Pradilla y Ayerbe founded the town of Villa de San Lorenzo de Barichara, after the Guane word *barachalá,* meaning 'place of relaxation.'

The town's natural beauty, temperate climate and bohemian lifestyle have long attracted visitors. In recent years Barichara has become a magnet for affluent Colombians. Compared to Villa de Leyva, Barichara is more upscale but less touristy. It is, without a doubt, one of the most beautiful small colonial towns in Colombia.

◎ Sights & Activities

The main attraction of Barichara is its architecture.

Catedral de la Inmaculada
Concepción   CHURCH
(Parque Principal; ⊙5:45am-7pm) This 18th-century sandstone church is the most elaborate structure in town, looking somewhat too big for the town's needs. Its golden stonework (which turns deep orange at sunset) contrasts with the whitewashed houses surrounding it. The building has a clerestory (a second row of windows high up in the nave), which is unusual for a Spanish colonial church.

Capilla de Jesús
Resucitado   CHURCH, CEMETERY
(cnr Carrera 7 & Calle 3) Since restored, this cemetery chapel unfortunately lost a part of its bell tower when it was damaged by light-

Barichara

ning. Do try and visit the cemetery next to the chapel, noted for interesting tombs elaborated in stone, which you can see from the entrance even when it's closed.

Casa de Cultura MUSEUM
(Calle 5 No 6-29; admission COP$1000; ⊙8am-noon & 2-6pm Wed-Mon) This colonial house laid out around a fine patio and situated on the main square features a mishmash collection of fossils, Guane pottery, paintings, typewriters, tools and other tchotchkes.

Parque Para Las Artes PARK
A lovely little park decorated with water features and statues carved by local sculptors, and an outdoor amphitheater that occasionally hosts live music concerts. From the park you can enjoy breathtaking views of the neighboring valley.

Fundación San Lorenzo TOURS
(Taller de Papel; www.fundacionsanlorenzo.wordpress.com; Carrera 5 No 2-88; tour COP$2000) This

small paper factory offers visitors a fascinating glimpse into the four-month-long process of making artisanal paper from *fique,* a natural fiber that grows in the leaves of the Andean *fique* plant. The resulting stationery and paper products are great souvenirs.

🛏 Sleeping

Barichara isn't the cheapest (budget travelers are better off staying in San Gil) but the town rewards those who hang around. Prices where not noted here can spike 30% or more during *temporada alta* (high season), roughly December 20 to January 15 and Semana Santa. During high season reservations are a must.

★Tinto Hostel HOSTEL $
(☑726-7725; www.hostaltintobarichara.com; Carrera 4 No 5-39; dm from COP$20,000, s/d from COP$40,000/60,000; @🛜🛒) Barichara's best hostel occupies a great multilevel home. There are three dorms and three privates with rustic bathrooms, vaulted ceilings and hot water. The common areas – guest kitchen with artsy ceramic pottery, lounge, hammock space and terrace – are all wonderful, and the last has expansive town views. Artistic touches throughout. Tuck in and stay awhile.

Color de Hormiga Hostel HOSTEL $
(☑726-7156; www.colordehormiga.com; Calle 6 No 5-35; dm/s/d COP$20,000/50,000/60,000; 🛜) This charming hostel is one of Barichara's best. Small, green-accented rooms surround a leafy courtyard and offer little design touches like wall-hung chairs for bedside tables and modern bathrooms. The only pity is the dreaded cold, one-spigot showers.

La Mansión de Virginia GUESTHOUSE $
(☑315-625-4017; www.lamansiondevirginia.com; Calle 8 No 7-26; s/d Mon-Thu COP$40,000/50,000, Fri-Sun COP$50,000/100,000, all incl breakfast; 🛜) A tranquil, friendly establishment with clean, comfy rooms with TV and recently renovated private bathroom and requisite courtyard.

**★Color de Hormiga Posada
Campestre** GUESTHOUSE $$
(☑315-297-1621; www.colordehormiga.com; Vereda San José; r per person incl breakfast COP$70,000; 🛜) After operating Santander's most popular restaurant of the same name for years, Chef 'Jorge Hormiga' hung up his apron, then turned his attention to his countryside *finca,* a wonderful four-room

WORTH A TRIP

EL CAMINO REAL TO GUANE

Don't miss the spectacular hike to the tiny hamlet of Guane on the historic **El Camino Real**. This ancient stone-paved road was built by the indigenous Guane people and rebuilt continuously over the centuries. It was declared a national monument in 1988. From Barichara, the 9km easy hike takes about two hours to complete. The trail is mostly downhill, occasionally crossing over the modern highway to Guane. You'll begin the hike by climbing down the rim of a canyon and then traversing a valley filled with cacti and trees, occasionally encountering grazing goats or cows but rarely other humans. Notice the many fossils embedded in the stone road. El Camino Real begins at the north end of Calle 4, where a sign marks the beginning of the trail.

In the sleepy town, the handsome main square features a fine rural church, the **Santa Lucía Iglesia**, built in 1720. Across the square is the unique **Museum of Paleontology & Archaeology** (Carrera 6 No 7-24; admission COP$2000; ☺8am-noon & 2-6pm), with a collection of more than 10,000 fossils, a 700-year-old mummy, a few conehead skulls, Guane artifacts and religious art. The curator locks the front door and gives a personal tour (in Spanish) whenever someone shows up, so just hang tight.

During daylight most travelers opt to hike to Guane and catch a bus back. Buses to Barichara depart from Guane's plaza 10 times daily between 6am and 6:15pm (COP$1800, 20 minutes).

Don't forget water, sunscreen and proper footwear.

guesthouse. Set on a 29-hectare nature reserve where he breeds thousands of the region's famous *hormigas culonas* (fat-bottom ants; see p111), the rustic rooms here feature boutique beds, memorable outdoor bathrooms and rain-style showers.

Jorge does expectedly exquisite meals here (COP$15,000) and is an all-around great host. It's an 800m walk uphill along the Camino Real past astounding views; the path begins on the southern edge of Calle 7 near the new Coliseo Puente Grande (marked by a spray-painted rock). Or take a *moto-carro* (autorickshaw) for COP$8000.

Hotel Coratá HISTORIC HOTEL **$$**
(☎726-7110; hotelcorata@hotmail.com; Carrera 7 No 4-08; s/d with bathroom COP$80,000/120,000, s without bathroom COP$50,000; @☎) Aficionados of historical residences will fall in love with Coratá, a 300-year-old building decorated with antiques and wood furnishings. The rooms have vaulted ceilings, TV and private bathrooms and there's outstanding town views from the breakfast patio.

Carambolo GUESTHOUSE **$$**
(☎316-701-6200; www.elcarambolo.com; Calle 5 No 3-27; s/d COP$70,000/130,000; ☎) The four rooms at this discreet guesthouse surround a starfruit tree from which it gets its name – and its juices. The friendly host is the difference here.

La Nube Posada BOUTIQUE HOTEL **$$$**
(☎726-7161; www.lanubeposada.com; Calle 7 No 7-39; s/d/ste COP$224,000/259,000/775,862; ☺☎) Hidden behind the simple exterior, this old colonial home has been transformed into an unassuming boutique hotel with sleek, minimalist decor. The eight simply furnished rooms, with queen-sized beds and vaulted ceilings with exposed wood beams, surround an abstract courtyard with rotating art exhibitions.

The on-site gourmet Colombian bar/restaurant is one of the best in town and it boasts a 14-country rum collection under lock and key. A new annex houses suites and a spa. The one outright flaw is the bathrooms – they are fine for a Holiday Inn, but you deserve better in Barichara.

✖ Eating & Drinking

Barichara has a good selection of international flavors and traditional regional dishes like *cabrito* (grilled baby goat). The regional specialty is the famous *hormigas culonas*. There is practically no nightlife. A few corner shops sell aguardiente, beer and the local specialty, *chicha de maíz*, an alcoholic drink made from maize, and there are a couple of *casitas* (vendors) clinging to the canyon edge along Calle del Mirador that are well worth a late-afternoon beer with breathtaking views.

Shambalá
VEGETARIAN $

(Carrera 7 No 6-20; mains COP$11,000-20,000; 12:30-4pm & 6-9:30pm Thu-Tue;) Tiny and extremely popular cafe doing tasty made-to-order, mostly vegetarian dishes. Pick from wraps, rices and pasta in Mediterranean, Indian or Thai styles (you can add chicken or shrimp) and chase it with excellent juices, teas and the like.

El Compa
COLOMBIAN $

(Calle 5 No 4-48; meals COP$8000-18,000; 8am-6pm) The best local restaurant – unpretentious, not touristy and not particularly service-oriented, it does 15 or so workhouse Colombian meals. Tasty *cabrito* as well as *sobre barriga* (flank steak), trout, chicken, *carne oreada* etc are all served piled with a host of sides such as salad, yuca, *pepitoria* (goat innards, blood, seasoned rice – we passed on that!) and potatoes.

Filomena
CAFE $

(Carrera 9 No 6-34; panini COP$10,000-16,000; 6-10pm Tue-Fri, 1-10pm Sat & Sun;) A cafe offering rich paninis, burgers and salads – grab one to go for the hike to Guane.

★ Ristorante Al Cuoco
ITALIAN $$

(312-527-3628; Carrera 6A No 2-54; mains COP$19,000-28,000; noon-9:30pm) This fairly elegant one-man Italian show is run out of the home of an amicable Roman chef. Though the menu is limited (a few types of ravioli, cannelloni, a couple of mains and two desserts), the house-made pasta excels, both as a deviation from the status quo and as a culinary journey to the Mother Boot. Reservations recommended on weekends and holidays.

7 Tigres
PIZZA $$

(Calle 6 No 10-24; pizza COP$14,000-16,000; 6-9:30pm Mon-Thu, noon-4pm & 6-10pm Fri-Sun) A good traveler staple for thin-crust pizzas. The Mediterranea, with eggplant, olives, tomatoes, oregano and pesto, is best in show.

Iguá Náuno
BAR

(Calle del Mirador & Carrera 7; 4:30-11pm) This is the one spot where the town's trendy gather for drinks. It's not even a dedicated bar, but imported beers (good *micheladas*), a few cocktails and an atmospheric garden a watering hole does make. Folks eat here, too, and there's a fair selection of vegetarian dishes.

🔒 Shopping

Barichara has many boutique shops and galleries and is well known for its fine stonework. There are several stone-carving shops along Calle 5 where you can buy sculptures and other stone goods.

ℹ Information

There are two ATMs on the plaza.

4-72 (Carrera 6 No 4-90; 8am-noon & 2-6pm) Post office.

Police (726-7173; Carrera 7 No 5-51) The tourism police also sometimes operate from a kiosk on Parque Principal.

Tourist Office (315-630-4696; www.barichara-santander.gov.co; Carrera 5; 9am-5pm Wed-Mon) Located at the entrance to town from San Gil.

ℹ Getting There & Away

Buses shuttle between Barichara and San Gil every 30 minutes from 5am to 6:45pm (COP$4200, 45 minutes). They depart from the **Cotrasangil bus office** (726-7132; www.cotrasangil.com; Carrera 6 No 5-70) on the main plaza. There are 10 buses to Guane (COP$1800, 15 minutes) per day between 5:30am and 5:45pm.

BARICHARA'S BOOTYLICIOUS BUGS

Of Colombia's culinary traditions, perhaps none is as peculiar as Santander's delicacy, *hormigas culonas* – literally, fat-bottom ants. The tradition dates back more than 500 years when indigenous Guane people cultivated and devoured ants for their supposed aphrodisiac and healing properties. The giant dark-brown colored ants are fried or roasted and eaten whole, or ground into a powder. Containers of fried ant snacks are sold in just about any corner shop in Santander, but especially Barichara, San Gil and Bucaramanga. They are normally in season during spring, but can now be found year-round. They taste like, well, crunchy dirt mixed with old coffee grounds. It's definitely an acquired taste – but one you must attempt to acquire.

Parque Nacional del Chicamocha

Halfway between San Gil and Bucaramanga is the spectacular canyon of Río Chicamocha and the **Parque Nacional del Chicamocha** (www.parquenacionaldelchicamocha.com; Km54, Vía Bucaramanga-San Gil; adult/child COP$17,000/11,000; ⊙10am-6pm Wed-Fri, 9am-6pm Sat & Sun; 🖟), nicknamed 'Panachi.' The windy, cliff-hugging road between the two cities is one of the most scenic drives in Santander.

Opened in 2006, the park houses a **Museum of Guane Culture**, several restaurants, a 4D cinema, an ice rink, children's playground, a forgettable **ostrich farm** (admission COP$2000; 🖟) and the **Monumento a la Santandereanidad** commemorating the revolutionary spirit of Santanderians. But the real attraction here is the majestic canyon itself. The best views on land are from the **mirador**, providing a 360-degree vantage of the area. Or for a real bird's-eye view, the new 6.3km-long, 22-minute **teleférico** (return cable-car ticket incl park entrance COP$42,000; ⊙9-11am & 1-5:30pm Wed & Thu, 9am-4:30pm Fri-Sun; 🖟) descends to the base of the canyon then ascends to the top of the opposite rim, Mesa de los Santos (see the boxed text, p116). Adrenaline junkies can extreme swing (COP$12,000), zipline (COP$22,000) or paraglide (COP$170,000), which is an astonishing and peaceful ride; and enjoy the latest attraction, a US$6 million **water park**.

Any bus between San Gil and Bucaramanga will drop you off at the park. To get back to either city, walk down to the highway and flag a passing bus. For those heading north, a better option is to just go to the parking lot near the park entrance and look for the frequent Cotrasangil buses to Bucaramanga (COP$10,000, one hour), which ply the road and look for passengers every 30 minutes.

Bucaramanga

📍7 / POP 524,000 / ELEV 960M

With a greater metropolitan population of about one million people, Bucaramanga, the capital of Santander, is one of the largest cities in Colombia, surrounded by mountains and packed with uninspiring skyscrapers.

Buca, as it's known to locals, was founded in 1622 and developed around what is today the Parque García Rovira, but most of its colonial architecture is long gone. Over the centuries the city center moved eastward, and today Parque Santander is the heart of Bucaramanga. Further east are newer, posh neighborhoods peppered with hotels and nightspots.

Dubbed 'The City of Parks,' Buca is filled with lovely green spaces and is a suitable spot to recharge your urban batteries. It comes to life at night, when dozens of clubs, hundreds of bars and 10 universities don their party hats.

◉ Sights & Activities

Museo Casa de Bolívar   MUSEUM
(Calle 37 No 12-15; admission COP$2000; ⊙8am-noon & 2-6pm Mon-Fri, 8am-noon Sat) Housed in a colonial mansion where Bolívar stayed for two months in 1828, this museum displays various historic and archaeological exhibits, including weapons, documents, paintings, and mummies and artifacts of the Guane people who inhabited the region before the Spaniards arrived.

Mercado Central   MARKET
(cnr Calle 34 & Carrera 16; ⊙4am-6pm Mon-Sat, to 2pm Sun) Buca's colorful, well-organized central market is worth a stroll, especially for its 4th-floor food court with all manner of local eats and mountain vistas to boot.

Colombia Paragliding   PARAGLIDING
(📱312-432-6266; www.colombiaparagliding.com; Km2, Vía Mesa Ruitoque) Bucaramanga's most popular sport is paragliding. The hub for this high-flying activity is atop the Ruitoque mesa. Colombia Paragliding offers 10-/20-/30-minute tandem rides for COP$50,000/80,000/100,000, or go all-out and become an internationally licensed paragliding pilot; 12-day courses including lodging begin at COP$2,800,000. Owner/instructor Richi speaks English and is a well-known Buca character.

🛌 Sleeping & Eating

Kasa Guane Bucaramanga   HOSTEL $$
(📱657-6960; www.kasaguane.com; Calle 49 No 28-21; dm from COP$23,000, s/d with bathroom COP$65,000/85,000, without bathroom COP$40,000/65,000; @🛜) Two helpful English lads manage this Buca staple, better known as KGB, located in one of the nicest neighborhoods in town. It offers dorms and private rooms, hot-water bathrooms (no, really), kitchen and laundry facilities, hammocks, a satellite TV room and pool-table terrace – there's even nice-smelling soap!

GIRÓN

The cobbled streets, horse carts and lazy atmosphere of whitewashed **San Juan de Girón** are a world away in time, but just 9km from bustling Bucaramanga. The pleasant town was founded in 1631 on the banks of the Río de Oro. In 1963 it was declared a national monument. Today it's a magnet for artists and day-trippers, anxious to escape the city but in exchange for an increase in temperature – Girón sits in a breezeless hole in the valley and is baking most of the year.

Take the time to stroll about Girón's narrow cobblestone streets, looking at whitewashed old houses, shaded patios, small stone bridges and the waterfront *malecón* (promenade). The **Catedral del Señor de los Milagros** on Parque Principal (the main plaza) was begun in 1646 but not completed until 1876. Don't miss the pleasant plazas, **Plazuela Peralta** and **Plazuela de las Nieves**, which features a charming village church, the 18th-century **Capilla de las Nieves**.

There are frequent city buses from Bucaramanga (COP$1850) to Girón. A taxi from Bucaramanga is a fixed COP$26,000.

Meanwhile, the bar has become quite the happening spot on weekends, when tourists and locals alike line up to get in. There's a COP$10,000 consumption charge at the door, COP$2000 of which goes to their local social project, Goals for Peace. Cheers for charity!

Nest
HOSTEL $$

(☑678 2722; www.thenesthostel.com; Km2 Via Mesa Ruitoque; dm/s/d per person COP$35,000/70,000/95,000; @🖥🏊) This fly-site hostel is located next to Colombia Paragliding's launch pad, 20 minutes' drive from downtown and perched on a hilltop with amazing views of the city. The majority of guests are paragliding students, but it's also a good choice for anyone seeking peace and quiet.

Rates include breakfast and laundry services, and there's a wonderful kitchen for guests plus a small pool.

Cure Cuisine
LEBANESE $

(Carrera 37 No 41-08; mains COP$1500-6500, combos COP$12,000-22,000; ⊙11am-10pm) Lebanese-descended Colombians do a commendable job at this clean-cut Middle Eastern that's just a step above fast food. Falafel, shawarma, kibe, tabbouleh, baklava – it's all here and accompanied nicely with excellent toasted almond rice. The cheese and onion *fatayers* (small fried pastry pies) are especially tasty.

★Mercagán
STEAK $$

(www.mercaganparrilla.com; Carrera 33 No 42-12; steaks COP$18,500-39,000; ⊙11:30am-11pm Tue, Wed & Fri, to 3pm Mon & Thu, to 4pm Sun) Often touted as the best steak in the whole of Colombia, this traditional *parrilla* run in four locations by four brothers *is* all it's cracked up to be: perfect slabs of meat from their own farm come in 200g, 300g or 400g sizes (good luck!), served on sizzling iron plates.

It's all about the *lomo finito* (tenderloin). Don't let them butterfly it – you want it *'ien bloque!'* The second location on nearby **Parque San Pío** (Carrera 34 No 44-84; ⊙11am-11pm Mon & Thu, to 3pm Tue & Wed, to midnight Fri & Sat, to 10pm Sun) should be open on nights this one is closed.

La Cevicheria
SEAFOOD $$

(www.lacevicheria.co; Carrera 37 No 52-17; ceviche COP$19,500; ⊙noon-10pm Mon-Thu, to 11pm Fri & Sat, 6-10pm Sun; 🖥🏊) Colorful, cute and happening, this build-your-own ceviche and salad spot is a great escape from meat, rice and yuca. There are four predetermined choices, which is the way to go to avoid a head explosion laboring over the perfect combination. Great house-concocted juices, teas and smoothies, too.

🍷 Drinking & Nightlife

Bucaramanga comes to life when the sun goes down. *La vida nocturna* (the nightlife scene) attracts clubbers from around the region. Calle 48 between Carreras 34 and 39 is a sure bet for happening options. For a more traditional night out (think salsa, vallenato and merengue), head to Zona Rosa (between Calles 34 and 36 around Carrera 32).

Things change here quicker than a baby's diaper, so what was hot when we came through will probably be closed when you arrive, but stick to the aforementioned addresses and you'll have a good time.

Bucaramanga

500 m
0.25 miles

El Parque del Agua (500m)

AMERICA

Calle 34
Calle 35
Calle 36
Calle 37
Calle 39
Calle 41
Calle 42
Calle 44
Calle 45
Calle 48
Carrera 34

10

4

9

5

8

6

Parque San Pío

Parque Las Palmas

Calle 44

SOTOMAYOR

Buses to Girón & Bus Terminal

La Cevichería (250m)

Copetran Ticket Office

Sky Bar (1.6km)

3

Calle 49

Carrera 33

Calle 32
Zona Rosa
Carrera 31
LA AURORA
Carrera 30
Carrera 29
Calle 31

Carrera 29

7

Calle 37 Bus Stop

Parque Mejores Públicas

Calle 27A

Carrera 28
Carrera 27
Calle 34 Bus Stop
Metrolínea Line

Av González Valencia

Calle 45
Calle 48

NUEVO SOTOMAYOR

Calle 50
Parque Turbay Bus Stop

Tourism Police

Parque de Los Niños Bus Stop

Parque de Los Niños

Carrera 26
Carrera 25
Carrera 24
Carrera 23

ANTONIA SANTOS

Museo de Arte Moderno de Bucaramanga

BOLIVAR

Av La Rosita

Calle 35
Calle 36
Calle 37

Parque Bolívar

Carrera 22
Carrera 21

Calle 45

Calle 22
Calle 24
Calle 28
Calle 30

ALARCÓN

Av Quebrada Seca

Calle 31
Calle 34

Parque Antonia Santos

Carrera 20
Carrera 19
Carrera 18

Parque Centenario

Colectivos
Parque Santander

Catedral de la Sagrada Familia

CENTRO

Calle 39

Bus Terminal (4km); Girón (9km): (15km)

GRANADA

Calle 22
Calle 24
Calle 28

Metrolínea Line

Calle 30
Calle 31
Carrera 17
Carrera 16

Carrera 15

Carrera 14
Carrera 13
Carrera 12

Calle 35
Calle 36
Calle 37

San Mateo Station

Chorreras-Centro Station

Calle 41
Calle 42

Carrera 33
Carrera 10
Carrera 9

Parque García Rovira

GARCIA ROVIRA

Capilla de los Dolores

Carrera 11

2

Bucaramanga

Coffeehouse San Fernando CAFE
(Carrera 29 No 41-40; coffee COP$2000-10,000; ⊙10am-8pm; 🛜) 🌿 Rainforest Alliance–certified coffee from Mesa de Los Santos. Good espresso.

La Birrería 1516 BAR
(Carrera 36 No 43-46; beers COP$4500-22,000; ⊙10am-midnight Mon-Thu, to 1:30am Fri & Sat) Kick back with a good selection of imported standards and domestic craft brews (Bogotá's Tres Marías is the house draft) on the breezy outdoor patio at this sophisticated pub/restaurant. The food is distinctly average.

Vintrash BAR
(Calle 49 No 35A-36; cover Fri & Sat COP$10,000; ⊙4-11pm Mon-Wed, to midnight Thu, to 3am Fri & Sat; 🛜) Among vintage oil barrels, hanging bicycles and a wisp of street cred, this bar sucks in the indie cool kids and those drawn to them for great but at times outlandish music (Tuesday night classics jump from NKOTB to New Order) and alternative attitude.

Sky Bar BAR
(Transversal Oriental & Calle 93, 18th fl; cocktails COP$18,000-20,000; ⊙9:30am-10:30pm Sun-Thu, to 11:30pm Fri & Sat) Bucaramanga's trendiest bar is on the 18th floor of the new Holiday Inn (never thought we'd write *that!*). It's an open-air affair decked in white with stupendous city views. Definitely a nice spot for a drink.

La 33 CLUB
(Carrera 33 No 44-27; cover COP$10,000-15,000; ⊙9pm-3am Fri & Sat) Hot-to-trot under-thirty-somethings pack in this rambunctious *rumba* hotspot some 400-strong on weekends, one of the hottest clubs in town at the time of research (read: subject to change *yesterday*). Salsa, merengue and – sigh – reggaeton rule the rhythms over three floors and the sunken dance floor.

ⓘ Information

There is no shortage of ATMs; many are clustered near Parque Santander along Calle 35, and in Sotomayor on Carrera 29.

Clínica Foscal (www.foscal.com.co; Av El Bosque No 23-60) The best hospital in Bucaramanga, located in Floridablanca. Bilingual staff.

Tourism Police (☑634-5507; www.imct.gov.co; Parque de Los Niños; ⊙8am-noon & 2-7pm) At the Biblioteca Pública Gabriel Turbay, the tourism police pull double-duty here, surprisingly well. There are maps, brochures, a little English and lots of willingness to help. There are also Puntos de Información Turística (PIT) locations at the airport and bus terminal.

ⓘ Getting There & Away

AIR
The Palonegro airport is on a *meseta* (plateau) high above the city 30km west in Lebrija. The landing here is quite breathtaking. The airport is served by most major Colombian cities as well as internationally from Panama City.

Colectivo taxis (COP$10,000; ⊙6am-6pm Mon-Sat) to the airport park off Parque Santander on Carrera 20 and leave every 15 minutes between 5am and 6pm. A taxi from the city center is a fixed COP$32,000.

BUS
Bucaramanga's **Terminal TB** (☑637-1000; www.terminalbucaramanga.com; Transversal Central Metropolitana) is situated southwest of the city center, midway to Girón; frequent city buses marked 'Terminal' go there from Carrera 15 (COP$1850) or take a taxi (COP$7000 to COP$8000). **Copetran** (☑644-8167; www.copetran.com.co) is the big bus company here, serving most major destinations such as Bogotá (COP$60,000, 10 hours), Cartagena (COP$90,000, 13 hours), Medellín (COP$70,000, eight hours), Santa Marta (COP$70,000, 11 hours), Pamplona (COP$30,000, five hours) and Cúcuta (COP$36,000, six hours). **Cootrasangil** (www.cotrasangil.com) heads to San Gil (COP$15,000, 1½ hours) via Parque Nacional del Chicamocha (COP$10,000, one hour). Cootraunidos has hourly buses to Ocaña (COP$40,000, five hours) for onward transportation to Playa de Belén.

If you're heading toward Venezuela, it's quicker to catch a bus from **El Parque del Agua** (Diagonal 32 No 30A-51), where they leave every 30 minutes (COP$35,000, six hours).

WORTH A TRIP

THE ROCK SHELTER

Santander's best view for the peso is a little high-adventure hostel called **Refugio La Roca** (☑ 313-283-1637; www.refugiolarocacolombia.com; Km22.7 Mesa de Los Santos; campsite COP$15,000, dm COP$25,000, r with bathroom COP$90,000-120,000, without bathroom COP$75,000; @ 🛜) 🎿, on Mesa de Los Santos, the mountain plateau at the opposite end of the Parque Nacional del Chicamocha's *teleférico*. Not only does the mesa offer far more to do than Chicamocha (rock climbing, hiking, waterfalls, coffee *fincas*) in a far less Disneyfied way, the hostel, built completely with natural materials, sits literally on the edge of the ridge, built right into the rock in some cases. Views are predictably jaw-dropping, especially from the private rooms with open-air bathrooms that make using the restroom a postcard-worthy experience. The fiercely sustainable hostel is located next to La Mojarra, the best rock-climbing spot in the area, and climbing courses are on offer. Alexandra and Ricardo, the young couple who run the place, also offer rappelling, highline, yoga, a properly trained chef in the kitchen (mains COP$10,000 to COP$22,000), and a whole lot of homespun hospitality.

To get there from Bucaramanga, catch Metrolínea P8 heading south on Carrera 33 in the city to Piedecuesta, where direct **La Culona** (☑ 7-655-1182; Carrera 6 No 12-60) buses to Los Santos leave hourly from 6am to 7:45pm (COP$7000, 1½ hours). Ask the bus driver to let you off at La Mojarra/Refugio La Roca. From San Gil, take the *teleférico* – it ends 12km south of the hostel (they'll pick you up for COP$25,000).

🛈 Getting Around

METROLÍNEA

Metrolínea (www.metrolinea.gov.co; ⊙ 5am-10:30pm Mon-Fri, to 9:30pm Sat-Sun), modeled on Bogotá's TransMilenio, covers the city of Bucaramanga to Piedecuesta, while subsequent phases to Girón, Ciudadela Real de Minas and along Carrera 33 remain under construction. The main lines run north–south along Carrera 15 and Carrera 27 (along the latter, they remain traditional bus stops rather than stations). Of little use yet to tourists, it's mainly used en route to Mesa de los Santos.

A single ride costs COP$1700 but you must purchase a *Tarjeta Inteligente* (COP$3000) if you want to board outside dedicated stations.

NORTE DE SANTANDER

Norte de Santander is where the Cordillera Oriental meets the hot, lowland plains that stretch into neighboring Venezuela. The scenic road from Bucaramanga climbs to 3300m at the provincial border town of Berlin before it begins its rapid descent toward Venezuela, calling at pleasant Pamplona along the way. Nearly 300km northeast, tiny Playa de Belén stands out as the department's most picturesque moment.

Pamplona

☑ 7 / POP 55,300 / ELEV 2290M

Spectacularly set in the deep Valle del Espíritu Santo in the Cordillera Oriental is colonial-era Pamplona, founded by Pedro de Orsúa and Ortún Velasco in 1549, and a delightful town of old churches, narrow streets and bustling commerce. With an average temperature of just 16°C, it's a welcome respite from the heat of nearby Bucaramanga and Cúcuta, and a nice stopover if you're en route to or from Venezuela. Unfortunately, an 1875 earthquake wiped out a good part of the town. Today, the inviting plaza is a mix of reconstructed colonial and modern architecture and there's a surprising number of trendy cafes, bars and restaurants considering its size and location.

👁 Sights

Pamplona has quite a collection of museums and almost all are set in restored colonial houses. There are some 10 old churches and chapels in town, reflecting Pamplona's religious status in colonial days, though not many have retained their splendor.

Museo de Arte Moderno Ramírez Villamizar   MUSEUM
(www.mamramirezvillamizar.com; Calle 5 No 5-75; admission COP$1000; ⊙ 9am-noon & 2-6pm Tue-Sun) In a 450-year-old mansion, this

museum has about 40 works by Eduardo Ramírez Villamizar, one of Colombia's most outstanding artists, born in Pamplona in 1923. The collection gives an insight into his artistic development from expressionist painting of the 1940s to geometric abstract sculpture in recent decades.

Museo Arquidiocesano de Arte Religios MUSEUM
(Carrera 5 No 4-53; admission COP$2000; ☺10am-noon & 3-5pm Wed-Sat & Mon, 10am-noon Sun) Features religious art comprising paintings, statues and altarpieces collected from the region. There is an especially impressive silver collection.

GETTING TO VENEZUELA

As far as border towns go, **Cúcuta** could be worse. Though it's a hot and muggy mess, it's a big city with all manner of restaurants, modern shopping malls, decent hotels, trendy neighborhoods (especially those saddled up against Av Libertadores) and an airport (which is to say, it offers more than most South America borders). The notoriously chaotic bus station is likely all you'll see of it, though. By 2016, a new modern bus terminal/shopping plaza will open 9km north of town. Until then, you're stuck with this one.

If you're heading to Venezuela, **Expresos Bolivarianos** (every 20 minutes between 5am and 5:30pm) and **Corta Distancia** (every eight minutes between 5am and 6:30pm) operate buses to San Antonio del Táchira in Venezuela from *Muelle de Abordaje* (Boarding Zone) 1 inside the terminal (COP$1400, 30 minutes). Private taxis go for around COP$10,000 to COP$12,000 (though you will be offered much higher fares than that!). Get your Colombian exit stamp at **Migración Colombia** (🗐7-573-5210; www.migracioncolombia.gov.co; CENAF – Simón Bolívar) on the left just before the bridge. From there, walk across or grab a moto-taxi (COP$3000).

As of August 2014, Colombia and Venezuela mutually agreed to close the border between 9:30pm and 4:30am in order to combat large-scale smuggling of gasoline and basic foodstuffs, which are subsidized by the Venezuelan government and very cheap in Venezuela, but were being smuggled into Colombia and sold at far higher prices. Plan accordingly and check to see if the situation has changed by the time you need to cross. Once in Venezuela, pop into the immigration building for entrance formalities at the **SAIME** (🗐0276 771 1321; www.saime.gob.ve; Carrera 9 btwn Calles 6 & 7; ☺24hr) office in central San Antonio del Táchira (not the SAIME office right at the bridge). It's best to have the moto-boys take you all the way there.

Move your watch forward 30 minutes when crossing from Colombia into Venezuela. Nationals of the US, Canada, Australia, New Zealand, Japan, the UK and most of Western and Scandinavian Europe don't need a visa to enter Venezuela. At time of research, direct buses to Caracas were suspended due to an increase in military checkpoints and the closure of the border at night – the bus station in San Antonio was all but abandoned. You must take a bus from **La Plaza de PTJ** (Carrera 7 & Av Venezuela) in San Antonio, three blocks northeast of SAIME (more convenient, anyway), to San Cristóbal (BsF40, one hour) and switch for a bus to Caracas from there.

If possible, take as many US dollars as possible to Venezuela, which can either be shockingly expensive (at the official exchange rate) or quite a bit more down to earth (on the active black market, called *dólar paralelo*). It isn't difficult to find someone to exchange US dollars at the black market rate – check www.dollar.nu for current *dólar paralelo* rates to avoid getting fleeced.

If you must sleep in the border area, Cúcuta has more choice than San Antonio. A couple of options in the area:

Hotel Mary (🗐7-572-1585; www.hotelmarycucuta.com; Av 7 No 0-53, Cúcuta; d/tr COP$75,000/97,000, s/d/tr with fan COP$50,000/60,000/75,000; ❄@🖀) Alluring website photography notwithstanding, Mary is a secure 56-room layover hotel across the street from the bus station.

Hotel Don Jorge (🗐7-771-1932; hoteldonjorge@hotmail.com; cnr Calle 5 & Carrera 9, San Antonio del Táchira; d/tr/q/ste BsF550/600/750/800; ❄🖀) Clean, neat and to-the-point, the Don Jorge has had more than 20 years to get it right, and continues to deliver well-maintained, good-value rooms, even if they refuse to show you one.

GRAN COLOMBIA OR BUST!

About 10km southeast of Cúcuta on the road to the Venezuelan border is the sedate suburb of **Villa del Rosario**. Here, Colombia's founding fathers met in 1821 to draw up the constitution of the new country of Gran Colombia, and inaugurate Simón Bolívar as its first president. History buffs will want to take a look.

The site of this important event in Colombia's history has been converted into a park, the **Parque de la Gran Colombia**. The park's central feature is the ruin of **Templo del Congreso**, the church (built in 1802) where the sessions of the congress were held. The original church was almost completely destroyed by the 1875 earthquake and only the dome was rebuilt. A marble statue of Bolívar has been placed in the rebuilt part of the church.

To get to the Parque de la Gran Colombia from Cúcuta, take the bus to San Antonio del Táchira (COP$1400), which passes the park on the way to the border. Don't take buses marked 'Villa del Rosario' – they won't bring you anywhere near the park.

Casa Colonial   MUSEUM
(Calle 6 No 2-56; ⊗8am-noon & 2-6pm Mon-Fri)
FREE One of the oldest buildings in town, Casa Colonial dates from the early Spanish days. The collection includes pre-Columbian pottery, colonial sacred art, artifacts of several indigenous communities including the Motilones and Tunebos (the two indigenous groups living in Norte de Santander department), plus antiques.

Catedral   CHURCH
(Parque Agueda Gallardo) The 17th-century Catedral was badly damaged during the earthquake of 1875 and altered in the reconstruction. The five-nave interior (two outer aisles were added at the beginning of the 20th century) is rather austere except for the magnificent main retable that survived the disaster. The central figure of San Pedro was made in Spain in 1618.

🛏 Sleeping & Eating

1549 Hostal   GUESTHOUSE $$
(📋568-0451; www.1549hostal.com; Calle 8B No 5-84; s/d incl breakfast COP$80,000/130,000; @🛜) Pamplona's most discerning option is a friendly seven-room boutique guesthouse in a colonial home on a pleasant side street with a good bar/restaurant. Rooms are a tad tiny, but character-driven touches like local art, creative bric-a-brac, candles and bathrobes give it a leg up in both design and intimacy. Staff lays it on extra thick for foreigners.

El Solar   HOTEL $$
(📋568-2010; www.elsolarhotel.com; Calle 5 No 8-10; r per person from COP$60,000; 🛜) The cheaper bottom-floor rooms here are simpler; up the creaky staircase, the more expensive 2nd floor has modern rooms with fantastic windows and big kitchens. El So-

lar has an excellent bar-restaurant that is warmed by a cozy, hanging fire pit at night (the town's most popular *menú del día* – get there before 1pm or forget it!)

London Coffee   CAFE $
(Carrera 6 No 8-20; coffee COP$1000-4000; cocktails COP$10,000-12,000; ⊗1:30-11:30pm Sun-Thu, to 1am Sat; 🛜) The town's best cafe, a small and trendy little number with good espresso, cocktails, imported beers, sweet and savory waffles, tapas and a gourmet *michelada* menu.

★Piero's   ITALIAN $$
(Carrera 5 No 8B-67; pizza COP$13,000-35,000; pasta COP$9000-17,000; ⊗5-11:30pm Mon-Sat, noon-3pm & 5-11:30pm Sun) Who knows how an actual Italian ended up here, but he did, and now there is great pizza and pasta to show for it. Oddly, though, the classics are missing (where is the pizza margarita?), but what's here, somewhat curbed for Colombian tastes, is solid, including great pastas.

There is also pizza, sweets and fresh baked goods at the attached Caffè Rimaní.

ℹ Information

ATMs cluster around Parque Agueda Gallardo.
4-72 (Calle 8 No 5-33; ⊗8am-noon & 1-6pm Mon-Fri, 9am-noon Sat) Post office.

ℹ Getting There & Away

Pamplona's bus terminal is just 750m east of the main square.

Pamplona is on the Bucaramanga–Cúcuta route. Cotranal goes to Cúcuta (COP$15,000, two hours) every 20 minutes. There are regular Bucaramanga buses (COP$25,000, 4½ hours). There are several direct buses per day to Bogotá (COP$55,000, 14 hours) as well as the Caribbean coast. For Ocaña, for onward travel to Playa de Belén, switch in Cúcuta, where Cootraunidos buses depart every 30 minutes for Ocaña (COP$35,000, five hours).

Right-side bus windows afford dramatic views along the recently paved and spectacular road from Bucaramanga to Pamplona. Passengers prone to motion or altitude sickness should consider taking Dramamine or similar medication. And bring a sweater.

Playa de Belén

⏱ 7 / POP 8395 / ELEV 1450

The tiny color-coordinated patrimonial *pueblo* of Playa de Belén evokes a perfectly chiseled chin, dramatically carved out of an otherworldly landscape created by eroded rock formations in the far north of Norte de Santander. The gorgeous and sleepy village saddles right up against Área Natural Única Los Estoraques, one of Colombia's smallest protected areas, and everything in the village – the architecture, the streets, the sidewalks – is planned, right down to the carefully placed potted wall plants that pepper the outside of the buildings around town.

Playa de Belén is not a Colombian secret, but very few foreigners make it this far north in Norte de Santander. If you go, you'll find a friendly village unaffected by international tourism.

◉ Sights

Área Natural Única Los
Estoraques   NATIONAL PARK

(⊙9am-5pm) This 6-sq-km protected area, one of Colombia's smallest, is an otherworldly delight of eroded and weathered brownstone rock formations sprouting skyward – columns, pedestals and caves – that have formed over time due to rainfall and tectonic shifts. If you use your imagination, it's vaguely reminiscent of Cappadocia (without all the folks living in fairy chimneys). The park is 350m north of where the pavement ends on Carrera 3. Technically the park was closed at the time of research, but you can still go in. A few guides hang around working for tips only and can guide you on a walk through the area. Beware of the snakes!

Mirador Santa Cruz   LOOKOUT

For a bird's-eye view of the *pueblo* and surrounding rock formations, head up to this lookout point above town, a straight 15-minute ascent east on Calle 4.

🛏 Sleeping & Eating

Casa Real   GUESTHOUSE $

(☎318-278-4486; karo27_03@yahoo.es; Vereda Rosa Blanca; r per person with meals COP$50,000) Still a work in progress when we came through, this small *finca* offers simple but friendly cheapies. It's a trade-off – you're outside the idyllic *pueblo,* but there's something to be said for the outdoor patio and guest kitchen, which have views across to Los Estoraques. It's a 700m walk from town north along Carrera 1.

Hotel Orquídeas Plaza   HOTEL $

(☎313-830-0442; Av Los Fundadores No 0-71; s/d/tr COP$35,000/70,000/90,000; 🛜🍴) A friendly option at the entrance to town. There's nothing notable about the rooms themselves, but there's a pool under the nose of a few interesting rock formations.

Hospedaje la Morisca   GUESTHOUSE $$

(☎313-369-5123; www.posadaenlaplaya.com; Calle Central 5-65; r per person COP$70,000; 🛜) The coziest spot in the village, with six rooms decked out in dark hardwood furniture surrounding a tiny brick courtyard. Breakfast is an additional COP$8000.

Los Arrayanes   COLOMBIAN $

(Carrera 3 No 1-57; meals COP$7000-10,0000; ⊙8:30am-10pm) Although this is a distinctly average spot for sustenance and there are better restaurants (Donde Edgar, for example), many open on weekends only, whereas Los Arrayanes opens daily.

ⓘ Information

The nearest ATM is in Ocaña.

Tourist Information (☎317-644-8177; pitplayadebelen@gmail.com; cnr Calle 1 & Carrera 2; ⊙9am-noon & 3-6pm Mon, Thu & Fri, 9am-noon & 2-5pm Sat & Sun) Well-stocked and eagerly staffed tourist information – they're even active on Twitter!

ⓘ Getting There & Away

Cootrans Hacaritama (☎314-215-5316; Carrera 4 No 5-01) has four set van departures daily to Ocaña from Playa de Belén (COP$6000, 45 minutes) at 5:30am, 6am, 8am and 2:30pm, which return from Ocaña when full. Otherwise, *colectivo* taxis leave when full for the same price until 5pm. Coming from Cúcuta or Bucaramanga, you don't have to go all the way to Ocaña – ask the driver to drop you off at the crossroads for Playa de Belén, where moto-taxis hang about the store across the road and can take you the remaining 11km (COP$5000, 15 minutes), even with luggage.

Caribbean Coast

Best Places to Eat

➡ Ouzo (p145)

➡ El Santíssimo (p134)

➡ El Fuerte (p164)

➡ La Cevichería (p133)

➡ Josefina's (p168)

Best Places to Stay

➡ Hotel Casa San Agustin (p132)

➡ Dreamer (p153)

➡ Casa Marco Polo (p131)

➡ Finca Barlovento (p152)

➡ Masaya (p144)

Why Go?

Sun-soaked and stewed in culture, Colombia's dramatic Caribbean coastline is its dazzling crown, capping the country with myriad ecosystems, from the dense jungles of the Darién Gap on the border with Panama to the barren desert of La Guajira near Venezuela.

The crown jewel along the coast is Cartagena, a colonial city with a beauty and romance that's unrivaled anywhere in Colombia, despite the enormous numbers of visitors it attracts. A yet undiscovered version can be enjoyed by journeying inland to find gorgeously isolated colonial Mompox, a sleepy hamlet lost in the jungle and whose star is truly in the ascendant. Other attractions are more natural: the Parque Nacional Natural (PNN) Tayrona, a wonderful stretch of perfect beach and virgin rainforest, and the thrilling and arduous Ciudad Perdida (Lost City) trek, which will satisfy adventurers wanting to discover the remnants of an ancient civilization against a stunning mountain backdrop.

When to Go
Cartagena

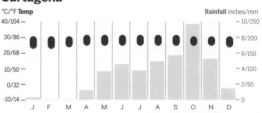

Dec & Jan The beaches are at their best at Christmas as the humidity drops.

Feb Barranquilla's Carnaval is an insane four-day Mardi Gras celebration.

Sep & Oct Prices are at their lowest and you'll have many places to yourself.

CARTAGENA & AROUND

The capital of the Bolívar department, Cartagena has a raw beauty and historical significance. It's also a major port and the gateway to offshore destinations such as the northern section of Parque Nacional Natural (PNN) Corales del Rosario y San Bernardo and sleepy down-shore towns like Mompox.

Cartagena

☑5 / POP 944,000 / ELEV 2M

Cartagena de Indias is the undisputed queen of the Caribbean coast, a fairy-tale city of romance, legends and superbly preserved beauty lying within an impressive 13km of centuries-old colonial stone walls. Cartagena's old town is a Unesco World Heritage Site, a maze of cobbled alleys, balconies covered in bougainvillea, and massive churches that cast their shadows across plazas.

But then there is the outer town, full of traffic, the working class, and a chaotic nature that can leave you dazed and confused in minutes. It is here that Cartagena becomes a typical workhorse South American city. To the south, the peninsula of Bocagrande – Cartagena's Miami Beach – is where fashionable *cartagenos* sip coffee in trendy cafes, dine in glossy restaurants and live in the upscale luxury condos that line the area like guardians to a New World.

Cartagena is a place to drop all sightseeing routines. Instead, just stroll through the old town day and night. Soak up the sensual atmosphere, pausing to ward off the brutal heat and humidity in one of the city's many open-air cafes.

Holding its own against Brazil's Ouro Preto and Peru's Cuzco for the continent's most enthralling and righteously preserved colonial destination, Cartagena is hard to walk away from – it seizes you in its aged clutches and refuses to let go.

History

Cartagena was founded in 1533 by Pedro de Heredia on the site of the Carib settlement of Calamari. It quickly grew into a rich town, but in 1552 an extensive fire destroyed a large number of its wooden buildings. Since that time, only stone, brick and tile have been permitted as building materials.

Within a short time the town blossomed into the main Spanish port on the Caribbean coast and the major northern gateway to South America. It came to be the storehouse for the treasure plundered from the local population until the galleons could ship it back to Spain. As such, it became a tempting target for all sorts of buccaneers operating on the Caribbean Sea.

In the 16th century alone, Cartagena suffered five sieges by pirates, the most famous (or infamous) of which was led by Sir Francis Drake. He sacked the port in 1586 and 'mercifully' agreed not to level the town once he was presented with a huge ransom of 10 million pesos, which he shipped back to England.

It was in response to pirate attacks that the Spaniards built up a series of forts around the town, saving it from subsequent sieges, particularly from the biggest attack of all, led by Edward Vernon in 1741. Blas de Lezo, a Spanish officer who had already lost an arm, a leg and an eye in previous battles, commanded the successful defense. With only 2500 poorly trained and ill-equipped men, don Blas managed to fend off 25,000 English soldiers and their fleet of 186 ships. The Spaniard lost his other leg in the fighting and died soon after, but he is now regarded as the savior of Cartagena. You can see his statue outside the Castillo de San Felipe.

In spite of the high price it had to pay for the pirate attacks, Cartagena continued to flourish. The Canal del Dique, constructed in 1650 to connect Cartagena Bay with the Río Magdalena, made the town the main gateway for ships heading to ports upriver, and a large part of the merchandise shipped inland passed through Cartagena. During the colonial period, Cartagena was the most important bastion of the Spanish overseas empire and influenced much of Colombia's history.

The indomitable spirit of the inhabitants was rekindled again at the time of the independence movement. Cartagena was one of the first towns to proclaim independence from Spain, early in 1810, which prompted Bogotá and other cities to do the same. The declaration was signed on November 11, 1811, but the city paid dearly for it. In 1815 Spanish forces under Pablo Morillo were sent to reconquer and 'pacify' the town and took it after a four-month siege. More than 6000 inhabitants died of starvation and disease.

In August 1819, Simón Bolívar's troops defeated the Spaniards at Boyacá, bringing freedom to Bogotá. However, Cartagena had to wait for liberation until October 1821, when the patriot forces eventually took the

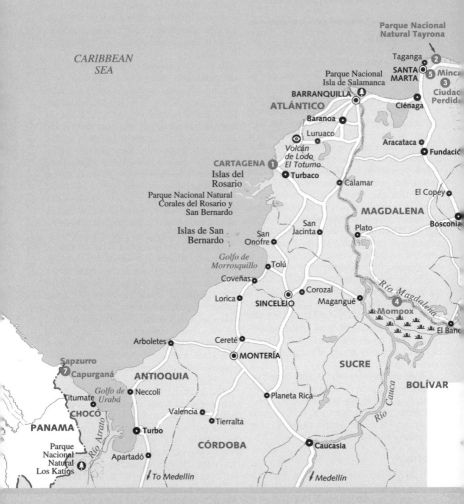

Caribbean Coast Highlights

1 Soak up the history as you stroll the colonial streets of old-town **Cartagena** (p121).

2 Beach-hop through **Parque Nacional Natural (PNN) Tayrona** (p150).

3 Trek through thick Colombian jungle to the mysterious **Ciudad Perdida** (p154), the former pre-Columbian capital of the Tayrona people.

4 Discover **Mompox** (p162), easily the region's most charming colonial town and site of a future tourism boom as word gets out.

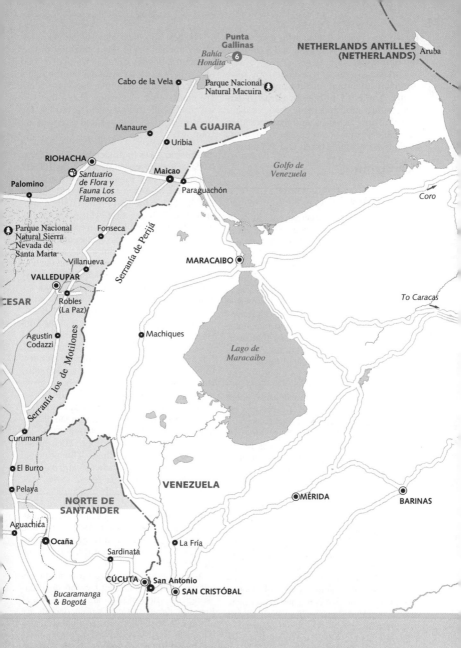

5 Escape the heat of the coast in the mountain town and chilled-out backpacker haunt of **Minca** (p146).

6 Traverse the feral seaside desertscape at **Punta Gallinas**

(p160), South America's stunning northernmost point.

7 Straddle the Colombia–Panama border in the tranquil villages and excellent beaches

around **Capurganá** and **Sapzurro** (p166).

city by sea. It was Bolívar who gave Cartagena its well-deserved name of 'La Heroica,' the Heroic City.

Cartagena began to recover and was once again an important trading and shipping center. The city's prosperity attracted foreign immigrants, and many Jews, Italians, French, Turks, Lebanese and Syrians settled here. Today their descendants own many businesses, including hotels and restaurants.

◉ Sights

◉ Old Town

Without a doubt, Cartagena's old city is its principal attraction, particularly the inner walled town consisting of the historical districts of El Centro and San Diego. El Centro in the west was traditionally home to the upper classes, and San Diego in the northeast was previously occupied by the middle classes. Both sections of the old town are packed with perfectly preserved colonial churches, monasteries, plazas, palaces and mansions, with balconies and shady patios that overflow with brightly colored flowers.

Getsemaní, the outer walled town, is less obviously impressive with its modest architecture, but as it's far more residential and less sanitized, it offers plenty of atmosphere and is well worth exploring. In recent years it has become the home of backpackers in the city, but gentrification is coming astonishingly quickly, and the area is full of trendy restaurants, packed cocktail bars and salsa clubs, and now almost as many boutique hotels as the inner walled town. A beautiful walkway, the **Muelle Turístico de los Pegasos**, links Getsemaní with the old town.

The old town is surrounded by **Las Murallas**, the thick walls built to protect the town against enemies. Construction began toward the end of the 16th century, after the attack by Francis Drake; until that time Cartagena was almost completely unprotected. The project took two centuries to complete due to repeated damage from both storms and pirate attacks. It was finally finished in 1796, just 25 years before the Spaniards were eventually expelled.

Las Murallas are an outstanding piece of military engineering, and are remarkably well preserved, except for a part of the walls facing La Matuna, which were unfortunately demolished by 'progressive' city authorities in the mid-20th century.

The best approach is to wander about leisurely about the old town, savoring the architectural details, street life and street food along the way. Don't just seek out the sights detailed in our recommendations – there are many interesting places that you will find while walking and exploring the charming streets, squares and alleyways on your own.

★**Palacio de la Inquisición**　MUSEUM
(Plaza de Bolívar; adult/child COP$16,000/13,000; ⊙9am-6pm) The Palace of the Inquisition may today be one of the finest buildings in the city, but in the past it housed the notoriously grizzly Inquisition, whose bloody task it was to stamp out heresy in colonial Cartagena. The palace is today a museum, displaying the Inquisitors' gnarly instruments of torture, some of which are quite horrific. The museum also houses pre-Columbian pottery and historical objects dating from both colonial and independence times, including arms, paintings, furniture and church bells.

Although the site was the seat of the Punishment Tribunal of the Holy Office from 1610, the palace wasn't completed until 1776. It is a good example of late-colonial architecture, noted particularly for its baroque stone gateway topped by the Spanish coat of arms, and the long balconies on the facade.

On the side wall, just around the corner from the entrance, you'll find a small window with a cross on top. Heretics were denounced here, and the Holy Office would then instigate proceedings. The principal 'crimes' were magic, witchcraft and blasphemy. When culprits were found guilty, they were sentenced to death in a public *auto-da-fé* (public execution of heretics). Five *autos-da-fé* took place during the Inquisition until independence in 1821. About 800 folk were condemned to death and executed. The Inquisition did not judge the indigenous people.

A good model of Cartagena from the beginning of the 19th century and an interesting collection of old maps of the Nuevo Reino de Granada from various periods are also on display. There are no English translations, but guides (COP$35,000 in English) are available. Go in a group if you can: these prices count for up to five people.

Convento & Iglesia de San Pedro Claver　MUSEUM
(☑664 4991; Plaza de San Pedro Claver; adult/child COP$9000/6000; ⊙9:30am-noon & 3-5pm Mon-

Fri) This convent was founded by Jesuits in the first half of the 17th century, originally as San Ignacio de Loyola. The name was later changed in honor of Spanish-born monk Pedro Claver (1580–1654), who lived and died in the convent. Called the 'Apostle of the Blacks' or the 'Slave of the Slaves,' the monk spent all his life ministering to the enslaved people brought from Africa. He was the first person to be canonized in the New World (in 1888).

The convent is a monumental three-story building surrounding a tree-filled courtyard, and much of it is open as a museum. Exhibits include religious art and pre-Columbian ceramics, and a new section devoted to Afro-Caribbean contemporary pieces includes wonderful Haitian paintings and African masks.

You can visit the cell where San Pedro Claver lived and died in the convent, and also climb a narrow staircase to the choir loft of the adjacent church. Should you need one, guides (COP$22,000 in English for a group of up to seven) are generally found by the ticket office. Iglesia de San Pedro Claver was completed in the first half of the 18th century. The church has an imposing stone facade, and inside there are fine stained-glass windows and a high altar made of Italian marble. The remains of San Pedro Claver are kept in a glass coffin in the altar. His skull is visible, making it an altar with a difference.

Plaza de Bolívar   PLAZA
Formerly the Plaza de Inquisición, this leafy and shaded plaza is surrounded by some of the city's most elegant balconied colonial buildings. It's one of Cartagena's most alluring plazas and offers wonderful respite from the Caribbean heat. A statue of the eponymous Simón Bolívar stands in the middle of the plaza.

Museo del Oro Zenú   MUSEUM
(Plaza de Bolívar; ⊘9am-5pm Tue-Sat, 10am-3pm Sun) FREE This museum is like a miniature version of Bogotá's world-class gold museum, Museum del Oro. Though small, it offers a fascinating collection of the gold and pottery of the Zenú (also known as Sinú) people, who inhabited the region of the present-day departments of Bolívar, Córdoba, Sucre and northern Antioquia before the Spanish Conquest. Some pieces are exquisitely detailed.

Should you be heading to Bogotá, this gold museum offers just a taste of the big-

ger and grander one there. It's also a superb spot to cool right down as the air-con is set to arctic levels.

Iglesia de Santo Domingo   CHURCH
(Plaza de Santo Domingo; adult/child COP$12,000 /8000; ⊘9am-7pm Tue-Sat, noon-8pm Sun) Santo Domingo is reputedly the oldest church in the city. It was originally built in 1539 in Plaza de los Coches, but the original building succumbed to fire and was rebuilt in its present location in 1552. Builders gave it a particularly wide central nave and covered it with a heavy roof, but it seems they were not too good at their calculations as the vault began to crack afterwards.

Massive buttresses had to be added to the walls to support the structure and prevent it from collapsing. The builders also had problems with the bell tower, which is distinctly crooked.

The interior is spacious and lofty. The figure of Christ carved in wood is set in the baroque altar at the head of the right-hand aisle. The floor in front of the high altar and in the two aisles is paved with old tombstones dating mostly from the 19th century.

The church was previously only open during Mass, but you can now take a 20-minute self-guided audio tour, offered in most European languages.

Puerta del Reloj   GATE
Originally called the Boca del Puente, this was the main gateway to the inner walled town and was linked to Getsemaní by a drawbridge over the moat. The side arches of the gate, which are now open as walkways, were previously used as a chapel and armory. The republican-style tower, complete with a four-sided clock, was added in 1888.

Plaza de los Coches   PLAZA
Previously known as Plaza de la Yerba, the triangular plaza just behind Puerta del Reloj was once used as a market for enslaved people. It is lined with old balconied houses with colonial arches at ground level. The arcaded walkway, known as El Portal de los Dulces, is today lined with confectionery stands selling local sweets. The statue of the city's founder, Pedro de Heredia, is in the middle of the plaza.

Plaza de la Aduana   PLAZA
This is the largest and oldest square in the old town and was used as a parade ground. In colonial times, all the important

Cartagena Old Town

CARIBBEAN COAST

CARIBBEAN SEA

Av Santander

Metrocar
Buses to
Bus Station

Las Murallas

Playa del Tejadillo

Del Tejadillo

Calle del Curato

Calle del Torno

Calle de las Bóvedas

43

Plaza de
San Diego

Stuard

48

SAN
DIEGO

30

6

39 17

18 31

Sargento
Mayor

C del Santísimo

C de los
7 Infantes

19

Estanco del
Aguardiente

Calle Merced

Calle del Cuartel

Calle San
Agustín
Chiquita

Plaza
Fernandez
de Madrid

47

Calle Don Sancho

21

EL
CENTRO

Calle Segunda de Badillo

29

Calle de
los Puntales

22

50

De la Factoría

55

La Soledad

35

Calle de
la Moneda

Calle de
la Bomba

Calle de
la Mantilla

65

36

Del Estanco del
Tabaco

Del Porvenir

Calle Primera
de Badillo

Av Carlos Escallón

Calle Gastelbondo

54

Plaza de
Santo Domingo

52

44

66

5

Calle De Ayos

42

Del Coliseo

Dolores

57

Calle de los
Estribos

28

Palacio de la
Inquisición

3

Proclamación Román

15

51

Calle Baloco

41

32 1

Calle de la
Inquisición

13

11

Velz Daníes

Candilejo

64

16

Plaza de los
Coches

Parque del
Centenario

Vicaria
Santa
Teresa

De las Damas

59

Playa de la Artillería

Sta Teresa

67

San Juan de Dios

14

Muelle
Turístico de
los Pegasos

Amargura

Plaza Santa
Teresa

12

4

10

Plaza de
la Aduana

63

Plaza de San
Pedro Claver

Centro de
Convenciones

Santa Orden

Av del Mercado

GETSEMANÍ

Parque
de la
Marina

Av Blas de Lezo

9

Calle Larga

40

60

Av del Arsenal

Bahía De
Las Ánimas

Av Santander

Bocagrande (1km)

governmental and administrative buildings were here. The old Royal Customs House has been restored and is now the City Hall. A statue of Christopher Columbus stands in the center of the square.

Museo de Arte Moderno
MUSEUM

(Museum of Modern Art; Plaza de San Pedro Claver; adult/child COP$5000/3000; ⊗9am-noon & 3-7pm Mon-Fri, 10am-1pm Sat, 4-9pm Sun) The Museum of Modern Art is a perfectly sized museum, housed in a beautifully converted part of the 17th-century former Royal Customs House. It presents rotating exhibitions from its own collection, including works by Alejandro Obregón, one of Colombia's most remarkable painters, who was born in Cartagena, and Enrique Grau, another local painter who left a legacy to the museum on his death. There's also a range of sculpture and abstract art – all well worth a look. The 2nd floor houses temporary exhibitions.

Museo Naval del Caribe
MUSEUM

(Calle San Juan de Dios No 3-62; adult/child/student COP$8000/4000/2000; ⊗9am-5:30pm) Opened in 1992 on the 500th anniversary of Columbus' discovery of the New World, the Naval Museum occupies a great colonial building, which was once a Jesuit college. It features, for the most part, a grand collection of reconstructed cityscapes and boat models from throughout the centuries, but woefully lacks much in the way of actual artifacts (although there are some nice torpedoes). It can be a little boring unless you're a naval history fanatic. Tours in English (COP$25,000) are available for the latter.

Catedral
CHURCH

(Calle de los Santos de Piedra; adult/child COP$12,000/8000 incl audio tour; ⊗10:30am-7pm; ℗) Work on Cartagena's cathedral began in 1575, but in 1586, while still under construction, it was partially destroyed by the cannons of Francis Drake, and was not completed until 1612. Alterations were made between 1912 and 1923 by the first archbishop of Cartagena, who covered the church with stucco and painted it to look like marble. He also commissioned the dome on the tower.

Restoration work has uncovered the lovely limestone on the building's exterior, and apart from the tower's top, the church has basically preserved its original form. It has a fortlike appearance and a simply decorated interior that features three naves and massive semicircular archways supported

CARIBBEAN COAST CARTAGENA

Cartagena Old Town

on high, stone columns. The main retable, worked in gold leaf, dates from the 18th century. You can take a self-guided audio tour that lasts about 25 minutes.

Iglesia de Santo Toribio de Mangrovejo
CHURCH

(Calle del Curato) This is one of the smaller of Cartagena's churches. Erected between 1666 and 1732, its ceiling is covered with Mudejar paneling. During Vernon's attack on the city in 1741, a cannonball went through a window into the church when it was filled with worshippers, but fortunately there were no casualties. The cannonball is now on display in a glassed niche in the left wall. The church was undergoing a full renovation in 2014, and should soon be looking superb again.

Las Bóvedas
HISTORIC BUILDING

(Playa del Tejadillo) These are 23 dungeons, built between 1792 and 1796, hidden within the 15m-thick city walls. These dungeons were the last major construction carried out in colonial times and were destined for military purposes. The vaults were used by the Spaniards as storerooms for munitions and provisions. Later, during the republican era, they were turned into a jail. Today they house rather touristy craft and souvenir shops.

Casa de Rafael Núñez   MUSEUM

(🕙 9am-5pm Tue-Fri, 10am-4pm Sat & Sun) `FREE`
This charming mansion, just outside the
walls of Las Bóvedas, was the home of the
former president, lawyer and poet Rafael
Núñez. He wrote the words of Colombia's
national anthem and was one of the authors
of the constitution of 1886, which was in use
(with some later changes) until 1991. The
beautiful white-and-green wooden mansion
is now a museum featuring some of Núñez's
documents and personal possessions.

It's hard not to envy his lovely outdoor
covered dining room or the huge walk-out
balcony. The chapel opposite the house,
known as the Ermita del Cabrero, holds his
ashes.

Monumento a la India Catalina   STATUE

The monument at the main entrance to the
old town from the mainland is a tribute to
the Carib people, who inhabited this land
before the Spanish Conquest. The lovely
bronze statue depicts Catalina, a beautiful
Carib woman who served as interpreter to
Pedro de Heredia upon the arrival of the
Spaniards. The statue was forged in 1974
by Eladio Gil, a Spanish sculptor living in
Cartagena.

Muelle Turístico   PORT

Often incorrectly referred to as Pegasos (giv-
en the close location of the two sites), this is
the old port of Cartagena on the Bahía de las
Ánimas. Not much goes on here now other
than the departure of tourist boats to Playa Blanca and Isla del Rosario (there's also
a cruise office here for bookings). The new
harbor where big ships dock is on Manga
Island.

👁 Spanish Forts

Cartagena's old city is a fortress in itself, yet
there are more fortifications built at strategic points outside the city.

★ Castillo de San Felipe de Barajas   FORTRESS

(Av Arévalo; adult/child COP$17,000/8000;
🕗 8am-6pm) The *castillo* is the greatest
fortress ever built by the Spaniards in any
of their colonies. It still dominates an entire section of Cartagena's cityscape today,
and should definitely be your first choice
of fortresses to visit. The original fort was
commissioned in 1630 and was quite small.
Construction began in 1657 on top of the
40m-high San Lázaro hill. In 1762 an exten-

sive enlargement was undertaken, which
resulted in the entire hill being covered over
with this powerful bastion.

It was truly impregnable and was never
taken, despite numerous attempts to storm
it. A complex system of tunnels connected
strategic points of the fortress to distrib-
ute provisions and to facilitate evacuation.
The tunnels were constructed in such a
way that any noise reverberated all the way
along them, making it possible to hear the
slightest sound of the approaching enemy's
feet, and also making it easy for internal
communication.

Some of the tunnels are lit and are open
to visitors – an eerie walk not to be missed.
Take an audio tour (COP$10,000 in English)
if you want to learn more about the curious
inventions of Antonio de Arévalo, the military engineer who directed the construction
of the fortress.

The fortress is a short walk from Getsemaní, but if you're in a hurry a taxi costs
COP$6000. Entrance is free the last Sun-
day of every month between February and
November.

Fuerte de San Sebastián del Pastelillo   FORTRESS

`FREE` This fort, on the western end of Manga Island, was constructed in the middle of
the 16th century as one of the town's first
defense posts. It's quite small and not particularly inspiring, but it's quite close to the
old town – just across the bridge from Getsemaní. Today the fort is home to the Club de
Pesca, which has a marina where local and
foreign boats anchor.

👁 Convento de la Popa

Convento de la Popa   CHURCH

(adult/child COP$8000/6000; 🕗 8am-6pm) On a
150m-high hill, the highest point in Cartagena, stands this convent. A beautiful image
of La Virgen de la Candelaria, the patroness
of the city, is in the convent's chapel, and
there's a charming flower-filled patio. There
is also a chilling statue of a speared Padre
Alonso García de Paredes, a priest who was
murdered along with five Spanish soldiers
for trying to spread the good word. The
views from here are outstanding and stretch
all over the city.

The convent's name literally means the
Convent of the Stern, after the hill's apparent similarity to a ship's back end. Founded
by the Augustine fathers in 1607, its official

name is actually Convento de Nuestra Señora de la Candelaria. Initially it was just a small wooden chapel, which was replaced by a stouter construction when the hill was fortified two centuries later, just before Pablo Morillo's siege.

There is a zigzagging access road leading up to the convent (no public transportation) and paths cutting the bends of the road. It takes 30 minutes to walk to the top, but it's not recommended for safety and climatic reasons – walking up would be equivalent to a trek in the desert! Take a cab and expect to pay up to COP$45,000. Haggle politely but insistently and you might get it for half that.

◉ Mercado Bazurto

Mercado Bazurto MARKET
(Av Pedro de Heredia; ⊘24hr) For adventurous souls only, Cartagena's labyrinthine central market is both dirty and enthralling, an all-out assault on your senses. If it's marketable, it's for sale here: there are endless stalls of fruits and vegetables, meat and fish, and plenty of options to grab a quick bite or juice up on a chilled beverage. Don't wear flashy jewelry and pay close attention to your camera and wallet. Grab a taxi (COP$7000 from the old town) and explore away.

If you can find it, look for Cecilia's restaurant, which sometimes serves up river turtle, shark and cow's tongue (it's in the area known as Pescado Frito – ask and people can direct you). You won't likely buy anything here, but it's a fascinating glimpse into the daily lives of real *cartagenos*.

🏃 Activities

Cartagena has grown into an important scuba-diving center, taking advantage of the extensive coral reefs along its coast. La Boquilla, just outside town, is also popular for kitesurfing.

Kitesurf Colombia KITESURFING
(☑311-410-8883; www.kitesurfcolombia.com; Carrera 9, behind the Edificio Los Morros 922, Cielo Mar) Kitesurfing school located beyond the airport off the main road to Barranquilla. It also offers windsurfing, surfing, kayaking and other activities from its beachside premises.

Diving Planet DIVING
(☑300-815-7169, 320-230-1515; www.divingplanet. org; Calle Estanco del Aguardiente No 5-09) This five-star PADI diving school offers two-tank dives in the Islas del Rosario including transportation, equipment, lunch and instructors for COP$300,000. Discounts are available if you book online.

Vélo Tours BIKE TOURS
(☑300-276-5036, 664-9714; Calle don Sancho; tours per person COP$80,000-100,000) This innovative bike tour agency offers tours of the city, nocturnal tours and tours of the fortifications and the nearby coastline, all by bike, as well as renting out bikes (COP$80,000 per 24 hours) for individual use.

🎓 Courses

Centro Catalina Spanish School LANGUAGE COURSE
(☑310-761-2157; www.centrocatalina.com; Calle de los 7 Infantes No 9-21) This recommended Spanish school has an enviable location right in the heart of the walled city. It offers a range of courses; a one-week course with 20 hours tuition, starts at US$229. Accommodations can also be arranged and a whole slew of activites is available.

Nueva Lengua LANGUAGE COURSE
(☑660-1736; www.nuevalengua.com; Calle del Pozo No 25-95, Getsemaní) Language courses at this casual school start for as little as US$200 per week for 15 hours of instruction.

🎊 Festivals & Events

Fiesta de Nuestra Señora de la Candelaria PROCESSION
(⊘Feb 2) On the day of Cartagena's patron saint a solemn procession is held at the Convento de la Popa during which the faithful carry lit candles. Celebrations begin nine days earlier, the so-called Novenas, when pilgrims flock to the convent.

Concurso Nacional de Belleza BEAUTY PAGEANT
(www.srtacolombia.org; ⊘Nov 11) The national beauty pageant celebrates Cartagena's independence day. Miss Colombia, the beauty queen, is elected as the high point of the event. The fiesta, which includes street dancing, music and fancy-dress parades, strikes up several days before the pageant and the city goes wild. The event, also known as the Carnaval de Cartagena or Fiestas del 11 de Noviembre, is the city's most important annual bash.

🛌 Sleeping

Cartagena has a reasonable choice of places to sleep and, despite its touristy status, its hotel prices remain reasonable compared to other large cities. If you're in a position to splash out, there is now an enormous number of beautifully restored colonial options that operate as luxury boutique hotels at the top end of the market. The tourist peak is from late December to late January, but even at this time you'll be able to find a room.

Most travelers stay within the walled city. In this area, Getsemaní is the main place to find budget accommodations, especially on Calle de la Media Luna, while El Centro and San Diego tend to host the more luxurious options.

Chill House   HOSTEL $
(📞660-2386; www.chillhousebackpackers.hostel.com; Calle de la Tablada, Parque Fernandez de Madrid, No 7-12, San Diego; dm from COP$21,000, r with/without air-con COP$90,000/70,000; ❄️🌐) You won't find a cheaper dorm room in the heart of the old town, and even though it's rather cramped here, there's a sociable vibe (and, weirdly enough, a weight machine in the lobby). The hostel is on a beautiful square near some good, cheap places to eat, which is good as there's no food provided on-site.

Casa Viena   HOSTEL $
(📞668-5048; www.casaviena.com; Calle San Andrés No 30-53, Getsemaní; dm COP$20,000, s/d COP$40,000/70,000, s/d without bathroom COP$35,000/50,000; ❄️@🌐) An old-school Austrian-run joint on a rowdy street in Getsemaní – earplugs are your friend. The busy dorm is cramped and needs a lick of paint, but you get free internet and coffee. It's sociable and there's a kitchen to use, and you won't find better conditions at other hostels at this price elsewhere in town.

★Casa Marco Polo   BOUTIQUE HOTEL $$
(📞316-874-9478; casamarcopolo@hotmail.com; Calle de los 7 Infantes No 9-89; s/d/tr incl breakfast COP$150,000/160,000/200,000; ❄️🌐) A superb deal in the old town, this beautiful private home is a gorgeously renovated and remodeled colonial house with just three individually designed guest rooms. Each is ensuite, wonderfully decorated with traditional arts and crafts and offers access to a great roof terrace. There's also both hot water and one of Colombia's best breakfasts to greet you in the morning.

★Hotel Casa del Mango   BOUTIQUE HOTEL $$
(📞660-6486; www.casadelmangocartagena.com; Calle del Espiritu Santo No 29-101; s/d incl breakfast COP$120,000/150,000; ❄️🌐🚻) One of Getsemaní's best midrange deals, this charming place is a beautifully rustic wooden creation within the walls of a colonial mansion. The most impressive rooms are the two at the front of the house, both of which are spread over two floors, and one of which has a private roof terrace and sleeps four. As they're partially open to the elements, however, these two rooms don't have air-con.

Casa Villa Colonial   HOTEL $$
(📞664-5421; www.casavillacolonial.com; Calle de la Media Luna No 10-89, Getsemaní; s/d COP$100,000/150,000; ❄️🌐) A complete bargain for the price – you'll get four-star personal service, beautiful communal areas with comfortable sofas, and silent air-con. The best rooms have small balconies onto the courtyard, and there's a small kitchen for guest use and endless great coffee.

El Genovés Hostal   HOSTEL $$
(📞646-0972; www.elgenoveshostal.com; Calle Cochera del Hobo No 38-27, San Diego; dm COP$30,000-35,000, r from COP$171,000, all incl breakfast; ❄️🌐🚻) A welcome addition to the hostels in San Diego, this charming, colorful place has a 12-bed and a four-bed dorm as well as a number of private double and triple rooms with own bathroom. The hostel surrounds a welcome plunge pool and is topped off with a small roof terrace. There's also a full communal kitchen.

Media Luna Hostel   HOSTEL $$
(📞664-3423; www.medialunahostel.com; Calle de la Media Luna No 10-46, Getsemaní; dm with/without air-con COP$35,000/30,000, r COP$120,000; ❄️@🌐🚻) This boutique hostel is undoubtedly the hub of the backpacking scene in Getsemaní. It is centered on its big courtyard and roof terrace, which is also home to the biggest single party in Cartagena each Wednesday night. Rooms are clean and well kept, with crisp linens and good mattresses. Look no further if you want to party.

El Viajero Cartagena   HOSTEL $$
(📞660-2598; www.hostelcartagena.com; Calle de los 7 Infantes No 9-45; dm from COP$36,000, d COP$170,000, s/d without bathroom COP$81,000/162,000, all incl breakfast; ❄️🌐) This massive backpacker blockbuster is both the most centrally located and one of the most social hostels in the city. All rooms have air-con – an absolute dream in this heat and at this price. The beds are firm, the kitchen is well organized and spotless, and there's a very friendly, social vibe in the lovely open courtyard.

Casa Relax
HOTEL **$$**

(📞 664-1117; www.cartagenarelax.com; Calle del Pozo No 29B-119, Getsemaní; r incl breakfast from COP$150,000; ❋🕾🏊) A good place to soak up some restored colonial atmosphere without taking out a second mortgage. Run by an occasionally brusque pipe-smoking French gentleman, Casa Relax is recommended mainly for its large swimming pool, pool table, communal kitchen and comical parrots.

Hostal Santo Domingo
HOSTEL **$$**

(📞 664-2268; hsantodomingopiret@yahoo.es; Calle Santo Domingo No 33-46, El Centro; s/d/tr incl breakfast COP$90,000/130,000/150,000; ❋🕾) Walk through a handicrafts shop to get to this friendly little place. If it were located in Getsemaní, it could only charge half this much for what is relatively simple accommodations, but it's on a beautiful street in the center of town and is steps away from some of the most beautiful buildings in Latin America.

★ Hotel Casa San Agustin
LUXURY HOTEL **$$$**

(📞 681-0000; www.hotelcasasanagustin.com; Calle de la Universidad; r incl breakfast from COP$740,000; ❋🕾🏊) Since opening in 2012, this superb addition to the city's hotel scene has already established itself as Cartagena's finest. Its central location would be wonderful anyway, but its unique building (through which the city's former aqueduct cuts over an angular swimming pool) creates such an unusual and atmospheric space that it's got the competition beaten.

Overflowing with formal, old-world fittings, such as its dazzling library, the hotel has unsurprisingly palatial rooms, including tiled marble bathrooms that heave with designer goodies and all of which boast a rain shower. In-room iPads, huge balconies and heavy wooden canopy beds complete the scene.

San Pedro Hotel Spa
BOUTIQUE HOTEL **$$$**

(📞 664-5800; www.sanpedrohotelspa.com.co; Calle San Pedro Martir No 10-85; r incl breakfast COP$490,000; ❋🕾🏊) A wonderful colonial mansion conversion, the San Pedro offers rooms full of antiques, a gorgeous roof terrace with a Jacuzzi as well as a small pool in the courtyard. Perhaps its most unique feature: a superb shared kitchen where you can live out your Masterchef fantasies. Your not inconsiderable nightly rate includes a free hand massage.

La Passion
HOTEL **$$$**

(📞 664-8605; www.lapassionhotel.com; Calle Estanco del Tabaco No 35-81, El Centro; r incl breakfast from COP$325,000; ❋🕾🏊) Run by a French movie producer and his Colombian partner, this republican-style home dating to the early 17th century features eight uniquely decorated rooms, some with Roman baths and outdoor showers. It's the canoe-swing in the courtyard, though, that really sets the eccentric, albeit stylish, tone. The pool and rooftop terrace with front-row views of the cathedral clinch it.

Hotel Casa Lola
HOTEL **$$$**

(📞 664-1538; www.casalola.com.co; Calle del Guerrero No 29-108, Getsemaní; r incl breakfast from COP$465,000; ❋🕾) This stylish 10-room boutique hotel is incense-infused and veers designwise between the artful and the garish. Its highlight is undoubtedly the multilevel roof terrace, complete with two small pools and wonderful city views. The rooms are gorgeous too, and the entire place is deceptively huge.

Bantú
HOTEL **$$$**

(📞 664-3362; www.bantuhotel.com; Calle de la Tablada No 7-62, San Diego; s/d incl breakfast from COP$466,000/556,000; ❋@🕾🏊) Two wonderfully restored 15th-century homes make up this lovely 23-room, open-air boutique hotel, rife with exposed-brick archways, original stone walls and lush vegetation. Smartly appointed rooms are full of local artistic touches that blend sympathetically with the old building. There is also a rooftop pool, a shower and a Jacuzzi – as well as ridiculously attired male staff members.

Casa Canabal
BOUTIQUE HOTEL **$$$**

(📞 660-0666; www.casacanabalhotel.com; Calle Tripita y Media No 31-39, Getsemaní; r incl breakfast from COP$340,000; ❋🕾🏊) Luxury without absurd cost can be found at this Getsemaní bolt-hole where sleek design combines with old-world care from attentive staff. Beautiful, minimalist rooms come with high ceilings, lots of wood and stylish bathrooms. The highlight is definitely the wonderful roof terrace, complete with bar, pool and spa (with a free welcome massage for each guest, naturally).

Centro Hotel
HOTEL **$$$**

(📞 664-0461; www.centrohotelcartagena.com; Calle del Arzobispado No 34-80, El Centro; s/d incl breakfast from COP$176,000/220,000; ❋🕾) The simple but clean Centro Hotel is perfectly located just steps from Plaza de Bolívar. Well-maintained rooms with lovely tiled floors are arranged around an open courtyard with a palm tree growing up through it, and some offer Juliette balconies that open over the street.

✖️ Eating

You can eat well in Cartagena, whether it be a COP$12,000 *comida corriente* (daily set menu) meal at midday in a busy local lunch spot or a gourmet blowout feast inside a colonial-era boutique hotel.

The city is also strong on street food: plenty of snack bars all across the old town serve typical local snacks such as *arepas de huevo* (fried maize dough with an egg inside), *dedos de queso* (deep-fried cheese sticks), empanadas (meat and/or cheese pastries) and *buñuelos* (deep-fried maize and cheese balls). Try typical local sweets at confectionery stands lining El Portal de los Dulces on the Plaza de los Coches.

In restaurants, you'll see the ubiquitous *arroz con coco* (rice sweetened with coconut) as an accompaniment to most fish and meat dishes. Fruit stalls are also everywhere (and are often mobile).

✖️ El Centro & San Diego

⭐**Crepe Xpress** CREPES **$**
(Calle Baloco No 220; crepes COP$6000-12,000; ⊙4-10pm) This charming little place serves up crepes that are the perfect combination of crispy outside and moist in the middle. You're free to design your own, though we're not sure you can actually top their spinach, cheese and caramelized onion. Don't even bother looking for better crepes in Cartagena, as you won't find them.

Espíritu Santo COLOMBIAN **$**
(Calle del Porvenir No 35-60; mains COP$10,000-14,000; ⊙11:30am-3:30pm) There's no telling from the outside, but this fiercely popular Centro lunch spot stretches back cavernously, and usually it feels as if half the city is in here for simple and damn tasty *comida corriente* each lunchtime. Staples include fish fillet in coconut milk, fried beef and some excellent salads. Portions are big and the value is terrific.

La Mulata COLOMBIAN **$**
(📞664-6222; Calle Quero No 9-58, El Centro; set meal COP$15,000; ⊙11:30am-4pm Mon-Sat; 🛜) Stylish *comida corriente* lunch option that's both outstanding and cheap. A daily set menu offers a handful of excellent choices and fresh juices in an atmosphere entirely

too hip for the price. The place has grown and grown since it began as a tiny place with just a few tables, but it remains one of the best deals in Cartagena.

Girasoles VEGETARIAN **$**
(📞664-5239; Calle de los Puntales No 37-01, San Diego; set meals COP$7000; ⊙7:30am-6pm Mon-Fri, 8am-4pm Sat; 🛜🍴) This vegetarian restaurant and health-food store does a set menu of animal-friendly options that changes daily.

⭐**La Cevicheria** SEAFOOD **$$**
(📞664-5255; Calle Stuart No 7-14, San Diego; mains COP$20,000-60,000; ⊙noon-11pm Wed-Mon; 🛜) This place is tiny and hidden, but its ceviche is the best this side of heaven, and its chili sauce would scare Lucifer. Each dish is prepared with panache and elegance: the octopus in peanut sauce is incredible, as is the black squid ink rice and Peruvian fish and shrimp ceviche.

Señor Toro STEAKHOUSE **$$**
(📞656-4077; Calle Santo Domingo No 35-55; mains COP$20,000-60,000; ⊙noon-midnight; 🛜) This centrally located steakhouse is the most rigorous in the city in terms of sourcing and preparing meat. Nowhere else will you find such perfectly cooked medium-rare porterhouse or entrecôte. There are also ceviche and burgers on the menu if steak isn't your thing.

El Bistro EUROPEAN **$$**
(📞664-1799; Calle de Ayos No 4-46, El Centro; sandwiches from COP$10,000, mains COP$18,000-47,000; ⊙9am-11pm Mon-Sat) An eclectic and popular place filled with curios, this charmer sells fresh bread and offers a full menu. Daily lunch specials include a soup to start as well as a filling main course. Do not miss the particularly good *limonada de coco* (coconut lemonade).

Pastelería Mila BAKERY **$$**
(Calle de la Iglesia No 35-76; breakfasts COP$14,000-20,000, lunches COP$11,000-30,000; ⊙9am-10pm Mon-Sat, 10am-8pm Sun; 🛜) Cartagena's fanciest patisserie serves up breakfasts and lunches at this fashionable spot in the heart of the old town. The distressed walls and wooden beams create a contemporary vibe, while the leather banquettes are more in the grand style. The combo breakfast (pancakes with *dulce de leche*, sour cream, scrambled eggs and crispy bacon) might be considered a crime in other, less permissive jurisdictions.

Sopa y Seco COLOMBIAN, ITALIAN **$$**
(☑660-2213; Calle del Cuartel No 36-17, El Centro; lunch mains COP$12,000-15,000, dinner mains COP$22,000-43,000; ☺noon-3pm & 6pm-midnight) By day this casual but nicely designed Colombian place serves up delicious, simple lunches (try the *filete de pescado al ajillo*, fish filet in garlic, or the house specialty if you have room: *pargo rojo*, whole red snapper). Come evenings another dining room opens as Italian restaurant Da Roberta Scacco Matto, which serves more upscale classic Italian dishes.

★**El Santísimo** COLOMBIAN, FUSION **$$$**
(☑550-1531; www.elsantisimo.com; Calle del Torno No 39-76, San Diego; mains COP$39,000-45,000; ☺noon-11pm Mon-Sat, 1-4pm & 7pm-midnight Sun) A charming and refined atmosphere greets you inside one of Cartagena's most innovative restaurants. The menu here is a trip through Colombian cuisine, combining ingredients and reinventing classics as it goes. Evening meal deals allow you two hours of all-you-can-drink alcohol, a good deal if you like wine with your dinner. Highly recommended for an impressive culinary experience.

Agua de Mar TAPAS **$$$**
(☑664-5798; Calle del Santísimo No 8-15; tapas COP$10,000-25,000; ☺☺) This gorgeous and inventive place is one of Cartagena's most interesting restaurants, featuring titular water features and a very cool gin bar (where the friendly owner will create a mind- and wallet-blowing gin-and-tonic combination just for you). The gourmet tapas menu is full of interesting flavor combinations, and is particularly strong on seafood, as well as having plentiful vegetarian choices.

La Vitrola SEAFOOD **$$$**
(☑660-0711; Calle Baloco No 2-01, El Centro; mains COP$25,000-70,000; ☺lunch & dinner) Perfectly lit and comfortably furnished, this 400-year-old colonial home converted to a seafood restaurant is famous – and deservedly so. The *mero* (grouper) *Don Román*, with a tamarind, *nam pla* (fish sauce) and chili sauce, is the standout dish, but do your mouth a favor and hit the teriyaki octopus, too. There's a great wine list and live Cuban music. No shorts.

✗ Getsemaní

★**Gastrolab Sur** CARIBBEAN, MEDITERRANEAN **$**
(Calle del Espiritu Santo No 29-140; mains COP$8000-16,000; ☺5-11pm) This gem of a place is easy to miss if you don't know it's there. In the beautifully lit pebbly back garden of the Ciudad Móvil cultural center, the humming heart of the revivified Getsemaní community, it serves up delicious *aranchinas* (rice balls) with various flavors (try the *tríptico*, a combination of all three), *bruschettas costeñas* and pizzas. The staff is super friendly and it's also a great place to come for drinks.

Restaurante Coroncoro COLOMBIAN **$**
(☑664-2648; Calle Tripita y Media No 31-28, Getsemaní; mains COP$7000-13,000; ☺7:30am-10pm) This Getsemaní *comida corriente* institution is always heaving with hungry locals filling up on cheap set meals and delicious daily specials.

Casa de las Novias BAKERY **$**
(Calle Larga No 8B-126; ☺8am-8pm; 🛜) A wonderfully bizarre place for a superb coffee and cake, this is actually a wedding planner with its own charming cafe attached. Relish the low, low air-con and sip macchiatos served up in dainty decorated porcelain cups while deciding upon the perfect dress for your special day.

Gato Negro CAFE **$**
(☑660-0958; Calle San Andrés No 30-39, Getsemaní; mains COP$6000-9000; ☺7am-2pm Mon-Sat; 🛜) A favorite Getsemaní option that concentrates on a plain and simple breakfast menu – omelettes, crepes, muesli and continental breakfasts are all available – but does it well. There's a set lunch, too, and it's all served up in a colonial house with contemporary art on the walls.

I Balconi PIZZA **$$**
(☑660-9880; Calle del Guerrero No 29-146, 2nd fl, Getsemaní; pizzas COP$12,500-26,000; ☺4pm-midnight Tue-Sun) Perched above Havana bar, this is where you'll find the best pizza in Cartagena. The Italian owner is so fanatical about quality ingredients that he has commissioned a local cheesemaker and schooled him in the ways of gorgonzola and parmesan. The results are great. Service is impeccable and the room is breezy with cool art on the walls.

La Guacha STEAK **$$$**
(☑664-1683; Calle del Espiritu Santo No 29-07, Getsemaní; mains COP$27,000-50,000; ☺6-11:30pm Mon-Sat; 🛜) Sometimes you just need a large, rare steak and a glass of decent Malbec. When that call comes, answer it here.

The breezy, elegant room is all high ceilings and exposed brick, and the meat is superlative (especially the *punta de anca*, or topside of rump) – it's served in stylishly hewn and artfully charred hunks that ooze flavor. A steal at this price.

🍷 Drinking & Nightlife

Cartagena's bar scene is centered on the Plaza de los Coches in El Centro for salsa and vallenato, while along Calle del Arsenal in Getsemaní the clubs are bigger and the prices higher. Weekends are best and the action doesn't really heat up until after midnight.

You can go on a night trip aboard a *chiva* (a typical Colombian bus) with a band playing vallenato and all-you-can-drink aguardiente (easy, now). *Chivas* depart from hotels in Bocagrande around 8pm for a three- to four-hour trip, and leave you at the end of the tour in a club. Most agencies and hostels can book this for you.

★ Café Havana   CLUB
(cnr Calles del Guerrero & de la Media Luna, Getsemaní; cover COP$10,000; ☺ 8pm-4am Thu-Sat, 5pm-2am Sun) Café Havana has it all: live salsa from horn-blowing Cubans, strong drinks, a gorgeous horseshoe bar surrounded by brilliant eccentrics, wood-paneled walls and a ceiling full of whirring fans. This was where Hillary Clinton chose to take the party during the Summit of the Americas in 2012, and rightly so; it's still the best bar in town.

★ Bazurto Social Club   CLUB
(www.bazurtosocialclub.com; Av del Centenario No 30-42; cover COP$5000; ☺ 7pm-3:30am Wed-Sat) Join the crowds at this wonderfully lively spot where locals dance in unison under an enormous glowing red fish to live *champeta* music; sip knock-out cocktails; and catch up on the local Getsemaní gossip. The music is great, and even if you don't feel like dancing, after a few drinks you'll find yourself being dragged in.

Laboratorio   COCKTAIL BAR
(Calle de la Media Luna No 10-20; ☺ 6pm-4am Tue-Sun; 🛜) This Media Luna place distinguishes itself with low lighting, bottles of pickles and other delicacies displayed on the walls, and a zinging cocktail list served up by charming and efficient staff. There's also a distinctly happy hour from 6pm to 10pm – what's not to love?

Tu Candela   CLUB
(☑ 664-8787; El Portal de los Dulces No 32-25, El Centro; ☺ 8pm-4am) Wall-to-wall reggaeton, vallenato, merengue and some decent salsa. Tu Candela is always cramped – but the atmosphere is cool and anything goes. This is the place that Barack Obama's errant Secret Service detail famously began their cocaine and prostitute exploits, and it's easy to see why: this place is off the hook.

Convert the cover charge to cocktails at the bar, and make sure Secret Service agents pay you up front.

Donde Fidel   BAR
(☑ 664-3127; El Portal de los Dulces No 32-09, El Centro; ☺ 11am-2am) The sound system here, when it kicks, has been known to reduce grown men to tears – as does the extraordinary salsa collection of Don Fidel himself. This is music of love, loss and lament. A Cartagena institution, it hosts smooching couples dancing in alcoves under portraits of the owner and various gurning megastars. The vast seated terrace is perfect for people-watching.

Bar Ético   CLUB
(Calle de la Media Luna No 10-56; cover COP$10,000; ☺ 9pm-3am) The darkness in this salsa club is split by spotlights picking out young dancing couples making the most of the free aguardiente that their COP$10,000 cover grants them. The back room features live music at weekends, and despite its location on the main backpacker strip, there's nary a non-Colombian to be seen here.

Il Italiano   CLUB
(☑ 664-7005; Av del Arsenal No 8B-137, Getsemaní; cover COP$15,000; ☺ 9pm-4am) This massive, multispace club is a curiosity. Is it a rock club? A salsa joint? A pumping house club? A vallenato hot spot? It's all of the above, and is as crowded as it is flirty. Try to ignore the decor and get on the floor instead.

Quiebra-Canto   CLUB
(☑ 664-1372; Camellon de los Martines, Edificio Puente del Sol, Getsemaní; ☺ 7pm-4am Tue-Sat) It gets tight with an eclectic crowd of all shapes and sizes at this excellent Getsemaní spot for salsa, son and reggae. It's on the 2nd floor overlooking Pegasos and the clock tower. Purists insist the salsa here is hotter than at rival bar Café Havana, but its crowd tends to be less exciting.

Café del Mar
BAR

(📞664-6513; Baluarte de Santo Domingo, El Centro; cocktails COP$18,000-35,000; ⏱5pm-late) Ocean breezes swoop in off the coast and bring a relaxing freshness to this touristy outdoor lounge perching on the western ramparts of the old city. Dress up a notch or two and be prepared to pay COP$10,000 for a beer if you want to blend in. The view is unbeatable.

La Casa de la Cerveza
BAR

(📞664-9261; Baluarte San Lorenzo del Reducto, Getsemaní; ⏱4pm-4am) A chic spot set high atop the city's walls with stupendous views out toward Castillo de San Felipe. Drinks are pricey – you're paying for the view.

☆ Entertainment

Cartagena's local soccer team, Real Cartagena, plays games at **Estadio Olímpico Jaime Merón León** (Villa Olímpico), located 5km south of the city. Games run throughout the year. Buy tickets at the stadium. A taxi there will cost around COP$12,000.

🛍 Shopping

Cartagena has a wide range of shops selling crafts and souvenirs, and the quality of the goods is usually high. The biggest tourist shopping center in the walled city is Las Bóvedas (p128), which offers handicrafts, clothes, souvenirs and the like. The best wares here are at **Artesanías India Catalina II** (No 6) for homewares and art; **D'Yndias** (No 15) for high-quality hammocks and handbags; and **La Garita** (No 23) for colorful kitchenware, T-shirts and better-quality general merchandise.

Ábaco
BOOKS

(📞664-8338; cnr Calles de la Iglesia & de la Mantilla; ⏱9am-9pm Mon-Sat, 3-9pm Sun) A good selection of books on Cartagena and a few English-language choices, including everything ever written by a certain Gabriel García Márquez. There's also Italian beer, Spanish wine and strong espresso.

Colombia Artesanal
HANDICRAFTS

(www.colombiaartesanal.com; Callejón de los Estribos No 2-78) A set of several stores in the old town offers an excellent selection of brightly hued Colombian handicrafts from all over the country. The salespeople are extremely knowledgeable and can offer fascinating insights into the making and history of each piece.

Upalema
HANDICRAFTS

(📞664-5032; Calle San Juan de Dios, Edificio Rincon No 3-99, El Centro; ⏱9:30am-10pm Mon-Sat, 10am-10pm Sun) For something unique, head here for exclusive artisan homewares and handicrafts that aren't reproduced anywhere on the street. It's pricey, but it's top-quality stuff, unrivaled elsewhere.

ℹ Information

DANGERS & ANNOYANCES

Cartagena is the safest metropolis in Colombia – around 2000 police officers patrol the old city alone. That said, don't flaunt your wealth, and stay alert at night in less populated areas such as Getsemaní and particularly La Matuna. You are more likely to be irritated by peddlers than become a victim of any crime. Aggressive hassling in the streets by unofficial vendors selling tourist tat, women or cocaine is definitely the No 1 nuisance here. A simple 'No quiero nada' ('I want nothing') should shoo them away.

EMERGENCY

Hospital Naval de Cartagena (📞655-4306; Carrera 2 No 14-210, Bocagrande; ⏱24hr) Hospital with hyperbaric chamber.

MONEY

Casas de cambio (currency exchanges) and banks are ubiquitous in the historic center, especially around Plaza de los Coches and Plaza de la Aduana. Compare rates before buying. There are many street 'moneychangers' fluttering around Cartagena offering fantastic rates; they are all, without exception, expert swindlers, so don't even think of changing money on the street. There's a real lack of ATMs in El Centro and San Diego; however, there's a proliferation on Av Venezuela.

POST

4-72 (Calle 8B, Edificio Villa Anamaria, Local 1, Bocagrande; ⏱8am-5pm Mon-Fri, to noon Sat) Post office.

TOURIST INFORMATION

Tourist Office (Turismo Cartagena de Indias; 📞660-1583; www.turismocartagenadeindias. com; Plaza de la Aduana; ⏱9am-noon & 1-6pm Mon-Sat, 9am-5pm Sun) The main tourist office has a friendly and helpful English-speaking staff. There are also small booths in Plaza de San Pedro Claver and Plaza de los Coches as well as the administrative offices at Muelle Turístico.

TRAVEL AGENCIES

Aventure Colombia (📞314-588-2378, 660-9721; www.aventurecolombia.com; Calle de la Factoría No 36-04; ⏱9am-noon & 2-7pm

Mon-Thu, 9am-7pm Fri & Sat) A superfriendly English-speaking French-Colombian outfit that offers excursions around Cartagena and the coast, including La Guajira, Ciudad Perdida and PNN Tayrona. Highly recommended.

VISA INFORMATION

Ministerio de Relaciones Exteriores (☑ 666-0172; Carrera 20B No 29-18, Pie de la Popa; ◷ 8am-noon & 2-5pm) Immigration and visa extensions office, located about 1km east of the old town. Plan on a half-day minimum to get it sorted.

❶ Getting There & Away

AIR

All major Colombian carriers operate flights to and from Cartagena. There are flights to Bogotá, Cali, Medellín, San Andrés and many other major cities. Internationally the city is connected to Panama, Miami, Fort Lauderdale and New York.

The terminal has four ATMs and a *casa de cambio* (in domestic arrivals), which changes cash and traveler's checks.

BOAT

Sailboat is a popular way to get to Panama. Various boats leave from Cartagena to Panama via the San Blas Archipelago and vice versa, but there is no set schedule. The trip normally takes five days and includes three days in San Blas for snorkeling and island-hopping. Trips tend to come in at around US$450 to US$650 all inclusive per person, but this varies as there are many factors involved.

Most boats arrive in the Panamanian ports of Portobelo or Porvenir. A few go to Colón, which is a tough town and a place where you should take taxis everywhere. It's easy to connect to Panama City from all three ports.

The industry has been transformed in recent years by **Blue Sailing** (☑ 321-687-5333, 310-704-0425; www.bluesailing.net; Calle San Andrés No 30-47), a Colombian-American run agency that has sought to legalize what has always been an unregulated business. Currently Blue Sailing represents 22 boats, and ensures all have proper safety equipment for open sea navigation. It also monitors boats' locations 24 hours a day and uses only licensed captains. It is therefore highly recommended to find a boat for the trip through Blue Sailing to ensure a safe and legal crossing. There is normally a daily departure, even in low season; simply email Blue Sailing with your preferred departure dates and staff will try to hook you up with a boat.

Other agencies in Cartagena offer boat crossings, but do ask to see evidence of safety equipment and the captain's license. Ideally also ask around and check online for any reviews of the boat and crew before committing to a crossing.

For those travelers with less than five days to spare, **Ferry Xpress** (☑ 368-0000; www.ferry xpress.com) offers a regular 1000-person passenger ferry service (seat/cabin one way US$99/155, 18 hours) between Cartagena and Colón. Ferries depart Cartagena Tuesdays and Thursdays, and return from Colón Mondays and Wednesdays. It's possible to take cars on the ferry.

BUS

If heading to Barranquilla or Santa Marta, the easiest option is to leave from the **Berlinastur Terminal** (www.berlinastur.com; off Calle 47 & Carrera 3), a short taxi ride from the old town. Air-conditioned minibuses depart from here every 20 minutes from 5am to 8pm, stopping first in Barranquilla (COP$18,000, two hours) and then in Santa Marta (COP$36,000, four hours).

An even better, but pricier option for this route is the **MarSol** (☑ 656-0302; www.transportes-marsol.net) bus between Cartagena and Santa Marta (COP$42,000, three hours). It picks you up from any hotel or hostel, skips Barranquilla entirely and then drops you at any hotel or hostel in Santa Marta. There are two buses a day; simply call at least a day ahead to reserve your seats.

For other destinations, including for cheaper tickets to Barranquilla and Santa Marta, you'll need to head to Cartagena's main bus terminal. It's on the eastern outskirts of the city, far away from the center – give yourself 45 minutes to get there in all but the darkest hours.

Several bus companies serve Bogotá and Medellín throughout the day. Among them, **Expreso Brasilia** (☑ 663-2119; www.expresobrasilia. com) heads to Bogotá (from COP$80,000, 18 hours, six buses daily) and Medellín (from COP$40,000, 12 hours, six buses daily). **Unitransco** (☑ 663-2067) serves Barranquilla (COP$12,000, 2½ hours, hourly) with continuing services to Santa Marta (COP$25,000, four hours, hourly). **Caribe Express** (☑ 371-5132) runs a 7am service to Mompox (COP$50,000, six hours, daily) and a 6:30am service to Tolú (COP$25,000, three hours, daily). There are additional buses to Barranquilla throughout the day, where you can change for Santa Marta. For Montería, Expreso Brasilia leaves every 45 minutes from 6:30am to 3:30pm (COP$50,000, five hours).

If you can't get a seat on the daily bus to Mompox and want to go the alternative route via Mangangue, **Torcoroma** (☑ 663-2379) leaves at 5:30am and every 30 minutes until noon (COP$40,000, three hours) and Expreso Brasilia departs at 10:30am (COP$40,000).

For Riohacha on La Guajira Peninsula, **Rapido Ochoa** (☑ 663-2119) has a couple of daily departures (COP$35,000, eight hours). This is the best way to get to Venezuela as well. Change in

Riohacha for services to Maracaibo, where you can pick up transport to Caracas.

On overland trips to Panama, head to Montería (COP$50,000, five hours), where you can switch for buses to Turbo (from COP$30,000, five hours). It's worth noting that if you do not leave Cartagena before 11am, you risk missing the last bus for Turbo and will have to sleep in Montería. From Turbo you can take the boat to Sapzurro the following morning, from where there are regular launches to Obaldia.

❶ Getting Around

TO/FROM THE AIRPORT

The 3km trip to and from the airport in Crespo is serviced by frequent local buses. There are also *colectivos* to Crespo (COP$1500), as well as nicer air-conditioned shuttles called Metrocar (COP$2000), both of which depart from Monumento a la India Catalina. (For Metrocar, look for the green-signed buses.)

By taxi, there's a surcharge of COP$4000 on airport trips. It costs COP$9000 to COP$12,000 from the center to the airport, while coming from the airport into town there's a flat fee of COP$10,000 to Getsemaní, San Diego and El Centro.

TO/FROM THE BUS STATION

Large green-and-red-signed Metrocar buses shuttle between the city and the bus terminal every 15 to 30 minutes (COP$2500, 40 minutes). In the center, you can catch them on Av Santander. A taxi from the bus station to El Centro costs COP$15,000 plus an additional COP$5000 after 8pm.

Fuerte de San Fernando & Batería de San José

On the southern tip of the Isla de Tierrabomba, at the entrance to the Bahía de Cartagena through the Bocachica strait, lies **Fuerte de San Fernando** (admission COP$9000). This fort, together with **Batería de San José** on the opposite side of the strait, once guarded access to the bay. A heavy chain was strung between the two forts to prevent surprise attacks in the 1700s.

Originally, there were two gateways to Cartagena Bay – Bocachica and Bocagrande. Bocagrande was partially blocked by a sandbank and two ships that sank there. An undersea wall was built after Vernon's attack in order to strengthen the natural barrage and to make the channel impassable to ships. It is still impassable today and all ships and boats have to go through Bocachica.

The fort of San Fernando was built between 1753 and 1760 and was designed to withstand any siege. It had its own docks, barracks, sanitary services, kitchen, infirmary, storerooms for provisions and arms, two wells, a chapel and even a jail, much of which can still be seen today.

The fortress can be reached only by water. Water taxis departing from Muelle Turístico de la Bodeguita (p129) in Cartagena do the journey for COP$10,000. If you require a guide, plan on an additional COP$10,000.

Islas del Rosario

This archipelago, about 35km southwest of Cartagena, consists of 27 small coral islands, including some tiny islets. The archipelago is surrounded by coral reefs, where the color of the sea ranges from turquoise to purple. The whole area has been declared a national park, the PNN Corales del Rosario y San Bernardo. Sadly, warm water currents have eroded the reefs around Islas del Rosario, and the diving is not as good as it once was. But water sports are still popular and the two largest islands, **Isla Grande** and **Isla del Rosario**, have inland lagoons and some tourist facilities, such as hotels and a resort.

Tours

The usual way to visit the park is on a one-day boat tour of the islands. Tours depart year-round from the Muelle Turístico de la Bodeguita (p129) in Cartagena. Boats leave between 8am and 9am daily and return roughly between 4pm and 6pm. The cruise office at the *muelle* (pier) sells tours (COP$70,000 per person). There are also a number of smaller operators offering tours from the pier, often at lower prices. Popular budget hotels in Cartagena sell tours too, and may offer lower prices – COP$40,000 is common. Tours usually include lunch, but do not include port taxes and the national park entrance fees and aquarium entry; check with your tour operator to confirm.

The boats all take a similar route to the islands, though it may differ a little between small and large boats. They all go through the Bahía de Cartagena and into the open sea through the Bocachica strait, passing between Batería de San José and, directly opposite, the Fuerte de San Fernando. The boats then cruise among the islands (there is generally Spanish narration along the way) and stop at the tiny **Isla de San Martín**

Around Cartagena

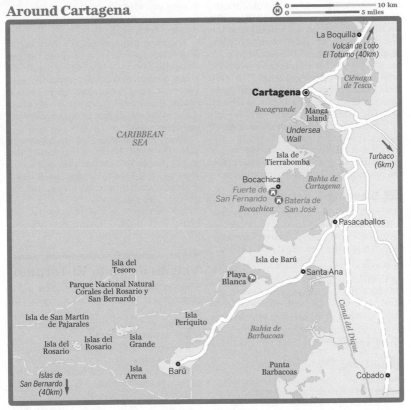

de Pajarales. Here there is an aquarium (COP$30,000) and a shady wooded area to chill out in for those who opt not to visit the aquarium, or you can have a swim while you hang around and wait for the trip to continue. The boats then take you to **Playa Blanca** on the Isla de Barú for lunch and two hours or so of free time.

🛏 Sleeping & Eating

The islands have some tourist infrastructure so you can stay overnight, go sunbathing, swimming, diving or snorkeling, or just take it easy in a hammock.

Eco Hotel Las Palmeras　　GUESTHOUSE $$
(📲 314-584-7358; Isla Grande; hammock/r per person incl full board COP$70,000/110,000) 🍃 This Isla Grande ecotourism option is run by the charming Ana Rosa. It's all very basic and rustic, but it's a wonderful place to disconnect from the world. Canoe tours are offered

of the nearby lagoons; there's good snorkeling nearby; and you're just a five-minute walk away from Playa Bonita, the best beach on the island.

Hotel San Pedro de Majagua　　HOTEL $$$
(📲 650-4460; www.hotelmajagua.com; Isla Grande; r & bungalows from COP$380,000; 🌀🛜) This high-end option offers stays on Isla Grande in chic stone bungalows with fiber-woven roofs and minimalist decor. There are two beaches and a restaurant. It's a very fabulous experience and feels much like being on a private island.

Playa Blanca

Playa Blanca lives up to its name – it is indeed a lovely stretch of sugary sand and one of the finest beaches around Cartagena. But development is encroaching and it can feel extremely overcrowded during high season.

The beach is located about 20km southwest of Cartagena, on the Isla de Barú. It's usually a stop for boat tours heading to the Islas del Rosario; when the boat tours arrive, peddlers descend upon the tourists, which has the potential to turn an otherwise idyllic beach into a two-hour challenge. The only thing worth buying is *cocada,* a sweet coconut treat that comes in a variety of flavors. To be fair, though, this is how folks here earn their living, as invasive as their hawking of wares may sometimes seem.

This spot is also good for snorkeling, as the coral reef begins just off the beach. You can rent gear for COP$5000 on the beach.

🛏 Sleeping & Eating

The beach has some rustic places to stay, and before 10am and after 4pm the place is wonderfully deserted. A few restaurants serve up fresh fish and rice for around COP$20,000.

La Estrella   CABIN $
(☑ 312-602-9987; hammock COP$10,000; d from COP$50,000) If you want to stay close to the water, Jose, a friendly local, offers nice tents under thatched roofs that sleep three to four people, typical hammocks (with mosquito net) and a sand-floored hut or two.

❶ Getting There & Away

The easiest way to get to the beach is on a tour, but you'll find it far more peaceful at other times. Head to Av El Lago, behind Cartagena's main market, Mercado Bazurto, in a taxi (COP$7000), and ask the driver to let you off at the boats to Playa Blanca. Boats depart (when full) between 7:30am and 9:30am daily except Sundays. The trip takes one hour. Expect to pay COP$25,000, but never pay anyone until you reach the beach.

Alternatively, buses (COP$1500) marked 'Pasocaballos' leave throughout the day from the corner of Av Luis Carlos Lopez and Calle del Concolon in La Matuna. Ask the driver to let you off at the ferry across Canal del Dique (COP$1500). Once on the other side, take a moto-taxi (COP$15,000) to Playa Blanca. This route takes about three hours.

La Boquilla

A small fishing village and kitesurfing haven, La Boquilla sits 7km north of Cartagena at the northern tip of a narrow peninsula, bordered by the sea on one side and the Ciénaga de Tesca on the other. If you get up at 4am, you can catch locals at the *ciénaga* (shallow lake or lagoon) working with their famous *atarrayas* (round fishing nets) that are common in Colombia, particularly on the Caribbean coast.

There's a pleasant place known as **El Paraíso**, a five-minute walk from the bus terminus, where you can enjoy a day on the beach. You can also arrange a boat trip with the locals along the narrow water channels cutting through the mangrove woods to the north of the village. Negotiate the price, and pay upon return.

There is a collection of restaurants in **palm-thatched shacks** on the beach. These attract people from Cartagena on weekends; most are closed at other times. Fish is usually accompanied by *arroz con coco* and *patacones* (fried plantains).

Frequent city buses run to La Boquilla from India Catalina in Cartagena (COP$2000, 30 minutes).

Volcán de Lodo El Totumo

About 50km northeast of Cartagena, a few kilometers off the coast, is an intriguing 15m mound that looks like a miniature volcano. However, instead of erupting with lava and ashes, it spews forth mud.

The crater is filled with lukewarm mud, which has the consistency of cream. You can climb into the crater and frolic around in a refreshing mud bath; the mud contains minerals acclaimed for their therapeutic properties. Once you've finished, go and wash off in the lagoon, just 50m away.

The volcano is open from dawn to dusk and you pay a COP$5000 fee to have a bath. Bring plenty of small bills to tip the various locals who will pamper you during your time here – massaging you rather inexpertly, rinsing you off, holding your camera and taking photos. All in all, it's a lot of fun.

❶ Getting There & Away

El Totumo is on the border of the Atlántico and Bolívar departments, roughly equidistant between Barranquilla and Cartagena. The latter is far more popular as a jumping-off point for the volcano as it has better public transportation than Barranquilla and numerous tours.

A tour is by far the most convenient and fastest way of visiting El Totumo, and no more expensive than doing it on your own. Several tour operators in Cartagena organize minibus trips to the volcano (COP$30,000 to COP$40,000, depending on whether lunch is included). Tours can easily be purchased through almost any hotel.

NORTHEAST OF CARTAGENA

The departments of Atlántico and Magdalena sit northeast of Cartagena, where the highest coastal mountain range in the world, the Sierra Nevada de Santa Marta, begins to rise from the sea. The increasingly charming Santa Marta, a coastal colonial city, and the beautiful coastal and mountainous attractions around it – namely Parque Nacional Natural (PNN) Tayrona and Ciudad Perdida – are some of Colombia's most visited attractions.

Santa Marta

📝 5 / POP 448,000 / ELEV 2M

Santa Marta is South America's oldest surviving city and the second-most important colonial city on Colombia's Caribbean coast. But despite its long history and charming center, it gets a bad rap from many travelers, who rightly cite its unsightly urban sprawl and terrible traffic as reasons not to hang about here. The secret to Santa Marta is to use it for what it does well: hotels, restaurants and bars, and then get out to the slew of superb destinations nearby during the daytime. It's as a base that Santa Marta excels: come here for a destination in itself and you can easily be disappointed.

That said, following the pedestrianization of several streets in the center of town and the renovation of the lovely Parque de los Novios, Santa Marta is slowly gaining a bit more of its own charm, and you might well find yourself spending more time here than you imagined. The climate is hot, but the heat here is drier than Cartagena, and the evening sea breeze cools the city and makes it pleasant to wander about.

History

Rodrigo de Bastidas planted a Spanish flag here in 1525, deliberately choosing a site at the foot of the Sierra Nevada de Santa Marta to serve as a convenient base for the reputedly incalculable gold treasures of the indigenous Tayronas.

As soon as the plundering of the Sierra began, so did the inhabitants' resistance. By the end of the 16th century the Tayronas had been wiped out and many of their extraordinary gold objects (melted down for rough material by the Spaniards) were in the Crown's coffers.

BARRANQUILLA: COLOMBIA'S BIGGEST PARTY

Barranquilla is a hardworking industrial port town laid out in a tangled ribbon along mangroves and the Caribbean Sea, sweltering and hustling in the blinding sun, and is mainly dedicated to making money. It's notable for being the birthplace of Colombian pop goddess Shakira and for its annual **carnaval** (www.carnavaldebarranquilla.org; ⊘ Feb) – once a year the town clocks off, checks in its commonsense at the door, puts on its glad rags and goes wild as it throws the country's biggest street party.

This Mardi Gras celebration is second in size only to that in Rio de Janeiro, making it South America's second-most important carnival. It's held in February on the four days before Ash Wednesday, so the date changes each year. Much like the carnival in Rio de Janeiro, there are street bands, masquerade and fancy dress, live performances and a riotous, slightly unhinged atmosphere as the town drinks and dances itself into the ground. It can be rough and ready, and you need to keep an eye on your possessions and your companions, but let your hair down and it could be a highlight of your trip.

Barranquilla is a huge urban sprawl, with its fair share of unsafe barrios. Most of the cheap accommodations can be found around Paseo Bolívar (Calle 34), but this area is seedy – just check the number of army personnel present even during the day. If you'd like to stay in a more pleasant environment, try El Prado. However, if you're coming for carnaval, be sure to secure your hotel reservations months in advance, or you'll have no chance at all. One place we recommend highly among Barranquilla's otherwise lackluster accommodations scene is the charming Italian-run **Meeting Point Hostel** (📝 320-502-4459, 318-2599; ciampani@gmail.com; Carrera 61 No 68-100; dm/r from COP$15,000/40,000; ❀ 🛜).

There's little reason to visit Barranquilla outside of Mardi Gras madness. At any other time of the year, you'll likely only visit the bus station on your way to much more agreeable Santa Marta or Minca, and your experience of Barranquilla will simply be of its bad traffic.

Santa Marta

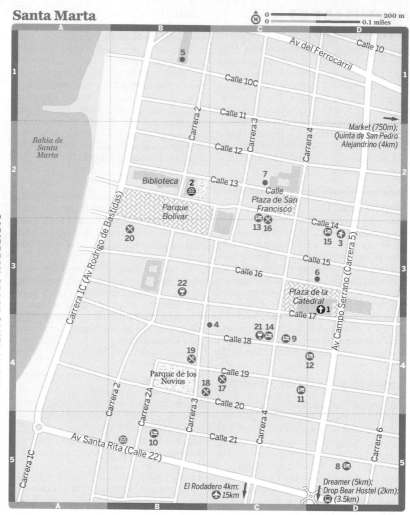

Santa Marta was also one of the early gateways to the interior of the colony. It was from here that Jiménez de Quesada set off in 1536 for his strenuous march up the Magdalena Valley to found Bogotá two years later.

Engaged in the war with the Tayronas and repeatedly ransacked by pirates, Santa Marta didn't have many glorious moments in its colonial history and was soon overshadowed by its younger, more progressive neighbor, Cartagena. An important date remembered nationwide in Santa Marta's history is December 17, 1830, when Simón Bolívar died here, after bringing independence to six Latin American countries.

⊙ Sights

The principal tourist seaside boulevard is Av Rodrigo de Bastidas (Carrera 1C), which is alive until late at night. From here there's a good view over the bay and a small, rocky island – El Morro – offshore.

Most tourist activity occurs between the waterfront and Av Campo Serrano (Carrera 5), the main commercial street. The beach resort of El Rodadero, 5km south of the center, is popular with Colombian holiday-

Santa Marta

makers. Buses shuttle frequently between the center and El Rodadero; the trip takes 15 minutes.

Museo del Oro
MUSEUM

(Calle 14 No 1-37; ⊙ 11am-6pm) **FREE** The Gold Museum is in the fine colonial mansion known as the Casa de la Aduana (Customs House) and was fully renovated in 2014. It has an interesting collection of Tayrona objects, mainly pottery and gold, as well as artifacts of the indigenous Kogi and Arhuaco. Don't miss the impressive model of Ciudad Perdida, especially if you plan on visiting the real thing.

Catedral
CHURCH

(cnr Carrera 4 & Calle 17) This massive white-washed cathedral claims to be Colombia's oldest church, but work wasn't actually completed until the end of the 18th century, and thus reflects the influences of various architectural styles. It holds the ashes of the town's founder, Rodrigo de Bastidas (just to the left as you enter the church). Simón Bolívar was buried here in 1830, but in 1842 his remains were taken to Caracas, his birthplace.

Quinta de San Pedro Alejandrino
MUSEUM

(🖉 433-1021; www.museobolivariano.org.co; Av Libertador; adult/child COP$12,000/10,000; ⊙ 9:30am-4:30pm) This hacienda on the outskirts of town is where Simón Bolívar spent his last days and died. At the time the hacienda was owned by a Spanish supporter of Colombia's independence cause. He invited Bolívar to stay and take a rest at his home before his intended journey to Europe. Several monuments have been built on the grounds in remembrance of Bolívar, the most imposing of which is a massive central structure called the **Altar de la Patria**.

Just to the right of this is the **Museo Bolivariano**, which features works of art donated by Latin American artists, including those from Colombia, Venezuela, Panama, Ecuador, Peru and Bolivia, the countries liberated by Bolívar.

Highlights among the wares in the house include an absolutely decadent marble bathtub. The hacienda was established at the beginning of the 17th century and was engaged in cultivating and processing sugarcane. It had its own *trapiche* (sugarcane mill) and a *destilería* (distillery).

The outstanding grounds, home to Santa Marta's 22-hectare **Jardín Botánico**, are also worth a stroll. Some of the property's trees alone warrant a trip out here. The *quinta* is in the far eastern suburb of Mamatoco, about 4km from the city center. To get here, take the Mamatoco bus from the waterfront (Carrera 1C); it's a 20-minute trip (COP$1500) to the hacienda.

👉 Tours

Santa Marta's tour market revolves around Ciudad Perdida treks, but the same agencies who offer these can also arrange various other hiking trips, plus bird-watching, mountain biking and visits to Minca and PNN Tayrona. Speak (in Spanish) with **José 'Chelo' Gallego** (🖉 316-232-5366; jose087301@hotmail.com) for tailor-made trips to the mountains. He's an expert with many years' experience. Other highly recommended agencies for local tours include **Aventure Colombia** (🖉 430-5185; www.aventurecolombia. com; Calle 14 No 4-80) and Expotur (p157).

🛏 Sleeping

There has been a real boom in both hostels and boutique hotels in Santa Marta recently, so you'll have plenty of choice. Be warned that it's considered unwise to walk in some streets north of Calle 10C after dark.

Dreamer
HOSTEL $

(☑433-3264; www.thedreamerhostel.com; Diagonal 32, Los Trupillos, Mamatoco; dm from COP$20,000, d from COP$70,000; 🌐🎤⌨) A very high-end, self-contained and intelligently designed hostel with rooms clustered around one of Santa Marta's best swimming pools. Even the dorms get air-con, a clean shared bathroom and good beds. It's hugely popular with discerning travelers. The Italian owners oversee the kitchen, so the food is fantastic, too.

It's a little way out of town, but in fact it's really well located for trips to Ciudad Perdida, PNN Tayrona, Minca and some of the better beaches in the area, meaning you don't have to face the crush of the city's traffic every time you head somewhere.

Drop Bear Hostel
HOSTEL $

(☑435-8034; www.dropbearhostel.com; Carrera 21 No 20-36; dm with air-con/fan COP$28,000/22,000, r with air-con/fan COP$90,000/75,000; 🌐@🎤⌨) Although it's housed in the former mansion of a drug cartel family, there couldn't be anything less shady about this bright and breezy hostel. Ask for a tour if you're interested – Australian owner Gabe believes there's still money hidden somewhere in the walls. Despite being located in a somewhat inconvenient suburb, the big rooms, great pool and superfriendly atmosphere keep travelers returning. A taxi here from the center is COP$6000.

Some of the private rooms, barely changed since their '80s heyday, are quite fabulous, and you might find you have a bathroom larger than most hotel rooms in Colombia. Definitely a quirky place, it's a good mix of a chill-out and party hostel, and will appeal to anyone who enjoys character.

Aluna
HOSTEL $

(☑432-4916; www.alunahotel.com; Calle 21 No 5-72; dm COP$25,000, s/d COP$70,000/90,000, without air-con COP$50,000/70,000; 🌐🎤) A lovely hotel with nicely proportioned dorms, cosy private rooms and spacious, breezy communal areas. The well-equipped kitchen has lockers, and the best book exchange on the coast speaks of an intelligent, widely read crowd. Ask owner Patrick about his place up in nearby Paso del Mango, which is a bird-watcher's paradise. Breakfast can be had in the ground-floor cafe, but isn't included.

★ Masaya
BOUTIQUE HOSTEL $$

(☑423-1770; www.masaya-experience.com; Carrera 14 No 4-80; dm COP$22,000-33,000, r incl breakfast COP$110,000-140,000; 🌐@🎤⌨) This fabulous addition to the hostel scene takes some beating. It's a clever and stylish multilevel conversion of an old mansion in the center of town, and has a bunch of superb-value dorms and gorgeous private rooms for those on a more generous budget. There's a busy rooftop bar, three plunge pools, a large outdoor kitchen and activities galore. Breakfast on the roof is an extra COP$7500 for those staying in dorms. The staff is kind and knowledgeable and the vibe superb.

★ La Casa del Farol
BOUTIQUE HOTEL $$

(☑423-1572; www.xarmhotels.com; Calle 18 No 3-115; r/ste incl breakfast from COP$160,000/350,000; 🌐🎤⌨) This 12-bedroom boutique hotel inside a mansion that dates from 1720 is run by the energetic Sandra, a Barcelona native who is quietly revolutionizing Santa Marta's hotel scene. The large rooms are individually decorated and named after a different city, and all have ancient tiled floors, high ceilings and roof beams. Staff is uniformed and the epitome of polite.

The rooms share a fantastic roof terrace with sumptuous cathedral views and plenty of recliners for lazy sunbathing. Sandra also runs **Casa del Agua** (☑432-1572; www.lacasadelagua.com.co; Calle 18 No 4-09; 🌐🎤⌨), **Casa del Arbol** (☑422-4817; www.lacasadelarbol.com.co; Calle 21 No 3-115; 🌐🎤⌨) and **Casa del Piano** (☑423-1572; www.xarmhotels.com; Calle 19 No 4-76; 🌐🎤⌨), three similarly priced and stylish converted mansions in the city center.

La Brisa Loca
HOSTEL $$

(☑431-6121; www.labrisaloca.com; Calle 14 No 3-58; dm with/without air-con from COP$35,000/20,000, r with/without bathroom COP$100,000/80,000; 🌐@🎤⌨) The 'crazy breeze' is the choice for a young, festive lot who crowd into the 100 or so beds here. Dorms run from four to 10 beds, and there's an array of private rooms too, all with firm beds, high ceilings, ancient tilework, and in-room lockers that even allow you to charge you phone securely while you're out. The hostel is centered on the lively bar, which has a friendly vibe, a pool table and lewd cartoons on the wall. New rooms have recently been added to the rooftop, which hosts big parties at the weekends. Look out for super-helpful, razor-witted Lola on the front desk, a very reliable source of information on Santa Marta.

A RITUAL HIGH: COCA LEAVES

As you travel up and down the Caribbean coast, you might see Kogi people hopping on local buses with bags full of seashells. But they're not collecting them as ornaments. The indigenous groups of the Sierra Nevada de Santa Marta collect them for a sacred, ritualized method of consuming coca known as the *poporo*.

The active alkaloids in coca leaves are a powerful stimulant when chemically refined into cocaine. When the leaves are chewed alone, they have little effect. However, when chewed together with an alkaline substance, their active ingredients are multiplied, enabling users to walk many kilometers without rest or food, even at altitude – handy if you live in the world's highest coastal mountain range.

For the *poporo*, thousands of seashells called *caracucha* are collected, roasted over a fire and then pounded into a fine powder. This powder is then placed into a hollowed-out gourd, known as a *totuma*, which represents femininity. Men receive this as they come of age.

Women of these tribes collect coca leaves and dry them by placing them into *mochilas* (bucket-shaped, woven shoulder bags) packed with hot stones. Men then take a large wad of leaves, put them in their mouths, and dip a small stick into the *totuma* to gather some of the powdered shell, which they suck off the stick. Any excess spittle and powder mix is wiped back on the outside of the gourd, causing it to grow – symbolizing wisdom. They then chew the mixture for up to 30 minutes, as their basified saliva causes the coca leaves to release their active components, giving users a slightly cocaine-like high. It is believed the *poporo* instills knowledge, just as reading a book or going to college increases students' intelligence.

Casa Verde HOTEL **$$**
(☏ 431-4122; www.casaverdesantamarta.com; Calle 18 No 4-70; r incl breakfast COP$174,000-232,000 ste COP$290,000; ❋🛜☷) If you're what the relaxed and attentive live-in owner calls 'a retired backpacker,' then this cute six-room spot – with pebble-lined walls and floors, smart bathrooms, crisp bed linen, and intelligently designed and pristinely whitewashed rooms – is for you. Lounge in the cooling pool near the lobby to feel more than a little like a Roman emperor.

✖ Eating

Santa Marta has some of the best food on the coast. An influx of Latin and North American restaurateurs has simplified the menus, focusing on ambience, classic cooking and stylish presentation. There's a huge number of places to choose from around Parque de los Novios.

★ Ouzo MEDITERRANEAN **$$**
(☏ 423-0658; Carrera 3 No 19-29, Parque de los Novios; mains COP$17,000-38,000; ☺ 6-11pm Mon-Sat; 🛜) Ouzo offers a stripped-back, classic Greek and Italian menu that includes superb pizza from a wood-fired oven and a good wine list. The octopus is slow-cooked for two hours in a garlicky broth, then slammed on the coals to sear and seal in the flavor. Great service, and a superbly designed interior means the heat stays in the kitchen.

El Bistró INTERNATIONAL **$$**
(Calle 19 No 3-68; mains COP$18,000-30,000; ☺ 11am-11pm; 🛜) A charming new venue just off Parque de los Novios, El Bistró has a fully translated menu that includes classics such as steak tatare, lamb shank, filet mignon and a delicious array of fish and seafood. The portions are big and there's great people-watching from the sidewalk tables.

Agave Azul MEXICAN **$$**
(☏ 431-6121; Calle 14 No 3-58; mains COP$18,000-25,000; ☺ dinner Mon-Sat; 🛜) OK, so you're not in Mexico. But bite into a perfect tostada that totters with toppings including the town's most tender meat; the sweetest, most buttery avocados; and a tart, crispy salad, and you might be forgiven for thinking you are. Presentation is superbly delicate. Steaks are amazing, too.

Radio Burger BURGERS **$$**
(Parque de los Novios; mains COP$15,000-25,000; ☺ 5-11pm; 🛜) This curious little restaurant is actually the site of Santa Marta's first-ever radio station, and it's now a burger-producing homage to the fact, crammed with antique radios. The burgers are delicious and there's a great outdoor seating area right on the square.

Tierra Negra COLOMBIAN $$$
(☑ 422-8421; www.tierranegra.co; Calle 15 No 1C-40, Parque Bolívar; mains COP$28,000-50,000; ◷ noon-3pm & 7pm-midnight Mon-Sat; 🕾) You have to know about this gorgeous place, tucked away up an unassuming staircase on Santa Marta's main square. Inside you'll find a beautiful dining space, both indoor and out, and a sumptuously inventive menu that's heavy on the seafood, but also has an impressive 'tierra' section too, such as braised lamb in peach sauce. One of the city's best.

🍷 Drinking & Nightlife

Parque de los Novios serves as an informal gathering place where young and old can crack a cold beer, meet friends, flirt and gossip before heading out to drink and dance till the dawn breaks.

Crabs BAR
(Calle 18 No 3-69; ◷ 8pm-3am Wed-Sat) A perenially busy bar with pool table, outdoor smoking terrace, decent-priced beers and spirits, and video screens paying homage to some of the more obscure monsters of rock.

La Puerta CLUB
(Calle 17 No 2-29; ◷ 6pm-1am Tue & Wed, to 3am Thu-Sat) Students and gringos eye each other up and get happily trashed in a beautifully benign Colombian style. Soca, salsa, house, hip-hop and reggae warm up the packed dance floor. The gusting fans surrounding it will make you and other dancers look dramatically windswept and much more attractive – especially after half a bottle of aguardiente.

ⓘ Information

4-72 (☑ 421-0180; Calle 22 No 2-08; ◷ 8am-noon & 2-6pm Mon-Fri, to noon Sat) Post office.
Aviatur (☑ 423-5745; www.new.aviatur.com; Calle 15 No 3-20; ◷ 8am-noon & 2-4pm Mon-Fri) Make reservations here for the concession's camping and higher-end options (Ecohabs) in PNN Tayrona.
Fondo de Promoción Turística de Santa Marta (☑ 422-7548; www.fonprotursantamarta.com; Calle 10 No 3-10, El Rodadero; ◷ 8am-noon & 2-6pm Mon-Fri, 8am-noon Sat) Santa Marta's member-based tourism office provides the best information for travelers.
Policía Nacional (☑ 421-4264; Calle 22 No 1C-74)

ⓘ Getting There & Away

AIR
The airport is 16km south of the city on the Barranquilla–Bogotá road. City buses marked 'El Rodadero Aeropuerto' will take you there in 45 minutes from Carrera 1C. Flights include Bogotá and Medellín.
Avianca (☑ 421-4018; www.avianca.com; Carrera 2A No 14-47; ◷ 8am-6pm Mon-Fri, 9am-1pm Sat)
Viva Colombia (www.vivacolombia.org; airport)

BUS
The bus terminal is on the southeastern outskirts of the city. Frequent minibuses go there from Carrera 1C in the center, or you can take a cab (COP$6000).

The main bus companies all offer several daily connections to the following:
Barranquilla COP$12,000, two hours, hourly
Bogotá COP$80,000, 18 hours
Cartagena COP$25,000, four hours, hourly until 5:30pm
Medellín COP$110,000, 15 hours

There are also buses to Riohacha (COP$20,000, 2½ hours) every 30 minutes until 5pm, all of which continue to Maicao (COP$25,000, four hours), the last Colombian town before the border with Venezuela. Here you can change for buses to Maracaibo (Venezuela). Don't linger much beyond the bus station – safety has improved dramatically in Maicao, but it remains the distribution center for all sorts of contraband from Venezuela.

There are also six daily direct buses to Tolú (COP$50,000, seven hours) and three to Bucaramanga (COP$80,000, nine hours).

Transport also leaves from the market in Santa Marta, found at Calle 11 and Carrera 12, a short walk from the city center.

Minca

☑ 5

Perched 600m high up in the Sierra Nevada above Santa Marta, Minca is a small mountain village famous for organic coffee and, perhaps more importantly, for much cooler temperatures than sweaty Santa Marta. The town is delightful, and has in the past few years grown hugely as a traveler destination, attracting backpackers who want a week or two off from the ardors of the road. It's a great base for mountain biking, birdwatching and hiking in the Sierra Nevada, offering fresh mountain air, more than 300 bird species nearby and sumptuous views.

🏃 Activities

Bird-watching and mountain biking are the two most popular activities here.

Marcos Torres López   BIRD-WATCHING
(☑ 314-637-1029;   marcostorres92@yahoo.com.co) Marcos doesn't speak English, but he has the sharpest eye in Minca, so much so that he gets international clientele traveling to bird-watch with him. He charges just COP$150,000 for a full-day bird-watching trip to El Dorado, including lunch and transport.

Francisco Troncoso   BIRD-WATCHING
(☑ 422-0500, 317-851-3155;   francisco_troncoso@hotmail.com) Francisco Troncoso is a well-established English-speaking bird-watching guide. He charges COP$205,000 per day, or COP$325,000 including transport.

Jungle Joe Minca Adventures   TOURS
(☑ 317-308-5270; www.junglejoeminca.com) Joe Ortiz can fix you up for a day of tubing, canyoning, horseback riding, rappelling, mountain biking or bird-watching. English speaking and very helpful, Joe gets wonderful reviews from past clients.

Lucky Tours   MOUNTAIN BIKING
(☑ 310-397-5714) Based in the Tienda Café de Minca, this mountain-bike specialist outfit is run by Andrés, who can take you on some superb trips, including the Kraken, a ride that takes you through 11 different ecosystems, and the Clockwork Orange, another world-class bike route.

Fidel Travels   TOURS
(☑ 311-683-2099; www.fideltravels.com) Fidel Travels has an office just by the church and offers bird-watching tours, visits to La Victoria coffee farm and trips to El Pozo Azul, a gorgeous spot for swimming.

🍴 Sleeping & Eating

Minca is full of guesthouses and small hotels, so finding accommodations is rarely problematic.

★Casa Elemento   RETREAT $
(☑ 313-587-7677, 311-655-9207; www.casaelemento.com; above Minca; dm COP$25,000, d from COP$70,000; 🐕) When they say 'above Minca' they are *not* kidding – just getting to this fantastic place is a great adventure and ensures that only the truly intrepid arrive. Created and run by an international crew,

Casa Elemento has an incredible position with extraordinary views and is the perfect place to escape the world. From Minca, it's a 30-minute, COP$15,000 motorbike ride.

The accommodations are simple and hostel-like, with a small pool, toilets that have views direct into the jungle and a busy restaurant-bar-hangout. The centerpiece is an enormous hammock where a dozen people can comfortably fit and drink in the views, and there are also zip wires between trees connecting platforms that are perfect for bird-watching. There's no wireless, which makes for an extremely social atmosphere, and otherwise the main activity seems to be disconnecting from the world.

Walk back down to Minca by all means, but only masochists walk up – take a motorbike.

Casa Loma   HOSTEL $
(☑ 313-808-6134; www.casalomaminca.com; hammock COP$15,000, r without bathroom from COP$65,000) Up the hillside beyond the church, this rustic place looks like one giant tree house. It has wonderful valley views, and a young and friendly management team. The rooms all come with mosquito nets, and look like something you might have dreamed about living in when you were aged 12. It's hard to beat the *mirador* room, though, with its fabulous balcony.

There's an on-site Italian restaurant, and more rooms are under construction a little further up the hillside.

Hotel Minca   HOTEL $$
(☑ 317-437-3078; www.hotelminca.com) This 13-room place is the closest thing Minca has to a formal hotel. It has large, simple rooms in a colonial-style building that was once a convent, surrounded by thick vegetation. Breakfast on the balcony is an incredible spectacle as hundreds of hummingbirds come to feed from sugar water put out for them by staff.

Lazy Cat   INTERNATIONAL $
(Calle Principal Diagonal; mains COP$12,000-20,000; 🕐 noon-10pm Sat-Thu, from 8am Dec-Feb; 🛜) This expat-run backpacker favorite is a great spot in the center of town for quesadillas, salads or a gourmet burger. There's a balcony overlooking the valley below, and the eponymous lazy cat can usually be found lounging around the place somewhere. Don't miss the fabulous mango cheesecake. In high season, set breakfasts cost COP$8000.

★**Casa d'Antonio** SPANISH $$$
(☑312-342-1221; www.hotelrestaurantecasadan
tonio.com; mains COP$22,000-58,000; ⊘lunch
& dinner; ☎) A five-minute walk from the
center of Minca, you'll find Antonio's charm-
ing house, where the Málaga native prepares
delicious Spanish-style seafood such as *pael-
la de mariscos* (COP$48,000 for two) or *pul-
po a la gallega* (Galician-style octopus) and
serves it up on his porch. Antonio also offers
good-value accommodations (COP$35,000
per person). Take the pathway that runs up-
hill from the Hotel Minca.

Do not miss the show-stopping lemon pie.

❶ Getting There & Away

Minca-bound *colectivos* (midsized buses) and
shared taxis (COP$7000, 45 minutes) leave
from outside the market on the corner of Calle
11 and Carrera 12 in Santa Marta. A faster option
for the same price is taking a moto-taxi to Minca.
However, these depart from Yucal, a barrio on
the outskirts of town, so you need to take a
COP$6000 taxi from anywhere in Santa Marta
to get there.

Taganga
☑5 / POP 5000

Taganga is something of a cautionary tale
about the overdevelopment of small towns.
What was once a tiny fishing village, set in a
beautiful, deep, horseshoe-shaped bay 5km
northeast of Santa Marta, seemed to have
hit the jackpot when it became a big back-
packer destination a decade ago. It drew a
diverse crowd of locals and travelers, and
led to the creation of a new middle-class of
hostel, restaurant and other small-business
owners. Business was booming, but many
locals found it hard to get a slice of the pie;
as a result, drugs began to be sold to the
backpackers, and this further socially frag-
mented the tiny place.

Over the past few years, Taganga has gone
from a near obligatory stop on the gringo
trail to a rather depressing place that looks
in part like a bomb has hit it. Poverty is rife,
the streets are unsafe after dark and it feels in-
creasingly like a town divided. That said, there
are still a number of travelers who continue to
come here for cheap accommodations, party-
ing and diving, as well as those who appreci-
ate the small-town vibe here in contrast to the
big-city feel of nearby Santa Marta.

The beach here is dirty and you're unlike-
ly to want to swim, but the beaches of PNN
Tayrona are just a short boat trip away, and

the diving remains cheap. For our money,
you're far better off in Santa Marta, PNN
Tayrona or Minca, but there are two excel-
lent restaurants here, and some travelers
still enjoy Taganga's vibe.

☂ Activities

Taganga is a popular scuba-diving center,
with plenty of dive schools offering dives and
courses. Four-day open-water PADI courses
range from COP$600,000 to COP$750,000,
but beware of the many cowboy operators.

Aquarius Diving Club DIVING
(☑422-2263; www.aquariusdivingclub.com; Calle
13 No 2-06) A five-star PADI diving center
right in the heart of the town. Charg-
es COP$150,000 for a two-tank dive and
COP$650,000 all-inclusive for open-water
courses.

Poseidon Dive Center DIVING
(☑421-9224; www.poseidondivecenter.com; Calle
18 No 1-69) Well-equipped and experienced
dive school; the open-water courses cost
COP$720,000.

☞ Tours

Taganga remains a popular and competitive
place to buy Ciudad Perdida tours.

Expotur TOURS
(☑421-9577; www.expotur-eco.com; Calle 18 No
2A-07) The Taganga office of this excellent
Santa Marta–based agency sells Ciudad
Perdida treks, tours of La Guajira and PNN
Tayrona as well as mountain-biking and
bird-watching trips.

Magic Tour TOURS
(☑317-679-2441, 421-9429; www.magictourcolom
bia.com; Calle 14 No 1B-50) ✐ This is the Tagan-
ga sales office for this well-regarded Santa
Marta travel agency. It offers tours to Ciudad
Perdida, La Guajira and PNN Tayrona.

Turcol TOURS
(☑421-9027; www.turcoltravel.com; Calle 19 No
5-40) One of the longest-established agen-
cies running tours to Ciudad Perdida. It also
runs tours to PNN Tayrona and La Guajira.

🛏 Sleeping

Casa de Felipe HOSTEL $
(☑316-318-9158, 421-9120; www.lacasadefelipe.
com; Carrera 5A No 19-13; dm COP$20,000-23,000,
s/d from COP$50,000/60,000, apt COP$100,000;
@☎) This French-run hostel is the best
budget option in town. It's also very secure,

ARACATACA: MAGIC & REALITY

Welcome to Macondo. Locals, maps, bus drivers and government officials will tell you it's really named Aracataca, and residents themselves rejected a name change in a 2006 referendum, but anyone who has read Gabriel García Márquez's masterpiece, *One Hundred Years of Solitude,* might be interested to know that the great author's place of birth was also the inspiration for the fictional town of Macondo, so beautifully described in the novel.

While Cartagena and Mompox are the main Gabriel García Márquez destinations in Colombia, with gorgeous Mompox looking today pretty much as Macondo is described, Aracataca is a place for diehard fans to head to. The workaday and largely modern place may not have much in terms of atmosphere or architecture, but it boasts the interesting and well-curated **Casa Museo Gabriel García Márquez** (☑ 5-425-6588; Carrera 6 No 5-46; ⊙ 8am-1pm & 2-5pm Tue-Sun) FREE.

The museum is housed in a reconstruction of the house in which García Márquez was born in 1927; the original house was sold by the family and knocked down decades ago. However, even though it's a fake, the buildings have been carefully re-created. Panels in each room describe various scenes from books that were set there and link the building's history to Gabo's work.

It's possible to visit Aracataca independently by bus from Santa Marta's market (COP$8000, 1½ hours). Alternatively, a recommended tour guide is **Darlis Contreras** (☑ 300-343-7366); she doesn't speak English but can show you around the rest of the town and point out other Gabriel García Márquez-related sights if your Spanish is up to it.

though be sure to take a taxi here after dark. It's in a beautiful house on lush grounds above the bay, and boasts great staff, pleasant rooms, a good bar, a kitchen, cable TV, numerous hammocks, an excellent breakfast and friendly folk from around the world.

Divanga GUESTHOUSE **$$**
(☑ 421-9092; www.divanga.com; Calle 12 No 4-07; dm COP$32,000-44,000, s/d per person incl breakfast from COP$74,000/94,000; ❄ ☎) Another French-run place not short on atmosphere – colorful local artworks don the walls and doors of the rooms, most of which surround a swimming pool. There's a rooftop deck and bar that catches a lovely sea breeze. It's more tranquil than Casa de Felipe, so opt to stay here if that's a priority.

✖ Eating

There are a couple of outstanding restaurants here, as well as plenty of cheap eats along the seafront.

★ Babaganoush INTERNATIONAL **$$**
(Carrera 1C No 18-22; mains COP$15,000-25,000; ⊙ noon-11pm Wed-Mon; ☎) This cosy rooftop restaurant has great bay views and an eclectic menu that keeps the crowds returning again and again. Try the excellent pumpkin soup, the perfectly cooked filet mignon or the sublime Thai green curry. It's up the hillside on the road toward Santa Marta.

Pachamama FRENCH **$$**
(☑ 421-9486; Calle 16 No 1C-18; mains COP$15,000-30,000; ⊙ 6-11pm Mon-Sat; ☎) You'll find Pachamama down a quiet backstreet in a small walled compound. With Tiki stylings and a laid-back vibe, it's like an indoor beach bar – but casual as it may be, the French chef has produced one of the most creative menus on the coast. The langoustines in bacon and tarragon are sensational, and the tuna carpaccio is perfect.

ℹ Information

In recent years Taganga's security situation has seriously deteriorated. Be careful at any time of day, and don't leave the main streets if you're on your own. Do not try to walk to Playa Grande, even though it's only a 15-minute stroll from the town; there have been numerous reports of robberies in broad daylight here. Always take taxis after dark.

There's only one ATM in Taganga, and it's always broken or empty. The nearest reliable ATMs are in Santa Marta.

The tourist information point is directly on the beachfront as you arrive from the main road.

ℹ Getting There & Away

Taganga is easily accessible; there are frequent minibuses (COP$1500, 15 minutes) from Carreras 1C and 5 in Santa Marta. A taxi costs COP$10,000.

From Taganga there's a daily boat to Cabo San Juan del Guía in PNN Tayrona. This leaves at 11am each day, and returns at 4pm from Cabo San Juan, though in the high season the boat makes three trips in both direction per day. The one-way cost is COP$45,000; the trip takes an hour and boats leave from the tourist information point. Note that you'll have to pay the PNN Tayrona entry fee (adult/student and under 26 years COP$38,000/7500) when you arrive.

Parque Nacional Natural (PNN) Tayrona

🕗 5 / POP 5000

One of Colombia's most popular national parks, Tayrona grips the Caribbean coast in a jungly bear hug at the foot of the Sierra Nevada de Santa Marta. The park stretches along the coast from the Bahía de Taganga near Santa Marta to the mouth of the Río Piedras, 35km to the east, and covers some 12,000 hectares of land and 3000 hectares of sea.

The scenery varies from sandy beaches along the coast in the north to rainforest at an altitude of 900m on the southern limits of the park. The extreme western part is arid, with light-brown hills and xerophytic plant species such as cacti. The central and eastern parts of the park are wetter and more verdant, largely covered by rainforest. May, June and September to November are the wettest periods. At least 56 endangered species call the park home, but most stay out of sight, deep within the forest.

The region was once the territory of the Tayrona people, and some archaeological remains have been found in the park. The most important of these are the ruins of the pre-Hispanic town of Pueblito (called Chairama in the indigenous language), considered to have been one of Tayrona's major settlements. The remains of more than 500 dwellings were discovered, estimated to have been home to 4000 people at one point in history.

For many travelers the park's biggest attraction is its gorgeous beaches, which are set in deep bays, backed by mountains and shaded by coconut palms. However, vicious currents mean that most are not suitable for swimming, though you can take a dip and snorkel (with great care) at a select few. Look out for the red flags and never go in the water where you see them; many foolhardy swimmers drown each year. Snorkeling gear is available for rental in the park. Mosquito repellent is essential and be wary of snakes in the area.

One important thing to keep in mind: high season attracts huge numbers of people. By far the best time to visit is the low season (February to November). Otherwise, be prepared for the possibility that much of Tayrona's undeniably world-class charms may be lost in the crowds.

◎ Sights

The PNN Tayrona can be entered at several different points, but wherever you enter, you'll need to pay the entrance fee (adults/ under 26 and students COP$38,000/7500). This entry fee is valid for as long as you care to stay inside the park, and you can also leave the park and re-enter at another entrance until 5pm on the day of purchase. Upon entering you may be searched for al-

Parque Nacional Natural Tayrona

cohol and glass bottles, neither of which are permitted in the park.

Tayrona's eastern part features most of the park's attractions and tourist facilities, and is by far the most popular and visited area of the park. Its main gateway is **El Zaíno**, 34km east of Santa Marta on the coastal road to Riohacha.

From El Zaíno, a 4km paved side road goes northwest to **Castilletes**, the longest beach in the park and the first place you can turn in for the night. A van plies the route constantly and charges just COP$2000.

A few more kilometers down the road is **Cañaveral**, also on the seaside. Here you'll find a campground, upscale cabañas (cabins) and a restaurant. The beaches in Cañaveral are very beautiful – golden sand and blue water – but there is no shade, and swimming can be dangerous because of treacherous offshore currents.

From Cañaveral, most visitors take a 45-minute walk west along a trail to **Arrecifes**, where there are budget lodgings and eating facilities – nowadays these are the best value and best managed in the park. Bear in mind that sea currents here are just as dangerous as those in Cañaveral, although decent, safe beaches are found nearby. If you don't want to walk to Arrecifes from Cañaveral, horses are available (COP$20,000 one way).

From Arrecifes, a 10-minute walk will take you to **La Aranilla**, a gorgeous, tiny cove framed by massive boulders, with chunky sand and glints of fool's gold dancing in the water. A 20-minute walk northwest along the beach will bring you to **La Piscina**, a deep bay with quiet waters, which are reasonably safe for swimming and snorkeling.

Another 20-minute walk by path will take you to **Cabo San Juan del Guía**, a beautiful cape with an absolute knockout beach. It's by far the most crowded area of the park. There is a restaurant and campsite here, including hammocks in a curious structure on a rock in the middle of the beach, where it's possible to spend a very atmospheric night.

From the cape, a scenic path goes inland uphill to **Pueblito**, providing some splendid tropical-forest scenery. It will get you to Pueblito in a bit more than an hour, but this path is definitely more challenging than others in the park – the majority of the uphill climb is over stones, some of them massive. It is not an easy trail and you can forget about it when it rains or if you have a large pack.

Not much of Pueblito's urban tissue has survived, apart from small fragments of the stone paths and foundations of houses, but it's worth seeing, especially if you aren't planning a trip to Ciudad Perdida.

From Pueblito, a path continues southwest to Calabazo on the main road. After five minutes, the path splits to the right down to **Playa Brava**.

Other entrances to the park include **Palangana**, from where it's possible to access **Bahía Neguange** by a rather rough road if you have your own transport. From Bahía Neguange, there are launches that take you to the nearby **Playa Cristal**, a gorgeous palm-fringed beach with several seafood restaurants, where you can enjoy fresh fish and a cold beer after your swim. Launches cost COP$70,000 per boat round trip – agree a time for your pickup with the captain as they constantly go back and forth.

🛏 Sleeping & Eating

Castilletes, the first point reached after entering from El Zaíno, offers peaceful camping with sea views. Cañaveral is favored by the well-to-do; Arrecifes is mainly popular with families and those wanting peace, quiet and clean bathrooms; while Cabo San Juan del Guía is the most popular spot with backpackers.

🛏 Castilletes

Camping Castilletes　　CAMPGROUND $
(📞313-653-1830;　www.campingcastilletespnn
tayrona.blogspot.com; campsite/tent per person COP$15,000/25,000) This campground sits on 1.5km of beach that is also the park's

Playa Brava
Cabo San Juan del Guía
La Piscina
Pueblito
Arrecifes
Cañaveral
Castilletes
Los Naranjos
Calabazo
Río Piedras
El Zaíno
Riohacha (175km)

0 — 5 km
0 — 2.5 miles

most popular spot for sea-turtle nesting. The beach is swimmable in September and October (other months are only safe for advanced swimmers). It's a good choice if you want to dump your bags and crash out.

Cañaveral

Campsite CAMPGROUND $

(campsite per person COP$15,200) This campground is right next door to horse stables, so you won't be taking in any tropical sea breezes. It's run by travel agency Aviatur; sites here can be booked at Aviatur's offices in Santa Marta (p146), through its office in Bogotá, or you can just turn up – but you'll need to bring your own tent.

Ecohabs CABINS $$$

(344-2748; www.aviaturecoturismo.com; 4-person cabañas incl breakfast from COP$642,000;) This colony of luxurious cabañas is a five-minute walk from the car park that marks the end of the drivable road into the national park. Each two-story cabaña is in the style of a Tayrona hut, has a minibar, a large shaded terrace, small flat-screen TVs and spectacular views. It's by far the nicest spot to stay, but it's overpriced.

Arrecifes

Camping Don Pedro CAMPGROUND $$

(317-253-3021, 315-320-8001; campingdonpedro@hotmail.com; hammocks COP$12,000, campsite per person with/without tent hire COP$14,000/12,000, cabañas incl breakfast COP$100,000) Of the three places to stay and eat in Arrecifes, this is the best. It's reached via a 300m split off the main trail just before Arrecifes. The spacious grounds are well maintained and have an abundance of fruit trees. Cooking facilities are available to guests, while excellent meals, including superb fresh fish, cost an average COP$12,000. The welcome is warm.

Yuluka CAMPGROUND $$$

(344-2748; www.aviatur.com; hammocks COP$30,000, campsite per person COP$15,000, 6-person cabañas incl breakfast from COP$432,000) This is by far the best option for campers, who can enjoy five-star bathrooms and a gourmet restaurant (although your main course may cost more than your bed for the night). The cabins, which sleep up to six people, are of high quality, though they lack sea views. You need to book via Aviatur (p146) in Santa Marta – walk-ins are not accepted.

Cabo San Juan del Guía

Camping Cabo San Juan del Guía CAMPGROUND $$

(314-385-2546, 312-604-2941; www.cecabosanjuandelguia.com.co; campsite COP$15,000, hammocks with/without view COP$25,000/20,000, r COP$150,000) Most backpackers end up at this campground, which has the air of a music festival in high season. There are two gorgeous swimming beaches here as well as a restaurant. For COP$25,000, you can sleep in the hammocks high atop the *mirador* on the rocks above the beach, giving fantastic views of the sea, beaches and mountains.

There are also two private double rooms on the top floor of the *mirador*.

Playa Cristal

Estadero Doña Juana SEAFOOD $$

(mains COP$20,000-40,000; 11am-4pm low season, 7am-4pm high season) Take a boat from Bahía Neguange over to gorgeous Playa Cristal (also known locally as Playa del Muerto – which translates to Beach of the Dead – little wonder they decided on a name change) and head straight for Doña Juana's makeshift beach restaurant. You'll be taken to the kitchen, shown various fish and asked to choose one, and it will arrive 20 minutes later, mouthwateringly prepared.

Los Naranjos

★**Finca Barlovento** HOTEL $$$

(313-293-6733; http://barloventotayrona.com; s/d COP$250,000/270,000) The single most beautiful spot in the area – and perhaps in all of Colombia – is just outside PNN Tayrona at Playa Los Naranjos. In this spectacular setting, where the Río Piedras bursts out of the Sierra Nevada and empties into the Caribbean, sits an architecturally unique home, clinging to a cliff face.

Finca Barlovento features open-air beds that jut out on a deck over the sea, so the waves crash right under your mattress. The food is simply sensational.

Palomino

5 / POP 4000

Palomino doesn't look like much as you pass through it on the main Santa Marta–Riohacha highway, but lurking on one side of its urban sprawl is one of Colombia's most perfect beaches, while on the other are the dramatic Sierra Nevada Mountains, a place the Wayuu people still guard carefully from outsiders. Palomino makes a great base from which to explore both, with a number of great places to stay and a backpacker vibe you'll not find in many other places along the coast.

The town lies between the Ríos San Salvador and Palomino, which flow from the Sierra Nevada de Santa Marta. Along its beaches you'll find Wayuu indigenous fisherfolk using traditional nets, while in its mountainous hinterland the Wayuu live their traditional way of life as they have done for centuries. With seven different ecosystems between the beach and the glaciers of the Sierra Nevada, it's no surprise that ecotourism is slowly coming into its own here.

Be aware that swimming from the beach in Palomino is only rarely possible, as currents are treacherous: look out for the red flags, and do not go into the water if they're flying. Take care at other times too. Thus the real reason to come to Palomino is to get into the mountains, for which the town makes a great base.

🛏 Sleeping & Eating

Unless otherwise stated, our recommended places to stay are on the beach, and all can arrange trips into the mountains for activities, including hiking, tubing or white-water rafting.

La Casa de Rosa CAMPGROUND $
(📞315-445-9531; campsite with/without tent hire COP$8000/6000, hammocks COP$8000) This is the simplest campsite on the coast, with bucket showers drawn from a well. The two twinkly eyed sisters, Milena and Paolina, are sweeter than *panela* (raw sugarcane juice) and will make you supper if you order in the morning. If Milena *really* likes you, she might kill you a cockerel.

Jaguar Azul HOSTEL $
(📞313-800-9925; www.jaguarazulpalomino.com; dm COP$20,000, s/d COP$50,000/60,000; 🛜) 🍃 It's a rather different approach to tourism that you'll find here. This place is not on the beach, but on the other side of the main road, in a barrio of Palomino known as La Sierrita. Here you'll find simple fan-cooled accommodations, a shared kitchen and a big garden that's full of fruit trees and backed by the mountains.

Instead of attracting beach bums, this place draws travelers interested in making it into the mountains, so it's a great place from which to arrange tours and activities. It's poorly signed – as you enter Palomino from Santa Marta, turn right by the gas station on your right-hand side; the hostel is on your left further down the road.

★Dreamer HOSTEL $$
(www.thedreamerhostel.com; dm COP$25,000, d from COP$110,000; 🛜🏊) This excellent new hostel on the beach is run by the same team running the original Dreamer in Santa Marta. Centered on a large garden with a fantastic pool, the tile-floored rooms here are spacious and have thatched roofs. There's a really social vibe, plenty of activities to keep you occupied, a busy bar and a superb restaurant that's busy all day.

Reserva Natural El Matuy CABINS $$
(📞315-751-8456; www.elmatuy.com; cabañas per person incl full board COP$170,000) There are two types of gorgeously rustic beach cabaña here, all with embroidered bedspreads, outdoor bathrooms and showers, and porches with hammocks. The newer ones sleep up to six people, while the older ones have a maximim of three. With light provided by candles only and no way to charge your cell phone or devices, this is a place to totally disconnect from the world.

Finca Escondida HOSTEL $$
(📞310-456-3159, 315-610-9561; www.chillandsurfcolombia.com; hammocks COP$15,000, dm COP$25,000, r from COP$80,000; 🛜) Run by a friendly international crowd, this large beachfront complex includes a number of rooms in various shapes and sizes, the better of which are huge and enjoy large balconies. The feel is rustic, with wooden buildings set in grounds full of fruit trees. A host of activities from surfing to pilates is offered, making it a firm backpacker favorite.

The attached restaurant, which has tables on the beach, is one of the best in town, and does excellent fresh fish and seafood served with ice-cold beers.

La Sirena LODGE $$
(📞310-718-4644; www.ecosirena.com; r/cabaña incl breakfast from COP$80,000/120,000; 🛜) 🍃 Airy beachside cabins with lots of space and a healthy, holistic vibe. The rooms have outdoor bathrooms and mosquito nets, and the larger cabañas are well worth the extra money. It's set amid a peaceful garden and takes

its enviornmental impact seriously. There's a minimum two-night stay (three in high season). The small, mainly vegetarian cafe here also comes highly recommended.

Hukumeizi HOTEL $$
(☎315-354-7871; www.turismoguajira.com; cabañas per person incl full board/breakfast COP$250,000/ 150,000; ☎☒) Fluttering white curtains lead the way into vast, minimally decorated rooms that are effectively open to the elements. The beds are huge; the showers are ultramodern; and even the beachside sofas are shaded. There's a great garden, a super beach-proximate pool and a suitably dramatic entrance to the entire place.

Suá COLOMBIAN $$
(mains COP$12,000-28,000; ⊙noon-9pm Wed-Sun) On the main road through town, Suá is one of the few restaurants in Palomino not associated with a hotel. The fare is inventive, with a fully translated English menu that includes specialties such as lion fish in a coconut, orange and ginger sauce; prawns marinated in garlic, sea salt and butter; and beef loin in a red wine and spice sauce.

It's poorly signed, but you'll find it across the road from the Ayatawacoop gas station.

❶ Getting There & Away

To get here, take the Mamatoco bus from the market in Santa Marta (COP$7000, two hours). Jump out at the gas station, and walk down to the beach or grab a moto-taxi to drive you the 500m there (COP$2000). Buses and motorbikes run all day and until late at night.

Ciudad Perdida

What could be more mysterious than the discovery of an ancient abandoned city? Ciudad Perdida (literally 'Lost City') was lost around the time of the Spanish conquest and only 'discovered' again in the 1970s. Deep in the Sierra Nevada de Santa Marta mountains, it remains only accessible on foot by doing what is easily one of Colombia's most exciting and breathtaking hikes. Known by its indigenous name of Teyuna, it was built by the Tayrona people on the northern slopes of the Sierra Nevada de Santa Marta. Today, it's one of the largest pre-Columbian towns discovered in the Americas.

The city was built between the 11th and 14th centuries, though its origins are much older, going back to perhaps the 7th century. Spread over an area of about 2 sq km, it is the largest Tayrona city found so far; it was most probably their biggest urban center and their major political and economic center. Some 2000 to 4000 people are believed to have lived here.

During the Conquest, the Spaniards wiped out the Tayronas, whose settlements disappeared without a trace under lush tropical vegetation. So did Ciudad Perdida, until its discovery by *guaqueros* (grave robbers) in the early 1970s. It was a local man, Florentino Sepúlveda, and his two sons Julio César and Jacobo, who stumbled upon this city on one of their grave-robbing expeditions.

Word spread like wildfire and soon other *guaqueros* came to Ciudad Perdida. Fighting broke out between rival gangs, and Julio César was one of the casualties. In 1976 the government sent in troops and archaeologists to protect the site and learn its secrets, but sporadic fighting and looting continued for several years. During this time, the *guaqueros* dubbed the site the Infierno Verde (Green Hell).

Ciudad Perdida lies on the steep slopes of the upper Río Buritaca valley at an altitude of between 950m and 1300m. The central part of the city is set on a ridge from which various stone paths lead down to other sectors on the slopes. Although the wooden houses of the Tayrona are long gone, the stone structures, including terraces and stairways, remain in remarkably good shape.

There are around 170 terraces, most of which once served as foundations for the houses. The largest terraces are set on the central ridge and these were used for ritual ceremonies. The vast majority of the site is totally unexcavated, as the indigenous people will not allow further investigation.

Archaeological digs have uncovered Tayrona objects (fortunately, the *guaqueros* didn't manage to take everything). These are mainly various kinds of pottery (both ceremonial and utilitarian), goldwork and unique necklaces made of semiprecious stones. Some of these objects are on display in the Museo del Oro (p143) in Santa Marta and in Bogotá. It's a good idea to visit the museum in Santa Marta before going to Ciudad Perdida.

☞ Tours

Previously, just the one agency, Turcol, had access to Ciudad Perdida. However, in 2008 the Colombian military cleared out the paramilitaries in the area, which has effectively

THE LOST CIVILIZATION

In pre-Columbian times, the Sierra Nevada de Santa Marta on the Caribbean coast was home to various indigenous communities, of which the Tayrona, belonging to the Chibcha linguistic family, was the dominant and most developed group. The Tayrona (also spelt Tairona) are believed to have evolved into a distinctive culture since about the 5th century AD. A millennium later, shortly before the Spaniards came, the Tayrona had developed into an outstanding civilization, based on a complex social and political organization and advanced engineering.

The Tayronas lived on the northern slopes of the Sierra Nevada, where they constructed hundreds of settlements, all of a similar pattern. Due to the rugged topography, a large number of stone terraces supported by high walls had to be built as bases for their thatched wooden houses. Groups of terraces were linked by a network of stone-slab paths and stairways.

Recent surveys have pinpointed the location of about 300 Tayrona settlements scattered over the slopes, once linked by stone-paved roads. Of all these, Ciudad Perdida (Lost City), discovered in 1975, is the largest and is thought to have been the Tayrona 'capital.'

Tayrona was the first advanced indigenous culture encountered by the Spaniards in the New World, in 1499. It was here in the Sierra Nevada that the conquerors were for the first time astonished by the local gold, and the myth of El Dorado was born.

The Spaniards crisscrossed the Sierra Nevada, but met with brave resistance from the indigenous people. The Tayronas defended themselves fiercely, but were almost totally decimated in the course of 75 years of uninterrupted war. A handful of survivors abandoned their homes and fled into the upper reaches of the Sierra. Their traces have been lost forever.

CARIBBEAN COAST CIUDAD PERDIDA

opened up the route to Ciudad Perdida to healthy competition. There are now four main agencies, based in Santa Marta and Taganga, guiding groups of travelers on the four- to six-day hike to the ancient ruins. You cannot do the trip on your own or hire an independent guide. If you're not sure about the legitimacy of your guide or agency, be sure to ask for the OPT (Operación de Programas Turísticos) certificate, the essential document needed by any guide.

Once the market opened in 2008, the race to the bottom began, and prices and quality fell. The government intervened by regulating prices and service, and the official price of the tour is now set at COP$700,000 – pay any less and the money will be taken from your guide's fees, health insurance or life insurance.

The price includes transportation, food, accommodations (normally mattresses with mosquito nets, though some agencies still use hammocks on one night), porters for your food, non-English-speaking guides and all necessary permits. The price does not go down if you complete the walk in fewer days. Most groups tend to do the trek in four days, but less fit walkers and those who want to take their time often do it in five. Six-day trips are the maximum; we recommend the four-day version.

Take the strongest mosquito repellent you can find and reapply it every few hours. Local brand Nopikex is excellent and will protect you better than many stronger, foreign brands. Take some long pants and a long-sleeved T-shirt, both of which are advisable at Ciudad Perdida itself, where the mosquitoes are particularly hungry.

Tours are in groups of four to 15 people, and depart year-round as soon as a group is assembled. In the high season, expect a tour to set off every day. In the low season, the agencies tend to pool resources and form a joint group, even if each agency still has its own guides. Other companies are middle-people for these agencies and there's really no reason to use them.

Do note that all access to Ciudad Perdida is closed (and thus no hikes depart) for the first half of September each year, when the indigenous peoples meet to perform cleansing ceremonies at the site.

The Hike

After meeting in Santa Marta in the morning, you'll be driven to the village of El Mamey (also known as Machete), the end of the road from Santa Marta, where you'll have a leisurely lunch before setting off. The walk normally takes 1½ days uphill to Ciudad

HIKING TO CIUDAD PERDIDA: WHAT TO BRING

The following items are broken down into the essential and less essential. Be aware that most camps have some kind of generator-powered recharging facilities, so it's not ridiculous to bring your phone and charger (for taking photos, at least – there is no mobile reception along the way!). However, do carry as little as possible, as you'll find the trip miserable if you take too much.

Must Have

➡ Flashlight

➡ 1.5L water bottle

➡ Insect repellent

➡ Sunscreen

➡ Long pants

➡ A different T-shirt for each day's walking

➡ Multiple pairs of socks and underwear

➡ Two pairs of shoes (ideally walking shoes for the hiking and strap sandals for river crossings)

➡ Multiple plastic bags (very useful for carrying wet clothing)

➡ Towel

➡ Ciprofloxacin and Loperamide (antibiotic and anti-diarrhea medicines)

Nice to Have

➡ Playing cards

➡ Band Aids or bandages for blistered feet

➡ Peaked cap

➡ Waterproof bag cover

➡ Sweatpants or pyjamas for the evenings

➡ Zip-lock bags to keep things dry

➡ Antihistamine pills to soothe mosquito bites, and cream to treat blisters

➡ Five extra pairs of socks

➡ A book or journal for the evenings

➡ Earplugs (for the communal sleeping experience)

Perdida, with a half-day at the site on the morning of the third day, then one full day's walking back downhill that is split over two days. The round trip covers 40km. In the dry season, the schedule can vary. Ask your tour company for a detailed itinerary. You walk in and out along the same route, which is a shame; travel agencies are continuing to negotiate with the indigenous people to grant access to a different route out.

The hike is challenging, but not mercilessly so; although each day covers only 5km to 8km, it's nearly all very steep ascent or descent. If you've never hiked before in your life, you'll find it tough, but even unfit first-timers complete the journey. At times, you will be scrambling alongside vertiginous river banks, clutching on to vines, and most people find carrying a stick helps with balance. Rainy season brings its own challenges, such as surging rivers; heavy, boot-caking mud; and collapsed walkways.

There are significant uphill slogs that can be brutal in the scorching jungle heat. When the sun isn't blazing, it's likely to be muddy, so you'll trade sweat for loose traction. The driest period is from late December to February or early March. Depending on the season, on day three you might have to cross the Río Buritaca multiple times, at times waist-deep, and finally, you will have to slog up Ciudad Perdida's mystical but slippery moss-strewn rock steps – 1260 of them in total – that lead to the site.

Along the way, the food is surprisingly good and the accommodations are comfortable, often located by rivers where you can cool off in natural swimming pools. The scenery is (obviously) nothing short of astonishing: this is a walk that is done at least as much for the journey as for the destination and, many veterans would argue, sometimes much more.

The site itself, a high plateau surrounded by blindingly brilliant jungle, is fascinating, and you will likely only be sharing it with your group and the few Colombian soldiers stationed there when you arrive.

It's important to be aware that the mountains are sacred to all the indigenous people that live there, so it's essential to leave absolutely no litter (and by all means pick up any you find on the route), and behave with respect within the Ciudad Perdida site.

Tour Operators

★**Expotur** HIKING TOURS
(☑ 420-7739; www.expotur-eco.com; Carrera 3 No 17-27, Santa Marta) The only agency that sends an English translator with every group, Expotur is also exemplary in terms of how it treats its staff and is one of only two agencies to pay their guides' social security contributions. It works with certified indigenous guides, with whom radio contact is maintained during the hike, and has a decade of experience offering Ciudad Perdida tours.

There are also offices in Taganga (p148) and Riohacha (p158).

Magic Tours HIKING TOURS
(☑ 421-5820; Calle 16 No 4-41, Santa Marta) A very highly recommended operator, Magic Tours has led the way in terms of treating its guides well, providing them with social security coverage, health care and pensions, while also doing much to ensure that tourism benefits the indigenous communities it affects. Guides are from the mountains, and are knowledgeable and certified. There's also an office in Taganga (p148).

Guias y Baquianos Tours HIKING TOURS
(☑ 431-9667; www.guiasybaquianos.com; Hotel Miramar, Calle 10C No 1C-59, Santa Marta) Located inside Hotel Miramar, this was the original agency to offer treks to Ciudad Perdida. Using guides that have at least a decade of experience (and often twice that), the company has strong relationships to the indigenous communities with which it works. Many of the guides themselves have farms in the Sierra Nevada.

Turcol HIKING TOURS
(☑ 421-2256; www.turcoltravel.com; Calle 13 No 3-13 CC San Francisco Plaza, Santa Marta) This agency has the most experience on the Ciudad Perdida route, starting in the 1990s, and has professional guides who work hard with its groups. It also has an office in Taganga (p157).

❶ Getting There & Away

Ciudad Perdida lies about 40km southeast of Santa Marta. It's hidden deep in the thick forest amid rugged mountains, far away from any human settlement, and without access roads. The only way to get there is by foot. The trail begins in El Mamey, a 90-minute drive from Santa Marta.

LA GUAJIRA PENINSULA

English pirates, Dutch weapons smugglers and Spanish pearl-hunters have all tried to conquer the Guajira Peninsula – a vast swath of barren sea and sand that is Colombia's northernmost point – but none were able to overcome the indigenous Wayuu people, who wisely traded with, or waged war upon, the invaders.

The Wayuu's complex and autonomous political and economic structures meant they were ready to mount a staunch defense of their lands – on horseback and, to the surprise of the Spanish, with firearms.

This is a diesel-and-dust landscape with more than a whiff of lawlessness. Its symbol might be a plastic bag caught in a bush. Smugglers shuttle back and forth to Venezuela, shipping their wares to the rest of Colombia and beyond. And then there's the Wayuu, living autonomously on the edge of the continent in small familial villages known as *rancherías*.

The peninsula is split into three sections: Southern Guajira, home to its capital, Riohacha; Middle Guajira, on the border with Venezuela; and Upper Guajira, where you'll find end-of-the-world paradises such as Cabo de la Vela and Punta Gallinas, the latter an immaculate collision of desert and sea that is the Caribbean coast's most remarkable setting.

Riohacha

📍5 / POP 213,000

Riohacha is the gateway to the northern, semiarid desert region of La Guajira, and was traditionally the end of the line. But as ecotourism in the peninsula has developed in recent years, Riohacha has become an unlikely mini traveler hub and you may well find yourself spending the night here on the way to or from more isolated and beautiful parts of Colombia. The town isn't teeming with things to do, but it's pleasant enough; there's a 5km-long beach strewn with palm trees, and the long pier, constructed in 1937, makes for a lovely evening stroll.

◉ Sights & Activities

The beachfront Calle 1 is the town's main thoroughfare, with Riohacha's main plaza, **Parque José Prudencio Padilla**, sitting two blocks inland between Carreras 7 and 9. The **Catedral de Nuestra Señora de los Remedios**, which has featured a venerated image of the Virgin on its high altar since colonial times, is also here.

The 1.2km-long **walking pier**, constructed in 1937, is an impressive work of maritime architecture. On weekend evenings, the **malecón** (boardwalk) and its parallel street, Carrera 1, fill with revelers taking in the waterfront restaurants and bars. Unless it's raining, you'll find Wayuu women in traditional clothing, selling handicrafts.

The main attraction around Riohacha itself is a trip out to the **Santuario de Flora y Fauna Los Flamencos** FREE, a 700-hectare nature preserve 25km from town in Camarones, which you'll pass if you're arriving here from Santa Marta. Pink flamingos inhabit this tranquil area in great numbers: up to 10,000 in the wet season (September through to December), and bunches of up to 2000 can usually be seen in one of the four lagoons within the park.

Admission to the park is free, but if you want to see the flamingos, you'll need to take a canoe (COP$30,000 for one to three people, and COP$15,000 per extra person) out on the water. The skippers usually know where the birds are hanging out, but will not take you if they are beyond a reasonable distance. Be warned – if it's not flamingo season, there's very little else to see here.

Tours

Expotur   ADVENTURE TOURS
(📍728-8232; www.expotur-eco.com; Carrera 3 No 3A-02) This outpost of the excellent Santa Marta–based agency specializes in tours to Punta Gallinas and all over the La Guajira Peninsula. It has excellent relationships with the Wayuu people and offers English-speaking guides.

Kaí Ecotravel   ADVENTURE TOURS
(📍311-436-2830; www.kaiecotravel.com; Hotel Castillo del Mar, Calle 9A No 15-352) This excellent agency opened La Guajira to ecotourism and has spent years fostering relationships with the Wayuu, allowing access to Punta Gallinas and PNN Macuira, both Wayuu-controlled. It's the best source for tours on the peninsula as well as homestays with indigenous families, and offers transportation-only deals to Cabo de la Vela if it has spare seats.

🛏 Sleeping & Eating

La Casa de Mamá   GUESTHOUSE $
(📍727-2859; Calle 9 No 3-51; r with air-con/fan COP$70,000/40,000; 🅿🛜) Mamá's digs are, at least until somebody opens a hostel here, the best value in town. Rooms are simple, but all have their own bathrooms. It's a friendly, family environment and you're able to use the kitchen to self-cater if you wish.

Taroa Hotel   HOTEL $$$
(📍729-1122; www.taroahotel.com; Calle 1 No 4-77; s/d incl breakfast COP$193,000/235,000; 🅿🛜) This brand-new 'lifestyle hotel' has raised the bar several notches in sleepy Riohacha. Here you have a modern, luxury hotel run by an all-Wayuu staff, but with a thoroughly international approach. Overlooking the beach, this tower block has enormous rooms, all with minibars, flat-screen TVs, coffee machines and balconies. It's the perfect place to recharge before a La Guajira trip.

Donde Aurora   COLOMBIAN $
(Carrera 8, btwn No 23-24; mains COP$8000; ⏰6:30-9:30pm) If you want to try *friche,* the Wayuu delicacy of goat stewed in its own blood and guts, take a cab here – but beware, it sells out by 7pm most nights. Donde Aurora is a tin-roofed shack with no sign, no name, no number and no menus, but the food is fantastic.

La Casa del Marisco SEAFOOD $$

(Calle 1 No 4-43; mains COP$20,000-40,000; ⊙11am-10pm; 🐟) This place, right on the seafront, packs in locals all day long with its deliciously prepared sea-plucked fish and seafood. Specialties include several types of fish casserole, *calamari al gusto* and *fritura de mariscos* (fried seafood).

Mantequilla WAYUU $$

(Calle 7 No 11-138; mains COP$15,000-25,000; ⊙11am-3pm & 6-10pm Mon-Thu, 11am-10pm Fri-Sun; 🐟) This bright and clean place won't win an award for character any time soon, but its meaty menu will be welcomed by anyone who has overdosed on fish and seafood on the coast. Also on the eclectic (and not particularly Wayuu) menu are wraps, sandwiches and pasta grills.

ℹ Information

Tourist Office (📞727-1015; Carrera 1 No 4-42; ⊙8am-noon & 2-6pm Mon-Fri) Located on the waterfront, this extraordinarily nice tourism office can help you with lodging, restaurants and information on trips deeper into La Guajira. Beautiful Wayuu handbags and hammocks are also for sale.

ℹ Getting There & Away

AIR

The airport is 3km southwest of town. A taxi costs COP$6000 from town. **Avianca** (📞727-3627; www.avianca.com; Calle 7 No 7-04; ⊙8am-6pm Mon-Fri, 9am-1pm Sat) operates two flights daily to and from Bogotá.

BUS

The bus terminal is at the corner of Av El Progreso and Carrera 11, about 1km from the center. A taxi to the bus station is COP$5000.

Expreso Brasilia (📞727-2240) has buses to Santa Marta (COP$18,000, 2½ hours) and Barranquilla (COP$25,000, five hours) every 30 minutes; hourly services to Cartagena (COP$35,000, seven hours) and services every 45 minutes to Maicao (COP$9000, one hour), on the border with Venezuela. There's a daily bus to Bogotá (COP$90,000, 18 hours) at 3:30pm, which also passes through Valledupar (COP$25,000, four hours).

Coopetran (📞313-333-5707) offers similar services to Santa Marta, Cartagena and Bogotá. It also has a twice-daily connection to Bucaramanga (COP$85,000, 12 hours).

Cootrauri (📞728-0000; Calle 15 No 5-39) runs *colectivos*, leaving as they fill up, every day from 5am to 6pm to Uribia (COP$12,000, one hour), where you switch for the final leg to Cabo

de la Vela (COP$10,000 to COP$15,000, 2½ hours). Just let the driver know you are heading to Cabo and they will drop you off at the switch point. The last car for Cabo de la Vela leaves Uribia at 1pm. Private rides to Cabo are available (COP$400,000; haggle and you might get it for less) and will take you and three friends there and back in a day, rushing through the highlights at break-neck speed, which kind of misses the point. You can also hitch a lift with Kaí Ecotravel (p158) for COP$50,000 if they have a spare seat; rides depart daily.

To visit Santuario de Fauna y Flora Los Flamencos, you must catch a *colectivo* from the Francisco El Hombre traffic circle, next to Almacen 16 de Julio, bound for the town of Camarones. The driver will drop you at the entrance to the park.

Cabo de la Vela

📷 5 / POP 1500

The remote Wayuu fishing village of Cabo de la Vela, 180km northwest of Riohacha, was until recently little more than a dusty rural community of Wayuu living in traditional huts made from cactus, right up against the sea. But in the last couple of years Cabo has become a hotbed of ecotourism and now boasts a wealth of indigenous-style accommodations. Still, the village has electricity by generator only and there are few fixed phone lines, internet or any of life's other distractions. The surrounding area is a highlight of the Upper Guajira and one of the most starkly beautiful spots in Colombia. The cape for which it's named is full of rocky cliffs above and sandy beaches below, all set against a backdrop of stunning desert ochers and aquamarines.

However, if you're looking for peace, Cabo is best avoided around Easter, December and January, when Colombians arrive to party.

◉ Sights & Activities

Wayuu and tourists alike head to **El Faro**, a small light tower on the edge of a rocky promontory, for postcard-perfect sunsets. The view is indeed stunning. It's a 45-minute walk from town, or you can wrangle a ride with a local for COP$30,000 or so for a round trip. Take plenty of water, insect repellent and a hat.

Just beyond El Faro is **Ojo del Agua**, a nicely sized crescent-shaped dark-sand beach bound by 5m-high cliffs. The beach gets its name from a small freshwater pool that was discovered here, a deeply sacred site for Wayuu.

But the jewel of the area is **Playa del Pilón**, far and away the most beautiful beach in Cabo. Here you'll find a startling rust-orange collection of sand backed by craggy cliffs that glow a spectacular shade of greenish-blue, especially at sunrise and sunset. In wet season, add in lush desert flora and fauna to the mix and the whole scene is rather cinematic (though in high season, you must add in 1000 tourists on the small beach and a few kitesurfers). **Pilón de Azucar**, a 100m hillside, looms over the beach and provides the area's most picturesque viewpoint, the whole of Alta Guajira displayed before you with the Serranía del Carpintero mountain range in the distance. Picture a tropical beach on the rocky coast of Ireland and you have an idea of the scene here. A statue of **La Virgen de Fátima**, erected here in 1938 by Spanish pearl-hunters, stands at the top of the viewpoint as the patron saint of Cabo.

Cabo de la Vela is also a notable center for kitesurfing. **Kite Addict Colombia** (320-528-1665; www.kiteaddictcolombia.com) offers personalized courses with one-on-one tuition and all equipment necessary at COP$100,000 per hour. You'll find it on the seafront next to the sign 'Area de Kite Surf.'

Sleeping & Eating

There are more than 60 rustic posadas (inns) in Cabo de la Vela that are part of a government-sponsored ecotourism project. Lodging is generally in Wayuu huts fashioned from *yotojoro*, the inner core of the cardon cactus that grows in the desert here. You can choose between smaller hammocks, larger and warmer traditional Wayuu *chinchorros* (locally crafted hammocks) or beds with private bathrooms (though note that running water is scarce). Bring your own towel. Nearly all posadas double as restaurants, and more or less serve the same thing – fish or goat in the COP$10,000 to COP$15,000 range and market-price lobster.

Posada Pujuru   GUESTHOUSE $
(300-279-5048, 310-659-4189; posadapujuru@gmail.com; hammocks/chinchorros COP$10,000/15,000, s/d COP$25,000/50,000) This *posada ecoturística* offers 10 well-constructed huts for private rooms, and luggage lockers for those in hammocks. The generators run from 6pm to 10pm and the restaurant (mains COP$10,000 to COP$15,000) serves up a tasty *pargo rojo* (red snapper), though the shrimp and rice is greasy and best avoided. You'll find it on the seafront.

Hostería Jarrinapi   GUESTHOUSE $
(311-683-4281; hammocks COP$15,000, r per person COP$35,000, mains COP$15,000-40,000) One of the more central options in Cabo, this place has very nicely maintained public areas and spotless rooms with tiled floors (a big deal in these parts!). A front desk and running water make you feel almost like you're in an actual hotel. The generators pump all night – meaning your fan whirs and you can sleep.

Ranchería Utta   GUESTHOUSE $
(313-817-8076, 312-678-8237; www.rancheriautta.com; hammocks/chinchorros/cabañas per person COP$15,000/22,000/35,000) The cabañas here adjoin each other and offer little privacy through their 'walls,' but they're right on the beach and quietly located outside of the town. A clean, well-run option that is popular with small groups en route to Punta Gallinas. There's a decent restaurant on-site, too.

❶ Getting There & Away

Arriving in Cabo de la Vela is not the easiest trip you'll make in Colombia, so most folks come on an organized tour. That said, it's possible to come on your own: from Riohacha, you must catch a *colectivo* at Cootrauri (p159) to Uribia; it will depart as it fills up every day from 5am to 6pm (COP$12,000, one hour). The driver will let you out in front of Panadería Peter-Pan, from where trucks and 4WDs leave for Cabo (COP$10,000 to COP$15,000, 2½ hours). Non-4WD vehicles are a definite no-go.

Punta Gallinas

Punta Gallinas is South America's most northerly point and offers one of the continent's most dazzling landscapes. This is the beauty of remote, wild simplicity and so will not appeal to all. Its access point, **Bahía Hondita**, is where burnt-orange cliffs surround an emerald bay with a wide and wild beach, beyond which a large colony of pink flamingos make their home. Otherwise the bay is home to just eight Wayuu families, who dwell in a feral desertscape peppered with vibrant green vegetation and shared only with herds of goat and locusts.

As the continent gives way to the Caribbean, massive sand dunes toppling 60m in height push right up against the shimmering turquoise sea like a five-story sand tsunami in reverse. This is **Playa Taroa**, Colombia's most beautiful and least trampled-upon beach, accessed by sliding down a towering sand dune right into the water.

As you walk back through the desert at dusk, check out the ancient smashed ceramic pots and the rubbish piles of burnt conches – evidence of simple dinners eaten round campfires thousands of years ago.

🛏 Sleeping & Eating

There are just a couple of sleeping and eating options around Punta Gallinas, though none of them are actually at the point themselves, but a short 4WD drive away overlooking Bahía Hondita.

Hospedaje Alexandra   GUESTHOUSE **$**
(☎318-500-6942, 315-538-2718; hospedaje alexandra@hotmail.com; hammocks/chinchorros/ cabañas per person COP$15,000/20,000/30,000) Has a wonderful position right on the bay, with views to wild flamingos and thick mangrove forests below. It has basic but charming huts and superb food.

Hospedaje Luzmila   GUESTHOUSE **$**
(☎312-626-8121, 312-647-9881; luzmilita10@ gmail.com; hammocks/chinchorros per person COP$15,000/20,000, r per person COP$30,000) Luzmilla offers jaw-dropping bay views and accommodations which, while modern, are still fairly basic.

ℹ Getting There & Away

There is virtually no way to reach Punta Gallinas without the help of an organized tour, though it is technically possible: for much of the year 4WD vehicles from Cabo de la Vela can make the three- to four-hour drive to La Boquita, the top of the bay across the water from the posadas. With advance notice, someone from the posadas can come and pick you up from there by boat (it's free for guests). When roads are impassable due to rains, access is by three-hour boat ride from Puerto Bolívar, a short drive from Cabo de la Vela near the El Cerrejón coal mine. Contact Aventure Colombia (p136) in Cartagena, or Kaí Ecotravel (p158) or Expotur (p158) in Riohacha to make the trip.

VALLEDUPAR

Valledupar lies in the long, fertile valley formed by the Sierra Nevada de Santa Marta to the west and Venezuela's Serranía del Perijá to the east. It has remained off the traveler radar as it's not a hugely touristic town, and was landlocked during the darker days of the Colombia civil conflict, when the town was held virtual hostage by the guerrillas that controlled the mountains.

With its small, well-preserved colonial center, some great outdoors activities nearby and a bustling nightlife, Valledupar is quietly growing as a traveler destination.

This is cattle-and-cowboy country, and in some ways it could be claimed to be the cultural heart of Colombia. Valledupar is mythologized and venerated by Colombians as the birthplace and cradle, the nursery and university of vallenato, the coast's ubiquitous, manic, accordion-driven folk music that sings of love, politics and the pain of losing your woman (or horse) to another man.

🏃 Activities

Valledupar is a place to chill out, relax and recharge. It makes a great stop if you're completing a circuit around Santa Marta, La Guajira Peninsula and Mompox.

Balneario La Mina   SWIMMING
(COP$7000) 🏊 The Río Badillo carves a bizarre, brain-like path through the riverbed down from the Sierra Nevada to make this a great swimming hole. Take plenty of strong insect repellent and beware the surging currents in wetter months. Take a *colectivo* from Carrera 6 in the center of town to Atanquez and jump out at La Mina; service runs from 11am to 2pm. To return take a mototaxi for COP$10,000, no later than 4pm.

There's a really worthwhile women's cooperative here, run by Maria Martinez, whom everyone calls La Maye. All proceeds benefit local women who lost their husbands and sons in the years of conflict, and the woven bags are of very high quality. She also serves a cheap (COP$10,000) fantastic *sancocho de gallina,* or cockerel stew, cooked over a wooden fire and served in the yard of her simple home.

Balneario Hurtado   SWIMMING
On Sundays and holidays, the *vallenatos* come here to bathe in the Río Guatapurí, cook and socialise. There are a few simple restaurants and wandering snack vendors, and all in all it's a superchilled family day out. It lies alongside the Parque Lineal; buses head there from Cinco Esquinas in the center of town.

🎉 Festivals & Events

Festival de la Leyenda Vallenata   MUSIC
(🗓Apr) The city's Festival de la Leyenda Vallenata is a four-day orgy of vallenato and Old

Parr whisky – the favored tipple here. The latter is so beloved that locals call the town Valle de Old Parr.

🛏 Sleeping & Eating

Room prices quadruple – and book out a year in advance – during the city's Festival de la Leyenda Vallenata in April.

★ **Provincia Hostel**   HOSTEL $$
(☑ 580-0558; www.provinciavalledupar.com; Calle 16A No 5-25; dm/s/d/tr COP$23,000/60,000/ 80,000/100,000; ❄️ 🛜) Friendly, safe, clean and charming, this is the best place in town whatever your budget. The private rooms lack natural light, and can get some noise from the kitchen and social area right outside, but are superbly comfortable, while the dorms are great value. Bicycle rental is also available and the owner can give great day-trip advice.

Compae Chipuco   COLOMBIAN $
(Carrera 6 No 16-05; mains COP$7000; ⊙ 7am-8pm) Just off Plaza Alfonso López you'll find this charmer, where you can sit under the massive mango tree and chow down on a seriously good *comida corriente,* which includes fish, meat and chicken options every day. Whip-cracking service, hearty food and simple flavors.

El Varadero   CUBAN $$$
(☑ 570-6175; Calle 12 No 6-56; mains COP$30,000-40,000; ⊙ noon-3pm & 6-10pm; 🛜) Cuban seafood is the fare in this restaurant, where photographs of local celebrities deck the walls. And it is very good seafood indeed: the lobster salad to start is great, as are the garlic mussels. To complete the continent-hopping menu, try the seafood Al Macho, served Peruvian-style with yellow peppers.

❶ Getting There & Away

The **bus station** (Carrera 7 & Calle 44) is a 30-minute taxi ride (COP$5000) from the center, or take any bus with 'Terminal' as its destination from Carrera 7 and Calle 17. Buses go to the following:
Bucaramanga COP$80,000, eight hours
Cartagena COP$40,000, 5½ hours
Medellín COP$100,000, 12 hours
Mompox COP$60,000, five hours
Riohacha COP$20,000, three hours
Santa Marta COP$22,000, two hours

SOUTHEAST OF CARTAGENA

The area to the southeast of Cartagena is dominated by the giant Río Magdalena, and is a thickly forested and sparsely populated place. The single traveler drawcard here is the gorgeous colonial town of Mompox, a time capsule of Colombia's past and a place well worth making the effort to see.

Mompox

Less an incurable medieval disease and more a wormhole into the past, Mompox is one of Colombia's most perfectly preserved colonial towns. Remotely located deep inland on the banks of the Río Magdalena, Mompox (also called Mompos) has essentially been in decline since river transport patterns changed in the mid-19th century, leaving the town – quite literally – a backwater. Its similarities to García Márquez's fictional town of Macondo are striking, and Mompox is indeed a far better place to soak up the atmosphere of *One Hundred Years of Solitude* than García Márquez's hometown of Aracataca.

The 21st century finds this forgotten gem finally rising again, with a steady proliferation of boutique hotels and restaurants opening in recent years. It's easily the most charming town in northern Colombia, its decaying facades and multicolored churches reminiscent more of Havana old town than of polished and buffed Cartagena. Best of all, its distance from the tourist trail means that it has a wonderfully undiscovered atmosphere, and you can often feel like pretty much the only visitor in town.

History

Founded in 1540 by Alonso de Heredia (brother of Cartagena's founder, Pedro de Heredia) on the eastern branch of the Río Magdalena, Mompox was an important trading center and active port through which all merchandise from Cartagena passed via the Canal del Dique and the Río Magdalena to the interior of the colony. The town flourished, minted coins for the colony, and became famous for its goldsmiths, traces of which can be found today in the town's superb filigree jewelry. Mompox declared its independence in 1810, the first town in Colombia to do so.

Toward the end of the 19th century, shipping was diverted to the other branch of the river, the Brazo de Loba, bringing the town's prosperity to an end and leaving it isolated.

◉ Sights

The best thing to do here is wander the gorgeously decaying streets, stroll along the Río Magdalena's fine embankment and take in the colors, sounds and smells.

River embankment Carrera 1 is known locally as Calle de la Albarrada, while the town's main thoroughfare, Carrera 2, is known to most people as Calle del Medio.

Iglesia de Santa Bárbara   CHURCH
(Carrera 1 & Calle 14) Dating from 1613, this unusual riverside church is undoubtedly the most striking building in Mompox, with its wide-eyed lions and griffins, its strange balcony-ringed bell tower, and its population of bats and swallows that stream in and out during evening mass.

Museo del Arte Religioso   MUSEUM
(Carrera 2 No 17-07; admission COP$4000; ⊙8-11:45am & 2-4pm Tue-Sat) Mompox's main museum is a glorious collection of religious paintings, gold and silver crosses and other religious objects all displayed in several rooms of a gorgeous colonial mansion.

Palacio San Carlos   HISTORIC BUILDING
(Carrera 2 & Calle 18) A former Jesuit convent that's now the town hall, this fine building dates from 1600 and has a notable statue of a freed slave with broken chains outside it. The line *'Si a Caracas debo la vida, a Mompox debo la gloria'* (If to Caracas I owe my life, then to Mompox I owe my glory) comes from Bolívar himself and refers to the fact that some 400 men from Mompox formed the basis of his victorious revolutionary army.

Cementerio Municipal   CEMETERY
(Calle 18; ⊙8am-noon & 2-5pm) Mompox's cemetery is one of the most striking spots in town to visit. Whitewashed graves and slots for remains are stacked high atop each other, sometimes six together, forming a wall of tombstones around a central chapel.

⚜ Festivals & Events

Two annual events are well worth traveling here for: the town's **Semana Santa** celebrations are some of the most elaborate in the country, while the newly inaugurated **Mom-** pox **Jazz Festival**, held in early October, is one of Colombia's best small music events.

⨶ Sleeping

There are a number of boutique hotels in town catering to wealthy weekenders, while budget travelers are also covered.

Hostal La Casa del Viajero   HOSTEL $
(☑684-0657;   www.hotelenmompos.besaba. com; Carrera 2 No 13-54; dm with/without air-con COP$20,000/25,000, r COP$35,000; ❀ ⧈) This spacious and friendly traveler hangout has all you need for a cheap stay in Mompox: a shared kitchen, a patio strewn with hammocks, a central location and roomy dorms – one with a great walk-out balcony. There's even a karaoke machine for those long Momposina nights.

★La Casa Amarilla   BOUTIQUE HOTEL $$
(☑310-606-4632, 685-6326; www.lacasaamarilla mompos.com; Carrera 1 No 13-59; dm/s/d/tr/q/ ste incl breakfast COP$25,000/90,000/145,000/ 175,000/200,000/185,000; ❀ ⧈) This beautiful hotel was created by a British journalist and his Momposina wife inside a restored 17th-century mansion overlooking the river. It has several wonderfully atmospheric rooms, as well as a couple of roomy upstairs suites that are perfect for romantic stays.

Breakfast is a friendly, communal affair, served up by smiling staff on a large dining table in the kitchen overlooking the courtyard garden. Staff members speak English, are a mine of useful information about Mompox and will do their very best to make you feel totally at home here. Reservations are advised.

Hotel Portal de la
Marquesa   BOUTIQUE HOTEL $$$
(☑685-6221; www.hotelportaldelamarquesa.com; Carrera 1 No 15-27; r/ste incl breakfast COP$179,000/ 208,000; ❀ ⧈) This impressive riverside building is one of Mompox's finest, and the conversion to a hotel has been quite stunning, not least in the gorgeous public areas. The rooms – of which there are just three, plus a suite with its own plunge pool – are great too, though the shiny modern floors and the odd Ikea piece don't do them any favors.

✦ Eating

Comedor Costeño   COLOMBIAN $
(Carrera 1 No 18-45; mains COP$7000; ⊙7am-5pm) This rustic riverfront restaurant in the

market area serves wonderful set meals, including *bocachico* fish numerous ways. The delicious, wholesome food includes various meat and fish dishes doused in housemade *ají picante* (hot pepper sauce). Lunch plates also come with an excellent soup, salad and the usual three starches.

★ **El Fuerte**   EUROPEAN $$$
(✒685-6762, 314-564-0566; Carrera 1 No 12-163; mains from COP$40,000; ☉dinner Fri-Sun) If at all possible, time your visit to Mompox to coincide with the weekend, when the town's best restaurant is (usually) open. With its beautifully crafted interior, charmingly multilingual host and superb menu of largely homemade specialties, it really is a highlight of the town itself. Try the excellent pizza, lovingly prepared pasta and mind-blowing desserts.

In low season it's important to reserve a table to ensure that they know you're coming, while in high season it's essential to reserve a table as it's nearly always full. Look for the giant fork on the river embankment to find it.

🛈 Getting There & Away

Mompox is remote, there's no denying that, but it can be reached by direct bus from Cartagena, or, with some extra effort, from elsewhere. Most travelers come to Mompox from Cartagena with Caribe Express (p137), which runs a daily bus at 7am (COP$50,000, eight hours).

If you can't get a seat on Caribe Express, there's an alternative route via Magangué: Torcoroma (p137) leaves Cartagena at 5:30am and every 30 minutes until noon (COP$40,000, three hours) and Expreso Brasilia (p137) goes at 10:30am (COP$40,000, three hours). When the bus arrives in Magangué, continue walking down the road and around to the right at the river and buy a ticket for a *chalupa* (boat) to Bodega (COP$7000, 20 minutes, frequent departures until about 3pm). The ticket booth is located across from El Punto del Sabor. Once in Bodega, hop in a *colectivo* to Mompox (COP$12,000, 45 minutes). There may also be direct *chalupas* from Magangué to Mompox. It's also possible to travel to Magangué from Medellín (COP$103,000, 12 hours, departs 8:45am daily).

Buses run to El Banco Magdalena from Santa Marta (COP$35,000, six hours, 1pm) and from Bogotá (COP$100,000, 14 hours, 5pm). In both cases, once you arrive in El Banco you need to take one of the waiting 4x4 jeeps (COP$35,000 per seat, 1½ hours) to get to Mompox.

SOUTHWEST OF CARTAGENA

Unspoiled beaches and the road less traveled characterize the Caribbean coast southwest of Cartagena, an area that, due to security concerns, has seen little international tourism in the last two decades. Secure and at the ready these days, areas like Tolú and the Islas de San Bernardo, which previously catered to Colombians only, are now wide open for foreign exploration. There is quite a notable change in the landscape here from the northern coast through the departments of Sucre, Córdoba, Antioquia and Chocó. Swampy pasturelands dotted with billowing tropical ceiba trees, ground-strangling mangrove trees and crystalline lagoons flank the seaside around the Golfo de Morrosquillo; while the jungle near the Darién Gap rides right up against cerulean waters and beaches where the Golfo de Urabá gives way to Panama, near the serene villages of Capurganá and Sapzurro.

Tolú

✒5 / POP 48,000

You'd never know it, but the tranquil *pueblo* of Tolú, the capital of the Golfo de Morrosquillo, is one of Colombia's most visited tourist destinations. Colombians flock here throughout the high season for its small-town feel, the beaches and natural playground, but there's rarely a foreigner in sight. The rest of the year, it's a fun spot to get off the gringo trail and holiday like the locals. Tolú is a small town where residents choose bicycles over vehicles, and bicycle taxis, known as *bicitaxis,* are an art form: each one is decked out with individual personality and flair – and features massive, cranked-up speakers playing salsa and reggaeton.

Tolú's lengthy *malecón,* full of seaside bars, restaurants and small artisan stalls, makes for a fun stroll, but the main draw for foreign tourists is the town's proximity to Islas de San Bernardo, part of Parque Nacional Natural (PNN) Corales del Rosario y San Bernardo. Here the picturesque beaches on Isla Múcura, wrought with mangroves and postcard-perfect palm trees, are some of the coast's most idyllic.

◉ Sights & Activities

Tolú is the main jumping-off point for day tours to Islas de San Bernardo. In high season, the town swells with Colombian tourists who come to eat and drink along the coast of the Golfo de Morrosquillo, which runs from here to Coveñas. In Coveñas there is less infrastructure but better beaches, many of which are dotted with thatched-roof tables fit for drinking an afternoon away.

For a bit of nature, the wonderful **La Ciénega de Caimanera** sits halfway between Tolú and Coveñas. This 1800-hectare nature preserve is a part-freshwater, part-saltwater bog with five varieties of mangroves. The red mangroves' roots twist and tangle in and out of the water like hyperactive strands of spaghetti. The canoe trip here is a pleasant and beautiful way to live an hour and a half of your life, meandering through artificial mangrove tunnels and sampling oysters right off the roots.

To reach the Ciénega, grab any bus (COP$2000) heading toward Coveñas and ask to be let off at La Boca de la Ciénega. Canoe guides wait for tourists on the bridge, and charge COP$20,000 for one to two people and as little as COP$8000 per person for larger groups.

Tolú's beaches aren't up to much – head 20km south to Coveñas for more agreeable patches of sand. **Playa Blanca** is accessed via moto-taxi from Coveñas. *Colectivos* depart every 10 minutes daily (COP$2500) from near Supermercado Popular at the corner of Carrera 2 and Calle 17 in Tolú. Or go for **Punta Bolívar**, five minutes away from Coveñas by moto-taxi (COP$4000).

🛏 Sleeping & Eating

The town is full of hotels used by Colombian holidaymakers. There's little reason to stay here overnight, but you may need to en route to the Islas de San Bernardo. Do not leave Tolú without eating the country's most sublimely perfect *arepa*, filled with egg and spiced meat, from Doña Mercedes' food stand on the southeast corner of the square next to the Expreso Brasilia office. Crunchy, savory perfection.

Villa Babilla   HOSTEL **$**
(☎312-677-1325;   www.villababillahostel.com;
Calle 20 No 3-40; s/d from COP$40,000/60,000;
🛜) Three blocks from the waterfront, this German-run hostel/hotel offers a friendly space highlighted by its thatched-roof outdoor TV lounge. There's a kitchen, laundry service and free coffee all day. There's no sign outside but it's the tallest building on the block.

El Velero   HOSTEL **$$**
(☎312-658-0129, 286-0058; info@hostalvelero.com; Carrera 1 No 9-30; s/d COP$50,000/80,000; ❄🛜🏊) The 'sailboat' is right on the seafront and has the waves at its door. The welcome is warm and the rooms are very comfortable; all boast TVs, fridges and sparkling bathrooms.

La Red   SEAFOOD **$$**
(cnr Calle 20 & Carrera 2; mains COP$8000-30,000; ☺breakfast, lunch & dinner) Go for the red snapper in garlic and butter here – it was swimming offshore a few hours earlier. Service could most kindly be described as leisurely, while the decor is tortoise-shell chic.

ℹ Information

Hospital de Tolú (☎288-5256; Calle 16 No 9-61; ☺24hr)

Mundo Mar (☎288-4431; www.clubnauticomundomartolu.com; Carrera 1 No 14-40) This well-run agency does daily tours departing at 8:30am to Islas de San Bernardo for COP$35,000. You'll be back by 4pm.

Tourist Office (☎286-0599; Carrera 2 No 15-40; ☺8am-noon & 2-6pm) Located in the *alcaldía* (town hall) on the west side of Plaza Pedro Heredia. Opens when the fancy takes them.

ℹ Getting There & Away

Expreso Brasilia/Unitransco (☎288-5180), **Rapido Ochoa** (☎288-5257) and **Caribe Express** (☎288-5223) share a small bus station on the southwest side of Plaza Pedro de Heredia. Buses depart hourly for Cartagena (COP$30,000, three hours) and Montería (COP$20,000, two hours). If you are continuing on to Turbo and the Panamanian border beyond, you must take a bus to Montería and switch there for Turbo.

Islas de San Bernardo

The 10 archipelagoes that make up the Islas de San Bernardo, set off the coast of Tolú, are a far more spectacular and interesting addition to the PNN Corales del Rosario y San Bernardo than their neighbors to the north, the Islas del Rosario.

Carib *indígenas* (indigenous Caribbeans) once called the islands home, but they are more trampled on today by vacationing Colombians, who have done well to keep the islands a secret from foreign tourists. Known for their crystalline waters, mangrove lagoons and white-sand beaches, these picturesque islands stand out on the

Caribbean coast as a little oasis of rest and relaxation.

Tours

Day tours to the archipelago depart daily from the Muelle Turístico in Tolú at around 8:30am. The full day includes a fly-by of one of the world's most densely populated islands, **Santa Cruz del Islote**, where up to 1000 people, mostly fisherfolk, live in a tropical aquatic shantytown measuring just 1200 sq meters; and **Isla Tintípan**, the largest of the archipelago's islands.

Most of the tourism infrastructure is on **Isla Múcura**, where tours stop for three hours of free time. Here you can rent snorkeling equipment for COP$5000, kick back and have lunch and a beer (not included in the tour), or simply wander around the mangroves. The best beach and the best for snorkeling is **Isla Palma**, where the tour concludes at the aquarium, which is more of a rustic zoo than a waterworld (though there is a foggy-windowed aquarium here). You'll also find monkeys, pink flamingos, loads of birds (including many loose macaws) and even a buffalo! It's strange, but sort of interesting.

Sleeping & Eating

In high season reservations are a must, and you should expect considerable price hikes.

Donde Wilber   CABINS **$$**
(📞 316-605-5840; Isla Múcura; cabins per person COP$30,000, incl full board COP$90,000) For the only budget accommodations on the islands, ask for Angelo at the Isla Múcura dock, and he'll take you through the village to a bunch of very ramshackle seaside shacks and a rustic cabin. It's one-star at best, but it's relaxed and friendly, and it's owned by locals, which means your money isn't siphoned off the island. Donde Wilber can arrange fishing trips and snorkeling, and the view is spectacular.

Punta Faro   HOTEL **$$$**
(📞 in Bogotá 1-616-3136; www.puntafaro.com; Isla Múcura; r per person incl full board COP$590,000; ❋ 🛜) The smartest hotel in the archipelago makes liberal use of mangrove wood in its beautiful lobby and bedroom furniture, and caters to wealthy Colombians and business travelers. There's a private beach, three restaurants, two bars and transportation from Cartagena. Equipment such as kayaks and snorkeling gear is included in the price.

Turbo

📍 4 / POP 140,000

Part of the department of Antioquia and 373km northwest of Medellín, Turbo is a gritty port that you'll have to overnight in if you want to catch a boat to Capurganá or Sapzurro. There's absolutely nothing to keep you here, and you shouldn't stray from your hotel after dark.

Sleeping & Eating

There are a number of small and largely indistinguishable cafes along the waterfront by the docks where you can eat from around 5am until dusk.

Hotel El Velero   HOTEL **$$**
(📞 312-618-5768, 827-4173; Carrera 12 No 100-10; r from COP$80,000; ❋ 🛜) A moment's walk from the dock where the boats leave for Capurganá, this modern place is definitely the best place to stay in Turbo. Its rooms are small but very comfortable, with crisp linen bedding and well-stocked minibars. It can feel like a little slice of heaven after the long journey to Turbo.

Getting There & Away

From Cartagena, you must catch a bus before 11am to Montería (COP$50,000, five hours) and switch for the bus to Turbo (COP$30,000, five hours). In Turbo, there is no central bus station but most of the companies of concern are located on Calle 101. Returns to Montería run from 4:30am to 4pm. Buses head to Medellín hourly from 5am to 10pm (COP$62,000, eight hours) from Turbo.

Boats to Capurganá (COP$55,000, 2½ hours) and Sapzurro (COP$60,000, 2½ hours) leave daily from the port from 7am.

Capurganá & Sapzurro

📍 4 / POP 2000

Colombia ends its extraordinary Caribbean coastline with a flourish: these two idyllic, laid-back villages and their surrounding beaches are hidden in an isolated corner of Colombia's northwest and make up two of the country's most wonderful – and least visited – highlights. Backed by jungled mountains, washed by deep blue waters, the villages attract a crowd of locals seeking refuge from the chaotic mainstream of Colombian life. Do yourself a favor and make time to join them.

GETTING TO PANAMA

It is not possible to drive from Colombia to Panama – the Pan-American Hwy does not extend through the Darién Gap. Various maniacs have ignored the dangers and attempted crossing the 87km distance in all-terrain vehicles and even on foot, risking encounters with guerrillas, paramilitaries or narcotraffickers.

It is possible and fairly safe, however, to reach Panama (mostly) overland, with just a few sea trips and a short flight. At the time of research the following route was secure and calm, but always check ahead for security updates before setting out, and stick to the coast.

➡ Make your way to Turbo. The Medellín–Turbo route (COP$62,000, eight hours) is safe now – but daytime travel is still advised. From Cartagena, you have to go to Montería (COP$50,000, five hours) and change there for Turbo (COP$30,000, five hours). Buses run regularly from 7am to 5pm, and you have to leave Cartagena before 11am to avoid getting stuck overnight in Montería. You have to spend the night in Turbo, which isn't a particularly wonderful experience, but it's all part of the adventure.

➡ Catch a boat from Turbo to Capurganá (COP$55,000, 2½ hours). Arrive at least an hour early to secure a ticket. Hang on to your hat – this can be a bumpy ride. There is a 10kg baggage limit – COP$500/kg overcharge applies.

➡ Take a boat from Capurganá to Puerto Olbaldía in Panama (COP$30,000, 45 minutes). But first, get your Colombian exit stamp at **Ministerio de Relaciones Exteriores** (🖉 311-746-6234; www.migracioncolombia.gov.co; ◷ 8am-5pm Mon-Fri, 9am-4pm Sat), near Capurganá's harbor, one day before departure (the office will not be open on the morning you leave). Boats depart Capurganá every day, at 7:30am, so be at the docks for 7am. This is another dicey journey, depending on sea conditions.

➡ Obtain your Panama entry stamp at Panamanian immigration in Puerto Olbaldía. Then fly to Panama City's domestic Albrook terminal with **Air Panama** (🖉 in Panama +507-316-9000; www.flyairpanama.com). There are two to three daily flights. Puerto Olbaldía has very little to offer tourists. Avoid spending any more time than necessary there, and head straight to Panama City.

CARIBBEAN COAST CAPURGANÁ & SAPZURRO

Part of the adventure is in getting here: both Capurganá and Sapzurro are only accessible by a lengthy boat trip from Turbo, or by a tiny plane from Medellín. Consequently, their beaches remain Colombia's least overrun. The tourism here has been 90% homegrown, due to access and security issues in the past. But that's all changed now, and both towns are delightfully safe, and tourism is booming.

A visit here is a grand alternative to the beaches of PNN Tayrona, which can be uncomfortably crowded in high season. It's easy to let a few days drift into a week as you explore the excellent beaches and nature walks in the area. The coral reef here is fantastic and there are now several diving schools exploring the coast and logging new sites.

For those making the overland trek to or from Panama, these two relaxed villages make for an ideal spot to break your journey, with blazing white beaches and a wealth of nature-related activities in the vicinity. Just remember to bring enough cash – there are no ATMs in either village.

Activities

Capurganá has better diving than the coast's main diving destination, Taganga, with a better-preserved reef and visibility up to 25m common from August to October. The sea is rough from January to March. At **Dive & Green** (🖉311-578-4021, 316-781-6255; www.diveandgreen.com) and **Centro de Buceo Capurganá** (🖉314-861-1923; centrodebuceocapurgana@gmail.com; Luz de Oriente), two-tank dives cost between COP$170,000 and COP$190,000, while one night dive costs COP$110,000.

ℹ Information

Capurganá Tours (🖉824-3173) Friendly English-speaking agency that can book flights in Panama and excursions in the area. They can do cash advances on credit cards (handy given there are no banks in Capurganá) and arrange transportation from Turbo throughout Colombia.

Minsterio de Relaciones Exteriores (🖉311-746-6234; Capurganá; ◷8am-5pm Mon-Fri, 9am-4pm Sat) Immigration services for those heading to Panama. It's on the main drag. Opening hours are, let's say, flexible.

❶ Getting There & Away

Boats to Capurganá (COP$55,000, 2½ hours) and Sapzurro (COP$60,000, 2½ hours) leave daily from the port at Turbo from 7am. There is often more than one boat each day, sometimes as many as four or five, but the 7am boat is – weather permitting – always running. Boats can fill up quickly with locals – arrive at least an hour early, or if possible reserve a seat the day beforehand to ensure you can get a place. It can be a wet and sometimes bumpy journey, so throw your luggage in a trash bag (vendors sell them for COP$1000). Be sure to take your passport and plenty of cash with you, as there are no ATMs in Capurganá or Sapzurro. When you return, studiously avoid the clamoring locals who want to 'help' you to your bus. They work on commission and will fleece you.

Searca (www.searca.com.co) and **TAC** (www.taccolombia.com) operate flights from Medellín (COP$400,000 one way) on Mondays and Fridays in low season, and up to three flights daily in high season.

San Blas Tours (📲 321-505-5008; www.sanblasadventures.com) offers tours to the Kuna Yala in Panama, departing from Sapzurro, or border crossings if you're headed that way. You'll need to get your exit stamp in Capurganá.

Capurganá

Capurganá sits at the northwest edge of Colombia's Chocó department at the entrance to the Golfo de Urabá. It offers more tourism infrastructure than Sapzurro – there is no shortage of accommodations and the town remains supremely relaxed, except during Semana Santa and in November and December.

◎ Sights & Activities

El Cielo, a one-hour jungle hike into the mountains from Capurganá, passes several natural swimming pools and waterfalls along a trail where you might see howler and squirrel monkeys, toucans and parrots. The pleasant coastal hike to **Aguacate** (one hour) stops at quiet beaches along the way, while the wonderful **Playa Soledad** can be accessed by a three-hour walk east of Capurganá, or on a short boat trip negotiated with one of the fishers on Capurganá's main beach.

🍽 Sleeping & Eating

Restaurants are scarce in Capurganá, so most of the hotels offer all-inclusive packages, though there are a few budget options around the soccer field. Hotel owners often hang around the dock, waiting for passengers. They're a cool bunch, not hustlers.

For a late drink, check out the bars circling the soccer field.

★ Posada del Gecko   GUESTHOUSE $
(📲 313-651-6435, 314-525-6037; www.posadadelgecko.com; s/d/tr/q COP$25,000/70,000/95,000/120,000; 🛜) A friendly guesthouse with simple wooden rooms that are great value; smarter options include rooms with air-con and private bathrooms, too. The owner organizes three-day trips to the San Blas Islands for US$185. The attached bar-restaurant serves authentic pizza and pastas and is a fine place for a drink; it has an impressively indie playlist.

Hostal Capurganá   HOSTEL $
(📲 316-482-3665; www.hostalcapurgana.net; Calle de Comercio; dm COP$18,000, r incl breakfast per person COP$35,000) On the main street, just back from the dock, this excellent option has six rooms, each with fan, private bathroom and access to a charming courtyard garden. This is the only place in town that takes credit cards, should you have failed to bring enough cash. Its clued-up staff is good at helping with onward travel bookings as well.

Campamento Wittenberg   HOTEL $
(📲 311-436-6215; hammocks COP$10,000, r per person COP$20,000) A friendly French-owned joint right on the border of Panama, where you can find a basic room or two, cheap, healthy breakfasts, fishing trips and sailing courses. The owner has been in Colombia for years and is friendly, professional and very helpful.

Luz de Oriente   HOTEL $$
(📲 310-371-4902; www.luzdeoriente.com; Playa Blanca; r per person incl half board COP$72,000; 🛜) Right on the harbor, Luz de Oriente's fan-cooled rooms are clean and tidy, and all have sea views. They do a mean mojito in the bar, and you feel right in the center of things, just seconds from the beach.

★ Josefina's   SEAFOOD $$
(mains COP$20,000-40,000; ⏱noon-9:30pm) Scour the entire coast and you won't find better seafood – or a more wonderful welcome – than at Josefina's. Her crab in spicy coconut-cream sauce, served in impossibly crispy, wafer-thin plantain cups, is superb, as is the *crema de camarón* (cream of shrimp soup) and her take on *langostinos* (crayfish). You'll find Josefina in an unremarkable hut on the main beach in Capurganá.

Sapzurro

If you're headed this way, chances are it's to find tranquillity and isolation while enjoying the spectacular natural world. As such, Sapzurro is the most alluring destination on this stretch of Colombia's coastline: with no airport, just a couple of daily boats to the 'mainland' and an atmosphere that feels like nobody is on a schedule of any kind, this is one of the most wonderfully laid-back places in the country.

The town beach is lovely, but a short hike over the hillside into Panama takes you to the most famous beach in the area, **La Miel** (bring your ID – there's a military checkpoint). It's a quick walk up a series of steep steps across the border and back down the other side (turn right at the bottom of the hill and follow the sidewalk). The small beach offers perfect white sand, cerulean waters, and a couple of small places to eat fresh fish and drink a cold beer.

🛏 Sleeping & Eating

La Gata Negra   GUESTHOUSE $
(☑ 320-610-5571; www.lagatanegra.net; Sapzurro; r per person COP$20,000-45,000) This Italian-run guesthouse is in a gorgeous timber chalet set back a short distance from the town beach. The three rooms share bathrooms and are fan cooled. Prices vary according to season and how many are sharing; the cabaña sleeps four in a double bed and two bunks. The Italian home cooking, courtesy of owner Giovanni, is another draw.

Zingara   GUESTHOUSE $
(☑ 320-687-4678; www.hospedajesapzurrozingara. com; r per person COP$25,000-45,000; 🕾) Owner Clemencia will make you feel instantly welcome in this rustic wooden guesthouse. The two rooms here are on the mountainside and have private bathrooms, mosquito nets and balconies surrounded by fruit trees. The top room is the best: it sleeps five and has a huge balcony with gorgeous views. Find the guesthouse on the pathway that leads to the climb up to the Panamanian border.

★ La Punta del Arrecife   GUESTHOUSE $$
(☑ 320-687-3431, 314-666-5210; luzdelaselva52@ yahoo.es; r per person incl breakfast COP$65,000) Built over a reef at the edge of the village (follow the raised walkway out of town), this wonderful place is set in a gorgeously overgrown garden and is presided over by Rubén and Myriam, two charming and funny re-

WORTH A TRIP

THE GOLFO DE URABÁ

The Golfo de Urabá has a few tiny towns nestled on the fringes of the Darién Gap. **Acandí**, **Triganá** and **San Francisco** have decent, affordable accommodations, quiet beaches and amazing hiking. All are accessible by boat from Turbo.

In Acandí, in March, April and May, hundreds of leatherback turtles, measuring up to 2m in length and weighing up to 750kg come ashore and lay their eggs.

For accommodations in tiny San Francisco, try **Ralle's Hostel** (☑ 314-703-5151; dm COP$25,000, cabin per person COP$50,000). In Triganá, try **Hostería Triganá** (☑ 314-615-6917) or the **Anayansi Cabañas** (☑ 320-697-9025). Both have rooms and cabins for less than COP$40,000 per person, depending on the season.

cluses from the modern world. They host guests in gorgeous, simple rooms that are crafted from wood and full of tasteful arts and crafts. They grow much of their own food here, and encourage guests to disconnect as much as possible. It's a short walk from the beach at Cabo Tiburón, and there's great snorkeling to be had on the reef itself.

★ La Posada   HOSTEL $$
(☑ 312-662-7599; www.sapzurrolaposada.com; Sapzurro; s/d from COP$65,000/130,000, camping or hammocks per person COP$10,000) The most comfortable and well-run spot in town has beautiful gardens with flourishing guava, coconut and mango trees; open-air showers for campers; and beautiful, airy rooms with wooden floors, exposed beams and hammocks on the balconies. Owner Mario speaks great English, and his wife prepares meals (mains COP$17,000 – call ahead if you plan to eat). Mario is planning to build several tree-house rooms, and is the person to talk to locally to arrange sailings to Cartagena (24 hours by sailboat), various Panamanian ports and to the Islas de San Bernardo.

Restaurante Doña Triny   COLOMBIAN $
(set meals COP$17,000; ⊙ noon-9pm) Facing you as you get off the launch from Capurganá, this local fish restaurant is demonstrably popular, with locals and visitors alike crowding in. The set meal includes a soup, a fish or seafood main course and some kind of dessert.

San Andrés & Providencia

Best Places to Eat

➡ Restaurante La Regatta (p178)

➡ Caribbean Place (p184)

➡ Gourmet Shop Assho (p177)

➡ Donde Francesca (p179)

➡ Café Studio (p185)

Best Places to Stay

➡ El Viajero San Andrés (p175)

➡ Deep Blue (p184)

➡ Frenchy's Place (p183)

➡ Casa Harb (p176)

➡ Sirius Hotel (p185)

Why Go?

The archipelago of San Andrés and Providencia is geographically located near to Nicaragua, historically tied to England and politically part of Colombia. While these pristine islands may lack an untainted pedigree, their diverse history and picture-postcard setting make them Colombia's most interesting paradise.

Here you'll find isolated beaches, unspoiled coral reefs and an alluring island flavor, and with just a little digging the 300-year-old English-Creole-speaking Raizal culture emerges.

San Andrés, the largest island in the archipelago, and its commercial and administrative hub, attracts many tourists seeking duty-free shopping sprees. The crowds, however, are not difficult to escape.

Providencia offers the same turquoise sea and extensive coral reefs, but it's much less commercialized and its colonial heritage is still thriving in small hamlets of colorful wooden homes peppered about the island.

When to Go
San Andrés

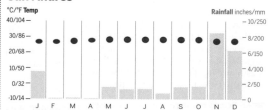

Jan–Jun During the dry season you can avoid the Caribbean's hurricanes.

Apr–Jul Crab migration season – roads in Providencia can be closed to protect them!

Jun–Dec Prices are much lower outside the Christmas peak on both islands.

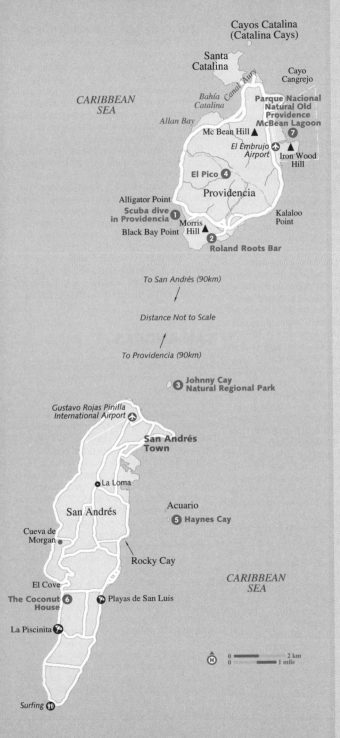

Cayos Catalina
(Catalina Cays)

Santa
Catalina

CARIBBEAN
SEA

Bahía
Catalina

Canal Aury

Cayo
Cangrejo

Allan Bay

Parque Nacional
Natural Old
Providence
McBean Lagoon

Mc Bean Hill ▲

❼

El Embrujo
Airport ✈

Iron Wood
Hill

El Pico ▲ ❹

Providencia

Alligator Point
**Scuba dive
in Providencia** ❶

Kalaloo
Point

Morris
Black Bay Point Hill ▲

Roland Roots Bar

To San Andrés (90km)

Distance Not to Scale

To Providencia (90km)

❸ **Johnny Cay
Natural Regional Park**

Gustavo Rojas Pinilla
International Airport ✈

**San Andrés
Town**

● La Loma

San Andrés

Acuario
● ❺ **Haynes Cay**

Cueva de
Morgan ●

Rocky Cay

El Cove

CARIBBEAN
SEA

The Coconut ❻
House

❼● Playas de San Luis

La Piscinita ❼●

Ⓝ 0 ——— 2 km
   0 ——— 1 mile

Surfing ❿

San Andrés & Providencia Highlights

❶ **Scuba dive** (p178) into Providencia's blue waters, gawking at Colombia's prettiest coral reefs and marine life.

❷ Groove to reggae rhythms over Old Milwaukee's at **Roland Roots Bar** (p184).

❸ Dig your toes into the pristine sands of beautiful **Johnny Cay** (p173), part of the 4-hectare Johnny Cay Natural Regional Park.

❹ Trek through iguana country to **El Pico** (p181) for stunning views of Providencia.

❺ Swim with the stingrays at sunset off **Haynes Cay** (p175).

❻ Marvel at the **Coconut House** (p177) and nature garden at West View.

❼ Explore the thick mangrove swamps of Providencia's beautiful **Parque Nacional Natural Old Providence McBean Lagoon** (p180) by boat.

History

The first inhabitants of the islands were probably a group of Dutch colonists who made their home on Providencia toward the end of the 16th century. In 1631 they were expelled by the English, who effectively colonized the islands. The English brought with them enslaved black people from Jamaica and began to cultivate tobacco and cotton. The Raizal people are the product of intermingling between the British and their slaves. The Spanish, irate at the English success on the islands, unsuccessfully invaded the archipelago in 1635.

Because of their strategic location, the islands provided convenient shelter for pirates waiting to sack Spanish galleons bound for home, laden with gold and riches. In 1670 legendary pirate Henry Morgan established his base on Providencia, and from here he raided both Panama and Santa Marta. Legend has it that his treasures are still hidden on the island.

Shortly after Colombia achieved independence, it laid claim to the islands, although Nicaragua fiercely disputed its right to do so. The issue was eventually settled by a treaty in 1928, which confirmed Colombia's sovereignty over the islands.

Geographic isolation kept the islands' unique English character virtually intact, though things started to change when a flight service connected the islands to the mainland in the 1950s. In 1954 a government plan to make the islands a duty-free zone brought with it tourism, commerce, entrepreneurs and Colombian culture, which slowly began to uproot the 300-year-old Raizal identity, pushing it aside in favor of big tourism bucks. Unprepared and unqualified to make a living from tourism, locals were caught off-guard.

In the early 1990s the local government introduced restrictions on migration to the islands in order to slow the rampant influx of people and to preserve the local culture and identity. Yet Colombian mainlanders account for two-thirds of San Andrés' population. English and Spanish have been the two official languages since 1991.

The tourist and commercial boom caused San Andrés to lose much of its original character; it's now a blend of Latin American and English-Caribbean culture, though there is a movement to restore Raizal roots in San Andrés. Providencia has preserved much more of its colonial culture, even though tourism is making inroads into the local lifestyle.

Although the political status of San Andrés and Providencia is unlikely to change, Nicaragua continues to press the issue of its sovereignty over the islands at the International Court of Justice in the Hague. The court reaffirmed Colombia's sovereignty over the main islands in 2007, but said it would rule on the maritime boundary and secondary islands at a later date, undetermined at the time of research.

In 2005 the Seaflower Marine Protected Area (MPA) was established to strengthen protection of key ecosystems in the marine area of the Seaflower Biosphere Reserve. The MPA includes 65,000 sq km of crystalline waters that are zoned for a variety of uses ranging from complete protection to controlled fishing. The objective of this multiple-use MPA is to foster sustainable development in the archipelago by strengthening conservation of marine biodiversity and promoting sustainable use. The Seaflower is Colombia's first MPA and is the largest in the Caribbean.

SAN ANDRÉS

8 / POP 68,000

Just 150km east of Nicaragua and some 800km northwest of Colombia, the seahorse-shaped island of San Andrés counts 27 sq km of cultural tug-of-war as both its asset and its handicap. Covered in coconut palms, San Andrés, the largest island in the archipelago, is indeed paradisiacal Caribbean, but not everything here is crystal clear.

Take the downtown area, for instance, at the northern end of the island. Colombians call it El Centro, but the island's English-speaking Raizal people refer to it as North End. The cultural elbowing escalates from there. What's not up for debate, however, is that the commercialized area of town won't be splashed across any postcards anytime soon – it's an uninspiring collection of concrete blocks housing one duty-free shop after another, only broken up by the occasional hotel or restaurant.

All is not lost on San Andrés, however. A charming brick promenade lines the waterfront, and it's a lovely spot to enjoy a drink or take an evening stroll. And paradise is little more than a canoe paddle away: the endlessly idyllic Johnny Cay sits off in the distance, just 1.5km from shore. In high season it can feel as crowded as the Mediterranean, but otherwise Johnny Cay is the archipelago's finest moment.

San Andrés is best appreciated outside of the downtown hubbub. A 30km scenic paved road encircles the island, and several minor roads cross inland. There are two other small towns: La Loma (The Hill) in the central hilly region and San Luis on the eastern coast, both far less tourist-oriented than San Andrés Town and boasting some fine English-Caribbean wooden architecture. Excellent scuba-diving and snorkeling opportunities abound all around the island – visibility and temperature here are nearly unrivaled in the Caribbean.

It only takes a day or two to suss out the Raizal from the Colombians. At just one-third of the island's population, Raizals are now an ethnic minority, but their fading Creole culture – descended from English settlers, African slaves and West Indians from other islands – is what gives San Andrés its unique character, different from that of mainland Colombia.

⊙ Sights

Johnny Cay Natural Regional Park   BEACH
This protected 4-hectare coral islet sits about 1.5km north of San Andrés Town. It's covered with coconut groves and surrounded by a lovely, white-sand beach. The sunbathing is good, but be careful swimming here as there are dangerous currents. The cay can fill up far beyond capacity, as tourists fight for space with an estimated 500 iguanas that call it home. Food is available. Boats leave from the main San Andrés Town beach (round trip COP$15,000). The last boat back is at 5pm in high season, 3:30pm in low.

La Piscinita   BEACH
(West View; admission COP$2000) Also known as West View, and located just south of El Cove, La Piscinita is a good site for snorkeling. It has usually calm water, plenty of fish (which will eat out of your hand) and some facilities, including a restaurant with traditional local food and snorkel rental. When the sea is rough, you can only feed the fish from land.

La Loma   VILLAGE
This small town in the inner part of San Andrés, also known as the Hill, is one of the most traditional places here. It's noted for its Baptist church, the first established on the island (in 1847). In 1896 the church was largely rebuilt in pine brought from Alabama. Definitely take a stroll – it's the least Colombian-influenced part of the island.

San Andrés

0 — 2 km
0 — 1 mile

Providencia (90km)

Johnny Cay Natural Regional Park

Gustavo Rojas Pinilla International Airport

SAN ANDRÉS TOWN

Casa Harb

See San Andrés Town Map (p174)

Posada Nativa Green Sea

La Loma

Chamay's Nautica

Baptist Church

San Andrés

Acuario

Hotel Playa Tranquilo

Cueva de Morgan

Cocoplum Hotel

Haynes Cay

Grog

Las Canteras

Rocky Cay

San Andrés Divers

SAN LUIS

EL COVE

El Radar

San Luis Village Hotel

La Piscinita

Coconut House

Playas de San Luis

Vía Tom Hooker

Nirvana

CARIBBEAN SEA

Hoyo Soplador

Cayo Bolívar (25km)

Hoyo Soplador   GEYSER
At the southern tip of the island, the Hoyo Soplador is a small geyser where sea water spouts into the air (up to 20m at times) through a natural hole in the coral rock. This phenomenon occurs only at certain times, when the winds and tide are right. An international surf contest is held nearby in January.

San Luis   VILLAGE
Located on the island's east coast, San Luis boasts white-sand beaches and some fine traditional wooden houses. The sea here is good for snorkeling, though conditions can be a little rough. San Luis has no center as

San Andrés Town

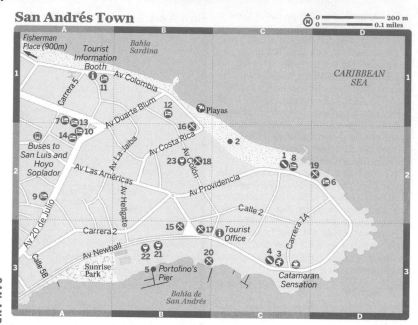

such, and is really just a 3km string of mostly ramshackle houses along the coast, but it's a tranquil alternative to San Andrés Town.

Acuario
BEACH
Next to Haynes Cay, off the east coast of San Andrés, Acuario is frequently visited by tourists by boat (round trip COP$15,000). The surrounding sea is shallow and calm, and good for snorkeling. If you forget to bring your snorkeling gear, you can rent some here on the beach.

Cayo Bolívar
ISLAND
This pristine slice of Caribbean fantasy, 25km from San Andrés, is a tiny island covered in palms and surrounded by white-sand beaches. Known to Raizals as Courtown Cay, it's visitable on a day trip. There are no facilities on the island – this is proper Robinson Crusoe territory, so ensure your tour includes lunch and drinks, and bring sunscreen as there's little shade.

Cueva de Morgan
CAVE
(admission COP$5000) This is the cave where Welsh pirate Henry Morgan is said to have buried some of his treasure. The cave is 120m long, but it's filled with water, so you see only its mouth. You can't enter the cave, and there's not much to see here anyway, yet

the magic of alleged riches draws in plenty of tourists. Additional distractions include traditional *mento* dancers shaking it to calypso and *Schottische*, a sort of island polka.

🏃 Activities

Due to the beautiful coral reefs all around, San Andrés is an important diving center, with more than 35 dive spots.

Banda Dive Shop
DIVING
(☑ 513-1080; www.bandadiveshop.com; Hotel Lord Pierre, Av Colombia, San Andrés Town) Extra-friendly dive shop offering two-tank dives for COP$180,000 and PADI open-water certification for COP$800,000. Best choice on the island.

Chamay's Nautica
WATER SPORTS
(☑ 513-2077; Via San Luis Km4, San Luis) The go-to shop for water sports. DIY rental possibilities per hour include kayaking (COP$30,000), windsurfing (COP$80,000) and kitesurfing (COP$110,000).

Karibik Diver
DIVING
(☑ 318-863-9552, 512-0101; www.karibikdiver.com; Av Newball No 1-248, San Andrés Town) This small German-run school provides quality equipment and personalized service. A two-tank

San Andrés Town

dive is COP$180,000 all inclusive. PADI certification costs COP$770,000.

San Andrés Divers   DIVING
(☑ 312-448-7230; www.sanandresdivers.com; Av Circunvalar, Km9) Though not as centrally located as other dive shops on the island, this large shop and school has a great reputation and offers PADI certification for COP$800,000. A two-tank dive with all equipment included is COP$160,000. The office is located at the Hotel Blue Cove, while the training pool and dive center can be found further down the main road.

⟲ Tours

Coonative Brothers   BOAT TOURS
(☑ 512-2522, 512-1923) On San Andrés Town's beach, this boating co-op provides trips to Johnny Cay (COP$10,000) and Acuario (COP$10,000), plus a combined tour to both cays (COP$15,000). It also offers an 8am-to-5pm day trip to Cayo Bolívar (COP$170,000 including lunch), which runs daily from Tuesday to Saturday.

San Andrés Diving & Fishing   WILDLIFE TOURS
(☑ 316-240-2182; sanandresfishing@gmail.com; 3hr tours COP$75,000) The name says it all, really. Jaime Restrepo runs a very popular tour to swim with the stingrays at Haynes Cay, and throws in some deep-water snorkeling and brews on top of the package. It's somewhat casual and limited to groups of 10. The tour leaves at 2:15pm from Portofino's Marina at Barracuda Park in San Andrés Town and it's important to reserve.

Crucero Rivel   BOAT TOURS
(☑ 512-8840; Av Newball, San Andrés Town) Offers daily tours that combine Acuar-

io and Johnny Cay and leave at 8:30am (COP$20,000). Also run a day trip to Cayo Bolívar (COP$180,000) that includes lunch and drinks.

🛏 Sleeping

The overwhelming majority of the island's accommodations can be found in San Andrés Town. There are some hotels in San Luis, but elsewhere there are very few places to stay. For the most part, accommodations on the island are more expensive than on the mainland, although there are now a couple of hostels for those on a tighter budget. Rates rise during high season.

🛏 San Andrés Town

El Viajero San Andrés   HOSTEL $$
(☑ 512-7497;   www.elviajerohostels.com; Av 20 de Julio 3A-12; dm/r incl breakfast COP$35,000/140,000; ❋ 🛜) The first hostel on the island is also a great place to stay, with a lively bar, attentive staff full of informed advice, and a convenient location in the center of San Andrés Town. All dorms have private bathrooms and air-con, and the clean, simple – if rather bare – rooms have plasma TVs and five-star mattresses.

Apartahotel Tres Casitas   HOTEL $$
(☑ 512-5813;   www.apartahoteltrescasitas.com; Av Colombia No 1-60; r per person incl half board COP$120,000; ❋ 🛜 ⊠) A cute yellow-and-blue clapboard hotel with extra-large rooms, all with kitchenettes and separate living areas. Rates include breakfast and dinner, and some rooms have balconies over the sea. Definitely one of the more charming options in San Andrés Town.

Cli's Place
GUESTHOUSE **$$**

(📞512-0591; luciamhj@hotmail.com; Av 20 de Julio No 3-47; s/d/tr COP$70,000/130,000/180,000; ❄️🛜) This Raizal-run place is part of the island's *posada nativa* program, where you bed down with locals. English-speaking Cli has eight simple rooms, some with kitchenettes. It's reached via the alley next to the park across from Pollo Kikiriki. Breakfast costs an extra COP$10,000 per person.

Posada Henry
GUESTHOUSE **$$**

(📞512-6150; libiadehenry@hotmail.com; Av 20 de Julio No 1-36; s/d COP$40,000/80,000) This centrally located guesthouse is a part of the *posada nativa* program, which allows travellers to stay with locals on the island. The fan-cooled, tile-floored rooms all have bathrooms and fridges and are decorated in bright island colors. Breakfast is not available.

Red Cay Hotel
HOTEL **$$**

(📞512-4349; www.hotelredcay.com; Av 20 de Julio; s/d COP$70,000/140,000) Despite its scrappy exterior, the rooms here are decent, with Arctic-level air-con, and small but clean and well-equipped rooms in the center of town. There's a rooftop bar, but no breakfast.

Hotel Portobelo
HOTEL **$$**

(📞512-7008; www.portobelohotel.com; Av Colombia No 5A-69; s/d incl breakfast COP$165,000/240,000; ❄️🛜) This unassuming beachside hotel is one of four properties run by the same management along the beachfront. The simple rooms, some with sea views (COP$50,000 and about 20 sq meters extra) have cable TVs and new air-conditioners. It's all about the location.

Hotel Mary May Inn
HOTEL **$$**

(📞512-5669; www.marymayinn.com; Av 20 de Julio 3-74; s/d COP$85,000/120,000; ❄️🛜) This small and friendly place offers nine simple but cozy rooms in a pleasant courtyard location two blocks from the beach. The interior design offers a trip back to the 1950s.

Decameron los Delfines
BOUTIQUE HOTEL **$$$**

(📞512-4083; www.decameron.com; Av Colombia No 16-86; r per person all inclusive COP$349,000; ❄️🛜🏊) The first boutique hotel on the island, as well as within the Decameron chain, this stylish 36-room hotel is quiet, discreet and very popular with couples. It features an over-water restaurant, a small pool and smart furniture, all housed in a design-forward structure that wouldn't be out of place in Los Angeles.

Noblehouse Hotel
HOTEL **$$$**

(📞512-8264; www.sanandresnoblehouse.com; Av Colón No 3-80; s/d incl breakfast COP$189,000/200,000; ❄️🛜) This Italian-run operation likes to mix its decors: New England Leaf Peeping one moment, Moorish Seaside the next. The 15 large and kitschy rooms are comfortable and spacious, though most have no daylight. Despite this, it's a good option if you want to be in San Andrés Town and the staff is super helpful. It's one block from the beach.

🏝 San Andrés Island

There are a number of hotels and guesthouses outside San Andrés Town, most of which are located on the coastal road. These tend to be better value than hotels in town, and possess a quieter, more Caribbean atmosphere.

Posada Nativa Green Sea
GUESTHOUSE **$**

(📞512-6313, 317-751-4314; Harmony Hall Hill; r per person COP$40,000; ❄️) Run by the fabulous Flory Perez, who has never left the island in her life, these small, simple self-catering cottages offer privacy and peace rather than luxury. You do get a small terrace and a kitchen, however, and the pleasure of Flory's wonderful welcome.

Casa Harb
HOTEL **$$$**

(📞512-6348; www.casaharb.com; Calle 11 No 10-83; d incl breakfast from COP$890,000; ❄️🛜🏊) Located in an impressive republican-style mansion behind the airport, this is probably San Andrés' most luxurious hotel. The five suites are individually designed with very Asian aesthetics (think lots of dark-wood furniture) and feature deep soaking tubs. As its price tag suggests, it caters to an exclusive market.

Hotel Playa Tranquilo
BOUTIQUE HOTEL **$$$**

(📞513-0719; www.playatranquilo.com; Km 8, Via El Cove; r incl breakfast COP$290,000-350,000; ❄️🛜🏊) Buddha overlooks a small pool here and sets the tone for this boutique place, which has gorgeous rooms that combine modern and traditional touches. Kitchens and communal sitting areas are on offer in some rooms, which means it's a great place to come with kids. There's also a dive school on-site, though the beach of the hotel's name is nowhere in evidence: it's got a great seafront location, but there's no sand.

Cocoplum Hotel
HOTEL **$$$**

(📞513-2121; www.cocoplumhotel.com; Via San Luis No 43-39; s/d incl breakfast

COP$194,000/264,000; ❋🛜❋) On a gorgeous private white-sand beach shaded with palm trees, this multicolored low-key beach resort sports Caribbean architecture. There's a restaurant that serves fresh meals all day, and it's also open to nonguests. Rocky Cay, a good spot for snorkeling, is nearby.

San Luis Village Hotel HOTEL $$$
(📇 513-0196; www.hotelsanluisvillage.com; Av Circunvalar No 71-27, San Luis; s incl breakfast COP$341,000-390,000, d incl breakfast COP$410,000-460,000; ❋🛜❋) Right on the sea and with the beach at your doorstep, this very comfortable 18-room hotel has luxuries including hot water, flat-screen TVs and private balconies or terraces for each room. At this price it's not a great bargain, but it's one of the best options on the island if you want to be on the beach.

Eating

The Creole-Caribbean influence means staples include breadfruit, which takes the place of *patacones* (fried plantains) as the starch of choice, and ubiquitous conch. Be sure to try the most traditional dish, rundown (or 'rondon' in the local Creole), a soupy dish of lightly battered fish, plantains, yucca and other gooey starches, all slow-cooked in a healthy dose of coconut milk. You'll find the more upmarket offerings in San Andrés Town, while on the rest of the island you'll find lots of delightfully simple fresh fish and seafood on offer.

🍴 San Andrés Town

★ Gourmet Shop Assho EUROPEAN $$
(Av Newball; mains COP$30,000-60,000; ⏲12:30pm-midnight Mon & Wed-Sat, from 4:30pm Tue, from 6pm Sun; 🕿) A surprise find in San Andrés Town, this strangely named place stands out with its delightful decor and impressive menu: instead of the usual grilled meats with rice and plantain, here you'll find rare steak, beautifully seasoned seafood dishes, and a range of salads and vegetarian options. There's an excellent wine list and the best coffee on the island to boot.

Miss Celia O'Neill Taste SEAFOOD $$
(Av Colombia; mains COP$20,000-40,000; ⏲lunch & dinner) A good choice for native food such as rondon, stewed crab and stewed fish, served within a colorful home with a large garden and patio. It's across from the Club Náutico.

Perú Wok PERUVIAN $$
(www.peruwok.com; Av Colombia No 00001, Big Point; mains COP$20,000-40,000; ⏲lunch & dinner; 🕿) This new place serves up a big choice of Peruvian-Asian fusion food from an easy-to-use pictorial menu, including ceviches, seafood, rice dishes, wok dishes and grills. The sleek, modern design sets it apart from much of the competition and you can choose between the cool dining room or the breezy sea-view terrace.

Mr Panino ITALIAN $$
(Edifico Breadfruit, local 106-107, Av Colón; mains COP$15,000-40,000; ⏲lunch & dinner) Parma

SAN ANDRÉS & PROVIDENCIA SAN ANDRÉS

THE HOUSE OF COCONUT

Behind the Restaurant West View (where you can get a mean rondon for COP$26,000), you'll find a curious **house** and ecopark project run by the courtly and welcoming Mr Forbes. The house, every single part of it, including all of its decorations, are made of coconut. The floor, the walls, the ceilings, the beds, the desk, the chairs, the lamps, the fan blades, the curtains, the curtain poles, the door handles, the coat hooks, the false flowers in the vases, the vases themselves: all are made of a coconut-derived product. Even the light switches are crafted from the wood of the coconut tree, which Mr Forbes (it felt unseemly to ask his Christian name) says is the most useful tree on earth.

Over a glass of delicious coconut wine, he tells us that every part of the tree can be used from the minute it is planted until it dies 50 years later. He has yearned to build this dream coconut house for his entire life, ever since he was punished by his father as a boy for stealing two coconuts. His punishment? To stand holding two coconuts at head height, arms outstretched to his left and right, for the entire day.

He is the architect, designer, carpenter and builder of the house. It stands in a peaceful garden surrounded by the trees and fruit bushes of the islands, with coconuts, of course, very strongly represented. Guests can stay here, he says, but it was impossible, even after several more glasses of coconut wine, to get him to agree a price. Though he did climb a coconut tree and toss a few coconuts down.

DIVING ON SAN ANDRÉS & PROVIDENCIA

Divers will delight over the underwater viewing opportunities off both San Andrés and Providencia. While diving courses may be cheaper on the mainland at Taganga, the richness of the corals and the variety of the marine life here rivals almost any place in the Caribbean.

Both San Andrés and Providencia have extensive coral reefs – 15km and 35km respectively. The reefs on both islands are notable for their sponges, which appear in an amazing variety of forms, sizes and colors. Other aquatic inhabitants include barracudas, sharks, turtles, lobsters, rays and red snappers. Wreck divers will want to check out the two sunken ships, the *Blue Diamond* and *Nicaraguense,* off the coast of San Andrés.

The top five dive spots:

Palacio de la Cherna A wall dive southeast of San Andrés that begins at 12m and drops off some 300m more. Midnight parrot fish, tiger fish, king crabs, lobsters and even nurse and reef sharks are common sightings.

Cantil de Villa Erika Southwest of San Andrés. Depths range from 12m to 45m along this colorful reef full of sponges, soft and hard corals, sea turtles, manta and eagle rays, and sea horses.

Piramide A shallow dive inside the reef on San Andrés' north side, this is a haven for stingrays. The quantity of fish, octopus and moray eels make it one of the most active spots on the island.

Tete's Place Large schools of mid-sized goat fish, grunt fish, schoolmasters and squirrel fish frequent this aquarium-like site 1km offshore at Bahía Suroeste in Providencia.

Manta's Place Despite its name, there are no manta rays at this Providencia site but rather southern stingrays with wingspans of up to 5m. As you survey the sands between coral mounds, you pass over fields of ghost feather dusters, where brown garden eels withdraw into the sand for protection as you near them.

ham, real cheese and an Italian specialty deli with sandwiches, pasta, risotto and a beautiful octopus carpaccio: despite the touristy sounding name, this place in San Andrés Town is the real deal, and the olive-oil drenched panini are superb.

★**Restaurante La Regatta**　SEAFOOD $$$
(☑512-0437; www.restaurantelaregatta.com; Av Newball; mains COP$30,000-80,000; ☺lunch & dinner; ☑) The islands' best restaurant, La Regatta is housed on a wooden pontoon structure over the sea at the Club Náutico in San Andrés Town. Despite a healthy dose of pirate kitsch, it has a formal, white-linen tablecloth atmosphere and the food is heavenly. The coconut-curry *marinera* is nothing short of perfection. Book a table for the evenings.

Fisherman Place　SEAFOOD $$$
(☑512-2774; Av Colombia; mains COP$15,000-50,000; ☺noon-4pm) This open-air, beachside San Andrés Town restaurant is a great way to support local fisherfolk and eat well. Rondon and fried fish are the most popular dishes, but the lobster is the clear winner for the price.

Mahi Mahi　THAI $$$
(Hotel Casablanca, Av Colombia; COP$25,000-85,000; ☺lunch & dinner; ☑) This chic Thai spot on the waterfront, part of Hotel Casablanca, provides a welcome break from Colombian staples with its seasoned curries and island-tinged dishes. As well as the cheaper Thai menu, there's a pricey Colombian seafood menu, too.

✗ San Andrés Island

Grog　SEAFOOD $$
(Rocky Cay; mains COP$20,000-35,000; ☺10am-6pm Wed-Mon) With shade-dappled tables scattered all over the beach, this friendly little locale does a mean range of seafood dishes, including ceviche, rice and wok dishes, and tasty starters. Unsurprisingly, the titular drink (represented here by Aguila and Club Colombia) is also very popular.

Restaurante West View　SEAFOOD $$
(☑513-0341; Circunvalor Km11, West View; mains COP$20,000-45,000; ☺9am-6pm) This West View option looks ordinary but the food stands out. Try the filet of fish – and do not

miss the attached flourishing nature garden, which has an example of every fruit tree that grows on the island.

★ Donde Francesca
SEAFOOD $$$

(San Luis; mains COP$28,000-50,000; ⊘9am-6pm; 🐾) Right on the beach, this breezy place may be little more than a shack, but it serves up absolutely delicious traditional Caribbean food such as *langostinos al coco* (breaded crayfish deep fried with coconut), *pulpo al ajillo* (octopus cooked in garlic) and tempura calamari. There are showers and changing facilities, so you can combine a meal with a swim.

El Paraíso
SEAFOOD $$$

(San Luis; mains COP$25,000-50,000; ⊘9am-5pm; 🐾) On a great strip of white-sand beach, El Paraíso is a slightly more upmarket restaurant than some of the simpler beach shacks, but its fresh seafood is of the same excellent quality. There are shower and changing facilities here, and so it's a great spot to hang out for the day.

☆ Entertainment

There are many nightspots in San Andrés Town along the eastern end of Av Colombia, but expect drunk holidaying Colombians and ear-bleeding music. We recommend some of the better options.

Banzai
COCKTAIL BAR

(Av Newball, local 119, San Andrés Town; ⊘7pm-2am) If you want a late-night drink without going to a club, Banzai is a great cocktail bar that's popular with locals. The well-mixed drinks are served expertly to a reggae backbeat, and it's chic without being over-fancy.

Blue Deep
CLUB

(Sunrise Beach Hotel, Av Newball, San Andrés Town; cover after 11pm COP$15,000; ⊘9:30pm-3am Thu-Sat) The biggest disco in town holds 700 sweaty bodies. There is live music (salsa and reggaeton), which provides the soundtrack for a decent mix of locals and tourists, all stumbling about after too many frothy rum punches.

Éxtasis
CLUB

(☑512 3043; Hotel Sol Caribe San Andrés, Av Colón, San Andrés Town; cover COP$25,000; ⊘9:30pm-3am Mon-Thu, to 4am Fri & Sat) A good disco, with TV screens (soccer, of course) and three rows of lounge chairs for those who prefer voyeurism. You can recoup COP$12,000 of the cover in cocktails.

❶ Information

4-72 (Av Newball, Edificio Cámara de Comercio, local 101, San Andrés Town; ⊘8am-noon & 2-6pm Mon-Fri, 8am-noon Sat) Post office.

Tourist Office (Secretaría de Turismo; ☑513-0801; Av Newball, San Andrés Town; ⊘8am-noon & 2-6pm Mon-Fri) Across from Restaurante La Regatta, the staff here speaks English and is very helpful. It also has a tourist information booth (cnr Avs Colombia & 20 de Julio).

❶ Getting There & Away

AIR

San Andrés airport, Gustavo Rojas Pinilla International Airport (also known as Aeropuerto Internacional Sesquicentenario), is northwest of the town center. You must buy a tourist card (COP$44,000) on the mainland before checking in for your San Andrés–bound flight. Airlines that service San Andrés include **Avianca** (☑512-3349; Av Colón, edificio Onaissi, San Andrés Town; ⊘8am-noon & 2-6pm Mon-Fri, 8am-1pm Sat) and **Copa** (☑512-7619; www.copaair.com; Sucursal Centro Comercial San Andrés, San Andrés Town; ⊘8am-noon & 2-6pm Mon-Fri, 9am-1pm Sat).

There are direct connections to the following:
Barranquilla From COP$320,000
Bogotá From COP$400,000
Cali From COP$430,000
Cartagena From COP$365,000
Medellín From COP$390,000
Panama City From COP$525,000

Satena (☑512-3139; www.satena.com; Gustavo Rojas Pinilla International Airport) operates two flights per day between San Andrés and Providencia in low season (round trip from COP$400,000) and up to six in high season. Decameron's affiliated airline **Searca** (www.searca.com.co) also flies the route.

BOAT

Catamaran Sensation (☑318-347-2336, 310-223-5403; Bay Point Bdg, suite 6, Av Newball; ticket one way COP$65,000) provides a service from San Andrés to Providencia four times a week in both directions. It departs from the Muelle de la Casa de Cultura, in front of the sales office, at 7:30am on Monday, Wednesday, Friday and Sunday, and returns at 3:30pm on the same day. The journey takes three hours, and can be extremely rough. It's possible to visit Providencia on a day trip with this service, but we don't advise this; Providencia deserves to be seen and enjoyed over several days. Indeed, with just a few hours on the island you might wonder what all the fuss is about.

SAN ANDRÉS & PROVIDENCIA SAN ANDRÉS

Tickets can often sell out, even in low season, so it's important to call ahead and book your places.

ⓘ Getting Around

TO/FROM THE AIRPORT

San Andrés' airport is in San Andrés Town, a 10-minute walk from the town center, or an expensive COP$15,000/7000 ride by taxi/moto-taxi. If you don't have much luggage, it's an easy walk: turn left out of the terminal building, then turn right onto the main road, which will become Av Colombia. There's a left luggage room at the airport (COP$4000 per item per 24 hours).

BUS

Local buses circle the island; they also ply the inland road to El Cove. They are the cheapest way to get around (per ride COP$2000) unless you want to walk. They can drop you off close to all the major attractions.

A bus marked 'San Luis' travels along the east-coast road to the southern tip of the island; take this bus to San Luis and the Hoyo Soplador. The bus marked 'El Cove' runs along the inner road to El Cove, passing through La Loma. It'll drop you in front of the Baptist church, within easy walking distance of Cueva de Morgan and La Piscinita. You can catch both buses at the end of Carrera 5 in San Andrés Town.

SCOOTER

The best way to travel independently around the island is by scooter (from COP$60,000 per day) or golf buggy (from COP$100,000 per day). Many of the rental businesses are on Av Newball in San Andrés Town and are concentrated around the tip of the island. Most will also deliver to your hotel. Shop around as prices and conditions vary. One place we recommend is **Rent A Car Esmeralda** (☑315-303-7037; Av Colombia).

TAXI

A taxi to take you for a sightseeing trip around the island will cost around COP$70,000.

BICYCLE

Cycling around San Andrés is a great way to get a feel for the island. Roads are paved and there is little traffic to contend with. Prices start at around COP$10,000/20,000 per half-/full day.

PROVIDENCIA

☑8 / POP 5000

Providencia, 90km north of San Andrés, is a wonderfully remote and traditional Caribbean island with breathtaking scenery,

gorgeous golden-sand beaches, friendly locals and superb diving. Best of all, it's a pain to get to, ensuring that you'll never have to share this slice of paradise with the package-holiday crowd: the only way to reach Providencia is by a short flight in a rickety 20-seater plane or on a three-hour catamaran ride, both from San Andrés.

What tourism industry does exist here can be found in the tiny hamlets of Aguadulce and Bahía Suroeste on the west coast. Here you'll find small cottages, hotels and cabañas strung along the road, and a handful of restaurants. While you can see virtually the whole island in a day, travelers end up staying longer than they expected, spending their time scuba diving, hiking or simply lying in a hammock with a Club Colombia.

Without a direct connection to the Colombian mainland, the island hasn't seen nearly the same levels of cultural invasion as San Andrés, leaving its traditions and customs more or less intact. You'll still hear the local English Creole spoken all over the island, and road signs direct you with the old English names for towns, rather than their Spanish equivalents. All this combined with gorgeous topography standing sentinel over swaths of turquoise-blue sea gives Providencia no small claim to being paradise.

◉ Sights

Providencia's best beaches are Bahía Suroeste, Bahía Aguadulce, and Bahía Manzanillo at the southern end of the island. Note that local road signs use the English names (South West Bay, Fresh Water Bay, Manchaneel Bay respectively), which can be confusing.

Parque Nacional Natural (PNN) Old Providence McBean Lagoon   PARK

(admission COP$14,500) To protect the habitat, a 10-sq-km area in the island's northeast was established in 1995. About 10% of the park's area covers a coastal mangrove system east of the airport; the remaining 905 hectares cover an offshore belt including the islets of Cayo Cangrejo and Cayo Tres Hermanos. An 800m-long ecopath helps you identify different species of mangroves and the fauna that inhabit them.

Santa Catalina   ISLAND

Some tiny, deserted beaches exist on the island of Santa Catalina. It's worth a look if only to see Morgan's Head, a rocky cliff in the shape of a human face, best seen from the water. An underwater cave is at the base of the cliff. The shoreline changes considerably with the tides; during high-tide, beaches get very narrow and some totally disappear. To explore the island's attractive coastline, take the path to the left after the pontoon bridge.

Lighthouse   GALLERY
(www.lighthouseprovidencia.com; High Hill; ☉5-9pm Mon-Sat) With a great lookout to the sea, this community-run arts space serves as a small educational center, gallery, cafe and hangout. It shows documentaries on a projector after dark (ask to see the fascinating – if bizarre – doc about the local crab migration); serves up good coffee and a range of island snacks; and promotes environmental awareness.

🏃 Activities

Diving & Snorkeling
Snorkeling and diving are the island's two biggest single attractions. Diving trips and courses can be arranged with recommended local operators.

Sirius Dive Shop   DIVING
(📞514-8213; www.siriusdivecenter.com; Bahía Suroeste) Sirius Dive Shop is located in Bahía Suroeste on the grounds of the Sirius Hotel and offers an open-water or advanced course for COP$750,000. A two-tank dive with quality equipment is COP$170,000. Night dives are also offered (COP$170,000).

Felipe Diving Shop   DIVING
(📞514-8775; www.felipediving.com; Aguadulce) You can rent snorkeling gear in Aguadulce (COP$10,000). Diving trips and courses can be arranged with this recommended local operator run by a native Raizal. An open-water or advanced course can be arranged for COP$800,000.

Sonny Dive Shop   DIVING
(📞318-274-4524;   www.sonnydiveshop.com; Aguadulce) Sonny's Dive Shop in Aguadulce offers an open-water or advanced course for COP$800,000. Two-tank dives cost COP$160,000.

Hiking
The mountainous interior of the island is impressive in terms of its vegetation and small animal life, making it great for walking. There's perhaps nowhere else in Colombia that you will see so many colorful lizards scampering through bushes. Beware of a common shrub with spectacular horn-like thorns; ants living inside have a painful bite. Mosquitoes also abound on the island's interior.

Don't miss a trip to **El Pico Natural Regional Park** for outstanding 360-degree views of the Caribbean from El Pico (360m). The most popular trail begins in Casabaja. Ask for directions as several paths crisscross on the lower part (further up there are no problems), or ask in Casabaja for a guide. Some locals will take you up for a small fee. It is a steady 90-minute walk to the top. Carry plenty of drinking water – there is none along the way.

🎎 Festivals & Events

Crab Migration   NATURE
(☉Apr-Jul) This event takes place twice a year for a week or two between April and July. First, the adult black crabs descend to the beaches and lay their eggs, before returning to the mountainside. Then several weeks later the juvenile crabs leave the sea and follow in their path. Roads are usually closed for days at a time to provide safe crossing for the crabs.

Getting around the island is very tough at this time; the result is always utter paralysis, but it's fascinating. The crabs are around at other time of the year, too, so keep a look out.

Cultural Festival   CULTURAL
(☉Jun) Providencia's major cultural event takes place in the last week of June. It includes music and dance, a parade of motorcycles and, just for kicks, an iguana beauty pageant.

🛏 Sleeping & Eating

Generally speaking, accommodations and food are expensive on Providencia, even more so than on San Andrés. For self-caterers, there are rather pricey supermarkets with an unsurprisingly limited range in both Aguadulce and Santa Isabel.

🛏 Aguadulce

This 20-house hamlet offers peace, quiet and a charming beach. There are more than a dozen places to stay at, many with their own restaurants. For better or worse, the Decameron chain has taken over most of the best spots, so independent travelers can be shut out in high season – it's always a good idea to book ahead.

Providencia

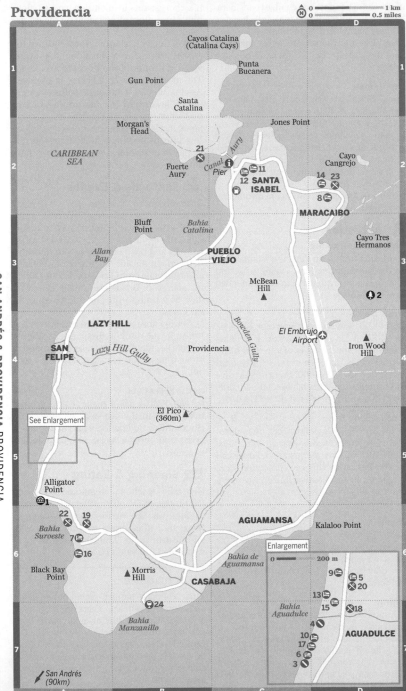

0 — 1 km
0 — 0.5 miles

Cayos Catalina
(Catalina Cays)

Punta
Bucanera

Gun Point

Santa
Catalina

Morgan's
Head

Jones Point

CARIBBEAN
SEA

21

Fuerte
Aury

Pier

Canal Aury

11
12

SANTA
ISABEL

Cayo
Cangrejo

14   23

8

MARACAIBO

Bluff
Point

Bahía
Catalina

Cayo Tres
Hermanos

Allan
Bay

PUEBLO
VIEJO

McBean
Hill

2

LAZY HILL

Lazy Hill Gully

El Embrujo
Airport

Iron Wood
Hill

SAN
FELIPE

Providencia

Broeden Gully

See Enlargement

El Pico
(360m)

Alligator
Point

1

22   19

7

Bahía
Suroeste

16

Black Bay
Point

Morris
Hill

AGUAMANSA

Kalaloo Point

Bahía de
Aguamansa

Enlargement

200 m

9   5
20

CASABAJA

Bahía
Aguadulce

13
15
4

18

24

Bahía
Manzanillo

AGUADULCE

10
17
6
3

San Andrés
(90km)

Providencia

Mr Mac HOTEL **$$**
(📞 316-567-6526, 316-695-9540; posadamister-mack@hotmail.com; Aguadulce; r per person with kitchen & fan/air-con COP$50,000/70,000) Mr Mac is the island's cheapest option, and even if you get rather damp and aged rooms, it's still a good deal. The green painted timber house is over the water, with hammocks strewn along the veranda. Rooms are large, and the better ones come with air-con and kitchenettes. It's possible to swim here, although there's no beach.

★ Frenchy's Place APARTMENT **$$$**
(📞 315-709-6910, 318-306-1901; estemayo29@gmail.com; Aguadulce; apt COP$180,000) Run by Parisienne Marie (known as 'Frenchy'), this charmingly rustic, wood-crafted apartment is perhaps the most characterful place to stay on the island. There's a gorgeous balcony overlooking the sea, two bedrooms (one double, one single), a full kitchen,

bathroom, and a living area crammed full of knickknacks. Book in advance for this little-known island secret.

Cabañas Aguadulce CABINS **$$$**
(📞 514-8160; www.cabanasaguadulce.com; r per person incl breakfast COP$120,000; ❄🛜🏊) Each of these comfortable white, yellow and blue cabañas has a rather cutesy local animal name, its own shady terrace and two floors with beds on the upper level. There's a small fish-shaped pool and a chilled-out on-site restaurant as well. It works out as a good deal for singles.

Sol Caribe Providencia HOTEL **$$$**
(📞 514-8036; www.solarhoteles.com; Aguadulce; r per person incl breakfast COP$155,000; ❄🛜🏊) Following the island's kaleidoscopic color scheme, this bright yellow hotel is the most upmarket in Aguadulce. There's a pleasant seaside restaurant, rooms with nice hard-wood furniture and colorful Caribbean art. It's right off the beach.

Cabañas Miss Elma HOTEL **$$$**
(📞 310-566-3773; Aguadulce; r per person incl breakfast COP$130,000; ❄🛜) Right on Agua-dulce's small but lovely beach, this friendly family-run place has colorful common areas and a wonderfully casual seaside restaurant. The rooms are spacious; some have sea views; and all have fridges.

Posada del Mar HOTEL **$$$**
(📞 514-8454; www.posadadelmarprovi-dencia.com; Aguadulce; s/d incl breakfast COP$120,000/200,000; @🛜) This Decameron-affiliated place still feels small scale, though it's rather larger than you'd expect a genuine posada (inn) to be. It's brightly painted and well maintained; its rooms have smallish balconies overlooking the sea; and there's a garden from where you can swim.

Hotel El Pirata Morgan HOTEL **$$$**
(📞 514-8232; www.elpiratamorganhotel.org; Agua-dulce; s/d incl breakfast COP$158,000/198,000; ❄🛜🏊) A solid option in the 'town' center, with the best-stocked supermarket on the island just across the road. It lacks the Car-ibbean flair of the other options and has rather dated interiors, but the welcome is friendly and the rooms are clean. The hotel restaurant is one of the few places on the is-land open on Sundays.

Blue Coral Pizza PIZZA **$$**
(📞 514-8224; Aguadulce; mains COP$15,000-40,000; ⊙5-10pm Wed-Mon) A fairly low-cost

SAN ANDRÉS & PROVIDENCIA PROVIDENCIA

ROLAND ROOTS BAR

Don't leave Providencia without visiting the ridiculously atmospheric **Roland Roots Bar** (🕿 514-8417; Bahía Manzanillo; ⊙ 10am-midnight, until 2am Fri & Sat), which has booths fashioned from bamboo under ramshackle thatched roofs spread among the sands, all set to a booming reggae soundtrack. Roland is famous for his late-night parties and his *coco locos* – jazzed-up piña coladas served in coconuts. There's also good food available (mains COP$15,000 to COP$40,000) – so all in all, it's unmissable.

outdoor option, this relaxed place does panini and seafood as well as the titular pizza. It's also one of the few places open on Providencia's very quiet Sunday evenings.

★Caribbean Place   SEAFOOD $$$
(🕿 311-287-7238; Aguadulce; mains COP$30,000-75,000; ⊙ 12:30-4pm & 7-10pm Mon-Sat) Follow the wine-bottle-strewn pathway that leads to this charming place, and discover one of the island's culinary highlights. Though the wonderful seafood isn't cheap, Bogotá-trained chef Martin Quintero has succeeded in producing serious food in a casual atmosphere. Highlights include black crab cooked many ways, craw fish, shrimp and various seafood casseroles. Reservations are a good idea.

🛏 Santa Isabel, Santa Catalina & Maracaibo

Strangely, Santa Isabel doesn't see much tourism, despite its gorgeous location in a picturesque bay attached by a pontoon bridge to the little island of Santa Catalina. Its lack of a beach might be the explanation, but it's well worth coming up here to wander around the quaint town, and take a walk around Santa Catalina. Just down the road, sleepy Maracaibo has a growing number of hotels.

Hotel Flaming Trees   HOTEL $$
(🕿 514-8049; Santa Isabel; s/d COP$60,000/120,000; 🌀) Named after the brightly hued trees in the garden here, this rather charming pink-and-blue painted place is the best choice in Santa Isabel; it offers nine spacious timber-floor rooms

with fridges, TVs and local art. Breakfast is COP$12,000 extra.

Hotel Old Providence   HOTEL $$
(🕿 514-8691; grecy06@hotmail.com; Santa Isabel; s/d/tr COP$70,000/120,000/150,000; 🌀) This hotel offers good-sized, decent rooms, with tiled floors, fridges and cable TVs. Some even come with balconies. The public areas have definitely seen better days.

Posada Coco Bay   GUESTHOUSE $$
(🕿 311-804-0373; posadacocobay@gmail.com; Maracaibo; s/d from COP$90,000/140,000; 🌀 🛜) A gorgeous, rustic spot with a view of Cayo Cangrejo and hammocks on the timber balconies, this is a good choice for a chilled island vibe. The ship-shape rooms come with mosquito nets and some even have kitchens. While there's no beach here, it's still possible to swim.

Deep Blue   LUXURY HOTEL $$$
(🕿 514-8423; www.hoteldeepblue.com; Maracaibo; s/d/ste incl breakfast from COP$395,000/560,000/705,000; 🌀 🛜 🏊) Providencia's smartest hotel by some distance, the Deep Blue offers 13 spacious rooms complete with marble floors, rain showers, flat-screen TVs and L'Occitane bathroom products. The higher categories even have mini-infinity pools on their balconies and there's a rooftop jacuzzi with amazing views towards Cayo Cangrejo. There's no beach in Maracaibo Bay itself.

Other extras include free kayaks and a free 10am shuttle service to any beach on the island, with a 4pm pickup.

Don Olivio   SEAFOOD $$
(Santa Catalina; set meals COP$20,000; ⊙ lunch) Serving up delicious seafood and other homemade dishes on the terrace of a local house on the island of Santa Catalina, Don Olivio is a great place for a relaxed lunch while exploring this lovely place.

Restaurante Deep Blue   CARIBBEAN $$$
(Maracaibo; mains COP$25,000-70,000; ⊙ noon-10pm) Not only does it have a gorgeous view towards Cayo Cangrejo, this place also boasts a very impressive and inventive menu. We can highly recommend the *canastillas de mariscos* (plantain baskets filled with fish, shrimp and calamari, bathed in a tomato-and-chive sauce with coconut milk and coconut rice). Service can be slow, though, so don't come expecting to eat in a hurry.

⌷ Bahía Suroeste

This gorgeous bay and surrounding village is the second most popular tourist destination after Aguadulce, but it has only a couple of hotels. Still, the palm-lined beach is nothing short of paradisiacal, and with two of the best restaurants in town here, it's a great spot for true escape. If you're on the island on a Saturday afternoon, be sure to come here for the weekly bareback horse race along the beach. It starts around 2pm.

Sirius Hotel   HOTEL **$$$**
(☑ 514-8213; www.siriushotel.net; Bahía Suroeste; s/d cabañas incl breakfast from COP$105,000/170,000, s/d incl breakfast from COP$130,000/230,000; ❄️ 🛜) This shabby place was clearly once a brightly designed and much cared-for property. Its rooms are still extremely clean, but it's in good need of some paint and a modernisation. That said, it's perfect if you want to spend quiet days on the gorgeous beach doing nothing. Request one of the rooms with a sea view for great sunsets.

Cabañas Miss Mary   HOTEL **$$$**
(☑ 514-8454; www.hotelmissmary.com; Bahía Suroeste; s/d incl breakfast COP$120,000/200,000; ❄️ 🛜) Miss Mary provides nicely dressed-up rooms right on the beach, each with large patios and hammocks. There's cable TV and ever-elusive hot water. It's comfortable here and the rooms with sea views are great, but it doesn't exactly ooze character.

★ Café Studio   SEAFOOD **$$**
(☑ 514-9076; Bahía Suroeste; mains COP$23,000-50,000; ⊙ 11am-10pm Mon-Sat) The island's best restaurant is run by a Canadian–Raizal couple and the food is an absolute delight, both memorable and reasonably priced. Highlights include the island-style crab, lobster tails in garlic sauce and Wellington's conch, which is cooked in a housemade Creole sauce made with wild basil from the garden. Save room for the mind-blowingly good cappuccino pie!

El Diviño Niño   SEAFOOD **$$**
(Bahía Suroeste; mains COP$20,000-44,000; ⊙ noon-6pm) A simple restaurant on Providencia's best beach, this place is a gorgeous spot for a long lunch with waves lapping at your feet. Feast on fresh fish, lobster, crab or just order the superb seafood *plato mixto* and a cold beer. The loud music is a shame at such a peaceful spot, but hey, you're in Colombia.

ℹ Information

The island's only two ATMs, as well as it's only **gas station**, can also be found in Santa Isabel.
Tourist Office (☑ 514-8054; Santa Isabel; ⊙ 9am-noon & 2-5pm Mon-Fri) Near the pier.

ℹ Getting There & Away

Satena (p179) and **Searca** (www.searca.com. co) both fly between San Andrés and Providencia (round trip from COP$400,000) twice daily in low season, several more in high season. It's important to buy your ticket in advance in the high season, and note that the luggage allowance is 10kg; you'll need to pay for any extra.

Catamaran Sensation (p179) also connects Providencia to San Andrés four times a week in each direction.

ℹ Getting Around

TO/FROM THE AIRPORT

Vehicles congregate at the airport waiting for incoming flights and ask for a flat fare of COP$23,000 for any distance. To avoid overpaying, walk a bit further from the airport and wave down a *colectivo* or pickup truck passing along the road; there's a standard COP$2500 fare. This might not be the best solution if you are carrying lots of bags, though. Aguadulce and Bahía Suroeste are a 15-minute ride by *colectivo* from the airport.

COLECTIVO

Getting around the island isn't the easiest thing to do without your own transportation. *Colectivos* run hourly along the road in both directions; it's COP$2500 for a ride of any distance. As there are such big gaps between the buses, locals will often stop and offer you a ride.

TAXI

Taxis are hard to come by and are quite expensive compared to on the mainland. From the airport, count on COP$25,000 to Santa Isabel or Aguadulce. The bottom line is that if you call, you'll pay for it; if you can spare the time to wait for a ride, it'll be much cheaper.

SCOOTER

The best way to get about is to hire a scooter (COP$70,000 per day). This can be done at **Moto Rent Airport** (☑ 315-308-9566, 514-8943), a house next to the airport (turn left onto the main road and it's the second house on your left), as well as at Hotel El Pirata Morgan (p183) in Aguadulce and at Cabañas Miss Mary (p185) in Bahía Suroeste. You can also hire golf carts (COP$180,000 per day) at **Providencia Tours** (☑ 314-310-1326) in Aguadulce. The only gas station on the island is on the outskirts of Santa Isabel.

Medellín & Zona Cafetera

Best Places to Eat

➡ Carmen (p196)
➡ Helena Adentro (p222)
➡ Itaca (p196)
➡ La Fogata (p219)
➡ Verdeo (p195)

Best Places to Stay

➡ Hotel Casa Victoria (p195)
➡ 61 Prado (p193)
➡ Finca Villa Nora (p220)
➡ Ciudad de Segorbe (p222)
➡ Hacienda Venecia (p211)

Why Go?

Welcome to *país paisa – paisa* country – a vibrant region made up of coffee plantations and flower farms, lush cloud forest, dynamic student towns and the busy city of Medellín. It is one of Colombia's most dynamic regions, and is not to be missed.

In Medellín, the country's second-largest metropolis, towers soar skyward in the center of a deep valley, concrete examples of the ambition that has placed the city at the vanguard of Colombia's revival. It is an attractive city that seduces most travelers instantly, with its just-perfect climate, great restaurants, museums, public artwork and thumping discos.

Further south is the Zona Cafetera, a rich tapestry of historic villages, charming coffee farms, fantastic nature reserves and grand mountain peaks. Coffee is more than a cash crop here – it is a way of life. You'll never look at your morning cup the same way again.

When to Go
Medellín

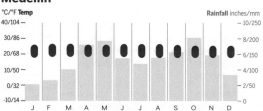

Jan–Mar Clear conditions expose the peaks of Parque Nacional Natural (PNN) Los Nevados.

Aug The streets of Medellín explode with the vibrant colors of the Feria de las Flores.

Oct–Dec Coffee pickers mass on farms throughout the Zona Cafetera for the main harvest.

National, State & Regional Parks

The big daddy of national parks here is Parque Nacional Natural (PNN) Los Nevados, which soars at more than 5000m. Recinto del Pensamiento, Los Yarumos and Reserva Ecológica Río Blanco, near Manizales, boast beautiful species of orchids and butterflies. East of Pereira are the rarely visited Santuario Otún Quimbaya and Parque Ucumarí. Further south, don't miss the stunning Valle de Cocora, near Salento, with its soaring wax palms.

❶ Getting There & Around

Medellín airport is the main international hub of the area. Pereira and Armenia airports also both receive international flights. The region is well serviced by buses to Bogotá, Cali and the Caribbean coast.

Avoid long-distance road travel during torrential rains (most likely during April/May and September/October) as landslides are common.

MEDELLÍN

📕 4 / POP 3 MILLION / ELEV 1494M

Medellín packs the punch of a city twice its size. Situated in a narrow valley, the city's skyline reaches for the heavens, setting highrise apartment and office buildings against a backdrop of jagged peaks in every direction. Its pleasant climate gives the city its nickname – the City of Eternal Spring – and the moderate temperatures put a spring in the locals' steps, at work and at play. It's a bustling city of industry and commerce, especially textile manufacturing and exported cut flowers. On the weekends Medellín lets its hair down, and the city's many discos attract the beautiful people.

The city sprawls north and south along the valley floor. Slums hug the upper reaches of the hills. True to its *paisa* (people of Antioquia) roots, Medellín affects an indifference to the rest of Colombia, and puts on metropolitan airs – the traffic officers wear Italian-style round, boxy hats; many discos prefer techno or reggaeton to salsa and vallenato; and the city looks overseas for the inspiration for its next great public-works project.

History

Spaniards first arrived in the Aburrá Valley in the 1540s, but Medellín was not founded until 1616. Historians believe that many early settlers were Spanish Jews fleeing the Inquisition. They divided the land into small haciendas (country estates), which they farmed themselves – something that was very different from the slave-based plantation culture that dominated much of Colombia. With their focus on self-reliance, these early *paisas* came to be known as hard workers with a fierce independent streak – traits they've exported throughout the Zona Cafetera.

Medellín became the capital of Antioquia in 1826 but long remained a provincial backwater, which explains why its colonial buildings are neither sumptuous nor numerous. The city's rapid growth began only at the start of the 20th century, when the arrival of the railroad, together with a highly profitable boom in coffee production, quickly transformed the city. Mine owners and coffee barons invested their profits in a nascent textile industry, and their gamble paid off. Within a few decades, Medellín had become a large metropolitan city.

By the 1980s the city's entrepreneurial spirit was showing its dark side. Under the violent leadership of Pablo Escobar, Medellín became the capital of the world's cocaine business. Gun battles were common, and the city's homicide rate was among the highest on the planet. The beginning of the end of the violence came with Escobar's death in 1993, and today Medellín is one of the most accessible destinations in the country.

◉ Sights

★ **Plazoleta de las Esculturas**   PLAZA
(Plaza Botero; Map p194) This public space in front of the Museo de Antioquia is home to 23 large bronze sculptures by renowned local artist Fernando Botero. For more Botero, check out the iconic **La Gorda**, in front of the Banco de la República in Parque Berrío. There are three more Botero sculptures in Parque San Antonio, including the **Pájaro de Paz** (Bird of Peace), which sits alongside its earlier incarnation that was destroyed in a terrorist bomb attack.

★ **Cerro Nutibara**   LOOKOUT
(Map p190) On top of this 80m-tall hill, 2km southwest of the city center, sits the kitschy **Pueblito Paisa**, a miniature version of a typical Antioquian township. Views across the city from the adjacent platform are stunning. Next to the lookout you'll find the **Museo de la Ciudad** (Map p190; admission COP$1000;

Medellín & Zona Cafetera Highlights

1 Crane your neck to see the tops of the majestic wax palms in the **Valle de Cocora** (p223).

2 Ride the Metrocable high above the rooftops of **Medellín** (p187), then explore the city's many fine restaurants and bars.

3 Head out into the plantation and pick your own coffee in the **Zona Cafetera** (p205).

4 Bathe in piping-hot thermal springs high in the mountains at **Termales San Vicente** (p217).

5 Spend the night in **Río Claro** (p205), your hotel room open to the jungle, the river roaring below.

6 Hike among the mighty glaciers of **Parque Nacional Natural Los Nevados** (p212).

7 Scale the **Piedra del Peñol** (p201) for amazing views over the Embalse Guatapé.

8 Sip a mug of local arabica in the vibrant central plaza in **Jardín** (p203).

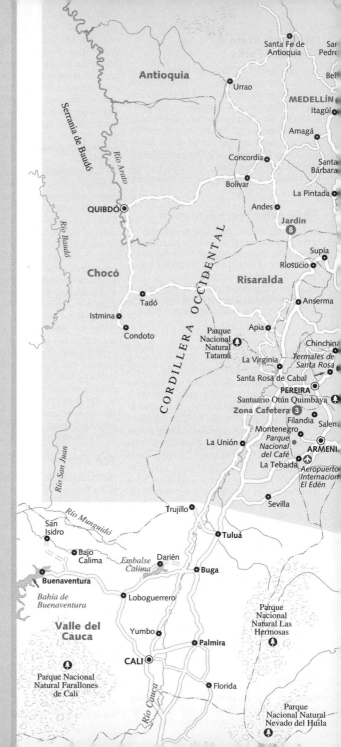

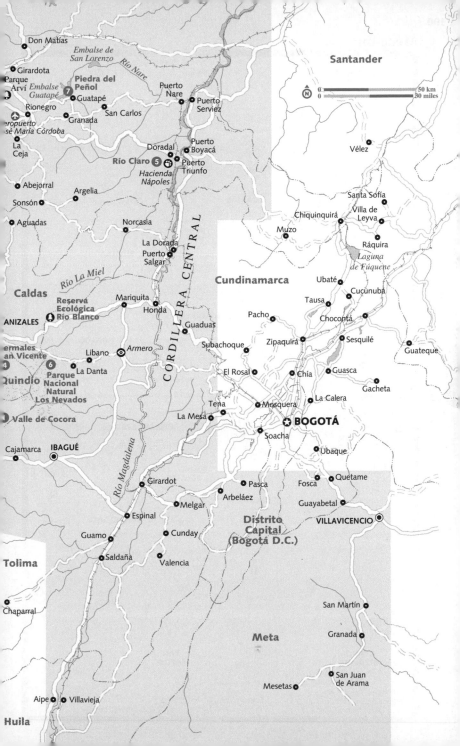

Medellín

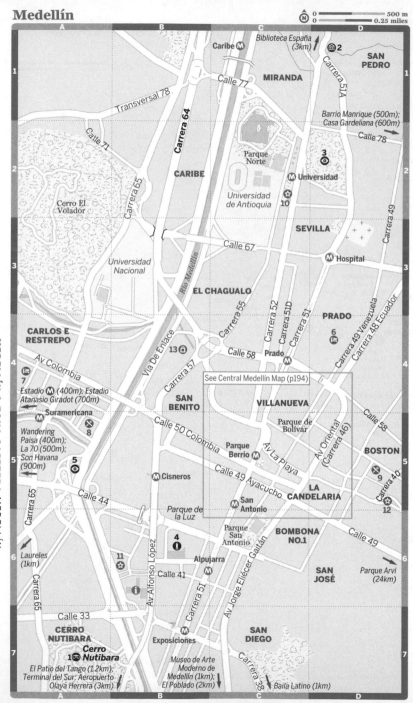

0 — 500 m
0 — 0.25 miles

Caribe Ⓜ

Biblioteca España (3km)

🏛 2

SAN PEDRO

Calle 77

MIRANDA

Transversal 78

Carrera 64

Carrera 51A

Barrio Manrique (500m); Casa Gardeliana (600m)

Calle 78

Carrera 65

Parque Norte

CARIBE

3 ◎

Cerro El Volador

Ⓜ Universidad

Universidad de Antioquia

☆ 10

SEVILLA

Carrera 49

Calle 67

Universidad Nacional

Río Medellín

Ⓜ Hospital

EL CHAGUALO

Carrera 55

Carrera 52

Carrera 51D

Carrera 51

PRADO

Carrera 49 Venezuela

Carrera 48 Ecuador

6 🏛

CARLOS E RESTREPO

Vía De Enlace

13 🏠

Calle 58

Prado Ⓜ

Av Colombia

7 🏛

Carrera 57

SAN BENITO

VILLANUEVA

Calle 58

Estadio Ⓜ (400m); Estadio Atanasio Girardot (700m)

Ⓜ Suramericana

8

Calle 50 Colombia

Parque de Bolívar

Av Oriental (Carrera 46)

BOSTON

Wandering Paisa (400m); La 70 (500m); Son Havana (900m)

5 ◎

Parque Berrío Ⓜ

Av La Playa

9 🍴

Carrera 40

Ⓜ Cisneros

Calle 49 Ayacucho

LA CANDELARIA

☆ 12

Carrera 69

Calle 44

Parque de la Luz

Ⓜ San Antonio

See Central Medellín Map (p194)

Laureles (1km)

4 ℹ

Parque San Antonio

BOMBONA NO.1

Calle 49

Carrera 65

11 ☆

Alpujarra Ⓜ

Av Alfonso López

Calle 41

Av Jorge Eliécer Gaitán

SAN JOSÉ

Parque Arví (24km)

ℹ

Carrera 51

Calle 33

CERRO NUTIBARA

1 ◎ Cerro Nutibara

Ⓜ Exposiciones

SAN DIEGO

Carrera 38

El Patio del Tango (1.2km); Terminal del Sur; Aeropuerto Olaya Herrera (3km)

Museo de Arte Moderno de Medellín (1km); El Poblado (2km)

Baila Latino (1km)

Medellín

◎ **Top Sights**
1 Cerro Nutibara A7

◎ **Sights**
2 Casa Museo Pedro Nel Gómez D1
3 Jardín Botánico D2
4 Monumento a la Raza B6
Museo de la Ciudad .... (see 1)
5 Plaza de Toros A5

🛏 **Sleeping**
6 61 Prado D4
7 Palm Tree Hostal A4

🍴 **Eating**
8 Ciao Pizza Gourmet A5
9 Itaca D5

🎭 **Entertainment**
10 Parque de los Deseos C2
11 Teatro Metropolitano B6
12 Teatro Pablo Tobón Uribe D5

🛍 **Shopping**
13 Plaza Minorista José María Villa B4

⊙ 10am-6pm), a small museum dedicated to the history of Medellín and mainly showcasing old photographs of the city.

Take a taxi to the top and walk back down to check out the **Parque de las Esculturas**, which contains modern abstract sculptures by South American artists.

Museo de Antioquia   MUSEUM
(Map p194; 251-3636; www.museodeantioquia.org.co; Carrera 52 No 52-43; admission COP$10,000; ⊙ 10am-5:30pm Mon-Sat, to 4:30pm Sun) In the grand art deco Palacio Municipal, Colombia's second-oldest museum (Museo Nacional in Bogotá is the oldest) is also one of its finest. The collection includes pre-Columbian, colonial and modern art collections, as well as many works donated by native son Fernando Botero.

Parque Arví   PARK
(www.parquearvi.org; Veredas Mazo & Piedras Blancas, Santa Elena) ∅ Accessible by the fantastic new Cable Arví Metrocable (Linea L) from the Santo Domingo interchange (COP$4600 one way, 15 minutes), Parque Arví is a big chunk of mountain wilderness in Santa Elena that makes a great escape from the city. Inside the boundaries of the 17.61-sq-km reserve are hiking trails, canopy lines, lakes and a *mariposario* (butterfly enclosure). Free guided walks leave every hour from 10am to 3pm from the tourist information point. The cable car is closed for maintenance on Mondays. Attractions are spread out so it's best to arrive early.

Biblioteca España   BUILDING
(385-6717; Carrera 33B No 107A-100; ⊙ 8am-7pm Mon-Fri, 11am-5pm Sun) Constructed high on the mountainside in a marginalized neighborhood, this huge library is one of Medellín's most recognized landmarks and an emblem of the city's revival. At the time of research the entire structure was cloaked in a protective net after serious structural issues were identified, but it's still worth a trip up here to see another side of the city and take in the views from the adjacent park. It's next to the Santo Domingo Metrocable interchange.

Jardín Botánico   GARDENS
(Map p190; www.botanicomedellin.org; Calle 73 No 51D-14; ⊙ 9am-5pm) FREE One of Medellín nicest green spaces, the botanic gardens covers 14 hectares, showcases 600 species of trees and plants, and includes a lake, a herbarium and a butterfly enclosure. A couple of hours here offers a fine respite from the bustle of the city. The gardens are easily accessed from the nearby metro stop Universidad.

Museo de Arte Moderno de Medellín   GALLERY
(444-2622; www.elmamm.org; Carrera 44 No 19A-100; admission COP$8000; ⊙ 9am-5:30pm Tue-Fri, 10am-5:30pm Sat, 10am-4:30pm Sun) In a refurbished industrial building in Ciudad del Río, 'El MAMM' showcases changing exhibitions of contemporary art. A large new wing that is to house the permanent collection was under construction at the time of research.

Casa Museo Pedro Nel Gómez   MUSEUM
(Map p190; 444-2633; Carrera 51B No 85-24; ⊙ 9am-5pm Mon-Sat, 10am-4pm Sun) FREE Located in the house where the artist lived and worked, this interesting museum has an extensive collection of pieces by prolific local painter Pedro Nel Gómez (1899–1984), as well as occasional major exhibitions. It also hosts regular art workshops.

Basílica de la Candelaria   CHURCH
(Map p194; cnr Carrera 50 & Calle 51) Medellín's most important church stands guard over Parque Berrío, and was constructed in the 1770s on the site of an earlier wooden structure. It features a German-made pipe organ brought to the city by boat up the Río Magdalena and then on horseback.

Ermita de la Veracruz CHURCH

(Map p194; cnr Calle 51 Boyacá & Carrera 52 Carabobo) Constructed with funds from European immigrants, this fine colonial church was inaugurated in 1803. It features a stone facade and a white-and-gold interior.

Monumento a la Raza MONUMENT

(Map p190; Calle 44, Centro Administrativo La Alpujarra) Rodrigo Arenas Betancur's most impressive work in Medellín tells the story of Antioquia in dramatically twisting metal.

Catedral Metropolitana CHURCH

(Map p194; Carrera 48) Overlooking Parque de Bolívar, Medellín's neo-Romanesque cathedral was completed in 1931. Its spacious but dim interior has Spanish stained-glass windows.

Activities

There are strong thermal winds around Medellín, making it a fine paragliding spot. All the paragliding companies operate out of San Felix in Bello. Take a bus (COP$2800, 45 minutes) from the Terminal del Norte. A taxi will cost around COP$35,000.

Zona de Vuelo PARAGLIDING

(☑ 388-1556, 312-832-5891; www.zonadevuelo.com; Km5.6 Via San Pedro de los Milagros) This experienced operator offers tandem flights (from COP$85,000 to COP$105,000) and 15-day courses (COP$1,500,000).

Psiconautica ADVENTURE SPORTS

(☑ 426-4948, 312-795-6321; www.aventurapsiconautica.com; Km5.6 Via San Pedro de los Milagros) In the same complex as Zona de Vuelo, this one-stop adventure shop specializes in rock climbing, canyoning and abseiling as well as paragliding. Its experienced bilingual guides arrange mountaineering and trekking trips around the country.

Courses

Universidad EAFIT LANGUAGE COURSE

(☑ 261-9399; www.eafit.edu.co; Carrera 49 No 7 Sur-50) Private university offering intensive and semi-intensive Spanish study in a group setting. Individual tuition is also available.

Baila Latino DANCE COURSE

(☑ 448-1338; www.academiabailalatino.com; Carrera 43 No 25A-233; individual classes per hour COP$45,000, group classes per month COP$65,000) Learn salsa and other tropical rhythms with friendly and enthusiastic instructors.

Tours

Real City Tours GUIDED TOURS

(☑ 319-262-2008; www.realcitytours.com) Run by enthusiastic young locals, this company offers a free walking tour through the city center with detailed explanations in English of the stories behind the main points of interest. Tips for the guides are encouraged. It also runs a paid fruit-themed tour to Medellín's largest market. You need to reserve online to secure your spot.

Paisa Road GUIDED TOURS

(☑ 317-489-2629; www.paisaroad.com) Runs the original Pablo Escobar–themed tour (COP$40,000) as well as sociable football tours (COP$50,000) on weekends where you'll sit among the most passionate supporters at a national league match.

Festivals & Events

Festival Internacional de Tango DANCE

(www.festivaldetangomedellin.com; ☺ Jun) The city celebrates its love for tango with competitions, concerts and workshops.

Festival de Poesía de Medellín LITERATURE

(www.festivaldepoesiademedellin.org; ☺ Jul) This fine international festival attracts poets from all corners of the globe.

Feria de las Flores CULTURAL

(www.feriadelasfloresmedellin.gov.co; ☺ Aug) This week-long festival is Medellín's most spectacular event. The highlight is the Desfile de Silleteros, when up to 400 campesinos (peasants) come from the mountains to parade along the streets with flowers on their backs.

Festival Internacional de Jazz MUSIC

(Medejazz; www.festivalmedejazz.com; ☺ Sep) Many North American bands come for this festival. There are usually a couple of free concerts.

Alumbrado Navideño RELIGIOUS

(☺ Dec & Jan) A colorful Christmas illumination of the city, with thousands of lights strung across streets and alongside the Río Medellín.

Sleeping

El Poblado has quickly become the place to stay for most travelers. It is close to the bars and restaurants, and is usually safe, even late at night. Those not interested in partying, or who want a less-sanitized experience of Medellín, may like to stay in the more rough-and-

PROFITING FROM PABLO

Even after his death, infamous cocaine warlord Pablo Escobar Gaviria keeps on making money. When backpackers started flowing back into Medellín – something only made possible by the fall of the Medellín Cartel boss – a couple of young local entrepreneurs sensed an opportunity. They began running Escobar-themed tours, visiting the pivotal places from his bloody reign over the city: his luxurious homes and offices, the suburban house where he was shot, and his grave. More mainstream tour operators soon latched on, and even members of Escobar's family have begun running tours where you can discuss the *capo's* (boss's) favorite things with his brother.

Needless to say, plenty of Colombians are unimpressed with what they see as the glorification of a bloodthirsty terrorist who blew up planes and once paid his henchmen for every police officer they killed. Others accept that Escobar is an important historical figure and compare the tours to those dedicated to mobsters in Chicago.

Most tours last around half a day, but note that prices and quality vary widely. If you do decide to take an Escobar-themed tour, Paisa Road gets positive reviews for its informative and impartial tours.

You can get an even better idea of the sheer scale of Escobar's wealth, ambition and questionable taste at **Hacienda Nápoles** – site of a huge farm four hours from Medellín. This he turned into a private kingdom complete with several mansions, a bullring, and exotic pets including giraffes, zebras and several hippopotamuses.

When the government turned up the heat on Escobar, Hacienda Nápoles was abandoned. The hippos went feral but somehow survived and now take center stage at a new safari-themed **adventure park** (☑1800-510-344; www.haciendanapoles.com; admission COP$32,000-60,000) that has opened on the site. It is a truly bizarre place where you can walk through Escobar's abandoned mansion and look over his bombed-out vehicles while a concrete Tyrannosaurus rex bellows out in the distance. There are also rides for the kids, a water park and a butterfly enclosure alongside some graphic displays on the violence that accompanied Escobar's reign. It's worth checking out for weirdness factor alone.

The turnoff to Hacienda Nápoles is 1km from Doradal on the Medellín–Bogotá highway. From here to the park gate is a further 2km down an unpaved road. A taxi from town costs COP$10,000. Ask for the driver's number for the round-trip journey. The park can easily be visited on a day trip from Río Claro.

tumble center. A middle option is the area around 'La Setenta', which is less flashy than Poblado yet more orderly than the center.

Black Sheep
HOSTEL **$**

(Map p198; ☑311-1589, 317-518-1369; www.black sheepmedellin.com; Transversal 5A No 45-133; dm COP$22,000-25,000, s/d COP$60,000/80,000, without bathroom COP$50,000/65,000; @🛜) Conveniently located close to the Poblado metro, this well-run hostel has a pleasant social vibe without being rowdy. There are a variety of common areas, including a lovely new terrace, and a good selection of comfortable, modern, private rooms. The knowledgeable staff is particularly helpful in arranging activities and onward travel plans. The on-site Spanish lessons get top reviews.

61 Prado
GUESTHOUSE **$**

(Map p190; ☑254-9743; www.61prado.com; Calle 61 No 50A-60; s/d/ste COP$55,000/75,000/85,000; @🛜) This elegant place in the historic Prado neighborhood is a great base from which to explore the sights around the center. Carefully renovated rooms are spacious with high ceilings and touches of art throughout. The candlelit dining room is a fine place to enjoy a meal from the on-site restaurant. Guests can use the well-equipped kitchen.

Casa Kiwi
HOSTEL **$**

(Map p198; ☑268-2668; www.casakiwi.net; Carrera 36 No 7-10; dm COP$20,000-24,000, s/d COP$60,000/80,000, without bathroom COP$40,000/60,000; @🛜🏊) With an enviable location on the edge of the *zona rosa* in El Poblado, Casa Kiwi is a popular choice among those keen to sample Medellín's famous nightlife. There are a variety of elegant private rooms alongside more standard dorms. The appealing common areas include a spacious terrace, a cinema-like TV room, a rooftop dipping pool, a vibrant bar and a fantastic deck overlooking the street.

MEDELLÍN & ZONA CAFETERA MEDELLÍN

Central Medellín

Also organizes adventurous full-day rafting trips (COP$180,000) to the Río Buey and Río San Juan in rural Antioquia.

Wandering Paisa
HOSTEL $

(☑436-6759; www.wanderingpaisahostel.com; Calle 44A No 68A-76; dm COP$21,000-25,000, s/d COP$55,000/60,000; @🛜) Right by the bars and restaurants of La 70, this dynamic hostel is a great choice for those wanting to find a middle ground between the bright lights of El Poblado and the chaos of downtown. There is a small bar and the enthusiastic management is constantly arranging social events and group outings. Bikes are available to explore the neighborhood.

Grand Hostel
HOSTEL $

(Map p198; ☑444-6612; www.grandhostelmedellin.com; Transversal 6 No 45-70; dm COP$20,000-25,000, s/d COP$70,000/90,000, without bathroom 50,000/60,000; 🛜) A quiet option close to the Poblado metro, this friendly place is

popular with mellow travelers looking for a homely base. The rooms in the main part of the house are bright and comfortable; however, the privates with shared bathroom in the rear are dark and lack ventilation.

Palm Tree Hostal
HOSTEL $

(Map p190; ☑444-7256; www.palmtreemedellin.com; Carrera 67 No 48D-63; dm COP$25,000, r without bathroom COP$66,000; @🛜) In a middle-class neighborhood close to the metro and plenty of cheap eateries, Medellín's original backpacker hostel has simple but comfortable rooms and friendly staff.

Happy Buddha
HOSTEL $$

(Map p198; ☑311-7744; www.thehappybuddha.co; Carrera 35 No 7-108; dm/r/tw incl breakfast COP$30,000/110,000/120,000; 🛜) Boasting top-notch facilities and a sleek, modern design, this new hostel on the edge of the zona rosa in El Poblado has quickly become a popular choice for those looking for both

Central Medellín

nightlife and comfort. The common areas include a pleasant terrace and a lounge with sofas, ping pong and a pool table. Added extras include a free weekly BBQ and dance classes.

In House Hotel HOTEL $$
(Map p198; ✆444-1786; www.inhousethehotel. com; Carrera 34 No 7-109; s/d/tr incl breakfast COP$138,000/155,000/212,000; @🛜) This excellent-value small hotel stands out from the crowd in busy Poblado. Its stylish, bright rooms feature pine furniture, work desks and big windows. Service is friendly and professional, and a continental breakfast is included. Rooms at the front have private balconies while those at the rear are quieter.

Hotel Casa Victoria HOTEL $$$
(✆268-5099; www.hotelcasavictoria.com; Carrera 32 No 1 Sur-13; s/d/ste incl breakfast COP$168,240/175,240/226,240; ❄@🛜) Located on a hillside below El Tesoro, this fine hotel offers spacious rooms with wooden floors and huge windows offering great views over the city. The suites open onto private terraces. Offers discounts on weekends.

Hotel Dann Carlton HOTEL $$$
(Map p198; ✆444-5151; hotelesmedellin. danncarlton.com; Carrera 43A No 7-50; s/d

COP$229,000/363,000, ste from COP$621,000; ❄🛜❄) This professionally run hotel is a cut above the rest with quality accommodations and plenty of extras such as fresh tropical fruits and elegant flower displays. The suites in particular are huge, with attached sitting room, walk-in closet and massive bathroom.

🍴 Eating

El Poblado is full of upscale restaurants. Southwest of the center, the Laureles neighborhood around Av Nutibara has many unpretentious eateries. Self-caterers should check out the **Plaza Minorista** (Map p190; cnr Carrera 57 & Calle 55) – a large covered market full of fresh fruit and vegetables.

El Poblado

Cafe Zorba INTERNATIONAL $
(Map p198; Calle 8 No 42-33; pizza COP$11,500-18,500; ◷5-11:45pm; 🛜) Nestled on the edge of Parque La Presidenta, this fashionable open-air cafe serves up excellent pizzas, salads and dips as well as delicious desserts. It's also a great place to enjoy an after-dinner drink.

El Taxista COLOMBIAN $
(Map p198; Carrera 43B No 10-22; meals COP$6500; ◷7am-4pm) Tradespeople sit shoulder-to-shoulder with sharp-suited business folk at this no-nonsense diner near Parque Poblado. It serves cheap and cheerful *paisa* favorites from a tiny kitchen full of frantically frying women.

Verdeo VEGETARIAN $$
(Map p198; www.ricoverdeo.com; Carrera 35 No 8A-3; mains COP$14,500-21,800; ◷noon-10pm Tue-Sun, to 4pm Mon; 🍴) 🍃 You don't have to be vegetarian to enjoy the creative dishes on offer at this groovy Poblado restaurant. Take your pick from delicious vegetarian shawarma, burgers, ravioli and salads. The attached grocer is a great place to pick up organic veggies, tofu and other products not found in local supermarkets.

Il Castello ITALIAN $$
(Map p198; ✆312-8287; Carrera 40 No 10A-14; mains COP$16,000-28,000; ◷noon-2:30pm & 6-10:30pm Mon-Sat) For authentic, quality Italian food, look no further than this unpretentious bistro. The pizzas are tasty but it is the pastas that really excel, especially the ravioli. Accompany your meal with a bottle from the extensive wine list.

MEDELLÍN & ZONA CAFETERA MEDELLÍN

Mondongos COLOMBIAN $$
(Map p198; www.mondongos.com.co; Calle 10 No
38-38; mains COP$21,000-28,000; ⊗11:30am-
9:30pm Mon-Sat, to 8pm Sun) Medellín families
flock to this unremarkable-looking eatery to
fill up on *sopa de mondongo* (tripe soup).
It is served with avocado, banana, lemon
and *arepas* (corn cakes), which are added or
dunked in the bowl according to each din-
er's personal ritual. For the full experience,
come for Sunday lunch. There is another
branch on La 70.

Bahía Mar SEAFOOD $$
(Map p198; Calle 9 No 43B-127; mains COP$20,000-
40,000; ⊗noon-10pm Mon-Sat, to 3pm Sun) This
top-notch seafood place serves a variety of
dishes in an unpretentious Caribbean setting.

★**Carmen** INTERNATIONAL $$$
(Map p198; ☑311-9625; www.carmenmedellin.com;
Carrera 36 No 10A-27; mains COP$39,000-50,000;
⊗noon-3pm Mon, noon-3pm & 7-10:30pm Tue-Fri,
7-10:30pm Sat) Run by an American-Colombian
couple, both of whom are Cordon Bleu chefs,
Carmen prepares sophisticated international
cuisine with a heavy Californian influence.
The restaurant itself is made up of distinct
dining zones – an intimate dining room over-
looking the open kitchen, a conservatory and
a rear patio. The English-speaking waiters
can offer recommendations for wine to ac-
company your meal from the extensive list.
Reservations are essential.

Central Medellín

★**Itaca** COLOMBIAN $
(Map p190; Carrera 42 No 54-60; set lunch
COP$8500, mains COP$10,000-25,000; ⊗noon-
3pm & 6-10pm Mon-Sat, noon-5pm Sun) It doesn't
look like much but this tiny hole-in-the-wall
restaurant on the outskirts of downtown
prepares fantastic gourmet plates bursting
with flavor at bargain prices. There is no
menu; just tell friendly chef Juan Carlos
what you like and he will whip up a mod-
ern Colombian classic from his collection of
market-fresh ingredients. There's no sign –
look for the blue door.

Try a portion of the homemade sausages –
which have been proclaimed the best in An-
tioquia.

Salón Versalles COLOMBIAN $
(Map p194; www.versallesmedellin.com; Pasaje
Junín 53-39; meals COP$13,900; ⊗7am-9pm Mon-
Sat, 8am-6pm Sun) Famous for its scrumptious
Argentine-style empanadas, this Medellín

institution also serves up a good set meal
and is a great place to take a rest from
the bustle of the center. It is frequented by
everyone from hard-up pensioners to young
entrepreneurs and is worth checking out
just to observe the crowd.

Ciao Pizza Gourmet ITALIAN $$
(Map p190; cnr Calle 49 & Carrera 64A, Carlos E
Restrepo; mains COP$12,000-27,000; ⊗noon-
9:30pm Mon-Sat, to 7:30pm Sun) Sit outside on
the small plaza at this neighborhood restaurant to enjoy wonderful pizzas and homemade pastas cooked to perfection by the
Italian chef. It's hidden in a residential area
behind the Suramericana building.

Café Colombo Credenza COLOMBIAN $$$
(Map p194; Carrera 45 No 53-24, 10th fl; mains
COP$23,000-31,000; ⊗noon-10pm Mon-Sat) On
the top floor of the building housing the
Centro Colombo Americano, this casual bis-
tro serves up quality meals along with great
views of the city. It's a great spot for cocktails
early in the evening.

🍷 Drinking & Nightlife

The city's *zona rosa* is around Parque Lleras
in El Poblado, a dense tangle of upscale res-
taurants and bars. A bunch of Medellín's
most exclusive bars are located in and
around the **Río Sur** (Carrera 43A No 6 Sur-26)
mall on a stretch of Av El Poblado known as
the Milla de Oro (Golden Mile). Less showy
are the bars around La 33 and La 70 near the
Laureles neighborhood. For a more bohemi-
an experience, check out the options around
Parque del Periodista in the center.

Many late-night options are clustered in
the former industrial neighborhood of Bar-
rio Colombia and on the Autopista Sur – the
southern highway out of town.

Pergamino CAFE
(Map p198; www.pergamino.co; Carrera 37 No 8A-
37; ⊗8am-9pm Mon-Fri, 9am-9pm Sat) It's worth
the effort to wait in line for a drink at this
popular cafe, which serves up the best coffee
in Medellín. There is a full range of hot and
cold beverages, all made with top-quality
beans sourced from small farms around the
country. You can also buy coffee in bags to
take home.

Trilogia Bar CLUB
(www.trilogiabar.com; Carrera 43G No 24-08;
⊗8:30pm-3:30am) For a dynamic night out,
head to this friendly club in Barrio Colombia
where bands perform Colombian crossover

music from a revolving stage while tipsy locals sing along. Come with a group, and make reservations on the website to avoid missing out.

El Acontista
BAR

(Map p194; www.elacontista.com; Calle 53 Maracaibo No 43-81; ☺closed Sun) Attracting an intellectual crowd, this chilled bar-cafe near Parque del Periodista is a great place for drinks and conversation. There is live jazz on Mondays and a bookstore upstairs.

Calle 9 + 1
BAR

(Map p198; Carrera 40 No 10-25; ☺9pm-late) Set around a spacious covered courtyard, this hip alternative hangout has DJs spinning independent electronic music to an arty crowd, and a different vibe to most of the mainstream bars in the Parque Lleras area.

Son Havana
CLUB

(Carrera 73 No 44-56; ☺8:30pm-3am Wed-Sat) The bar of choice for serious salsa fans, this popular place just off La 70 has a great tropical vibe. The small dance floor fills up fast, so most patrons end up dancing around the tables. It's pretty dark so you don't need to worry too much if you lack the moves. It gets packed on Thursdays and Saturdays for its live band performances.

Berlín
PUB

(Map p198; ☎266-2905; Calle 10 No 41-65; ☺6pm-2am) The only real pub in El Poblado, Berlín comes complete with dingy lighting, pool tables and rock classics. It's a welcome respite from the neon-clone bars that dominate the area.

Eslabon Prendido
CLUB

(Papayera; Map p194; Calle 53 No 42-55; ☺9pm-3am) Hugely popular with backpackers and Medellín's expat community, this unpretentious salsa bar attracts a crowd on Tuesdays and Thursdays for its live band. The vibe is very sociable; you don't need to bring a dance partner.

Luxury
CLUB

(Carrera 43G No 24-15; ☺10:30pm-4am Thu-Sun) One of the hottest clubs in Barrio Colombia, Luxury is full of young *paisas* grinding to reggaeton and hip-hop. Avoid the upstairs VIP area – the ground floor is where the action is at. Turn up well tipsy unless you actually enjoy reggaeton.

COUNTING CALORIES: BANDEJA PAISA

The artery-busting *bandeja paisa* (*paisa* tray) is famed across Colombia as the most typical plate of Antioquia and the Zona Cafetera. What is harder to get consensus on is what it actually consists of. The dish has its origins among poor farmers who would eat one high-calorie meal a day to give them energy to work in the cool mountain climates. These days there are many variations of the dish served in restaurants all over the country. However, among purists, for a plate to be worthy of the name it must include white rice, red beans, ground meat, pork rinds, avocado, fried eggs, plantains, sausage, *arepas* (corn cakes), *hogao* (warm tomato chutney) and black pudding. It must also all be squeezed onto one oval-shaped plate.

Bendito Seas
CLUB

(Map p198; Calle 10A No 38-21; ☺10pm-4am Thu-Sat) This unpretentious club a couple of blocks from Parque Lleras packs in a young crowd that come to dance to crossover and reggaeton, especially on Thursdays when there is an open bar.

☆ Entertainment

Cinema

Teatro Lido
CINEMA, THEATER

(Map p194; ☎251-5334; www.medellincultura. gov.co; Carrera 48 No 54-20) On Parque de Bolívar, this refurbished theater has regular free screenings of documentaries and alternative films as well as concerts and other events.

Parque de los Deseos
CINEMA

(Map p190; ☎516-6404; www.fundacionepm.org. co; Carrera 52 No 71-11) Bring something soft to sit on for the free open-air cinema at this sleek, all-concrete space across from the Jardín Botánico. Films are usually shown at 6:30pm on Tuesdays and weekends.

Tango

Once the preferred dance of the we're-not-really-Colombian *paisas,* it now lingers on in the memories of the older generation, and those with a taste for nostalgia.

El Poblado

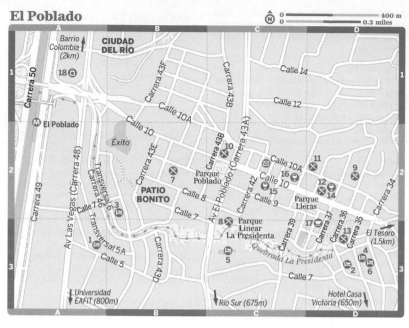

El Poblado

Casa Gardeliana   DANCE
(☏ 444-2633; Carrera 45 No 76-50; admission free; ☺ 9am-5pm Mon-Fri) Located in Barrio Manrique, the Casa Gardeliana was Medellín's main tango venue for years, hosting tango bands and dance shows. It still holds events occasionally but is now basically a small tango museum and dance academy offering group classes (COP$33,000 per month) as well as personalized instruction (COP$40,000 per hour).

El Patio del Tango   DANCE
(☏ 235-4595; www.patiodeltango.com; Calle 23 No 58-38; mains COP$28,000; ☺ noon-8pm Mon-Wed,

noon-1:30am Thu-Sat) Now tango's major stage in Medellín, this steak restaurant is decorated like a typical Buenos Aires tango dive. Make reservations in advance for the live shows on Fridays and Saturdays. It's located a couple of blocks from the zoo.

Sports
Medellín has two soccer teams, **Independiente Medellín** (DIM; www.dimoficial.com) and **Atlético Nacional** (www.atlnacional.com. co). Both play at **Estadio Atanasio Giradot** near the aptly named Estadio metro station.

The greater metropolitan area of Medellín also has its own team, **Envigado Fútbol**

Club (www.envigadofutbolclub.net), which plays in the southern municipality of Envigado.

Theater

Medellín has the liveliest theater scene outside of Bogotá.

Teatro Metropolitano　　　　THEATER
(Map p190; ☑ 232-2858; www.teatrometropolitano. com; Calle 41 No 57-30) Medellín's largest and most modern theater hosts concerts, opera and ballet and is home to Medellín's Philharmonic Orchestra.

Teatro Pablo Tobón Uribe　　　THEATER
(Map p190; ☑ 239-7500; www.teatropablotobon. com; Carrera 40 No 51-24) This is Medellín's major mainstream theater.

🛍 Shopping

Centro Comercial Palacio
Nacional　　　　　　　　SHOPPING CENTER
(Map p194; cnr Carrera 52 & Calle 48) A palatial building from 1925 in the center, it has been transformed into a shopping mall with more than 200 budget shops (most selling clothing and footwear). The area around the Palacio, nicknamed El Hueco (The Hole) by locals, features plenty of bargain stores.

Centro Artesanal Mi Viejo
Pueblo　　　　　　　　　HANDICRAFTS
(Map p194; Carrera 49 No 53-20; ◷9am-7:30pm Mon-Thu, to 8pm Fri & Sat, 10am-6pm Sun) This tourist-oriented handicraft market has a wide selection of souvenirs, including hammocks, bags and traditional clothing.

Mercado de San Alejo　　　　MARKET
(Map p194; Parque de Bolívar; ◷1st Sat each month) This colorful craft market is great for cheap buys or simply for strolling around.

Centro Commercial
Monterrey　　　　　　　　ELECTRONICS
(Map p198; Carrera 48 No 10-45) Large mall full of cut-priced electronics.

❶ Information

There are numerous ATMs throughout the city including at Parque Berrío in the center, along Av El Poblado and around Parque Lleras.

Medellín makes it easy to get tourist information through a network of Punto Información Turísticas (PIT), operated by courteous and knowledgeable bilingual staff. In addition to those we list, there are also branches in Pueblito Paisa and in each of the airports and bus terminals.

---

❶ WHAT'S ON IN MEDELLÍN

Planepoly (www.planepoly.com) A comprehensive website with event and cinema listings.

Opcion Hoy (www.opcionhoy.com) Local entertainment listings with a cultural focus.

Medellín en Escena (www.medellin enescena.com) For local theater event listings.

Medellín Zona Rosa (www.medellin-zonarosa.com) Concert schedules and nightlife.

4-72 (Map p198; Calle 10A No 41-11; ◷8am-noon & 1-6pm Mon-Fri, 9am-noon Sat) Post office in El Poblado.

Clínica Las Vegas (☑ 315-9000; www.clini calasvegas.com; Calle 2 Sur No 46-55) Professional private medical facility. Staff speaks some English.

Clínica Medellín (☑ 311-2800; www.clinica medellin.com; Calle 7 No 39-290) Private clinic in El Poblado where the staff speaks some English. There is another branch in central Medellín.

Migración Colombia (☑ 345-5500; www. migracioncolombia.gov.co; Calle 19 No 80A-40, Barrio Belén; ◷8am-4pm Mon-Fri) For visa extensions. From El Poblado take the Circular Sur 302/303 bus heading south along Av Las Vegas.

PIT Plaza Botero (Map p194; www.medellin. travel; cnr Carrera 51 & Calle 53; ◷8am-5pm Mon-Sat) Tourist office just outside the Plazoleta de las Esculturas.

PIT Plaza Mayor (Map p190; ☑ 261-7277; www. medellin.travel; Calle 41 No 55-80; ◷8am-6pm Mon-Fri) The main tourist office in the Palacio de Exposiciones.

❶ Getting There & Away

AIR

Medellín has two airports. All international flights and domestic flights to major cities depart from **Aeropuerto Internacional José María Córdoba**, 35km southeast of the city near the town of Ríonegro. Buses shuttle between the city center and the airport every 15 minutes (COP$8600, one hour, 5am to 9pm). The **bus stop** (Map p194; Carrera 50A No 53-13) in town is behind the Hotel Nutibara. A taxi will set you back COP$60,000.

The smaller **Aeropuerto Olaya Herrera** is next door to Terminal del Sur bus station. Regional domestic flights leave from here, including services to destinations in El Chocó.

BUS

Medellín has two bus terminals. **Terminal del Norte**, 3km north of the city center, handles buses to the north, east and southeast, including Santa Fe de Antioquia (COP$13,000, two hours), Cartagena (COP$130,000, 13 hours), Santa Marta (COP$130,000, 16 hours) and Bogotá (COP$60,000, nine hours). It is easily reached from El Poblado by metro (alight at Caribe) or by taxi (COP$12,500).

Terminal del Sur, 4km southwest of the center, handles all traffic to the west and south, including Manizales (COP$35,000, five hours), Pereira (COP$35,000, five hours), Armenia (COP$40,000, six hours) and Cali (COP$50,000, nine hours). From El Poblado it's a quick taxi ride (COP$6000).

ℹ Getting Around

BICYCLE

Medellín has a fledgling free public bicycle system called **Encicla** (www.encicla.gov.co). Visitors are able to take out bicycles for short trips using their passport. A network of new bicycle paths are planned for the second phase of the project. Check the website for station locations.

BUS

Medellín is well serviced by buses, although most travelers will find the metro and taxis sufficient for their needs. The majority of routes originate on Av Oriental and from Parque Berrío. Buses stop running around 10pm or 11pm.

METRO

Medellín's **Metro** (www.metrodemedellin.gov. co; single ticket COP$1900; ☺ 4:30am-11pm Mon-Sat, 5am-10pm Sun) is Colombia's only commuter rail line. It opened in 1995 and consists of a 23km north–south line and a 6km east–west line. Trains run at ground level except for 5km through the central area where they go on elevated tracks. The metro company also operates three cable car lines, called Metrocable, built to service the impoverished barrios in the surrounding hills and Park Arví in Santa Elena. The rides themselves afford magnificent views and make for a lovely way to check out the town. The two main Metrocable lines are included in the price of a metro ticket, while the Arví line is separate.

TAXI

Taxis are plentiful in Medellín and all are equipped with meters. Minimum charge is COP$4700. A taxi from the center to El Poblado will cost around COP$10,000.

AROUND MEDELLÍN

Guatapé

📷 4 / POP 4230 / ELEV 1925M

The pleasant holiday town of Guatapé is located on the shores of the Embalse Guatapé, a sprawling artificial lake. It is known for the frescolike adornment of its traditional houses. Brightly painted bas-relief depictions of people, animals and shapes cover the lower half of many houses.

Guatapé makes a great day trip from Medellín (it's a two-hour bus ride away), but there is enough here to keep you entertained a bit longer if you fancy a peaceful break from the city. Visit on the weekend if you want to experience the festival atmosphere when the town is packed with Colombian tourists or during the week to explore the surrounding nature at a more relaxed pace.

◉ Sights

A block south from the main square is **Calle de los Recuerdos**, a cobblestone street that angles uphill and showcases the best example of the local frescoes.

Iglesia del Calma   CHURCH

The Iglesia del Calma features a Greco-Roman exterior and a polished wood interior. It was built in 1811 as a form of penance, or so the story goes, by a man who killed an orange thief.

Casa del Arriero   NOTABLE BUILDING

(Carrera 28) The oldest and biggest house in Guatapé is still occupied by descendants of the original owners. They usually leave their front door open so visitors can wander into the central courtyard. Take note of the ornate, painted folding doors as you enter. Very typical of Guatapé.

🏃 Activities

A number of boating companies on the *malecón* (promenade) take turns running trips out onto the water. The standard tours swing past La Cruz (a monument to the flooded town of old Peñol mistakenly believed by many to be part of the old church) and Isla de las Fantasias. Most large boats have big sound systems and a dance floor but do not make any stops where you are able to disembark. All charge around COP$10,000 per person and sell cheap drinks.

It is also possible to charter smaller boats (COP$90,000 for up to six passengers) to see the sights on a private tour. Stops include a visit to a museum dedicated to the creation of the lake and, upon request, Pablo Escobar's abandoned farm, Finca La Manuela, where you can get a drink at the refurbished disco-bar.

A **canopy ride** (per ride COP$10,000; ☉1-6pm Mon-Fri, 9am-6pm Sat-Sun) runs along the lake shore from a large hill near the entrance to town. A hydraulic system pulls clients up to the hill from the *malecón* – there's no need to walk up the hill.

🛏 Sleeping & Eating

Prices listed are for weekend stays; most places offer discounts during the week.

★**El Encuentro**   HOSTEL $
(☎311-619-6199;   www.hostelelencuentro.com;
Vereda Quebrada Arriba; dm COP$22,000, s/d from COP$55,000/65,000, ste from COP$95,000; 🛜)
Combining a peaceful ambience, spectacular views and gardens that slope down to a private swimming area, this place feels more like a fancy retreat than a hostel. Some of the elegant rooms have private balconies overlooking the lake. The staff organizes interesting treks in the surrounding mountains. It's a 10-minute walk from town – take a moto-taxi (COP$3000) if you have bags.

Guatatur   HOTEL $$
(☎861-1212; www.hotelguatatur.com; s/d from COP$50,000/100,000, ste COP$224,000; 🛜)
This modestly priced resort near the plaza specializes in weekend package deals for visitors from Medellín; during the week you can snag great deals. Several of the rooms have views of the lake, and the suites have Jacuzzis and even lovelier views.

Donde Sam   INDIAN, INTERNATIONAL $$
(Calle 32 No 31-57; set lunch COP$8000, mains COP$18,000-22,000; ☉9am-9pm) This spacious 2nd-floor restaurant has great views of the lake and even better food. Choose from a variety of authentic, freshly prepared Indian and Thai classics as well as some Italian, Chinese and Mexican dishes. Vegetarians are well catered for and prices are very reasonable for the quality.

La Fogata   COLOMBIAN $$
(mains COP$13,000-20,000; ☉7am-9pm) Right opposite the lake with an elevated, open-air dining area, this popular place does quality *paisa* food, including filling breakfasts

(COP$9000). Go for the *trucha* (trout), or if you're really hungry, a *bandeja paisa*.

ℹ Information

There are two ATMs in town; near the plaza and next to the bus station.

Tourist Office (☎861-0555; Alcaldía; ☉8am-1pm & 2-6pm) The office in the *Alcaldía* (town hall) on the main square dispenses advice during the week. On weekends, a small shack on the waterfront takes over the role and another branch opens at the entrance to La Piedra.

ℹ Getting There & Away

If you're coming on a day trip from Medellín, it makes sense to climb Piedra del Peñol before venturing onward to Guatapé, as it can get cloudy and rain in the afternoon. Buses to and from Medellín (COP$12,000, two hours) run about once an hour. *Colectivos* (shared minibuses or taxis) shuttle frequently between the turnoff to Piedra del Peñol and Guatapé (COP$1500, 10 minutes) or you can take a moto-taxi all the way to the entrance (COP$10,000).

If returning to Medellín from Guatapé on the weekend, be sure to buy your round-trip ticket immediately upon arrival, as buses fill up fast. The ticket office is on the waterfront.

Piedra del Peñol

ELEV 2100M

Also known as El Peñon de Guatapé, thanks to the fierce rivalry between the towns it straddles, this 200m-high **granite monolith** (El Peñon de Guatapé; per climb COP$10,000; ☉8am-5:40pm) rises from near the edge of the Embalse Guatapé. A brick staircase of 659 steps rises up through a broad fissure in the side of the rock. From the top there are magnificent views of the region, the fingers of the lake sprawling amid a vast expanse of green mountains.

Coming from Medellín, don't get off the bus in the town of Peñol – ask the driver to let you off at 'La Piedra,' which is another 10 minutes down the road. Take the road that curves up past the gas station (1km) to reach the parking lot at the base of the rock. Taxi drivers and horse owners will try to convince you that it's a long, exhausting climb but while it's steep, it's not far.

At the base there are a host of restaurants, tourist shacks selling knickknacks and numerous restaurants serving lunch (from COP$8000 to COP$12,000). At the top of the rock, shops sell fruit juice, ice cream and *salpicón* (fruit salad in watermelon juice).

Santa Fe de Antioquia

📋 4 / POP 23,600 / ELEV 550M

This sleepy colonial town is the region's oldest settlement and was once the capital of Antioquia. Founded in 1541 by Jorge Robledo, the clock stands still at 1826, the year the government moved to Medellín. Because it was eclipsed for so long by its neighbor 80km southeast, its colonial center never fell to the wrecking ball and today it looks very much like it did in the 19th century. The narrow streets are lined with whitewashed houses, all single-story construction and many arranged around beautiful courtyards. You'll also see elaborately carved – and typically Antioquian – woodwork around windows and doorways.

It makes a great day trip from Medellín. Don't miss sampling *pulpa de tamarindo,* the beloved sour-sweet candy made with tamarind from the surrounding valley.

⊙ Sights

Puente de Occidente   BRIDGE
This unusual 291m bridge over the Río Cauca is 5km east of town. When completed in 1895, it was one of the first suspension bridges in the Americas. José María Villa, its designer, was also involved in the creation

of the Brooklyn Bridge in New York. It's a boring and hot 45-minute walk downhill. You're best to take a moto-taxi (round trip COP$15,000). The driver will wait while you walk across.

Be sure to climb the dirt path behind the entrance for complete aerial photos of the bridge.

Iglesia de Santa Bárbara   CHURCH
(cnr Calle 11 & Carrera 8; ⊙5-6:30pm & Mass Sun morning) Built by Jesuits in the mid-18th century, Santa Fe's most interesting church has a fine, baroque facade. The interior has an interesting, if time-worn, retable over the high altar.

Museo Juan del Corral   MUSEUM
(📞853-4605; Calle 11 No 9-77; ⊙9am-noon & 2-5:30pm, closed Wed) FREE Visit this interesting museum dedicated to the history of the region in order to check out the perfectly preserved colonial mansion it is set in.

Museo de Arte Religioso   MUSEUM
(📞853-2345; Calle 11 No 8-12; admission COP$3000; ⊙10am-1pm & 2-5pm Fri-Sun) This museum occupies the former Jesuit college constructed in the 1730s, next door to Iglesia de Santa Bárbara. It has a fine collection of colonial religious art, including paintings by Gregorio Vásquez de Arce y Ceballos.

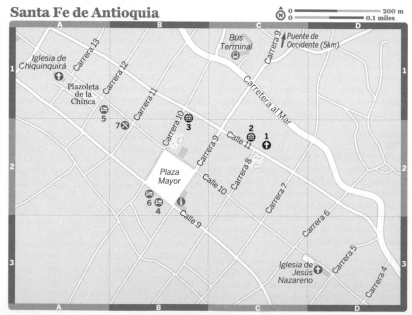

Santa Fe de Antioquia

✨ Festivals & Events

Semana Santa RELIGIOUS
(Holy Week; ⊙Easter) Like most traditional towns dating from the early days of the Spanish Conquest, Santa Fe celebrates Semana Santa with pomp and solemnity. Book accommodations in advance.

Fiesta de los Diablitos CULTURAL
(⊙Dec) The town's most popular festival is held annually over the last four days of the year. It includes music, dance, parades and – like almost every party in the country – a beauty contest.

🛏 Sleeping & Eating

Most people come to Santa Fe as a day trip, but the town has more than a dozen hotels catering to all budgets. Weekend prices are listed; discounts are common during the week.

Hotel Plaza HOSTEL $
(✉853-2851; Plaza Mayor; r per person COP$35,000; 🖥) Set in an old colonial building on the main square, this budget hotel is good value considering the location. The recently renovated rooms are generally cool but many don't have windows and the toilets are literally in the shower.

Hotel Caserón Plaza HOTEL $$
(✉853-2040; www.hotelcaseronplaza.com.co; Plaza Mayor; r COP$150,000-216,000; ✳🖥🏊) On the town's main square, this inn was once home to a member of the local gentry. Rooms are arranged around an attractive courtyard, and there's a nice pool and garden at the back. The upstairs rooms are more spacious and have mountain views although all have tiny bathrooms. During the week it's a good deal; at weekends it's overpriced.

Air-conditioning costs COP$10,000 extra. Day-trippers can get a meal and pool access for COP$30,000.

★**Hotel Mariscal Robledo** HOTEL $$$
(✉853-1563; www.hotelmariscalrobledo.com; cnr Carrera 12 & Calle 10; r per person incl 2 meals COP$190,000; 🅿✳@🖥🏊) Occupying a privileged place on the Parque de la Chinca, Santa Fe's finest hotel oozes character. The spacious rooms are packed with antiques, most of which are for sale, and reflect a simple colonial elegance. There is a rooftop viewpoint, a fantastic large swimming pool and a pretty interior courtyard. The biggest negative: electric showers.

Restaurante Portón del Parque COLOMBIAN $$
(✉853-3207; Calle 10 No 11-03; mains COP$22,000-28,000; ⊙noon-8pm) Occupying an elegant colonial house with high ceilings and a flowery courtyard, this restaurant is widely considered the best in town. The walls are covered with some pretty shoddy artwork but the kitchen prepares quality traditional food and international favorites.

ℹ Information

Bancolombia (Carrera 9 No 10-72) ATM half a block from the main plaza.
Punto Informacion Turistica (PIT; ✉853-4139; Plaza Mayor; ⊙8am-noon & 2-6pm) Has useful information on where to stay and can also direct you to local craftspeople and jewelry makers.

ℹ Getting There & Away

There are hourly buses (COP$10,000, two hours) and minivans (COP$14,000, 1½ hours) to/from Medellín's Terminal del Norte. The last van back to Medellín leaves around 7:30pm.

Jardín

📋4 / POP 14,100 / ELEV 1750M
The self-proclaimed most beautiful town in Antioquia, Jardín is an enchanting agricultural settlement boasting brightly painted two-story houses surrounded by small coffee farms that cling impossibly to the slopes of majestic green mountains.

At the center of town life is the breezy cobblestone plaza dominated by the immense neo-Gothic church. It is chock full of colorful wooden tables and chairs where fruit sellers hawk delicious cocktails and old-timers converse between measured sips of coffee. In the evenings it seems like the entire community comes out to socialize over a drink, while portly middle-aged men in sombreros make their finely groomed horses dance laps around them.

But a visit here is not just about small-town charm. Explore the spectacular nearby countryside and you'll find hidden caves, waterfalls and top-notch bird-watching as well as a wide array of adventure-sport opportunities.

◉ Sights

★ **Cerro Cristo Rey** LOOKOUT
You'll spot this lookout point with its white Christ statue from the center of Jardín. Take the modern cable car (round trip COP$5000) up for fantastic views of town and the mountains beyond. There is a shop at the top selling cold beers and snacks.

Basílica Menor de la Inmaculada Concepción CHURCH
Towering over the central plaza, this imposing neo-Gothic church seems more than a little out of place in such a small town. Its gray granite walls topped with aluminum spires contrast markedly with the colorful surrounds. The striking blue interior features gold-plated arches and capitals.

🏃 Activities

Cueva del Esplendor HIKING, HORSEBACK RIDING
(admission COP$6000) Located at 2200m, this spectacular cave has a 10m waterfall gushing through a large hole in the roof. The cave is only accessible on horseback or on foot along muddy, sometimes narrow mountain paths. The entrance is around a three-hour hike from town or two hours on horseback.

The cascade begins about 70m above the entrance, falling in various stages before pouring into a small pool at the bottom of the cave, throwing up clouds of mist. It's possible to take a dip but the water is ice-cold.

Expect to pay COP$60,000 to COP$65,000 per person for the trip on horseback including a traditional lunch. Recommended guides include **Bernardo Lopez** (📞314-714-2021), who will pick you up in town with the horses. Another good option is **Jaime Marín** (📞314-780-4070, 313-719-1017), who will drive you in a jeep to his farm, from where it's a one-hour ride to the entrance.

Condor de los Andes ADVENTURE TOURS
(📞310-379-6069; condordelosandes@colombia.com; Carrera 6 No 1-100) This dynamic adventure company offers a range of high-adrenaline activities around town including abseiling in Cueva del Esplen-

dor (COP$97,000) and Cascada la Escalera (COP$65,000). Also runs authentic coffee tours and an informative city tour. There is a comfortable hostel on-site, too, with rooms set in a lovely colonial building surrounding a pretty garden (dorms COP$25,000, rooms per person COP$35,000 to COP$40,000). It's right at the entrance to town.

Tienda de Parapente PARAGLIDING
(📞311-362-0410; armandovuelo@gmail.com; Calle 15, Av la Primavera; tandem flights COP$80,000; ⊙10am-6pm) Soar over lush green mountains and the neat tiled roofs of town in tandem paragliding flights. To find the office, walk for five blocks up the hill behind the church.

🛏 Sleeping & Eating

Adventure company Condor de los Andes offers comfortable hostel rooms.

For a local-style snack, head to the central plaza in the evening for some *callo y oreja frito* (fried pig's ear and bovine intestines) fresh from the bubbling vats of oil in the rows of food carts.

Balcones del Parque HOTEL $$
(📞845-6844; www.balconesdelparque.com; Calle 9 No 2-75; r per person incl meals COP$60,000-80,000; 🛜) On a corner opposite the central plaza (known as 'the park'), this good-value hotel offers neat rooms with high wood ceilings, although the bathrooms are a bit poky. Ask for a room with a balcony; the internal ones can be dark. Prices are reduced during the week.

Hotel Jardín HOTEL $$
(📞310-380-6724; www.hoteljardin.com.co; Carrera 3 No 9-14; r/apt per person COP$40,000/50,000; 🛜) Right on the central plaza, this colorfully painted hotel has rooms and apartments with kitchens, all set around a lovely courtyard. There is a wonderful wide balcony overlooking the park and a rear porch with mountain views. Some of the rooms on the lower floor lack natural light; try to get one upstairs with a window to the street.

Hostal Selva y Cafe HOSTEL $$
(www.hostalselvaycafe.co; Casa del Lago, Vereda La Salada; dm/s/d COP$27,000/80,000/90,000; 🛜) This small hostel a short walk from town has a tranquil natural setting and comfortable accommodations in a cozy two-story house. The staff organizes plenty of interesting activities including bird-watching trips into the cloud forest, nature hikes, yoga

classes, horseback riding and coffee tours. It's a 15-minute walk from town; otherwise, take a moto-taxi (COP$3000).

Pastellate   INTERNATIONAL $
(Carrera 4 No 3-45; mains COP$7000-12,000; ☺noon-8:30pm Tue-Sun) A cute cafe serving an array of delicious light meals at reasonable prices. The desserts are top-notch, too.

🏠 Shopping

Dulces del Jardín   SWEETS
(dulcesdeljardin@hotmail.com; Calle 13 No 5-47) This cavity-inducing sweets factory is famous throughout Antioquia for its wide variety of *arequipe* (a sweet dessert of milk and sugar), conserves and fruit candies.

ℹ Information

Bancolombia (Calle 8 No 3-33) ATM on the plaza.

Punto Informacíon Turistica (cnr Carrera 3 & Calle 10; ☺9am-1pm & 2-5pm, closed Tue) Helpful tourist office around the corner from the church.

ℹ Getting There & Away

Around a dozen buses (COP$18,000, three hours) head daily to Jardín from Medellín's Terminal del Sur. In Jardín the buses depart from the offices on Calle 8. Make sure to purchase your round-trip ticket in advance as seats sell out during peak periods.

If you are continuing south to the Eje Cafetera (Coffee Axis) in the Zona Cafetera, **Rapido Ochoa** (☑845-5051; Calle 8 No 5-24) has a direct service to Manizales (COP$37,000, five hours) at 6:25am. Alternatively, take the bus to Río Sucio (COP$19,000, three hours) and pick up a connection to Manizales there.

Río Claro

ELEV 350M

Set 2km south of the Medellín–Bogotá highway, three hours east of Medellín and five hours west of Bogotá, is the **Reserva Natural Cañon de Río Claro** (☑313-671-4459, 4-268-8855; www.rioclaroelrefugio.com; Km152 Autopista Medellín–Bogotá; admission COP$10,000, campsite per person COP$15,000, r per person incl 3 meals COP$80,000-140,000). Here the river has carved a stunning canyon from its marble bed. You can visit a spectacular cave, go white-water rafting, canopying, or just swim and hike along its banks. It's also a favorite spot for bird-watchers, who come to see everything from hummingbirds to herons.

The reserve offers a variety of accommodation options. The most impressive lie a 15-minute walk upriver from the restaurant – rooms face the open jungle, and you'll fall asleep to the roar of the river beside you and the loud thrum of crickets in the night. You'll wake to see mist rising up through the jungle-clad canyon. Book in advance to make sure you get a river view. There is also a motel-style property at the edge of the highway, but it is not surrounded by nature and suffers from constant highway road noise.

Be sure to visit the **Caverna de los Guácharos** (guided tour COP$20,000), a spectacular nearby cave. Cavern after cavern soar high and hollow like great cathedrals. A 1km-long stream runs through the cave. The entrances are guarded by shrill, shrieking flocks of guácharos, a batlike nocturnal bird. You'll be given a life vest and be expected to swim part of the way.

You can also go rafting (COP$25,000), but it's more a gentle cruise through some gorgeous scenery; hard-core rafters may be disappointed. Canopy cables crisscross the river, and make for a diverting afternoon zipping through the jungle (COP$20,000).

Bring a swimsuit, towel and flashlight. On weekends the reserve is often full of Colombian high-school students – you may prefer to come during the week. Beer is for sale in the restaurant but hard liquor is forbidden.

ℹ Information

The reserve is 24km west of Doradal, where you will find a couple of budget hotels and internet cafes near the main plaza. The closest ATM is in Puerto Triunfo, a further 15 minutes east by taxi or bus.

ℹ Getting There & Away

Many Medellín–Bogotá buses, with the exception of some of the bigger express services, will drop you at the reserve's entrance. From any other direction, look for transportation to Doradal, from where you can pick up a bus to the main gate (COP$5000, 20 minutes).

ZONA CAFETERA

Colombia is famous for its coffee, but nowhere is the prized bean more important than in the departments of Caldas, Risaralda and Quindío, which together make up the heart of the Zona Cafetera, also called the Eje Cafetero (Coffee Axis). Here you'll find jeeps packed with mustachioed coffee pickers; poncho-wearing senior citizens gossiping in cafes; and, of course, endless cups of piping hot arabica. Many working *fincas* (coffee farms) have embraced tourism and welcome visitors onto their plantations to learn all about the coffee-growing process. It is particularly interesting to visit during the harvests (April to May, October to December) when the farms are a hive of activity.

The region was colonized by *paisas* in the 19th century during the *colonización antioqueña,* and to this day remains culturally tied to Medellín in everything from its traditional architecture to its cuisine. It is an area of spectacular natural beauty. There are stunning vistas everywhere – Salento, in particular, and the adjacent Valle de Cocora, are jaw-dropping. Parque Nacional Natural (PNN) Los Nevados soars above 5000m and offers trekking opportunities through the striking *páramo* (high-mountain plains).

Manizales

✒6 / POP 388,530 / ELEV 2150M

The northern point of the Eje Cafetero (Coffee Axis), Manizales is a pleasantly cool, midsized university town, surrounded on all sides by green mountain scenery. The capital of the Caldas department, Manizales was founded in 1849 by a group of Antioquian colonists looking to escape the civil wars of that time. The town's early development was hindered by two earthquakes in 1875 and 1878, and a fire in 1925. For this reason there's not a lot of historical interest left – the real attractions are the surrounding nature activities and the town's vibrant nightlife.

◉ Sights

★ Monumento a Los Colonizadores   MONUMENT
(Av 12 de Octubre, Chipre) Located atop a hill in the neighborhood of Chipre, this massive monument to the city's founders was crafted from 50 tonnes of bronze. It's an impressive work, but the real attraction here is the spectacular views over town and to Parque Nacional Natural (PNN) Los Nevados.

Torre Panoramico   LOOKOUT
(Av 12 de Octubre, Chipre; admission COP$3000; ⊙9am-9pm) The 30m-high spaceshiplike lookout point has 360-degree views of the

dramatic mountainous terrain surrounding the city. To get here, take any bus from Cable Plaza to Chipre; they leave constantly.

Plaza de Bolívar   PLAZA
The city's main square has the mandatory statue of Bolívar by Rodrigo Arenas Betancur, here known as Bolívar-Cóndor since the sculptor endows Colombia's founder with distinctly birdlike features. The Palacio de Gobierno, a pretty, neoclassical confection built in 1927, stands on the northern side of the plaza.

Catedral de Manizales   CHURCH
(tower access adult/child COP$10,000/7000; ⊙9am-8pm) Plaza de Bolívar's south side is dominated by the odd but impressive Catedral de Manizales. Begun in 1929 and built of reinforced concrete, it is among the first churches of its kind in Latin America. Its main tower is 106m high, making it the highest church tower in the country. You can climb to the top for great views of the city.

Iglesia de Inmaculada Concepción   CHURCH
(cnr Calle 30 & Carrera 22) Built at the beginning of the 20th century, this elegant church has a beautiful carved-wood interior reminiscent of a ship's hull.

🏃 Activities

Manizales is a good place to organize treks in the PNN Los Nevados.

Kumanday Adventures   ADVENTURE TOURS
(☎315-590-7294, 887-2682; www.kumanday.com; Calle 66 No 23B-40) This full-service adventure company in the hostel of the same name runs treks in PNN Los Nevados and mountaineering trips nationwide. It also offers scenic mountain-bike tours through nearby coffee farms, a high-adrenaline downhill run from the edge of Nevado del Ruiz (4050m) back to Manizales, and three-day cycling trips through the Andes. Mountaineering gear and tent rental is available.

Ecosistemas   ADVENTURE TOURS
(☎312-705-7007, 880-8300; www.ecosistemastravel.com.co; Carrera 21 No 20-45) An experienced outfitter offering excursions and multiday tours to PNN Los Nevados, including hikes to the summits of Nevado Santa Isabel and Nevado del Tolima. Also specializes in visits to local coffee farms.

✨ Festivals & Events

Feria de Manizales   CULTURAL
(☻Jan) At Manizales' annual festival you'll find the usual assortment of parades, crafts fairs and, of course, a beauty pageant.

Festival Internacional de Teatro   THEATER
(☻Aug) Held annually since 1968, this is one of two important theater festivals in Colombia (the other is in Bogotá). The festival lasts about a week and includes free street performances.

🛏 Sleeping

Most accommodations are located in the Cable Plaza area, where you will find a large shopping mall and most of the city's best restaurants.

Mountain Hostels   HOSTEL $
(✉887-0871, 887-4736; www.manizaleshostel.com; Calle 66 No 23B-91; dm COP$20,000-23,000, s/d/t COP$60,000/65,000/90,000; ☏) A short walk from the *zona rosa* (nightlife zone), this fine choice spread over two buildings is one of the few hostels where backpackers and Colombian travelers mix. There are a variety of social areas including rear patios with hammocks, and the staff is helpful in organizing activities around town. The rooms in the reception building are the most comfortable.

Kumanday Hostal   HOSTEL $
(✉315-590-7294, 887-2682; www.kumanday.com; Calle 66 No 23B-40; dm incl breakfast COP$25,000, s/d incl breakfast COP$50,000/70,000; ☏) Friendly, compact hostel near the *zona rosa* with simple but clean and comfortable rooms.

Estelar Las Colinas   HOTEL $$$
(✉884-2009; www.hotelesestelar.com; Carrera 22 No 20-20; s/d COP$160,000/218,000; P☏) The poshest place in the center, this modern glass-and-concrete hotel isn't pretty to look at, but it has large, comfortable rooms, plus a fine restaurant. Prices include a generous buffet breakfast. Rooms on the upper levels have better views and more natural light. On weekends discounts are available.

Varuna Hotel   HOTEL $$$
(✉881-1122; www.varunahotel.com; Calle 62 No 23C-18; s/d COP$203,000/251,000; ☏) A popular business-traveler option, this modern hotel offers minimalist rooms with polished wood floors a short walk from Cable Plaza. It has a restaurant serving breakfast, lunch and dinner. Ask for an upstairs room with a view. On weekends prices are reduced.

🍴 Eating

La Suiza   BAKERY $
(Carrera 23 No 26-57; mains COP$8500-17,500; ☻9am-8:30pm Mon-Sat, 10am-7:30pm Sun) This scrumptious bakery does great pastries and even homemade chocolate. It also does tasty breakfasts, plus light lunches, such as mushroom crepes and chicken sandwiches. There's another branch near Cable Plaza.

Rushi   VEGETARIAN $
(Carrera 23C No 62-73; meals COP$7000-9000; ☻8am-9pm Mon-Sat; ✎) Hip vegetarian restaurant serving up great juices and interesting meat-free dishes prepared before your eyes in the open kitchen. The changing lunch menu is top value.

Spago   ITALIAN $$
(✉885-3328; Calle 59 No 24A-06; mains COP$17,000-33,000; ☻noon-3pm & 6-10pm Mon-Sat) Manizales is a bit limited when it comes to international dining, but this modern bistro delivers with great home-style Italian food. The flavors here are subtle, the ingredients fresh and the staff professional. Has a fair selection of wines.

🍷 Drinking & Nightlife

The main *zona rosa* is along Av Santander near Cable Plaza. There is a bunch of old-style tango bars on so-called Calle de Tango (Calle 24). Check out **Los Faroles** (Calle 24 No 22-46; ☻8pm-2am Fri-Sat) and neighbouring **Reminiscencias** (Calle 24 No 22-42; ☻9pm-2am Fri-Sat). Wear dress shoes or you ain't getting in.

Bar La Plaza   CAFE, BAR
(Carrera 23B No 64-80; ☻11am-11pm Mon-Wed, to 2am Thu-Sat) Delicatessen by day, bar by night; this is the place to start your evening. Fills up fast and by 9pm you'll have to wait for a table. The music isn't too loud, so you can converse. There's a young, student vibe, and it offers gourmet sandwiches (COP$5900 to COP$14,800) and snack platters of quality salami and cheese to help line your stomach. Does good cocktails.

Prenderia   BAR
(Carrera 23 No 58-42; ☻8pm-2am Thu-Sat) Wonderfully relaxed bar where talented local musicians play to an older, laid-back crowd. Try the lethal *carajillo* – strong espresso spiked with rum – and try not to slide off the bar stools.

Manizales

Zona Rosa Inset

4

Aguas de Manizales

Av Kevin Ángel

Cable Plaza

Carrera 23 (Av Santander)

Calle 61

13

Carrera 23C

15

Calle 65A

9

Calle 61

Calle 65

10

Calle 11

Calle 62

Palo Grande

Carrera 25

Calle 66

11

Calle 59

14

17

Calle 67

PALERMO

DELICIAS

Calle 30

Calle 29

Calle 28

Calle 27

Calle 45B

See Zona Rosa Inset

La Nubia (8km)

Recinto de Pensamiento (11km)

Terminal (3km)

Carrera 26A

Calle 38

Av Paralela

Carrera 21

Carrera 23

Calle 34

Calle 33

Calle 32

Calle 31

Calle 30

CAMPOAMOR

Calle 29

Calle 33B

Tourist Office

19

3

Carrera 20

Carrera 21

Carrera 22

Carrera 23

Carrera 24

Carrera 25

Carrera 26

Carrera 12

Carrera 13

Carrera 14

Carrera 15

Carrera 16

Carrera 17

Carrera 18

Calle 27

Calle 26

Calle 25

Calle 24

Calle 23

Calle 22

Calle 21

12

18

16

5

23

2

8

7

CENTRO

Calle 24

Calle 23

Calle 22

Calle 21

Calle 20

SAN ANTONIO

Calle 19

Calle 18

Calle 17

Calle 16

Calle 15

Calle 14

Calle 13

Calle 12

Calle 11

Carrera 20

Carrera 21

Carrera 22

Carrera 23

Carrera 25

Carrera 26

Calle 19

Calle 18A

Calle 18

Calle 17

Calle 16

Carrera 9B

Calle 20

Calle 19

Carrera 13A

Carrera 14

Carrera 15

Carrera 16

Carrera 17

Carrera 18

Calle 14

Calle 13

LAS AMERICAS

Av Gilberto Alzate

Av Centenario

LOS AGUSTINOS

Calle 12

Calle 10

Calle 6

Calle 6

Calle 5A

Calle 5

Calle 4A

Calle 4

Calle 3B

Carrera 11

Carrera 12

Carrera 13

Carrera 10

Calle 12B

Calle 12

Calle 9

Av 12 de Octubre

Carrera 8

Calle 9

Monumento a Los Colonizadores

1

6

Carrera 16

Carrera 22

Carrera 24

Calle 24

500 m

0.25 miles

500 m

0.25 miles

Manizales

Bar C   CLUB
(Via Acueducto Niza; ⊙9pm-5am Thu-Sat) When
all the bars in Manizales close at 2am, anyone left standing comes here. Set up on a
mountaintop about 3km east of Cable Plaza, its gives great views of the city and the
stars. DJs play mostly Colombian crossover
to please the late-night student crowd.

☆ Entertainment

Teatro Los Fundadores   THEATER
(☑878-2530; www.ccclosfundadores.com; cnr
Carrera 22 & Calle 33) Manizales' leading mainstream theater; it also has a cinema.

❶ Information

The area around the central market just north of
the city is a favored hangout for thieves and is
best avoided.

Mind the unpainted sidewalk traffic pylons; you
are likely to bang your shins at least once.

There are several ATMs inside Cable Plaza.
4-72 (Carrera 23, No 60-36; ⊙8am-noon &
1-6pm Mon-Fri, 9am-noon Sat)
Banco de Bogotá (cnr Carrera 22 & Calle 22)
Central location; has an ATM.
Tourist Office (☑873-3901; www.ctm.gov.co;
cnr Carrera 22 & Calle 31; ⊙7am-7pm) Tourist
office with enthusiastic staff and plenty of
maps and brochures.

❶ Getting There & Away

AIR
Aeropuerto La Nubia (☑874-5451) is 8km
southeast of the city center, off the road to
Bogotá. Take the urban bus to La Enea, then
walk for five minutes to the terminal, or grab a
taxi (COP$10,000). Delays and cancellations

are common because of fog, so don't book tight
connections out of here.

BUS
Manizales' sparkling modern **bus terminal**
(☑878-7858; www.terminaldemanizales.com;
Carrera 43 No 65-100) is located south of the
center and is linked to the downtown area by an
efficient cable car (COP$1500) that offers great
views of the city. A second cable car line runs
from the terminal across to Villa María on the
far side of the valley. If you are staying by Cable
Plaza, it is easier to take a taxi direct from the
terminal (COP$6500).

Buses depart regularly to Cali (COP$38,000,
five hours), Bogotá (COP$50,000, eight hours)
and Medellín (COP$35,000, five hours).

Minibuses to Pereira (COP$9000, 1¼ hours)
and Armenia (COP$17,000, 2¼ hours) run every
15 minutes or so.

Around Manizales

◎ Nature Reserves

Recinto del Pensamiento

Set in the cloud forest 11km from Manizales,
this **nature park** (☑6-889-7073; www.recinto
delpensamiento.com; Km11 Vía al Magdalena; admission with/without telesilla COP$17,400/13,000;
⊙9am-4pm Tue-Sun) has a fine *mariposario*,
several short walks through an impressive
orchid-populated forest, and a medicinal
herb garden. You'll also see plantations of
guadua and chusqué (two kinds of Colombian bamboo). There's even a *telesilla* – a kind

COLOMBIAN COFFEE

Colombia is the third-largest coffee exporter in the world and the only big producer that grows arabica beans exclusively. The coffee bean was brought to Colombia from Venezuela in the early 18th century by Jesuit priests. It was first cultivated in the area that is now Norte de Santander before spreading throughout the country.

Local conditions proved ideal for growing arabica coffee. Colombia's location near the equator means that coffee can be grown high in the mountains, where the beans mature more slowly. This results in a harder, more dense bean that provides consistent flavor when roasted. Frequent rainfall in the region sees bushes that are almost always flowering, which enables two harvests a year. And the plants thrive in the region's volcanic soils, which contain a high amount of organic material.

The main varieties of arabica coffee grown in Colombia are Tipica, Bourbon, Maragogipe, Tabi, Caturra and Colombia. As the beans on a single plant mature at different times, all Colombian coffee needs to be handpicked. This job is performed by small armies of *recolectores* (coffee pickers) that travel from region to region according to the harvests.

The heavy rainfall means that beans cannot be dried in the open like in other coffee-producing regions. Colombian beans are wet-processed or 'washed,' with the fruit surrounding the bean being removed prior to drying. This process takes much of the acidity out of the bean and gives the end product a richer aroma.

While the country is a major coffee producer, outside the Zona Cafetera Colombians are not huge coffee drinkers and almost all the best beans are picked for export. If you want to purchase coffee to take home, it's best to visit some farms yourself and buy single-origin beans direct from the growers.

of chair lift – to take you up the mountain slope on which the park sits.

Admission includes 2½ hours of mandatory guide service; a couple of the guides speak some English. There's impressive birdlife here – book in advance for bird-watching tours (COP$8000) from 6am to 9am. Wear brown or green clothes and bring binoculars.

To get here, take the bus marked Sera Maltería from Cable Plaza in Manizales (COP$1550, 30 minutes, every 10 minutes), or take a taxi (COP$8000).

Reserva Ecológica Río Blanco

Three kilometers northeast of Manizales lies this 3600-hectare cloud forest reserve (2150m to 3700m). It is an area of high biodiversity and protects numerous endangered species, including the oso andino (spectacled bear). There are 362 species of bird present in the park, including 13 of Colombia's endemics. It attracts bird-watchers from around the world, but even the amateur will be delighted by the quantities of hummingbirds, butterflies and orchids you'll see in the peaceful calm of this cloud forest. It makes a great half-day excursion – best in the morning, as it often rains in the afternoon.

Before you can visit you must request permission (free) two days in advance from the tourism office in **Aguas de Manizales** (311-775-5159, 887-9770; practi_cuencas@ aguasdemanizales.com.co; Av Kevin Ángel No 59-181). It will organize the services of a local birding guide (Spanish/English per half day COP$30,000/45,000), who will meet you at the entrance and take you into the reserve. If you just want to hike, a guide for the two-hour exploration trail costs COP$20,000 per group.

It is possible to stay within the reserve in typical houses (rooms per Colombian/ foreign visitor COP$35,000/70,000). Budget meals (COP$8500 to COP$13,500) can be organized with local residents. You'll need to book accommodations in advance, but if you stay you don't need to obtain visitors permission.

A taxi to the main gate from Manizales will cost around COP$25,000. Get the number of your driver for the round trip; there is next to no traffic up here.

Los Yarumos

Set on a hill with great views over Manizales, this 53-hectare municipal **adventure park** (6-875-3110; Calle 61B No 15A-01; 8:30am-5:30pm Tue-Sun) has panoramic views of the city, forest trails and canopy lines. There are numerous short walks you can do through mature secondary forest including a two-hour guided hike to four small waterfalls (COP$8000). Other activities include abseiling (COP$15,000) and a vertigo-inducing 80m-high Tibetan bridge above the forest canopy (COP$6000).

It's also a great place to just come and chill on a clear afternoon, when you can see the peaks of PNN Los Nevados.

A new cable car links the park directly with Cable Plaza but has been plagued by technical problems and runs irregularly. Otherwise it's a 40-minute walk or COP$4000 in a taxi.

◎ Coffee Farms

Hacienda Venecia

This **hacienda** (☎320-636-5719; www.haciendavenecia.com; Vereda el Rosario, San Peregrino; main house r with/without bathroom COP$250,000/340,000, hostel dm COP$30,000, r with/without bathroom COP$95,000/80,000; ☒) has won numerous awards for its coffee. It offers a coffee tour (COP$45,000) in English that includes an informative presentation about Colombian coffee, an introduction to coffee cupping, a class in coffee preparation and a walking tour through the plantation. You can use the pool afterwards, and a typical lunch is available for COP$12,000. The tour price includes transport to/from your hotel in Manizales.

The plantation is centered around a well-preserved *paisa* farm house with majestic views that has been converted into a lovely boutique hotel. The gardens are well kept, and there's a pond with lily pads and a round blue pool. The rooms are full of books, antiques and old photographs, while the wraparound veranda has hammocks and rocking chairs to rock away the evening.

There are also less atmospheric but clean and comfortable budget accommodations in a new building across the river from the main house, which also has its own swimming pool.

Hacienda Guayabal

This slow-paced working **coffee farm** (☎314-772-4900; www.haciendaguayabal.com; Km3 Vía Peaje Tarapacá, Chinchiná; r per person incl breakfast COP$60,000, full board COP$95,000; ☒) near Chinchiná is a great place to come and unwind surrounded by *cafetero* culture. It runs a coffee tour (Spanish/English COP$30,000/35,000) that follows the coffee process from the plant to the cup. It is a bit

more personal than those offered by some of the larger outfits and the guides are very keen to share their knowledge. Bags of coffee are available to purchase as souvenirs.

Make sure you stay for lunch – the traditional farm-style food here is absolutely delicious and vegetarians are well catered for. You can hang around afterwards to use the pool. There is also fine bird-watching here – ask for the bird list, which contains more than 120 species documented on the farm.

If you want to stay longer, it offers simple, functional accommodations in a modern house set up on a hill with magnificent views over the surrounding plantations.

To get here, take any bus from Manizales to Chinchiná (COP$3000, 30 minutes), then from the main plaza in Chinchiná take the bus marked 'Guayabal Peaje' (COP$1100, 10 minutes, every 15 to 30 minutes). Ask the driver to let you off before the toll booth at the 'Tienda Guayabal'; from here it's a 1km walk down the small road between the houses.

◎ Thermal Baths

Termales El Otoño

This high-end resort and **thermal spa complex** (☎6-874-0280; www.termaleselotono.com; Km5 Antigua Vía al Nevado; admission per day COP$30,000; ☺7am-midnight) has a number of large thermal pools and is surrounded by impressive mountain peaks. The onsite hotel has rooms ranging from generic hotel-type offerings to luxurious cottages with wooden ceilings, open fireplaces and private thermal spas. You don't need to be a hotel guest to use the pools; you can come just for the day. It is a little too busy and developed to be a real nature experience but it is still a relaxing day away from the city.

Another cheaper set of pools, **Ecotermales El Otoño** (admission COP$15,000/20,000; ☺1-10pm Tue-Thu, to midnight Fri, 10am-midnight Sat, 9am-10pm Sun), on the other side of the car park, are arguably nicer with less concrete around and more dramatic mountain views, but during peak periods you'll share them with hordes of visitors. There are three pools here, with the one at the top closest to the entrance being the hottest. They are surrounded by breezy wooden shelters and there is a cafe serving meals and booze.

To get here take the bus (COP$1650, 30 minutes) from Av Kevin Ángel below Cable Plaza or Carrera 20 in central Manizales.

A taxi from Cable Plaza will set you back around COP$15,000.

Termales Tierra Viva

These small **thermal baths** (☑6-874-3089; www.termalestierraviva.com; Km2 Vía Enea-Gallinazo; admission COP$12,000-14,000; ☺9am-11:30pm) are located on the edge of Río Chinchiná just outside Manizales. There are two thermal baths made of rocks set among a pretty garden that attracts hummingbirds and butterflies. There is an excellent elevated, open-air restaurant and a small spa offering massages. The baths are quiet during the week, but on the weekends it can feel a little overcrowded.

If you want to stay out here, the four chic, modern rooms with bamboo features and big windows overlooking the river are a fine deal (rooms COP$165,000).

To get here take the Enea–Gallinazo bus (COP$1650) from downtown Manizales. By taxi it is around COP$10,000.

Parque Nacional Natural (PNN) Los Nevados

ELEV 2600–5325M

Following a spine of snow-covered volcanic peaks, this 583-sq-km **national park** (www.parquesnacionales.gov.co; admission Colombians/foreigners COP$14,000/37,500) provides access to some of the most stunning stretches of the Colombian Andes. Its varied altitude range encompasses everything from humid cloud forests and *páramo* to glaciers on the highest peaks. The main peaks, from north to south, are El Ruiz (5325m), El Cisne (4750m), Santa Isabel (4965m), El Quindío (4750m) and El Tolima (5215m).

Thirty-seven rivers are born here, providing water to 3.5 million people in four departments. The glaciers in the park have been receding, however, and research is underway to measure the impact on the environment.

The best months to see snow in Los Nevados are October and November and from March to May. Outside of those times, you're more likely to get the dry, windy conditions favorable to trekking and clear views.

At the time of research, most of the northern section of the park around Nevado del Ruiz remained off-limits because of volcanic activity. The restrictions remain liable to change. Check on the situation in Manizales before heading out.

Fortunately for nature lovers, the southern part of the park remains open and offers a variety of breathtaking day trips and multiday treks. The main access points are from Potosi near Santa Rosa de Cabal; the Refugio La Pastora in the Parque Ucumarí, from where a 12km trail goes uphill to the magnificent Laguna del Otún; and Valle de Cocora near Salento, where a path heads uphill to the *páramo* around Paramillo del Quindío (4750m).

Tours

Public transportation to most entry points of the park is nonexistent. While it's possible to hike into the park from either Parque Ucumarí or Valle de Cocora, it's often more convenient to organize a package including guides and transportation in Manizales or Salento.

Both Ecosistemas (p206) and Kumanday Adventures (p206) in Manizales offer day trips to Nevado del Ruiz and Nevado de Santa Isabel, as well as multiday hikes through the park and ascents of the various other peaks. It's possible to take a hiking tour beginning in Manizales and finishing in Pereira or Valle de Cocora near Salento. Ask the company to forward your backpack so that you don't have to double back.

In Salento, **Paramo Trek** (☑311-745-3761; paramotrek@gmail.com) offers a variety of hikes in the park entering through Valle de Cocora.

Nevado del Ruiz

This is the highest volcano of the chain. Its eruption on November 13, 1985, killed more than 20,000 people and swept away the town of Armero on the Río Lagunillas. El Ruiz had previously erupted in 1845, but the results were far less catastrophic; today, the volcano continues to grumble, resulting in restrictions on activities in this part of the park.

The principal access road into the park is from the north. It branches off from the Manizales–Bogotá road in La Esperanza, 31km east of Manizales. The entrance to the park is at Las Brisas (4050m), where you'll need to register at the rangers' office.

At the time of research, access was only permitted from Thursday to Sunday between 8am and 2pm, with all visitors having to leave the park by 3:30pm. Furthermore, visitors were only permitted to travel a short 5km stretch of road through the *páramo* to Valle de las Tumbas (4350m). While tour operators are still running trips (COP$100,000 to COP$130,000) to this part of the park,

Parque Nacional Natural Los Nevados

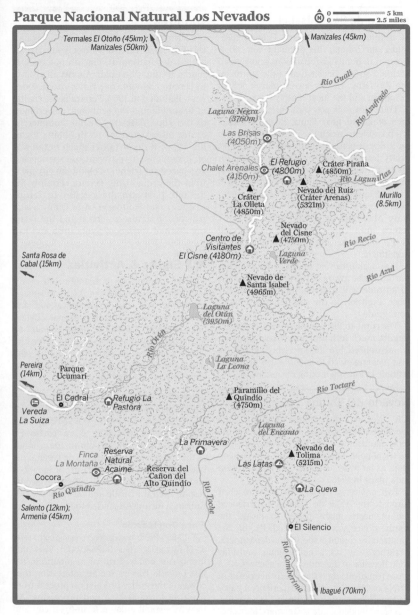

tours are targeted at the package-tour crowd. Visitors spend the entire trip in vehicles; it's not permitted to get out and hike even short distances.

If restrictions are lifted, it should be possible to explore more of the area. The vol-

cano actually has three craters: Arenas, La Olleta and Piraña. It is possible to summit the main one, Arenas (5321m). The extinct Olleta crater (4850m), on the opposite side of the road, is covered with multicolored layers of sandy soil and normally has no snow.

Nevado de Santa Isabel

Straddling the departments Caldas, Risaralda and Tolima, this dormant volcano is covered in domelike formations and topped with a 2-sq-km glacier that is the source of the Río Otún. It's the lowest glacier left in Colombia and the most rapidly retreating.

The volcano is accessed through the village of Potosí near Santa Rosa de Cabal. It's possible to reach the edge of the glacier on a day trip from Manizales although it's pretty intense: you'll travel in a vehicle for about three hours along an unsealed road to a height of 4050m before hiking uphill through stunning *páramo* for another three hours to the snow line. The trips usually leave Manizales at around 5am and don't return until 7pm. Expect to pay around COP$160,000 per hiker, including breakfast and lunch.

If you plan to visit on a day trip, it's important to be aware of the effect the change in altitude will have on your stamina. Pay close attention to the recommendations of your guide.

The climb to the summit (4965m) does not require much technical experience, although it's advisable to hire an experienced guide. It's also recommended to spend a day or two at altitude before attempting the ascent.

Nevado del Tolima

The Nevado del Tolima (5215m), the second-highest volcano in the chain, is the most handsome of all with its classic symmetrical cone. On a clear day it can be seen from as far away as Bogotá. Its last eruption took place in 1943.

For novice climbers, it's best reached through the Valle de Cocora. Experienced mountaineers might prefer to tackle the southern face accessible through Ibagué, the unattractive capital of the Tolima department.

Either way it's a challenging multiday trek. Because of the state of the glaciers, it's a more technical climb than the other peaks in PNN Los Nevados, and an experienced guide and mountaineering equipment is essential. A recommended guide is **German 'Mancho'** (☏312-211-7677, 312-268-4130; La Primavera), who is based at the small mountain lodge at La Primavera and grew up in the area. In Ibagué, try **David 'Truman' Bejarano** (☏313-219-3188, 315-292-7395), an experienced mountain guide who also offers trips to other peaks around the country.

Pereira

☏6 / POP 457,000 / ELEV 1410M

Hardworking Pereira is not your typical tourist destination. In fact it's not really a tourist destination at all. Almost all visitors to Pereira come for one thing – to do business. Founded in 1863, Pereira is the capital of Risaralda and the economic powerhouse of the Zona Cafetera – a hot commercial center most noted for its throbbing nightlife. While it doesn't offer much in the way of attractions, if you want to experience a fast-paced yet friendly Colombian city away from the gringo trail, Pereira certainly fits the bill. It is also the gateway to Parque Ucumarí and Santuario Otún Quimbaya, a pair of top nature reserves, and the relaxing thermal springs of Santa Rosa and San Vicente.

◉ Sights & Activities

The downtown area is notably thin on attractions. In the middle of the main square, presiding over the city's commerce and interaction, sits Rodrigo Arenas Betancur's **Bolívar Desnudo** (Plaza Bolívar), an 8.5m-high, 11-tonne bronze statue of the Liberator, naked on horseback, urging his stallion forward with a manic passion, buttocks clenched to his plunging mount.

Jardín Botánico   GARDENS
(☏321-2523; www.utp.edu.co/jardin; Vereda la Julita; admission 1-3 visitors COP$20,000, 4-plus visitors per visitor COP$6000; ⊗8am-4pm Mon-Fri, 9am-1pm Sat, 11am-1pm Sun) Within the grounds of the Universidad Tecnológia de Pereira, the botanic gardens has orchids, exotic bamboos and medicinal plants, and offers a welcome respite from the hustle and bustle of the city. Entrance includes a guided tour.

Finca Don Manolo   FARM
(☏313-655-0196; www.cafedonmanolo.com; Vereda El Estanquillo; tour COP$20,000) Visit this family-run coffee farm on a mountainside just outside Pereira for an interesting tour covering the entire production process from planting to harvesting and processing. Afterwards you'll enjoy a farm-fresh cup and a brownie while taking in the great views. You'll be shown around by friendly owner don Manolo, so call ahead to make sure he is home.

A taxi from town costs around COP$8000 or look for the bus marked 'Vereda El Estanquillo' at the terminal.

🛏 Sleeping

Kolibrí Hostel
HOSTEL $

(☑331-3955; www.kolibrihostel.com; Calle 4 No 16-35; dm COP$22,000, r with/without bathroom COP$65,000/50,000; 🛜) With a great location just off the main *zona rosa,* this top new hostel offers everything budget travelers need. There is a variety of comfortable rooms and a great terrace with mountain views. The enthusiastic owners are particularly helpful in arranging activities around town and beyond. For a tasty budget meal, check out the chilled open-air restaurant out the front.

Hotel Cumanday
HOTEL $

(☑324-0416; Carrera 5 No 22-54; s/d COP$35,000/45,000; 🛜) A step up from the rest of the downtown budget options, this small, neat hotel is great value with hot water, cable TV and a laundry service. Go for a room at the back overlooking the rear patio.

Hotel Condina
HOTEL $$

(☑333-4484; www.luxorhoteles.com; Calle 18 No 6-26; s/d with air-con COP$99,000/119,000, with fan COP$83,000/107,000; P ❄ 🛜) On a bustling traffic-free street in the heart of downtown, this midsized hotel offers outstanding value. Bright, modern rooms have big, spotless bathrooms, work desks and even a pillow menu. The facilities are way above what you would normally expect at this price.

Hotel Abadia Plaza
HOTEL $$$

(☑335-8398; www.hotelabadiaplaza.com; Carrera 8 No 21-67; s/d incl breakfast COP$232,200/238,200; ❄@🛜) This stylish place right in the center of town is a top choice for comfort and professional service. You'll find original art on the walls, a well-equipped gym, and plush rooms with marble bathrooms and noiseproof windows. Prices drop by around a third on weekends.

🍴 Eating

⭐Vegetariano La 23
VEGETARIAN $

(Calle 23 No 9-60; meals COP$6000-9500; ⊙11am-2pm Mon-Fri; 🍴) Up an unmarked staircase in a nondescript house in the center, this homely vegetarian restaurant is a local institution, serving up delicious meat-free meals to those in the know. The menu is constantly changing but always features a wide variety of grains and farm-fresh vegetables.

Grajales Autoservicios
CAFETERIA $

(Carrera 8 No 21-60; mains COP$10,000; ⊙24hr) At this large 24-hour self-service restaurant-cum-bakery you can put together your own lunch or dinner at the buffet. It's also a good option for breakfast.

El Mirador
ARGENTINE $$$

(☑331-2141; www.elmiradorparrillashow.com; Entrada Av Circunvalar Calle 4; mains COP$24,000-38,000; ⊙11am-11pm Mon-Thu, to 1am Fri & Sat) This upmarket open-air restaurant sits outside the city on top of a mountain overlooking the twinkling lights of Pereira. The food is for the most part Argentine and there is an extensive wine list.

🍷 Drinking & Entertainment

The Sector Circunvalar is full of bars and small discos and is now Pereira's principal party spot, while downtown has a number of bars popular with a bohemian crowd. The late-night action is a little way outside of the city in La Badea.

⭐Rincón Clásico
BAR

(cnr Carrera 2 & Calle 22; ⊙4-11pm Mon-Sat) Music lovers of all ages descend on this diminutive corner bar to drink and sing along to tango, bolero and other classics from the elderly owner's collection of 7000 records. Don Olmedo has been spinning tunes here for more than half a century. He'll play anything as long as it's classic – don't go asking for reggaeton!

El Parnaso
BAR

(Carrera 6 No 23-35; ⊙2pm-midnight Mon-Sat) Walk down the long corridor to emerge in this arty garden bar with an open fireplace. It serves tasty pizzas and burgers, and the hip indie-rock soundtrack is restrained enough to enjoy a conversation.

Bar Celona
BAR

(Av Circunvalar No 1-76, La Rebeca; ⊙3pm-2am) At the far end of Av Circunvalar, this unpretentious drinkery plays a crowd-pleasing mix of Latin and international hits; don't be surprised if the crowd joins in on the chorus to a favorite song. The pleasant courtyard out the back is a lively place to start your evening and there are plenty of TVs to catch sporting events.

Leña Verde
SALSA CLUB

(La Badea; ⊙9pm-6am Fri & Sat) Great for people-watching, this popular *salsateca* (salsa dance club) attracts all types, from baggy-trousered homeboys to smooth romantics with tight shirts and perfectly manicured mustaches. But everyone has one goal – to get blind drunk and dance all night. Bring a dance partner – it's not the safest place to be hitting on strangers.

❶ Information

There are numerous ATMs in the bus station, around Plaza Bolívar and on the Av Circunvalar.

4-72 (Carrera 9 No 21-33; ☺8am-noon & 2-6pm Mon-Fri, 9am-noon Sat)

Tourist Office (☎324-8753; www.pereiracul turayturismo.gov.co; cnr Carrera 10 & Calle 17; ☺8am-noon & 2-6pm Mon-Fri) In the Centro Cultural Lucy Tejada. There is another branch in the airport.

❶ Getting There & Away

AIR

Pereira's international **Aeropuerto Matecaña** (☎314-8151) is 5km west of the city center, 20 minutes by urban bus; a taxi costs COP$12,000. Copa has direct flights to Panama.

BUS

The **bus terminal** (☎321-5834; Calle 17 No 23-157) is 1.5km south of the city center. Many urban buses will take you there in less than 10 minutes. There are regular departures to Bogotá (COP$50,000, nine hours). A number of buses go to Medellín (COP$35,000, six hours) and Cali (COP$24,000, four hours). Minibuses run every 15 minutes to Armenia (COP$7000, one hour) and Manizales (COP$9000, 1¼ hours).

❶ Getting Around

Pereira's **Megabus** (www.megabus.gov.co; single ticket COP$1800) system runs across town and out to Dosquebradas. It's similar to Bogotá's TransMilenio and Cali's Mio, but on a smaller scale.

The taxi minimum is COP$4000 with a COP$700 surcharge after 7pm.

Termales de Santa Rosa

☎6 / ELEV 1950M

These spectacular **thermal springs** (☎320-680-3615, 364-5500; www.termales.com.co; admission adult/child Fri-Sun COP$42,000/21,000, Mon-Thu COP$30,000/15,000; ☺9am-10pm) are located at the foot of three adjacent waterfalls, the largest 170m high. Opened in 1945 and built in the style of a Swiss chalet, the hotel and tourist complex have the air of another place and time. There is one large pool open to the general public, while hotel guests have exclusive access to a medium-sized pool under the original water source and two smaller baths. There is also a full spa service, bar and cafeteria.

The on-site **Hotel Termales** (☎321-799-8186, 365-5500; www.termales.com.co; r per person incl breakfast COP$100,000-170,000; 🅿🛆) has three separate wings. Accommodations in the original house – Casa Finca – seem overpriced considering the worn conditions and that many rooms have shared showers. The accommodations in the adjacent Montañas block are only slightly more expensive but are far superior with more space and waterfall views. The most luxurious rooms are in the Cabaña block, which has a private thermal pool on an elevated deck overlooking the river. Discounts are available during the week.

Owned and managed by Hotel Termales, the **Termales Balneario** (☎314-701-9361; www.termales.com.co; admission adult/child COP$32,000/16,000; ☺9am-10pm), 1km back down the road towards town, are cheaper and no less impressive than Santa Rosa, with a 25m-waterfall splitting into various streams as it crashes down next to four thermal pools. There is more green space and less concrete here. A bar-cafe serves food, beer and liquor to crowds of local visitors.

There are no accommodations on-site for these pools, but several small hotels cluster 500m from the entrance. Check out friendly **Cabaña El Portal** (☎320-623-5315; r per person COP$30,000). It has hot water and satellite TV, and also serves hearty budget meals. Ask the staff about horseback-riding trips (COP$15,000 per hour) in the surrounding countryside.

Further down the road, just outside Santa Rosa de Cabal, **Mamatina** (☎311-762-7624; mamatina.src@hotmail.com; La Leona Km1 Via Termales; s/d incl breakfast COP$35,000/70,000, ste COP$120,000) offers modern, comfortable accommodations with views over the surrounding farms. The popular grill restaurant here is a great place to try *chorizos santarosanos* – regarded as the best sausage in Colombia.

❶ Getting There & Away

The thermal pools are 9km east of Santa Rosa de Cabal, off the Pereira–Manizales road. Urban buses (COP$1300, 45 minutes) leave from the main plaza in Santa Rosa de Cabal every two hours from 6am to 6pm, returning an hour later from the Hotel Termales.

There is frequent daytime Santa Rosa–Pereira bus service (COP$2500, 40 minutes). Buses to Manizales (COP$7000, one hour) stop at the gas station on the Pereria–Chinchiná road, four blocks from the plaza.

Termales San Vicente

☑ 6 / ELEV 2250M

Set at the head of a steep, forested valley and straddling a cold creek, these **thermal pools** (www.sanvicente.com.co; admission adult/child COP$30,000/12,000, r per person incl breakfast COP$74,000-198,000; ☺ 8am-midnight) are only 18km east of Santa Rosa de Cabal but feel a world away. There are five thermal pools (37°C), two of which are reserved for hotel guests. Most visitors hang around in the concrete main pool, but the natural Piscina de las Burbujas near the entrance is far nicer. A short walk further down the valley lies the spectacular Pozos del Amor, where the thermal waters mix with the rushing stream to create amazing natural spas surrounded by thick forest – it is hard to imagine a more romantic setting.

The complex also has three natural saunas, built over 80°C to 90°C hot springs, and a full range of spa treatments. There is a wide range of accommodations on offer. Cabins range from split-log rustic to modern minimalist with working fireplaces and private thermal pools. Most have electric shower heads. There are also less appealing hotel-style accommodations and some budget rooms above the reception. Rates include admission and breakfast.

The baths are operated from the **booking office** (☑ 333-6157; Av Circunvalar No 15-62; ☺ 8am-5pm Mon-Fri, to 3pm Sat) in Pereira, where you can make inquiries. A day package for visitors (adult/child COP$60,000/40,000) includes round-trip transportation from Pereira, admission, lunch and a refreshment. The bus leaves from the office at 8am and returns at 5pm. Alternatively, you can hire a jeep from the market – La Galería – in Santa Rosa de Cabal (COP$50,000 one way for up to 6 passengers).

Santuario Otún Quimbaya

This nature reserve 18km southeast of Pereira protects a 489-hectare area of high biodiversity between 1800m and 2400m. Set on the Río Otún, it boasts more than 200 species of birds and butterflies and two rare species of monkey, among other wildlife. The reserve has several hiking trails along the river and through the forest; Spanish-speaking guides are available (COP$40,000 to COP$45,000 per group).

You'll pay the admission fee (COP$5000) at the **visitor center** (Vereda La Suiza; dm/r/tw COP$32,000/70,000/80,000), which also provides accommodations and meals. There are electric showers (24-hour electricity) but no central heating, and fires are not allowed. Alcohol is also prohibited. Ask for a room on the 2nd floor – rooms have small balconies facing the forest and birdsong. Reservations can be made through the excellent community tourism organization **Yarumo Blanco** (☑ 310-379-7719, 314-674-9248; www.yarumoblanco.co).

Transporte Florida (☑ 334-2721; Calle 12 No 9-40, La Galería, Pereira) offers daily *chiva* (typical Colombian bus) services (COP$4000, 1½ hours) at 7am, 9am and 3pm, with an extra service at noon on weekends, from Pereira to the visitor center in the small municipality of Vereda La Suiza. The 9am and 3pm services continue past the visitor center to El Cedral, where they immediately turn around and head back. The *chiva* terminal is in a dangerous part of town; ask your taxi driver to take you all the way into the parking area.

Parque Ucumarí

Established in 1984 just outside the western boundaries of the PNN Los Nevados, this 42-sq-km reserve protects a rugged, forested land around the middle course of the Río Otún, about 30km southeast of Pereira. More than 185 species of bird have been recorded here.

The cabins at **Refugio La Pastora** (dm/campsite per person COP$22,000/5000), at an elevation of 2500m, are at the heart of the park and offer dormitory accommodations and excellent budget meals. The ambience here is particularly laid-back; ask the guy who runs the place to build a bonfire – BYO wine and marshmallows.

There are ecological paths traced through verdant hills, where you can see lush vegetation and spot some of the park's rich wildlife or check out the large waterfall about 30-minutes' walk from the base.

From La Pastora you can hike up Río Otún, leading through a gorge to PNN Los Nevados. You can even get to **Laguna del Otún** (3950m) but it's a 12km, six- to eight-hour walk uphill. It's possible to do the round trip within a day, though it's a strenuous hike. It's better to split the trek and stay in a tent or at the simple house of 'Los Machetes,' a famously hospitable local family. If you do stay longer, you can also make some side excursions in the *páramo*. Conditions are harsh up here – you'll need to take a guide to show you the way.

There is no phone reception in the park itself but you can call Yarumo Blanco (p217) in advance to make your reservations for the *refugio* and organize guides for the trek. It is also able to organize guides (COP$100,000 per day) and rent tents for treks to Lago del Otún and beyond.

To get here from Pereira, take the Transporte Florida (p217) *chiva* to El Cedral (COP$5800). From there it's a 5km, 2½-hour walk, or rent a horse (COP$20,000 one way).

Armenia

🗹6 / POP 290,000 / ELEV 1640M

Armenia feels more like a big town than a departmental capital, far more slow-paced than its coffee-country rivals Manizales and Pereira. There is not much in the way of attractions here for visitors. Devastated by an earthquake in 1999 that flattened much of the city center, Armenia has never fully recovered. The center of the city is makeshift – check out the hastily reconstructed cathedral, made of prefab concrete slabs – and the de facto center has moved north of downtown, along Av Bolívar.

Most travelers will pass through Armenia only long enough to change buses; however, the city has a fine museum and excellent botanical gardens, which make it interesting enough for a day or so.

◎ Sights

Jardín Botánico del Quindío   GARDENS
(🗹742-7254; www.jardinbotanicoquindio.org; Km3 Via al Valle, Calarcá; admission adult/child COP$17,000/8000; ⊙9am-4pm) Armenia's excellent 15-hectare botanical garden has the best *mariposario* in the Zona Cafetera. The 680-sq-meter butterfly house is in the shape of a giant butterfly and houses up to 2000 of the insects (up to 50 different species). There's also a 22m-tall lookout tower, plus ferns, orchids, a guadua (bamboo) forest and an extensive collection of palm species.

To get here, take the bus marked 'Mariposario' (COP$1600, 40 minutes) from Plaza de la Constitución in central Armenia or along Av Bolívar.

Admission includes the services of a guide – they are all volunteers so tips are appreciated. The best time to visit is in the morning when the butterflies are most active.

Museo del Oro Quimbaya   MUSEUM
(🗹749-8169; museoquimbaya@banrep.gov. co; Av Bolívar 40N-80; ⊙10am-5pm Tue-Sun) **FREE** Check out the bling-bling of the pre-Columbian Quimbaya culture at this excellent gold museum that also houses a fine ceramics collection. It's in the Centro Cultural, 5km northeast of the center. Grab bus 8 or 12 northbound on Av Bolívar.

Parque de la Vida   PARK
(🗹746-2302; cnr Av Bolívar & Calle 7N; admission COP$1000; ⊙7am-7pm) If all the concrete is getting too much, stop by this tranquil park located in a valley in the middle of the city. It features both gardens and forested areas, as well as several small lakes and a fast-flowing stream. Keep an eye out for the guatin (a kind of large rodent); they may nick your picnic lunch.

🛏 Sleeping

Casa Quimbaya   HOSTEL $
(🗹732-3086; www.casaquimbaya.com; Calle 16N No 14-92; dm COP$23,000, s/d COP$50,000/70,000; @🛜) With a handy location near the university, bars and restaurants, this relaxed place is the budget travelers' choice in town, although the popular bar downstairs can make it a little noisy. Where it does excel is with the obliging management, who is able to help arrange activities throughout the department.

Hotel Casa Real   HOTEL $
(🗹734-0606; Carrera 18 No 18-36; s/d COP$25,000/31,000; 🛜) Located above some shops in a busy commercial street, this friendly hotel is nothing fancy, but it offers amenities not usually found at this price, including hot water, cable TV and wi-fi. The rooms at the back are quieter, while those at the front have more natural light.

FESTIVALS & EVENTS

Desfile de Yipao (⊙Oct) Charge your camera batteries – this is one photo op you don't want to miss. An important part of Armenia's annual birthday celebration, the Yipao is a fantastic parade in which local working jeeps are loaded down with tonnes of plantain, coffee and household goods, and paraded through town – sometimes on two wheels.

Armenia Hotel
HOTEL **$$$**

(📞746-0099; www.armeniahotelsa.com; Av Bolívar No 8N-67; s/d/tr COP$199,000/254,000/310,000; ❄@🛜) The best hotel in town, the Armenia has nine floors built around a vaulted interior atrium with a glass ceiling. The rooms are spacious, decked out with stylish guadua (bamboo) furniture, and many offer great views of the Cordillera Central or the city. There is a heated outdoor pool and a full-service restaurant downstairs.

Eating

There are plenty of cheap eats in the center during the day and also around the Universidad de Quindío, where numerous bars and small eateries pursue the student market.

Natural Food Plaza
VEGETARIAN **$**

(www.naturalfoodplaza.com; Carrera 14 No 4-51; mains COP$9000-15,000; ⏰7:30am-6:30pm, closed Sat; 🖊) An oasis in a city of slim pickings for herbivores, this delicious vegetarian cafe prepares an excellent lunch buffet (COP$9000), as well as great burgers and vegetarian versions of typical dishes.

La Fonda Antioqueña
COLOMBIAN **$**

(Carrera 13 No 18-59; mains COP$12,000-15,000; ⏰8am-6pm Mon-Sat, to 3pm Sun) A block from Plaza de Bolívar is this fine *paisa* restaurant. It serves lovingly prepared traditional fare, including *bandeja paisa* and, on weekends, *sancocho* (soup or stew). The *almuerzo ejecutivo* (executive lunch; COP$7000) changes daily and is a great deal. Be sure to try *mazamorra,* a typical dish made from cooked corn served with a splash of milk and *panela* (raw sugarcane juice).

La Fogata
COLOMBIAN **$$**

(Carrera 13 No 14N-47; mains COP$23,000-34,000; ⏰noon-10pm Mon-Sat, to 5pm Sun) This fine restaurant is one of Armenia's most famous eateries and with good reason. It does excellent steaks and seafood as well as *vuelve a la vida,* a fish soup rumored to be an aphrodisiac. Also has a good selection of wines.

🍷 Drinking & Entertainment

Armenia has a lively bar scene, although not as good as coffee-country rivals Manizales or Pereira. The area around the Universidad de Quindío northeast of the center on the road to Pereira has several cheap bars. Most of the late-night options are in the *zona rosa* up on a hill outside town.

★La Fonda Floresta
BAR

(Av Centenario; ⏰8pm-3am Fri & Sat) Set up like a traditional Antioquian village with old antiques hanging from the ceiling and party lights everywhere, this popular bar draws a mixed crowd, who come to sit around small tables and drink. Once suitably hammered, they then turn the entire place into one big dance floor. It's a 10-minute taxi ride from the center.

Club 3:00AM
CLUB

(Km1 Via Circasia; ⏰2:30pm-7:45am Fri & Sat) Just outside the town boundaries – and thus not restricted by licensing laws – this spot is where the hip crowd goes to keep the party going after everything else closes.

ℹ Information

4-72 (Calle 22 No 15-17; ⏰8am-6pm Mon-Fri, 9am-noon Sat)

Banco AV Villas (cnr Carrera 14 & Calle 15N) ATM in the north of town.

Banco de Bogota (Calle 21 No 17-02) ATM in center of town.

Tourist Office (Corporación de Cultura y Turismo; Plaza de Bolívar; ⏰9am-noon & 2-5pm) On the 4th floor of the Gobernación del Quindío building, this tourist office has very helpful staff and lots of information. There are also convenient tourist-information points in the bus terminal and airport.

ℹ Getting There & Around

AIR

Aeropuerto Internacional El Edén (p322) is 18km southwest of Armenia near the town of La Tebaida. A taxi will set you back around COP$26,000. Spirit has direct flights to Fort Lauderdale, Florida.

BUS

The **bus terminal** (www.terminaldearmenia. com; Calle 35 No 20-68) is 1.5km southwest of the center and can be reached by frequent city buses that run along Carrera 19 (COP$1500).

There are plenty of buses to Bogotá (COP$40,000, eight hours), Medellín (COP$35,000, five hours) and Cali (COP$22,000, 3½ hours). Regular minibuses run to Pereira (COP$8000, one hour) and Manizales (COP$17,000, 2½ hours).

TAXI

During the day the downtown area is full of merchants and shoppers but after dark security is an issue. Taxis are a cheap and secure way to get to your destination. The minimum fare is COP$3500.

Around Armenia

Tiny Quindío department packs plenty into its modest boundaries with enchanting coffee farms, phenomenal vistas and fun theme parks that appeal to visitors of all ages.

Coffee-farm tourism began here, and there are hundreds of *fincas* (farms) catering to a variety of tastes, mostly Colombian. Numerous publications catalog and rate them. The Armenia tourist office has a lengthy list of options. Also check out **Haciendas del Café** (www.clubhaciendasdelcafe.com).

◉ Sights & Activities

Recuca   FARM
(☎ 310-830-3779; www.recuca.com; Vereda Callelarga, Calarcá; tours COP$18,000; ☉ 9am-3pm) This innovative coffee farm offers tours that provide insight into life on a *finca*. Visitors get to throw on traditional clothes, strap on a basket and hit the plantation to pick their own beans before returning to the hacienda to learn about the coffee-making process. You can also learn some traditional dances. It's more than a little cheesy but is also good fun.

It's best to reserve in advance if you want lunch (COP$14,000).

From Armenia, take any bus (COP$1600) from the terminal to Río Verde and ask to be let off at the entrance to the farm. From here it is a 2km walk through some plantain farms or ask the watchman to call for a jeep (COP$8000 per vehicle). A taxi from Armenia should cost around COP$30,000.

Parque Nacional del Café   AMUSEMENT PARK
(☎ 6-741-7417; www.parquenacionaldelcafe.com; Km6 Via Montenegro; admission COP$23,000-56,000; ☉ 9am-4pm Wed-Sun) This theme park has surprisingly little to do with coffee, but does have a roller coaster and a waterslide. There's also a small coffee museum, some bumper cars and a horseback-riding trail. At the entrance, an 18m lookout tower has great views over Armenia. A cable car offers bird's-eye views of the park, and links the museum with a recreation of a typical Quindian town. Buses depart Armenia bus terminal every 15 minutes (COP$2000, 30 minutes, 7am to 6pm).

🛏 Sleeping

Hacienda Combia   FARMSTAY **$$**
(☎ 6-748-8403; www.combia.com.co; s/d incl breakfast from COP$113,000/144,000; @🛜🏊) This professionally run hotel on a large working coffee farm near Armenia's Jardín Botánico del Quindío has fantastic mountain views and top-notch facilities, including an infinity pool and spa. It doesn't have the intimacy of some smaller farms but you won't find better comfort for the price and the coffee here is the real deal – it has been produced by the same family for four generations.

The rooms in the old farmhouse have more character than those in the new wing. There is a spacious open-air restaurant serving typical meals. A polished, high-end coffee tour (COP$95,000, four hours) is also open to nonguests. A taxi here from Armenia costs around COP$25,000.

Finca Villa Nora   FARMSTAY **$$$**
(☎ 311-389-1806, 310-422-6335; www.quindiofin cavillanora.com; Vereda la Granja, Quimbaya; s/d incl breakfast & dinner COP$220,000/320,000; 🏊) Located between Armenia and Pereira, this coffee, avocado and guava farm offers

---

WILLYS JEEP: AN ICONIC RIDE

If you spend any time at all in the Zona Cafetera, it is highly probable that you will take at least a couple of rides in a classic WWII Willys jeep.

These veterans don't just look great parked in formation around the town plaza – they are still the main form of transportation in rural parts of the Zona Cafetera. Willys are used to transport everything from passengers to pigs, *platano* (plantain), furniture and, of course, coffee. And, unlike buses, a Willys jeep is never really full – don't be surprised if your driver packs in 16 passengers or more.

The first jeeps to arrive were army surplus models sent from the US in 1950. In order to sell the vehicles to farmers in the Zona Cafetera, a kind of traveling jeep show was created: expert drivers maneuvered the vehicles up and down the stairs in front of the town churches and moved loads through obstacle courses in the plazas. The locals were sold instantly – and so began a love affair that lasts to this day.

Willys jeeps are such an integral part of rural Colombian culture that a 'yipao' – which means a jeep full – is a legitimate measure of agricultural products in Colombia (it's about 20 to 25 sacks of oranges).

comfortable accommodations in a beautiful old white-and-red-trimmed farmhouse that has a wide wraparound veranda. The owners run both the lodging and the farm, providing personalized attention to guests. It's a tranquil option that is full of character. Staff can arrange a private transfer from Armenia or Pereira airports.

Salento

📍6 / POP 4000 / ELEV 1900M

Set amid gorgeous green mountains 24km northeast of Armenia, this small town survives on coffee production, trout farming and, increasingly, tourists, who are drawn by its quaint streets, typical *paisa* architecture and its proximity to the spectacular Valle de Cocora. It was founded in 1850, and is one of the oldest towns in Quindío.

The main drag is Calle Real (Carrera 6), which is full of *artesanías* (local craft stalls) and restaurants. At the end of the street are stairs leading up to Alto de la Cruz, a hill topped with a cross. From here you'll see the verdant Valle de Cocora and the mountains that surround it. If the skies are clear (usually only early in the morning), you can spot the snowcapped tops of the volcanoes on the horizon.

🏃 Activities

Horseback riding is a popular activity in Salento; however, there have been some accidents involving tourists riding here. Go with an experienced guide, and if your travel insurance doesn't cover horseback riding, make sure your guide has a policy.

Álvaro Gomez HORSEBACK RIDING
(☎759-3343, 311-375-8293) An experienced horseback-riding guide who runs trips to several nearby waterfalls, along an old, unfinished railway track, plus a longer day trip up into Cocora and multiday adventures. He charges COP$40,000 per person for a half-day trip.

Kasa Guadua HIKING
(☎313-889-8273; www.kasaguaduanaturalreserve.org) About a 30-minute walk from town, this private nature reserve protects 14 hectares of tropical Andean cloud forest. The enthusiastic owners lead informative guided hikes (COP$15,000 to COP$25,000 per visitor) along several trails. Accommodations in innovative elevated cabañas (cabins) surrounded by forest were under construction when we visited.

Los Amigos TEJO
(Carrera 4 No 3-32; ⊗3-11pm) If you are in the mood to drink beer and throw rocks at gunpowder, do as the locals do and head to this atmospheric *tejo* club. Wear your best moustache!

👉 Tours

A number of local coffee farms run tours for visitors keen to learn about the process. Recommended farms are in the rural area near Vereda Palestina. It's about a 45-minute, mostly downhill walk from town. From the central park in Salento, walk north for a block, then west across the yellow bridge and keep following the main road.

From there, it's possible to walk for 30 minutes down into the valley to Boquia on the Armenia–Salento road and take the regular bus service (COP$1000) back to Salento. A private jeep from Salento to the farms near Vereda Palestina costs around COP$24,000.

Don Elías Organic Farm COFFEE TOURS
(near Vereda Palestina; tour COP$5000) Charismatic local coffee grower don Elías offers an enthusiastic guided tour of his traditional organic farm. If your language skills permit, go for the original Spanish-language tour with don Elías himself.

El Ocaso COFFEE TOUR
(☎310-451-7194; www.fincaelocasosalento.com; near Vereda Palestina; tour COP$8000) The most polished coffee tour around Salento is set on an expansive farm with fine coffee bushes and a pretty old farmhouse. You'll visit the plantation and then follow the process of preparing the beans for market. Tours last around an hour and begin at 9am, 11am, 1pm and 3pm. On weekends the tour is offered in English.

🛏 Sleeping

Tralala HOSTEL $
(☎314-850-5543; www.hosteltralalasalento.com; Carrera 7 No 6-45; dm COP$20,000-22,000, s/d COP$50,000/65,000, without bathroom COP$40,000/50,000; 🛜) In a brightly renovated colonial house, this small, well-run hostel was clearly created by someone who knows exactly what travelers want. Facilities include comfortable mattresses, piping-hot showers, two kitchens, an extensive DVD library and fast wi-fi. And there is even rubber-boot rental for muddy treks.

FILANDIA

Slow-paced Filandia is a traditional coffee town that is every bit as charming as its popular neighbor Salento, just a short distance away, but gets a fraction of the visitors. It has some of the best-preserved architecture in the region, as well as the **Colina Iluminada** (Km1 Via Quimbaya; admission COP$3000; ⊘2-7pm Mon-Fri, 10am-7pm Sat & Sun) *mirador* (lookout), an impressive 19m-tall wooden structure that offers breathtaking views over three departments and, on a clear day, Parque Nacional Natural (PNN) Los Nevados.

Numerous small **coffee farms**, many of which welcome visitors, surround the town. You can arrange visits and accommodations at the **tourist office** (☑6-758-2195; Calle 6 No 6-04; ⊘7am-noon & 1:30-4:30pm Mon-Fri) inside the Alcaldia building around the corner from the plaza. The office can also organize horseback-riding trips (COP$25,000).

Nature lovers should be sure to check out the **Cañon del Río Barbas** and **Reserva Natural Bremen – La Popa**, undeveloped forested areas full of birdlife that offer the chance to spot howler monkeys. **Turaco** (☑315-328-0558; turaco@hotmail.es; Calle 7 No 4-51) offers guided hikes to both reserves as well as trips to local waterfalls and coffee farms. Expect to pay around COP$80,000 for up to five hikers.

There are several great-value accommodations in town, the best of which is the tranquil **La Posada del Compadre** (☑315-354-5253; Carrera 6 No 8-06; r incl breakfast COP$60,000-70,000), set in a lovingly restored colonial house with amazing mountain views from the rear deck. For budget digs, check out **Hostal Colina de Lluvia** (☑312-715-6245; aguadelluvia@outlook.com; Carrera 4 No 5-15; dm COP$25,000, r with/without bathroom COP$65,000/45,000). Foodies should make sure to visit **Helena Adentro** (Carrera 7 No 8-1 ;mains COP$9000-18,000; ⊘noon-10pm Wed-Thu, to midnight Fri, to 1am Sat), a hip bar-restaurant serving outstanding modern Colombian cuisine and great cocktails.

Filandia is famous for its woven baskets, an art that can be traced back to those once used by coffee pickers to collect the harvest. To find out more, visit the **Centro de Interpretación de la Cestería de Bejucos** (☑312-234-4055; cnr Carrera 5 & Calle 6, Casa del Artesano; ⊘2-6pm) **FREE** in the center, a kind of museum-gallery dedicated to the craft. Alternatively, pass by the many workshops in Barrio San Jose, where you can buy direct from the *artesanos* (craftspeople) and even learn to make your own basket.

Buses run to/from Armenia (COP$4200, 45 minutes) every 20 minutes until 8pm. There is also a direct service to Pereira (COP$5300, one hour) every hour until 7pm. Coming from Salento, you can pick up a bus at Las Flores where the Salento road joins the main highway.

La Floresta Hostel
HOSTEL $

(☑759-3397; www.laflorestahostel.com; Carrera 5 No 10-11; dm COP$18,000-20,000, s/d COP$44,000/54,000, without bathroom COP$34,000/44,000; 🛜) In a new building just across the yellow bridge from the center of Salento, this friendly locally owned hostel is excellent value. Rooms are well equipped and comfortable, and the ample garden, where you're able to pitch a tent, has hammocks and mountain views. La Floresta also rents decent bicycles for exploring the area.

★ Ciudad de Segorbe
HOTEL $$

(☑759-3794; www.hostalciudaddesegorbe.com; Calle 5 No 4-06; s/d incl breakfast COP$70,000/95,000; 🅿🛜) While the elegant rooms with wooden floors and tiny balconies overlooking the mountains in this two-story house are an excellent deal, it is the wonder-fully warm Spanish-Colombian hosts that make this small and peaceful hotel really stand out from the pack. An excellent breakfast is served in the interior courtyard.

La Serrana
HOSTEL $$

(☑316-296-1890; www.laserrana.com.co; Km1.5 Via Palestina; dm COP$23,000-25,000; s/d COP$80,000/85,000, without bathroom COP$70,000/75,000; 🅿🛜) On a peaceful hilltop dairy farm with stunning views across the valley, this hostel has top-notch facilities and a fantastic atmosphere. The restaurant prepares good budget meals and there is a lovely yard in which to pitch a tent. There are also luxurious permanent tents (single/double/triple COP$65,000/70,000/80,000). It's well worth the 20-minute walk from town. If you've heavy bags, hire a jeep (COP$6000).

🍴 Eating & Drinking

On weekends the plaza explodes with food stalls that prepare local specialties such as trout and crispy *patacones* (fried plantains) smothered in *hogao* (warm tomato chutney).

La Eliana INTERNATIONAL $
(Carrera 2 No 6-65; mains COP$10,000-14,000; ⊙noon-9pm) Prepares quality breakfasts plus gourmet pizzas, sandwiches and, if you're in the mood for something different, real Indian curries. The portions are generous and prices are very reasonable for the quality involved. Try the delicious orange brownies.

Rincón del Lucy COLOMBIAN $
(Carrera 6 No 4-02; meals COP$6000) Sit at great tree-trunk slabs of tables to eat the best-value meal in town: fish, beef or chicken served with rice, beans, plantain and soup.

Billar Danubio Hall BAR
(Carrera 6 No 4-30; ⊙8am-midnight Mon-Fri, to 2am Sat & Sun) This is every Latin small-town fantasy rolled into one. Old men in non-ironic ponchos and cowboy hats sip aguardiente (anise-flavored liquor) as they play dominos. The clientele breaks into ragged harmony whenever an anthem of heartbreaking personal relevance is played. It's a bastion of unreconstructed male behavior, so women may be treated as a curiosity, but these are total gentlemen.

Café Jesús Martín CAFE
(www.cafejesusmartin.com; Carrera 6A No 6-14; ⊙8am-8pm) This groovy cafe serves top-quality espresso coffee roasted and prepared in the owner's factory. It's got a distinctly upper-crust feel to it; don't expect to see too many local farmers drinking here. Also serves wine, beer and light meals. Ask about the high-end coffee-tasting tours.

Donde Mi Apá BAR
(Carrera 6 No 5-24; ⊙4-11pm Mon-Thu, 1pm-2am Sat, 1-11pm Sun) This is the place where hardworking mountain folk come to get seriously smashed after a tough day at the office. The cozy interior is full of assorted antiques/junk from all over the Zona Cafetera, and behind the bar there is an extraordinary collection of 18,000 pieces of worn vinyl covering all genres of *musica vieja* (old music).

ℹ️ Information

Banco Agrario de Colombia (Carrera 7) ATM on the plaza.
Bancolombia (Carrera 6) ATM on the plaza.

ℹ️ Getting There & Away

Minibuses run to/from Armenia every 20 minutes (COP$3800, 45 minutes, 6am to 8pm). Buses leave from the plaza, except on Sunday when you need to go to the bus office on Carrera 2. You can also take a taxi direct from Armenia (30 minutes, COP$50,000).

There is a direct bus service from Pereira (COP$6000, 1½ hours) at 6:50am, 11:30am, 1:30pm and 4:30pm during the week. Buses leave Salento for Pereira at 7:50am, 12:50pm, 2:50pm and 5:50pm. On the weekends buses ply this route every hour. Coming from Pereira, you can also take an Armenia-bound bus to Los Flores and cross the road to grab a Salento-bound bus from Armenia.

Valle de Cocora

In a country full of beautiful landscapes, Cocora is one of the most striking. It stretches east of Salento into the lower reaches of PNN Los Nevados, with a broad green valley framed by sharp peaks. Everywhere you'll see palmas de cera (wax palms), the largest palm in the world (up to 60m tall). It's Colombia's national tree. Set amid the misty green hills, they are breathtaking to behold.

The most popular walk is the 2½-hour walk from the small hamlet of Cocora to the **Reserva Natural Acaime** (admission incl refreshment COP$5000). As you arrive in Cocora, the trail is on the right-hand side as you walk into the valley and away from Salento. The first part of the trail is through grassland, the second through dense cloud forest. At Acaime you can get a hot chocolate (with cheese), and you'll see plenty of hummingbirds. Basic accommodations are available.

About 1km before you reach Acaime, there's a turnoff to **Finca La Montaña**, an energy-sapping one-hour hike up a fairly steep mountainside, from where you can take an easy downhill trail back to Cocora (1½ hours). It is worth the extra effort to complete the loop, rather than tracking back along the same path, as the trail offers spectacular views of the valley from above and takes you right among the wax palms. It is possible to rent horses in Cocora for a guided ride to Acaime (COP$45,000 per person).

Jeeps leave Salento's main square for Cocora (COP$3400, 30 minutes) at 6:10am, 7:30am, 9:30am, 11:30am, 2pm and 4pm, coming back an hour later. There are additional services on weekends. You can also contract a jeep privately for around COP$27,000.

Cali & Southwest Colombia

Best Places to Eat

➡ Hotel Camino Real (p239)
➡ Platillos Voladores (p230)
➡ Lulodka (p230)
➡ Donde Richard (p243)

Best Places to Dance

➡ Zaperoco (p230)
➡ New York (p239)
➡ Tin Tin Deo (p231)
➡ Viejoteca Pardo Llada (p231)

Why Go?

Out of the way and with a reputation for security problems, southwest Colombia is often overlooked by travelers, but this fascinating region warrants an appearance on all itineraries. It's an authentic land of contrasts: Andean and African, modern and pre-Columbian. It stimulates the senses at every opportunity and leaves intrepid visitors with countless tales of classic travel experiences.

Security has improved markedly and destinations that were once off-limits are being put back on the map by adventurous trailblazers. Here you will find the best archaeological sites in the country and some of its finest colonial architecture. It's a region of immense biodiversity where you can pass through desert, jungle and *páramo* (high-mountain plain) ecosystems in just one day. Nature lovers will find active volcanoes, thermal springs and spectacular mountain ranges all easily accessible from thriving metropolitan centers famed for their vibrant culture.

When to Go
Cali

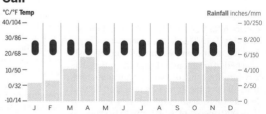

Aug Afro-Colombian rhythms take over Cali during the Festival Petronio Álvarez.

Jul–Sep Thermal winds pack an extra punch for the best kite-surfing on Lago Calima.

Dec & Jan Clear skies make for pleasant hiking in Parque Nacional Natural (PNN) Puracé.

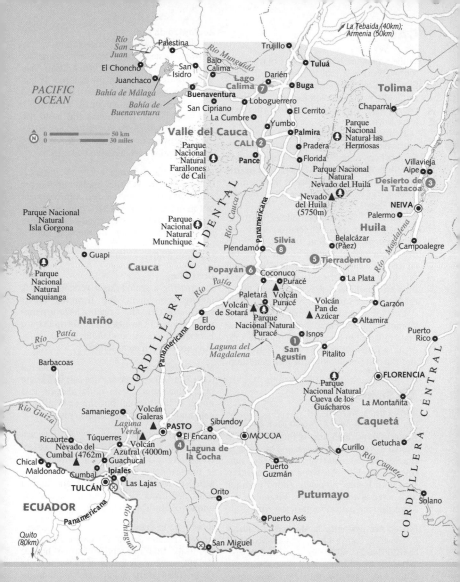

Cali & Southwest Colombia Highlights

① Gawk at giant pre-Columbian sculptures in phenomenal natural settings at **San Agustín** (p241).

② Learn to swivel your hips and boogie in the sweaty salsa joints of **Cali** (p226).

③ Stargaze in Colombia's tiniest desert, the **Desierto de la Tatacoa** (p247).

④ Take a boat ride on **Laguna de la Cocha** (p252) and visit cloud-forest-clad Isla Corota.

⑤ Hike the spectacular hills of **Tierradentro** (p245) to visit ancient underground tombs.

⑥ Wander through the elegant streets of **Popayán**

(p235) to check out its imposing colonial mansions.

⑦ Pick up thermal winds rolling off the cloud-covered mountains while kitesurfing **Lago Calima** (p233).

⑧ Get up close to the indigenous Guambiano culture at the market in **Silvia** (p238).

CALI

🔲 2 / POP 2.5 MILLION / ELEV 969M

While it may not have the looks to front the tourist brochure, Cali is the kind of place that provides all the substance. It's a hot, gritty city with a passion for life that draws you in and stays with you long after you leave town.

It is not an easy place to get to know – tourism doesn't seem to be high on anyone's agenda here – but if you make the effort you will find great nightlife, good restaurants and plenty to do, especially in the evening, when a cool mountain breeze dissipates the heat of the day.

Cali is rich in Afro-Colombian heritage; nowhere is the nation's racial diversity and harmony more apparent than here. From the impoverished barrios to the slick big clubs, everyone is moving to one beat, and that beat is salsa. Music here is much more than entertainment, it is a unifying factor that ties the city together.

Caleños (Cali residents) are proud of their vibrant culture and have a rebellious attitude that's reflected in the city's catchphrase: '*Cali es Cali y lo demás es loma, ¿oís?*' (Cali is Cali, and the rest [of Colombia] is just mountain, ya hear?).

◉ Sights

Iglesia de la Merced　　　　CHURCH
(cnr Carrera 4 & Calle 7; ⊘ 6:30-10am & 4-7pm) Begun around 1545, this is the city's oldest church. It's a lovely whitewashed building in the Spanish colonial style, with a long, narrow nave, and humble wood and stucco construction. Inside, a heavily gilded baroque high altar is topped by the Virgen de las Mercedes, the patron saint of the city.

Museo Arqueológico la Merced　　MUSEUM
(🔲885-4665; Carrera 4 No 6-59; admission adult/child COP$4000/2000; ⊘9am-1pm & 2-6pm Mon-Sat) Housed in the former La Merced convent, Cali's oldest building, this interesting museum contains a collection of pre-Columbian pottery left behind by the major cultures from central and southern Colombia.

**Museo de Arte Moderno
La Tertulia**　　　　GALLERY
(🔲893-2939; www.museolatertulia.com; Av Colombia 5 Oeste-105; admission COP$4000; ⊘10am-6pm Tue-Sat, 2-6pm Sun) Presents exhibitions of contemporary painting, sculpture and photography. It's a 15-minute walk from the city center along the Río Cali.

Zoológico de Cali　　　　ZOO
(🔲488-0888; www.zoologicodecali.com.co; cnr Carrera 2A Oeste & Calle 14 Oeste; admission adult/child COP$15,000/10,000; ⊘9am-4:30pm) This large zoo is the best in the country. It has a good collection of species indigenous to Colombia, including chiguiros (capybaras), oso hormigueros (anteaters) and monkeys, and a *mariposario* (butterfly enclosure). It's 2km southwest of the center in Barrio Santa Teresita and is best accessed by taxi.

Iglesia de San Antonio　　　CHURCH
Constructed in 1747, this small church is set atop a hill, the Colina de San Antonio, west of the old center. It shelters valuable *tallas quiteñas*, 17th-century carved-wood statues of the saints, representing the style known as the Quito School. The park surrounding the church offers great views of the city.

Cristo Rey　　　　MONUMENT
Resembling a scaled-down version of Rio's famous monument, this towering Christ statue atop Cerro las Cristales affords panoramic views of the city. A round-trip taxi up here should cost around COP$50,000. Walking here is not recommended.

Museo del Oro　　　　MUSEUM
(Calle 7 No 4-69; ⊘10am-5pm Tue-Sat) **FREE** One block east from Iglesia de la Merced, this museum has a small but fine collection of gold and pottery of the Calima culture.

Iglesia de San Francisco　　　CHURCH
(cnr Carrera 6 & Calle 10) This neoclassical construction dating from the 18th century is most renowned for the adjacent **Torre Mudéjar** (cnr Carrera 6 & Calle 9), an unusual brick bell tower that is one of the best examples of Mudejar architecture in Colombia.

Iglesia de la Ermita　　　CHURCH
(cnr Av Colombia & Calle 13) Overlooking the Río Cali, this neo-Gothic church houses the 18th-century painting of *El Señor de la Caña* (Lord of the Sugarcane); many miracles are attributed to the image.

🏃 Activities

Colombia Walking Tours　　GUIDED TOURS
(🔲310-398-5513; www.colombiawalkingtours.com) **FREE** This group of enthusiastic young guides offers a free walking tour around the city center on Monday and Friday at 4pm beginning from outside the Iglesia de la Merced. It also offers a number of other on-demand tours around Cali.

Club Social Los Amigos TEJO
(☎442-1258; Calle 49 No 8A-23; ⊙3pm-midnight Tue-Sun) This large, working-class bar east of the center has three *canchas de tejo,* as well as *canchas de sapo* (which involves throwing metal discs into holes in a wooden target box) and billiards. A taxi here will cost around COP$10,000.

Hiking

No trip to Cali is complete without visiting **Cerro de las Tres Cruces**, three crosses that tower over the city. The views here are spectacular. It's a hefty two- to three-hour walk round trip from Granada heading northwest – bring plenty of water – or take a taxi (COP$35,000).

Marker **Km18** lies 18km west of the city. There are numerous bars and restaurants here. At 1800m it's pleasantly cool, and the nearby cloud forest is an Important Bird Area (see www.mapalina.com for details of the species found here) with high biodiversity. The walk from here to the small town of **Dapa** (four hours) – off the Cali–Yumbo road – is a pleasant stroll. There are numerous crossroads – always take the left-hand fork.

There are regular bus services to Km18 from the bus terminal (COP$2000, 45 minutes). Buses and jeeps service Dapa every half hour (COP$3500, 30 minutes) from Sameco in the north of Cali.

Courses

Many visitors come to Cali to learn to dance salsa, whether it be the city's own high energy version or more traditional styles. There are many professional salsa schools around town, each with their own character and methodology. Expect to pay from COP$35,000 to COP$50,000 per hour for private lessons with discounts offered if you pay for packets of classes in advance.

Recommended schools include **Son de Luz** (☎370-2692; www.sondeluz.co; Carrera 28 No 6-118) and **Compañía Artística Rucafé** (☎556-0300; www.rucafe.com.co; Carrera 36 No 8-49, El Templete), which specializes in Salsa Casino. Those on a budget should check out the popular group classes at **Manicero** (☎314-658-7457; Calle 5 No 39-71).

If you already have some skill and want to perfect your moves, **Swing Latino** (☎374-2226; www.elmulatoysuswinglatino.com; Carrera 31 No 7-25) is a high-end school that receives significant international recognition. It offers individual classes (COP$75,000 per hour) and group classes organized by level. Prices drop dramatically if you purchase a packet of lessons.

For language courses, head to **Universidad Santiago de Cali** (☎518-3000, ext 421; www.usc.edu.co; cnr Calle 5 & Carrera 62), which runs a respected Spanish program for foreigners.

Festivals & Events

★**Festival de Música del Pacífico Petronio Álvarez** MUSIC
(www.festivalpetronioalvarez.com; ⊙Aug) A festival of Pacific music, heavily influenced by the African rhythms brought by the many slaves that originally populated the Pacific coast. *Caleños* turn up en masse for nonstop dancing and copious amounts of *arrechón* (a sweet artisanal alcohol).

Festival Mundial de Salsa DANCE
(www.mundialdesalsa.com; ⊙Sep) Amazing dancers from Cali and beyond take to the stage in colorful costumes during this competitive salsa event.

Calle del Arte CULTURAL
(⊙Sep) San Antonio hosts this street-closing festival with music, *artesanías* (local crafts), theater, dance and food.

Feria de Cali CULTURAL
(www.feriadecali.com; ⊙Dec) Cali's big bash is from Christmas to New Year, with parades, music, theater, a beauty pageant and general citywide revelry.

Sleeping

For a taste of Cali's colonial origins, lay your head in laid-back San Antonio; if you are after nightlife head for Granada.

Guest House Iguana HOSTEL $
(☎382-5364; www.iguana.com.co; Av 9N No 22N-46; dm COP$19,000-21,000, s/d COP$50,000/60,000, without bathroom COP$40,000/50,000; @ 🛜) This laid-back hostel has a variety of comfortable accommodations spread over two adjoining houses. There is a pleasant garden area, helpful management and free salsa classes several times a week. It's north of the center, within walking distance of the restaurants in Granada and Chipichape.

La Maison Violette HOSTEL $
(☎371-9837; www.maisonviolettehostel.com; Carrera 12A No 2A-117; dm COP$23,000, s/d COP$65,000/75,000, ste COP$85,000; 🛜) A new arrival in San Antonio, this hostel has tastefully decorated rooms, spacious suites

Cali

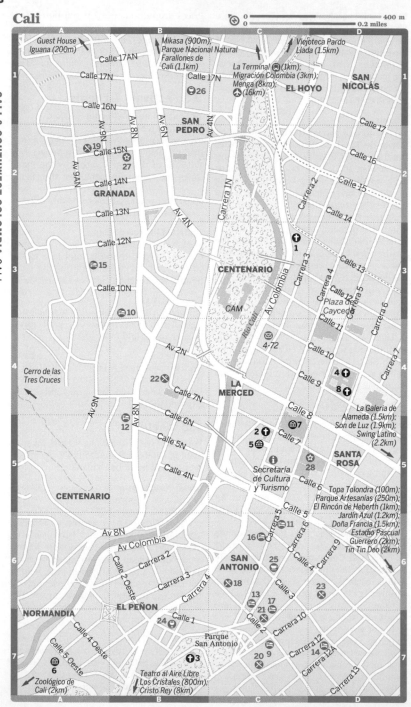

Guest House Iguana (200m)

Mikasa (900m);
Parque Nacional Natural
Farallones de
Cali (1.1km)

Viejoteca Pardo
Llada (1.5km)

La Terminal (1km);
Migración Colombia (3km);
Menga (8km);
(16km)

EL HOYO

SAN
NICOLÁS

SAN
PEDRO

GRANADA

CENTENARIO

CAM

Rio Cali

LA
MERCED

CENTENARIO

SANTA
ROSA

La Galeria de
Alameda (1.5km);
Son de Luz (1.9km);
Swing Latino
(2.2km)

Secretaría
de Cultura
y Turismo

Topa Tolondra (100m);
Parque Artesanías (250m);
El Rincón de Heberth (1km);
Jardín Azul (1.2km);
Doña Francia (1.5km);
Estadio Pascual
Guerrero (2km);
Tin Tin Deo (2km)

SAN
ANTONIO

NORMANDIA

EL PEÑON

Parque
San Antonio

Cerro de las
Tres Cruces

Teatro al Aire Libre
Los Cristales (800m);
Cristo Rey (8km)

Zoológico de
Cali (2km)

Cali

and a rooftop terrace with panoramic views of the city.

Café Tostaky   HOSTEL $
(📞 893-0651; www.tostakycali.com; Carrera 10 No 1-76; dm COP$20,000, s/d without bathroom COP$35,000/50,000; @🛜) Right in the heart of San Antonio, this popular hostel has basic but functional rooms, good hot water and a kitchen you can use. Downstairs it runs a chilled cafe that serves crepes, sandwiches and good coffee. Worth visiting even if you're not staying here.

La Casa Café   HOSTEL $
(📞 893-7011; lacasacafecali@gmail.com; Carrera 6 No 2-13; dm COP$18,000, s/d without bathroom COP$25,000/40,000; @🛜) For an old-school, no-frills backpacking experience head to this groovy cafe-bar which rents good-value dorm beds and private rooms on the 2nd floor of its colonial building.

Jardín Azul   GUESTHOUSE $$
(📞 556-8380; www.jardinazul.com; Carrera 24A No 2A-59; r COP$115,000-165,000; 🛜🏊) Set in a converted house on a hill near the colonial sector east of the center, this spotless small hotel has spacious, bright rooms with big beds and imported cotton sheets. Some rooms have private balconies and views of the city. There is a small pool set in an appealing garden that attracts plenty of birds.

El Viajero   HOSTEL $$
(📞 893-8342; Carrera 5 No 4-56; dm COP$23,000-25,000, s/d COP$75,000/100,000, without bath-room COP$47,000/88,000; 🛜🏊) In a renovated colonial house, El Viajero is a popular choice among young travelers looking for a social vibe. The private rooms are a little on the small side, but the large pool in the rear courtyard provides respite from the heat and the adjacent bar area is lively in the evenings. There are regular free dance classes.

La Casa Azul   GUESTHOUSE $$
(📞 374-4766; www.lacasaazulhotelbotique.com; Av 4N No 5-09, Centenario; r incl breakfast COP$100,000; ❄) Conveniently located in Centenario within walking distance of many attractions, this modern guesthouse has large air-conditioned rooms with flat-screen TVs and big beds. Prices include an ample breakfast.

Posada San Antonio   HOTEL $$
(📞 893-7413; www.posadadesanantonio.com; Carrera 5 No 3-37; s/d/tr incl breakfast COP$100,000/120,000/150,000; @🛜) Set in an old colonial building in San Antonio, this peaceful hotel has spacious rooms with private bath and cable TV set around a pleasant courtyard. There are also cheaper, less atmospheric rooms around the rear patio.

Ruta Sur   HOSTEL $$
(📞 893 6946; hostalrutasur@gmail.com; Carrera 9 No 2-41; s/d COP$75,000/95,000) This homely, welcoming hostel in San Antonio is popular with travelers looking for a quiet base in a central location. Rooms are tastefully decorated but the bathrooms are tiny.

Casa de Alférez
HOTEL $$$

(☑393-3030; www.movichhotels.com; Av 9N No 9-24; r COP$179,000-330,000, ste COP$500,000; ✳@) This ultraluxurious hotel offers elegant rooms with king-sized beds, spacious bathrooms and French windows that open onto small balconies on a lovely, tree-lined street.

Now Hotel
BOUTIQUE HOTEL $$$

(☑488-9797; www.nowhotel.com.co; Av 9AN No 10N-74, Granada; r COP$521,000; ✳@☎✉) This arty boutique hotel has an industrial-chic theme with plenty of metal, mesh, polished concrete and colored glass. The rooftop pool and bar area is a great place for a cocktail in the early evening.

Eating

The best cheap eats in town are at **La Galería** (food market; cnr Calle 8 & Carrera 26) in Alameda, a colorful local market with plenty of small lunch counters serving seafood and *comidas típicas* (typical food).

El Buen Alimento
VEGETARIAN $

(☑375-5738; Calle 2 No 4-53; set meal COP$10,000, mains COP$12,500-15,500; ☺11:30am-10pm Mon-Sat, to 5pm Sun; ☑) This hip vegetarian restaurant serves excellent meat-free versions of Colombian classics, as well as creative fusion dishes such as Mexican lasagna and great fresh juices.

Doña Francia
ICE CREAM $

(Carrera 27 No 3-100; snacks COP$2000-5000; ☺8am-7pm) Sit on benches outside this Cali institution and enjoy sensational juices, sorbets and possibly the best *salpicón* (fruit salad) in all of Colombia. It's one block east from Parque del Perro.

Zahavi
BAKERY $

(Carrera 10 No 3-81; pastries COP$2000-6000; ☺11am-8pm Mon-Fri, 8am-7:30pm Sat & Sun) This posh bakery in San Antonio serves excellent coffee, rich gooey brownies and delicious gourmet sandwiches.

★Lulodka
FUSION $$

(Calle 2 No 6-17; set meals COP$15,000, mains COP$14,000-28,000; ☺10am-3:30pm & 6-11pm Mon-Sat) You won't find better value for your peso than at this groovy fusion restaurant in a lovely colonial house. The gourmet set lunches include soup, salad, main course, fresh juice and dessert. Everything is cooked to perfection with delicately balanced flavors and textures. Try the signature 'Lulodka' – a lulo-based beverage mixed with vodka.

El Zaguán de San Antonio
COLOMBIAN $$

(Carrera 12 No 1-29; mains COP$25,000; ☺noon-midnight) This San Antonio institution serves big portions of traditional *valle-caucana* food (food from the Valle del Cauca department) and excellent fresh juices. The food is delicious but the real reason to come here is for the amazing view from the rooftop, which is also a great place for a drink.

★Platillos Voladores
FUSION $$$

(☑668-7750; www.platillosvoladores.com.co; Av 3N No 7-19; mains COP$27,000-45,000; ☺noon-3pm & 7-11pm Mon-Fri, 1-4pm Sat) Cali's best fine dining experience, Platillos Voladores offers an interesting and varied menu of beautifully presented gourmet dishes combining Asian, European and local influences, served in either the outdoor garden area or one of several air-conditioned dining rooms. Wash your meal down with an offering from the impressive wine list. Reservations are essential.

El Solar
ITALIAN $$$

(Calle 15N No 9-62; mains COP$28,500-44,000; ☺noon-3pm & 6-11pm) This hugely popular restaurant serves consistently excellent Italian and international dishes in a large courtyard. On the menu are fresh homemade pastas, risottos, gourmet pizzas and salads. There is also a fine selection of seafood with sauces made from local seasonal fruits.

🍺 Drinking & Nightlife

Most *caleños* don't really go out to drink, they go out to dance. For a more low-key night out head to Parque del Perro, where you can take your pick from numerous small bars or go totally local and simply drink in the park. Just north of the Cali municipal boundary is Menga, where numerous discos are open till dawn. Further afield is Juanchito, where several big *salsatecas* (salsa dance clubs) cluster.

★Zaperoco
SALSA CLUB

(www.zaperocobar.com; Av 5N No 16-46; ☺9pm-late Thu-Sat) If you only visit one salsa bar in Cali, make sure it's Zaperoco. Here the veteran DJ spins *salsa con golpe* (salsa with punch) from old vinyl while rows of industrial fans try in vain to keep the place cool. Somewhere under the mass of moving limbs there is a dance floor – but we've never worked out exactly where it is.

It's a high-energy place – a night out here will burn more calories than a half-marathon in the tropics.

Tin Tin Deo
SALSA CLUB

(www.tintindeocali.com; Calle 5 No 38-71; ⊗8pm-late Thu-Sat) This iconic, unpretentious 2nd-floor salsa joint features a large dance area overseen by posters of famous salsa singers. While it sometimes feels like an expat hang-out (especially on Thursdays), it's an excellent place for novice dancers to get on the floor. There is no need to bring a dance partner, you'll find plenty of volunteers among the friendly regulars.

Viejoteca Pardo Llada
SALSA CLUB

(Av 2N No 32-05; cover COP$5500; ⊗ 2-7pm Sun) Hosted in a lovely open-air dancehall upstairs at the senior citizen's association, this is Cali's original and best *viejoteca* (seniors disco), where the city's old timers dress up in their best threads and show off their impressive salsa moves. It's great to come and observe over a beer even if you don't dance. It's near the Parque del Avión.

Mikasa
BAR

(Calle 26N No 5AN-51; ⊗9pm-3am Thu-Sat) An alternative for those who don't breathe salsa, this hip bar has skilled DJs spinning all kinds of music, an outdoor dance area with retractable roof and an open air terrace upstairs. Don't be put off by the commando security team – inside it's actually quite chilled.

El Rincón de Heberth
BAR

(Carrera 24 No 5-32; ⊗8pm-3am Thu-Sat) In a shop front in a strip mall, this humble salsa bar is an unlikely hit but it packs a crowd who come for the great music and laid-back vibe. Most sit outside and drink in the street where it's fresher until a particular song inspires them to take to the steamy dance floor.

Macondo
CAFE

(Carrera 6 No 3-03; ⊗11am-11pm, from 4pm Sun) This San Antonio institution does great coffee and a wide range of desserts. It also serves beer and wine till late. Try one of the scrumptious cocktails.

Topa Tolondra
BAR

(Calle 5 No 13-27; ⊗ 6pm-late Thu-Mon) Humble small salsa bar with a fun ambience near Loma de la Cruz. The tables are all pushed right up against the walls leaving the concrete floor free to get your boogie on.

La Colina
BAR

(Calle 2 Oeste No 4-83) Friendly neighborhood shop-bar hybrid in San Antonio. Cheap beer and classic salsa and bolero.

CALI'S CARROT LAW
....

Closing time in Cali is referred to as the *ley zanahoria* (carrot law), because you'd have to be boring as a carrot to go home that early (at present, 3am on weekends).

Lolas
CLUB

(www.lolasclub.com.co; Antiguo via Yumbo; cover COP$10,000; ⊗ 9pm-late Thu-Sat) Set in a huge white dome in Menga, the inside of this prestigious club is like something out of a big-budget house video, with glamorous young *caleñas* dancing on tables while high-tech lasers slash through clouds of smoke. Groups of unaccompanied men won't get in.

☆ Entertainment

Cinema

For thought-provoking films, check the program of the **Cinemateca La Tertulia** (☎893 2939; www.museolatertulia.com; Av Colombia No 5 Oeste-105; admission COP$5000), which generally has two shows daily from Tuesday to Sunday. Also attracting crowds for its free art-house screenings is **Lugar a Dudas** (☎668 2335; www.lugaradudas.org; Calle 15N No 8N-41; ⊗11am-8pm Tue-Fri, 4:30-8pm Sat) FREE.

Soccer

Cali has two *fútbol* (soccer) teams: **Deportivo Cali** (www.deportivocali.co) plays in the top flight and **America de Cali** (www.america.com.co) languishes in the lower divisions. Home matches are generally played in the city at **Estadio Pascual Guerrero** (cnr Calle 5 & Carrera 34). To get here take the Mio which passes right outside.

Theater

Teatro Municipal
THEATER

(☎881-3131; www.teatromunicipal.gov.co; Carrera 5 No 6-64) Completed in 1918, the city's oldest existing theater is used for various artistic forms, including musical concerts, theater and ballet. If there is nothing going on, you can ask the security officer to show you around.

Teatro al Aire Libre Los Cristales
THEATER

(☎558-2009; Carrera 14A No 6-00) Frequent free concerts are held at this open-air amphitheater.

Delirio
PERFORMING ARTS

(☎893-7610; www.delirio.com.co; Calle 69N No 4N-98; tickets COP$150,000) ✔ You'll need to plan well in advance to see Cali's legendary salsa circus but it's well worth the effort. Think street circus meets flashy dance club and you'll have some idea of what to expect from this explosive celebration of *caleña* culture that takes place once a month in a big top in the Parque del Amor. Admission is restricted to adults.

🛍 Shopping

Parque Artesanías   MARKET
(⊙10am-8pm) On Loma de la Cruz, this is one of Colombia's best *artesanía* markets. You'll find authentic, handmade goods from the Amazon, Pacific coast, southern Andes and even Los Llanos.

ℹ Information

DANGERS & ANNOYANCES

During the day, the city center is alive with street vendors and crowds. After dark and on Sunday it can get dodgy. Also avoid the area east of Calle 5 and along the Río Cali at night. Take a taxi and take extra care with your belongings.

MEDICAL SERVICES

Centro Medico Imbanaco (☎ 682 1000; www. imbanaco.com; Carrera 38A No 5A-100) Respected professional private medical facility.

MONEY

Most of the major banks have offices around Plaza Caycedo in the center and on Av Sexta (Av 6N).

Banco de Occidente (Av Colombia 2-72) Most secure ATM close to San Antonio. Avoid banks in the center at night.

POST

4-72 (Carrera 3 No 10-49; ⊙8am-noon & 2-6pm Mon-Fri, 9am-noon Sat) Post office.

TOURIST INFORMATION

Secretaría de Cultura y Turismo (☎ 885 6173; www.cali.gov.co/turista; cnr Calle 6 & Carrera 4; ⊙8am-noon & 2-5pm Mon-Fri, 10am-2pm Sat) City tourist information office.

VISA INFORMATION

Migración Colombia (☎ 397 3510; www. migracioncolombia.gov.co; Av 3N 50N-20, La Flora; ⊙8am-noon & 2-5pm Mon-Fri) For visa extensions.

ℹ Getting There & Away

Alfonso Bonilla Aragón Airport (p322) is 16km northeast of the city, off the road to Palmira. Minibuses between the airport and the bus terminal run every 10 minutes until about 8pm (COP$5000, 45 minutes), or take a taxi (around

COP$55,000). There are direct international flights from Cali to Miami, Madrid and destinations in Central and South America.

The bus terminal, **La Terminal** (www.terminal cali.com; Calle 30N No 2AN-29), is 2km north of the center. It's a sweaty walk in Cali's heat – take a taxi (COP$6000 to COP$8000).

Buses run regularly to Bogotá (COP$65,000, 12 hours), Medellín (COP$50,000, nine hours) and Pasto (COP$40,000, nine hours). Pasto buses will drop you off in Popayán (COP$15,000, three hours) or you can take the hourly minibuses there (COP$16,000). There are regular departures to Armenia (COP$21,000, four hours), Pereira (COP$24,500, four hours) and Manizales (COP$38,000, five hours).

ℹ Getting Around

Cali's air-conditioned bus network, the **Mio** (www.mio.com.co), will remind many of Bogotá's TransMilenio. The main route runs from north of the bus terminal along the river, through the center and down the entire length of Av Quinta (Av 5). Other routes spread out across the city. It costs COP$1600 per ride.

Taxis are fairly cheap in Cali. The minimum fare is COP$4200 and there is a COP$1100 surcharge at night.

AROUND CALI

Parque Nacional Natural (PNN) Farallones de Cali

This 1500-sq-km national park protects the headlands around Cali. During the height of the armed conflict it was closed and has yet to be officially reopened to visitors.

At the time of research, security was still an issue in some areas and ecological protection measures were also in place to protect the delicate ecosystem, making the majority of the park off-limits to travelers. The only path that was accessible was the full-day hike to Pico de Loro, accessible by hiring a guide in the community of Pance. Studies were underway in order to re-open the five-day hike to Pico de Pance, PNN Farallones' iconic peak, so check the latest at the **park office** (☎2-667-6041; Calle 29N No 6N-43; ⊙8am-noon & 2-4pm Mon-Fri) in Cali before heading out.

At research time no entrance fees were being charged to the park but this is likely to change when it is officially reopened.

Pance

📍 2 / POP 2000 / ELEV 1550M

This small holiday town surrounded by imposing mountains on the eastern edge of PNN Farallones is full of holiday *fincas* (farms) and is popular with *caleños* looking to cool off in the town's crystal clear river. The weather is a pleasantly fresh change from the heat of Cali. On the weekend its one street opens and all the bars and restaurants are in full flower. During the week it's empty and you'll struggle to even get a meal.

In addition to swimming in the river or one of the streams, you can also do a day hike to some nearby waterfalls, or organize a longer trek into PNN Farallones de Cali.

Pico de Loro is a seven-hour round-trip hike west from Pance. Expect to pay around COP$80,000 per group for a local guide to show you the way. In order to hike the trail, you must enter the park before 10am, so it's best to stay in Pance the night before.

To visit the nearby waterfalls, you'll need to get advanced permission and pay an entrance fee (adult/child COP$4700/2300) at the office of the **Corporación Autónoma Regional del Valle de Cauca** (📞 620-6600; www.cvc.gov.co; Carrera 56 No 11-36) in Cali, which administers the area. From Pueblo Pance, walk 1km downhill to the bridge and turn right. Follow the road 3km uphill to El Topacio, where you will find a visitor center and you will be met by a guide. There are two short trails to explore here: the Barranquero trail leads to a 40m waterfall while the Naturaleza trail ends at a 130m cataract. Also ask about visiting La Nevera (The Refrigerator), a pristine swimming hole fed by fresh mountain waters.

🛏️ Sleeping & Eating

Reserva Natural Anahuac CAMPGROUND $
(📞 556 6894; www.reservanatuanahuac.com.co; Vereda El Pato, Pance; campsite per person with/without tent rental COP$18,000/9000, r per person Mon-Sat COP$9000, Sun COP$28,000; 🐕) Anahuac is a small private nature reserve amid secondary forest next to Río Pance. There are a variety of very basic rooms in a couple of worn lodge buildings, but the tiny two-story *bohíos* (huts) by the river will appeal most to travelers as they offer more privacy.

Alternatively just come out for the day (admission COP$6000) to take a dip in the pools – some of which are fed by the water from the river.

★ La Fonda Pance HOSTEL $$
(📞 558-1818, 317-664-3004; www.lafondapance. com; contiguo al Finca Nilo; campsite per person with/without tent hire COP$15,000/10,000, dm COP$20,000, r with/without bathroom COP$80,000/50,000; @ 🛜 🐕) Hands down the best choice for travelers in the area, La Fonda is a relaxing spot with comfortable modern rooms, mountain views and a huge garden divided by a gurgling stream. There's also an outdoor Jacuzzi to soak in after a long hike and a refreshing natural pool fed by waters rushing down from the surrounding peaks.

Meals are served and the friendly management can organize guides for treks in the area. It's 200m before the Topacio turnoff.

ℹ️ Getting There & Away

Minibuses head to Pance roughly every hour (COP$2300, 1½ hours) between 5:15am and 8pm from outside the bus terminal in Cali. They are marked 'Recreativo' and 'Pueblo Pance.'

Lago Calima

This artificial reservoir attracts kitesurfers and windsurfers from around the world for its year-round winds. The lake covers the flooded Darién valley of Río Calima, and was built in 1965. Some 86km north of Cali, its temperate climate also attracts *caleños* looking to cool off on weekends. The green hills that surround the lake are populated with holiday *fincas*.

Most tourist activity stretches along the northern bank of the lake, from the small town of Darién at the eastern end to the dam to the west. There's no beach; launching points are from grassy slopes that lead down to the water.

Because transportation is infrequent in the area, Lago Calima makes a difficult day trip. You're better off coming for a day or two, especially on the weekend, when the many visitors give the place a party atmosphere.

Darién

📍 2 / POP 7000 / ELEV 1800M

This small town has a few budget hotels, a couple of supermarkets, a few ATMs, a couple of internet cafes and, on the weekends, several lively discos. Most everything clusters within two or three blocks of Parque Los Fundadores, the main plaza. Of interest is the **Museo Arqueológico Calima** (📞 253-3496; www.inciva.org; Calle 10 No 12-50;

admission adult/child COP$3000/2000; ⊘8am-5pm Mon-Fri, 10am-6pm Sat & Sun), where you'll find a collection of almost 2000 pieces of pre-Columbian pottery. Darién is a perfectly pleasant little town, but a trip to Lago Calima is the drawcard.

🏃 Activities

Kitesurfing & Windsurfing

There are numerous schools offering classes and rentals. Most also offer accommodations. Expect to pay roughly COP$60,000 per hour for windsurfing instruction and COP$90,000 to COP$100,000 per hour for kitesurfing instruction. Kite rentals go for around COP$60,000 per hour.

Cogua Kiteboarding   KITESURFING
(☑318-608-3932, 253-3524; www.coguakiteboard ing.com; Calle 10 No 4-51) In addition to offering kiteboarding classes, the young owner of this laid-back outfit also runs a kiteboard factory, where he makes custom boards from coconut fiber and guadua (a type of bamboo). Visitors are welcome to drop by the factory to find out about the process or even to design their own board.

Budget accommodations are available in town for clients and it also offers stand-up paddle (SUP) rentals.

Escuela Pescao
Windsurf y Kitesurf   WINDSURFING, KITESURFING
(☑316-401-6373, 311-352-3293; www.pescaowind surfing.com) This outfit sits in a big warehouse on the edge of the lake. The wheelchair-bound former champion kitesurfer gives classes on the shore before sending students out onto the water with an instructor. It offers accommodations (per person students/visitors COP$20,000/35,000) in the warehouse in tents with mattresses and sleeping bags.

Boat trips

Many captains offer excursions on the lake from the Entrada 5 port just outside town. Expect to pay around COP$8000 per person or rent the entire boat for COP$50,000 to COP$60,000. One well-established operator is **El Arriero Paisa** (☑315-439-5939; www.elar rieropaisa.com.co; Entrada 5; ⊘7am-6pm), which also runs a small resort and a restaurant overlooking the lake.

🛏 Sleeping & Eating

La Casa del Viento   HOSTEL $
(☑315-265-6540; www.lacasadelviento.com.co; Carrera 6 No 12-40; dm/r COP$30,000/65,000)

Darién's only hostel has comfortable rooms and friendly management that organizes kitesurfing lessons as well as land-based alternatives involving beefed-up skateboards and buggies. It also offers parasailing over the surrounding countryside.

Hostería Los Veleros   HOTEL $$$
(☑684-1000; www.comfandi.com.co; s/d/tr incl 2 meals COP$197,600/235,000/275,600; 🐾) The best hotel on the lake, Los Veleros is part of the Comfandi complex, and prices include two meals and admission to the recreation center and pools. Some of the rooms have balconies with spectacular views of the lake. Packed on the weekend; during the week you'll have the place to yourself.

El Fogón de la Abuela   COLOMBIAN $
(Calle 9 No 5-58; set meals COP$7500, mains COP$17,500; ⊘7am-8pm) This cheap restaurant a couple of blocks from the park does a filling set meal.

Meson llama   COLOMBIAN $$
(☑667-9703; www.mesonilama.com; mains COP$19,000-22,000; ⊘7:30am-7pm Mon-Fri, to 9pm Sat & Sun) About 10km from Darién is this large, exposed-timber restaurant with great views of the lake. It does all the basics very well – *sancocho* (typical Colombian soup), *churrasco* (grilled meat) baby beef and trout. It also has a variety of comfortable accommodations on the lakeshore.

🛈 Getting There & Away

There is a frequent direct bus service to/from Cali (COP$13,600, 2½ hours) during the day. Coming from the north, get off in Buga and grab the half-hourly service to Darién (COP$6800, 1½ hours).

Note that there are two bus routes that come out from Cali to Lago Calima and Darién. They cost the same. If you're going direct to Darién, ask for the bus via Jiguales; for the kitesurfing/ windsurfing schools, ask for the bus that goes *'por el lago'* ('along the lakeshore').

🛈 Getting Around

There are no taxis in Darién. Jeeps hang out on the main square, and can take you around town and along the lake shore, but these are expensive (around COP$15,000 to Comfandi).

Minibuses shuttle between Darién and the dam at Lago Calima (COP$1500), past the kite schools, from 7am to 7pm on the hour. You can also jump on buses heading to Buga/Cali – but make sure they are taking the lake exit.

CAUCA & HUILA

These two departments are home to Popayán, one of Colombia's most charming colonial cities, plus two of the country's most important archaeological sites – San Agustín and Tierradentro. Here you'll also find the peculiar Desierto de la Tatacoa, a striking anomaly near Neiva, halfway between Bogotá and San Agustín.

In the days of river travel in Colombia, both Cauca and Huila were major hubs of commerce. The introduction of the railroad and highways in the early 20th century stunted their growth, and these days a sleepy languor envelops the region.

Popayán

📞 2 / POP 266,000 / ELEV 1760M

This small colonial city is famous for its chalk-white facades (its nickname is 'La Ciudad Blanca,' or 'the White City'), and is second only to Cartagena as Colombia's most impressive colonial settlement. It sits beneath towering mountains in the Valle de Pubenza, and for hundreds of years was the capital of southern Colombia, before Cali overtook it.

The town was founded in 1537 by Sebastián de Belalcázar, and became an important stopping point on the road between Cartagena and Quito. Its mild climate attracted wealthy families from the sugar haciendas of the hot Valle de Cauca region. In the 17th century they began building mansions, schools and several imposing churches and monasteries.

In March 1983, moments before the much-celebrated Maundy Thursday religious procession was set to depart, a violent earthquake shook the town, caving in the cathedral's roof and killing hundreds. Little damage is visible today.

The city has numerous universities and during the day the streets of the old center are filled with students.

⦿ Sights

Iglesia de San Francisco   CHURCH

(cnr Carrera 9 & Calle 4; guided tour COP$2000) The city's largest colonial church is also its most beautiful. Inside are a fine high altar and a collection of seven unique side altars. The 1983 earthquake cracked open the ossuary, revealing six unidentified mummies. Two are left, and when guides are available, it is possible to visit them on a one-hour guided tour of the church. Ask in the office to the left of the entrance.

Museo Guillermo Valencia   MUSEUM

(Carrera 6 No 2-69; ⦿10am-noon & 2-5pm Tue-Sun) FREE This late-18th-century building is full of period furniture, paintings, old photos and documents that once belonged to the Popayán-born poet who lived here. It has been left more or less as it was when Valencia died in one of the upstairs bedrooms.

Casa Museo Mosquera   MUSEUM

(Calle 3 No 5-38; admission COP$2000; ⦿9am-noon & 3-5pm) This interesting museum is housed in an 18th-century mansion that was once home to General Tomás Cipriano de Mosquera, who was Colombia's president on four occasions between 1845 and 1867. The original French crystal chandelier in the dining room was transported from the Caribbean to Popayán by mule. Note the urn in the wall; it contains Mosquera's heart.

Puente del Humilladero   BRIDGE

Popayán's emblematic landmark, this 240m-long, 11-arch brick bridge was constructed in the mid-19th century to improve access to the center from the poor northern suburbs. It dwarfs the adjacent Puente de la Custodia, a pretty stone bridge constructed in 1713 to allow priests to cross the Río Molino to bring the holy orders to the sick.

Museo de Historia Natural   MUSEUM

(museo.unicauca.edu.co; Carrera 2 No 1A-25; admission COP$3000; ⦿9-11am & 2-4pm) One of the best of its kind in the country, this museum on the grounds of the university is noted for its extensive collection of insects, butterflies and, in particular, stuffed birds.

Museo Arquidiocesano de Arte Religioso   MUSEUM

(Calle 4 No 4-56; admission COP$5000; ⦿9am-12:30pm & 2-6pm Mon-Fri, 9am-2pm Sat) You don't have to be an expert on religious art to be impressed by this collection of paintings, statues, altar pieces, silverware and liturgical vessels, most of which date from the 17th to 19th centuries.

Iglesia La Ermita   CHURCH

(cnr Calle 5 & Carrera 2) Constructed in 1546, Popayán's oldest church is worth seeing for its fine main retable and the fragments of old frescoes, which were only discovered after the earthquake.

Catedral   CHURCH

(Parque Caldas) The neoclassical cathedral is the youngest church in the center, built between 1859 and 1906 on the site of a

Popayán

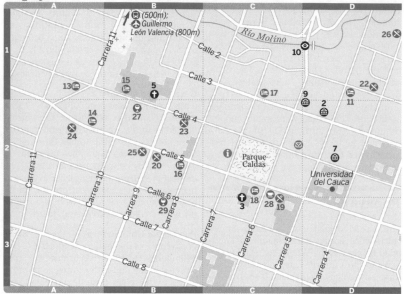

previous cathedral, which had been completely destroyed by an earthquake.

Viewpoints
The **Capilla de Belén**, a chapel set on a hill just east of the city center, offers nice views over the town. **El Morro de Tulcán**, a hill topped with an equestrian statue of the town's founder, provides even better vistas. It's said to be the site of a pre-Columbian pyramid and is a good place to watch the sunset. Both sights are isolated and robberies have been reported – don't carry any valuables.

🏃 Activities

Popayan Tours   ADVENTURE TOURS
(📞831 7871; www.popayantours.com) Offers a variety of adventurous tours outside Popayán, including a downhill mountain-bike run from the Coconuco thermal springs.

⭐ Festivals & Events

Semana Santa   RELIGIOUS
(Holy Week; ☉Easter) Popayán's Easter celebrations are world-famous, especially the nighttime processions on Maundy Thursday and Good Friday. Thousands come from all over to take part in this religious ceremony and the accompanying festival of religious music. Book accommodations well in advance.

Congreso Nacional Gastronómico   FOOD
(www.gastronomicopopayan.org; ☉Sep) Top chefs from a different country each year are invited to come and cook up a storm in the first week of September. Admission to all of the week's events costs COP$350,000.

🛏 Sleeping

Hosteltrail   HOSTEL $
(📞831-7871; www.hosteltrail.com; Carrera 11 No 4-16; dm COP$20,000, s/d COP$45,000/65,000, without bathroom COP$35,000/50,000; @ 🖥) Popayán's most popular budget choice, Hosteltrail is a friendly, modern place on the edge of the colonial center with everything weary travelers need. There is fast internet, express laundry, a fully equipped kitchen and eager staff with a wealth of local know-how.

Parklife Hostel   HOSTEL $
(📞300-249-6240; www.parklifehostel.com; Calle 5 No 6-19; dm COP$20,000, s/d COP$45,000/55,000, without bathroom from COP$35,000/48,000; @ 🖥) You'd be hard pressed to find a hostel with a better location than Parklife – it's attached to the cathedral wall. The house has plenty of its original style; there are wood floors, chandeliers and antique furniture. It's an atmospheric place – you can hear the

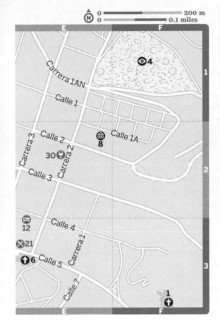

Popayán

church choir from the communal lounge. The front rooms have superb views over Parque Caldas.

Hostel Caracol HOSTEL $
(☑820-7335; www.hostelcaracol.com; Calle 4 No 2-21; dm COP$20,000, s/d without bathroom COP$35,000/50,000; @☎) In a renovated colonial house, this homely hostel is popular with laid-back independent travelers. It has smallish but comfortable rooms set around a pleasant courtyard common area and plenty of information about attractions and entertainment in town.

Casa Familiar Turística HOSTEL $
(☑824-4853; casafamiliarturistica@hotmail.com; Carrera 5 No 2-07; dm COP$15,000, s/d COP$30,000/35,000; ☎) Popayán's original budget digs are a good option for those looking to immerse themselves in local culture – you are basically sharing the house with a Colombian family. Rooms are basic but spacious and you can use the kitchen.

★ Hotel Los Balcones HOTEL $$
(☑824-2030; www.hotellosbalconespopayan.com; Carrera 7 No 2-75; s/d/apt COP$73,700/137,500/171,000; @☎) Climb 200-year-old stone stairs to your room in this regal 18th-century abode. The place has an almost

medieval feel with old wooden furniture, stuffed eagles and a maze of corridors. In the lobby, MC Escher sketches hang next to a case of ancient pottery and plush leather furniture. The rooms on the top floor are quieter.

Hotel La Plazuela HOTEL $$
(☑824-1084; www.hotellaplazuela.com.co; Calle 5 No 8-13; r incl breakfast COP$116,000; ☎) In a beautiful, whitewashed mansion complete with a lovely courtyard, this classy hotel has been fully refurbished but still has much of the original, antique furniture. The front rooms have effective soundproof windows and provide views of Iglesia San José.

Hotel Colonial HOTEL $$
(☑831-7848; hotelcolonial@hotmail.es; Calle 5 No 10-94; s/d/tr COP$55,000/75,000/120,000;

WORTH A TRIP

SILVIA

A picturesque mountain town 53km northeast of Popayán, **Silvia** is the center of the Guambiano region. The Guambiano people don't live in Silvia itself, but in the small mountain villages of Pueblito, La Campana, Guambia and Caciques. The whole community numbers about 12,000.

The Guambiano are considered one of the most traditional indigenous groups in Colombia. They speak their own language, dress traditionally and still use rudimentary farming techniques. They're also excellent weavers.

On Tuesday, market day, they come to Silvia to sell fruit, vegetables and handicrafts. This is the best time to visit the town. Almost all the Guambiano come in traditional dress; men in blue skirts with a pink fringe and bowler hats, women in hand-woven garments and beaded necklaces, busily spinning wool. They come in *chivas* (colorful buses) and congregate around the main plaza. They don't like cameras, and may be offended if you take their picture; respect their culture and keep your gear in your bag.

The market begins at dawn and goes until the early afternoon. It is not a tourist market – fruit and vegetables, raw meat, discount clothing and shoes dominate – but you may find a poncho or sweater that takes your fancy.

From the main plaza, walk uphill to the church for 360-degree views of the surrounding countryside. Down by the river you can rent horses to ride around a small lake or up the mountain to another lake high in the clouds.

Buses depart Popayán roughly every hour (COP$7000, 1½ hours), with extra early-morning services on Tuesday. From Cali, take a Popayán-bound bus as far as Piendamó (COP$12,000, two hours), from where you can pick up an onward bus to Silvia (COP$3000, 30 minutes).

@ 🛜) Recently renovated, this efficient small hotel in a colonial house in the center is good value. The rooms have comfortable beds, flat-screen TVs and spotless bathrooms, although they can be a little noisy when the hotel is busy. Ask for a room upstairs.

Hotel Dann Monasterio　　HOTEL **$$$**
(📞 824 2191; www.hotelesdann.com; Calle 4 No 10-14; s/d COP$222,720/288,840, ste COP$362,000-436,000; @ 🛜 🌊) This Franciscan-monastery-turned-hotel offers elegant but not particularly luxurious rooms set around a vast arcaded courtyard. It's an impressive building full of character but rooms vary in quality so ask to see a few options. The wi-fi struggles to penetrate the thick adobe walls, although ethernet cables are available.

🍴 Eating

Popayán is known throughout Colombia for its flavorful typical cuisine. Look out for *carantantas,* a kind of corn chip, and *empanadas de pipián,* fried potato pastries served with a spicy satay-style peanut sauce. Refreshing traditional drinks include *champús,* a maize beverage with lulo and pineapple, and *salpicón payanese,* an icy concoction made from fresh blackberries.

Tienda Regional del Macizo　　COLOMBIAN **$**
(Carrera 4 No 0-42; meals COP$3500; ☉ 8am-4pm) This small cafe is part of an organization that works to develop markets for farmers in the Macizo Colombiano. Needless to say the absurdly cheap lunches are made with the freshest ingredients and are bursting with flavor.

Mora Castilla　　CAFE **$**
(Calle 2 No 4-44; snacks COP$2500-4000; ☉ 9am-7pm) This tiny cafe prepares excellent traditional food including *salpicón payanese, champus, tamales* (steamed cornmeal dough) and *carantantas.* If you're still hungry, pop next door to sample some of doña Chepa's famous *aplanchados* (flat pastries).

Sabores del Mar　　SEAFOOD **$**
(Calle 5 No 10-97; lunch COP$6000; ☉ 7am-8pm) Run by an energetic family from Guapi, this tiny nautical-themed place serves a great-value seafood lunch. Try the fillets of toyo (a kind of shark).

Tequila's　　MEXICAN **$**
(Calle 5 No 9-25; set lunch $6500, mains COP$10,000-20,000; ☉ noon-10pm) Run by a Mexican expat and his local wife, this small restaurant in the center prepares up good-value Mexican favorites.

La Fresa   CAFE $
(Calle 5 No 8-89; snacks COP$200-2000; ⊘7am-7pm) A grimy corner store with a couple of plastic tables, La Fresa is famed throughout Popayán for its delicious *empanadas de pipián*. Most locals wash them down with a *malta* (a malt-based soda).

La Semilla Escondida   FRENCH $$
(Calle 5 No 2-26; mains COP$10,000-25,000; ⊘noon-3pm Mon, noon-3pm & 6-10pm Tue-Sat) This bright bistro in one of Popayán's oldest streets prepares great savory and sweet crepes as well as pasta dishes. The gourmet set lunch (COP$7700) is fantastic value.

Restaurante Italiano   ITALIAN $$
(Calle 4 No 8-83; mains COP$15,000-26,000; ⊘noon-10pm) Swing open the saloon doors of this Swiss-owned Italian joint and you'll find great pizza and pasta as well as authentic fondue for those cool mountain nights. The set meal (COP$7500) is one of the best of its kind in Colombia.

Hotel Camino Real   FRENCH, COLOMBIAN $$$
(☑824-3595; Calle 5 No 5-59; mains COP$25,000-35,000; ⊘noon-3pm & 6-10pm) The owners of this hotel are key players in the Congreso Nacional Gastronómico and their passion for food is evident in the interesting menu, which combines French and Colombian elements. Every plate here is of the highest quality. Go for one of the excellent set menus (COP$45,000), which include two appetizers, a main, cheeses and a fruit mousse. Reservations are recommended.

▼ Drinking & Nightlife

In the evenings impoverished students descend on the Pueblito Patojo, an outdoor model town below El Morro de Tulcán, to shoot the breeze and down BYO booze. Most of Popayán's late-night action congregates on the highway out of town.

Wipala   BAR
(Carrera 2 No 2-38; ⊘2:30-9:30pm Mon-Thu, to 11:30pm Fri & Sat; ☏) Groovy cafe-bar with a small garden that serves organic local coffee, *hervidos* (fruit infusions) and its own energy drink made with coca tea, ginger and ginseng. It also serves a good veggie burger. Come for the entertainment, which could be anything from belly dancing to rock.

New York   SALSA CLUB
(Contiguo Salon Communal, Barrio Pueblillo; ⊘9pm-3am Thu-Sun) On the outskirts of town, this vibrant neighborhood salsa place is as authentic as it gets. Take a seat in one of the vintage booths beneath the hundreds of old LPs, plastic toys and portaits of salsa heroes that are plastered all over the walls and ceiling. It's in a rough neighborhood; get a taxi (COP$6000) right to the door.

El Sotareño   BAR
(Calle 6 No 8-05; ⊘4pm-1am Mon-Thu, to 3am Fri & Sat) In a busy street in the center, this cozy Popayán classic plays tango, bolero and ranchera on scratched old vinyls.

Capriccio Café   CAFE
(Calle 5 No 5-63; ⊘9:30am-12:30pm & 2-8pm Mon-Sat) Popular cafe that roasts coffee from rural Cauca and prepares great iced drinks.

Bar La Iguana   BAR
(Calle 4 No 9-67; ⊘noon-late) The place to go in the center to show off your salsa moves. Sometimes has live bands.

❶ Information

There are many ATMs around Parque Caldas.
4-72 (Calle 4 No 5-74; ⊘9am-5pm) Post office.
Migración Colombia (☑823-1027; Calle 4N No 10B-66; ⊘9am-noon & 2-5pm) Visa extensions.
Policía de Turismo (☑822-0916; Carrera 7 No 4-36) Tourist office on main plaza.

❶ Getting There & Away

AIR
Aeropuerto Guillermo León Valencia is right behind the bus terminal, 1km north of the city center. Avianca flies three times a day direct to Bogotá.

BUS
The **bus terminal** is 1km north of the city center. There are frequent services to Cali (COP$16,000, three hours). Direct buses to Bogotá (COP$85,000, 12 hours) and Medellín (COP$70,000, 11 hours) depart in the evenings.

There are regular minibuses to San Agustín (COP$30,000, five hours). Buses to Tierradentro (COP$22,000, five hours) leave at 5am, 8am, 10:30am, 1pm and 3pm. The 10:30am service takes you all the way to the Museo Arqueológico entrance.

There are hourly buses to Pasto (COP$32,000, six hours) and Ipiales (COP$40,000, eight hours). Security on the road from Popayán to the Ecuadorean border has improved and robberies are no longer common although night buses are still required to travel in convoy for part of the journey as a precaution. It's best to travel during the day if possible.

Coconuco

There are two thermal springs near the town of Coconuco (2360m), in the mountains outside Popayán on the road to San Agustín. On weekends they are packed with kids and rum-soaked parents; during the week they are all but empty. The weather here is decidedly cool, which makes the springs even more enjoyable.

On weekends people come to party while loud music blares at **Agua Hirviendo** (☑ 314 618 4178; admission COP$7000; ☺ 24hr). You read that right, a 24-hour thermal spring. The complex is run by the local indigenous community and has two large thermal pools and several small baths plus a natural sauna. An adjacent restaurant serves meals until late.

Surrounded by splendid mountain scenery, nearby **Termales Aguatibia** (☑ 315-578-6111; www.termalesaguatibia.com; admission COP$12,000; ☺ 8am-6pm) has plenty of green space although most of the pools here are warmish rather than hot. It has four thermal pools, a mud spring and a 53m-long 'toboggan' – a butt-bruising concrete slide.

During the week there is hourly transportation from Popayán to Coconuco (COP$4000, one hour, 31km), more on the weekends. From here you can grab a jeep (COP$10,000 per vehicle) or a moto-taxi (COP$3000) to the baths.

PARQUE NACIONAL NATURAL (PNN) PURACÉ

Forty-five kilometers east of Popayán along the unpaved road to La Plata lies this 830-sq-km **national park** (Resguardo Indígena Puracé; ☑ 313-680-0051, 521 2578; Colombian/foreigner COP$5000/10,000; guide per group COP$35,000; ☺ 8am-6pm). The vast majority of the park lies within the *resguardo* (official territory) of the Puracé indigenous group.

At the time of research, the indigenous community had taken control of the park following a dispute with the national government over its management. If you ask at any national park or official government tourist office they will tell you that the park is closed, however the community is still accepting visitors and is dedicated to expanding its fledgling ecotourism program. In addition to your entrance fee, each group is required to hire an indigenous guide (COP$35,000 per group) to explore the park.

PNN Puracé is the only place in Colombia you can see Andean condors in the wild. Nearly a dozen of the great vultures were reintroduced to the park – three remain. The guides will tempt them down with food so you can see them up close.

In good weather you can summit **Volcán Puracé** (4750m), the highest of the seven volcanoes in the Coconuco range. It's about five hours up and three hours down along an often muddy trail. Because of the difference in altitude from Popayán the last part of the trek is quite difficult. The best time to climb is December and January; the weather from June to August can be foul. Consider spending the night before in a cabin to get an early start to the day.

The visitor center (3350m) rents unheated **cabins** (r per person COP$20,000) and serves budget meals; there's no hot water, but some cabins have working fireplaces.

To get here, take any La Plata–bound bus to the **Cruce de la Mina** (COP$12,000, 1¼ hours). If you are coming for the day, it's best to take the first bus at 4:30am or at the latest the 6:45am service.

From Cruce de la Mina it's a 1.5km walk uphill to the **Cruce de Pilimbalá** where you turn left and walk another 1km for the visitor center. There is usually a guide waiting at the bus stop to show you the way.

About 8km past the Cruce de la Mina are the **Termales de San Juan** (3200m), which bubble up amid an otherworldly *páramo* (high-mountain plain) setting – spectacular. Unlike Coconuco, these thermals aren't for bathing. The pools are outside the indigenous territory and you'll find a ranger station here staffed by officials from Parques Nacionales who may restrict access depending on the state of negotiations over the park. Ask in Popayán before heading out.

The last bus back to Popayán passes the Cruce de la Mina at around 5pm. Bring food, water, warm clothes, sunscreen and a copy of your passport.

San Agustín

📌 8 / POP 31,300 / ELEV 1695M

Five thousand years ago, two indigenous cultures lived in the adjacent river valleys of the Magdalena and the Cauca. Divided by uncrossable peaks, the rivers were their highways, and here, near San Agustín, within several days' march of each other, lie the headwaters of both rivers. It is here that those two civilizations met to trade, to worship, and to bury their dead.

The volcanic rocks thrown great distances by the now-extinct nearby volcanoes proved irresistible to the local sculptors, who set about working them into grand monuments. The result is more than 500 statues (the largest is 7m high) scattered over a wide area in the lush green hills surrounding San Agustín. Many of them are anthropomorphic figures, some realistic, others resembling masked monsters. There are also sculptures depicting sacred animals such as the eagle, jaguar and frog. Archaeologists have also uncovered a great deal of pottery, but very little in the way of gold – unlike the Tayrona on the Caribbean coast, these people had no gold to mine.

Little else is known about the peoples of San Agustín. They didn't have a written language and had disappeared many centuries before the Europeans arrived. But their legacy is one of the most important archaeological sights on the continent – a mystical place in a spectacular landscape that is well worth making a detour for.

◉ Sights

You'll need two full days (or three more relaxed ones) to see the main archaeological sites – with one day for the archaeological park and the horseback trip to El Tablón, La Chaquira, La Pelota and El Purutal (a four-hour round trip), and one day for a jeep tour to El Estrecho, Alto de los Ídolos, Alto de las Piedras, Salto de Bordones and Salto de Mortiño (six hours).

Upon paying your admission at either the Parque Arqueológico or Alto de Los Ídolos you will be given a 'passport,' which is valid for entrance to both sites for two consecutive days.

It is highly recommended to visit the more remote sites with a local guide – there is little in the way of signs or explanations outside the Parque Arqueológico. In addition, there have been reports of robberies in remote areas around some of the sites.

The official rate for a certified guide is COP$60,000 per half day; slightly more for an English-speaking guide. You can rent horses for around COP$30,000 per half day, plus you'll be expected to pay for the guide's horse (thus making it cheaper to go in a group). Jeep tours to the more remote sites go for around COP$150,000 to COP$180,000 per day (maximum five people), not including a specialist guide.

★ **Parque Arqueológico**   ARCHAEOLOGICAL SITE
(www.icanh.gov.co; adult/child/student COP$20,000/5000/10,000; ⊙8am-4pm) The 78-hectare archaeological park is 2.5km west of the town of San Agustín. There are in total about 130 statues in the park, either found in situ or collected from other areas, including some of the best examples of San Agustín statuary. Plan on spending around three hours in the park. Reputable guides congregate around the museum.

At the entrance to the park is the **Museo Arqueológico**, which features smaller statues, pottery, utensils, jewelry and other objects, along with interesting background information about the San Agustín culture.

Besides the various clusters of statues (called *mesitas*) is the Fuente de Lavapatas. Carved in the rocky bed of the stream, it is a complex labyrinth of ducts and small, terraced pools decorated with images of serpents, lizards and human figures. Archaeologists believe the baths were used for ritual ablutions and the worship of aquatic deities.

From here, the path winds uphill to the Alto de Lavapatas, the oldest archaeological site in San Agustín. You'll find a few tombs guarded by statues, and get a panoramic view over the surrounding countryside.

Alto de los Ídolos   ARCHAEOLOGICAL SITE
(adult/child/student   COP$20,000/5000/10,000; ⊙8am-4pm) Located across the Río Magdalena 4km southwest of San José de Isnos (a clutch of houses 26km northeast of the town of San Agustín), this is the second-most important archaeological park in the region. It's home to the largest statue in the San Agustín area, which is 7m tall but with only 4m visible above ground.

Alto de las Piedras   ARCHAEOLOGICAL SITE
This site is 7km north of Isnos and has tombs lined with stone slabs, some of which still show traces of red, black and yellow coloring. One of the most famous statues, known as Doble Yo, is here; look carefully as

San Agustín

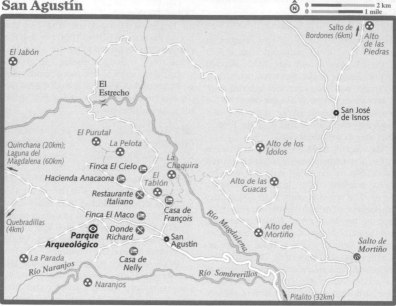

there are actually four figures carved in this statue. You'll also find an intriguing statue of a female figure in an advanced state of pregnancy.

El Tablón, La Chaquira, La Pelota & El Purutal ARCHAEOLOGICAL SITES

These four sites are relatively close to each other; most people visit as part of a horseback-riding tour. Don't miss La Chaquira, with divinities carved into the mountain face. It overlooks the stunning gorge of the Río Magdalena.

Other sights

There are several more archaeological sites to see if you are not in a hurry, including **La Parada**, **Quinchana**, **El Jabón**, **Naranjos** and **Quebradillas**. Apart from its archaeological wealth, the region is also noted for its natural beauty, and features two spectacular waterfalls, **Salto de Bordones** and **Salto de Mortiño**. It's also worth a walk or ride to **El Estrecho**, where the Río Magdalena passes through a 2.2m narrows. All these sights are accessible by road or on horseback.

🏃 Activities

One of the best ways to explore the mountains surrounding San Agustín is on horseback. Unlike in some parts of the country,

the horses available to tourists here are more often than not in excellent condition. You can travel by horseback to some of the archaeological sites around town or head out on some epic multiday adventures.

A recommended tour leader is **Francisco 'Pacho' Muñoz** (☎311-827-7972) – you can usually find him hanging around at Finca El Maco. In addition to guiding you around San Agustín, Pacho can also take you to Laguna del Magdalena, Tierradentro or, if you are willing to purchase horses, will even lead you all the way to Ecuador.

Laguna del Magdalena HORSEBACK RIDING

An interesting horseback-riding trip is the three-day journey to Laguna del Magdalena (3327m), the birthplace of the Río Magdalena, 60km from San Agustín in the Macizo Colombiano. The region was historically infested by guerrillas but is now considered safe. The trip takes three to five days depending on the route, and costs around COP$150,000 per person per day, fluctuating with group size.

Magdalena Rafting RAFTING

(☎311-271-5333; www.magdalenarafting.com; Calle 5 No 16-04) The Río Magdalena offers challenging white-water rafting through some phenomenal landscapes. Magdalena Rafting offers 1½-hour tours (COP$50,000 per person) with Classes II to III rapids for novices, and full-day, Class V tours (COP$120,000) for experienced pros. Minimum four people per group. It also offers kayaking classes.

🛏 Sleeping

There are numerous budget hotels in the center of town. Right on the main plaza you'll find the comfortable **Hotel Hipona Plaza** (📞314-454-8497; www.hiponaplazahotel. com; Calle 3 No 13-24; s/d COP$30,000/60,000), which offers the best-value digs in the center. Alternatively, **Residencias El Jardín** (📞314-488-6220; Carrera 11 No 4-10; r per person with/ without bathroom COP$22,000/17,000, cabaña s/d COP$30,000/50,000; 📶) offers cheap rooms in a spacious old house near where the bus pulls in.

You'll enjoy your time in San Agustín more if you stay outside the center of town in one of the many charming rural properties available.

Finca El Maco　　　　　　　　HOSTEL $
(📞320-375-5982, 837-3847; www.elmaco.ch; campsite per person COP$10,000, dm COP$18,000, s/d from COP$44,000/63,000; @📶) This tranquil hostel has a variety of cabins set amid a pretty garden. The restaurant serves homemade organic yogurt and an excellent curry. The owner can organize trips throughout the region. Take the road to the Parque Arqueológico and turn right at the Hotel Yalconia. From here it's a 400m walk uphill. Take a taxi (COP$7000) if you have luggage.

Casa de François　　　　　　　HOSTEL $
(📞837-3847; www.lacasadefrancois.com; campsite per person COP$10,000, dm COP$19,000, r with/ without bathroom COP$50,000/40,000, cabaña COP$80,000; 📶) 🌿 Set in a garden just above town overlooking the hills, this creative, ecological hostel is constructed of glass bottles embedded in rammed-mud walls. The breezy, elevated dormitory has fantastic views and there is a spacious shared kitchen. The small restaurant serves up a variety of quality meals and snacks.

Casa de Nelly　　　　　　　　HOSTEL $
(📞310-215-9067; www.hotelcasadenelly.co; Vereda LaEstrella;dmCOP$18,000,s/dCOP$35,000/70,000, without bathroom COP$25,000/50,000; 📶) The original San Agustín hostel has friendly management and a range of comfortable accommodations set around one of the prettiest gardens in town. There is a spacious so-

cial area with an open fireplace and outdoor barbecue area.

Hacienda Anacaona　　　　　　HOTEL $$
(📞311-231-7128; www.anacaona-colombia.com; Via al Estrecho; s/d/tr COP$70,000/120,000/150,000; 📶) This peaceful colonial-style hotel is one of the most comfortable options in the area. It is set amid a well-maintained garden and has good views. Prices include a hearty breakfast. Staff will pay for your first taxi on arrival.

Finca El Cielo　　　　　　　　HOTEL $$
(📞313-493-7446; www.fincaelcielo.com; Via al Estrecho; r per person incl breakfast COP$60,000) This pretty posada built of guadua on the road to El Estrecho has tremendous views out over the surrounding misty green hills. The friendly owners live on the ground floor and prepare good home-cooked meals with advance notice.

🍴 Eating

Pasteleria Le Péché Mignon　　　FRENCH $
(Calle 5 No 16-09; pastries COP$3000-3500; ⊙1-7pm Wed-Sun) Locals and visitors alike love this French bakery that serves up fancy cakes and pastries made fresh every morning.

★Donde Richard　　　　　　COLOMBIAN $$
(📞312-432-6399; Vía al Parque Arqueológico; mains COP$24,000; ⊙8am-6pm Wed-Mon) This grill restaurant on the road to the Parque Arqueológico serves up the best food in town, with generous portions of quality roast meats, steaks and a variety of fish dishes prepared in the open kitchen. A great spot for lunch on the way back from the park.

El Fogón　　　　　　　　　COLOMBIAN $$
(📞320-834-5860; Calle 5 No 14-30; mains COP$18,000-20,000; ⊙7am-9pm) A local institution, El Fogón serves up big portions of Colombian favorites and an excellent-value set lunch (COP$6000). There is another branch close to the Parque Arqueológico.

Restaurante Italiano　　　　　ITALIAN $$
(📞314-375-8086; Vereda el Tablón; mains COP$16,000-23,000; ⊙noon-9:30pm Tue-Sun, to 6pm Mon) A little way out of town, this unpretentious restaurant serves authentic traditional Italian plates, including a selection of homemade pastas. A taxi here costs around COP$4000.

MOCOA: JUNGLE ROUTE TO ECUADOR

If you are planning to travel from San Agustín to Ecuador, you don't need to return to Popayán. Just four hours from Pitalito (just east of San Agustín) by bus, the department of Putumayo is a land of rushing rivers, dense jungle and amazing wildlife. If you are not going to get to Leticia this trip, it is well worth making a detour to this accessible corner of the Amazon. The departmental capital is Mocoa. The town itself is an unremarkable agricultural center, but there is great nature right on the doorstop, including dozens of waterfalls, refreshing swimming holes and excellent trekking.

Next to one of Mocoa's best swimming holes to the southeast of the center, the atmospheric **Casa del Río** (⌂8-420-4004; www.casadelriomocoa.com; Vereda Caliyaco, via Mocoa-Villagarzón; dm/s/d COP$18,000/35,000/43,000; @🛜) has comfortable rooms in a lush garden full of birds. Keep an eye out for the tiny monkeys.

From Mocoa you can head to Pasto (COP$35,000, six hours) on the Trampolin de la Muerte (Trampoline of Death) – one of the most dangerous and spectacular roads on the continent. It is an unpaved, single-carriage road with sheer 400m drops into rocky ravines the entire way. When you meet oncoming traffic you often have to navigate this treacherous track in reverse! It is considered safer to travel in a pickup than by bus. It's just two hours to the border from Pasto. Alternatively, you can take a bus to the border at San Miguel (COP$27,000, six hours) and cross into Ecuador near the town of Nueva Loja (Lago Agrio), which boasts good access to the Ecuadorean Amazon and from where there are bus services and flights to Quito.

The security situation around San Miguel remains unsettled, although many visitors have crossed the border here without problems. Check the situation with the authorities in Mocoa before setting out and only travel during the day.

🍷 Drinking & Nightlife

El Faro   BAR
(Carrera 13 No 6-50; ⊙5-11:30pm Tue-Sun) This laid-back bar has an arty vibe that is conducive to conversation over beers or cocktails. It also serves up San Agustín's best pizzas from the wood-burning oven in the courtyard.

Macizo Coffee   CAFE
(Calle 2 No13-17; coffee COP$3000-6000; ⊙8:30am-8pm) On the central plaza, this popular cafe serves up a wide variety of beverages using certified coffee from local farms. There are another couple of branches in the Parque Arqueológico.

🛍 Shopping

Farmers come to buy and sell at San Agustín's Monday market at **La Galería** (cnr Calle 3 & Carrera 11; ⊙5am-4pm). It's a raucous scene with few tourists. If you miss the Monday market, the marketplace is open the rest of the week, but is a more subdued affair.

ℹ Information

Local touts pushing hotels and 'cheap' tours hang around in the center and often hustle passengers from arriving intercity buses. Contract professional guides and jeeps through your hotel or at the archaeological park.

Banco de Bogotá (Calle 3 No 10-61) ATM.

Oficina de Turismo (⌂320-486-3896; Carrera 11 No 3-61; ⊙8am-noon & 2-5pm Mon-Fri) Tourist office inside the Casa de Cultura.

ℹ Getting There & Away

Bus company offices are on the corner of Calle 3 and Carrera 11 (known as Cuatro Vientos). There are regular minibuses to Neiva (COP$28,000, four hours), Popayán (COP$30,000, five hours) and Cali (COP$40,000, eight hours). There are several buses in the early morning and evening to Bogotá (COP$50,000, 11 hours).

If you prefer a bit more comfort, **Colombia on the Road** (⌂837-3437; www.colombia ontheroad.com) offers a door-to-door van service to Popayán (COP$40,000) and Cali (COP$70,000).

The road to Popayán passes through the spectacular *páramo* landscapes of Parque Nacional (PNN) Puracé. Do not travel on this route at night as robberies have been reported.

For Tierradentro, go to Pitalito (COP$6000, 45 minutes) and change for La Plata (COP$25,000, 2½ hours), where you can get a bus or *colectivo* to San Andrés (COP$10,000, 2½ hours).

Arriving from Popayán, buses with few passengers will drop you at the crossroads 5km from town and pay your taxi fare to San Agustín. The taxi drivers often take you direct to a hotel they work with – be firm about where you want to go.

❶ Getting Around

Around a dozen taxis service San Agustín. They can take you around town and, more importantly, to your lodging outside of town. The rates are fixed but confirm what you'll pay before you get in.

A bus runs the 2km to the park every 15 minutes (COP\$1200) from the corner of Calle 5 and Carrera 14. *Colectivos* ply the nearby country roads and are an alternate way of getting to and from some of the rural hotels.

Tierradentro

📙2 / ELEV 1750M

Tierradentro is the second-most important archaeological site in Colombia (after San Agustín) but gets surprisingly few visitors. Located well off the beaten track down some rough dirt roads, it is a peaceful place with friendly locals and awe-inspiring archaeological wonders. Where San Agustín is noted for its statuary, Tierradentro is remarkable for its elaborate underground tombs. So far, archaeologists have discovered about 100 of these unusual funeral temples, the only examples of their kind in the Americas. There is a fabulous walk you can do that takes in all the major tomb sites amid gorgeous mountain scenery.

❍ Sights

Scattered across the hills around the town of San Andrés de Pisimbalá, Tierradentro consists of five separate sites, four with tombs and one with an above-ground statuary, plus two museums.

Measuring from 2m to 7m in diameter, the tombs are scooped out of the soft volcanic rock that forms the region's undulating hillsides. They vary widely in depth; some are just below ground level, while others are as deep as 9m. The domed ceilings of the largest tombs are supported by pillars. Many are painted with red and black geometric motifs on white backgrounds.

Little is known about the people who built the tombs and the statues – the Páez (or Nasa) indigenous group that lives in the area today is not thought to be connected to the ruins. Most likely they were of different cultures, and the people who scooped out the tombs preceded those who carved the statues. Some researchers place the 'tomb' civilization somewhere between the 7th and 9th centuries AD, while the 'statue' culture appears to be related to the later phase of

San Agustín development, which is estimated to have taken place some 500 years later.

The ticket office for the **Parque Arqueológico** (Archaeological Park; 📞311-3900-324; www.icanh.gov.co; adult/child/student COP\$20,000/5000/10,000; ⊙8am-4pm) is inside the museum complex. You will be given a 'passport' that enables access to both museums and the tombs. It is valid for two consecutive days. It is worth visiting the museums before heading out to the tombs as there is not much in the way of explanation at the sites themselves.

A 25-minute walk uphill from the museums is the little town of **San Andrés de Pisimbalá**. The town's main attraction, a beautiful thatched adobe **church**, had been torched by arsonists and restoration efforts had yet to get underway when we visited.

Burial Sites & Statues

You can visit all the burial sites in Tierradentro on a full-day, 14km walk. The walk takes you through some spectacular scenery, and it's well worth doing the entire loop. You can follow the loop in either direction, but if you are beginning at the museums it is recommended to head out counterclockwise, otherwise you will have a tough uphill climb at the beginning of the hike. It is also possible to begin the hike from town and pay your entry fee at the first archaeological site you visit.

Only some of the tombs have electric lighting so bring a flashlight (torch) for better viewing. The tombs are open from 8am to 4pm.

Going counterclockwise, a 20-minute walk uphill from the museums is **Segovia** (1650m), the most important burial site. There are 28 tombs here, some with well-preserved decorations. Twelve of the tombs have electric lighting.

A 15-minute walk uphill from Segovia brings you to **El Duende** (1850m), where there are four tombs, though their decoration hasn't been preserved. From here it's a 25-minute walk along the road to **El Tablón** (1700m), which has nine weather-worn stone statues, similar to those of San Agustín, excavated in the area and now thrown together under a single roof. The site is poorly signposted; it is behind an adobe house with a tin roof perched on a hill on the left side of the road. You can also get to El Tablón via the path off the main San Andrés road.

Continue into town. Next to the restaurant La Portada you'll find the path to **Alto de San Andrés** (1750m), with six large

Tierradentro

tombs; two have remarkably well-preserved paintings. One of the tombs is closed because of structural instability and humidity, and another has caved in completely.

El Aguacate (2000m) is the most remote burial site, but has the best views. From Alto de San Andrés it's a 1½-hour walk, then downhill another 1½ hours to the museums. There are a few dozen tombs, but most have been destroyed by *guaqueros* (tomb raiders). Only a few vaults still bear the remains of the original decoration.

Museums

Museo Arqueológico   MUSEUM
Dedicated to the civilization behind the tombs, this museum contains pottery urns used to keep the ashes of the deceased. There are also miniature models of what the tombs may have looked like when they were freshly painted.

Museo Etnográfico   MUSEUM
With a focus on post-Tierradentro indigenous communities, the Museo Etnográfico has utensils and artifacts of the Páez people, and exhibits from colonial times, including a *trapiche* (sugarcane grinder), *bodoqueras* (blow-dart guns) and traditional clothing.

🛏 Sleeping & Eating

🛏 Parque Arqueológico

There are half a dozen basic lodgings and one hotel clustered within the 500m stretch uphill of the museums. Many are run by endearing senior citizens – there's not much going on for young folk around here. All the budget options charge COP$10,000 to COP$15,000 per person.

Hospedaje Tierradentro   GUESTHOUSE **$**
(☑313-651-3713; alorqui@hotmail.com; Tierradentro; r per person COP$15,000) Offers the most privacy of the budget choices, with spotless, freshly painted rooms located in a new building in the garden of the main house.

Hotel El Refugio   HOTEL **$**
(☑321-811-2395; hotelalbergueelrefugio@gmail. com; Tierradentro; s/d/tr COP$45,000/63,000/ 80,000; ☒) The most luxurious option in the area, this community-run hotel has comfortable, if a little generic, rooms with mountain views, cable TV and a big pool.

Mi Casita   GUESTHOUSE **$**
(☑312-764-1333; Tierradentro; r per person COP$12,000) A popular choice, with extreme-

Tierradentro

ly friendly owners and a pleasant garden with mountain views.

**Residencias y Restaurante
Pisimbalá** GUESTHOUSE $
(☎311-605-4835, 321-263-2334; Tierradentro; r per person with/without bathroom COP$15,000/ 10,000) The rooms here are set inside the family house and all have private bathrooms. Also serves cheap meals, including options for vegetarians, and artisanal fruit wines.

Residencias Lucerna GUESTHOUSE $
(Tierradentro; r per person COP$10,000) This simple place near the museums is so old school it doesn't even have a phone, but it does have a kitchen you can use.

Super Jugos BREAKFAST $
(Tierradentro; juices COP$2000; ☺8am-6pm) To fuel up for the hike, head to Super Jugos in front of the park entrance for fresh juices and homemade yogurt.

🛏 San Andrés de Pisimbalá

If you are going to be here for a while, you may prefer to stay in San Andrés de Pisimbalá.

★La Portada GUESTHOUSE $
(☎311-601-7884; laportadahotel.com; San Andrés de Pisimbalá; s/d COP$30,000/35,000, without bathroom COP$15,000/20,000) Right by where the bus stops in town, this wooden lodge has large, clean rooms with hot-water bathrooms downstairs and cheaper rooms with shared cold-water bathrooms upstairs. It also serves the best food in town in its

breezy restaurant – try the homemade ice cream. The friendly owners can organize guides and horse rental.

Residencia El Viajero GUESTHOUSE $
(☎321-349-4944; Calle 6 No 4-09, San Andrés de Pisimbalá; r per person COP$12,000) Near the football field, Residencia El Viajero offers basic rooms with shared bathroom in the sweet elderly owner's home.

ℹ️ Information

At the time of research there was still some occasional guerrilla activity around Tierradentro. It's worth checking on the situation with the Tourist Police in Popayán before heading out.

There is no tourist office or bank near Tierradentro. In San Andrés, **Puerta Virtual** (via Sta Rosa, San Andres de Pisimbalá; per hour COP$1500; ☺9am-8pm Mon-Sat) offers a surprisingly speedy internet connection and calls.

ℹ️ Getting There & Away

Arriving at Tierradentro, most buses will drop you at El Crucero de San Andrés, from where it's a 20-minute walk uphill to the Tierradentro museums and another 20 minutes to San Andrés. Very irregular *colectivos* (COP$1000) make the trip. Otherwise a moto-taxi costs COP$3000.

A direct bus to Popayán (COP$22,000, four hours) leaves San Andrés de Pisimbalá at 6am and passes in front of the museums. There are other buses to Popayán (9am, 11am, 1pm and 4pm) from El Crucero de San Andrés.

Buses and pickups leave San Andrés de Pisimbalá at 6:30am, 8am, noon and 4pm for La Plata (COP$10,000, two hours), where you can pick up connections to Bogotá, Neiva for the Desierto de la Tatacoa and Pitalito for San Agustín.

Desierto de la Tatacoa

Halfway between Bogotá and San Agustín lies the Tatacoa Desert. It is a striking landscape of eroded cliffs and gullies, sculpted by the infrequent rain. Because of the dry, clear conditions, lack of light pollution and location at the equator, Tatacoa is a great spot for stargazing – the skies above both the northern and southern hemispheres are spread out for all to see.

Tatacoa isn't really a desert, although the thermometer says otherwise – it can hit 50°C at times. It's technically semi-arid dry tropical forest, averaging 1070mm of rain per year. Surrounded by mountains in every direction, the peaks around Nevado de Huila (5750m) grab most of the incoming precipitation, leaving 330-sq-km Tatacoa arid. The result is an ecosystem unlike anywhere else in Colombia – there are scorpions and weasels, fruit-bearing cacti, and at least 72 bird species have been spotted here.

To get to Tatacoa, you'll have to pass through Neiva, the hot capital of the Huila department and a port on the Río Magdalena. There's not much of interest in Neiva, instead take a *colectivo* to Villavieja, an hour's ride northwest. You can spend the night in Villavieja or, better yet, spend the night in the desert.

Be sure to bring sturdy shoes (there are cactus spines on the ground) and a flashlight (torch).

Villavieja

🏛 8 / POP 7338 / ELEV 440M

This small desert town was founded in 1550 and has largely been forgotten about since. A few families continue to eke out a living herding goats, but many have turned to tourism. On weekends and holidays it is often visited by *bogotanos* (residents of Bogotá) looking to warm up but on other occasions you'll have the place to yourself.

⊙ Sights & Activities

The region used to be a sea bed and contains numerous important fossils from the Miocene era; paleontologists continue to work in La Venta, a remote region of the desert. You can see some of their findings, including the bones of an armadillo the size of a tractor, at the Museo Paleontológico (🏛 879-7744, 314-347-6812; admission COP$2000; ⊙ 8:30am-noon & 2-5pm) on the main square. The helpful staff also act as a de facto tourist office as the official one run by the tourist police is rarely open.

As you leave town you'll pass through Bosque del Cardón, a small cactus forest. Four kilometers from Villavieja is El Cusco, where you'll find the Observatorio Astronómico de la Tatacoa (🏛 312-411-8166; www.tatacoa-astronomia.com; El Cusco; viewings COP$10,000; ⊙ visitors center 10am-9pm). The visitors center here can arrange guides to explore the area. The observatory is open to the public from 7pm to 9pm, when local astronomer Javier Fernando Rua Restrepo (🏛 310-465-6765) shows visitors around the sky using two tripod telescopes. Call ahead to check conditions. Every July at the new moon, university groups and Colombian

stargazing enthusiasts congregate here for a four-day, three-night Fiesta de Estrellas (Star Party).

A lookout point across the road from the observatory has impressive views, and is a fine place to watch the sunset. Below the lookout are the Laberintos del Cusco (Cusco Labyrinths), a striking mazelike landscape of undulating red rock formations that seem totally out of place in tropical Colombia.

Four kilometers past the observatory is Ventanas, a lookout point so named for its commanding views out over the desert. Another 5km takes you to Los Hoyos, where there is a swimming pool fed by a natural spring deep in a barren gray valley.

🛏 Sleeping & Eating

There are several basic hotels in town but most travelers prefer to spend the night in the desert itself. Most desert accommodations are basically four concrete walls with a corrugated tin roof, and charge around COP$25,000 per person. All serve basic meals (COP$7000 to COP$15,000).

Villa Paraiso HOTEL $
(🏛 879-7727; hotelvillaparaisovillavieja@gmail.com; Calle 4 No 7-69, Villavieja; s/d COP$20,000/50,000) The best choice in town, Villa Paraiso offers neat rooms with private bathrooms, split-system air-con and cable TV set around a pleasant patio area. The friendly management are particularly helpful.

Campground Observatorio CAMPGROUND $
(🏛 312-411-8166; Cusco, Tatacoa; campsite per person COP$7000) Behind the observatory is a large campsite with room for 40 tents. You can also rent a hammock for COP$10,000 and string it up outside on the Greek pillars on the front porch. The building is powered by solar panels.

Estadero Doña Lilia GUESTHOUSE $
(🏛 313-311-8828; Observatorio, 400m E, Tatacoa; r per person COP$25,000) The closest lodgings to the observatory, Estadero Doña Lilia has comfortable rooms and impressive views. It serves delicious meals. Try the goat – a local specialty.

Noches de Saturno GUESTHOUSE $
(🏛 313-305-5898; Observatorio, 700m E, Tatacoa; r per person COP$25,000, campground with/without tent rental per person COP$10,000/5000; ⊠) A short walk from the observatory, this place has a nice shady garden and a pool. The simple clean rooms catch a bit of breeze and

some afford nice views. There is also an area to pitch tents. Visitors can use the pool for COP$4000.

Estadero Villa Marquez LODGE $
([☎] 311-883-1570; Observatorio, 1.8km E, Tatacoa; campsite per person COP$8000, campsite with tent rental d COP$20,000, s/d COP$30,000/50,000, d tepee COP$35,000; [✿]) The family behind Villavieja's famous Conserves del Desert have packed up shop and moved into the desert. The good news is they are still making cactus-based delights including sweets, pickled cactus heart and wine (8.7% alcohol). They also offer a variety of accommodations including small concrete tepees (not for the claustrophobic) and basic cabañas.

All accommodations here include access to a good-sized pool, and special meals are offered for vegetarians.

★ El Peñon de Constantino LODGE $$
([☎] 317-698-8850, 310-255-5020; elpenonconstantino@hotmail.com; Observatorio, 2km E, Tatacoa; campsite/hut per person COP$10,000/25,000, luxury tent d/tr COP$80,000/100,000; [✿]) This safari-style lodge 2km past the observatory offers the freshest and most comfortable accommodations in the desert, with cute rammed-earth and bamboo huts and canvas perma-tents. All have external bathrooms. There is also a shady social area and prices include access to a well-maintained, rock-walled pool fed by a natural spring in the gully below.

Meals (COP$16,000 to COP$20,000) are served in the open-air dining area. It's a further 1.2km down the path after the entrance on the main road – make sure your ride takes you all the way.

Sol y Sombra COLOMBIAN $
(Calle 4 No 7-41, Villavieja; meals COP$5000-6000; [⊙]7am-8pm) For a tasty meal in the center of town. It prepares simple breakfasts and a variety of Colombian favorites.

Rincón de Cabrito SWEETS $
(Observatorio, 1km E, Tatacoa; snacks COP$3000-8000; [⊙]6am-9pm) About 1km from the observatory heading away from town you'll find this food stand that sells goat's-milk cheese and *arequipe* (a sweet dessert of milk and sugar).

❶ Information

There are a couple of internet cafes near the park charging around COP$1200 per hour for access.

Banco Agrario (Calle 4 No 4-30; [⊙]8am-1pm Mon-Fri) The only ATM in town – don't rely on it.

❶ Getting There & Away

Vans hop the 37km between Neiva and Villavieja (COP$6000, one hour) from 5am to 7pm. They leave with a minimum of five passengers; there are frequent services in the early morning and late afternoon, but during the day you could wait an hour or two.

There are frequent services between Bogotá and Neiva (COP$45,000, six hours). There are several buses a day direct to San Agustín (COP$30,000, four hours). For Tierradentro, change at La Plata (COP$20,000, four hours).

❶ Getting Around

There is a handful of moto-taxis in town that charge a stiff COP$20,000 to take up to three people to the observatory. A couple of places around town rent bicycles or you could walk the 4km, but take note that there's no shade, shelter or water on the way.

Several of the posadas in the desert rent horses for COP$10,000 to COP$15,000 per hour. Expect to pay around COP$50,000 per person for a full guided trip on horseback to the attractions.

NARIÑO

Welcome to Ecuador – almost. Nariño is Colombia's most southwesterly department, and the Ecuadorean influence here is strong.

The Andes here loom high and forbidding on their southerly march. The 'volcano alley' that runs the length of Ecuador begins here – pleasant Pasto, the departmental capital, sits a mere 8km from an active volcano covered in patchwork farmland.

Most people visit the region only to cross the border, but it's worth spending a few days here. Pasto has a compact center that's worth a stroll, Laguna de la Cocha is enchanting, and the towering Santuario de Las Lajas near Ipiales is an astonishing sight to behold.

Pasto

[☎]2 / POP 411,706 / ELEV 2551M
Just two hours from Ecuador, Pasto is the capital of the department and the logical jumping-off point for the border. It is a pleasant enough city with several fine colonial buildings as well as a bustling downtown area, but there is little here to hold

Pasto

◉ Sights
1 Iglesia de San Juan Bautista A2
2 Museo del Oro B3

🛏 Sleeping
3 Hotel Casa Lopez B3
4 Koala Inn A3

🍴 Eating
5 Caffeto...A2
6 Salón Guadalquivir B2

🍸 Drinking & Nightlife
7 Andina Peña Bar B2
8 Cola de Gallo.......................................A2

putedly the oldest surviving two-story house in Colombia.

Museo del Oro   MUSEUM
(Calle 19 No 21-27; ⊙10am-5pm Tue-Sat) **FREE** For insight into the pre-Columbian cultures of Nariño, check out this museum's small but interesting collection of indigenous gold and pottery.

Iglesia de San Juan Bautista   CHURCH
Grand on the outside, gold encrusted inside, this fine church on Pasto's main square is a fine example of colonial baroque architecture.

🛏 Sleeping

Koala Inn   HOSTEL **$**
(☑722-1101; hotelkoalainn@hotmail.com; Calle 18 No 22-37; s/d COP$30,000/45,000, without bathroom COP$20,000/40,000; 🖥) Set in a large colonial house with wooden floors, Pasto's only hostel is cheap, friendly and centrally located. The rooms are spacious and have cable TV, although those by the street can be noisy.

Hotel Sello Dorado   HOTEL **$**
(☑721-3688; hotelsellodorado@hotmail.com; Calle 13 No 14-19; s/d COP$30,000/40,000; 🖥) Surrounded by car-parts outlets and walking distance from the center, this new hotel does not have the most romantic location but offers fantastic value. The cozy, brand-new rooms have faux wooden floors, comfortable mattresses, piping-hot water and flat-screen TVs.

★ Hotel Casa Lopez   HOTEL **$$**
(☑720-8172; hcasalopez@gmail.com; Calle 18 No 21B-07; s/d/tw COP$122,000/157,000/162,000; 🖥) In a perfectly restored colonial home in the center, this family-run hotel is in a league

most travelers' attention for more than an overnight stop.

Nature lovers, however, might consider a longer stay as Pasto is surrounded by some spectacular countryside and is a good base for visiting Laguna de la Cocha, Laguna Verde and the restless Volcán Galeras.

The weather here is cool – so cool, in fact, you'll see *helado de paíla* being prepared fresh on the streets; it's traditional ice cream made in a copper tub sitting on a platform of ice.

◉ Sights

Museo Taminango de Artes y Tradiciones   MUSEUM
(☑723-5539; museotaminango@gmail.com; Calle 13 No 27-67; adult COP$2000; ⊙8am-noon & 2-6pm Mon-Fri, 9am-1pm Sat) This museum has a hodgepodge of antiques but is worth seeing since it's housed in a meticulously restored *casona* (large house) from 1623, re-

of its own in terms of comfort, service and attention to detail. Set around a pretty courtyard, the charming rooms have polished wooden floors and antique furnishings.

The affable owners are some of the most accommodating hosts around – don't be surprised if they pop around with a hot-water bottle or a cup of hot chocolate in the evening.

Eating

Nariño is the only place in Colombia where eating *cuy* (guinea pig) is mainstream. For fast food Nariño style, visit a *picanteria* – popular diners that serve *lapingachos* (grilled potato cakes topped with different kinds of meats).

Salón Guadalquivir   CAFE **$**
(Calle 19 No 24-84; snacks COP$600-3300, set meals COP$6800, mains COP$12,500-16,500; ⏱8am-12:30pm & 2:30-7:30pm Mon-Sat) This cozy cafe on the plaza serves classic *pastuso* (local cuisine) plates, including *empanadas de anejo* (small fried pastries), *quimbilitos* (sweet pastries of raisin, vanilla and sweet corn) and *envueltas de chocolo* (sweet corn cakes), in addition to good-value set meals.

Asadero de Cuyes Pinzón   COLOMBIAN **$$**
(☑731-3228; Carrera 40 No 19B-76, Palermo; cuy COP$32,000; ⏱1-9pm Mon-Sat, noon-2pm Sun) *Pastusos* (residents of Pasto) get dressed up to eat at this place about 1.5km north of the center of town. There's only one thing on the menu: *asado de cuy* (grilled guinea pig). The best way to get the meat off the bone is to eat with your hands – you'll be given plastic gloves. One *cuy* is big enough for two.

Caffeto   CAFE **$$**
(www.krkcaffeto.com; Calle 19 No 25-62; mains COP$8500-19,000; ⏱8am-10pm Mon-Sat) This fancy bakery-cafe does gourmet sandwiches, omelets and salads. The cakes are stupendous, and it does enormous ice-cream sundaes and serves real espresso coffee. Enough to satisfy even the most jaded traveler's inner yuppie.

Drinking & Nightlife

Andina Peña Bar   BAR
(cnr Calle 19 & Carrera 25, Centro Commercial San Sebastián de Belalcázar; ⏱7pm-late Thu-Sat) An underground Andean-themed bar playing crossover music. For cheap thrills seek out the open bar of *guayusa* (Thursday and Friday 7pm to 11pm, COP$6000 to COP$7000), a hot alcoholic beverage made with local spirits.

Cola de Gallo   BAR
(☑722-6194; Calle 18 No 27-47; coffee COP$2500-4800, cocktails COP$15,500-18,000; ⏱3-8pm Mon-Wed, to 1am Thu Sat) Down one of 80 different cocktails or a steaming mug of locally sourced gourmet coffee while listening to a hip jazz/blues/world music soundtrack at this swanky cafe-lounge.

Shopping

The city is known for *barniz de Pasto,* a traditional indigenous craft that uses processed vegetable resins from the Amazon region to decorate wooden objects in colorful patterns. Items can be bought at **Barniz de Pasto Obando** (☑722-4045, 301-350-0030; Carrera 25 No 13-04; ⏱8:30am-12:30pm & 2:30-6:30pm Mon-Fri, 9am-12:30pm & 3-6:30pm Sat), where you can also arrange to watch the artisans work.

🛈 Information

Most of the banks are around Plaza de Nariño.
4-72 (Calle 15 No 22-05; ⏱8am-6pm Mon-Fri, 9am-noon Sat) Post office.
Nariño Tourist Office (Oficina Departmental de Turismo; ☑723-4962; www.turismonarino. gov.co; Calle 18 No 25-25; ⏱8am-noon & 2-6pm

---

CARNAVAL DE BLANCOS Y NEGROS

Pasto's major event is **Carnaval de Blancos y Negros** (www.carnavaldepasto.org), held on January 5 and 6. Its origins go back to the times of Spanish rule, when slaves were allowed to celebrate on January 5 and their masters showed approval by painting their faces black. On the following day, the slaves painted their faces white.

On these two days the city goes wild, with everybody painting or dusting one another with grease, chalk, talc, flour and any other available substance even vaguely black or white in tone. It's a serious affair – wear the worst clothes you have and buy an *antifaz,* a sort of mask to protect the face, widely sold for this occasion. Asthmatics should not attend – you'll be coughing up talcum powder for days afterwards.

Mon-Fri) Dedicated to attractions around the department of Nariño. Looks flash but is a bit short on practical details.

Pasto Tourist Office (Punto Información Turistica; 722-1979; culturapasto.gov.co; cnr Calle 19 & Carrera 25; 8am-noon & 2-6pm) Tourist office covering attractions within the city.

❶ Getting There & Away

AIR

The airport is 33km north of the city on the road to Cali. *Colectivos* (COP$10,000, 45 minutes) for the airport leave from Plaza de Nariño at the corner of Calle 18 and Carrera 25. A taxi will cost COP$35,000 to COP$40,000.

BUS

The **bus terminal** (www.terminaldepasto. com) is 2km south of the city center. Frequent buses, minibuses and *colectivos* go to Ipiales (COP$6000 to COP$8000, 1½ to two hours); sit on the left for better views. Plenty of buses ply the spectacular road to Cali (COP$40,000, nine hours). These buses will drop you off in Popayán (COP$30,000, six hours). More than a dozen direct buses depart daily to Bogotá (COP$90,000, 20 hours).

Laguna de la Cocha

2 / ELEV 2760M

Set amid rolling green hills, and often shrouded in mist, this spectacular lake is a must-do day trip on your visit to Pasto. You can take a boat ride around the lake, stopping at Isla Corota (corota@parquesnacionales.gov.co; admission COP$1000) along the way. The island is a national park, and at an altitude of 2830m offers a rare glimpse of a well-preserved, evergreen cloud forest.

There's a small chapel and a biological research station on the island; a 550m-long boardwalk takes you the length of the island to a *mirador* (lookout). Boats to Isla Corota cost COP$25,000 for up to 10 people. The boat will wait for you and take you on a circle of the island on the way back.

🛏 Sleeping & Eating

At the mouth of the Río Encano, where it empties into the lake, you will find numerous basic hotels and restaurants serving roast chicken, *sancocho* (soup) and of course trout, which is farmed along the shores of the lake.

On the lakeshore there are a number of more upmarket options, the best known of which is the **Hotel Sindamanoy** (721 8222; reservas@hotelsindamanoy.com; s/d/tr/ste COP$120,000/165,000/212,000/220,000; 🐕), a faux-Swiss chalet which boasts a spectacular location overlooking Isla Corota. While the views are impressive, the rooms are a bit worse for wear. The elegant **restaurant** (mains COP$18,000-24,500), however, is a fine spot for a meal.

A short distance away, the **Chalet Guamuez** (721-9308; www.chaletguamuez.com; r with/without fireplace COP$205,200/147,200, cabaña COP$207,400; 🐕), known locally as Chalet Suizo, is in better nick, with tidy rooms overlooking a garden that runs down to the lake. The pricier options have a private fireplace and small balconies.

It's possible to reach either hotel by taxi from El Encano (COP$7000 to COP$8000) or by boat from the port for around COP$30,000 including a trip to Isla Corota.

VOLCÁN GALERAS

Just 8km from the center of Pasto, Volcán Galeras (4267m), one of Colombia's most active volcanoes, continues to rumble and threaten. The upper part of the volcano is preserved as a **national park** (admission COP$2000), while its lower slopes are a patchwork of farms and bright-green pastureland.

The majority of the park is closed to the public due to volcanic activity, however the area around Telpis is open to visitors. Here you will find the Laguna de Telpis, a mystical lake surrounded by *páramo* (high-mountain places) at more than 3000m.

To visit from Pasto, take a taxi to Yacuanquer (COP$3500) from the parking lot in front of the bus terminal then continue in either a moto-taxi or *colectivo* (minibus; both cost COP$2000) to the village of San Felipe. In San Felipe you will need to contract a guide (COP$20,000 per group of up to 15) for the three-hour hike to the *mirador* (lookout). It's easiest to arrange this through **Parques Nacionales** (732-0493, 313-733-3911, 314-796-4085; galeras@parquesnacionales.gov.co; Carrera 41 No 16B-17, Barrio El Dorado) in Pasto before heading out.

Good shoes and cold-weather gear are essential for this hike.

LAGUNA VERDE

You'll see photos of this striking emerald-green lake high in the Andes all over Nariño. It sits in the crater of the extinct Volcán Azufral (4000m), near Túquerres (3070m) – the highest major town in Colombia – and can be visited on a day trip from either Pasto or Ipiales, but you'll want to set out early.

Upon arrival in Túquerres, you'll need to hire a taxi (round trip COP$50,000) for the 30-minute trip to 'La Cabaña' (3600m) where the trail begins. It's advisable to arrange a time in advance with your driver for the return trip. Solo travelers could also take a motorcycle taxi (around COP$20,000 round trip). At the entrance there are bathrooms and a little shop where you'll pay a small admission fee. From here it's a 6km hike taking 1½ to two hours up a gentle incline to the lookout at the crater's edge. If you want to get closer, a steep path leads 700m down into the crater to the lake's edge.

While the hike is not particularly long, the high altitude makes it challenging, especially the climb back up from the lakeshore to the lookout. Allow around five hours for the round trip from El Refugio. Bring good cold-weather gear and wear plenty of layers. It can get warm while hiking, but the weather changes very quickly and the wind can be extremely cold. It's also important to bring sunscreen even if it's overcast.

Buses to Túquerres depart from both Pasto (COP$6000, 1¾ hours) and Ipiales (COP$7000, 1½ hours).

❶ Getting There & Away

Shared taxis to Río Encano by the lake (COP$4000, 40 minutes) leave from the Plaza de Carnaval in central Pasto and behind the Hospital Departmental (corner Calle 22 and Carrera 7). The taxis seat four people; if you're in a hurry, pay for all four seats.

Ipiales

🚐 2 / POP 123,341 / ELEV 2900M

Only 7km from the Ecuador border, Ipiales is an uninspiring commercial town driven by trade across the frontier. There is little to see or do here; a short side trip to the Santuario de Las Lajas is the real drawcard, although the Panamericana from Pasto is also thrilling.

🛏 Sleeping & Eating

There are few good reasons to spend the night in Ipiales. Pasto is a far nicer city, and those wanting to visit Las Lajas will find cheap, decent accommodations right next to the sanctuary there.

For some typical grub head to Barrio El Charco, where there are almost a dozen places selling barbecue *cuy* – they're flattened out and cooked over an open fire on a mechanical spit that resembles a macabre rodent Ferris wheel.

Gran Hotel HOTEL **$**
(📞 773-2131; granhotel_ipiales@hotmail.com; Carrera 5 No 21-100; s/d/tr COP$35,000/50,000/90,000; 🛜) Located in a commercial neighborhood a short walk from the center, this friendly new hotel has simple, spotless rooms with plasma screens and hot water. Some rooms can be a little noisy so ask to see all the options.

Hotel Belmonte HOTEL **$**
(📞 773-2771; Carrera 4 No 12-111; s/d COP$16,000/26,000; 🛜) The longtime backpackers' choice in Ipiales, this welcoming family-run institution is fairly old-school, with worn fittings, electric showers and small TVs, but it's cheap, clean and secure. Try to nab a room with a bathroom – they are the same price as those with shared facilities.

Hotel Los Andes HOTEL **$$**
(📞 773-4338; hotellosandes@gmail.com; Carrera 5 No 14-44; s/d/tr COP$62,500/93,200/127,600; @🛜) The largest place in town, Los Andes has 33 rooms around an interior courtyard. A loud TV in the lobby echoes up to the rooms. Some of the rooms have street views – not necessarily an improvement.

❶ Information

Artesys (Calle 12 No 6-16; per hour COP$1300; ⏱ 8am-10pm) Internet.
Banco de Bogota (Carrera 6 No 13-55) On Plaza la Pola.

❶ Getting There & Away

AIR

The airport is 7km northwest of Ipiales, on the road to Cumbal, and is accessible by taxi

GETTING TO ECUADOR

Passport formalities are processed at the border in Rumichaca, situated between Ipiales and Tulcán in Ecuador. The border is always open and the procedure is straightforward.

Frequent shared taxis travel the 2.5km from Ipiales to Rumichaca from around 5am to 8pm, leaving from the bus terminal (COP$1600) and the market area near the corner of Calle 14 and Carrera 8 (COP$1500). A private taxi is COP$7000. After crossing the border on foot, take another *colectivo* (shared minibus or taxi) to Tulcán (6km). On both routes, Colombian and Ecuadorean currency is accepted.

There are no direct flights from Ipiales to Ecuador, but you can easily get to Tulcán, from where Tame has daily flights to Quito. Heading to Tulcán from the border, you pass the airport 2km before reaching town.

(COP$15,000). Satena (p324) has flights to Bogotá three times a week; book early for a better price.

BUS

Ipiales has a new, large bus terminal about 1km northeast of the center. Urban buses can take you into the center of town (COP$1000), or grab a taxi (COP$3000).

There are several companies running buses to Bogotá (COP$100,000, 22 hours) and Cali (COP$45,000, 11 hours). All will drop you in Popayán (COP$30,000, eight hours).

There are plenty of buses, minibuses and *colectivos* to Pasto (COP$6000 to COP$8000, 1½ to two hours). They all depart from the bus terminal. Sit on the right for better views.

Santuario de Las Lajas

ELEV 2600M

Built on a stone bridge spanning a deep gorge at the village of Las Lajas, the neo-Gothic Santuario de Las Lajas is a strange but spectacular sight. On Sunday the place is full of pilgrims and vendors selling ice cream and souvenirs; during the week it gets hardly any visitors. The pilgrims place their faith in the Virgin Mary, whose image is believed to have emerged from an enormous vertical rock 45m above the river sometime in the mid-18th century. Plaques of thanksgiving line the walls of the canyon, many from prominent Colombian politicians.

The church is directly against the rocky wall of the gorge where the image appeared. A gilded painting of the Virgin, accompanied by Santo Domingo and San Francisco, has been painted directly on the rocks just to be sure there is no confusion. The first chapel was built in 1803; today's church, designed by Nariño architect Lucindo Espinoza, was built between 1926 and 1944.

In the lower floors of the church a **museum** (admission COP$2000; ⊘8:30am-5pm) has exhibits on the history of the church plus some religious art. The best views of the church are found by the waterfall on the far side of the canyon.

🛏 Sleeping & Eating

Santuario de Las Lajas is easily accessible from Ipiales but if you want to stay on site there are a number of basic hotels located down the first set of stairs to the left as you walk towards the church from the road. Across the stone bridge there is a restaurant with a fine view of the church – but it only opens during peak periods. Otherwise there are numerous basic eateries lining the path down from the village.

Casa Pastoral HOTEL $
(☑318-370-2651; s/d/tr/q COP$12,000/18,000/36,000/48,000) Run by nuns for a long time, this large, simple hotel caters to both pilgrims and casual visitors. Some rooms have views of the church and all have private bathrooms with hot water. A large cafeteria serves simple budget meals (COP$4000 to COP$6000). Take the first set of stairs on your left as you walk downhill toward the church. Bookings are recommended.

ℹ Getting There & Around

The sanctuary is 7km southeast of Ipiales. Shared taxis and vans run regularly from the corner of Carrera 6 and Calle 4 in Ipiales (COP$2000, 20 minutes) and from the town's bus station (COP$2000, 15 minutes). Pay for all four seats if you're in a hurry or alternatively a regular taxi from anywhere in Ipiales will cost around COP$9000. On Sundays there are direct shared taxis from Pasto if you prefer the greater creature comforts that the city offers.

Pacific Coast

Best Places to Stay

➡ Morromico (p264)

➡ El Cantil Ecolodge (p264)

➡ El Almejal (p261)

Best Places to Spot Whales

➡ Parque Nacional Natural (PNN) Ensenada de Utría (p261)

➡ Juanchaco & Ladrilleros

➡ El Valle

Why Go?

There are few destinations as ruggedly spectacular as the Pacific region of Colombia. This is where the jungle not so much meets the sea as comes crashing headlong into it. It is a place where waterfalls pour out of forest-covered bluffs onto spectacular gray-sand beaches, thermal pools lie hidden in dense jungle and tiny indigenous villages cling to the edge of wild rivers; where whales and dolphins frolic so close to shore you can admire them from your hammock and majestic sea turtles come even closer. There are plenty of comfortable ecoresorts throughout the region and you will find budget guesthouses in the many friendly Afro-descendant communities whose residents eke out a living from fishing and agriculture.

Difficult access and a lack of infrastructure has kept the crowds at bay, but this can't last. Make sure you visit before package tourism takes hold.

When to Go
Buenaventura

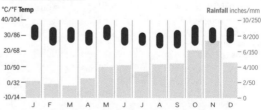

Jan–Mar Lighter rains make for better hiking and other outdoor activities.

Jul–Oct Humpback whales arrive in the region after an epic journey from Antarctica.

Sep–Dec Watch giant marine turtles scramble up beaches where they were born to lay their eggs.

Pacific Coast Highlights

1 Linger amid tropical gardens on the gray-sand beaches of **Guachalito** (p264).

2 Spot humpback whales at **Parque Nacional Natural (PNN) Ensenada de Utría** (p261).

3 Surf the Pacific's 2m waves near **El Valle** (p260).

4 Dive with hundreds of hammerhead sharks at **Isla Malpelo** (p268), Colombia's most remote scuba destination.

5 Relax in piping-hot thermal pools deep in the jungle near **Jurubidá** (p263).

6 Travel up the **Río Joví** (p264) in dugout canoes to remote waterfalls.

7 Hike from **Bahía Solano** (p257) to swimming holes cloaked in virgin forest.

8 Fly through the jungle on a motorcycle-powered rail trolley at **San Cipriano** (p268).

9 Paddle through the maze of mangroves around **Ladrilleros** (p266).

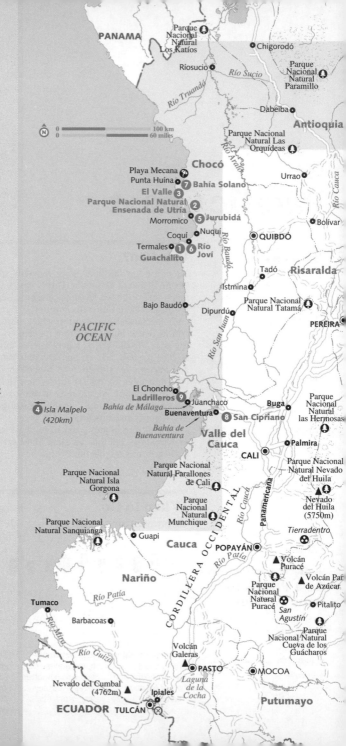

National, State & Regional Parks

Parque Nacional Natural (PNN) Isla Gorgona and Parque Nacional Natural (PNN) Isla Malpelo are both protected marine parks boasting interesting diving. Parque Nacional Natural (PNN) Ensenada de Utría, halfway between El Valle and Nuquí, attracts whales in season that play in a narrow bay just a few hundred meters offshore. You may also spot them around Parque Nacional Natural (PNN) Uramba Bahía Málaga, Colombia's most accessible chunk of Pacific wilderness.

ⓘ Dangers & Annoyances

Security in this region has improved dramatically, but guerrilla and paramilitary groups remain active in remote areas, especially around Tumaco near the Ecuadorean border and in the northern reaches of El Chocó near Panama.

When we visited the areas covered in this book were all calm, but you may wish to check on the latest situation before planning your visit.

ⓘ Getting There & Around

Only the Cali–Buenaventura highway links the Pacific coast to the rest of Colombia. From Buenaventura boats travel up and down the coast, although most travelers to the Chocó arrive by light plane via Medellín. It's also possible to reach here on very irregular boat services from Panama.

There is only one, very short road on the entire Pacific coast. Almost all local travel is in small boats that connect villages to transportation hubs. Wrap your luggage in plastic garbage bags to prevent a thorough soaking. Many villages and resorts don't have docks so you're likely to get a little wet when disembarking; wear shorts and sandals.

CHOCÓ

El Chocó is one of the wettest places on earth. On average, it receives 16m to 18m of rain per year. This defines the region, the people and its culture. When the sun shines, it's too hot to move too fast, and when it rains – almost every day – no one wants to go out and get wet. No wonder people joke about *hora chocoana* (Chocó time). Life here is slow.

The region is sparsely populated and remains covered in dense jungle. Pre-2001 it was a popular tourist destination but then the civil war arrived, destabilizing the area, and tourist arrivals plummeted. There is now a sizable Colombian military presence in the area and the situation has improved dramatically. You will see the occasional military patrol on the beach, but it's all fairly unobtrusive.

El Chocó is not a cheap destination. Transportation here is mostly in small boats that are much pricier than a comparable journey by bus. Furthermore, accommodations here are far more expensive than similar options elsewhere in Colombia. However, budget travelers should not be totally discouraged. With a bit of planning, a willingness to prepare your own basic meals and a flexible itinerary, it is possible to discover this amazing region without breaking the bank.

Bahía Solano

📋 4 / POP 9200

Bahía Solano is the largest settlement on the Chocó coast. It is famous for its deepsea sportfishing – some of the best in the world – and as a base to go whale-watching. It sits at the mouth of the Río Jella and faces north into the ocean. The town itself doesn't have a beach, although at low tide it's possible to walk around the bay to one and there are many nice stretches of sand just a short boat ride away.

⊙ Sights & Activities

Near the south end of town flows the Quebrada Chocolatal. You can hike upriver for about half an hour to the **Cascada Chocolatal**, a waterfall that empties into an icy-cold swimming hole where the jungle towers over you on both sides of the riverbank in a cascade of flowers and birdsong. On the same hillside closer to the waterfront an overgrown path leads upward to a small shrine to the Virgin Mary that offers great views over the town and the beach.

Right in front of the airport is the entrance to **Salto del Aeropuerto**, an impressive high-volume waterfall that pours into a deep, crystal-clear swimming hole where you can spot giant freshwater shrimp. It's about 15 minutes' walk back from the road.

There is good **scuba diving** in 150m-deep Bahía Solano. The warship *Sebastián de Belalcázar,* which survived the attack on Pearl Harbor, was sunk near Playa Huína to create an artificial reef (Buqué Hundido). Cave divers may like to explore the caves near Cabo Marzo. There are two dive operators in town; expect to pay around COP$220,000 for two

WARDING OFF THE EVIL EYE

Cabalonga, a hard nut grown in the Chocó, is worn on a necklace by indigenous children to ward off the *mal de ojo* (evil eye) that some elderly women are thought to possess.

immersions. **Posada del Mar** (☑314-630-6723; www.posadadelmarbahiasolano.com; Barrio El Carmen) has enthusiastic management and offers packages with dives and accommodations; by the bridge over the river, **Cabo Marzo** (☑314-861-8742; blackmarlin19@hotmail.com) offers similar dives but is less organized.

Colombia's Pacific coast is one of the best places in South America to pull in record-breaking blue marlin and sailfish. Expect to pay around COP$1,800,000 per day for four to five anglers. A recommended skipper is **Vicente Gonzalez** (☑320-694-5256).

🛏 Sleeping & Eating

All the hotels in the town itself are down by the waterfront in Barrio El Carmen. If you're after a cheap, local meal, head to the no-name shacks near the hospital where you can get fried fish and *patacones* (fried plantains).

★Posada del Mar   GUESTHOUSE $
(☑314-630-6723; www.posadadelmarbahiasolano.com; r per person COP$42,000, s/d without bathroom COP$25,000/45,000; 🛜) The best budget option in town has a number of brightly painted wooden huts dotted around a pleasant garden and cheaper rooms with shared bathrooms on top of the reception. Add COP$30,000 to the price for three tasty meals. The friendly owners organize whale-watching tours (COP$70,000) and are a wealth of information about attractions in the area.

Hotel Balboa Plaza   HOTEL $$
(☑682-7401; hotelbalboa@hotmail.com; Carrera 2 No 6-73; s/d from COP$70,000/110,000; 🌬) Built by Pablo Escobar, the Balboa remains the largest hotel in town. It's a bit ragged around the edges but remains good value. The bright, spacious rooms feature split-system air-conditioning and many have private balconies. There's no hot water but you don't really need it here. Visitors can use the large pool for COP$5000.

Rocas de Cabo Marzo   HOTEL $$$
(☑682-7525; www.posadaturisticarocasdecabomarzo.com; s/d incl meals COP$110,000/200,000; @) One of the few people who speaks English in the zone, the attentive owner of this small, comfortable hotel organizes sportfishing trips and offers guide services in the surrounding area. The food here is excellent and there's a nice terrace upstairs with views over the park to the bay. Accepts credit cards.

Restaurante Cazuela   SEAFOOD $$
(mains COP$15,000-30,000; ⊙8am-9pm) It doesn't look like much but this tiny restaurant with a handful of plastic tables serves up a wide variety of excellent seafood dishes including *ollitas en salsa* (whelks in sauce) and tuna steaks. Don't expect much in the way of vegetables on your plate. It's in front of the Banco Agrario.

La Casa Negra   SEAFOOD $$
(mains COP$13,000-22,000; ⊙7am-3:30pm & 5-9pm) In a new wooden house in front of the park a block back from the bay, this unsigned restaurant is popular with locals for its tasty seafood plates and typical Colombian meat dishes.

🛍 Shopping

You'll find a good variety of *artesanías* (handicrafts) in Bahía Solano including some produced by local indigenous peoples. Worth a look are the carvings of *tagua,* a hard palm resin sometimes called 'vegetable ivory.' The small *artesanía* shop at the airport has a good selection of products.

ℹ Information

4-72 (⊙8am-noon & 2-6pm Mon-Sat) The local postal agent is located in a shop opposite the back gate of the Balboa Plaza.

Banco Agrario de Colombia (⊙8-11:30am & 2-4:30pm Mon-Fri) The only bank in town, with the only ATM on the Chocó coast. It's sometimes empty – don't rely on it.

Ministerio de Relaciones Exteriores (☑321-271-7745; www.migracioncolombia.gov.co; ⊙24hr) Processes entry/exit stamps. In Barrio El Carmen.

Soluciones JG (per hr COP$2000; ⊙8am-9pm) Bahía's only real internet cafe. It's on the same block as the bank.

Super Giros (⊙7:30am-8pm Mon-Sat, 9am-noon Sun) You can receive domestic wire transfers here. Opposite Hotel Bahía.

ℹ Getting There & Away

AIR
Aeropuerto José Celestino Mutis is serviced by Satena (p324) and ADA (p324), although both companies have suspended services on occasion due to the poor condition of the runway. When the airlines pull out, a posse of charter pilots pick up the slack in their tiny prop planes.

The airport's nickname is 'Sal Si Puedes' (Get Out If You Can). Because of heavy rain, planes are sometimes unable to leave. It would be unwise to book international connections for the same day you leave Bahía Solano.

A moto-taxi to/from the airport costs COP$3000 per person.

BOAT
It's possible to travel to Buenaventura on the cargo boats that bring in supplies. The journey takes about 24 hours, generally leaving in the afternoon (both ways), depending on the tides.

The most regular service is the Bahía Cupica run by **Transportes Renacer** (☎ 2-242-0518, 315-402-1563; Muelle El Piñal). It leaves Buenaventura on Tuesday in the afternoon and returns from Bahía Solano on Saturday around noon. It costs COP$150,000 for a *camarote* (bunk bed) including meals. Call in advance to confirm departures, as you don't want to get stuck in Buenaventura.

You can travel onward to Panama (six to eight hours). Boats usually run around once a fortnight to Jaqué, Panama. Expect to pay around US$100 per person. Among the captains making the trip are **'Profesor' Justino** (☎ 313-789-0635), a veteran of the route who travels with a slow but steady philosophy that avoids unnecessary bumps.

Be sure to stamp out of Colombia at the Migración Colombia office in Bahía Solano before leaving town. To enter Panama you'll need a yellow fever vaccination and enough cash to prove you can travel onward (a minimum of US$500). Once you reach Jaqué and stamp in to Panama, there are flights (US$90) three times a week to Panama City with Air Panama. There is also a boat service once a week for around US$20.

TAXI & TUK-TUK
For travel to/from El Valle, shared taxis (COP$10,000, one hour) leave opposite the school when full. An express trip in a *tuk-tuk* costs COP$30,000.

Around Bahía Solano

Punta Huína
A 20-minute boat ride takes you to this pretty beach with a mixture of gold and black sand. It's lined with coconut palms and several modest resorts. A small indigenous community lives here, along with descendants of African slaves. Punta Huína has no phone signal, but a **Vive Digital** (per hr COP$1000; ◷8am-noon & 2-6pm Mon-Sat) kiosk offers satellite phone calls and internet access.

There are several jungle walks you can do in the vicinity, including to **Playa de los Deseos**, **Cascada El Tigre** and **Playa Cocalito**.

There is no public transportation to Punta Huína, but all the hotels we've listed offer transportation. Otherwise, if you hang around the Bahía Solano wharf at lunchtime you should be able to grab a ride with local villagers (COP$10,000). You can also hire an express boat (COP$100,000).

🛏 Sleeping

Los Guásimos RENTAL HOUSE $
(☎ 320-796-6664; r per person COP$30,000) One of the best deals on the entire Pacific coast, this small house sits alone on a hill across the river at the end of the beach. It sleeps up to 10, but if you have six or more you get the entire place. It has a large deck with magnificent views and a small kitchen to prepare meals.

Most locals don't know it by name – ask around for Pambelé, the owner. He also rents tent space behind his bar by the river and runs cheap diving trips.

Choibana LODGE $$
(☎ 2-321-8819, 312-548-2969; www.choibana.com; r per person COP$50,000-60,000) On a private beach backed by thick jungle, this atmospheric wooden lodge is a great place to take it easy. The pick of the rooms are in the romantic hut set on stilts over a rocky outcrop away from the main house – the views from the bed are phenomenal. Rates include breakfast. It is located on the other side of the headland at the far end of Playa Huína. During low tide it's possible to walk to the village. Return transportation from Bahía Solano is COP$30,000 per visitor.

Cabañas Brisas Del Mar HOTEL $$
(☎ 312-898-6724; r per person incl meals COP$70,000-80,000) This full-service budget choice has numerous wooden rooms above the family home. Some rooms are better than others and not all have private bathrooms so ask to look around. There are great views of the ocean from the balcony and a breezy kiosk right on the beach. The prices

include transportation from Bahía Solano, a boat trip and guided hike.

Playa de Oro Lodge HOTEL $$$
(🖉 in Medellín 4-361-7809; www.hotelesdecostaa-costa.com; r per person incl meals COP$188,000) This family-oriented resort surrounds a small garden with a playground for the kids. Each room has a small wooden balcony with a hammock, and 2nd-floor rooms have good views of the sea. The big bar area also boasts excellent views and is a great place for an evening drink.

Pacific Sailfish GUESTHOUSE $$$
(🖉 314-375-0941; pacific.sailfish21@gmail.com; r per person incl meals COP$120,000; 🕿) Run by a Spanish sportfishing enthusiast and his Colombian wife, this lodge in the village has a variety of neat wooden rooms with small private bathrooms, and arranges sportfishing excursions throughout the region. Prices include meals and return transportation from Bahía Solano.

Playa Mecana

A 25-minute boat ride from Bahía Solano lies **Playa Mecana**, a lovely long beach strewn with coconut palms. Here you can visit the nonprofit **Jardín Botánico del Pacífico** (🖉 321-759-9012; www.jardinbotanico delpacifico.org; r per person COP$195,000), a 170-hectare nature reserve running alongside the Río Mecana made up of mangroves, virgin tropical forest and a botanical garden of native plants and trees. Its staff include members of the local Emberá indigenous group who can take you on fantastic treks (COP$15,000 to COP$50,000 per visitor) through the property. There are three main circuits ranging from two to six hours' duration. They can also take you on boat rides up the river into their traditional lands and organize whale-watching excursions. The management also organize snorkeling and scuba-diving trips, while there is great bird-watching right by the lodge.

If you want to stick around a while, there are simple but functional rooms available in the main lodge. They are not particularly spacious but there is a lovely wide deck and you didn't come all this way to be cooped up inside! There are also a couple of more secluded private cabañas surrounded by nature further along the beach. Accommodations prices include meals and transportation to/from Bahía Solano.

It is possible to walk here from Bahía Solano but you must leave at or before low tide *(mareada baja)*. It's an hour's walk each way. Alternatively, call for a boat to pick you up (COP$60,000 per boat for up to eight passengers).

El Valle

🖉 4 / POP 3500

On the southern side of the peninsula from Bahía Solano sits its smaller neighbor, El Valle. At the west end of town is the pleasant Playa Almejal, a wide black-sand beach with fine surf and decent accommodations. El Valle is a good jumping-off point to visit Ensenada de Utría. It's also a good place to observe sea turtles during nesting season (September to December) and to spot whales just off the coast.

◉ Sights & Activities

Estación Septiembre WILDLIFE RESERVE
(🖉 321-793-7746, 314-677-2488) 🏖 On Playa Cuevita, 5km south of El Valle along the coast, is the turtle-nesting sanctuary and research station of Estación Septiembre. From June to December sea turtles arrive to lay eggs. The best time to see them is at night. The conservation project is run by the community organization Caguama – visitors are essential to keep it running. Entry is by voluntary donation. There are cabins you can stay in (per person with/without meals COP$80,000/40,000) if you want to spend some time here.

You can walk to the sanctuary from El Valle (two hours) either along a bush track or along the beach. If you take the beach, you will wade across a couple of waist-deep rivers, while a guide (COP$20,000) is recommended for the bush route. The staff can also organize nighttime turtle-watching tours departing from El Valle.

Cascada del Tigre OUTDOORS
(admission COP$5000) A tough four-hour walk north of El Valle through the jungle and along the shore takes you to Cascada del Tigre, an impressive waterfall with a swimming hole where you can bathe. Local guides charge around COP$40,000 per person. It's an exhausting full-day excursion if you travel both ways on foot – consider hiring a boat (COP$100,000 per group) for the return leg.

You can get a typical lunch (COP$10,000) beside the waterfall and at the time of research the owner was constructing an area for accommodations in hammocks and tents.

🛏 Sleeping & Eating

Posada Ecoturistica El Valle   HOTEL $
(📞310-472-0114; ecohotelvalle@gmail.com; r with/ without bathroom COP$35,000/25,000) This home-style posada (inn) is your best budget option in the town. The smaller rooms share an interior shower block, and there's a breezy terrace with hammocks upstairs. The owners also operate a pair of spacious cabañas near Playa Almejal.

Humpback Turtle   HOSTEL $$
(📞312-756-3439; thehumpbackturtle@gmail.com; campsite COP$15,000, hammock COP$15,000, dm COP$30,000, r per person COP$45,000) One of the most remote hostels in Colombia, this hip place at the end of Playa Almejal is right on the beach beside a pair of waterfalls. Accommodations are in a collection of wooden huts surrounded by a veggie garden; all have shared bathrooms. The thatched-roof bar area is a great place to chill when the rains come down. There is an open-air kitchen for guests and cheap fish meals are available. The managers rent boards and offer surfing tours in the surrounding area.

Posada El Nativo   GUESTHOUSE $$
(📞310-381-4729; r per person incl meals COP$60,000) For budget accommodations with a local flavor, head to this pair of thatched cabañas set in a lush garden about 100m back from the beach, run by tourism legend 'El Nativo' and his wife. To get here, cross the bridge on the left after the Telecom office and follow the road around.

El Almejal   HOTEL $$$
(📞412-5050; www.almejal.com.co; cabañas per person COP$144,000-230,000) The most luxurious option in the Bahía Solano area, El Almejal is set on an 8-hectare nature reserve halfway down Playa Almejal. The cabañas here have the most ingenious design – the walls of the lounge area open completely, allowing a breeze to pass through. Meals are served in a spacious open-air dining area.

A small creek spills into an artificial swimming hole near the back of the cabins; select a cabin nearby for the soothing sound. Concrete stairs behind the hotel lead uphill to a tranquil yoga area and lookout point from where you can sometimes spot whales.

Rosa del Mar   COLOMBIAN $
(mains COP$10,000; ⊙7am-8pm) In the street in front of the church, Doña Rosalia cooks up the best meals in town. Sit down and enjoy fresh seafood in her living room in front of the TV.

🍸 Drinking & Nightlife

El Mirador   BAR
(⊙10am-6pm Sun) Built on top of a rocky outcropping in the middle of Playa Almejal is El Mirador, one of Colombia's most spectacular bars. You can sit at the makeshift tables and suck down rum while the stereo blasts vallenato and reggaeton at the crashing waves.

ℹ Information

There is no longer a tourist information office in town although the staff at the Parques Nacionales office may be able to answer questions about the area.

There are a couple of no-name internet places charging around COP$2000 per hour for frustratingly slow access.

ℹ Getting There & Away

Shared taxis to Bahía Solano (COP$10,000, one hour) leave when full from outside the billiards hall. Services are more frequent in the morning.

Small boats leave for Nuquí (COP$60,000, 1½ hours) on Monday and Friday afternoons. The departure times depend on the tides.

Taxis and jeeps run from town to Playa Almejal – driving all over an important turtle-nesting beach. Do the turtles a favor and walk – it's not far.

Parque Nacional Natural (PNN) Ensenada de Utría

This **national park** (admission Colombians/ foreigners COP$14,500/38,000) surrounding a narrow inlet is one of the best places to see whales close-up from land. During the calving season they enter the *ensenada* (inlet) and play just a few hundred meters from shore. The **Centro de Visitantes Jaibaná** (s/d COP$130,000/189,000), on the eastern shore of the *ensenada*, has refurbished cabins for up to 30 people. Prices include all meals, snorkeling and kayaks. It's run by local community organization Mano Cambiada (p263), which manages all bookings.

With advance notice staff can organize diving in and around the park. There are a number of short walks you can do in the nearby mangroves and surrounding jungle, and at night you may see glow-in-the-dark mushrooms.

The public boats from Nuquí to El Valle/ Bahía Solano can drop you at the park for COP$60,000. If you have a group, a private transfer costs COP$250,000 to COP$350,000 from Nuquí or El Valle.

Alternatively, the park can organize a guide to take you on foot from El Valle to Lachunga at the mouth of the Río Tundo at the northwestern corner of the *ensenada* (COP$50,000, four hours). From here you can be picked up in a boat (COP$15,000 per person) and taken to the visitors center.

Nuquí

📞 4 / POP 8000

Midway along the Chocó coast is the small town of Nuquí. It boasts a wide beach right in front of town and a long, rugged stretch of sand across the river. A short boat ride away the secluded beach of Guachalito has some of the best resorts along this coast. A number of indigenous communities live up the Nuquí river but are not in the business of receiving visitors.

The town itself is paved with a mixture of concrete and gravel, but has no car traffic. It isn't a particularly attractive place but it's a convenient base from which to explore the gorgeous surrounding area. There is no bank or ATM here.

⊙ Sights & Activities

Playa Olímpica   BEACH
Just south of the mouth of the Río Nuquí, rugged Playa Olímpica stretches as far as the eye can see. A local named Señor Pastrana can paddle you across the river in his dugout canoe (COP$5000). To find him, walk south along the main beach road, past the church; he lives a block from the river in a peach-colored house.

Transporte Ecce Homo   BOAT TRIPS
(📞683-6124, 314-449-4446) With an office near the park, Transporte Ecce Homo offers boat trips all around the region. Sample itineraries include PNN Utría via Playa Blanca and Morromico (COP$60,000), mangroves and thermal pools at Jurubidá (COP$40,000), and to Guachalito including Cascada de Amor and Las Termales (COP$50,000). Prices are per person based on a group of six passengers (varying by group size and gasoline cost).

They also organize express transportation and have some basic rooms with kitchen access for rent in the office.

🛏 Sleeping

Most hotels cluster at the northern end of town, near the beach. There are a number of simple posadas in town.

Hotel Palmas del Pacifico   GUESTHOUSE $
(📞683-6010, 314-753-4228; r per person COP$35,000) The best budget choice in town is a block back from the beach and offers simple wooden rooms with soft mattresses and private bathrooms and a terrace with hammocks and sea views. It's not luxurious – you're not guaranteed a shower head or toilet seat – but it's clean and tranquil.

Go for a room upstairs at the front for fresh breeze.

Donde Jesusita   GUESTHOUSE $
(r per person COP$20,000) This simple guesthouse close to the dock is run by the grandmother of tourism in the Nuquí area. She is getting on a bit now but is a real character and a warm host. The place could do with an overhaul but the rooms upstairs have nice views of the river.

Hotel Nuquí Mar   HOTEL $$
(📞609-1074; www.hotelnuquimar.com; r per person COP$90,000-140,000) On the beach just past the football field, this hotel has appealing all-wood rooms with screens on the windows and sparkling tiled bathrooms. The suite on the top floor has a large private balcony. Prices include breakfast.

🍴 Eating

At the airport local women sell *mecocadas* (COP$1500), a tasty confection of coconut and guava paste.

Aqui es Chirringa COLOMBIAN $
(meals COP$12,000; ⏱7am-8pm) The entire family seems to work the kitchen at this simple open-air eatery around the corner from the airport. It serves good-sized plates of tasty Colombian cuisine served with a bowl of fish soup.

Doña Pola COLOMBIAN $
(📋683-6254; meals COP$11,000; ⏱7am-9pm) Down a side street between the hospital and the football field, Doña Pola cooks up hearty home-style meals.

🏠 Shopping

Artesanías Margot HANDICRAFTS
(⏱8am-5pm) Next to the airport, this small *artesanías* shop has a great selection of wooden carvings and other local arts and crafts. You might even spot an authentic blow-dart gun.

ℹ️ Information

There is no bank or ATM in Nuquí so bring sufficient funds. A couple of internet cafes offer sluggish access for around COP$2000 an hour if you're desperate to get online.

Mano Cambiada (📋313-759-6270; corporacionmanocambiada@yahoo.es; ⏱hours vary) A community-based tourism organization that runs the accommodations and services in Parque Nacional Natural Utría. Staff also offer general tourism information about the region and can organize tours in many communities.

Super Giros (📋683-6067; ⏱8am-noon & 2-6pm) You can receive domestic wire transfers here.

ℹ️ Getting There & Away

Aeropuerto Reyes Murillo (📋683-6001) is serviced by **Satena** (📋1 800 091 2034; www.satena.com) and **ADA** (📋4-444-4232; www.ada-aero.com), with flights to Medellín and Quibdó.

Transporte Yiliana (Donde Sapi; 📋314-764-9308, 311-337-2839) offers boat services to El Valle (COP$60,000, 1½ hours) and, depending on demand, onto Bahía Solano (COP$70,000, two hours) on Monday and Friday. Boats usually leave early in the morning.

Several cargo boats service Nuquí from Buenaventura. The recommended *Valois Mar* departs Nuquí every 10 days. Ask around town for **Gigo** (📋312-747-8374), the owner. It's a 16-hour trip and costs COP$120,000 including meals. In Buenaventura the *Valois Mar* leaves from Maderas del Patía wharf on Av Simón Bolívar.

Around Nuquí

Jurubidá

This colorful community of brightly painted houses, 45 minutes from Nuquí by boat, has plenty of attractions but doesn't receive many visitors. The bay in front of the village is dominated by the Archipelago de Jurubidá – a collection of spectacular rock formations covered in forest. When the tide drops, a natural pool forms in the rocks on one of the islands.

Grupo Los Termales, a local cooperative, can organize guides to the **Termales de Jurubidá** (COP$10,000 per person), a pair of thermal pools surrounded by dense jungle. The trip involves a short canoe ride and a beautiful walk alongside a crystal-clear river. The cooperative can also organize canoe trips through the mangroves (COP$10,000 to COP$20,000 per person), whale-watching (COP$120,000 per boat) and boat trips to an indigenous community a couple of hours upriver (COP$150,000 per boat).

There is no scheduled public transportation here but there are usually villagers traveling most days to/from Nuquí. Most boats dock at the Almacén Wilmer Torres, a bar/grocery store in the center. The going rate is around COP$15,000 per person for the 45-minute trip. Alternatively, you can hire an express boat for around COP$150,000.

🛏️ Sleeping & Eating

Cabaña Brisa del Mar HUT $
(Donde Tita; 📋314-684-9401; r per person COP$25,000-30,000) The most secluded sleeping option, this tranquil spot near the river has simple rooms in a homely thatched-roof cabaña. There is a lovely small balcony with a hammock and beach views. A packet of three meals costs COP$28,000.

Restaurante Artesenal Jessica GUESTHOUSE $
(📋311-753-4110; r per person COP$20,000) Located in the center of town, this simple guesthouse offers a couple of rooms above the family home. There is a breezy porch and the owner makes interesting handicrafts. Meals are served in the open-air restaurant next door.

Cabaña Emberafro HUT $$
(📋313-776-849; nohepro@hotmail.com; r per person incl meals COP$70,000) Located right

WORTH A TRIP

COQUÍ & JOVÍ

This pair of friendly villages, 25 minutes by boat from Nuquí, both have community tourism organizations. In Joví, **Grupo de Guias Pichinde** (☎321-731-1092) can take you up the Río Joví in dugout canoes to the waterfalls of Chontadura and Antaral. Chontadura is closer, while Antaral has a greater quantity of water and a bigger swimming hole. It can also arrange visits to the indigenous villages along the river. In Coquí the **Grupo de Ecoguias** (☎310-544-8904) can arrange boat trips through the mangroves.

There are simple posadas in both villages offering very basic accommodations for around COP$30,000 per person. The Nuquí–Arusí boat can drop you in either village.

on the beach, this simple thatched-roof hut is set apart from town and catches a fresh breeze.

Morromico

Situated on a magnificent private beach protected by forested headlands, **Morromico** (☎312 795 6321; www.morromico.com; r per person COP$240,000-270,000) is a beautiful, small ecoresort surrounded by thick jungle, 10 minutes by boat from Jurubidá. The hotel is set in lush gardens framed by a pair of waterfalls where you can bathe in crystal-clear mountain waters. The stylish semi-open rooms let in the sounds of the jungle and are powered by a small hydroelectric plant. The charismatic owner organizes boat trips and some pretty hardcore treks through the mountains to local indigenous communities. Rates include three filling meals. Reservations are essential.

Guachalito

A half-hour boat ride west of Nuquí is Guachalito. It's a long beach, clear of flotsam and debris. There are orchids and heliconias everywhere, the jungle encroaches on the beach, platter-sized mushrooms grow on the trees and coconut palms sway over the gray sand.

The Gonzalez family inhabits the beach's east end. Several hotels are scattered along

8km of the beach to Las Termales. On the way you'll pass El Terco and El Terquito, two almost-islands that serve as landmarks. You can walk the length of the beach (1½ hours). It's best to set out when the tide is low.

A 1km (20-minute) walk from the Gonzalez settlement, 200m inland from the beach, is **Cascada de Amor**, where a pretty waterfall surrounded by jungle empties into a natural rock pool. A 10-minute walk uphill takes you to an even bigger and more beautiful waterfall, which splits in two streams before filling a swimming hole below.

🛏 Sleeping

Originally Guachalito referred only to the Gonzalez family settlement at the eastern end of the beach. Four generations live here, and their four posadas – run by competing siblings – offer a variety of accommodations ranging in price from COP$100,000 to COP$210,000 per person including all meals.

La Joviseña (☎314-683-8856; www.la jovisena.com; r per person COP$210,000) offers the most comfort, with well-constructed detached wooden cabins spread throughout a lush garden beside an elegant open-air restaurant. Prices include transportation to and from Nuquí. At **Mar y Río** (☎314-656-9688; elmardeldiego@gmail.com; r per person COP$120,000) you'll stay with the family and eat at their kitchen table. It's located in a quiet corner of the beach with a small stream rushing by. The new rooms beside the main house are more private but have less character.

Luna de Miel (☎311-602-3742, 314-431-2125; clunademiel@hotmail.com; r per person COP$120,000) has two rustic rooms and a pleasant balcony with great views. The owners run the tourist dock in Nuquí, where you can ask for information. **Peñas de Guachalito** (☎320-5671-356; r per person COP$100,000) offers simple concrete rooms by a tropical garden full of coconut palms.

To the west of the Guachalito settlement there are a number of ecohotels and resorts. Most offer packages including transportation from the airport, accommodations and food.

⭐**El Cantil Ecolodge**　　　HOTEL $$$
(☎448-0767; www.elcantil.com; r per person COP$327,000) The most luxurious hotel on this beach, El Cantil has six duplex cabins surrounded by papaya plants and coconut palms. The restaurant (famous for its food)

is perched atop a hill and has sweeping views. A small hydroelectric plant produces power for the restaurant; the cabins are lit by candles. Prices include meals and transportation to/from Nuquí.

Whale-watching expeditions can be organized and surfing guides can show you the best spots.

La Cabaña de Beto y Marta HOTEL **$$$**
(☑ 311-775-9912; betoymarta@hotmail.com; r per person incl meals COP$200,000) This delightful hotel owned by two *paisas* (people from Antioquia) has four secluded cabins with hammocks and chairs on the deck from which to watch the sunset. The whole thing is set amid a spectacular garden, which includes lots of fruits and vegetables you'll find on your plate come dinnertime.

Pijibá Lodge HOTEL **$$$**
(☑ 311-762-3763; r per person incl meals from COP$190,000) Set among lush gardens, the three duplex cabins of Pijibá are constructed entirely of natural materials and let in plenty of fresh air. The food here has an excellent reputation.

Piedra Piedra HOTEL **$$$**
(☑ 315-510-8216; www.piedrapiedra.com; r per person incl meals COP$190,000) Set on a hill, this intimate place feels less resort-like than its neighbors. It has a freshwater pool on a rocky outcrop with views of El Terco. You can pitch a tent but at COP$50,000 per head it's a bit pricey.

The owners also rent out a spectacular house next door perched high on a bluff overlooking the water.

Termales

The small village of Termales has a lovely wide stretch of gray-sand beach and a couple of places to stay for those who want to get close to the local culture. As the sun sets children play games of football on the beach while chickens dart across the pitch and, in the distance, older youth take to the waves on boards donated by a nonprofit surf project.

A gravel path leads 500m inland from the village's one road to **Las Termales** (admission COP$12,000; ⊙ 8am-6pm), a pair of thermal pools set by a rushing stream surrounded by jungle. The site has been tastefully developed by the community and features a large restaurant (meals COP$13,000) and spa area that only function during busy periods.

Local community organization **Cocoter** (☑ 310-419-4411; Oficina Corporación Comunitario) can organize guides for the half-day trek to Cascada Cuatro Encantos – a towering set of waterfalls with good swimming holes surrounded by lush jungle.

With cheaper – but still not cheap – accommodations than nearby resorts and a laid-back vibe, Termales makes a good base from which to explore the area. Featuring a large balcony overlooking the beach, the friendly **Refugio Salomon** (☑ 313-756-7970; r per person incl meals COP$90,000, meals COP$12,000-15,000) has simple rooms with private bathrooms and serves delicious home-style meals. On the other side of the path, **Donde Paulino** (☑ 321-778-1165; r per person incl meals COP$90,000) offers simple, clean wooden rooms with shared bathrooms upstairs in the family home.

There is no phone coverage in Termales but business owners generally check their phones regularly if you want to leave a message.

❶ Getting There & Away

The fast boat (COP$25,000, 45 minutes) from Nuquí to Arusí, west of Termales, can drop you anywhere along the way. It leaves Arusí on Monday, Wednesday and Friday mornings around 6am and returns about 1pm. There is a slower, less-punctual boat (COP$22,000, one hour) covering the same route on Tuesday, Thursday and Saturday.

SOUTH COAST

Buenaventura

☑ 2 / POP 327,000

The largest city on this coast, Buenaventura is Colombia's busiest port and if ever there was an example of the failure of the nation's economic growth to improve the lot of its poorest residents, it is here. More than 60% of Colombia's legal exports pass through these docks; yet Buenaventura remains dreadfully poor and underdeveloped. Much of the nation's illegal exports pass through here, too, with associated power struggles often leading to outbreaks of violence.

The only reason to come here is transportation. Most tourist traffic runs through the *muelle turístico* (tourist wharf). This part of town is quite safe, and many restaurants and hotels cluster nearby.

🛏 Sleeping

There are several comfortable hotels, including some with water views, in the area around the *muelle turístico*.

Hotel Titanic   HOTEL **$$**
(📞241-2046; hoteltitanic@gmail.com; Calle 1A No 2A-55; s & d COP$76,500, tw/tr 88,200/118,000; ✳️🛰) One block from the entrance to the tourist wharf is this five-story hotel that offers comfortable-enough rooms, although the small windows onto the corridor don't let in much natural light. The rooftop bar-restaurant has good views over the water.

Hotel Tequendama Estación   HOTEL **$$$**
(📞243-4070; www.sht.com.co; Calle 2 No 1A-08; s/d COP$201,700/217,800; @🛰🏊) The best hotel in town is a flashback to Colombia's flapper days. Built in the 1920s and since refurbished, this white neoclassical confection boasts deluxe rooms and verandas all the way around. The pool (open 9am to 6pm) is open to the public (adult/child COP$22,000/18,000).

ℹ Information

Buenaventura is Colombia's most troubled major urban area and while tourists who mind their own business are unlikely to have any problems, it's worth sticking to the area around the *muelle turístico* and exercising a little extra caution here.

Banco AV Villas (Calle 2 No 2A-46) ATM.
Bancolombia (cnr Calle 2 & Carrera 2a) ATM.
Ciber P@cífico (Calle 1 No 2-11; per hr COP$2000; ⊗8am-7:30pm Mon-Sat) Internet and phone calls; just outside the tourist wharf.

ℹ Getting There & Away

There are frequent bus services between Cali and Buenaventura (COP$19,000, four hours). The bus terminal is located in the center just a few blocks from the *muelle turístico*. From Cali sit on the left side of the bus for the best views.

Tourist speedboat services heading north and south depart from the *muelle turístico*. Cargo boats leave from El Piñal, an industrial area a COP$6000 taxi ride away.

Around Buenaventura

Juanchaco & Ladrilleros

📞2 / POP 3500
An hour's boat ride north of Buenaventura are **Juanchaco** and neighboring **Ladrill-**eros. Juanchaco faces Bahía Málaga and accumulates a fine collection of Buenaventura's garbage on its beaches. Ladrilleros, on the other side of the peninsula, faces the roaring open waves of the Pacific Ocean.

During the rainy season (or rather, rainier season, from August to November) the ocean comes crashing in with 2m- to 3m-high waves, making the area appealing to surfers.

Neither Juanchaco nor Ladrilleros have the kind of beaches to keep you lazing around, although they make a good base for exploring the surrounding **Parque Nacional Natural (PNN) Uramba Bahía Málaga** – one of Colombia's newest national parks. The protected area boasts wild landscapes that alternate between crashing waves dancing around jungle-clad rocky outcrops and lush secluded bays. There are no fees to enter the park.

The best beach in the area is north of Ladrilleros at **La Barra**, where the wide expanse of gray sand is overlooked by a small fishing community.

Both Juanchaco and Ladrilleros are popular weekend getaway spots for people from Cali; during the week you will likely have the places to yourself.

🏃 Activities

Juanchaco is a cheap place to join a whale-watching tour. Expect to pay COP$25,000 to COP$30,000 per visitor for about an hour on the water in a collective boat. Ask around the main wharf for departures.

Nativos   ADVENTURE TOURS
(📞317-297-3703; manuel.nativos@gmail.com; Ladrilleros; per person from COP$20,000) Enthusiastic local tour operator offering a variety of nature experiences, including a boat trip through the mangroves to a natural swimming hole and trips to La Barra. It's in front of the Iglesia Mary.

Pedro Romero   SURFING
(📞313-752-3170; Cabaña Villa Malaty, Vía La Barra, Ladrilleros; classes per hr COP$25,000) Friendly local Pedro Romero offers surfing classes and rents boards. He also offers kayaking trips in local estuaries and overnight camping trips in the bush. On weekends and holidays you'll find him on the beach; otherwise look for him at the address given here. He also offers cheap accommodations and campsites with kitchen access on his property on the road to La Barra.

MELODIES FROM THE FOREST

The Pacific region, like many parts of Colombia, is all about music and dance. But here the soundtrack for letting one's hair down is not booming reggaeton or salsa – many villages don't have electricity – it's the sweet acoustic tones of the *marimba de chonta*. Made from the wood of a spiny palm tree native to the zone and tubes of *guadua*, the *marimba de chonta* has a distinct sound famous throughout the country. The instrument has its origins in Africa and is part of the cultural heritage of that continent brought to the Pacific region by freed slaves. It is still made the traditional way in artisanal workshops throughout the region, but especially around Guapi and Tumaco.

The *marimba de chonta* is traditionally played hanging from the ceiling, although these days you often see it supported by a stand, and accompanied by percussion instruments including *bombos, cununos* and *guasas*. It is the main musical protagonist in *El Currulao* – the typical dance of the area.

The most convenient place to hear the *marimba de chonta* in all its glory is during the Festival Petronio Álvarez in Cali.

Sleeping & Eating

There are a dozen or more hotels in Ladrilleros; most are pretty basic. Half a dozen simple eateries serve budget meals of fish and rice. For a tasty snack try the shrimp empanadas (savory pastries) at Restaurante Delfin.

In La Barra a number of local families have constructed cabañas for visitors (rooms per person COP$15,000 to COP$25,000) and there are numerous places to pitch a tent (with/without tent rental from COP$12,500/5000 per person). Most accommodations and a couple of dedicated eateries here serve fish meals for around COP$12,000.

Hotel La Cooperativa GUESTHOUSE $
(321-854-7956; Ladrilleros; r per person COP$20,000) The standout option among the cheapies, La Cooperativa catches the breeze up on the bluff and has clean rooms with private bathrooms and solid walls (not to be taken for granted around here).

Aguamarina Cabañas HOTEL $$
(311-728-3213, 246-0285; www.reservaaguamarina.com; Ladrilleros; r/cabaña per person incl 2 meals COP$110,000/90,000;) This friendly, well-run place set on the ocean bluff has attractive two-story cabins and more modern air-conditioned hotel accommodations, along with a large swimming pool. Accepts credit cards.

Hotel Palma Real HOTEL $$
(317-502-5931; www.hotelpalmarealcolombia.com; Ladrilleros; r per person incl 2 meals COP$85,000;) This upscale hotel is popular with *caleños* on romantic getaways and has comfortable air-conditioned rooms with

wood floors and cable TV set around a pretty pool with a poolside bar.

Yubartas LODGE $$
(310-849-6741; Juanchaco; r per person incl 3 meals COP$90,000) Offering elegant wooden cabañas with private bathrooms set in a large garden, this lodge in Juanchaco is one of the most comfortable accommodations options on this side of the airstrip. The management organizes ecological activities around Bahía Málaga. It's in front of the air strip.

Drinking

Templo del Ritmo BAR
(Ladrilleros; noon-late Fri & Sat) On the bluff overlooking the sea, Templo del Ritmo cranks up the volume on weekends, when *caleños* come to party.

Information

There are no ATMs here, and few places accept credit cards. You'll find the nearest ATM just outside the *muelle turístico* in Buenaventura.

Both Ladrilleros and Juanchaco have internet cafes.

Getting There & Away

The most reliable boat operator on the *muelle turístico* is **Asturias** (313-767-2864, 240-4048; barcoasturias@hotmail.com). It offers daily services to Juanchaco (round trip COP$54,000, 1¼ hours) at 10am, 1pm and 4pm, returning at 8am, 1pm and 4pm. The round-trip fare is good for 15 days. The trip can be rough – sit at the back for a more comfortable ride.

From Juanchaco it's 2.5km to Ladrilleros. The road loops around a naval airbase that divides the two towns. You can walk (30 minutes), hop

ISLA MALPELO

This tiny, remote Colombian island has some of the best diving in the world. A World Heritage site, it's a mere 1643m long and 727m wide, and is 378km from the mainland. It is the center of the vast **Santuario de Flora y Fauna Malpelo** (☑1-353-2400 ext 138; ecoturismo@parquesnacionales.gov.co; admission per day on Colombian/foreign boat COP$88,500/165,500), the largest no-fishing zone in the Eastern Tropical Pacific, which provides a critical habitat for threatened marine species.

The diversity and, above all, the size of the marine life is eye-popping, and includes over 200 hammerhead sharks and 1000 silky sharks. It is also one of the few places where sightings of the short-nosed ragged-tooth shark, a deepwater shark, have been confirmed. The volcanic island has steep walls and impressive caves. The best time to see the sharks is January to March, when colder weather drives them to the surface to feed. A small contingent of Colombian soldiers guard Malpelo, and it's forbidden to set foot on the island.

The quality of the diving is matched only by the difficulty of getting there, and the difficulty of the diving itself. The island can only be visited as part of a live-aboard dive cruise. Travel time is 30 to 36 hours each way from Buenaventura, and there is no decompression chamber on the island. There are strong currents that pull you up, down and sideways – you may well surface kilometers from where you entered the water. Only advanced divers with experience and confidence should attempt this trip.

Boats from various countries offer this trip. Your cheapest option is the Colombian-flagged boats operating out of Buenaventura although they generally pack lots of divers onto each trip and do not usually carry nitrox. Expect to pay around COP$3,100,000 per diver for seven days of diving. One boat with regular departures is the *Maria Patricia* owned by Asturias (p267).

A step up in comfort are the international boats operating out of Panama. The most spacious is the **MV Yemaya** (☑in Panama 507-232-0215; www.coibadiveexpeditions.com) sailing out of Puerto Mutis, which has three kinds of double cabins and capacity for up to 16 divers. Another recommended option is the **Inula** (☑in Germany 49 5130 790326, in Panama 507-6672-9091; www.inula-diving.com), out of Puerto David, run by a very experienced German skipper. Prices range from US$3700 to US$4660 per diver excluding park fees for a 10-day trip including around six days diving.

Alternatively, contact **Pura Colombia Travel** (☑310-373-0113; www.puracolombia. com), a Medellín-based tour operator specializing in diving that has a lot of experience in Malpelo and maintains a list of pending departures.

on a motorcycle (COP$2000, five minutes) or wait for one of the jeeps to fill up (COP$2000 per person).

To get to La Barra you can either take a moto-taxi or a small boat along the river – both charge COP$15,000 per person. Alternatively, it's a 45-minute walk along a sometimes muddy track.

San Cipriano

☑2 / POP 500

This tiny Afro-Colombian town is as famous for its mode of arrival as for the town itself. Situated on the little-used Cali–Buenaventura railroad and 15km from the nearest road, residents have come up with ingenious homemade rail trolleys powered by motorcycles, the front wheel fixed in the air, the back wheel in contact with one of the rails. Passengers sit on small wooden benches as they fly through the lush jungle at ridiculous speed – a truly remarkable experience. There is only one track and many trolleys are deficient in the brakes department. While not common, crashes have been reported. Hold on tight and wear shoes so you can jump off in an emergency.

The town is in the middle of the jungle on the Pacific side of the mountain range. A nearby river with crystal-clear water makes for a relaxing swim. You can go inner-tubing along much of its length – many places rent tubes for around COP$5000. There are also several waterfalls you can walk to. Guides for treks charge around COP$20,000 per group.

It rains heavily here so bring wet weather gear. The Fundación San Cipriano charges COP$1500 admission to the area.

🛏 Sleeping & Eating

Half a dozen hotels offer very basic lodging. Most offer budget meals. On weekends a couple of bars blast out music for partying *caleños*.

Hotel David   GUESTHOUSE $
(☎312-815-4051; s/d without bathroom COP$15,000/25,000) Several hundred meters after you pay your admission fee you'll find this friendly place. It has simple rooms on the 2nd floor with bare concrete floors and tin roofs, which make the heavy rains even more atmospheric. The wooden walls ensure guests hear everything going on in the room next door. It serves some of the best food in town.

Hotel Ivankar   GUESTHOUSE $
(☎310-456-8120; s/d COP$25,000/50,000) The most comfortable hotel in town offers clean concrete rooms with private bathrooms and cable TV. Most only have a tiny window onto the corridor which means they don't get much natural light or breeze. Try to grab the front room, which has a window onto the street.

ℹ Getting There & Away

From Cali, take any bus heading to Buenaventura and get off at the junction to Córdoba (COP$18,000, three hours). From here it's a 1km walk downhill to the railway line.

The official fare for visitors on a rail trolley to San Cipriano is COP$5000 each way; locals pay less, which is why drivers like to compete to get travelers on board. Be prepared to be led down the hill by touts when you disembark the bus.

From Buenaventura, take the Ruta 5 bus marked Córdoba from the terminal (COP$2000, 45 minutes). The bus runs every half-hour or so. If you don't want to walk back uphill, you can grab this bus back to the junction.

Buenaventura taxis can also deliver you to Córdoba for COP$25,000 to COP$40,000.

Parque Nacional Natural (PNN) Isla Gorgona

In late 2014 an unprecedented FARC attack on **Parque Nacional Natural (PNN) Isla Gorgona** destroyed the security post on the island and resulted in the death of a police officer. As a consequence, the company running the tourist facilities pulled out and the government has closed the park to visitors. Once the security situation is resolved, it's possible that the facility will be reopened under new management. Check the latest with Parques Nacionales (p74) before making plans.

The two main reasons to visit the park are for scuba diving and whale-watching, preferably at the same time. Gorgona is not on any of the main shipping channels, so whales continue to come here every year to calve and raise their young.

The island is 38km off the coast and is 11km long by 2.3km wide. It is covered in young, secondary rainforest (the convicts chopped down most of the trees for cooking fuel), which harbors an abundance of poisonous snakes. Gorgona is also noted for a large number of endemic species. You'll see many monkeys, lizards, bats and birds. Sea turtles come during breeding season and lay eggs on the beaches.

Ironically, in darker times, Gorgona was one of the few safe places tourists could visit on the Pacific coast. Now that conditions have improved in other parts of the region, you'll find there are better beaches and wilder jungle elsewhere.

☞ Tours

For divers who don't want to stay on the island, boats out of Buenaventura offer weekend live-aboard diving trips, departing the *muelle turístico* on Friday night and returning Monday morning. The *Maria Patricia* (owned by Asturias (p267)) charges around COP$1,350,000 per diver, including four dives, meals, transportation and a visit to the island. Nondivers pay COP$800,000.

ℹ Information

Gorgona got its Greek-mythology-derived name for a reason: it's an island full of poisonous snakes. Bring good solid footwear if you plan to go on hikes or ask to borrow gumboots. Yellow fever vaccinations are essential – park guides may demand to see your certificate on arrival.

ℹ Getting There & Away

When the park is open, speedboats run to the island from the small town of Guapi (1¼ hours) on Mondays and Fridays.

There are a number of companies running covered speedboat services (COP$95,000, three to four hours) between Buenaventura and Guapi, including **Transporte Jomar** (☎313-761-7571, 313-715-3335; Muelle Turístico, Buenaventura) and **Embarcaciones Alfa** (☎316-842-9861, 241-7599; sheli2838@hotmail.com; Muelle Turístico, Buenaventura). Aeropuerto Juan Casino Solis in Guapi is serviced by **Satena** (☎1 800 091 2034; www.satena.com) with flights to Cali. TAC (p168) offers three flights a week to/from Popayán.

Amazon Basin

Includes ➡

Best Places to Eat

➡ El Santo Angel (p276)

➡ El Cielo (p276)

➡ Tierras Amazónicas (p276)

➡ Las Margaritas (p281)

➡ São Jorge (p278)

Best Places to Stay

➡ Reserva Natural Palmarí (p281)

➡ Malokas Napü (p280)

➡ Amazon B&B (p275)

➡ Waira Suites Hotel (p275)

➡ Mahatu Jungle Hostel (p274)

Why Go?

Amazon. The very word evokes images of pristine jungle, incredible wildlife and one famous river. The Amazon basin, which Colombians call Amazonia, is a 643,000-sq-km region accounting for a third of Colombia's total area – about the size of California. Visitors can never quite account for the strange exhilaration they feel when they come face-to-face with the rainforest for the first time.

With transportation limited to rivers that crisscross the jungle, indigenous groups deep in the jungle have managed to keep their cultures intact. But in the cities, many indigenous and mestizo (mixed race) people now live modern lifestyles, driving Yamahas and only breaking out their traditional garb and customs for the benefit of tourists. A visit here remains a transcendent experience, from thrilling rainforest treks to simple hammock siestas soundtracked by the otherworldly sounds of the jungle.

When to Go
Leticia

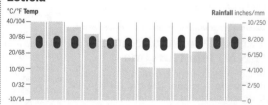

Sep–Nov Lower water levels afford excellent hiking and reveal white-sand beaches on the Río Yavarí.

Mar–May Get closer to the canopy in wet season, the climax of bird-watching and wildlife season.

Jul & Aug Loathe mosquitoes? The *terra firme* forest sees most retreat to the canopy.

Leticia

🎵 8 / POP 39,667 / ELEV 95M

As the capital city of the Amazonas province, Leticia is the largest city for hundreds of kilometers yet still looks and feels very much like a small frontier town. It's located on the Amazon River at the crossroads – or more accurately, the cross-river – point where Colombia, Brazil and Peru meet. Leticia is located about 800km from the nearest Colombian highway.

Leticia was founded in 1867 as San Antonio. The origin of its current name has been lost to history. In any case, it was part of Peru until 1922 when both countries signed a controversial agreement that ceded the land to Colombia. In 1932 a war broke out between Colombia and Peru, finally ending in 1933 after the League of Nations negotiated a cease-fire, ultimately awarding Leticia to Colombia. In the 1970s Leticia became a lawless hub of narcotics trafficking until

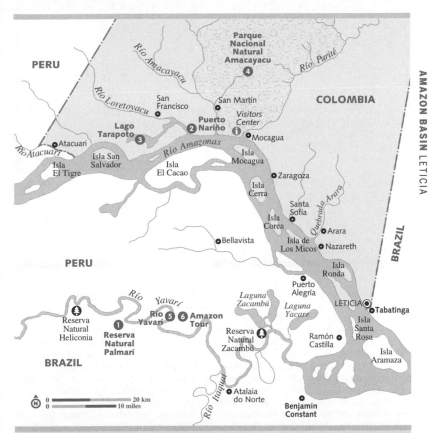

Amazon Basin Highlights

❶ Spend a few days observing abundant wildlife at the excellent **Reserva Natural Palmarí** (p281).

❷ Unwind in the car-free, sustainable and funky remote village of **Puerto Nariño** (p279).

❸ Spot pink and gray dolphins on the warm waters of the mighty **Lago Tarapoto** (p280).

❹ Be serenaded by parrots in the rainforest of **Parque Nacional Natural (PNN) Amacayacu** (p279).

❺ Slip silently into the jungle by canoe up the tributaries of the **Río Yavarí** (p281).

❻ Go beyond the lodges on a multiday **Amazon tour** (p273), where you'll really be welcomed to the jungle!

Leticia

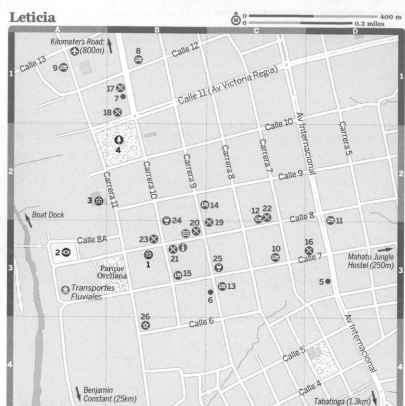

the Colombian army moved in and cleaned things up.

Leticia is on the banks of the Amazon on the Colombia–Brazil border. Just across the frontier sits Tabatinga, a Brazilian town much the same size as Leticia, with its own airport and port – the main gateway for boats downstream to Manaus. Visitors can freely move between the two cities as well as the Brazilian city of Benjamin Constant, 25km downstream, and the Peruvian island of Santa Rosa opposite Leticia/Tabatinga. Travelers wishing to venture further into either country must meet immigration requirements.

Despite oppressive heat, humidity and ferocious mosquitoes, Leticia makes a pleasant base for exploring the rest of the Amazon.

◉ Sights & Activities

★ **Mundo Amazónico**　　　　　　GARDENS
(☑ 592-6087, 321-472-4346; www.mundoamazon-ico.com; Km7.7, Vía Tarapacá; tours COP$10,000;

⊙8am-3pm) 🖉 This 29-hectare reserve was designed to preserve endangered flora and fauna of the Amazon, and functions as a center for environmental education. The extensive botanical gardens boast some 700 species of flora that can be visited on four differently themed tours (the botanical garden, sustainable processes, cultural scenarios and the aquarium), each lasting between 30 and 45 minutes.

You can combine as many tours as you like, and they'll even serve lunch for COP$20,000 per person if you'd like to make a day of it. Only two guides speak English though, so it's a good idea to call ahead and book. To get here from Leticia take any bus to Km7.7 and then follow the sign off the main road down the track for 10 minutes.

Museo Etnográfico Amazónico　　MUSEUM
(☑ 592-7729; Carrera 11 No 9-43; ⊙8:30-11:30am & 1:30-5pm Mon-Fri, 9am-1pm Sat) This small mu-

Leticia

seum located inside the dolphin-pink-colored Biblioteca del Banco de la República building has a small collection of indigenous artifacts including musical instruments, textiles, tools, pottery and weapons, and lots of ceremonial masks. It's all signed in English, and makes a good introduction to the indigenous cultures of the region.

Galería Arte Uirapuru MUSEUM
(Calle 8 No 10-35; ⊙ 8:30am-noon & 1-7pm Mon-Sat, 8:30am-noon Sun) Leticia's largest craft shop, selling artifacts from local indigenous groups, as well as a natural Amazonian pharmacy that includes herbal 'Viagra.' At the back of the shop is Museo Uirapuru, featuring a tiny exhibition of historic crafts (not for sale).

Parque Santander PARK
A visit to this park just before sunset makes for an impressive spectacle as you witness thousands of small screeching *pericos* (parrots) arriving for their nightly rest.

Reserva Tanimboca OUTDOORS
(📞592-7679, 310-791-7470; www.tanimboca.com; Km11, Vía Tarapacá; full-day pass COP$120,000, ziplining COP$65,000, kayaking COP$40,000; ⊙8am-4pm; 🛗) 🌿 Visitors can monkey around atop 35m-high trees, then slide 80m along ziplines from one tree to another through the beautiful forest canopy. There's also kayaking, or splurge for an overnight stay in one of two treehouses (per person including breakfast COP$110,000), which includes a nocturnal jungle hike. There is also the possibility of sleeping in hammocks

or beds in a dorm (per person hammock/bed COP$25,000/30,000). The reserve also arranges multiday jungle trips from its office in Leticia.

ⓕ Tours

The real jungle begins well off the Amazon proper, along its small tributaries. The deeper you go, the more chance you have to observe wildlife in relatively undamaged habitats and to visit indigenous settlements. This involves time and money, but the experience can be rewarding. A three- to four-day tour is perhaps the best way to balance the cost of the trip with the insight it will give you into the workings of the jungle, but it's also important to mention that expectations must be managed. Significant wildlife spotting is exceedingly rare in the Amazon: the animals aren't exactly social with people, they are hidden in the canopy, and encroachment by tourism and local customs and industry have driven populations of various animals to frighteningly low numbers. You have a reasonable chance of spotting macaws, monkeys and pink or gray dolphins in addition to numerous birds and the occasional odd fauna, but keep in mind the jungle is also about the sights, sounds and allure of one of the world's most fascinating and mysterious places.

Several companies organize multiday tours to the small nature reserves along the Río Yavarí on the Brazil–Peru border. Always agree on price, activities and duration before embarking on your trip. Avoid any unsolicited tour guides who approach you in the airport or streets.

Some highly recommended and experienced guides we can suggest include **Elaise Cuao** (☏ 311-828-7430; aguilaharpia@hotmail.es), who speaks English, Portuguese and a little French, and **Eliceo Matapi** (☏ 321-412-8372; elima725_2@hotmail.com), who speaks fluent English and is specialized in bird-watching and jungle adventures.

However, it's infrastructure that's vital in the jungle, and the following agencies run their own reserves.

Amazon Jungle Trips TOURS

(☏ 592-7377, 321-426-7757; www.amazonjungletrips.com.co; Av Internacional No 6-25) With more than 25 years of experience catering to backpackers, Amazon Jungle is one of the oldest and most reliable tour companies in Leticia. Owner Antonio Cruz Pérez speaks fluent English and can arrange individually tailored tours, including trips to the two very different reserves the company runs: Reserva Natural Zacambú and Tupana Arü Ü.

Zacambú is on the Río Yavarí in Peru, while Tupana Arü Ü is 60km upriver on the Amazon and deeper in the jungle. Both lodges are around an hour's boat ride from Leticia, though there's an extra 45-minute walk to Tupana Arü Ü from the river once you arrive at the settlement of La Libertad. A trip that includes a night or two at both reserves is optimal and surprisingly affordable at COP$250,000 per person per day and all-inclusive. Facilities are simple but include running water and mosquito nets, the food is good, guides are professional and the welcome is warm.

Selvaventura TOURS

(☏ 592-3977, 311-287-1307; www.selvaventura.org; Carrera 9 No 6-85) Owner Felipe Ulloa speaks English, Spanish and Portuguese and can arrange a variety of trips into the jungle to both high-forest and *igapó* (flooded) ecosystems, as well as selling tickets for various river trips into Peru and Brazil. The agency makes use of the Maloka jungle camp and the less remote Agape (at Km10).

From the latter it's possible to kayak down a small river to the Amazon proper: a good chance to see giant water lilies. Trips to Palmarí and Zacambú are also possible, staying with locals rather than in jungle camps to keep things affordable. For two people, you're looking at COP$1,300,000 per person for an all-inclusive five-day tour.

Tanimboca Tours TOURS

(☏ 592-7679; www.tanimboca.org; Carrera 10 No 11-69) In addition to the activities on offer at Reserva Tanimboca (p273) to the north of Leticia, the friendly folks here can organize boat or hiking trips into the jungle outside Leticia, including trips to indigenous villages. The owner speaks Serbian, German and English and several of the guides also speak English.

🛏 Sleeping

Note that prices can skyrocket during high season, especially around Christmas and Easter.

La Casa del Kurupira HOSTEL $

(☏ 592-6160, 311-287-1307; www.casadelkurupira.com; Carrera 9 No 6-85; dm COP$25,000, d COP$75,000, without bathroom COP$40,000-60,000; ☜) Operated by the owners of Selvaventura across the street (whose offices also function as a bar and social area for the hostel), this new hostel is very clean, bright and modern, with ceiling fans cooling the rooms and a large shared kitchen and roof terrace strewn with hammocks to chill out in. Laundry costs COP$10,000 and breakfast COP$7000.

Mahatu Jungle Hostel HOSTEL $

(☏ 311-539-1265; www.mahatu.org; Calle 7 No 1-40; dm COP$25,000, s/d COP$60,000/70,000; ☜🖥) You can begin your jungle exploration in Leticia at this beautiful hostel, which sits on 5 hectares, complete with duck- and geese-filled ponds, throngs of *pericos* and loads of exotic fruit trees – cashew, *asaí, cananguche* and *copasú* among them. Rooms are very simple and fan cooled with shared bathroom, but you're paying for the lush environs. Owner/philosopher Gustavo Rene is multilingual. It's a five-minute walk from the center of Leticia.

La Jangada GUESTHOUSE $

(☏ 312-361-6506, 311-498-5447; lajangadaleticia@gmail.com; Carrera 9 No 8-106; dm COP$25,000, s/d with bathroom COP$50,000/70,000, without bathroom COP$35,000/50,000; @☜) An excellent guesthouse run by a young Swiss-Colombian couple; the Swiss half has traversed 45,000km of Amazon rivers in his ecologically sound bicycle-powered boat, on which you can now do day tours (from COP$60,000). There's a five-bed dorm with a breezy balcony and hammock and a few private rooms with fan.

Hospedaje Los Delfines GUESTHOUSE **$**
(☏592-7488; losdelfinesleticia@hotmail.com; Carrera 11 No 12-85; s/d/tr COP$40,000/70,000/90,000; 🛜) Doña Betty extends a genial welcome to her guests at this budget 10-room place. With potable water treated on-site, a lovely garden full of fruit and flowers and friendly owners who are usually ready to do deals on room prices, this place is good value, although the fan-cooled rooms themselves are rather dark and pretty basic.

Omshanty LODGE **$**
(☏311-489-8985; www.omshanty.com; Km11 Vía Tarapaca; dm/s/d/tr/q COP$15,000/40,000/60,000/80,000/95,000) In a thick jungle setting and not strictly in Leticia itself, Omshanty is nevertheless an option to consider if you'd rather spend all your time in the Amazon in the jungle. The cabins sleep up to four and each has its own kitchen for self-caterers. Friendly English-speaking owner Kike organizes jungle excursions. It's possible to camp here too (COP$10,000 per person per night), but you'll need your own tent.

★ Amazon B&B B&B **$$**
(☏592-4981; www.amazonbb.com; Calle 12 No 9-30; s/d incl breakfast COP$102,000/169,000, cabaña s/d/tr COP$130,000/216,000/290,000; 🛜) Leticia's most charming and stylish option, this small hotel comprises six cabañas and four rooms surrounding a well-manicured garden. The cabañas are gorgeous and come with high ceilings, well-stocked minibars and small, enclosed terraces with hammocks. The decor in all rooms follows a minimalist-chic aesthetic previously unseen in town. There's also the Amazon Spanish College on the property.

Hotel Malokamazonas BOUTIQUE HOTEL **$$**
(☏592-6642, 311-474-3571; malokamazonasleticia@gmail.com; Calle 8 No 5-49; dm/s/d/tw/tr incl breakfast COP$45,000/60,000/120,000/140,000/180,000; 🌐🛜) This charming place has been thoughtfully designed, with nine comfortable and attractive rooms (including what must be the most spacious dorm in town) set amid a garden overflowing with orchids and fruit trees. There's an abundance of natural wood furniture and indigenous handicrafts, and the welcome is warm and professional.

Hotel de la Selva HOTEL **$$**
(☏314-803-4661; hoteldelaselvaleticia@hotmail.com; Calle 7 No 7-28; s/d with air-con COP$65,000/115,000, without air-con COP$50,000/95,000; 🌐🛜) The plant-filled entrance corridor and courtyard make this friendly place even more welcoming. There are 14 rooms, all with private bathroom, some even shaken up a bit with local handicrafts and *costilla* wood bedframes. Breakfast is an extra COP$8000 and the location is excellent.

Hotel Yurupary HOTEL **$$**
(☏592-6529, 311-505-6875; www.hotelyurupary.com; Calle 8 No 7-26; r incl breakfast COP$98,000-165,000; 🌐🛜🐾) The enormous tribal wood-work key-rings may be a little out of step with the gleamingly modern lobby, but this midrange place has some lovely traditional handicrafts in it too, and rooms are bright and comfortable. The outside courtyard features a great swimming pool, garden, bar and restaurant.

Waira Suites Hotel HOTEL **$$$**
(☏592-4428; www.wairahotel.com.co; Carrera 10' No 7-36; s/d incl breakfast COP$164,000/256,000; 🌐🛜🐾) Its sleek white building and fittings set it apart from the usual dusty Amazon hotels here, and so while it's definitely comfortable, some rooms are a little small and it's definitely a little overpriced. That said the pool is the best in town, set amid a new but growing garden, and staff are professional and polite.

🍴 Eating

Leticia's local specialty is fish, including the delicious *gamitana* and the overfished *pirarucú*, which is best avoided out of season as locals routinely ignore regulations preventing fishing for this species when it's spawning.

Prices tend to be a bit higher than in 'mainland' Colombia, but many restaurants serve cheap set meals. You can also find cheap eats at the **local market** (cnr Calle 8 & waterfront; ⏱5am-7pm).

La Cava Tropical COLOMBIAN **$**
(Carrera 9 No 8-22; set meals COP$7000; ⏱10am-6pm; 🌐) This open-air restaurant is the locals' lunchtime favorite. The set meals include a soup (often a tasty *sancocho*), small salad, a meat dish with a side of beans or veggies, and bottomless fresh juice at a very reasonable price. It can get quite crowded during the weekday lunch rush and there's an air-con section!

ⓘ DON'T MISS YOUR BOAT!

Tabatinga is one hour ahead of Leticia. Don't miss your boat!

Viejo Tolima   COLOMBIAN $
(Calle 8 No 10-20; mains COP$2500-15,000; ⊙8am-8pm Mon-Sat) This friendly, clean and atmospheric spot is a great place to come for an excellent breakfast (yummy *caldos* – soups) as well as fresh fruit juices and other local bites at any other time.

La Casa del Pan   BAKERY $
(Calle 11 No 10-20; breakfast COP$5000-10,000; ⊙7am-noon & 1-8pm) Facing Parque Santander, this friendly spot for a basic but filling breakfast of eggs, bread and coffee is a favorite with budget travelers.

Supermercado Hiper   SUPERMARKET $
(Calle 8 No 9-29; ⊙8am-6pm Mon-Sat) The best-stocked supermarket in town is a good place for self-caterers and anyone hoarding snacks for a jungle trip.

★El Santo Angel   INTERNATIONAL $$
(Carrera 10 No 11-119; mains COP$10,000-25,000; ⊙5pm-midnight Tue-Sat, noon-midnight Sun) This newcomer easily has the most varied and interesting menu in town; it includes wraps, nachos, salads, grills, panini, burgers and pizza. With inventive touches to the cooking and pleasant outside dining (avoid the sterile interior if possible), this may well be Leticia's best eating option.

Tierras Amazónicas   SEAFOOD, AMAZONIAN $$
(Calle 8 No 7-50; mains COP$15,000-20,000; ⊙11am-10pm Tue-Sun; ⊙) At first glance, this looks like an unapologetic tourist trap with walls covered in kitschy Amazonia knick-knacks and a huge metallic piranha sculpture greeting you at the entrance. Nonetheless, it's a fantastic place for a fun dinner. The specialty is fish, and that's what you should order. There's a full bar and occasional live music.

El Cielo   AMAZON FUSION $$
(Calle 7 No 6-50; mains COP$13,000-25,000; ⊙6-11pm Mon-Sat) Showcasing what it sees as the future of local cooking, this cool, creative space serves up *casabes* (mini pizzas made from yuca instead of flour) with imaginative toppings that combine all manner of local and national ingredients. The staff are friendly and the jungle-print-clad dining room is as close to designer as you'll get in these parts.

Restaurante Amektiar   COLOMBIAN $$
(Carrera 9 No 8-15; mains COP$10,000-30,000; ⊙noon-11:30pm; ✱⊙) Another welcome new arrival to Leticia, Amektiar serves up an array of dishes, from simple but vast *arepas* (corn cakes) and sandwiches to Mexican fast food and more elaborate *parrilla* (grill) dishes. It's throughly modern, with a nicely lit and welcomingly chilly interior, though the breezy terrace is good for evening dining.

 Drinking & Entertainment

Barbacoas   BAR, POOL HALL
(Carrera 10 No 8-28; ⊙10am-midnight) Unlike most Colombian billiards clubs that only cater to men, ladies are warmly welcomed at Barbacoas – probably because the pool tables are hidden in a separate back room. The sidewalk cafe is a pleasant place to people-watch over a beer.

Kawanna Bar   BAR
(Carrera 9 & Calle 7; ⊙6pm-midnight Sun-Thu, 6pm-2am Fri & Sat) A good spot for a relaxed beer on the terrace once the sun is setting; there's also dancing inside later on and at weekends.

Blue   CLUB
(Carrera 11 No 6-19; ⊙7pm-late Thu-Sat) Leticia's more upscale nightclub, which hosts a funny live-music mix on Thursday and Friday with Brazilian *pagoda* (a type of samba) and live reggaeton. On Saturdays DJs take over. It caters to a mix of well-to-do locals and tourists alike.

ⓘ Information

DANGERS & ANNOYANCES
A long-standing military presence in the region tries to keep Leticia/Tabatinga and the surrounding region safe, but there are issues. Former narcotraffickers, guerrillas, paramilitaries and *raspachines* (coca-plant harvesters) who have been re-inserted into mainstream society and now live on the outskirts of Leticia and Puerto Nariño run poker houses, dubious bars and the like around the city. Don't wander outside these urban areas on your own at night, especially on Leticia's infamous 'Los Kilometros' road. In Peru, narcotraffickers remain in business in this wayward corner of the country and have harassed tourists who have wandered off the beaten track. Tour operators and lodges in the region have been issued warnings about where they can and cannot bring tourists, so don't stray on your own beyond areas where local tourism guides normally operate.

EMERGENCY

Police (☑ 592-5060; Carrera 11 No 12-32) Between Calles 12 and 13.

MEDICAL SERVICES

San Rafael de Leticia Hospital (☑ 592-7826; Carrera 10 No 13-78) The only hospital in town.

MONEY

There are ATMs all over the center of town, but it's impossible to change traveler's checks here. To exchange currency, look for the *casas de cambio* on Calle 8 between Carrera 11 and the market. They change US dollars, Colombian pesos, Brazilian reais and Peruvian nuevos soles. Shop around as rates vary. Businesses in both Tabatinga and Leticia generally accept both reais and pesos.

Cambios El Opita (cnr Carrera 11 & Calle 8; ☺ 9am-5pm Mon-Sat) Currency exchange.

POST

4-72 (Calle 8 No 9-56; ☺ 8am-noon & 2-5pm Mon-Fri) Post office.

TOURIST INFORMATION

Tourist Office (Secretaría de Turismo y Fronteras; ☑ 592-7569; Calle 8 No 9-75; ☺ 7am-noon & 2-5pm Mon-Sat, 7am-noon Sun) Friendly, English-speaking. There is also a small booth at the airport during scheduled flights.

❶ Getting There & Away

The only way to get to Leticia is by boat or by air.

All foreigners must pay COP$20,000 tourist tax upon arrival at Leticia's airport, Aeropuerto Internacional Alfredo Vásquez Cobo, to the north of the town.

Avianca (☑ 592-6021; www.avianca.com; Alfredo Vásquez Cobo Airport; ☺ 8am-1.30pm Mon-Sat & 3-6pm Mon-Fri) and **Lan** (www.lan. com; Alfredo Vásquez Cobo Airport) have daily flights to Bogotá. Book early for the best rates.

Trip (www.voetrip.com.br) and **Tam** (www. tam.com.br) fly from Tabatinga International Airport to Manaus daily. The airport is 4km south of Tabatinga; *colectivos* marked 'Comara' from Leticia will drop you nearby. Don't forget to get your Colombian exit stamp at Leticia's airport and, if needed, a Brazilian visa before departure.

When departing Letica's airport, all foreigners must check in at the Ministry of Foreign Relations before proceeding through airport security, regardless of whether you've left Colombia or not; you'll be directed there at check-in if you haven't done it already – it's a painless procedure that takes a matter of seconds.

BORDER INFORMATION

Both locals and foreigners are allowed to come and go between Leticia, Tabatinga and Benjamin Constant and the surrounding Colombian, Brazilian and Peruvian jungle within an 80km radius of Leticia without visas or passport control, but if you plan on heading further afield, you must get your passport stamped at the Ministry of Foreign Relations office at Leticia's airport. Importantly, you must get a second stamp (from either the Brazilian or Peruvian authorities) within 24 hours, so plan carefully. If you have an early departure from Leticia by boat, you'll need to get your stamp at the airport the day before.

Citizens of some countries, including the USA, Canada, Australia and New Zealand, need a visa to enter Brazil and it may be costly. To avoid a lot of stress and heartache, it's strongly recommended to arrange your visa before arriving in

AMAZON BASIN LETICIA

GETTING TO PERU

High-speed passenger boats between Tabatinga and Iquitos (Peru) are operated by **Transtur** (☑ 3-412-2945; www.transtursa.com; Rua Marechal Mallet 248, Tabatinga) and **Transportes Golfinho** (☑ 313-202-6679; www.transportegolfinho.com; Rua Marechal Mallet 306, Tabatinga). Boats leave from Isla Santa Rosa daily around 5am except Monday, arriving in Iquitos about 10 hours later. Don't forget to get your Colombian exit stamp at the Leticia airport's Ministry of Foreign Relations office the day before departure. You can buy tickets through Selvaventura (p274) in Leticia, as neither company has an office in town at present.

The journey costs US$70 in either direction, including breakfast and lunch (mint-condition banknotes only; or COP$150,000). During dry season you can sometimes only access Isla Santa Rosa from Tabatinga's Porta da Feira, where water levels are always high. Check ahead. In fact, it's always easier in the middle of the night to go from Tabatinga, but taxi prices from Leticia can skyrocket to COP$30,000 for the ride.

Be warned: there are slower, cheaper boats to Iquitos, but they are not comfortable, barely seaworthy and should be avoided.

Note there are no roads out of Iquitos into Peru. You have to fly or continue by river to Pucallpa (five to seven days), from where you can go overland to Lima.

the Amazon. But if you must, bring a passport photo and yellow-fever vaccination certificate to the Brazilian consulate (p313). Processing time is one to three days, depending on volume. If you're coming from or going to Iquitos, get your entry or exit stamp at the **Policía Internacional Peruviano (PIP) office** (Isla Santa Rosa). Travelers coming here from Brazil may need to visit the **Colombian consulate** (📞 412-2104; Rua General Sampaio 623, Tabatinga; ⊗ 8am-2pm Mon-Fri) to get the necessary visa.

If you need a Colombian visa extension, there is no need to pay an extension fee. Simply stamp out and head to Brazil or Peru for one day and return for a fresh 60 days up to the allocable time per year.

ℹ Getting Around

The main mode of public transportation is by moto-taxi, the folks on motorcycles that zip around town with an extra helmet. The base rate is COP$2000. Frequent *colectivos* (COP$2000 to COP$6000) link Leticia with Tabatinga and the 'Kilometer' villages north of Leticia's airport. Standard taxis are pricier than in the rest of Colombia; a short ride from the airport to town runs COP$8000, to Tabatinga's airport COP$15,000 and to the Porto Bras in Tabatinga COP$10,000.

Tabatinga (Brazil)

📞 97 / POP 52,272 / ELEV 95M

This gritty, unattractive border town doesn't have much to offer in terms of tourist attractions. Most visitors are only here to catch a boat to Manaus or Iquitos, or they're on a quick border hop just to say they've been to Brazil. While it's distinctly less pleasant than Leticia, you might consider staying here if you're taking an early morning boat to Iquitos. Prices listed are in Brazilian reais, though Colombian pesos are accepted. Brazil's telephone country code is +55.

🛏 Sleeping

Avoid the hotels near the border; some of them double as brothels.

Novo Hotel HOTEL $
(📞 97-3412-3846; novohoteltbt@hotmail.com; Rua Pedro Texeira 9; s/d/tr COP$55,000/65,000/75,000; 🖤) Conveniently located just three blocks from Porta da Feira, this friendly, clean option is perfect if you're catching an early boat.

✕ Eating

★**São Jorge** PERUVIAN $$
(Av da Amizade 1941; mains R$20-40; ⊗ 9am-9:30pm Mon-Sat, to 6pm Sun) Locals on both sides of the border rave about the authentic ceviche at this simple Peruvian-run spot: the mountainous pile of excellent citrus-cooked fish and onions served on a bed of sweet potatoes and chunky corn serve two. It seems strange to walk from Colombia to Brazil for Peruvian ceviche, but that's the beauty of the tri-border!

Bella Epoca BRAZILIAN $$
(Rua Pedro Texeira 589; per kg R$22; ⊗ 11am-3pm) A passable Brazilian *por kilo* (pay-by-weight) restaurant, where you'll find various salads, mains and *churrasco* (grilled meats, including Brazil's tastiest cut, *picanha*).

🍷 Drinking & Nightlife

Scandalos CLUB
(cnr Av da Amizade & Rua Pedro Texeira; cover R$5; ⊗ 9pm-4am Fri & Sat) Some people in Tabatinga told us this club was 'un-Christian, immoral and homosexual,' which means, of course, it's awesome! Located about five blocks from the border, it attracts a young, sexy crowd dancing till dawn.

GETTING TO BRAZIL

Slow boats down the Amazon to Manaus (Brazil) leave from Tabatinga's port on Tuesday, Wednesday and Saturday at noon, though embarkation and customs checks begin from 9:30am. The journey to Manaus takes three days and costs R$200 if you bring your own hammock, or about R$800 to R$1000 for two people in a double cabin.

Traveling upstream from Manaus to Tabatinga, the trip usually takes six days, and costs R$200 in your hammock or R$900 to R$1300 for a double cabin.

Lancha Rápida Puma (📞 97-9154-2597; Tabatinga) runs high-speed boats to Manaus that depart Tabatinga on Friday and Sunday at 9am (R$430, 30 hours); embarkation and customs checks start from 6:30am.

It's easiest to get tickets for both boats from travel agencies in Leticia; they charge a commission, but it's worth paying.

ℹ Information

Tabatinga has a helpful, English-speaking **tourist information center** (Centro de Informação Turística; Av da Amizade s/n; ⊗ 8am-6pm Mon-Fri, to noon Sun), where you can pick up maps of the city and other helpful info.

Isla Santa Rosa (Peru)

Five minutes by boat from Leticia, this tiny island village on the Amazon River has a few rustic *hospedajes* (hostels) and some bars and restaurants, but not much else other than a sketchy reputation. About the only tourist attraction is the giant 'Welcome to Peru' sign. If you're traveling from or going to Iquitos, you'll need to come here and visit the **Policía Internacional Peruviano (PIP)** office to get an exit/entry stamp in your passport. Everything is located along the footpath through town. Water taxis (COP$3000) ply the Leticia–Isla Santa Rosa route from dawn to dusk in high-water season. In the dry season you'll often have to take a boat from Tabatinga to Isla Santa Rosa (COP$6000).

Parque Nacional Natural (PNN) Amacayacu

Sprawling across almost 300,000 hectares, **Parque Nacional Natural (PNN) Amacayacu** (☑8-520-8654; www.parquesnacionales.gov. co; adult/student & under 26 COP$38,000/7000) is an ideal spot from which to observe the Amazonian rainforest up close. About 75km upriver from Leticia, the park is home to 500 species of birds, 150 mammals and dozens of reptiles, including crocs, boas and anacondas. And millions of mosquitoes. Activities include kayaking, bird-watching and multiday hikes.

Visitor amenities include dorm lodges with shared bathrooms, seven luxury cabins with private bathrooms, and a good restaurant. The luxury hotel chain Decameron runs the park's tourist facilities, and with it comes sky-high prices. Simple dorm bunks cost COP$112,000 to COP$210,000 depending on the season; rooms start at COP$375,000 for a double.

High-speed boats to Puerto Nariño will drop you off at the visitor center (COP$24,000, 1½ hours from Leticia). Boats often fill up; buy your tickets in advance. To get back to Letitica, call **Transportes Fluviales** (☑8-592-5999, 8-592-6711) in Leticia

(inside the shopping mall on the waterfront; look for Cafeteria PAN Colombia) and reserve a seat on the boat back to town; you'll need to pay full price (COP$29,000), but it's the best way to ensure there's space on the boat. As a last resort, try flagging down one of the slow cargo ships or *peque-peques* (small motorized boats) back to Leticia.

Puerto Nariño

☑ 8 / POP 6000 / ELEV 110M

The tiny Amazonian village of Puerto Nariño, 75km upriver from Leticia, is living proof that humans and nature can peacefully coexist. Puerto Nariño has elevated the concept of green living to an art form. Motorized cars are banned (the only two vehicles here are an ambulance and a truck for collecting recycling). The spotless town is laid out on a grid of landscaped, pedestrian-only sidewalks. Every morning, citizen brigades fan out to tidy up the town.

The little town's ambitious recycling and organic waste management programs would put most world cities to shame. Trash and recycling bins are located on practically every corner. Rainwater is collected in cisterns for washing and gardening. Electricity comes from the town's energy-efficient generator, but only runs until midnight. Fall asleep to the sounds of jungle chit-chat and the pitter-patter of raindrops on tin roofs. It's such an aberration from established human population patterns in the Amazon that's it's worth making the trip here simply to see the village itself.

The majority of Puerto Nariño's residents are indigenous Tikuna, Cocoma and Yagua peoples. Their community experiment in ecological living has led to an important source of income: ecotourism. This tranquil town is a great base from which to visit beautiful Lago Tarapoto and the Amazon in general.

◉ Sights & Activities

An excellent local guide is jovial **Willinton Carvajal** (☑313-375-5788), who only speaks Spanish but gets the job done.

Mirador VIEWPOINT

(Calle 4; high/low season COP$7000/5000; ⊗6am-5pm) For a bird's-eye view of the village and the surrounding jungle and Amazon, climb the *mirador* tower, located on the top of a hill in the center of the village.

AMAZON BASIN ISLA SANTA ROSA (PERU)

Centro de Interpretación Natütama
MUSEUM

(admission COP$5000; ⊙9am-5pm Wed-Mon) The Centro de Interpretación Natütama has a fascinating museum with nearly 100 life-sized wood carvings of Amazonian flora and fauna. There's also a small turtle hatchery outside.

Fundación Omacha
MUSEUM

(www.omacha.org) 🥾 FREE Located on the riverfront just east of the docks is this conservation and research center working to save the Amazon's pink dolphins and manatees. There's a small display on the creatures and staff can help make arrangements to go wildlife spotting.

Lago Tarapoto
LAKE

Lago Tarapoto, 10km west of Puerto Nariño, is a beautiful jungle lake that is home to pink and gray dolphins, manatees and massive Victoria Regia water lilies. A half-day trip to the lake in a *peque-peque* can be organized from Puerto Nariño (COP$50,000 for up to four people), and is the main draw for visitors.

🛏 Sleeping

There are well over 20 accommodations options in town. You'll never have trouble finding somewhere to sleep. Some hotel owners hang out at the dock to meet the arriving boat from Leticia.

Malokas Napü
GUESTHOUSE $

(☑314-235-3782; www.maiocanapo.com; Calle 4 No 5-72; r per person with/without balcony COP$30,000/25,000; @) Our favorite hotel has the look and feel of a treehouse fort, surrounded as it is by a thickly forested garden. The rooms are simple but comfortable, with basic furnishings, fans and shared bathrooms with super-refreshing rain-style showers, and everyone who works here is above and beyond friendly. Try for rooms in the red-and-black-painted back building, which share a balcony with hammocks overlooking the courtyard garden and jungle. Breakfast is COP$10,000 extra.

Cabañas del Friar
CABAÑAS $

(☑311-502-8592; altodelaguila@hotmail.com; r per person COP$20,000) About 15 minutes west of town, famous friar Hector José Rivera and his crazy monkeys run this hilltop jungle oasis overlooking the Amazon. The complex includes several extremely simple huts, shared facilities and a lookout tower. The true joy of staying here is the playful interaction between the monkeys, dogs and macaws, and the utter isolation.

To get here, take the main street (parallel to the Amazon, two blocks back) west out of town across the bridge to the well-maintained sidewalk; keep left at the cemetery and walk through the high school campus (fascinating in itself), then turn right immediately after passing the school football pitch.

OFF THE BEATEN TRACK

SAN MARTIN DE AMACAYACU

Getting truly off the beaten path in the Colombian Amazon can be tricky, especially if you want to combine being in nature with experiencing the daily lives of the indigenous peoples of the region. One solution is a visit to the wonderful **Casa Gregorio** (☑310-279-8147, 311-201-8222; casagregorio@outlook.com; San Martin de Amacayacu; full board per person from COP$170,000), a small family-run hotel in the Tikuna indigenous community of San Martin de Amacayacu, surrounded by majestic rivers and impressive rainforest.

The guesthouse has just two double rooms in the main house and a separate cabin that sleeps five, and is fully integrated into the community rather than feeling enclosed or apart. Rates include full board, rubber boots, rain gear and drinking water and various nature activities, workshops and river trips. Prices range between COP$170,000 and COP$250,000 per person per day, depending on activities and number of travelers (maximum four per group). It gets rave reviews and feedback from travelers, many of whom return and develop strong links to the community here.

You'll need to book ahead to stay here as you need to be picked up on arrival. To reach Casa Gregorio from Leticia, take one of the three daily boats heading to Puerto Nariño and request the Bocana Amacayacu stop, from where you will be picked up by the Casa Gregorio staff (COP$30,000 per person).

Hotel Lomas del Paiyü HOTEL $
(☑ 313-871-1743, 313-268-4400; hotellomasdel
paiyu@yahoo.com; Calle 7 No 2-26; s COP$25,000-
35,000, d COP$50,000-80,000) This tin-roofed
22-room hotel is a reliable choice and has
quite a bit of rough charm. Some bathrooms
are almost as big as the rooms and while the
cheaper rooms come in the form of rustic
cabañas with communal hammocks, the
very nicest double has a gorgeous balcony
with town views.

Hotel Casa Selva HOTEL $$
(www.casaselvahotel.com;Carrera2No6-72;s/d/tr/q
incl breakfast COP$130,000/155,000/205,000/
254,000) Easily the grandest place in town,
the Casa Selva allows you to do the jun-
gle in some comfort, with 12 spacious and
comfortable rooms, lots of dark wood and
a prime position in the center of the village.

✖ Eating & Drinking

Puerto Nariño has one great restaurant,
quite simply where everyone goes. Some
hotels also do food. Other than that there
are a few fast-food joints and grocery stores
on the main road facing the river. 'Nightlife'
involves drinking at one of the hole-in-the-
wall bars fronting the basketball courts.

★ Las Margaritas COLOMBIAN $$
(Calle 6 No 6-80; set meals COP$15,000; ☺ 8am-
9pm) Hidden behind a picket fence under
a huge *palapa* (thatched roof) just beyond
the football pitch, Las Margaritas is the best
restaurant in town. Excellent home-cooked
meals are served buffet-style from traditional clay cookware, there's always a delicious
variety of local specialties and it's all shockingly tasty. The place can get swamped when
large tours come through town, though.

ℹ Information

There are no banks or ATMs in Puerto Nariño,
and credit cards are not accepted anywhere, so
bring plenty of cash from Leticia.
Compartel (cnr Carrera 6 & Calle 5; per hr
COP$2000; ☺ Mon-Sat) Provides internet
access plus local and international telephone
service.
Hospital (cnr Carrera 4 & Calle 5)
Tourist Office (☑ 313-235-3687; cnr Carrera
7 & Calle 5; ☺ 9am-noon & 2-5pm Mon-Sat)
Located inside the *alcaldía* (town hall building),
but there's a kiosk just outside on the riverfront.

ℹ Getting There & Away

High-speed boats to Puerto Nariño depart from
Leticia's dock at 8am, 10am and 2pm daily
(COP$29,000, two hours); round-trip boats to
Leticia depart at 7:30am, 11am and 4pm.

You can purchase tickets at **Transportes
Fluviales** (☑ 592-6752; Calle 8 No 11) near the
riverfront in Leticia. Boats can get very full, so
buy your tickets early or the day before.

Río Yavarí

Within reach of large stretches of virgin
forest, the meandering Río Yavarí offers
some of the best opportunities to see the
Amazon up close and undisturbed. A few
privately owned reserves provide simple
accommodations plus guided tours and activities, including kayaking, bird-watching,
dolphin-watching, jungle treks and visits to
indigenous settlements. The lodges provide
accommodations and food.

Costs take into account the number of
people in the party, length of stay, season
and number of guided tours; count on
COP$180,000 to COP$280,000 per person
per day. There are no regularly scheduled
boats, so you will have to arrange transportation with the reserves. Hiring a private
boat from Leticia is also an option – an extraordinarily expensive one. Expect to pay at
least COP$150,000 one way plus fuel (from
COP$250,000): it's therefore much better
to ensure that transportation is included in
your package.

Reserva Natural Palmarí

About 105km by river from Leticia, eco-
fierce Palmarí's rambling lodge and research
center sits on the high, south (Brazilian)
bank of the river, overlooking a wide bend
where pink and gray dolphins often gather.
It's the only lodge with access to all three
Amazonian ecosystems: *terra firme* (dry),
várzea (semiflooded) and *igapó* (flooded).

The lodge itself is rustic, much of it recently rebuilt after arsonists set fire to it in
2010. It has helpful employed from the
surrounding community (so no English,
but *mucho* authenticity and expertise), and
offers a wide choice of walking trips and
night treks, boat excursions and kayaking
trips, and excellent food served up by Brazilian kitchen staff. You'll find Palmarí offers
the best walking options around the region,
is the only option to encounter *terra firme*

forest and is the best spot in the region to see animals, including tapirs, and for the very lucky, jaguars.

Independent traveler rates include room and board (per night COP$275,000 for a bed or hammock) as well as all excursions and activities except the excellent, high-adrenaline canopying (COP$70,000). Nicer private cabañas with private bathrooms are reserved for guests on multiday packages that include transportation, but they are not a big enough step up to justify upgrading from the backpacker rate unless you just love pretty sinks.

The reserve is managed from Bogotá by owner **Axel Antoine-Feill** (📞310-786-2770, 1-610-3514; www.palmari.org; Carrera 10 No 93-72, Bogotá), who can speak several languages including English. His representative in Leticia is **Victoria Gomez** (📞310-793-2881), though Victoria only speaks Spanish.

Reserva Natural Zacambú

Zacambú is one of the reserves nearest to Leticia, about 70km by boat. Its lodge is on the Río Zacambú, a tributary of the Río Yavarí, on the Peruvian side of the river. The lodge is simple, with small rooms with shared bathrooms, and a total capacity of about 30 guests. Plan on COP$180,000 per person per night including food, excursions and transportation.

Zacambú sits on a flooded forest that is a habitat for many species of butterflies, but unfortunately is also a popular hangout for mosquitoes. Its proximity to Peruvian communities also means it's not the best spot for wildlife, though it's still easy to see dolphins, piranhas and caiman in the river, as well as a rich variety of birdlife in the jungle.

Both the lodge itself and tours are run from Leticia by Amazon Jungle Trips (p274).

Understand Colombia

Colombia Today

Years of violence and instability caused by paramilitaries, armed rebels and drug cartels are (largely) a thing of the past in Colombia today, with the country focused on bringing a final peace to the decades of conflict with the FARC rebels, which still sadly defines the country to many people. The reality of modern Colombia is very different, in fact: economically dynamic and fast changing, it's a nation where tourism is simply booming despite the not-inconsiderable problems and challenges still to solve.

Best on Film

Todos Tus Muertos (2011) Devastating critique of corruption and apathy in Colombia.

Apaporis (2010) Incisive documentary into indigenous Amazonian life.

Perro Come Perro (2008) Tarantino-esque gangster flick.

Maria Llena Eres de Gracia (2008) Moving tale of teen pregnancy and drug-trafficking.

Soñar No Cuesta Nada (2006) Colombian soldiers find millions of FARC dollars – and keep it.

Rosario Tijeras (2004) Vengeful hit-woman's thrilling tale.

Best in Print

One Hundred Years of Solitude (Gabriel García Márquez) Magic realist masterpiece.

Calamari (Emilio Ruiz Barrachina) Cartagena-set historical romance.

Beyond Bogotá – Diary of a Drug War Journalist in Colombia (Garry Leech) Essential reading for news that's not in the papers.

Delirium (Laura Restrepo) Explores personal and political madness in mid-'80s Bogotá.

Six Months on Minimum Wage (Andrés Felipe Solano) Life in a Medellín factory.

A Country on the Rise

Having largely overcome the instability and violence that has blighted it since the mid-20th century, Colombia is currently one of the most dynamic and fastest-growing economies in Latin America, overtaking its far more historically stable and developed neighbor Peru in 2014. Having avoided the recessions that have hit many Latin American economies in recent years, and also due in part to the high price of its main natural resources, oil and coal, Colombia looks set to continue growth at an impressive pace in the near future.

While it's undeniable that for many rural poor life has yet to improve, Colombia today is racing ahead to become one of the hottest, most exciting destinations on the continent, and tourism is playing an increasingly large role in that. Fresh from a great performance in the 2014 World Cup, Colombian confidence hasn't been so high in living memory, and most visitors will find this infectious.

This journey has been an arduous one, of course, and Colombia remains a nation beset by the demons of its past: memories of the Fuerzas Armadas Revolucionarias de Colombia (FARC; Revolutionary Armed Forces of Colombia) insurgency, paramilitary groups and violent drug cartels are never far from the minds of locals. But having largely driven the FARC deep into the jungle and simultaneously toward the negotiation table, the Colombian government is focused on bringing long-term peace to the country.

A Polarizing Peace Process

Harvard-educated Juan Manuel Santos became president of Colombia in 2010, following a landslide victory over a former mayor of Bogotá. Having been handpicked by his predecessor, Álvaro Uribe, and initially defining himself as a fierce and uncompromising opponent of the FARC, Santos actually oversaw the beginning of highly controversial negotiations with their representatives in Havana. The talks, aimed at de-arming the guerrilla group and bringing a final end to the decades of violence, infuriated Uribe, who quickly became Santos' fiercest critic.

Despite much popular opposition to the talks, Santos just managed to scrape a second term in the polarized 2014 presidential election, which highlighted the deep fissures within Colombian society. Up against the Uribe-endorsed Óscar Iván Zuluaga, Santos lost the first round, but managed to win the runoff with just 51% of the ballot to secure another four-year term. The election essentially became a referendum on whether the peace talks should continue or not, with Zuluaga promising to end them if he was elected.

Talks between government and FARC negotiators were still ongoing in late 2014, with enormous, albeit painful progress having been made. Colombians remain deeply divided about the ethics of negotiating with the armed group that has been responsible for thousands of deaths over the decades, but the country is at least united in desiring a lasting, long-term peace.

Free Trade?

Santos' close relationship with the United States reached its peak in 2012, when the US–Colombia Free Trade Agreement came into force. This treaty, which had been stalled in US Congress for years by Democrat concerns over human rights violations in Colombia, opened up the two economies to each other and removed tariffs and duties on around 80% of imports and exports between the two nations.

Yet it wasn't the untainted political win that Santos had hoped for; in 2011, police had confiscated and destroyed an entire town's rice harvest due to the farmers saving and reusing their own seeds as they had done for centuries, something that was deemed illegal under section 9.70 of the treaty. Instead they were expected to buy seeds anew from US companies such as Monsanto, something that led to a massive popular outcry at both the government and the use of force against farmers. Due to the public backlash section 9.70 was temporarily suspended in 2013, but it still remains in Colombian law. A series of nationwide Farmers' Strikes in 2013 spelled more trouble for Santos: despite claiming *'el tal paro nacional agrario no existe'* ('the so-called national farmers' strike doesn't exist'), he was then humiliatingly forced to negotiate to prevent national gridlock.

Colombian exports remain problematic of course; the country still produces an estimated 345 tonnes of cocaine annually, a subject of endless hand-wringing in Bogotá, and another blemish on the country's international reputation, even if it's now a smaller producer than both Bolivia and Peru. On his election

POPULATION: **48 MILLION**

AREA: **1.14 MILLION SQ KM**

GDP GROWTH: **4.2%**

UNEMPLOYMENT: **9.7%**

LIFE EXPECTANCY: **73 YEARS (MEN), 79 YEARS (WOMEN)**

if Colombia were 100 people

58 would be white & Amerindian
20 would be white
14 would be white & black
3 would be black & Amerindian
4 would be black
1 would be Amerindian

belief systems
(% of population)

90
Roman Catholic

8.1
Protestant

1.9
No religious beliefs

population per sq km

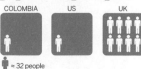

COLOMBIA   US   UK

≈ 32 people

Best Salsa Songs

El Preso (Fruko Y Sus Tesos)
La Pantera Mambo (La 33)
Rebelion (Joe Arroyo)
Oiga, Mira Vea (Orquesta Guayacan)
Gotas De Lluvia (Grupo Niche)

Etiquette

Fare haggling You can haggle gently on almost all intercity bus fares – you can often get a discount of up to 20%.

Buses Don't feel obliged to buy the small trinkets vendors will hand you on bus journeys.

Juice Wait for a top-up when you buy a juice in the street; it's called a *ñapa* and is customary.

Soup If you don't want soup with your lunch or dinner, order it *'seco'* (dry).

Drugs Don't take cocaine. There's much more fun to be had in Colombia, and the drug trade fuels the ongoing armed conflict.

to the presidency Santos called for a major rethink on the Drug War, arguing that as long as demand remains high in the US and Europe, production and supply will remain profitable, and pointing to the fact that despite various costly drives to eradicate crops and take out cartels, there has been little reduction in the overall levels of production, even with the advent of peace.

The Former Guerrilla in City Hall

Colombian politics remains volatile and unpredictable. When Gustavo Petro, ex-leader of the Movimiento 19 de Abril (M-19) leftist guerrilla movement that stormed Bogotá's Palace of Justice in 1985, became mayor of Bogotá in 2011, it was a shock to the country's political establishment. Petro's administration in Bogotá proved to be rather authoritarian as well as unpopular with residents of the capital, but it was his attempt to replace the private sector's role in Bogotá's waste collection with a publicly owned garbage-removal authority that spelled disaster for him. When garbage went uncollected on the streets (admittedly only for a couple of days), the mayor ended up buying trucks in order to forestall disaster.

Sometime later, Petro was removed from his post by the Office of the Inspector General of Colombia for overstepping his authority, and slapped with a 15-year ban on taking part in politics. The dismissal was approved by President Santos, a move that came back to haunt the president in April 2014, when Petro was reinstated as mayor of Bogotá following one of many legal challenges Petro's team launched against his dismissal. Despite the acrimony between the two, political necessity saw Santos and Petro subsequently burying the hatchet, with the latter endorsing the president in the 2014 elections. Only in Colombia...

History

Colombia's history is one of war and bloodshed. Whether it's the cruelty of the colonial conquests, the fight with Spain for independence, the ongoing 50-year civil war between the FARC guerrillas and the paramilitaries or the narco-chaos of the 1980 and '90s, Colombia has always been synonymous with violence. But this has receded in recent years, and Colombia today is a far safer place for its residents and for travelers, though never one where safety should be taken for granted.

Pre-Columbus Colombia

Set where South America meets Central America, present-day Colombia saw the continent's first inhabitants arrive between 12,500 and 70,000 years ago, having migrated from the north. Most – such as the ancestors of the Inca – just passed through. Little is known of the groups who did stick around (eg the Calima, Muisca, Nariño, Quimbaya, Tayrona, Tolima and Tumaco). By the time the Spaniards arrived, the first inhabitants were living in small, scattered communities, subsisting on agriculture or trade. They hardly rivaled the bigger civilizations flourishing in Mexico and Peru.

The area's biggest pre-Columbian sites (San Agustín, Tierradentro and Ciudad Perdida) were already long abandoned when the Spaniards arrived in the 1500s. Ciudad Perdida, the Tayrona jungle city, was built around 700 AD, with hundreds of stone terraces linked with stairways. The Muisca, one of the country's larger indigenous groups, occupied present-day Boyacá and Cundinamarca, near Bogotá (itself named from a Muisca word), and numbered 600,000 when the Spanish arrived.

The largest indigenous group between the Maya and Inca at the time of the Spanish Conquest, the Muiscas inspired El Dorado myths with their gold *tujos* (offerings), while their *chicha* (fermented-corn beer) still intoxicates Colombians today.

Spanish Conquest

Colombia is named after Christopher Columbus, even though the famous explorer never set foot on Colombian soil. One of Columbus' companions on his second voyage, Alonso de Ojeda, was the first recorded European to arrive in 1499. He briefly explored the Sierra Nevada de Santa Marta and was astonished by the wealth of the local indigenous people. The shores of present-day Colombia became the target of numerous expeditions by

TIMELINE	5500 BC	700 AD	1499
	Early groups of pre-Muisca begin moving to present-day Colombia. They continue to live in small, scattered, subsistence communities, while the Aztec and Inca established their empires.	The Tayrona begin building their largest city, the legendary Ciudad Perdida (or Lost City), in lush rainforest, which would be 'discovered' only in 1972.	On his second journey to the New World, Alonso de Ojeda lands at Cabo de la Vela – and a scientist onboard surprises the crew by discovering the place isn't actually Asia.

GOLD!

From day one of their arrival, tales of gold overwhelmed the conquistador mind-set. Eventually glimpses of gold artifacts – and stories of much more inland – gave birth to the myth of El Dorado, a mysterious jungle kingdom abundant in gold and, in some versions, surrounded by mountains of gold and emeralds. Long into the colonial period, the struggling Nueva Granada viceroyalty was based on a one-export economy: gold.

Eventually the legend became linked with the Muisca and their famous Laguna de Guatavita, which has suffered endless efforts to dig up enough wealth to change the world. Not much was ever found, alas. Read more in John Hemming's fascinating book, *The Search for El Dorado* (1978).

In a neat little historical dovetail, in recent years the FARC have turned away from white gold – cocaine – to the more traditional yellow variety as it is more lucrative, with the price of gold rocketing following the global financial crisis. This has led to environmental deterioration with illegal gold mining now a significant new threat to ecosystems.

The Explorers of South America (1972), by Edward J Goodman, brings to life some of the more incredible explorations of the continent, from those of Columbus to Humboldt, some of which refer to Colombia.

the Spaniards. Several short-lived settlements were founded along the coast, but it was not until 1525 that Rodrigo de Bastidas laid the first stones of Santa Marta, the earliest surviving European settlement in mainland South America. In 1533 Pedro de Heredia founded Cartagena, the strategic position and far better harbor of which quickly allowed it to become the principal trade center on the Colombian coast.

In 1536 an advance toward the interior began independently from three directions: under Gonzalo Jiménez de Quesada (from Santa Marta), Sebastián de Belalcázar (aka Benalcázar; from present-day Ecuador) and Nikolaus Federmann (from Venezuela). All three managed to conquer much of the colony and establish a series of towns, before meeting in the Muisca territory in 1539.

Of the three, Quesada got there first, crossing the Valle del Magdalena and Cordillera Oriental in 1537. At the time, the Muisca were divided into two rival clans – one ruled by the Zipa from Bacatá (present-day Bogotá), the other by Zaque in Hunza (present-day Tunja) – whose rivalry helped Quesada conquer both clans with only 200 men. Belalcázar, a deserter from Francisco Pizarro's Inca-conquering army, subdued the southern part of Colombia, founding Popayán and Cali. After crossing Los Llanos and the Andes, Federmann arrived in Bogotá shortly after Belalcázar. The three groups squabbled for supremacy until King Carlos V of Spain finally established a court of justice in Bogotá in 1550 and brought the colony under the control of the viceroyalty of Peru.

1537–38	1564	1717	1808
Conquistador Gonzalo Jiménez de Quesada twice founds a new settlement, Santa Fe de Bogotá. First, without permission from the Crown, in 1537, then with approval in 1538.	The Spanish Crown establishes the Real Audiencia del Nuevo Reino de Granada in Bogotá, subject to the viceroyalty of Peru in Lima.	Bogotá becomes capital of the viceroyalty of Virreinato de la Nueva Granada, an area that encompasses present-day Colombia, Ecuador, Venezuela and Panama.	Napoleon defeats Spanish King Ferdinand VII and installs his brother on the Spanish throne, sending a glimmer of possibility for independence-minded thinkers across South America.

The Colonial Era

In 1564 the Crown established a new authority, the Real Audiencia del Nuevo Reino de Granada, which had dual military and civil power and greater autonomy. The authority was run by a governor, appointed by the King of Spain. The Nuevo Reino at that time comprised present-day Panama, Venezuela (other than Caracas) and all of Colombia, except what is today Nariño, Cauca and Valle del Cauca, which were under the jurisdiction of the Presidencia de Quito (present-day Ecuador).

The population of the colony, initially consisting of indigenous communities and the Spanish invaders, diversified with the arrival of African slaves to Cartagena, South America's principal slave-trading port. During the 16th and 17th centuries the Spaniards shipped in so many Africans that they eventually surpassed the indigenous population in number. The emergence of *criollos* (locally born whites) added to the mix.

With the growth of the Spanish empire in the New World, a new territorial division was created in 1717, and Bogotá became the capital of its own viceroyalty, the Virreinato de la Nueva Granada. It comprised the territories of what are today Colombia, Panama, Ecuador and Venezuela.

Although the conquistador Sebastián de Belalcázar was rewarded for killing thousands of indigenous people, the Spanish Crown sentenced him to death for ordering the assassination of rival conquistador Jorge Robledo in 1546.

Independence from Spain

As Spanish domination of the continent increased, so too did the discontent of the inhabitants – particularly over monopolies of commerce and new taxes. The first open rebellion against colonial rule was the Revolución Comunera in Socorro (Santander) in 1781, which broke out against tax rises levied by the Crown. It began taking on more pro-independence overtones (and nearly taking over Bogotá) before its leaders were caught and executed. When Napoleon Bonaparte put his own brother on the Spanish throne in 1808, the colonies refused to recognize the new monarch. One by one, Colombian towns declared their independence.

In 1812 Simón Bolívar, who was to become the hero of the independence struggle, appeared on the scene. He won six battles against Spanish troops, but was defeated the following year. Spain recovered its throne from Napoleon and then set about reconquering the colonies, finally succeeding in 1817. Meanwhile, in 1815 Bolívar had retreated to Jamaica and taken up arms again. He went back to Venezuela, but Spanish forces were too strong in Caracas, so Bolívar headed south, with an army, and marched over the Andes into Colombia, claiming victory after victory.

The most decisive battle took place at Boyacá on August 7, 1819. Three days later Bolívar arrived triumphantly in Bogotá, having freed Colombia from Spanish rule – although some lesser battles were yet to come (including a victory at Cartagena in 1821).

During the colonial period, the local demographic picture became increasingly complex, as the country's three racial groups – mestizos (people of mixed European-indigenous blood), mulattos (people with European-African ancestry) and zambos (African-indigenous people) – mixed.

1819	1830	1880	1899
Simón Bolívar – crossing Los Llanos with an army of Venezuelans and Nueva Granadans from present-day Colombia – defeats the Spanish army at Boyacá and the Republic of Gran Colombia is founded.	Gran Colombia splits into Colombia (including modern-day Panama), Ecuador and Venezuela; Bolívar sends himself into exile; he dies in Santa Marta.	Colombia elects Dr Rafael Núñez, who helps ease tension between state and church with new 'regeneration' policies outlined in a constitution that will stay in place for over a century.	The three-year Thousand Days War between Liberals and Conservatives erupts around the country, providing a key backdrop for Gabriel García Márquez' One Hundred Years of Solitude.

THE FALL OF SIMÓN BOLÍVAR

Known as 'El Libertador,' Simón Bolívar led armies to battle the Spanish across northern South America, won the Colombian presidency, and ranks as one of the nation's great heroes. It's therefore surprising how it ended for him: humiliated, jobless, penniless and alone. He said, shortly before his death from tuberculosis in 1830, 'There have been three great fools in history: Jesus, Don Quixote and I.'

How did it happen? A proponent of a centralized republic, Bolívar was absent – off fighting back the Spanish in Peru and Bolivia – during much of his administration, leaving the running of the government to his vice president, and rival, the young federalist Francisco de Paula Santander, who smeared Bolívar and his ideas of being a lifetime president with the 'm' word: monarchist.

In 1828 Bolívar finally assumed dictatorship of a republic out of control, and restored a (hugely unpopular) colonial sales tax. Soon after, he narrowly escaped an assassination attempt (some believe Santander planned it) and a long-feisty Venezuela finally split from the republic. By 1830 Bolívar had had enough, abandoning the presidency – and then his savings, through gambling. He died a few months later.

The Formation of Political Parties

With Colombia independent, a revolutionary congress was held in Angostura (modern-day Ciudad Bolívar, in Venezuela) in 1819. Still euphoric with victory, the delegates proclaimed a new state, Gran Colombia, uniting Venezuela, Colombia, Panama and Ecuador (although Ecuador and parts of Venezuela were still technically under Spanish rule).

The Angostura congress was followed by another, held in Villa del Rosario, near Cúcuta, in 1821. It was there that the two opposing tendencies, centralist and federalist, first came to the fore. The two currents persisted throughout Bolívar's administration, which lasted to 1830. What followed after Bolívar's departure was a new (but not the last) inglorious page of Colombia's history. The split was formalized in 1849 when two political parties were established: the Conservatives (with centralist tendencies) and the Liberals (with federalist leanings). Fierce rivalry between these two forces resulted in a sequence of insurrections and civil wars, and throughout the 19th century Colombia experienced no fewer than eight civil wars. Between 1863 and 1885 alone there were more than 50 antigovernment insurrections.

In 1899 a Liberal revolt turned into the Thousand Days War, which resulted in a Conservative victory and left 100,000 dead. In 1903 the US took advantage of the country's internal strife and fomented a secessionist movement in Panama, then a Colombian province. By creating an independent republic there, the US was able to build and control a canal across

In his magic-realism novel *One Hundred Years of Solitude,* Gabriel García Márquez depicts the back-and-forth brutality of Liberal and Conservative rivalries and vendettas in ongoing conflicts from 1885 to 1902 in the fictional village of Macondo.

1903	1948	1964	1974
Long cut off from the rest of Colombia, Panama secedes from the country.	Likely Liberal presidential candidate, populist leader Jorge Eliécer Gaitán, is murdered leaving his office, setting off Bogotá and the country into bloody riots – the culprits are never identified.	The Colombian military drops napalm on a guerrilla-held area, giving rise to the Fuerzas Armadas Revolucionarias de Colombia (FARC); the Ejército de Liberación Nacional (ELN) and M-19 follow.	The National Front ends, and newly elected president Alfonso López Michelsen launches the first major counterinsurgency against all three main guerrilla groups.

the Central American isthmus. It wasn't until 1921 that Colombia eventually recognized the sovereignty of Panama and settled its dispute with the US.

The 20th Century: Sowing the Seeds

The turn of the 20th century saw Panama ceded from Gran Colombia, but there was a welcome period of peace, as the economy started to boom (particularly due to coffee) and the country's infrastructure expanded under the defused partisan politics of leader General Rafael Reyes. The brief lapse into a gentler world didn't last long, however. Labor tensions rose (following a 1928 banana strike) and the struggle between Liberals and Conservatives finally exploded in 1946 with La Violencia, the most destructive of Colombia's many civil wars to that point (with a death toll of some 200,000). Following the assassination of Jorge Eliécer Gaitán, a charismatic, self-made populist Liberal leader, more widespread riots broke out around the country (which came to be known as El Bogotazo in Bogotá – where Gaitán was killed – and El Nueve de Abril elsewhere). Liberals soon took up arms throughout the country.

Generations of Colombians remained divided into the two political camps and each held a deep mistrust of the opposition. It's believed that 'hereditary hatreds' helped fuel revenge attacks and were the cause of countless atrocities (including rapes and murders) committed over the course of the next decade, particularly in rural areas.

The 1953 coup of General Gustavo Rojas Pinilla was the only military intervention the country experienced in the 20th century, but the coup was not to last. In 1957 the leaders of the two parties signed a pact to share power for the next 16 years. The agreement, later approved by plebiscite (in which women were allowed to vote for the first time), became known as the Frente Nacional (National Front). During the life of the accord, the two parties alternated in the presidency every four years. In effect, despite the enormous loss of lives, the same people were returned

One of the best books on Colombia's history is David Bushnell's *The Making of Modern Colombia: A Nation in Spite of Itself* (1993), which follows colonization, partisan conflicts throughout independence and the emergence of cocaine politics in the 1980s.

COLOMBIAN COFFEE

Colombia's coffee boom began in the early 20th century, and found its exclamation point when Juan Valdez and his mule became the Colombian Coffee Federation's icon in 1959. (It was voted the world's top ad icon as recently as 2005.) In 2004 Valdez opened more than 60 cafes in Colombia, the US and Spain.

Despite competition from low-cost, lower-quality beans from Vietnam, Colombia's high-quality arabica-bean industry still employs around 570,000 and earns the country billions of dollars a year. Yet despite the ubiquity of the bean, Colombian coffee remains of generally poor quality in the country itself – forget strong espresso outside big cities and content yourself with a watery *tinto* (black coffee) instead.

1982	1982	1984	1990
Gabriel García Márquez wins the Nobel Prize in Literature. In his acceptance speech he remarks that while Europeans value the continent's art, they have no respect for its political movements.	Pablo Escobar is elected to the Colombian Congress; President Belisario Betancur grants amnesty to guerrilla groups and frees hundreds of prisoners; Colombia abandons plans to hold the World Cup.	Justice Minister Rodrigo Lara Bonilla is assassinated for supporting an extradition treaty with the US.	The M-19 demilitarizes; the cartels declare war on the government and the extradition treaty, and a government building near the Paloquemao market in Bogotá is destroyed by a bomb.

THE DISPLACED

Caught in the crossfire between paramilitaries and guerrilla forces, and sometimes outright targets in what the UN says is a 'strategy of war,' one in 20 Colombians (about four million, says the Internal Displacement Monitoring Centre) have become internally displaced since the 1980s, making Colombia home to more displaced persons than any country except Sudan.

Hundreds of people become displaced daily, forced out of their homes at gunpoint – usually stolen for the land, livestock or its location on drug transportation routes – but sometimes not until after a loved one is murdered. Most of the dispossessed are left to fend for themselves, living in tarp-covered huts outside the main cities. Those who are able to obtain new land frequently find it in areas with no infrastructure, schools or hospitals. Often, displaced children fall into a world of drugs and crime.

There has been some improvement in recent years with the introduction in 2011 of the Victims' Law, which aims to compensate and return land to those who had it stolen. Progress has been slow, inevitably, with the safety of returnees rather than huge numbers processed being the priority.

to power. Importantly, the agreement also disallowed political parties beyond the Liberals and the Conservatives, forcing any opposition outside of the normal political system and sowing the seeds for guerrilla insurrection.

The Birth of the FARC & Paramilitaries

While the new National Front helped ease partisan tensions between Conservatives and Liberals, new conflicts were widening between wealthy landowners and the rural mestizo and indigenous underclass, two-thirds of whom lived in poverty by the end of La Violencia. Splinter leftist groups began emerging, calling for land reform. Colombian politics hasn't been the same since. Much of what happened has been documented by international human rights groups such as Human Rights Watch.

For a simple, independent and readable account of the FARC's origins, aims and ideology, try *The FARC: The Longest Insurgency* by Gary Leech (2011).

New communist enclaves in the Sumapáz area, south of Bogotá, worried the Colombian government so much that its military bombed the area in May 1964. The attack led to the creation of the Fuerzas Armadas Revolucionarias de Colombia (FARC; Revolutionary Armed Forces of Colombia, led by Manuel Marulanda) and the more military-minded Jacobo Arenas. They vowed to overthrow the state and to redistribute land and wealth among the whole country, seizing it from Colombia's elites.

Other armed guerrilla groups included a fellow Marxist rival, the Ejército de Liberación Nacional (ELN; National Liberation Army), which

1993	1995	2000	2002
One-time Congress member – and a more famous cocaine warlord – Pablo Escobar is killed a day after his 44th birthday on a Medellín rooftop by Colombian police aided by the USA.	The towns of San Agustín and Tierradentro in Colombia's southwest, with their many mysterious statues, carvings and burial tombs, are added to the Unesco World Heritage Sites list.	Colombia and the USA agree on the expansive Plan Colombia to cut coca cultivation by 2005; the US eventually spends over US$6 billion with no drop in cocaine production over its first decade.	President Álvaro Uribe is elected on an uncompromising anti-FARC ticket; he launches an immediate and effective clampdown.

built its popularity from a radical priest, Father Camilo Torres, who was killed in his first combat experience. The urban M-19 (Movimiento 19 de Abril, named for the contested 1970 presidential election) favored dramatic statements, such as the robbery of a Simón Bolívar sword and seizing the Palace of Justice in Bogotá in 1985. When the military's recapture of the court led to 115 deaths, the M-19 group gradually disintegrated.

The FARC's fortunes continued to rise, though, particularly when President Belisario Betancur negotiated peace with the rebels in the 1980s. Wealthy landowners formed the Autodefensas Unidas de Colombia (AUC; United Self-Defense Forces of Colombia) or paramilitary groups, to defend their land in response to the FARC's advance. The roots of these groups – all generally offshoots of the military – began in the 1960s, but grew in the '80s.

Cocaine & Cartels

Colombia is one of the world's biggest suppliers of cocaine, despite exhaustive efforts to track down cartel leaders, drop devegetation chemicals on coca farms and step up military efforts. All for that little *Erythroxylum coca* leaf – which you can buy in its unprocessed form in some Colombia markets. When the first Europeans arrived, they at first shook their heads over locals chewing coca leaves, but when (forced) work output started to decline, they allowed its usage. Eventually the Europeans (and the world) joined in, and in the centuries to follow, Andean cocaine eventually found its way worldwide for medicinal and recreational use.

The cocaine industry boomed in the early 1980s, when the Medellín Cartel, led by former car thief (and future politician) Pablo Escobar, became the principal Mafia. Its bosses eventually founded their own political party, established two newspapers and financed massive public works and public housing projects. At one point, Escobar even stirred up secession sentiments for the Medellín region. By 1983 Escobar's personal wealth was estimated to be over US$20 billion, making him one of the world's richest people (number seven according to *Forbes* magazine).

When the government launched a campaign against the drug trade, cartel bosses disappeared from public life and even proposed an unusual 'peace treaty' to President Betancur. The *New York Times* reported in 1988 that the cartels had offered to invest their capital in national development programs and pay off Colombia's entire foreign debt (some US$13 billion). The government declined the offer, and the violence escalated.

The cartel–government conflict heated up in August 1989, when Liberal presidential candidate Luis Carlos Galán was gunned down by drug lords. The government's response was to confiscate nearly 1000 cartel-owned properties and sign a new extradition treaty with the US, which led to a cartel-led campaign of terror resulting in bombed banks,

Read personalized accounts of the poverty the displaced face in Alfred Molano's *The Dispossessed: Chronicles of the Desterrados of Colombia* (2005).

The official site of the Colombian embassy in the US can be found at www.colombiaemb.org. It has good up-to-date information on the country.

2004	2006	2006	2006
Carlos 'El Pibe' Valderrama, the flamboyantly coiffured midfielder, is included in Pelé's FIFA 100 list of greatest living footballers, chosen by the soccer legend to celebrate the 100th anniversary of FIFA.	Uribe is swept to power once more as his 'Democratic Security' policy brings stability and prosperity for many.	Up to 20,000 Autodefensas Unidas de Colombia (AUC; United Self-Defense Forces of Colombia) paramilitaries disarm in return for lenient sentences for their massacres and human rights abuses.	Shakira's 'Hips Don't Lie' breaks the 10-million mark in global sales and hits the number one spot in 25 countries – becoming the most successful song worldwide that year.

homes and newspaper offices, and, in November 1989, the downing of an Avianca flight from Bogotá to Cali, which killed all 107 onboard.

After the 1990 election of Liberal César Gaviria as president, things calmed briefly, when extradition laws were sliced and Escobar led a surrender of many cartel bosses. However, Escobar soon escaped from his luxurious house arrest and it took an elite, US-funded 1500-strong special unit 499 days to track him down, shooting him dead atop a Medellín rooftop in 1993.

Amid the violence, the drug trade never slowed. New cartels learned to forsake the limelight, and by the mid-1990s, guerrillas and paramilitaries chipped in to help Colombia keep pace with the world's rising demand.

> *Killing Pablo: The Hunt for the World's Greatest Outlaw* (2002), by Mark Bowden, is an in-depth exploration of the life and times of Pablo Escobar and the operation that brought him down. While the book has some reputed small inaccuracies, it is a thrilling crime read.

The War Heats Up

As communism collapsed around the globe, the political landscape for the guerrillas shifted increasingly to drugs and kidnapping (kidnapping alone, by one account, brought the FARC some US$200 million annually), and paramilitary groups aligned themselves with drug cartels and pursued the guerrillas with the cartels' blessing.

After September 11, 'terrorism' became the new buzzword applied to guerrillas, and even some paramilitaries. One group that made the US list of international terrorists, and which notoriously had been paid US$1.7 million by the Chiquita fruit company, was the infamous AUC. The firm paid a US$25 million dollar fine in US courts in 2007 for its repeated funding of the AUC.

Linked with cocaine since 1997, the AUC was inspired by paramilitary groups previously under the watch of the slain Medellín Cartel leader Rodríguez Gacha. The AUC was later run by brothers Fidel and Carlos Castaño, who set out to avenge their father, who was slain by guerrillas. The AUC, with a force of up to 10,000 troops, attacked campesinos (peasants) it alleged were guerrilla sympathizers. The guerrillas attacked any campesinos they said were AUC supporters.

> The CIA World Factbook website (www.cia.gov) has a breakdown of Colombian government, economy and population issues to keep you in the know.

When the Álvaro Uribe administration offered lenient sentences for paramilitaries or guerrillas who demobilized, AUC handed over their guns in 2006.

Uribe's Reign

Fed up with violence, kidnappings and highways deemed too dangerous to use, the nation turned to right-wing hardliner Álvaro Uribe – a politician from Medellín who had studied at Oxford and Harvard, and whose father had been killed by the FARC. Uribe ran on a full-on anti-guerrilla ticket during the testy 2002 presidential election. While his predecessor Andrés Pastrana had tried negotiating with the FARC and ELN, Uribe didn't bother, quickly unleashing two simultaneous pro-

2008	2008	2009	2009
The FARC is duped into handing over its highest-value hostage, French-Colombian presidential candidate, Ingrid Betancourt, to the Colombian army.	The FARC announces that its founder, Manuel 'Sureshot' Marulanda has died, aged 78, of a heart attack in the jungle.	The country's secret service is accused by the public prosecutor of tapping the phones of thousands of journalists, politicians, activists and NGO workers, and using the information to harass and threaten them.	The UN calls false positives 'systemic,' and confirms thousands of cases, vindicating claims made for years by NGOs dubbed as terrorist sympathizers by the Uribe government.

PLAN COLOMBIA

In 2000 the US entered the war against the drug cartels, with the controversial 'Plan Colombia,' concocted by the Bill Clinton and Andrés Pastrana administrations to curb coca cultivation by 50% within five years. As the decade closed, and with US$6 billion spent, even the normally rah-rah US International Trade Commission called the program's effectiveness 'small and mostly direct.' The worldwide street price for Colombian cocaine hadn't changed – indicating no lack of supply – and, after a few years of dipping coca cultivation, by 2007, a UN report concluded that cocaine production rose by 27% that year alone, rebounding to its 1998 level.

Originally the money was supposed to be split half-and-half between efforts to equip/train the Colombian military and developmental projects to offer campesinos (peasants) attractive alternatives to coca farming. It didn't turn out that way. Nearly 80% of the money ended up with the military (as well as helicopter-drop devegetation chemicals that infamously killed food crops, along with elusive coca crops). In 2007 a Pentagon official told *Rolling Stone* that Plan Colombia ended up being less about 'counternarcotics' than 'political stabilization,' in particular the ongoing fight with the FARC.

Emerging in the first decade of the century, new harder-to-track *cartelitos* (smaller sized Mafia groups) replaced the extinguished mega cartels (capped with the 2008 extradition to the US of Medellín narco-king don Berna). The *cartelitos* relocated to harder-to-reach valleys (particularly near the Pacific coast). Many are linked to the FARC, who tax coca farmers (earning the FARC between US$200 to US$300 million annually, according to the *New York Times*); other *cartelitos*, however, are linked with paramilitary groups.

As a result, Colombia still supplies about 90% of the USA's cocaine – often getting it there overland via Mexican cartels.

In Barack Obama's 2011 budget proposal, Plan Colombia was not specifically mentioned. Colombia continued to receive military aid, albeit 20% less than the previous year, at US$228 million.

grams: a military pushback of groups such as the FARC, and a demobilization offer for both sides.

Even Uribe's harshest critics acknowledge much overdue progress was made under his watch. From 2002 to 2008, notably, murder rates fell 40% overall and highways cleared of FARC roadblocks became safe to use.

In March 2008, Uribe approved a tricky bombing mission across Ecuador's border, resulting in the successful killing of FARC leader Raúl Reyes. The bombing mission, however, nearly set the region into broader conflict, with Venezuelan president Hugo Chávez immediately moving tanks to the Colombian border, but things soon settled – and Uribe's approval levels hit 90%.

2010	2010	2011	2011
Colombia receives 1.4 million foreign visitors, according to official statistics, shaking off its decades-long reputation as a danger zone as President Uribe's security measures hit home.	Juan Manuel Santos, from an influential family and former Defense Minister under Uribe, is elected as president in a landslide victory.	Alfonso Cano, leader of the FARC and its chief ideologue, is killed in a bombing raid, raising hopes of an end to the conflict.	A US–Colombia free trade deal is agreed to by US Congress after years of deliberation and delay over Democrats' concerns over human rights.

However, his presidency was ultimately tainted by scandal and by 2008, following his public feuds with the Colombian Supreme Court, 60 congressmen had been arrested or questioned for alleged 'parapolitics' links with paramilitaries.

The *falso positivos* (false positives) scandal, as documented by the UN in an in-depth 2010 report, showed how the Colombian military was incentivized to increase bodycount. From 2004, incidences of false positives – where army units killed innocent young men and claimed them as guerrillas killed in combat – soared. As the scandal grew, Uribe fired 27 officers in November 2008, and leading commander General Mario Montoya resigned.

During Uribe's presidency the Colombian army killed 3000 young, uneducated, innocent so-called 'false positive' campesinos in a strategy described by UN special rapporteur on extrajudicial executions, Phillip Alston, as 'systemic.'

Toward a Lasting Peace

After the constitutional court in 2010 refused to allow a referendum to let Uribe run for a third term, his defense minister Juan Manuel Santos was voted in by a landslide, and almost immediately claimed the single greatest victory ever won against the FARC: the killing of its new leader, Alfonso Cano.

Within days a new leader, Rodrigo Londoño Echeverri (alias Timochenko), on whose head the US has placed a US$5 million bounty, took control of the guerrilla organization. With a reputation as one of the organization's most bellicose minds, Timochenko stunned the nation by proposing peace talks with the government.

The Colombian government, war weary yet understandably suspicious, took a good deal of convincing that the offer of negotiations for a lasting peace were genuine. When negotiators from the administration finally sat down with representatives of the FARC in Havana in 2012, there was an outcry in the country, with many considering the move a betrayal of the victims of the conflict. This led to a polarizing presidential election and a country split down the middle as to whether the government should be pursuing the talks at all.

This complex process was still ongoing at the time of writing. By late 2014, the parties involved had come to provisional agreements on three of the five talking points, though a final resolution, to be ratified by the Colombian people in a referendum, is still a long way off. However, in a further boost to the peace process, the FARC announced an indefinite ceasefire against the Colombian army in December 2014. While this is the furthest any peace talks have ever got between the government and the FARC, there is still some distance left to go in bringing to an end a conflict that is half a century old.

There's little overt, official censorship in Colombia. But journalists, fearful of being targeted by bipartisan violence in the nation's ongoing civil conflict, routinely self-censor, says monitoring group Reporters Without Borders. It ranked Columbia 129th out of 179 countries in the NGO's 2013 survey of press freedom.

2012	2014	2014	2014
Negotiations between the Colombian government and the FARC aimed at bringing a lasting peace to Colombia begin in Havana, Cuba.	Colombia's most famous writer, Nobel laureate Gabriel García Márquez, dies in Mexico City.	Juan Manuel Santos wins a second term as president, defeating his opponent with just 51% of the vote.	The FARC announce an indefinite ceasefire against the Colombian army after two years of peace negotiations in Havana, Cuba.

Life in Colombia

Colombians are some of the warmest, most friendly and uncannily helpful people you'll encounter in South America. They handle life with good humor and a light-heartedness that is infectious. The country's geographical diversity – mountains and sea – has left discrete influences on the national psyche. While life is industrious and the Spanish crisp and formal in the Andean cities of Bogotá, Medellín and Cali, *costeños* (people from the coast) are more laid-back and speak a heavier-accented, more drawling Spanish.

Lifestyle & Attitude

Wealthy urban Colombians live a very different life to their poorer counterparts. Their children go to private schools, they treat intercity planes like taxis and whizz through city streets updating their Facebook statuses on their smartphones. They play golf in country clubs at weekends, and, more than likely, they own a small private *finca* (farm) where they occasionally indulge their rural fantasies.

Poorer Colombians buy their phone calls by the minute in the street, wait in interminable intercity and urban traffic jams, and dream of sending their children to any school at all. Indigenous people and those in isolated rural communities in areas where the civil conflict still grinds on are often focused on ensuring they have enough food to survive.

Between these extremes, Colombia boasts one of the largest middle-class populations in Latin America, where many of its neighbors suffer great disparity in wealth. The country's free-market policies and relatively low level of corruption have helped the middle class to flourish.

All Colombians, though, are bound by strong family ties, not just to immediate blood relatives but also to their extended family, and childless visitors over 21 years of age will be quizzed endlessly on their plans to start a family. And though the dominant faith is Catholicism, very few attend Mass.

Women are the heart of a Colombian household. Machismo may be alive and well outside the home, where men are unquestionably in charge, but inside the Colombian home, women rule the roost. That's not the only place they rule. Women make up a significant number of the country's high-ranking politicians and diplomats, including cabinet ministers and ambassadors. In fact, a quota law passed in 2000 requires that at least 30% of appointed positions in the executive branch be filled by women.

Try not to get uptight if a Colombian is late – anything up to 45 minutes – and don't take it personally; instead, perhaps go with the flow and enjoy a culture that truly believes that most things aren't worth rushing for! Bus timetables, in particular, are a laughable fiction.

Most Colombians don't use drugs, except perhaps students in major cities, though it's undeniable that many do love to drink – and how. The Carnaval de Barranquilla is a riot of licentiousness and rum-doused ribaldry.

Same-sex marriages came into being in Colombia in 2013, following a period of constitutional wrangling between the Constitutional Court and the country's Congress. There is still no formal legal mechanism for same-sex marriage, but they can now be created through court approval.

NATIONS WITHIN A NATION

Colombia may be an ethnic mixing pot that can put most countries to shame, but its indigenous people – yet another part of the jigsaw for first-time visitors to explore and encounter – remain in many cases nations apart, often somewhat or totally removed from the mainstream of Colombian society. Comprising around 1.4 million people and divided into 87 different tribes, including some that remain uncontacted, this flipside to mainstream Colombian society is fascinating to explore.

Some indigenous groups you're likely to encounter include the Ticuna in the Amazon, the Wiwa, Kogui and Arhuaco in the Sierra Nevada, the Waayu in La Guajira and the Muisca around Bogotá. Indigenous reserves make up an extraordinary third of the area of Colombia, the land being collectively owned by the indigenous communities there. Yet despite legal protections, indigenous groups have often borne the brunt of the violence in recent decades, their vast reserves making perfect hiding places for guerrillas, paramilitary groups and coca plantations. As if to add insult to injury, the Plan Colombia spraying of many rural areas by the US Air Force to destroy coca farms has also destroyed or damaged perfectly innocent crops that have long been cultivated by Colombia's native peoples, leaving many traditional societies without food.

People & Place: A Cultural Sancocho

The population is thought to be around 48 million today, although there hasn't been a census since 2005. This makes Colombia the third-most populous country in Latin America after Brazil and Mexico, and the figure is rising fast. The rate of population growth in 2013 remained high at 1.3%.

Each city in Colombia has its own unique cultural mix, making traveling here as satisfyingly varied as a rich *sancocho* (soup). Many European immigrants populated Medellín, while much of the population of Cali is descended from former enslaved people. Bogotá and the surrounding areas saw much intermarriage between European colonists and indigenous people, while Cali and the Caribbean and Pacific coasts have a high proportion of African-Colombians.

James Rodríguez, known simply to most Colombians as James (pronounced *Hames*), is currently the most famous footballer in the country and one of the most promising young players in the world. He played on the national team during the 2014 World Cup, becoming the highest scorer of the tournament.

Slavery was abolished in 1821, and the country has the largest black population in South America after Brazil. The last four centuries have seen plenty of intermarriage, meaning a great number of Colombians are mixed race; indeed it's quite a challenge to picture a 'typical' looking Colombian!

Balls & Bulls

Colombians love fútbol (soccer). The national league has 18 teams across the country, and attracts rowdy and boisterous crowds during the two seasons (February to June and August to December). The standard of play is often poor, making for comical, error-prone matches.

Animal-lovers will be disappointed to witness the popularity of bullfighting in Colombia, whether at formal events or at *correlejas,* the wild-side variant that sees amateurs pitting their addled wits against a charging *toro* (bull) with predictably gory consequences. The formal bullfighting season peaks during the holiday period between mid-December and mid-January, and attracts some of the world's best matadors. The January Feria de Manizales is of great appeal to aficionados. Cock-fighting is also wildly popular in rural areas.

After soccer, baseball is the second-most popular team sport in Colombia. Cycling is also hugely popular, with Bogotá's Ciclovía each Sunday bringing in thousands of cyclists and skaters to the city's roads, many of which are closed for the day.

The Arts

Ask most people to name three famous Colombian artists, and you'll get Gabriel García Márquez, sculptor Fernando Botero and Shakira. But Colombia's artists have a lot more to offer than magic realism, fat-bottomed statues and hip-swinging pop.

Music

Colombia is famous for its music, and silence is a very rare commodity, whether on the country's two coasts, in the highlands, in the capital, or on the vast plains that sweep towards Venezuela.

Vallenato, born a century ago on the Caribbean coast, is based on the German accordion. Carlos Vives, one of the best-known modern Latin musical artists, modernized the form and became a poster boy for the music. Vallenato's spiritual homeland is Valledupar. The style is not to everyone's taste, but if you leave Colombia without having danced to it a dozen times, you haven't really been there.

Cumbia, a lively 4/4 style with guitars, accordion, bass, drums and the occasional horn, is the most popular of the Colombian musical styles overseas. Groups such as Pernett and The Caribbean Ravers have modernized the sound, as have Bomba Estéreo, who also spiked the party with a dose of acid rock. The funkiest group of recent years has been Choc Quib Town, a Pacific coast hip-hop band, who mix incisive social commentary with tough beats.

Salsa spread throughout the Caribbean and in the late 1960s it hit Colombia, where it's been adopted and made its own. Cali and Barranquilla are its heartland, but it's loved everywhere. The country went into mourning when Joe Arroyo, known locally as El Joe, died in 2011. The modern, tough urban salsa style is best typified by La 33 of Bogotá.

Joropo, the music of Los Llanos, is accompanied by a harp, a *cuatro* (a type of four-string guitar) and maracas. It has much in common with the music of the Venezuelan Llanos. Chief proponents Grupo Cimarrón will dazzle you with their virtuosity and rapid footwork.

Colombia has also generated many unique rhythms from the fusion of Afro-Caribbean and Spanish influences, including *porro, currulao, merecumbe, mapalé* and *gaita.* The Cartagena-born sound of *champeta,* meanwhile, mixes African rhythms with a bumping, rough-cut, block-party attitude: check it out in Cartagena's less touristy clubs, such as Bazurto Social Club (p135). Reggaeton, with its thumping bass-snare loops, is popular as well, along with the rhythmically driven and heavy on the downbeat merengue.

Colombian Andean music is strongly influenced by Spanish rhythms and instruments, and differs noticeably from the indigenous music of the Peruvian and Bolivian highlands. Among typical old genres are the *bambuco, pasillo* and *torbellino,* instrumental styles featuring predominantly string instruments.

In the cities, especially Bogotá and Medellín, many clubs play techno and house; big-name international DJs sometimes play both cities.

Bogotá is Colombia's cultural capital. For a taste of what's on, check out www.culturarecreacionydeporte.gov.co.

The Bogotá Festival Iberoamericano de Teatro, the world's largest such event, was set up in 1976 by Colombia's most influential actress, Fanny Mikey (1930–2008). See www.festivaldeteatro.com.co for more.

Colombian Literature

Colombia's long (if modest) literary tradition began to form shortly after independence from Spain in 1819 and gravitated towards European romanticism. Rafael Pombo (1833–1912) is generally acclaimed as the father of Colombian romantic poetry and Jorge Isaacs (1837–95), another notable author of the period, is particularly remembered for his romantic novel *María,* which can still be spotted in cafes and classrooms around the country.

José Asunción Silva (1865–96), one of Colombia's most remarkable poets, is considered the precursor of modernism in Latin America. He planted the seeds that were later developed by Nicaraguan poet Rubén Darío. Another literary talent, Porfirio Barba Jacob (1883–1942), known as 'the poet of death,' introduced the ideas of irrationalism and the language of the avant-garde.

Talented contemporaries of literary Nobel Laureate Gabriel García Márquez included poet, novelist and painter Héctor Rojas Herazo, and Álvaro Mutis, who was a close friend. Of the younger generation, seek out the works of Fernando Vallejo, a highly respected iconoclast who has claimed in interviews that García Márquez lacks originality and is a poor writer. Popular young expat Santiago Gamboa has written travel books and novels; Mario Mendoza writes gritty, modern urban fiction; and Laura Restrepo focuses on how violence affects the individual and society – they are prolific writers who have each cranked out major works in recent years.

Art & Abstraction

Fernando Botero is to Colombian painting what Gabriel García Márquéz is to the country's literature – the heavyweight name that overshadows all others. Two other famous Colombian painters, often overlooked, are

GABRIEL GARCÍA MÁRQUEZ, COLOMBIA'S NOBEL LAUREATE

Gabriel García Márquez remains the titan of Colombian literature, despite his death in 2014. Born in 1928 in Aracataca, he wrote primarily about Colombia, despite actually living most of his life in Mexico and Europe.

García Márquez began as a journalist in the 1950s and worked as a foreign correspondent, criticizing the Colombian government and forcing himself into exile. His breakthrough novel came in 1967, with *One Hundred Years of Solitude*. It mixed myths, dreams and reality, and single-handedly invented the magic realism genre.

In 1982 García Márquez won the Nobel Prize in Literature. In the years following he created a wealth of fascinating work, including *Love in the Time of Cholera* (1985), a story based loosely on the courtship of his parents and *The General in his Labyrinth* (1989), which recounts the tragic final months of Simón Bolívar's life. *Strange Pilgrims* (1992) is a collection of 12 stories written by the author over 18 years. *Of Love and Other Demons* (1994) is the story of a young girl raised by her parents' slaves, set amid the backdrop of Cartagena's inquisition.

In 2012, García Márquez' brother revealed that Gabo, as he was affectionately known to Colombians, was suffering from dementia, accelerated by his chemotherapy for lymphatic cancer. Following his death in 2014, García Márquez was buried in Mexico City, with the presidents of both Colombia and Mexico in attendance. His home town, Aracataca, inspiration for the fictional Macondo in *One Hundred Years of Solitude,* held a symbolic funeral for him as well.

You'll find editions of García Márquez' works on sale in English all over Colombia, and while there's a good reconstruction of his family home that serves as a museum in his home town of Aracataca, the town itself will be a letdown for anyone wanting to get a geographic sense of García Márquez' books. For a better taste of Gabo's world, head to Cartagena or – better still – the isolated colonial town of Mompox, a modern-day Macondo that will delight any fan of *One Hundred Years of Solitude*.

FERNANDO BOTERO: LARGER THAN LIFE

Fernando Botero (b 1932) is the most widely recognized Colombian painter and sculptor. Born in Medellín, he had his first individual painting exhibition in Bogotá at the age of 19 and gradually developed his easily recognizable style – characterized by his figures' massive, almost obscene curvaceousness. In 1972 he settled in Paris and began experimenting with sculpture, which resulted in a collection of *gordas* and *gordos* (fat women and men), as Colombians call these creations.

Today, his paintings hang on the walls of world-class museums and his monumental public sculptures adorn squares and parks in cities around the globe, including Paris, Madrid, Lisbon, Florence and New York.

Moving from his typically safe subject matter in 2004, he shocked Colombia with a collection of works examining the country's civil war; and in 2005, he produced a controversial series of images that split critical opinion, featuring scenes from Iraq's Abu Ghraib prison, where US forces tortured and humiliated detainees. While some lauded Botero's move into more political matters, others regarded it as too little, too late, and still others thought this out-of-character development was inappropriate.

Omar Rayo (1928–2010), known for his geometric drawings, and Alejandro Obregón (1920–92), a Cartagena painter famous for his abstract paintings.

Colombia is also home to a good deal of colonial religious art. Gregorio Vásquez de Arce y Ceballos (1638–1711) was the most remarkable painter of the colonial era. He lived and worked in Bogotá and left behind a collection of more than 500 works, now distributed among churches and museums across the country.

Since the end of WWII, the most distinguished artists have been Pedro Nel Gómez, known for his murals, watercolors, oils and sculptures; Luis Alberto Acuña, a painter and sculptor who used motifs from pre-Columbian art; Guillermo Wiedemann, a German painter who spent most of his creative period in Colombia and drew inspiration from local themes (though he later turned to abstract art); Edgar Negret, an abstract sculptor; Eduardo Ramírez Villamizar, who expressed himself mostly in geometric forms; and Rodrigo Arenas Betancur, Colombia's most famous monument-maker.

These masters were followed by a slightly younger generation, born mainly in the 1930s, including artists such as Armando Villegas, a Peruvian living in Colombia, whose influences ranged from pre-Columbian motifs to surrealism; Leonel Góngora, noted for his erotic drawings; and the most internationally renowned Colombian artist, Fernando Botero.

The recent period has been characterized by a proliferation of schools, trends and techniques. Artists to watch out for include Bernardo Salcedo (conceptual sculpture and photography), Miguel Ángel Rojas (painting and installations), Lorenzo Jaramillo (expressionist painting), María de la Paz Jaramillo (painting), María Fernanda Cardozo (installations), Catalina Mejía (abstract painting) and Doris Salcedo (sculpture and installations).

Telenovelas (soap operas) are Colombia's cultural barometer. Although they aren't high art, they reflect the country's concerns and passions as faithfully as any documentary. One popular show was *Chepe Fortuna* (Fishing For Fortune), a gloriously improbable tale of love, politics, environmentalism and, er, mermaids.

The Natural World

From snowcapped, craggy Andean mountains and the vast plains of Los Llanos, to the lush tropical forests of the Amazon basin and rolling green valleys, Colombia is a mind-blowingly beautiful and varied country. And despite its relatively modest size, Colombia is the second-most biodiverse country on earth, after Brazil.

Gaviotas: A Village to Reinvent the World (1998), by Alan Weisman, tells the story of Colombian villagers who transformed their barren hamlet in Los Llanos into a global model for a sustainable community. See www.friendsofgaviotas.org for more information.

The Land

Colombia covers 1.14 million sq km, roughly equivalent to the combined area of California and Texas (or France, Spain and Portugal). It is the 26th-largest country in the world, and the fourth-largest in South America, after Brazil, Argentina and Peru.

While most people assume that Colombia is just a tropical land, the country's physical geography is amazingly varied. The country's environment is generally divided into five habitat categories: wet tropical forests, dry tropical forests, tropical grasslands, mountain grasslands, and deserts and scrublands.

The western part, almost half of the total territory, is mountainous, with three Andean chains – Cordillera Occidental, Cordillera Central and Cordillera Oriental – running roughly parallel north–south across most of the country. A number of the peaks are over 5000m, making them higher than anything in the USA. Two valleys, the Valle del Cauca and Valle del Magdalena, are sandwiched between the three cordilleras. Both valleys have their own eponymous rivers, which flow north, unite and eventually empty into the Caribbean near Barranquilla.

Apart from the three Andean chains, Colombia features an independent and relatively small range, the Sierra Nevada de Santa Marta, which rises from the Caribbean coastline to soaring, snowcapped peaks. It is the world's highest coastal mountain range, and its twin summits of Simón Bolívar and Cristóbal Colón (both 5775m) are the country's highest.

More than half of the territory east of the Andes is vast lowland, which is generally divided into two regions: Los Llanos to the north and the Amazon River basin to the south. Los Llanos, roughly 250,000 sq km in area, is a huge open swath of grassland that constitutes the Orinoco River basin. Colombians say it is like an internal, green sea. The Amazon region, stretching over some 400,000 sq km, occupies Colombia's entire southeast and lies in the Amazon basin. Most of this land is covered by a thick rainforest and crisscrossed by rivers, and remains totally cut off from the rest of the country by road, though this sadly doesn't stop illegal logging.

Colombia also has a number of islands. The major ones are the archipelago of San Andrés and Providencia (a long way off in the Caribbean Sea, 750km northwest of mainland Colombia), the Islas del Rosario and San Bernardo (near the Caribbean coast), and Gorgona and Malpelo (along the Pacific coast).

Wildlife

This huge variety of climatic and geographic zones and microclimates has spawned diverse ecosystems and allowed wildlife to evolve independently. And how. Colombia claims to have more plant and animal species per square kilometer than any other country in the world. Its variety of flora and fauna is second only to Brazil's, even though Colombia is seven times smaller than its neighbor.

Colombia is the only South American nation to have coastlines on both the Pacific Ocean and Caribbean Sea.

Animals

From pink dolphins to colorful parrots, tiny cats to giant rats, Colombia has some of the most diverse animal life on the planet. It has nearly 1700 recorded species of bird – 74 of which are native to the country – representing about 19% of all the birds on the planet. Colombia also has about 450 species of mammal (including 15% of the world's primates), 600 species of amphibian, 500 species of reptile and 3200 species of fish.

Some of the most interesting mammals include sleek cats such as the jaguar and the ocelot, red howler monkeys, spider monkeys, the three-toed sloth, giant anteaters, the goofy piglike peccary and tapir, and the hideous-looking capybara, or chiguiro, the world's largest living rodent that can grow to 48cm tall and weigh 55kg.

The waters of Colombia's Amazon are home to the famous rose-colored boto (Amazon River dolphin), the Amazonian manatee, and one of the most feared snakes, the anaconda *(Eunectes murinus)* that can grow to 6m (20ft).

Colombia's famous aviary includes 132 species of hummingbird, 24 species of toucan, 57 types of colorful parrot and macaw, plus kingfishers, trogons, warblers and six of the world's seven vultures, including the Andean condor – a national symbol of Colombia.

Bird-watching enthusiasts should pick up *A Guide to the Birds of Colombia* (1986) by Stephen L Hilty and William L Brown. Two great online resources for bird-watchers are www.colombiabirding.com and www.proaves.org.

There is also abundant marine life in the country's extensive river systems and along its two coastlines. The islands of San Andrés and Providencia boast some of the largest and most productive coral reefs in the Americas. In 2000 Unesco declared this area the Seaflower Biosphere Reserve in order to protect the ecosystem. The reefs are considered among the most intact in the Caribbean and play an important ecological role in the health of the sea. They provide feeding and nesting grounds for four species of endangered sea turtle and numerous types of fish and lobster. It has been determined that the health of certain fish stocks in the Florida Keys hinges directly on their ability to spawn in the Colombian reefs. The island of Providencia itself is home to the Providencia black crab *(Gecarcinus ruricola)*, a unique species of crab that lives on the land, but completes an extraordinary annual migration to the sea to lay and fertilize eggs.

THE GREAT PROVIDENCIA CRAB MIGRATION

It truly is one of the most extraordinary sights you'll ever see: for a whole week in April the uniquely terrestrial Providencia black crab comes down from its habitat in the mountains and makes its way awkwardly towards the sea, where the females lay their eggs and the males then fertilize them, before returning inland shortly afterwards. During this time, the one road that rings this tiny Caribbean island is closed, and life for many becomes very static and even quieter than usual, with islanders only able to move around the island on foot.

A few months later, usually in July, the hatched juvenile crabs, still tiny, crawl out of the sea and head to the mountains. During this second migration the island shuts down again, and the sound of rustling is permanent day and night as the tiny crabs make their inelegant way up the hillside in their millions. If you're lucky enough to arrive on Providencia during either of these times, you're in for an unforgettable, if Hitchcockian, experience.

Endangered Species

The vast savanna of Los Llanos is home to some of the most endangered species in Colombia. Among them is the Orinoco crocodile, which can reach 7m in length. According to the Nature Conservancy, only 1800 of these crocs remain in the wild, making it one of the most critically endangered reptiles in the world. Other endangered creatures from Los Llanos include the Orinoco turtle, giant armadillo, giant otter and black-and-chestnut eagle.

The cotton-top tamarin, a tiny monkey weighing just 500g, and its larger cousin, the brown spider monkey, are two of the most critically endangered primates in the world, according to the 2008 International Union for Conservation of Nature (IUCN) Red List of Threatened Species. Other critically endangered or endangered animals on the IUCN list include Handley's slender mouse opossum, mountain grackle and the mountain tapir. And two of the Amazon River's most famous residents, the pink river dolphin and the Amazonian manatee, are considered vulnerable.

Note that some remote restaurants and bars offer turtle eggs, iguanas and other endangered species on their menus. It's also worth noting that the pirarucú (a fish popular in the Amazon basin region around Leticia) has been subject to overfishing; locals routinely ignore regulations preventing fishing for this species when it's spawning. These animals are endangered and eating them may hasten their extinction. There are normally other fish available on menus in the Amazon.

The famous German geographer and botanist Alexander von Humboldt explored and studied regions of Colombia and described it all in amazing detail in *Personal Narrative of Travels to the Equinoctial Regions of America, During the Year 1799–1804.*

Plants

Colombia's flora is equally as impressive as its fauna and includes more than 130,000 types of plant, a third of which are endemic species. This richness does not convey the whole picture: large areas of the country, such as the inaccessible parts of the Amazon, have undiscovered species. It is estimated that, at a minimum, 2000 plant species have yet to be identified and an even greater number have yet to be analyzed for potential medicinal purposes.

GREEN FEVER

Colombia produces the largest percentage of the world's emeralds (50%; compared with Zambia's 20% and Brazil's 15%). Some estimate that the mines inside Colombia may actually contain up to 90% of the world's emerald deposits. This is good news for emerald prospectors but may not bode so well for the local environment – and perhaps Colombia as a whole. The fighting and destruction related to the production of these glamorous gems has had an impact on the country not so different from cocaine and heroin.

The main emerald-mining areas in Colombia include Muzo, Coscuez, La Pita and Chivor, all in the Boyacá department. Although the Muisca people mined emeralds in pre-Columbian times, the Spanish colonialists went crazy for the shiny green stones and greatly expanded the operations. They enslaved the indigenous locals to mine the gems and eventually replaced those workers with slave labor from Africa. Many of today's miners are the direct descendants of those slaves and live in only slightly better conditions.

The rich deposits in these areas have led to several environmental and social problems. Rampant digging has torn up the countryside and, in an attempt to find new digging sites or to improve their squalid living conditions, miners have continuously pushed further into the forest. Fierce battles have repeatedly been fought between rival gangs of miners, claiming lives and ravaging the mines. Between 1984 and 1990 alone, in one of the bloodiest 'emerald wars' in recent history, 3500 people were killed in Muzo. Yet 'green fever' continues to burn among fortune hunters and adventurers from all corners of the country and it may not stop until the last bewitching green gem is mined.

Colombia has some 3500 species of orchid, more than any other country. Many of them are unique to the country, including *Cattleya trianae*, the national flower of Colombia. Orchids grow in virtually all regions and climate zones of the country, but are mostly found in altitudes between 1000m and 2000m, particularly in the northwest department of Antioquia.

Further up into the clouds you will find the frailejón, a unique, yellow-flowering, perennial shrub that only grows at altitudes above 3000m. There are some 88 species of frailejón, most native to Colombia. You'll find them in protected places such as Sierra Nevada de Santa Marta, Sierra Nevada del Cocuy and Santuario de Iguaque.

National Parks

Colombia has 55 national parks, flora and fauna sanctuaries and other natural reserve areas, all administered by the government's **Parques Nacionales Naturales (PNN) de Colombia** (☑353 2400; www.parquesnacionales.gov.co).

Unfortunately, simply declaring an area a national park has not stopped guerrilla activity, drug cultivation, illegal ranching, logging, mining or poaching. Most parks in the Amazon basin (except Amacayacu) and along the Ecuadorian border should be considered off-limits. Other parks, such as Los Katios, a Unesco World Heritage Site near Darién Gap, are open but remain dodgy and access is limited; check the current security situation before proceeding.

On the bright side, many parks that were off-limits in recent years are now open for tourists and are included in our coverage. With the recent growth in tourism and ecotourism, the government is finally pumping pesos into its long-underfunded national parks system. New parks have recently opened and more are in the planning stages. Established parks are finally getting much-needed visitor amenities such as lodging and dining facilities, a rarity in Colombia.

This has not been without controversy. PNN has begun contracting with private companies to develop and operate tourist facilities inside some national parks, a move that some environmentalists fear will lead to overdevelopment. Some are concerned that prices will also increase and make the parks inaccessible to average Colombians. However, environmentalists have had some success checking such development. In 2011, plans for a gaudy seven-star hotel complex in Parque Nacional Natural (PNN) Tayrona were abandoned after pressure from environmental groups.

Colombia's most popular parks are situated along the country's pristine beaches. PNN Tayrona is by far Colombia's most popular national park, followed by Parque Nacional Natural (PNN) Corales del Rosario y San Bernardo and Parque Nacional Natural (PNN) Isla Gorgona.

Many other national parks offer just simple accommodations including basic cabins, dorms or campsites. Travelers wishing to stay overnight must book ahead with the PNN central office in Bogotá (p74). There are also PNN regional offices in most large cities and at the parks. Most parks have an admission fee, payable at the entrance or at a regional PNN office.

It is always a good idea to check ahead of time with tour agencies and the parks department for up-to-date security and weather conditions for any park before visiting.

Private Parks & Reserves

In recent years the number of privately owned and operated nature reserves has increased. These are run by individual proprietors, rural communities, foundations and nongovernmental organizations. Many are just small, family reserves, sometimes offering accommodations and food. About 230 of these private parks are affiliated with the **Asociación**

Colombia is the world's third-largest exporter of coffee (after Brazil and Vietnam). In 2010, eight million 60kg bags reaped the country US$2.8 billion – but the relentless rains of 2011 hit the 2012 production hard.

Colombia is the world's second-largest exporter of cut flowers, after the Netherlands. About US$1 billion worth of flowers are exported every year, mostly to the US. Americans buy 300 million Colombian roses on Valentine's Day. But the country cultivates more than 1500 different varieties of flower.

THE NATURAL WORLD NATIONAL PARKS

Red Colombiana de Reservas Naturales de la Sociedad Civil (http://resnatur.org.co).

Yet another new player on the park scene is the corporation. Future parks might look a lot more like the new Parque Nacional del Chicamocha (p112), near Bucaramanga. This for-profit, corporate-run resort opened in December 2006, at a reported cost of US$20 million. In addition to hiking and trekking opportunities, this commercial theme park features dozens of restaurants, cafes, thrill-rides, a zoo, cable cars and water park.

Environmental Issues

Many challenges remain, not least of which are the problems of climate change, habitat loss, and a loss of biodiversity through giant agribusiness megaplantations. The rapid push to develop a market-based economy and compete globally has put pressure on Colombia to build on its land and exploit its natural resources; farming, legal and illegal logging, mining and oil exploration are all a threat to Clombia's natural environment. Such deforestation has increased the rate of extinction for many plant and animal species and destabilized soils, leading to the silting of rivers and devastation of marine species.

Conservación Internacional is one of Colombia's most influential environmental advocacy groups. To learn more about its work, check out http://conservation.org.co.

Even more troubling is the environmental impact of the illegal drug trade. Other than cocaine, illegal cash crops include marijuana and opium poppies. Attempts to stop farmers cultivating coca simply cause the producers to relocate. They move higher up the slopes and to the more remote, virgin forests of the Andes (aided by an increase in opium cultivation, which favors higher altitudes) and deeper into parks and the Amazon basin. In addition, antidrug efforts by the Colombian government (and, in large part, funded by the US War on Drugs) have also taken some toll: the most common method of eradication has been aerial fumigation of coca fields; these hazardous herbicides destroy not just the coca plants, but surrounding vegetation as well, and no doubt seep into the watershed.

However, environmentalists now wield more clout in government policy. In 2006 then President Álvaro Uribe signed the controversial General Forestry Law that opened up the country's forests to logging. Colombian and international environmental groups sued the government – and won. The Colombia Constitutional Court in 2009 ruled that the Forestry Law was unconstitutional because indigenous communities were never consulted. Score one for the greens.

Survival Guide

Safe Travel

Few countries in Latin America or elsewhere have done more to turn around their own image than Colombia, which spent most of the 1980s and '90s as a woefully feared tourism black hole as an intertwined civil military conflict and international Drug War wreaked havoc on daily life. Today, most travelers will find Colombia safer on average than all of the country's immediate neighbors – an astonishing turnaround. Problems remain, however. Street crime is still an issue, and is on the rise in Bogotá, so vigilance and common sense are always required; and guerrillas, paramilitaries and narco-traffickers still linger in many Colombian departments (though they are being pushed further into hiding all the time). Keep your wits about you, avoid travel to dodgy parts of town and be extra vigilant after dark, and Colombia should offer you nothing but a good time.

Safe & Unsafe Areas

All the areas covered by us are generally safe from guerillas and paramilitary groups, and providing you do not wander far from what's included in our coverage, you aren't likely to run into any problems. If you're curious about an area that has been omitted, it's likely due to security issues. The Fuerzas Armadas Revolucionarias de Colombia (FARC) and/or paramilitaries maintain a presence in the Chocó, Cauca, parts of Nariño, rural parts of Huila, Putumayo, Meta, the jungle area east of the Andes (except for the area around Leticia) and parts of the northeast (especially Arauca), so avoid these areas where not covered by Lonely Planet.

Guerrilla & Paramilitary Activity

There are still isolated pockets of guerrilla activity in remote parts of Colombia, even though the FARC, the chief perpetrators of kidnapping in Colombia, have sworn off the practice now. The Ejército de Liberación Nacional; National Liberation Army (ELN) have yet to follow suit though. Going off the beaten track should be done with great caution, if at all. Your worst-case scenario is kidnapping, for financial or political ends. Half of Colombia is not currently covered by this guide, as the security situation remains dubious and tourist infrastructure currently simply does not exist: these areas include much of the west of the country and much of the Amazon region (though the area of the Amazon we cover is extremely safe).

Theft & Robbery

Theft is the most common travelers' danger. In general, the problem is more serious in the largest cities. The most common methods of theft are snatching your day pack, cell phone or camera, pickpocketing, or taking advantage of a moment's inattention to pick up your gear and run away.

GOVERNMENT TRAVEL ADVICE

Government websites with useful travel advisories:

Australian Department of Foreign Affairs (☑300-555-135; www.smartraveller.gov.au)

British Foreign Office (☑0845-850-2829; www.fco.gov.uk)

Canadian Department of Foreign Affairs (☑800-267-6788; www.travel.gc.ca)

US State Department (☑888-407-4747; http://travel.state.gov)

➡ Avoid wandering off the grid, especially without checking the security situation on the ground.

➡ Be cautious when using ATMs after dark, avoid doing so entirely on deserted streets.

➡ Carry a quickly accessible, rolled bundle of small notes in case of robbery.

➡ Avoid drug tourism.

➡ Be very wary of drinks or cigarettes offered by strangers or new 'friends.'

➡ Beware of criminals masquerading as plainclothes police.

➡ Be wary in Taganga, where the security situation has worsened in recent years. In particular, do not walk to the beaches beyond the town, where robberies have occurred in broad daylight, but take the boat instead.

➡ Avoid night travel between Popayán and San Agustín, as bus robberies are regular.

Distraction can often be part of the thieves' strategy. Thieves tend to work in pairs or groups, often on motorcycles; one or more will distract you while an accomplice does the deed. They may begin by making friends with you, or pretend to be the police and demand to check your possessions. Inside banks, pay special attention when withdrawing money from ATMs and be wary of criminals posing as bank employees and offering help – a common robbery tactic.

If you can, leave your money and valuables somewhere safe before walking the streets. In practice, it's good to carry a decoy bundle of small notes, a maximum of COP$50,000 to COP$100,000, ready to hand over in case of an assault; if you really don't have a peso, robbers can become frustrated and, as a consequence, unpredictable.

Armed hold-ups in the cities can occur even in some more upmarket suburbs. If you are accosted by robbers, it is best to give them what

they are after, but try to play it cool and don't rush to hand them all your valuables at once – they may well be satisfied with just your decoy wad. Don't try to escape or struggle – your chances are slim, and people have been murdered for pocket change. Don't count on any help from passersby.

Drugs

Cocaine and marijuana are cheap and widely available in Colombia's major cities. Purchasing and consuming drugs, however, is not a good idea. Many Colombians find Colombian drug tourism very offensive, especially in smaller towns. It's important to note the majority of Colombians don't consume drugs and many believe the foreign drug trade is responsible for Colombia's decades of violent conflict. So, asking after drugs, or openly using drugs, could land you in a lot of trouble (note: it's illegal to buy, sell or consume drugs in any quantity).

A recent rise in travelers coming to Colombia to use

ayahuasca (or *yagé* as it's often known in Colombia) is another worrying trend.The hallucinogenic drug, derived from various rainforest plants and used by Colombia's indigenous peoples in ceremonies for centuries, causes purging and vomiting alongside incredibly strong hallucinations. In 2014 a 19-year-old British backpacker died near Putumayo while trying the drug, and we strongly recommend that you avoid it.

Sometimes you may be offered drugs on the street, in a bar or at a disco, but never accept these offers. The vendors may well be setting you up for the police, or their accomplices will follow you and stop you later, show you false police documents and threaten you with jail unless you pay them off.

There have been reports of drugs being planted on travelers, so keep your eyes open. Always refuse if a stranger at an airport asks you to take their luggage on board as part of your luggage allowance.

Spiked Drinks

Burundanga is a drug obtained from a species of tree widespread in Colombia and is used by thieves to render a victim unconscious. It can be put into sweets, cigarettes, chewing gum, spirits, beer – virtually any kind of food or drink – and it doesn't have any noticeable taste or odor.

The main effect after a 'normal' dose is the loss of will, even though you remain conscious. The thief can then ask you to hand over your valuables and you will obey without resistance. Cases of rape under the effect of burundanga are known. Other effects are loss of memory and sleepiness, which can last from a few hours to several days. An overdose can be fatal.

COCAINE HOLIDAY? CONSIDER THE CONSEQUENCES

Drug tourism is an unfortunate reality in Colombia. And why not? Cocaine is cheap, right? *Not exactly.*

What may appear a harmless diversion directly contributes to the violence and mayhem that play out in the Colombian countryside every day. People fight and die for control of the cocaine trade. Purchasing and consuming cocaine helps finance that conflict. It's estimated that the Fuerzas Armadas Revolucionarias de Colombia (FARC) alone collects between US$200 and US$300 million per year from cocaine production.

Worse still, the byproducts from the production of cocaine are extremely damaging to the environment. The production process requires toxic chemicals such as kerosene, sulfuric acid, acetone and carbide, which are simply dumped afterward on the ground or into streams and rivers. Further, it's estimated that between 500 and 3000 sq km of virgin rainforest are cut down every year for coca production.

Colombia is one of the most beautiful countries in the world. The people, the music, the dancing, the food – there is already enough stimulation to overwhelm the senses.

Interacting with the Police & Military

While the Colombian military is highly trustworthy and the federal police have a reputation as untouchables, local cops have more of a mixed reputation. They don't get paid a lot of money, and incidents of bribery and bullying of tourists have been reported.

Always carry a photocopy of your passport with you, including your entry stamp (you're more likely to avoid trouble if you keep your papers in order), and never carry drugs of any kind, either on the street or when traveling.

In tourist areas, there are an increasing number of tourist police; many speak some English. They are uniformed and easily recognizable by the Policía de Turismo labels on their arm bands. At the first hint of trouble, go to them first if you can.

If your passport, valuables or other belongings are stolen, go to the police station and make a *denuncia* (report). The officer on duty will write a statement according to what you tell them. It should include the description of the events and the list of stolen articles. Pay attention to the wording you use, include every stolen item and document, and carefully check the statement before signing it. Your copy of the statement serves as a temporary identity document and you'll need to present it to your insurer to make a claim.

If you happen to get involved with the police, keep calm and be polite, and always use the formal *'usted'* (the word for 'you,' instead of *'tu'*). Keep a sharp eye out when they check your gear.

Scams

Under no circumstances should you agree to a search by plainclothes police officers asking to inspect your passport and money. Criminals masquerading as plainclothes police may stop you on the street, identify themselves with a fake ID, and then ask to inspect your passport and money. A common scam finds these 'officers' claiming your money is counterfeit, preceded by, of course, its confiscation (a variation on this scam involves jewelry as well). Legitimate Colombian police will never make such a request. Call out for uniformed police officers or decent-looking passersby to witness the incident, and insist on phoning a bona fide police station. By that time, the 'officers' will probably have discreetly walked away.

Overland Travel

Traveling overland in most parts of Colombia, especially during the day, should present no issues other than which iPod playlist you choose to drown out the bus driver's loud and questionable musical taste. In the past, taking night buses was not a good idea – the FARC used to control many of the major highways – but this is no longer the case. Night buses to most destinations are a comfortable way to avoid wasting a day in transit, plus you save the cost of a night's accommodation.

The only major routes on which you should avoid night travel are the road from Popayán to Pasto and the border with Ecuador; and to a lesser extent (though still troublesome) the route from Bucaramanga to Santa Marta. There is no longer guerrilla activity, but attacks and armed thieves stopping buses and robbing everyone on board have been reported.

Directory A–Z

Accommodations

There are three main kinds of accommodations in Colombia: backpacker hostels, budget hotels (frequented by Colombians) and top-end hotels. The few midrange hotels on offer tend to cater to Colombian business travelers.

Technically, foreigners are exempt from the 16% IVA (sales tax), but there seems to be universal confusion as to how that law is applied. For all intents and purposes, the posted price will be the price you pay, as the IVA is usually built into the posted price already, and only travelers who have booked and paid for a top-end hotel from abroad really have a shot at not paying IVA – even then the tax will have already been deducted from the posted price.

Camping

➡ For ages camping was out of bounds in Colombia. While the civil conflict continues to rage in remote regions of the country, more and more Colombians are strapping on a pack and getting reacquainted with their beautiful country.

➡ In many cases sleeping in a tent is considered a novelty, and many campgrounds charge more to pitch a tent than you would spend for a night in a hotel.

Hostels

➡ Backpacker tourism is booming in Colombia. All hostels have dorm beds for around COP$18,000 to COP$30,000, and most have a few private rooms for COP$50,000 to COP$80,000.

➡ Many of the most established hostels are members of the **Colombian Hostels Association** (www.colombianhostels.com). The most comprehensive listing of hostels is at www.hosteltrail.com.

Hotels

➡ Also sometimes called *residencias, hospedajes* or *posadas,* a hotel generally suggests a place of a higher standard, or at least higher prices. Cheaper accommodations are usually clustered around markets, bus terminals and in the backstreets of the city center. If you speak Spanish and wish to avoid the gringo trail, a budget private room with hot water, air-con and cable TV goes for between COP$25,000 and COP$30,000 – cheaper than a hostel.

➡ Midrange hotels are rare in Colombia. Prices tend to jump rapidly from budget cheapies to three- and four-star hotels, with little in between. Nevertheless, there are often a handful of hotels in the COP$75,000 to COP$180,000 range, usually in the city center, which cater primarily to Colombian business travelers.

➡ All the major cities have top-end hotels charging from COP$200,000 per night. The best choices of top-end hotels are in Bogotá, Medellín and Cartagena.

Resorts

➡ There are a handful of package-style resorts on the Caribbean coast and on San Andrés. Most are frequented by Colombians, rather than foreign package tourists, and are usually excellent value.

➡ The Pacific coast also has several good all-inclusives, but they are definitely for the more adventurous type as the area is quite remote and is heavily patrolled by the army.

BOOK YOUR STAY ONLINE

For more accommodations reviews by Lonely Planet authors, check out http://lonelyplanet.com/hotels/. You'll find independent reviews, as well as recommendations on the best places to stay. Best of all, you can book online.

➡ For a selection of some of the best small resorts, see www.posadasturisticas decolombia.gov.co.

➡ If you are booking a package resort deal from outside the country, you are exempt from the 16% IVA hotel tax. Some hotels may not know this rule, so be sure to ask for the discount.

Children

➡ Like most Latin Americans, Colombians adore children. Due to a high rate of population growth, children make up a significant proportion of the population, and they are omnipresent. Few foreigners travel with children in Colombia, but if you do plan on taking along your offspring, they will find plenty of local companions.

➡ Basic supplies are usually no problem in the cities. There are quite a few shops devoted to kids' clothes, shoes and toys; **Pepeganga** (www.pepeganga.com) in particular is recommended. You can also buy disposable diapers and baby food in supermarkets and pharmacies. Pick up a copy of Lonely Planet's *Travel with Children* for general tips.

Customs Regulations

➡ Colombian customs looks for large sums of cash (inbound) and drugs (outbound). If they have the slightest suspicion you are carrying either you can expect an exhaustive search of your belongings and your person. Expect to be questioned in Spanish or English by a well-trained police officer. The latest method is x-raying your intestines: if you look in any way out of the ordinary, or fail to give a convincing response to the officer's questions, they will x-ray you to see if you are a drug mule.

➡ You can bring in personal belongings and presents you intend to give to Colombian residents. The quantity, kind and value of these items shouldn't arouse suspicion that they may have been imported for commercial purposes. You can bring in items for personal use such as cameras, camping equipment, sports accessories or laptops without any problems.

➡ Be sure to hang onto your receipts for any big-ticket luxury items. Foreigners may request a refund of the 16% IVA (sales tax) on all goods purchased with a foreign credit card above COP$250,000 during their stay in Colombia. Get to the airport with plenty of time to submit your receipts to DIAN (Dirección de Impuestos y Aduanas Nacionales; the customs bureau) – you must do it *before* check-in.

Electricity

110V/60Hz

110V/60Hz

Embassies & Consulates

Most embassies and consulates are found in Bogotá, but a few countries also have consulates in other Colombian cities.

Argentine embassy (☑1-288-0900; www.ecolo.mrecic.gov.ar; Carrera 12 No 97-80, 5th fl, Bogotá)

Australian embassy (☑022-550-3500; www.chile.embassy.gov.au; Goyenechea 3621, 12th fl, Las Condes, Santiago, Chile) Australian embassy in Santiago handles services for Chile, Colombia, Ecuador and Venezuela.

Brazilian embassy (☑1-218-0800; www.bogota.itamaraty.gov.br; Calle 93 No 14-20, piso 8, Bogotá) Also in Leticia (☑8-592-7530; Calle 9 No 9-73).

Canadian embassy (☑1-657-9800; www.colombia.gc.ca; Carrera 7 No 114-33, Bogotá)

Ecuadorian consulate (☑1-212-6512; www.colombia.embajada.gob.ec; Calle 89 No 13-07, Bogotá) Also in Ipiales (☑2-773-2292; Carrera 7 No 14-10).

French embassy (☑1-638-1400; www.ambafrance-co.org; Carrera 11 No 93-12, Bogotá) Also in Bucaramanga (☑7-645-9393; www.bucaramanga.alianzafrancesa.org.co; Calle 42 No 37-19).

German embassy (☑1-423-2600; www.bogota.diplo.de; Calle 110 No 9-25, 11th fl, Edificio Torre Empresarial Pacífic, Bogotá)

Israeli embassy (☑1-327-7500; www.bogota.mfa.gov.il; Calle 35 No 7-25, piso 14, Bogotá)

Italian embassy (☑1-610-5886; www.ambbogota.esteri.it; Calle 93B No 9-92, Bogotá)

Japanese embassy (☑1-317-5001; www.colombia.emb-japan.go.jp; Carrera 7 No 71-21, torre B, 11th fl, Bogotá)

Netherlands embassy (☑1-638-4200; www.colombia.nlambassade.org; Carrera 13 No 93-40, oficina 201, Bogotá)

Panamanian embassy (☑1-257-5067; www.panamae nelexterior.gob.pa/bogota; Calle 92 No 7A-40, Bogotá) Also in Barranquilla (☑5-360-1870; Carrera 57 No 72-25, Edificio Fincar 207-208); Cali (☑2-486-1116; Av 6 No 25-58, piso 3); Cartagena (☑5-655-1055; Carrera 1 No 10-10, Bocagrande); Medellín (☑4-312-4590; Calle 10 No 42-45, oficina 266).

Peruvian embassy (☑1-746-2360; www.embajadadel peru.org.co; Calle 80A No 6-50, Bogotá) Also in Leticia (☑8-592-7755; Calle 11 No 5-32).

Spanish embassy (☑1-621-0809; www.exteriores.gob.es/embajadas/bogota; Calle 94A No 11A-70, Bogotá)

UK embassy (☑1-326-8300; www.ukincolombia.fco.gov.uk; Carrera 9 No 76-49, 8th fl, Bogotá)

US embassy (☑1-275-2000; http://bogota.usembassy.gov; Calle 24 bis No 48-50, Bogotá)

Venezuelan embassy (☑1-644-5555; www.colombia.embajada.gob.ve; Carrera 11 No 87-51, 5th fl, Edificio Horizonte, Bogotá) Also in Barranquilla (☑5-360-6285; Carrera 52 No 69-96); Cartagena (☑5-665-0382; Edificio Centro Executivo, Carrera 3 No 8-129, piso 14); Cúcuta (☑7-579-1951; http://cucuta.consulado.gob.ve; Av Camilo Daza at Calle 17, Cucutá); Medellín (☑4-444-0359; www.consulvenemedellin.org; Calle 32B No 69-59).

Food

Colombia is not a safe haven for gourmands (how many Colombian restaurants do you normally see around the world?). But that doesn't mean you won't be eating well – Colombia offers high-standard, filling food at great prices.

Colombians are blessed with a fertile country: fish and plantain on the coast; an eye-popping array of tropical fruit; coffee, chocolate and

EATING PRICE RANGES

The following price ranges refer to the cost of main dishes for lunch and dinner.

$	less than COP$15,000
$$	COP$15,000 to COP$30,000
$$$	more than COP$30,000

dairy in the mountains; and cheap, fresh vegetables and meat on all corners. The collective cuisine is known as *comida criolla* (Creole food).

There are plenty of budget places serving meals for COP$12,000 or less. Lunch is the easiest: known as *comida corriente* (literally 'fast food'), a two-course meal will consist of soup followed by rice, beans, choice of meat, a tomato salad and a glass of tropical fruit juice. Midrange restaurants (COP$15,000 to COP$30,000) tend to be a step up in quality and service, and meals in top-end restaurants generally cost more than COP$30,000.

Don't miss uniquely Colombian specialties *ajiaco* (an Andean chicken stew with corn, many types of potatoes, avocado, and a local herb known as guasca) and *bandeja paisa* (the 'paisa' platter'), a gut-busting mound of sausage, beans, rice, egg and *arepa* (ground maize flatbread) – Colombia's de facto national dish despite controversy that its prevalence rarely strays from Antioquia. On the street nationwide you'll find savory *arepas* of all

ilk (with cheese, with ham and eggs, with chicken), *mazamorra* (a maize-based beverage), empanadas (fried stuffed pastries), and fresh-squeezed orange juice and fruit salads. Regional options include *llapingachos* (fried potato cakes with meat) and *helado de paila* (ice cream whipped in a copper tin) in Nariño, ceviche on the Caribbean coast, and tamales in Tolima and Huila. There's also plenty for your sweet tooth: *obleas con arequipe* are thin wafers doused in milk caramel; and *cuajada con melao* is fresh cheese with melted jaggery.

In terms of fruit: zapote, nispero, lulo, uchuwa, borojo, curuba, mamoncillo. Confused? You will be. Don't try and translate these fruits – they're native to Colombia and you won't find them in many other places in the world.

Gay & Lesbian Travelers

→ Compared with some Latin American countries, homosexuality is well tolerated in Colombia (it was declared legal by the government in Bogotá in 1981). There is a substantial gay undercurrent in the major cities and as long as you don't broadcast the fact in public you are unlikely to be harassed. With popular apps such as Grindr for men, most contact is initiated online these days.

→ In 2011 Colombia's Constitutional Court ordered Congress to pass legislation addressing same-sex marriage by June 2013; if they did not, the ruling dictated same-sex couples would automatically receive all marital rights from that date forward. Congress failed to act and Colombia's first gay marriage was performed on July 24, 2013. Check the website www.guiagaycolombia.com for more information.

Health

Most visitors travel to Colombia without incident, but there are certain medical conditions to be aware of and several things you can do to prevent sickness. Most illnesses are the result of Colombia's tropical-zone location. If traveling anywhere along the coast or jungle, you can bank on little tropical nuisances – infected bug bites, rashes or heat exhaustion. Other, more dangerous afflictions, including malaria and yellow fever, can strike travelers who get further off the beaten track or spend a lot of time trekking through national parks. Dengue fever and the newest mosquito-borne threat, chikungunya, which arrived in 2014 on Colombian shores, are a risk in lowland population centers. Other problems can occur in the mountains, including *soroche* (altitude sickness).

The good news is that Colombia has some of the best medical care in South America.

CAFE COUNTRY

You think Colombia is *mucho famoso* for coffee, but in reality, it's really just famous for remarkable coffee marketing. The average everyday swill, called *tinto*, won't please connoisseurs (or anyone else). But Colombia is slowly trying to live up to its java reputation – single-origin coffeehouses with knowledgeable baristas are starting to pop up in bigger cities, with Bogotá leading the charge (p67).

Environmental Hazards

➡ Altitude sickness may develop in travelers who ascend rapidly to altitudes greater than 2500m, including those flying directly to Bogotá.

➡ Tap water in Bogotá and other big cities is safe to drink, but if you're pregnant or want to be more careful, use bottled water instead. In remote areas, water should be boiled or disinfected with iodine pills; or stick to bottled water.

Health Care

➡ Adequate medical care is available in major cities, but may be difficult to find in rural areas.

➡ For an online guide to physicians, dentists, hospitals and pharmacies in Colombia, go to the US embassy website (http://bogota.usembassy.gov/root/pdfs/medservices.pdf).

➡ If you develop a life-threatening medical problem, you'll probably want to be evacuated to a country with state-of-the-art medical care.

➡ For air ambulance service in Colombia, call **Aerosanidades** (☑300-222-1245; www.aerosanidadsas.com; Bogotá), which operates out of 14 airports in Colombia.

Infectious Diseases

➡ Dengue fever, a mosquito-born viral infection (transmitted by Aedes mosquitoes most commonly during the day and usually close to human habitations, often found indoors), is most often found in the departments of Santander, Tolima, Valle del Cauca, Norte de Santander, Meta and Huila.

➡ Malaria, also transmitted by mosquito bites, is prevalent in rural areas below 800m in Amazonas, Chocó, Córdoba, Guainía, Guaviare, Putumayo and Vichada.

➡ Yellow fever is a life-threatening viral infection transmitted by mosquitoes in forested areas, most notably above 2300m in many departments and Parque Nacional Natural (PNN) Tayrona and Ciudad Perdida. A yellow-fever vaccine is required for visitors to the national parks along the coastal regions. Travelers limiting their visit to the main cities and mountainous regions may not need to be immunized for yellow fever, but be aware that some countries, such as Australia, will not let you into the country if you're flying direct from Colombia without a yellow-fever vaccine. Check your country's government health information for specifics.

Insurance

➡ Ideally, all travelers should have a travel-insurance policy, which will provide some security in the case of a medical emergency, or the loss or theft of money or belongings. It may seem an expensive luxury, but if you can't afford a travel health insurance policy, you also probably can't afford medical emergency charges abroad if something goes wrong.

➡ If you need to make a claim on your travel insurance, you must produce a police report detailing loss or theft. You also need proof of the value of any items lost or stolen. Receipts are the best bet, so if you buy a camera for your trip, for example, hang on to the receipt.

➡ Colombian law stipulates that hospitals must treat you, whether or not you can pay. If you don't have the Spanish to insist on this right, you may have difficulty getting treatment.

➡ Worldwide travel insurance is available at www.lonelyplanet.com/travel-insurance. You can buy, extend and claim online anytime – even if you're already on the road.

Internet Access

➡ Colombia is a wired country. Internet is everywhere and cheap – rarely more than COP$2500 per hour.

➡ In smaller towns and more remote destinations, the government's ambitious and heralded Plan Vive Digital has brought free wi-fi to almost everywhere. You can usually stop by the local library to pick-up the password.

➡ Almost all hostels and hotels offer wi-fi. Shopping centers often have free wi-fi, major airports offer wi-fi, and so do most restaurants and cafes.

Language Courses

Universities and language schools in the larger cities run Spanish-language courses. It is generally cheaper and better value to arrange a private one-on-one tutor. Popular backpacker hotels are the best places to ask about independent teachers. Enrolling in a university course is useful if you want to extend your stay beyond the six months a tourist visa permits you.

Legal Matters

If arrested you have the right to an attorney. If you don't have one, one will be appointed to you (and paid for by the government). There is a presumption of innocence and you can expect a speedy trial.

The most common legal situation that travelers find themselves in involves drugs. In 2012, Colombia's Constitutional Court decriminalized the possession of small amounts of cocaine (1g or less) and marijuana (20g or less) for personal use, but that doesn't mean it's a good idea. Although

ORIENTATION

Colombian cities, towns and villages have traditionally been laid out on a grid plan. The streets running north–south are called Carreras, often abbreviated on maps to Cra, Cr or K, whereas those running east–west are called Calles, often labeled on local maps as Cll, Cl or C. This simple pattern may be complicated by diagonal streets, called either Diagonales (more east–west and thus like Calles), or Transversales (more like Carreras).

All streets are numbered and the numerical system of addresses is used. Each address consists of a series of numbers, eg Calle 6 No 12-35 (which means that it's the building on Calle 6, 35m from the corner of Carrera 12 toward Carrera 13), or Carrera 11A No 7-17 (the house on Carrera 11A, 17m from the corner of Calle 7 toward Calle 8).

The system is very practical and you will soon become familiar with it. It is usually easy to find an address. It's actually one of the most precise address systems in the world; if you have an address you can determine the location of the place with pinpoint accuracy.

In the larger cities the main streets are called Avenidas or Autopistas. They each have their own names and numbers, but are commonly known just by their numbers.

Cartagena's old town is the only Colombian city where centuries-old street names have withstood the modern numbering system. Streets in some other cities (eg Medellín) have both names and numbers, but elsewhere only numbers are used.

---

you cannot be criminally prosecuted, you may be ordered to receive physical or psychological treatment depending on your level of intoxication.

Maps

➡ It's difficult to find detailed maps of Colombia outside the country itself. In the USA, **Maps.com** (☎800-430-7532; www.maps.com) has an excellent supply of Colombian maps. A similarly extensive selection is available in the UK from **Stanfords** (☎020-7836-1321; www.stanfords.co.uk).

➡ Within Colombia, folded road maps of the country are produced by various publishers and are distributed through bookstores. Of special note is the Movistar **Guía de Rutas** (www.rutascolombia.com), a Spanish-language guidebook to Colombia with excellent maps. You can buy it at any tollbooth (ask the bus driver beforehand to buy it for you), or from a handful of better bookstores.

➡ The widest selection of maps of Colombia is produced and sold by the **Instituto Geográfico**

Agustín Codazzi (IGAC; ☎1-369-4000; www.igac.gov.co; Carrera 30 No 48-51, Bogotá), the government mapping body, which has its head office in Bogotá and branch offices in departmental capitals.

Money

➡ The Colombian peso (COP$) is the unit of currency in Colombia.

ATMs

➡ Almost all major banks have ATMs, and they usually work fine with cards issued outside Colombia (Bancolombia being the ornery exception for some folks). Cash machines affiliated with Banco de Bogotá, BBVA and ATH are best.

➡ Most banks have a maximum cash withdrawal limit of COP$300,000 per transaction, but it varies. Davivienda and Citibank allow double that from most branches, though it often doesn't work in practice. If you need more, just pull out twice, and be quick about it. The machines have very little tolerance for those that take their time navigating the menu – a second of

hesitation and it cancels the transaction!

➡ If you must use an ATM after dark, always use one inside a gas station. Some ATMs can be fussy if you do not have a chip-and-pin ATM card (we're talking to you, Americans!).

Cash

➡ There are paper notes of COP$1000, COP$2000, COP$5000, COP$10,000, COP$20,000 and COP$50,000. The most used coins are the COP$100, COP$200 and COP$500; the COP$20 and COP$50 are rarely seen outside of supermarkets, and some people may refuse to accept them. A new bimetallic COP$1000 coin was introduced in 2012.

Credit Cards

➡ Credit cards are common in Colombia and used extensively in the major cities and larger towns. When paying with a credit card, you will be asked, *¿a cuantas cuotas?'* (how many payments?). Colombian customers can choose to divide the payment over one to 24 months. Foreign cardholders should just say 'one.'

ORIENTATION
1	Calle 6 No 12-35	3	Diagonal 7 No 13-68
2	Carrera 11A No 7-17	4	Transversal 13 No 6-50

→ The most useful card for cash advances is Visa, as it's accepted by most banks. MasterCard is honored by a few banks. Other cards are of limited use.

→ You can get advance payments on cards from the cashier in the bank or from the bank's ATM. In either case you'll need your PIN.

International Transfers

→ If you need money sent to you quickly, **MoneyGram** (www.moneygram.com) and **Western Union** (www.westernunion.com) are your two principal options. MoneyGram is much cheaper, and is what most overseas Colombians use to send remittances home to their families.

→ Your sender pays the money, along with a fee, at their nearest MoneyGram or Western Union branch, and gives the details on who is to receive it and where. You can have the money within 15 minutes. When you pick it up, take along photo identification and the numbered password they'll give the sender.

→ Both services have offices in all the major cities and most smaller towns.

Moneychangers

→ You are better off using your ATM card in Colombia, as you will get a much better exchange rate. The US dollar is the only foreign currency worth trying to change in Colombia; expect dismal rates for euros, pounds sterling, Australian dollars etc.

→ Many but not all banks change money; in major cities and in border regions there are usually several *casas de cambio* (currency exchanges). Avoid changing money on the street. Most unofficial moneychangers are laundering drug money; the ones on the street can have fast fingers and often dodgy calculators, making it highly unlikely you'll get a fair deal. Though Peru is now the world's leader in producing the world's most counterfeit US notes, Colombia is considering a leader in that regard as well.

→ Your passport is required for any banking transaction. You'll also have to provide a thumbprint. There's a fair amount of paperwork involved in changing money (to prevent money laundering).

Tipping & Bargaining

→ A government regulation dictates that in midrange and top-end restaurants (anywhere there is a service charge), your waiter must ask you if they can add the 10% service charge to the bill. In midrange restaurants it's acceptable to decline to pay the service charge with a polite *'sin servicio, por favor'* if you are dissatisfied. In top-end restaurants refusing the pay the service charge is likely to bring a manager to your table to inquire what was wrong with your meal.

→ Bargaining is limited to informal trade and services, such as markets and street stalls.

→ In areas where taxis are not metered, especially the Caribbean coast, haggling is essential. If you don't like the price make a point of going to the next taxi in the queue.

Opening Hours

The office working day is typically eight hours long, usually from 8am to noon and 2pm to 6pm weekdays, but in practice offices tend to open later and close earlier. Most tourist offices are closed on Saturday and Sunday, and travel agencies usually only work to noon on Saturday.

Banks 9am to 4pm Monday through Friday, 9am to noon on Saturday, with variation by cities and rural areas, where banks sometimes close during lunch.

Bars and Nightclubs Bars usually open around 6pm until the law dictates they close (often 3am); nightclubs are generally open Thursday through Saturday from 9pm until very late.

Post Offices Postal hours vary widely. In Bogotá, many are open from 9am to 5pm Monday to Friday, with some branches also open on Saturday morning, but on the Caribbean coast many close for lunch.

Shops From 9am to 5pm Monday to Friday; some shops close for lunch. On Saturday most shops are open from 9am to noon, or sometimes until 5pm. Large stores and supermarkets usually stay open until 8pm or 9pm Monday to Friday; some also open Sunday.

Restaurants Those opening for lunch open at noon. Restaurants serving breakfast open by 8am. Most of the better restaurants in larger cities, particularly in Bogotá, tend to stay open until 10pm or later; restaurants in smaller towns often close by 9pm or earlier. Many don't open at all on Sunday. Most cafes are open from 8am until 10pm.

Post

➧ Colombia's official postal service is the spiffy new (though terribly named) **4-72** (www.4-72.com. co), which has turned the debilitating pension liabilities and inefficiency of Colombia's former government postal service, Adpostal (shut down in 2006), into a profitable and efficient business. There are also numerous private companies, including **Avianca** (www. aviancaexpress.com), **Deprisa** (www.deprisa.com) and **Servientrega** (www. servientrega.com).

➧ If you want to receive a package in Colombia, you have a choice. The sender can ship via a courier such as DHL, which guarantees fast, dependable delivery, but also guarantees Colombian customs will open the box and charge exorbitant duty. If you're not hurried, have the package sent via regular airmail (four to eight weeks).

➧ Identification is required to ship packages or letters from Colombia, so head to the post office with your passport.

Public Holidays

The following days are observed as public holidays in Colombia.

Año Nuevo (New Year's Day) January 1

Los Reyes Magos (Epiphany) January 6*

San José (St Joseph) March 19*

Jueves Santo & Viernes Santo (Maundy Thursday and Good Friday) March/April (Easter). The following Monday is also a holiday.

Día del Trabajo (Labor Day) May 1

La Ascensión del Señor (Ascension) May*

Corpus Cristi (Corpus Christi) May/June*

Sagrado Corazón de Jesús (Sacred Heart) June*

San Pedro y San Pablo (St Peter and St Paul) June 29*

Día de la Independencia (Independence Day) July 20

Batalla de Boyacá (Battle of Boyacá) August 7

La Asunción de Nuestra Señora (Assumption) August 15*

Día de la Raza (Discovery of America) October 12*

Todos los Santos (All Saints' Day) November 1*

Independencia de Cartagena (Independence of Cartagena) November 11*

Inmaculada Concepción (Immaculate Conception) December 8

Navidad (Christmas Day) December 25

* When the dates marked with an asterisk do not fall on a Monday, the holiday is moved to the following Monday to make a three-day long weekend, referred to as the *puente* (bridge).

In general, any holiday falling on a Tuesday (or Thursday) also turns the preceding Monday (or following Friday) into a holiday as well.

Solo Travelers

➧ Travelers on their own are unlikely to have any problems traveling in Colombia. There are hostels in all major cities and many smaller locales, and you'll often find yourself traveling with other foreigners you meet en route.

➧ If you are going to remote regions not frequented by or unused to foreign visitors, or if you're concerned about security in general, traveling with a friend will certainly ease your mind, and may lessen the likelihood of street crime.

Telephone

The telephone system in Colombia is modern and works well for both domestic and international calls. Telefónica Telecom is the national provider; ETB and Orbitel offer competing services. Public telephones exist in cities and large towns, but they are few and far between, and many are out of order. For directory assistance or information call ☑113.

Email cafes almost always have a few *cabinas* (telephone booths) where you can make local calls for around a few hundred pesos a minute. Most generally offer a fax service as well.

Cell Phones

Colombians love their cell (mobile) phones, and in urban areas almost everyone has at least one. The three major providers are **Claro** (www.claro.com.co), **Movistar** (www.movistar.co) and **Tigo** (www.tigo.com.co). Claro has the best nationwide coverage, and is the most useful to the traveler. Cell phones are cheap, and many travelers end up purchasing one – a basic, no-frills handset will set you back around COP$60,000 to COP$70,000, or you could bring your own cell phone from home and buy a Co-

SHOP TILL YOU DROP

Colombia is famous for everything from fat emeralds to massive hammocks. Here's a shopping list:

Emeralds Mined chiefly from the Muzo area, emeralds are sold in the flourishing emerald street market at the southwestern corner of Av Jiménez and Carrera 7 and nearby Plaza Rosario in Bogotá, where dozens of *negociantes* (traders) buy and sell stones – sometimes on the sidewalks. See p000.

Handicrafts Boyacá is the country's largest handicraft manufacturer, with excellent handwoven items, basketry and pottery. The Pacific coast also has an interesting selection of basketwork, plus the occasional blow-dart gun. Guapi is famous for its musical instruments, especially handmade drums. You may also find some good handwrought gold jewelry here. If you don't make it to the Pacific coast, the **Parque Artesanías** (☉10am-8pm) in Cali is a good place to shop.

Woodwork Pasto is known for its woodwork – decorative items are covered with *barniz de Pasto*, a kind of vegetable resin. Ceramic miniatures of *chivas* (traditional buses) have become a popular souvenir.

Hammocks These come in plenty of regional variations, from the simple, practical hammocks made in Los Llanos to the elaborate Wayuu-crafted *chinchorros*.

Ruanas Colombian woolen ponchos, known as *ruanas*, are found in the colder parts of the Andean zone. In many villages they are still made by hand with simple patterns and natural colors. Bogotá and Villa de Leyva are good places to buy them.

Mochilas The best and most fashionable *mochilas* (a kind of woven handbag) are those of the Arhuaco from the Sierra Nevada de Santa Marta. They are not cheap, but are beautiful and usually of good quality.

If you make any purchases above COP$250,000, use a foreign credit card and save your receipt. Foreigners can request the 16% IVA (sales tax) back.

---

lombian SIM card. A Claro SIM card, for example, costs COP$5000, which includes COP$1000 worth of prepaid calling minutes, though SIM costs vary by provider. Because it is expensive to call between networks you could, at least in theory, buy a SIM card for each of the three providers and swap them out to change networks.

Colombian cell-phone companies do not charge you to receive calls, only to make them. Street vendors selling *minutos* (minutes) are seen almost everywhere. Many corner stores also have cell phones you can use. These vendors purchase prepaid minutes in bulk, and it is always cheaper to make calls with them than to use credit on your own handset. For this reason many Colombians use their handsets to receive calls only and use street

vendors when they need to make calls.

Vendors generally have at least three cell phones – one for each network. The first three digits of the 10-digit number indicate the cell-phone provider, so state the prefix you're calling to and they'll give you the right phone. Expect to pay between COP$100 and COP$400 per minute for a call, depending on the network and provider.

To purchase a phone or SIM you'll need to show identification and proof of address (your hotel is fine). This is supposedly for security but in fact it's to prevent the street vendors from purchasing phones in bulk and competing with the cell-phone provider's own call centers. There have been cases of identity theft (they will photocopy your documents) so only purchase a

cell phone from a provider's official retail outlet.

Phone Codes

It is possible to call direct to just about anywhere in Colombia, but to call a cell phone from a landline, you will need to dial a prefix of ✆03 before the number (some landlines are blocked from calling cell phones); conversely, to dial a landline from a cell phone, you'll need to prefix the number with ✆03 + city code. Landline phone numbers are seven digits countrywide, while cell-phone numbers are 10 digits. Area codes are single digits.

All calls by default go through Telefónica Telecom (✆09). However, you can specify Orbitel (✆05) or ETB (✆07) by dialing that prefix immediately before the number. There's no need to worry much about this unless you're in Colombia long enough to own and operate your own landline.

Colombia's country code is ☑57. If you are dialing a Colombian number from abroad, drop the prefix of the provider (☑05, ☑07 or ☑09) and dial only the area code and the local number.

Time

➡ All of Colombia lies within the same time zone, five hours behind Greenwich Mean Time (GMT). There is no daylight-saving time.

Toilets

➡ There are a handful of public toilets in Colombia. In their absence use a restaurant's toilet. Museums and large shopping malls usually have public toilets, as do bus and airport terminals.

➡ You'll often (but not always) find toilet paper in toilets, so it's wise to carry some with you. Never flush toilet paper. The pipes are narrow and the water pressure is weak, so toilets can't cope with paper. A wastebasket is normally provided.

➡ The most common word for toilet is *baño*. Men's toilets will usually bear a label saying *señores*, *hombres* or *caballeros*, while the women's toilets will be marked *señoras*, *mujeres* or *damas*.

➡ Bus-station restrooms will usually charge COP$500 to COP$800 plus COP$200 for toilet paper. If you're a guy wanting to do some stand-up business, ask a bus-company employee where the driver's urinal *(orinario)* is, usually outside along a back wall, which they will sometimes let you use for free.

Tourist Information

Colombia has a number of good regional and national

websites offering information (sometimes in English) about what to do and where to stay. The country's principal portal is the excellent www.colombia.travel.

Visas

Nationals of some countries, including most of Western Europe, the Americas, Japan, Australia, New Zealand and South Africa, don't need a visa to enter Colombia; otherwise, expect a nominal visa fee.

All visitors get an entry stamp in their passport upon arrival and receive a 90-day tourist visa. Double-check your stamp immediately; errors are sometimes made.

If traveling overland, make sure you get an entry stamp or you'll have troubles later. Overstaying your welcome can result in heavy fines, and in some cases can result in being barred entry in the future. Similarly, make sure you get your departure stamp or there will be trouble the next time around.

Visa Extensions

Migración Colombia (☑511-1150; www.migracioncolombia.gov.co; Calle 100 No 11B-27; ⊘8am-4pm Mon-Fri) in Bogotá handles visa extensions for tourists via Centros Facilitadores de Servicios Migratorios offices around the country. Visitors on a tourist visa may extend up to an additional 90 days at the discretion of the officer. To apply for an extension, known as a *'Permiso Temporal de Permanencia,'* you'll be asked to submit your passport, two photocopies of your passport (picture page and arrival stamp) and two passport-sized photos, along with an air ticket out of the country in most cases. The fee of COP$78,300 must be deposited into the government bank account, which was Banco de Occidente in most areas (Banco de Bogotá in Maicao, Leticia and

Arauca) at the time of writing but often changes. Show up first to fill out forms, then they'll direct you to a nearby bank to pay the fee.

Expect the process to take an entire morning or afternoon. It can be done at any of the Centros Facilitadores de Servicios Migratorios offices in Colombia, which are present in all the main cities and some smaller towns (there is a list on the Migración Colombia website). You'll usually (but not always) get the extension on the spot; sometimes they'll take your fingerprints, send them to Bogotá for a background check and tell you to come back in a week. Fines for overstaying range from half of up to seven times the minimum salary (COP$589,500 as of 2013), depending on length of overstay.

Volunteering

Colombia offers a decent array of volunteering opportunities.

Techo (☑1-285-3057; www.techo.org) This youth-led organization works to transform slums into empowered communities across 19 Latin American countries, including Colombia. Volunteers help build houses with families living in extreme poverty.

Globalteer (☑+44-117-230-9998; www.globalteer.org) A registered UK charity that offers volunteer placements of one to 12 weeks in Medellín, working with street kids in schools, community projects and care homes. Costs are from £725 including accommodation and full in-country support.

FOR Peace Presence (☑+1-646-388-4057; www.peacepresence.org) Employs volunteers in Bogotá and San José de Apartadó in Urabá. The international team provides protective and political accompaniment for the leaders and residents of the Peace Community, supports Colombian conscientious objectors, and works with organizations protecting communities and the environment threatened by the extractive industry and the implementation of free-trade agreements. Suitable applicants serve for 12 months.

Let's Go Volunteer
(☑321-235-0846; www. letsgovolunteer.info; Carrera 5 sur No 22-40, Ibagué) A small, Colombian-based NGO that offers opportunities working with underprivileged children, women who want to leave prostitution, children living with HIV and the elderly. Costs range from one week (US$250) to one month (US$500) to nine months (US$3500).

Women Travelers

➡ Women traveling in Colombia are unlikely to encounter any problems.

➡ The usual caveats apply: bring your street smarts, don't wander alone in dodgy neighborhoods after dark, and keep an eye on your drink.

➡ Female travelers are also more likely to be victims of a bag-snatching or mugging attempt, as you will be perceived as less likely to fight back.

➡ Also be careful taking taxis alone after dark – while rare, there have been reports of taxi drivers raping single female passengers.

Work

➡ There is a growing demand for qualified English-language teachers in Colombia. Some schools may be willing to pay cash-in-hand for a short period of time, but for longer-term employment you will have to find a school willing to organize a work visa.

➡ As a general rule, the more popular the city is among travelers, the harder it will be to find employment; for example, Medellín is crammed with English teachers, while Cali is lacking.

➡ Don't expect to get rich teaching English: you're unlikely to make more than a few million pesos a month, and usually much less.

DIRECTORY A–Z WOMEN TRAVELERS

Transportation

GETTING THERE & AWAY

Flights, cars and tours can be booked online at lonelyplan et.com/bookings.

Entering the Country

Most travelers will arrive in Colombia by plane, or overland from Ecuador, Venezuela or Brazil. There are also numerous sailboats that bring travelers from Panama via the San Blas Islands.

You'll need a valid passport (with at least six more months of validity) and some nationalities will need a visa. Travelers receive a 90-day tourist visa, which can be extended another 90 days per calendar year. When arriving by plane (but not overland), you'll be given a customs form. You're supposed to keep this and return it at the time of your departure (or face a stiff fine), but no one

we know has ever been asked for this form when they left the country. Keep it with your passport just in case, though.

Air

Airports & Airlines

Colombia's biggest international airport is Bogotá's newly renovated **Aeropuerto Internacional El Dorado** (Map p46; www.elnuevodora do.com; Av El Dorado).

Other airports servicing international flights:

Aeropuerto Internacional El Edén (www.aeropuer toeleden.com) Armenia's airport is near the town of La Tebaida.

Aeropuerto Internacional José María Córdoba (www. aeropuertojosemariacordova. com; Medellín) Outside Medellín near the town of Rionegro.

Aeropuerto Internacional Rafael Núñez (www.sacsa. com.co; Cartagena)

Alfonso Bonilla Aragón Airport (Aeropuerto Palma-

seca; www.aerocali.com.co) Cali's airport is 16km northeast of town off the road to Palmira.

Camilo Daza International Airport (Barrio La Laguna, Cúcuta)

Ernesto Cortissoz Airport (www.baq.aero; Barranquilla)

Gustavo Rojas Pinilla International Airport (Aeropuerto Internacional Sesquicentenario; San Andrés)

Matecaña International Airport (Pereira)

Palonegro International Airport (Bucaramanga)

Tickets

Colombia requires, technically at least, that visitors have an onward ticket before they're allowed into the country. Airlines and travel agents quite strictly enforce this, and no one will sell you a one-way ticket unless you already have an onward ticket. Upon arrival in Colombia, however, hardly any immigration officials will ask you to present your onward ticket.

CLIMATE CHANGE & TRAVEL

Every form of transport that relies on carbon-based fuel generates CO_2, the main cause of human-induced climate change. Modern travel is dependent on airplanes, which might use less fuel per kilometer per person than most cars but travel much greater distances. The altitude at which aircraft emit gases (including CO_2) and particles also contributes to their climate change impact. Many websites offer 'carbon calculators' that allow people to estimate the carbon emissions generated by their journey and, for those who wish to do so, to offset the impact of the greenhouse gases emitted with contributions to portfolios of climate-friendly initiatives throughout the world. Lonely Planet offsets the carbon footprint of all staff and author travel.

Consider buying a fully refundable ticket with your credit card and requesting a refund upon arrival in Colombia. If arriving overland, a printout of an unpaid reservation may also be sufficient to get past the border guards. Scruffy-looking travelers are more likely to be asked to show an onward ticket than those who are neatly attired.

Onward Travel within South America

Airline tickets in South America are expensive. If you are traveling to Ecuador, Venezuela or Brazil, you will find it cheaper to fly domestically to the land border (Ipiales, Cúcuta or Leticia, respectively), cross the land border and take another domestic flight to your final destination.

That said, Bogotá is often the cheapest entry point to South America and there are plenty of intercontinental flights out of Bogotá, plus a few out of Cali and Medellín. You can fly Bogotá–Quito (from US$250) and Cali–Quito (from US$320), for example. Flights also connect Bogotá and Caracas (US$900), though seats in and out of Caracas are becoming harder and harder to come by.

Further afield, a flight to Santiago, Chile, will set you back around US$900, and to Buenos Aires US$800. Expect to pay around US$600 to São Paulo or Rio de Janeiro in Brazil. Of course, the fares above vary wildly depending on a number of factors.

Border Crossings

Colombia borders Panama, Venezuela, Brazil, Peru and Ecuador, but has road connections with Venezuela and Ecuador only. These are the easiest and the most popular border crossings.

You can also cross the border to Peru and Brazil at the three corners near Leti-

cia, and there is boat service to and from Panama and Ecuador.

Brazil & Peru

The only viable border crossing from these two countries into Colombia is via Leticia in the far southeastern corner of the Colombian Amazon. Leticia is reached from Iquitos (Peru) and Manaus (Brazil) by riverboat.

Ecuador

Virtually all travelers use the Carretera Panamericana border crossing through Tulcán (Ecuador) and Ipiales (Colombia). The part of the Panamericana between Pasto and Popayán has improved but buses still resort to banding together and traveling this sketchy stretch together; to avoid problems altogether and enjoy fantastic views, it's best to travel this road during the day.

It is theoretically possible to cross the border via skiff along the Pacific coast near Tumaco, but road access to Tumaco and the security situation in the city itself make it a place for travelers to avoid.

More iffy than off limits, there is also a crossing at San Miguel, Putumayo, that backpackers have begun to safely use, but check the situation on the ground with your hotel before proceeding as this area fluctuates often between acceptable and sketchy.

Panama

Numerous sailboats operate between the Panamanian

ports of Portobelo, El Porvenir or Colón and Cartagena. This is a popular form of intercontinental travel, and generally passes through (and stops in) the beautiful San Blas Islands along the way. Some boats operating from Cartagena's yacht clubs work on a fixed schedule, others leave when full. The entire Cartagena–San Blas–El Porvenir trip by sailboat ranges from between US$450 and US$650 all-inclusive. From El Porvenir, you'll need to carry on by speedboat to Carti or Miramar, from where you can continue overland to Panama City; or fly from El Porvenir.

Boats have traditionally been unregulated and safety is an issue. Cartagena-based **Blue Sailing** (Map p126; ☑321-687-5333, 310-704-0425; www.bluesailing.net; Calle San Andrés No 30-47), a Colombian-American-run agency, has begun to change that in recent years. At the time of research the company represented 22 boats, and they ensure that all of them have proper safety equipment for open sea navigation, monitor their boats' locations 24 hours a day and use only licensed captains.

For those in a hurry, **Ferry Xpress** (☑368-0000; www.ferryxpress.com) now offers a regular 1000-person passenger ferry service (seat/cabin US$99/155 one way, 18 hours) between Cartagena and Colón. Ferries depart Cartagena on Tuesday and Thursday, and return from Colón on Monday and

---

Wednesday. It's also possible to take cars on the ferry.

It is also possible to arrange transportation from Bahía Solano to Jaqué in Panama, although departures are infrequent. From here you can continue along Panama's Pacific coast to Panama City or fly.

Venezuela

There are four border crossings between Colombia and Venezuela. By far the most popular with travelers is the route via San Antonio del Táchira (Venezuela) and Cúcuta (Colombia), on the main Caracas–Bogotá road.

There is another reasonably popular border crossing at Paraguachón, on the Maracaibo (Venezuela) to Maicao (Colombia) road. Take this if you plan to head from Venezuela straight to Colombia's Caribbean coast. Buses and shared taxis run between Maracaibo and Maicao, and direct buses run between Caracas/Maracaibo and Santa Marta/Cartagena. Both Colombian and Venezuelan officials at the border will stamp your passport.

Not so popular is the crossing from Colombia's Puerto Carreño and either Puerto Páez or Puerto Ayacucho (both in Venezuela). Still less useful is the crossing from El Amparo de Apure (Venezuela) to Arauca (Colombia), a guerrilla-ridden region.

Tours

Some overland South American companies do visit Colombia, but not many. They are often constrained by their insurance coverage, which is void in any area deemed unsafe by the US State Department or UK Foreign Office.

Dragoman (www.dragoman.co.uk)

Exodus Travels (www.exodus.co.uk)

Intrepid Travel (www.intrepidtravel.com)

Last Frontiers (www.lastfrontiers.co.uk)

Wild Frontiers (www.wildfrontiers.co.uk)

GETTING AROUND

Air

➤ Prices are often fixed between the airlines, but it can be worthwhile checking out their websites just in case. Ticket prices to some destinations drop the last week or two before the date; for some other destinations, they may rise significantly.

➤ You can reserve and pay for domestic flights online with a foreign credit card.

➤ Some airlines offer packages to major tourist destinations (for example, Cartagena and San Andrés), which can cost not much more than you'd pay for air tickets only. If purchasing these package deals from another country you are exempt from the 16% IVA (sales tax) – be sure to ask for this discount, as many Colombians are unaware of it.

Airlines in Colombia

Colombia has several main passenger airlines and a handful of smaller carriers and charter airlines. The following fly a variety of routes:

ADA (☎4-444-4232; www.ada-aero.com) This Medellín-based carrier offers regional flights.

Avianca (☎1-401-3434; www.avianca.com) Long-time principal domestic airline (in partnership with Taca, often referred to as Aviancataca), with the widest network of both domestic and international routes.

Copa Airlines Colombia (☎1-320-9090; www.copaair.com) The second-biggest airline covers much the same domestic territory as Avianca.

EasyFly (☎1-414-8111; www.easyfly.com.co) A budget carrier offering regional flights.

LAN Colombia (☎1-800-094 9490; www.lan.com) Lan purchased Colombia's main budget carrier, Aires, and now flies to smaller regional localities in addition to department capitals.

Satena (☎1-800-091-2034; www.satena.com) The commercial carrier of the Colombian Air Force (FAC) services flights to the vast areas of the Amazon, Los Llanos and the Pacific coast; it lands at numerous small towns and villages that would be otherwise virtually inaccessible.

VivaColombia (☎4-444-9489; www.vivacolombia.co) Medellín-based upstart low-cost carrier serving many of Colombia's main destinations.

Bicycle

➤ Colombia is not the easiest of countries for cyclists, though the sport is wildly popular in certain regions (Boyacá, for example).

➤ Road rules favor drivers and you'll end up fighting traffic on main roadways. Never assume that a driver will give you right of way.

➤ On the plus side, most roads are paved and security is improving. Even the smallest towns will have a repair shop and you can get your bike fixed cheaply and easily.

➤ Bike rentals are uncommon but you can buy a bike almost anywhere.

➤ Colombian cities are becoming more bike-friendly, with new bike tracks and Ciclovia (the weekend closure of selected streets to cars and buses, making them tracks for cyclists and skaters instead).

Boat

➤ Cargo boats ply the Pacific coast, with the port of Buenaventura as their

Main Domestic Flights

hub. Travelers with sufficient time can get a bunk for travel to points north and south including to Nuquí and Bahía Solano.

➡ Before railroads and highways were built, river transportation was the principal means of transportation in mountainous Colombia. The only safe river journey you're likely to take is on the Amazon from Leticia, upriver to Iquitos, Peru or downriver to Manaus, Brazil.

➡ The Río Atrato and Río San Juan in the Chocó should both be avoided due to armed groups operating in the region.

Bus

Buses are the principal means of intercity travel, and go just about everywhere. Most long-distance intercity buses are more comfortable than your average coach-class airplane seat, and the

overnight buses sometimes have business-class-sized seats. Wi-fi is even beginning to make appearances on nicer buses (though it's often patchy or doesn't work at all). A word of warning: Colombian bus drivers turn the air-con up to arctic temperatures. Wear a sweater, a beanie and gloves, or better yet, bring a blanket. Bus drivers also tend to crank up the music and/or action movie (dubbed in Spanish) on the TV, even in the middle of the

COOL COLOMBIA TOURS

A number of domestic agencies offer interesting specialty tours nationwide. Be on the lookout for operators affiliated with **Acotur** (www.acotur.co), Colombia's Association for Responsible Tourism. Some favorites:

Awake Adventures (Map p56; ☑1-636-3903; www.awakeadventures.com; Carrera 11 No 98-46, Bogotá) Bogotá-based; offers good kayaking trips in the Amazon, on the Río Magdalena and other adventure opportunities.

Aventure Colombia (www.aventurecolombia.com) Bogotá (Map p50; ☑1-702-7069; www.aventurecolombia.com; Av Jimenez No 4-49, oficina 204); Cartagena (Map p126; ☑314-588-2378; Calle de la Factoria No 36-04); Santa Marta (Map p142; ☑5-430-5185; www.aventurecolombia.com; Calle 14 No 4-80) A good-time agency run by a charming French expat. It specializes in off-the-beaten-path destinations nationwide such as Punta Gallinas, indigenous homestays in the Sierra Nevada de Santa Marta, fascinating Caño Cristales in Meta, and adventure and ecotourism from the Caribbean coast to the Zona Cafetera and Parque Nacional Natural (PNN) Los Nevados to the Pacific coast.

Colombia 57 (☑6-886-8050; www.colombia57.com) This British-owned, Manizales-based tour operator specializes in custom-tailored tours.

Colombian Highlands (☑310-552-9079, 8-732-1201; www.colombianhighlands.com; Av Carrera 10 No 21-Finca Renacer) ✈ This highly regarded Villa de Leyva–based tour operator has gone national and now offers bespoke tours to Los Llanos, the Amazon (including Vaupés) and La Guajira, among others.

Colombian Journeys (Map p56; ☑1-618-0027; www.colombianjourneys.com; Carrera 13 No 90-36, oficina 701, Ed Blvd 90; ⊙8am-5pm Mon-Fri) Bogotá-based company offering multilingual tours countrywide.

De Una Colombia Tours (☑1-368-1915; www.deunacolombia.com; Carrera 26A No 40-18 Apt 202, La Soledad) This Dutch-owned company in Bogotá focuses on many far-flung destinations.

Expotur (www.expotur-eco.com) Santa Marta (Map p142; ☑5-420-7739; www.expotur-eco.com; Carrera 3 No 17-27); Taganga (☑5-421-9577; www.expotur-eco.com; Calle 18 No 2A-07); Riohacha (☑5-728-8232; www.expotur-eco.com; Carrera 3 No 3A-02) Professionally run agency particularly strong for trips to Ciudad Perdida and Punta Gallinas.

Mambe Travel (☑1-629-8880; www.mambe.org; Carrera 5 No 117-25, Bogotá) ✈ Bogotá-based sustainable tourism NGO that digs deeper into six off-the-beaten-track destinations: the Amazon, the Chocó, La Guajira peninsula, Sierra Nevada de Santa Marta, Vichada and Caño Cristales.

night. You may like to travel with earplugs.

It is common for buses to stop at *requisas* (military checkpoints), even in the dead of night. The soldiers at checkpoints will ask everyone to get off the bus, check everyone's identification, and then pat people down. They may look through your bags or, more rarely, do a strip search; or sometimes they ignore foreigners altogether.

Long-distance buses stop for meals, but not necessarily at mealtimes; it depends on when the driver is hungry or when the bus gets to a restaurant that has an arrangement with the bus company.

All intercity buses depart from and arrive at a *terminal de pasajeros* (passenger terminal). Every city has such a terminal, usually outside the city center, but always linked to it by local transportation. Bogotá is the most important bus transportation hub in Colombia, handling buses to just about every area of the country.

The highway speed limit in Colombia is 80km/h, and bus companies are obliged to put a large speedometer at the front of the cabin, so passengers can see how fast the bus is going (although in practice they are often broken or disabled). Bus company offices are also required by law to post their accident/fatality statistics at the ticket counter, which can give you a good idea of their safety record.

Classes

Most intercity buses are air-conditioned and have good legroom. On shorter routes (less than four hours), *busetas* (small buses) ply their trade. There are sometimes also vans, which cost more but are faster. In remote country areas, where the roads are bad, ancient *chivas* (a truck with a wooden carriage on the back with open rows of seats rather than a center aisle) service smaller towns, picking up and dropping off passengers along the way. The fastest service is called *Super Directo*.

Costs

Bus travel is reasonably cheap in Colombia. Depending on who you ask, bus prices can be negotiable outside of peak holiday times. Try your luck with a polite, *'Hay discuento?'* (Is there a discount?) or *'Cual es el minimo?'* (What is the minimum?), then work your way down the counters, indicating what the previously quoted fare was. You want to take the second-to-cheapest offer; there's usually something wrong with the cheapest bus.

When you get on a bus out on the road, you pay the fare to the *ayudante* (driver's sidekick). *Ayudantes* are usually honest, but it's worth knowing the actual fare beforehand to be sure you're not getting a gringo price.

Reservations

Outside of peak holiday periods (such as Christmas and Easter), reservations are not needed. Just rock up to the bus station an hour before you want to leave and grab the first bus going. On some minor routes, where there are only a few departures a day, it's worth considering buying your ticket several hours before the scheduled departure.

A common trick, especially with smaller buses, is to say they only need one passenger to leave, then they lock your bag in the back and you end up waiting an hour for the bus to leave, watching other buses leave before you do. Don't get into the bus or pay until you see the driver start the engine and prepare to leave.

Car & Motorcycle

Considering how cheap and extensive bus transportation is in Colombia, there is little reason to bring your own vehicle. What's more, the security situation remains dodgy in remote and rural parts of the country, substantially increasing the risk of vehicle theft and/or assault in isolated parts of the country. Check government websites for warnings before setting out anywhere remote.

In the cities, on the other hand, traffic is heavy, chaotic and mad. Driving 'manners' are wild and unpredictable. It takes some time to get used to the local style of driving. This applies to motorcycle travel as well.

Colombians drive on the right-hand side of the road and there are seatbelt requirements, so buckle up or risk a fine. The speed limit is 60km/h in the city and 80km/h on the highway. The nationwide highway police telephone number is ☑767.

If you do plan to drive in Colombia, bring your driver's license. The driver's license from your country will normally do unless it's one of non-Latin-alphabet origin, in which case, you'll need an International Driving Permit as well.

Bring Your Own Vehicle

➜ There's no way of bringing your vehicle to South America other than by sea or air, involving time, substantial cost and a lot of paperwork. You'll spend less (and be safer) traveling in Colombia by bus.

Rental

Several international rental car companies – **Avis** (www.aviscolombia.com) and **Hertz** (www.hertzcolombia.com.co) for example – are operating in Colombia. Expect to pay from COP$150,000 per day including Loss Damage Waiver, plus gasoline. You'll get better deals, as always, by booking online. Carefully check clauses pertaining to insurance and liability before you sign a rental contract. Pay close attention to any theft clause as it may load a large percentage of any loss onto the hirer. If you rent a car with tinted windows, you'll need a special document from the rental agency that police at checkpoints will ask for. Agencies don't generally volunteer the info so be sure to inquire.

Hitchhiking

➜ Hitchhiking in Colombia is uncommon and difficult. Given the complex internal situation, drivers don't want to take risks and simply don't stop on the road.

➜ Hitchhiking is never entirely safe, and we don't recommend it. Travelers who hitch should understand that they are taking a small but potentially serious risk.

Local Transportation

Bus

Almost every urban center of more than 100,000 inhabitants has a bus service, as do many smaller towns. The standard, speed and efficiency of local buses vary from place to place, but on the whole they are slow and crowded. City buses have a flat fare, so the distance of the ride makes no difference. You get on by the front door and pay the driver or the assistant. You never get a ticket.

In some cities or on some streets there are bus stops (*paraderos* or *paradas*), while in most others you just wave down the bus. To let the driver know that you intend to get off you simply say, or shout, *'por aquí, por favor'*

BUSING ABOUT, CHIVA-STYLE

The *chiva* is a Disneyland-style vehicle that was Colombia's principal means of road transportation several decades ago. Also called *bus de escalera* (which roughly translated means 'bus of stairs,' referring to the stairs along the side) in some regions, the *chiva* is a piece of popular art on wheels. The body is made almost entirely of wood and has wooden benches rather than seats, with each bench accessible from the outside. The body of the bus is painted with colorful decorative patterns, each different, with a main painting on the back. There are homebred artists who specialize in painting *chivas*. Ceramic miniatures of *chivas* are found in just about every Colombian handicraft shop.

Today, *chivas* have almost disappeared from main roads, but they still play an important role on back roads between small towns and villages. There are still a few thousand of them and they are most common in Antioquia, Huila, Nariño and on the Caribbean coast. *Chivas* take both passengers and any kind of cargo, animals included. If the interior is already completely packed, the roof is used for everything and everybody that doesn't fit inside.

Nighttime city tours in *chivas* are organized by travel agents in most large cities and have become a popular form of entertainment. There is normally a band on board playing local music, and a large stock of aguardiente (anise-flavored liquor) to create the proper atmosphere. The tour usually includes some popular nightspots and can be great fun.

(here, please), '*en la esquina, por favor*' (at the corner, please) or '*el paradero, por favor*' (at the coming bus stop, please).

There are lots of different types of local buses, ranging from old wrecks to modern air-conditioned vehicles. One common type is the *buseta* (small bus), a dominant means of urban transportation in cities such as Bogotá and Cartagena. The bus fare is somewhere between COP$600 and COP$1650, depending on the city and type of bus.

A bus or *buseta* trip, particularly in large cities such as Bogotá or Barranquilla, is not a smooth and silent ride but rather a sort of breathtaking adventure with a taste of local folklore thrown in. You'll have an opportunity to be saturated with loud tropical music, learn about the Colombian meaning of road rules, and observe your driver desperately trying to make his way through an ocean of vehicles.

Colectivo

Colectivo in Colombia can mean a midsized bus, a shared taxi, an overloaded

jeep, and everything in between. They are most popular in short intercity hops of less than four hours. Because they are smaller than regular buses, they can travel quicker, and charge around 30% more as a result. They often depart only when full.

In some cities they depart from and arrive at the bus terminal, but in smaller towns they are usually found in the main square. The frequency of service varies largely from place to place. At some places there may be a *colectivo* every five minutes, but elsewhere you can wait an hour or longer until the necessary number of passengers has been collected. If you're in a hurry you can pay for all the seats and the driver will depart immediately.

Mass Transit

➡ Mass transit is growing increasingly popular in Colombia. Bogotá boasts the TransMilenio, and Cali and Bucaramanga have similar projects, called the Mio and Metrolínea, respectively. Medellín has its famous Metro, the only commuter rail line in the country.

Pereira, too, offers the MegaBús system.

Motorcycles

➡ Some cities, especially in the north, use motorcycle-taxis, which are a quick way of getting around if you're on your own. These, however, are not the safest method of transportation and are even illegal in some places, including Cartagena (though no one seems to stop them).

➡ There may be options for renting a motorcycle, especially in resort-type areas such as San Andrés.

➡ Helmet laws are enforced, though not in San Andrés and Providencia.

Taxi

Taxis are cheap, convenient and ubiquitous in the major cities and most midsized towns. In the interior of the country all taxis have meters; on the Caribbean coast, it's haggle or pay extra, and many drivers are eager (especially in Cartagena) to see just how much they can take advantage of your naiveté. That said, a many taxi drivers are honest individuals; the better you speak Spanish, the more bargaining power you'll have, and the less likely you'll pay hyperinflated prices.

There are occasionally deceptive, untrustworthy individuals masquerading in fake taxis. This is rare, but if you are concerned, it is always safer to call for a taxi, which costs a mere few hundred pesos extra (or use an app). Taxi fares are always per taxi, never per number of passengers. Many taxis have somewhat flimsy doors – be kind, do not slam doors when getting into or out of the vehicle.

Don't use taxis with a driver and somebody else inside. While taxi drivers sometimes have a friend along for company or for security reasons, such a situation may be unsafe for you; this is a common robbery tactic. Taxi apps such as **Tappsi** (www.tappsi. co) and **Easy Taxi** (www. easytaxi.com) have drastically improved taxi security and should be used by all with a smartphone. They work in most of Colombia's major cities.

A taxi may also be chartered for longer distances. This is convenient if you want to visit places near major cities that are outside local transportation areas but too near to be covered by long-distance bus networks. You can also rent a taxi by the hour in the major cities – a good way to make your own impromptu tour. Expect to pay around COP$25,000 per hour for this service.

Tricycle Moto-Taxi

Chinese-made tuk-tuks are becoming increasingly popular in smaller tourist towns. Moto-taxis seat three and have a covered roof, plus a tarp that can be lowered around the sides in case of rain. You'll see these in Bari-chara, Mompox, Santa Fe de Antioquia, the Desierto de la Tatacoa and some of the small towns on the Pacific coast.

Train

Colombia has a nation-wide network of train track that is largely unused (or is overgrown or has been ripped up and sold off). The only train you're likely to board is **Turistren** (☑1-375-0557; www.turistren. com.co; round trip adult/child COP$43,000/27,000), which runs on weekends from Bogotá to Zipaquirá.

Those visiting San Cipriano, just off the Cali–Buenaventura highway, can enjoy the novel sensation of traveling on a railroad hand-cart (trolley) powered by a motorcycle.

Language

Latin American Spanish pronunciation is easy, as most sounds have equivalents in English. Also, Spanish spelling is phonetically consistent, meaning that there's a clear and consistent relationship between what you see in writing and how it's pronounced. Read our coloured pronunciation guides as if they were English, and you'll be understood. Note that kh is a throaty sound (like the 'ch' in the Scottish *loch*), v and b are like a soft English 'v' (between a 'v' and a 'b'), and r is strongly rolled.

There are some variations in spoken Spanish across Latin America, the most notable being the pronunciation of the letters *ll* and *y* – depending on where you are on the continent, you'll hear them pronounced like the 'y' in 'yes', the 'lli' in 'million', the 's' in 'measure' or the 'sh' in 'shut', and in Colombia you'll also hear them pronounced like the 'dg' in 'judge'. In our pronunciation guides they are represented with y because you're most likely to hear them pronounced like the 'y' in 'yes'.

The stressed syllables are indicated with an acute accent in written Spanish (eg *días*) and with italics in our pronunciation guides.

The polite form is used in this chapter; where both polite and informal options are given, they are indicated by the abbreviations 'pol' and 'inf'. Where necessary, both masculine and feminine forms of words are included, separated by a slash and with the masculine form first, eg *perdido/a* (m/f).

BASICS

Hello.	Hola.	o·la
Goodbye.	Adiós.	a·dyos
How are you?	¿Qué tal?	ke tal
Fine, thanks.	Bien, gracias.	byen gra·syas
Excuse me.	Perdón.	per·don
Sorry.	Lo siento.	lo syen·to
Please.	Por favor.	por fa·vor
Thank you.	Gracias.	gra·syas

You're welcome.	De nada.	de na·da
Yes.	Sí.	see
No.	No.	no

My name is ...
Me llamo ...   me ya·mo ...

What's your name?
¿Cómo se llama Usted? ko·mo se ya·ma oo·ste (pol)
¿Cómo te llamas? ko·mo te ya·mas (inf)

Do you speak English?
¿Habla inglés? a·bla een·gles (pol)
¿Hablas inglés? a·blas een·gles (inf)

I don't understand.
Yo no entiendo. yo no en·tyen·do

ACCOMMODATIONS

I'd like a room.	Quisiera una habitación ...	kee·sye·ra oo·na a·bee·ta·syon ...
single	individual	een·dee·vee·dwal
double	doble	do·ble

How much is it per night/person?
¿Cuánto cuesta por noche/persona? kwan·to kwes·ta por no·che/per·so·na

Does it include breakfast?
¿Incluye el desayuno? een·kloo·ye el de·sa·yoo·no

WANT MORE?

For in-depth language information and handy phrases, check out Lonely Planet's *Latin American Spanish Phrasebook*. You'll find it at **shop.lonelyplanet.com**.

KEY PATTERNS

To get by in Spanish, mix and match these simple patterns with words of your choice:

When's (the next flight)?
¿Cuándo sale   kwan·do sa·le
(el próximo vuelo)?   (el prok·see·mo vwe·lo)

Where's (the station)?
¿Dónde está   don·de es·ta
(la estación)?   (la es·ta·syon)

Where can I (buy a ticket)?
¿Dónde puedo   don·de pwe·do
(comprar un billete)? (kom·prar oon bee·ye·te)

Do you have (a map)?
¿Tiene (un mapa)?   tye·ne (oon ma·pa)

Is there (a toilet)?
¿Hay (servicios)?   ai (ser·vee·syos)

I'd like (a coffee).
Quisiera (un café).   kee·sye·ra (oon ka·fe)

I'd like (to hire a car).
Quisiera (alquilar   kee·sye·ra (al·kee·lar
un coche).   oon ko·che)

Can I (enter)?
¿Se puede (entrar)?   se pwe·de (en·trar)

Could you please (help me)?
¿Puede (ayudarme),   pwe·de (a·yoo·dar·me)
por favor?   por fa·vor

campsite	terreno de cámping	te·re·no de kam·peeng
cabin	cabaña	ka·ba·nya
hotel	hotel	o·tel
guesthouse	pensión	pen·syon
lodging/hostel	hospedaje	os·pe·da·khe
shelter	refugio	re·foo·khyo
youth hostel	albergue juvenil	al·ber·ge khoo·ve·neel
air-con	aire acondicionado	ai·re a·kon·dee·syo·na·do
bathroom	baño	ba·nyo
bed	cama	ka·ma
window	ventana	ven·ta·na

DIRECTIONS

Where's ...?
¿Dónde está ...?   don·de es·ta ...

What's the address?
¿Cuál es la dirección? kwal es la dee·rek·syon

Could you please write it down?
¿Puede escribirlo,   pwe·de es·kree·beer·lo
por favor?   por fa·vor

Can you show me (on the map)?
¿Me lo puede indicar   me lo pwe·de een·dee·kar
(en el mapa)?   (en el ma·pa)

at the corner	en la esquina	en la es·kee·na
at the traffic lights	en el semáforo	en el se·ma·fo·ro
behind ...	detrás de ...	de·tras de ...
far	lejos	le·khos
in front of ...	enfrente de ...	en·fren·te de ...
left	izquierda	ees·kyer·da
near	cerca	ser·ka
next to ...	al lado de ...	al la·do de ...
opposite ...	frente a ...	fren·te a ...
right	derecha	de·re·cha
straight ahead	todo recto	to·do rek·to

EATING & DRINKING

Can I see the menu, please?
¿Puedo ver el menú,   pwe·do ver el me·noo
por favor?   por fa·vor

What would you recommend?
¿Qué recomienda?   ke re·ko·myen·da

Do you have vegetarian food?
¿Tienen comida   tye·nen ko·mee·da
vegetariana?   ve·khe·ta·rya·na

I don't eat (red meat).
No como (carne roja). no ko·mo (kar·ne ro·kha)

That was delicious!
¡Estaba buenísimo!   es·ta·ba bwe·nee·see·mo

Cheers!
¡Salud!   sa·loo

The bill, please.
La cuenta, por favor. la kwen·ta por fa·vor

I'd like a table for ...	Quisiera una mesa para ...	kee·sye·ra oo·na me·sa pa·ra ...
(eight) o'clock	las (ocho)	las (o·cho)
(two) people	(dos) personas	(dos) per·so·nas

Key Words

appetisers	aperitivos	a·pe·ree·tee·vos
bottle	botella	bo·te·ya
bowl	bol	bol
breakfast	desayuno	de·sa·yoo·no
children's menu	menú infantil	me·noo een·fan·teel
(too) cold	(muy) frío	(mooy) free·o
dinner	cena	se·na

food	comida	ko·mee·da
fork	tenedor	te·ne·dor
glass	vaso	va·so
highchair	trona	tro·na
hot (warm)	caliente	kal·yen·te
knife	cuchillo	koo·chee·yo
lunch	almuerzo	al·mwer·so
main course	plato principal	pla·to preen·see·pal
plate	plato	pla·to
restaurant	restaurante	res·tow·ran·te
spoon	cuchara	koo·cha·ra
with	con	kon
without	sin	seen

Meat & Fish

beef	carne de vaca	kar·ne de va·ka
chicken	pollo	po·yo
duck	pato	pa·to
fish	pescado	pes·ka·do
lamb	cordero	kor·de·ro
pork	cerdo	ser·do
turkey	pavo	pa·vo
veal	ternera	ter·ne·ra

Fruit & Vegetables

apple	manzana	man·sa·na
apricot	damasco	da·mas·ko
artichoke	alcaucil	al·kow·seel
asparagus	espárragos	es·pa·ra·gos
banana	banana	ba·na·na
beans	chauchas	chow·chas
beetroot	remolacha	re·mo·la·cha
cabbage	repollo	re·po·yo
carrot	zanahoria	sa·na·o·rya
celery	apio	a·pyo
cherry	cereza	se·re·sa

SIGNS

Abierto	Open
Cerrado	Closed
Entrada	Entrance
Hombres/Varones	Men
Mujeres/Damas	Women
Prohibido	Prohibited
Salida	Exit
Servicios/Baños	Toilets

corn	choclo	cho·klo
cucumber	pepino	pe·pee·no
fruit	fruta	froo·ta
grape	uvas	oo·vas
lemon	limón	lee·mon
lentils	lentejas	len·te·khas
lettuce	lechuga	le·choo·ga
mushroom	champiñón	cham·pee·nyon
nuts	nueces	nwe·ses
onion	cebolla	se·bo·ya
orange	naranja	na·ran·kha
peach	melocotón	me·lo·ko·ton
peas	arvejas	ar·ve·khas
(red/green) pepper	pimiento (rojo/verde)	pee·myen·to (ro·kho/ver·de)
pineapple	ananá	a·na·na
plum	ciruela	seer·we·la
potato	papa	pa·pa
pumpkin	zapallo	sa·pa·yo
spinach	espinacas	es·pee·na·kas
strawberry	frutilla	froo·tee·ya
tomato	tomate	to·ma·te
vegetable	verdura	ver·doo·ra
watermelon	sandía	san·dee·a

Other

bread	pan	pan
butter	manteca	man·te·ka
cheese	queso	ke·so
egg	huevo	we·vo
honey	miel	myel
jam	mermelada	mer·me·la·da
oil	aceite	a·sey·te
pasta	pasta	pas·ta
pepper	pimienta	pee·myen·ta
rice	arroz	a·ros
salt	sal	sal
sugar	azúcar	a·soo·kar
vinegar	vinagre	vee·na·gre

Drinks

beer	cerveza	ser·ve·sa
coffee	café	ka·fe
(orange) juice	jugo (de naranja)	khoo·go (de na·ran·kha)
milk	leche	le·che
tea	té	te

(mineral) water	agua (mineral)	a·gwa (mee·ne·ral)
(red/white) wine	vino (tinto/ blanco)	vee·no (teen·to/ blan·ko)

EMERGENCIES

Help!	¡Socorro!	so·ko·ro
Go away!	¡Vete!	ve·te

Call ...!	¡Llame a ...!	ya·me a ...
a doctor	un médico	oon me·dee·ko
the police	la policía	la po·lee·see·a

I'm lost.
Estoy perdido/a.   es·toy per·dee·do/a (m/f)

I'm ill.
Estoy enfermo/a.   es·toy en·fer·mo/a (m/f)

It hurts here.
Me duele aquí.   me dwe·le a·kee

I'm allergic to (antibiotics).
Soy alérgico/a a   soy a·ler·khee·ko/a a
(los antibióticos).   (los an·tee·byo·tee·kos) (m/f)

Where are the toilets?
¿Dónde están los   don·de es·tan los
baños?   ba·nyos

SHOPPING & SERVICES

I'd like to buy ...
Quisiera comprar ...   kee·sye·ra kom·prar ...

I'm just looking.
Sólo estoy mirando.   so·lo es·toy mee·ran·do

Can I look at it?
¿Puedo verlo?   pwe·do ver·lo

I don't like it.
No me gusta.   no me goos·ta

How much is it?
¿Cuánto cuesta?   kwan·to kwes·ta

That's too expensive.
Es muy caro.   es mooy ka·ro

Can you lower the price?
¿Podría bajar un   po·dree·a ba·khar oon
poco el precio?   po·ko el pre·syo

There's a mistake in the bill.
Hay un error   ai oon e·ror
en la cuenta.   en la kwen·ta

ATM	cajero automático	ka·khe·ro ow·to·ma·tee·ko
credit card	tarjeta de crédito	tar·khe·ta de kre·dee·to
internet cafe	cibercafé	see·ber·ka·fe
market	mercado	mer·ka·do
post office	correos	ko·re·os
tourist office	oficina de turismo	o·fee·see·na de too·rees·mo

TIME & DATES

What time is it?	¿Qué hora es?	ke o·ra es
It's (10) o'clock.	Son (las diez).	son (las dyes)

morning	mañana	ma·nya·na
afternoon	tarde	tar·de
evening	noche	no·che
yesterday	ayer	a·yer
today	hoy	oy
tomorrow	mañana	ma·nya·na

Monday	lunes	loo·nes
Tuesday	martes	mar·tes
Wednesday	miércoles	myer·ko·les
Thursday	jueves	khwe·ves
Friday	viernes	vyer·nes
Saturday	sábado	sa·ba·do
Sunday	domingo	do·meen·go

January	enero	e·ne·ro
February	febrero	fe·bre·ro
March	marzo	mar·so
April	abril	a·breel
May	mayo	ma·yo
June	junio	khoon·yo
July	julio	khool·yo
August	agosto	a·gos·to
September	septiembre	sep·tyem·bre
October	octubre	ok·too·bre
November	noviembre	no·vyem·bre
December	diciembre	dee·syem·bre

TRANSPORTATION

boat	barco	bar·ko
bus	autobús	ow·to·boos
(small) bus/van	buseta	boo·se·ta
(traditional) bus	chiva	chee·va
plane	avión	a·vyon
(shared) taxi	colectivo	ko·lek·tee·vo
train	tren	tren

QUESTION WORDS

How?	¿Cómo?	ko·mo
What?	¿Qué?	ke
When?	¿Cuándo?	kwan·do
Where?	¿Dónde?	don·de
Who?	¿Quién?	kyen
Why?	¿Por qué?	por ke

first	primero	pree·*me*·ro
last	último	*ool*·tee·mo
next	próximo	*prok*·see·mo
A ... ticket, please.	Un boleto de ..., por favor.	oon bo·*le*·to de ... por fa·*vor*
1st-class	primera clase	pree·*me*·ra *kla*·se
2nd-class	segunda clase	se·*goon*·da *kla*·se
one-way	ida	*ee*·da
return	ida y vuelta	*ee*·da ee *vwel*·ta

I want to go to ...
Quisiera ir a ...   kee·*sye*·ra eer a ...

Does it stop at ...?
¿Para en ...?   *pa*·ra en ...

What stop is this?
¿Cuál es esta parada?   kwal es *es*·ta pa·*ra*·da

What time does it arrive/leave?
¿A qué hora llega/sale?   a ke o·ra ye·ga/*sa*·le

Please tell me when we get to ...
¿Puede avisarme cuando lleguemos a ...?   pwe·de a·vee·*sar*·me *kwan*·do ye·*ge*·mos a ...

I want to get off here.
Quiero bajarme aquí.   *kye*·ro ba·*khar*·me a·*kee*

airport	aeropuerto	a·e·ro·*pwer*·to
aisle seat	asiento de pasillo	a·*syen*·to de pa·*see*·yo
bus station	terminal terrestre	ter·mee·*nal*/ te·*res*·tre
bus stop	paradero/parada	pa·ra·*de*·ro/ pa·*ra*·da
cancelled	cancelado	kan·se·*la*·do
delayed	retrasado	re·tra·*sa*·do
platform	plataforma	pla·ta·*for*·ma
ticket office	taquilla	ta·*kee*·ya
timetable	horario	o·*ra*·ryo
train station	estación de trenes	es·ta·*syon* de *tre*·nes
window seat	asiento junto a la ventana	a·*syen*·to *khoon*·to a la ven·*ta*·na

I'd like to hire a ...	Quisiera alquilar ...	kee·*sye*·ra al·kee·*lar* ...
4WD	un todo-terreno	oon to·do·te·*re*·no
bicycle	una bicicleta	*oo*·na bee·see·*kle*·ta
car	un coche	oon *ko*·che
motorcycle	una moto	*oo*·na *mo*·to

NUMBERS

1	uno	*oo*·no
2	dos	dos
3	tres	tres
4	cuatro	*kwa*·tro
5	cinco	*seen*·ko
6	seis	seys
7	siete	*sye*·te
8	ocho	*o*·cho
9	nueve	*nwe*·ve
10	diez	dyes
20	veinte	*veyn*·te
30	treinta	*treyn*·ta
40	cuarenta	kwa·*ren*·ta
50	cincuenta	seen·*kwen*·ta
60	sesenta	se·*sen*·ta
70	setenta	se·*ten*·ta
80	ochenta	o·*chen*·ta
90	noventa	no·*ven*·ta
100	cien	syen
1000	mil	meel

child seat	asiento de seguridad para niños	a·*syen*·to de se·goo·ree·*da* pa·ra nee·nyos
diesel	petróleo	pet·*ro*·le·o
helmet	casco	*kas*·ko
hitchhike	hacer botella	a·ser bo·*te*·ya
mechanic	mecánico	me·*ka*·nee·ko
petrol/gas	gasolina	ga·so·*lee*·na
service station	gasolinera	ga·so·lee·*ne*·ra
truck	camión	ka·*myon*

Is this the road to ...?
¿Se va a ... por esta carretera?   se va a ... por es·ta ka·re·*te*·ra

(How long) Can I park here?
¿(Cuánto tiempo) Puedo aparcar aquí?   (*kwan*·to *tyem*·po) pwe·do a·par·*kar* a·*kee*

The car has broken down (at ...).
El coche se ha averiado (en ...).   el *ko*·che se a a·ve·*rya*·do (en ...)

I had an accident.
He tenido un accidente.   e te·*nee*·do oon ak·see·*den*·te

I've run out of petrol.
Me he quedado sin gasolina.   me e ke·*da*·do seen ga·so·*lee*·na

I have a flat tyre.
Se me pinchó une rueda.   se me peen·*cho* *oo*·na rwe·da

GLOSSARY

Spanish speakers wanting a complete reference to Colombian slang should pick up a copy of the *Diccionario de Colombiano Actual* (2005) by Francisco Celis Albán.

asadero – place serving roasted or grilled meats

AUC – Autodefensas Unidas de Colombia (United Self-Defense Forces of Colombia); a loose alliance of paramilitary squads known as *autodefensas*

autodefensas – right-wing squads created to defend large landowners against guerrillas, also called *paramilitares* or just *paras;* see also *AUC*

bogotano/a – person from Bogotá

buseta – small bus/van that is a popular means of city transport

cabaña – cabin, or simple shelter; usually found on beaches or up in the mountains

caleño/a – person from Cali

campesino/a – rural dweller, usually of modest economic means; peasant

casa de cambio – currency-exchange office

chalupa – small passenger boat powered by an outboard motor

chinchorro – hammock woven of cotton threads or palm fiber like a fishing net, typical of many indigenous groups; the best known are the decorative cotton hammocks of the Guajiros

chiva – traditional bus with its body made of timber and painted with colorful patterns; still widely used in the countryside

colectivo – shared taxi or minibus; a popular means of public transport

comida corriente – fast food; set lunch

costeño/a – inhabitant of the Caribbean coast

DAS – Departamento Administrativo de Seguridad; the security police, responsible for immigration (dissolved in 2011)

ELN – Ejército de Liberación Nacional (National Liberation Army); the second-largest guerrilla group after the FARC

FARC – Fuerzas Armadas Revolucionarias de Colombia; the largest guerrilla group in the country

finca – farm; anything from a country house with a small garden to a huge country estate

frailejón – *espeletia*, a species of plant; a yellow-flowering, perennial shrub that only grows at altitudes above 3000m, typical of the *páramo*

gringo/a – any white male/ female foreigner; sometimes, (but not always) used in a derogatory sense

guadua – the largest variety of the bamboo family, common in many regions of moderate climate

hacienda – country estate

hospedaje – lodging (in general); sometimes, a cheap hotel or hostel

indígena – indigenous; also indigenous person

IVA – *impuesto de valor agregado*, a value-added tax (VAT)

merengue – musical rhythm originating in the Dominican Republic, today widespread throughout the Caribbean and beyond

meseta – plateau

mestizo/a – person of mixed European-indigenous blood

mirador – lookout, viewpoint

muelle – pier, wharf

mulato/a – mulatto; a person of mixed European-African blood

nevado – snowcapped mountain peak

paisa – a person from Antioquia

paradero – bus stop; in some areas called *parada*

páramo – high-mountain plains, at an elevation of between 3500m and 4500m, typical of Colombia, Venezuela and Ecuador

piso – story, floor

poporo – a vessel made from a small gourd, used by the Arhuacos and other indigenous groups to carry lime; while chewing coca leaves, *indígenas* add lime to help release the alkaloid from the leaves; a sacred ritual of the indigenous people of the Caribbean coast

puente – literally 'bridge'; also means a three-day-long weekend (including Monday)

refugio – rustic shelter in a remote area, mostly in the mountains

reggaetón – a mix of hip-hop and Latin rhythms, it has a distinctly urban flavor with fast-paced danceable beats

salsa – type of Caribbean dance music of Cuban origin, very popular in Colombia

salsateca – disco playing salsa music

Semana Santa – Holy Week, the week before Easter Sunday

tagua – hard ivory-colored nut of a species of palm; used in handicrafts, mainly on the Pacific coast

tejo – traditional game, popular mainly in the Andean region; played with a heavy metal disk, which is thrown to make a *mecha* (a sort of petard) explode

Telecom – the state telephone company

vallenato – music typical of the Caribbean region, based on the accordion; it's now widespread in Colombia

Behind the Scenes

SEND US YOUR FEEDBACK

We love to hear from travelers – your comments keep us on our toes and help make our books better. Our well-traveled team reads every word on what you loved or loathed about this book. Although we cannot reply individually to postal submissions, we always guarantee that your feedback goes straight to the appropriate authors, in time for the next edition. Each person who sends us information is thanked in the next edition – the most useful submissions are rewarded with a selection of digital PDF chapters.

Visit **lonelyplanet.com/contact** to submit your updates and suggestions or to ask for help. Our award-winning website also features inspirational travel stories, news and discussions.

Note: We may edit, reproduce and incorporate your comments in Lonely Planet products such as guidebooks, websites and digital products, so let us know if you don't want your comments reproduced or your name acknowledged. For a copy of our privacy policy visit lonelyplanet.com/privacy.

OUR READERS

Many thanks to the travelers who used the last edition and wrote to us with helpful hints, useful advice and interesting anecdotes:

A Adam Norten, Aki Vilkman, Anika Sierk **B** Brian Fagan **C** Charles Petersen, Chris Davis, Christian Ehlermann, Claire Wilkinson, Conan Griffin, Cynthia Ord **D** David Dellenback, David Marshall, Dean Tysoe, Diego Garzón **E** Edith Delarue, Erik Bakker, Erik Janse, Evan Yost, Evelyne Eneman **F** Fetze Weerstra, France Francois **G** Giovanni Sabato, Gisela Cramer, Grant Butler, Gundula Zahn **H** Hanna Witek **I** Itsaso Urkiaga **J** Jason White, John Davis, John Garrison Marks, John Lundin, Jorge Wandurraga, Joris van den Broek, Juan Moreno, Julie Pimm **K** Karen Okamoto, Kirsten Vinther, Kristin Richter **L** Laura Farrell, Lauryn Drainie, Lea Mayer, Lonnie Carey, Luis Sarmiento, Luke Fadem **M** Maarten jan Oskam, Magda Bulska, Maria Alejandra, Matthijs van Laar, Michael Breen, Michael Oldre, Momi Zisquit **P** Patrick Ward, Paul Groenen, Per Andersen, Peter Borock, Pierre Raymond, Plecuy Reurner **R** Reinhard Enne, Richard Jenkins, Ronald Cannell **S** Sean Windsor, Sebastian Adamberry, Sebastian Werling, Sophie Balbo, Sophie Jarman, Stef Mertens, Susan Waldock **U** Uwe Lask **V** Valentina Botta **W** Wouter Bauhuis **Y** Yamid Puerto

AUTHOR THANKS

Alex Egerton

In Colombia thanks to the usual suspects: Olga Mosquera, Laura Cahnspeyer, Oscar Gilede, Melissa Montoya, Nicolas Solorzano, Richard, Felipe Goforit, Tyler, Alexa and Oscar Payan – *abrazos para todos.* Also a big shout to Kevin Raub, Tom Masters and MaSovaida for being wonderfully supportive colleagues. And big thanks to Kent *'¿Q mas?'* and Warren for the write-up pad.

Tom Masters

A huge debt of thanks first of all to Joe Kellner, who traveled with me for several weeks along the Caribbean Coast, patiently putting up with dawn starts, endless drives and my singing in the car: the drive to Turbo will not quickly be forgotten! Big thanks also to the teams at Expotur, particularly David Salas, the staff of Aventure Colombia, Sandra Rodil, Antonio Cruz Pérez, Richard McColl, Karelvis in Punta Gallinas, and last but not at all least, super co-authors Kevin and Alex.

Kevin Raub

Thanks to my wife, Adriana Schmidt Raub, who would surely appreciate Colombia's $2 freshly squeezed juices; MaSovaida Morgan; and my partners-in-crime, Alex Egerton and Tom Masters. On the road, Laura Cahnspeyer –

couldn't have done it without her! – Mathieu Perrot-Bohringer, Oscar Gilede, Mike Ceaser, Rodrigo Arias, Shaun Clohesy, Mike Anderson, Kat Hilby, Juan Ananda, Rodrigo Atuesta, Jorge Hormiga, Tim Woodhouse, Jorge Gomez, Richard McColl and Toya Viudes.

ACKNOWLEDGMENTS

Climate map data adapted from Peel MC, Finlayson BL & McMahon TA (2007) 'Updated World Map of the Köppen-Geiger Climate Classification', Hydrology and Earth System Sciences, 11, 163344.

Cover photograph: Plaza de Santo Domingo, Cartagena, Stefano Paterna/Alamy.

THIS BOOK

This 7th edition of Lonely Planet's *Colombia* guidebook was researched and written by Alex Egerton, Tom Masters and Kevin Raub. The previous edition was written by Kevin Raub, Alex Egerton and Mike Power. This guidebook was produced by the following:

Destination Editor
MaSovaida Morgan
Product Editor
Martine Power
Senior Cartographer
Mark Griffiths
Book Designer
Virginia Moreno
Assisting Editors Nigel Chin, Kate Evans, Kate James, Kate Mathews, Anne Mulvaney, Susan Paterson, Ross Taylor
Cover Researcher
Naomi Parker
Thanks to Sasha Baskett, Ryan Evans, Anna Harris, Diana Saengkham, Ellie Simpson, Tony Wheeler, Glenn van der Knijff

Index

NOTES

NOTES

Map Legend

Sights

- Beach
- Bird Sanctuary
- Buddhist
- Castle/Palace
- Christian
- Confucian
- Hindu
- Islamic
- Jain
- Jewish
- Monument
- Museum/Gallery/Historic Building
- Ruin
- Sento Hot Baths/Onsen
- Shinto
- Sikh
- Taoist
- Winery/Vineyard
- Zoo/Wildlife Sanctuary
- Other Sight

Activities, Courses & Tours

- Bodysurfing
- Diving
- Canoeing/Kayaking
- Course/Tour
- Skiing
- Snorkeling
- Surfing
- Swimming/Pool
- Walking
- Windsurfing
- Other Activity

Sleeping

- Sleeping
- Camping

Eating

- Eating

Drinking & Nightlife

- Drinking & Nightlife
- Cafe

Entertainment

- Entertainment

Shopping

- Shopping

Information

- Bank
- Embassy/Consulate
- Hospital/Medical
- Internet
- Police
- Post Office
- Telephone
- Toilet
- Tourist Information
- Other Information

Geographic

- Beach
- Hut/Shelter
- Lighthouse
- Lookout
- Mountain/Volcano
- Oasis
- Park
- Pass
- Picnic Area
- Waterfall

Population

- Capital (National)
- Capital (State/Province)
- City/Large Town
- Town/Village

Transport

- Airport
- Border crossing
- Bus
- Cable car/Funicular
- Cycling
- Ferry
- Metro station
- Monorail
- Parking
- Petrol station
- Subway/Subte station
- Taxi
- Train station/Railway
- Tram
- Underground station
- Other Transport

Note: Not all symbols displayed above appear on the maps in this book

Routes

- Tollway
- Freeway
- Primary
- Secondary
- Tertiary
- Lane
- Unsealed road
- Road under construction
- Plaza/Mall
- Steps
- Tunnel
- Pedestrian overpass
- Walking Tour
- Walking Tour detour
- Path/Walking Trail

Boundaries

- International
- State/Province
- Disputed
- Regional/Suburb
- Marine Park
- Cliff
- Wall

Hydrography

- River, Creek
- Intermittent River
- Canal
- Water
- Dry/Salt/Intermittent Lake
- Reef

Areas

- Airport/Runway
- Beach/Desert
- Cemetery (Christian)
- Cemetery (Other)
- Glacier
- Mudflat
- Park/Forest
- Sight (Building)
- Sportsground
- Swamp/Mangrove

OUR STORY

A beat-up old car, a few dollars in the pocket and a sense of adventure. In 1972 that's all Tony and Maureen Wheeler needed for the trip of a lifetime – across Europe and Asia overland to Australia. It took several months, and at the end – broke but inspired – they sat at their kitchen table writing and stapling together their first travel guide, *Across Asia on the Cheap*. Within a week they'd sold 1500 copies. Lonely Planet was born.

Today, Lonely Planet has offices in Franklin, London, Melbourne, Oakland, Beijing and Delhi, with more than 600 staff and writers. We share Tony's belief that 'a great guidebook should do three things: inform, educate and amuse'.

OUR WRITERS

Alex Egerton

Medellín & Zona Cafetera, Cali & Southwest Colombia, Pacific Coast A journalist by trade, Alex has worked in Latin America for more than a decade, regularly wandering the back roads from Mexico to Argentina. He is currently based in southern Colombia where he travels extensively and writes about the country for a variety of media. When not on the road researching guidebooks, you'll find him hiking around the remote landscapes of the upper Amazon, Chocó and southern mountains or working on his *tejo* technique closer to home. Alex also wrote the Itineraries, Colombia Outdoors and Regions at a Glance chapters.

Read more about Alex at:
lonelyplanet.com/members/alexegerton

Tom Masters

Caribbean Coast, San Andrés & Providencia, Amazon Basin Having traveled all over Latin America as a backpacker and later as a Lonely Planet author, Tom was thrilled to finally get to write about Colombia, a country he first visited in 2006. For this edition Tom traveled the Amazon Basin, dived and hiked in San Andrés & Providencia and drove almost 3000km up and down the Caribbean coastline, falling in love with Mompox, Sapzurro and Providencia in the process. You can find more of his work at www.tommasters.net. Tom also wrote the Need to Know, If You Like... and Month by Month chapters, all of the Understand features, plus the Safe Travel chapter.

Read more about Tom at:
lonelyplanet.com/members/tommasters

Kevin Raub

Bogotá; Boyacá, Santander & Norte de Santander Kevin Raub grew up in Atlanta and started his career as a music journalist in New York, working for *Men's Journal* and *Rolling Stone* magazines. He ditched the rock 'n' roll lifestyle for travel writing and moved to Brazil. He's done Colombia via government helicopter, on tour with DJ Paul Oakenfold and through jungles, over rivers and through woods. This is Kevin's 29th Lonely Planet guide. Follow him on Twitter (@RaubOnTheRoad) Kevin also wrote the Welcome to Colombia, Colombia's Top 21 Experiences, Directory and Transportation chapters.

Read more about Kevin at:
lonelyplanet.com/members/kraub

Published by Lonely Planet Publications Pty Ltd
ABN 36 005 607 983
7th edition – Aug 2015
ISBN 978 1 74220 784 1
© Lonely Planet 2015   Photographs © as indicated 2015
10 9 8 7 6 5 4 3 2 1
Printed in China